THOMAS AQUINAS

Contemporary Philosophical Perspectives

Edited by
Brian Davies

OXFORD
UNIVERSITY PRESS

2002

OXFORD
UNIVERSITY PRESS

Oxford   New York
Auckland   Bangkok   Buenos Aires   Cape Town   Chennai
Dar es Salaam   Delhi   Hong Kong   Istanbul   Karachi   Kolkata
Kuala Lumpur   Madrid   Melbourne   Mexico City   Mumbai   Nairobi
São Paulo   Shanghai   Taipei   Tokyo   Toronto

Copyright © 2002 by Oxford University Press, Inc.

Published by Oxford University Press, Inc.,
198 Madison Avenue, New York, New York 10016

www.oup.com

Oxford is a registered trademark of Oxford University Press

Library of Congress Cataloging-in-Publication Data
Thomas Aquinas : contemporary philosophical perspectives / edited by Brian Davies
p. cm.
Includes bibliographical references.
ISBN-13 978-0-19-515301-9

1. Thomas, Aquinas, Saint, 1225?–1274.   I. Davies, Brian, 1951–
B765.T54 T37 2002
189'.4—dc21   2001055168

Printed in the United States of America
on acid-free paper

For Margaret Urban Walker

with gratitude and affection

Credits

Chapter 1 originally appeared in James A. Weisheipl, *Nature and Motion in the Middle Ages* (Washington, D.C.: The Catholic University of America Press, 1985), pp. 177–201. Used by permission of the publisher.

Chapter 2 originally appeared in *Revue International de Philosophie* 52 (1998). Used by permission of the editor.

Chapter 3 originally appeared in S. Knuuttila and J. Hintikka (eds.), *The Logic of Being* (Dordrecht, The Netherlands: Kluwer Academic Publishers, 1986), pp. 181–200. Reprinted with kind permission from Kluwer Academic Publishers.

Chapter 4 originally appeared in *The New Scholasticism* 59 (1985). Reprinted by permission of the editors.

Chapter 5 originally appeared in *Medieval Philosophy and Theology* 4 (1994). Reprinted with the permission of Cambridge University Press.

Chapter 6 originally appeared in *Journal of the History of Philosophy* 22 (1984). Reprinted by permission of the editor.

Chapter 7 originally appeared in John F. Wippel, *The Metaphysical Thought of Thomas Aquinas* (Washington, D.C.: The Catholic University of America Press, 2000), pp. 442–500. Used by permission of the publisher.

Chaper 8 originally appeared in *Revue International de Philosophie* 52 (1998). Reprinted by permission of the editor.

Chapter 9 originally appeared in Anthony Kenny, *The Legacy of Wittgenstein* (Oxford: Blackwell, 1984), pp. 61–76. Reprinted by permission of the publisher.

Chapter 10 originally appeared in Timo Koistinen and Tommi Lehtonen (eds.), *Philosophical Studies in Religion, Metaphysics, and Ethics* (Helsinki: Luther Agricola Society). Reprinted by permission of the publisher.

Chapter 11 originally appeared in *The Monist* 80, 4 (1997), pp. 576–597. Copyright © *The Monist*, Peru, Illinois 64354. Reprinted by permission.

Chapter 12 is reprinted from "Being and Goodness," by Eleonore Stump and Norman Kretzmann in *Divine and Human Action: Essays in the Metaphysics of Theism*, Thomas V. Morris (ed.). Copyright © 1988 by Cornell University. Used by permission of the publisher, Cornell University Press.

Chapter 13 originally appeared in Norman Kretzmann and Eleonore Stump (eds.), *The Cambridge Companion to Aquinas* (Cambridge and New York: Cambridge University Press, 1993). Reprinted with the permission of Cambridge University Press.

Chapter 14 is reprinted from "Aquinas on the Passions," by Peter King in *Aquinas's Moral Theory: Essays in Honor of Norman Kretzmann* , Scott Macdonald and Eleonore Stump (eds.). Copyright © 1999 by Cornell University. Used by permission of the publisher, Cornell University Press.

Preface

The purpose of this book is twofold. Primarily, it aims to provide teachers and students of Aquinas with a convenient selection of some of the best philosophical essays on him published since *Aquinas: A Collection of Critical Essays*, edited by Anthony Kenny, appeared in 1969. But it is also intended to provide an introduction or guide to Aquinas's thinking in general—one of use to those who know little or nothing about it. For this reason, the essays included range across the main areas of Aquinas's philosophical interests. For this reason also, they come with a substantial introduction to his life and thought, a chronological list of his most significant writings, and a large bibliography.

No collection of essays can fully do justice to the enormous complexity and comprehensiveness of Aquinas's thought. And an enormous number of studies on Aquinas have appeared since the volume edited by Kenny. So selecting the following essays has not been an easy task. In making my selection I have aimed to include material which clearly explains aspects of Aquinas's thinking on all the philosophical topics which chiefly concerned him: logic, metaphysics, natural theology, the relationship between philosophy and theology, anthropology, philosophy of mind and action, ethics, and legal and political philosophy. I have also aimed to include philosophically perspicuous essays which engage with that thinking at a critical level. Most of the material that follows is therefore both expository and evaluative. While intended for a wide audience, it combines historical scholarship with rigorous philosophical discussion and thus should prove useful to professionals as well as to beginners.

For advice in the preparation of this book I am grateful to Gyula Klima, Brian Leftow, Robert Pasnau, Sara Penella, Martin Stone, and Eleonore Stump. For her editorial support, I am indebted to Cynthia Read of Oxford University Press. For her excellent work of copyediting, I am grateful to Pamela Bruton.

Contents

Contributors

BRIAN DAVIES is Professor of Philosophy at Fordham University.

SANDRA EDWARDS is Associate Professor of Philosophy at the University of Arkansas.

CHRISTOPHER HUGHES lectures in philosophy at King's College, London.

ANTHONY KENNY was formerly Master of Balliol College, Oxford, and Warden of Rhodes House, Oxford.

PETER KING is Professor of Philosophy and Adjunct Professor of Classics at the Ohio State University.

GYULA KLIMA is Associate Professor of Philosophy at Fordham University.

NORMAN KRETZMANN, who died in 1998, was Susan Linn Sage Professor of Philosophy at Cornell University.

SCOTT MACDONALD is Professor of Philosophy and the Norman K. Regan Professor in Christian Studies at Cornell University.

HERBERT MCCABE, who died in 2001, lectured in philosophy and theology at Blackfriars, Oxford.

PAUL E. SIGMUND is Professor of Politics at Princeton University.

ELEONORE STUMP is the Robert J. Henle Professor of Philosophy at St. Louis University.

RUDI A. TE VELDE lectures in philosophy at the Department of Theology of the Catholic University, Brabant.

HERMANN WEIDEMANN is Professor of Philosophy at the University of Bonn.

JAMES A. WEISHEIPL, who died in 1984, was Professor of the History of Medieval Science at the Pontifical Institute of Medieval Studies, Toronto.

JOHN F. WIPPEL is Professor of Philosophy at the Catholic University of America.

Thomas Aquinas

Introduction

I

Thomas Aquinas was the greatest European philosopher of the thirteenth century. Many would say that he was the greatest of all medieval thinkers. Yet his appeal and reputation have waxed and waned. In the period immediately following his death he had relatively few admirers willing to promulgate his teachings. And there were many anxious to censure it. In 1277 ideas thought to be his were ecclesiastically condemned in Paris and Oxford. His influence increased following his canonization in 1323. But his thinking never commanded anything like universal agreement in the Middle Ages. And though his impact on Roman Catholic teaching has been strong from the fifteenth century to the present, his work was largely ignored by the best known Western philosophers from the time of Descartes (1596–1650) to the middle of the twentieth century. Descartes himself sometimes mentions Aquinas with respect. But his most famous writings show little serious debt to Aquinas's major emphases. And some notable modern philosophical figures have been positively dismissive of Aquinas. According to Bertrand Russell (1872–1970), for instance: "There is little of the true philosophical spirit in Aquinas. He does not, like the Platonic Socrates, set out to follow wherever the argument may lead . . . Before he begins to philosophize, he already knows the truth; it is declared in the Catholic faith . . . The finding of arguments for a conclusion given in advance is not philosophy, but special pleading."[1]

Russell's opinion of Aquinas is still not uncommon. But it is now fair to say that it is increasingly under attack. For in the last few decades Aquinas has been more and more studied by professional philosophers, many of whom have come to view him as one of the most perceptive thinkers of all time. Hence, for example, a 1990 editorial comment in the journal *Philosophy* asserts that "St. Thomas Aquinas is a genius whose claim to that accolade is barely debatable."[2] Then again, according to Anthony Kenny, one of the most distinguished of contemporary analytical philosophers: "Aquinas is . . . one of the dozen greatest philosophers of the western world . . . His metaphysics, his philosophical theology, his philosophy of mind, and his moral philosophy entitle him to rank with Plato and Aristotle, with Descartes and Leibniz, with Locke and Hume and Kant."[3] Kenny views Aquinas as having something positive and valuable to contribute to contemporary discussions of key philosophical issues. And so do many others. The respect which Aquinas now commonly commands is evident from the large number of publications concerning him which appear almost daily. Translations of Aquinas into English have been increasingly emerging for a number of years. So have articles and many substantial volumes. Russell was a philosophical genius. But it is now widely recognized that Aquinas was as well.[4]

What has brought about this revival of respect? In Roman Catholic circles, a major cause was Pope Leo XIII's encyclical *Aeterni Patris* (1879), which presented Aquinas as an effective antidote to erroneous ideas and methodologies. This encyclical prompted the study of Aquinas in centers of religious education. It also inspired several generations of Catholic scholars to work on Aquinas and to recommend his principles. And its contents were effectively reiterated by the Second Vatican Council and by Pope John Paul II's encyclical *Fides et Ratio* (1998). But why has Aquinas come much more into vogue beyond an explicitly confessional context?

One reason lies in the fact that we are now much more informed about the mind of Aquinas than were people in the early years of the twentieth century. Since the time of *Aeterni Patris* (and especially since the 1920s) an enormous amount of careful critical work has been done on Aquinas's writings. This has allowed them to be properly viewed in their historical context and with attention to what they have to say in detail (as opposed to what it might be thought that they have to say from a reading of a paraphrase or manual abridgment). And this, in turn, has led people increasingly to realize that Aquinas was a complex and subtle thinker, one whose thought developed, one whose thought was decidedly less rigid and simplistic than, for example, some of his eighteenth-, nineteenth-, and early-twentieth-century critics supposed.

Another reason for the renewal of interest in Aquinas lies in the growth of twentieth-century analytical philosophy. Analytical philosophers have always placed a premium on logical rigor and detailed attention to linguistic usage. And concern with such matters is very much a feature of Aquinas's writings (as it is with that of medieval philosophers in general). Analytical philosophy finds natural conversational companions in thinkers such as Aquinas, and many analytical philosophers have come to realize as much. Some of them have also been led to a respect for Aquinas by to the work of Ludwig Wittgenstein (1889–1951). For many twentieth-century philosophers, Wittgenstein brilliantly showed that European philosophy from the time of Descartes was riddled with a large number of confusions and positive errors. Were these confusions and errors absent in earlier writers? Several contemporary thinkers (Kenny is a notable example) have concluded that they were, that they were notably absent in the writings of Aquinas, and that Aquinas is therefore someone with whom it is currently worth engaging.

But is he? The following essays offer answers to this question. They also provide accounts of Aquinas's thinking on topics which greatly preoccupied him. Together with the bibliographical information at the end of this book, readers should find them a helpful place to start when trying to make their own minds up on the significance of Aquinas. Several of the essays expound and consider what Aquinas has to say on matters to do with religious beliefs, such as belief in the existence of God or belief in life after death. But none of them explicitly deals with his discussions of specifically Christian doctrines, such as the doctrine of the Trinity or the doctrine of the Incarnation. That is unfortunate since these doctrines were of major importance to Aquinas and since some of his most interesting philosophical arguments are to be found in places where he turns to them. But Aquinas's writings run to thousands of pages, and space in this volume is limited.

II

What do we know about the life of Aquinas? Our sources for it are texts relating to his canonization process. There are also two early biographies: one by William Tocco, who knew Aquinas personally; the other by Bernard Gui, whose account depends partly on that of Tocco but may also incorporate reliable, independent information. But all of these documents leave us with many unanswered, and probably unanswerable, questions. Hence we find that the three most recent studies of Aquinas's life differ significantly on a number of matters.[5] They do so, for example, even when it comes to the year of Aquinas's birth, which can arguably be placed anywhere from 1224 to 1226.

Aquinas was born at Roccasecca in the (then) Kingdom of Naples. In 1230 or 1231 his family sent him to study at the abbey of Monte Cassino. But conflict between Emperor Frederick II and Pope Gregory IX made the abbey a center of imperial-papal rivalry. So in July 1239 Aquinas started to attend the recently founded university (or *studium generale*) in Naples. Here he began to learn about the writings of the Greek philosopher Aristotle (384–322 B.C.) and the Islamic and Jewish authors Averroes (c. 1126–c. 1198) and Maimonides

(1138–1204).[6] He also encountered the recently founded order of friars known as the Dominicans, which he joined sometime between 1242 and 1244.[7] After a troubled interlude during which his family tried to dissuade him from his Dominican associations, Aquinas studied in Paris, where he transcribed lectures of St. Albert the Great (c. 1198–1280) on Dionysius the Areopagite.[8] He subsequently moved to Cologne, where he continued to work under Albert, where he was probably ordained to the priesthood, and where he may also have completed his commentary on the Book of Isaiah and the short treatise *De principiis naturae*.[9]

Following his time in Cologne, Aquinas returned to Paris (possibly as early as 1251), where he formally began his teaching career. At the outset, he lectured on the Bible and the *Sentences* of Peter Lombard (c. 1095–1160).[10] In 1256 he became a master of theology, which again obliged him to discuss the Bible as well as to preside over a series of theological discussions referred to as "Quaestiones disputatae" (Disputed Questions). During this period of his life Aquinas also began to produce the earliest of the works for which he is best known today: a commentary on Lombard's *Sentences*, the Disputed Questions *De veritate* (*On Truth*), the work known as *De ente et essentia* (*On Being and Essence*), and a commentary on Boethius's *De trinitate* (*On the Trinity*). In addition, he started work on his lengthy *Summa contra Gentiles*.

A *summa* (summary) was an extended treatment of doctrinal matters set out in an orderly and comprehensive manner. It was a standard literary genre for medieval writers (on a variety of topics, not just philosophy and theology) from around the early twelfth century. Discussing the purpose of the *Summa contra Gentiles*, Aquinas says that he aims "by the way of reason to pursue those things about God which human reason is able to investigate."[11] A similar, though perhaps broader, intention can be detected in his *Summa theologiae*, which he began around 1265–68 but which remained unfinished at the time of his death. Commonly deemed to be Aquinas's greatest achievement, the *Summa theologiae* contains three long treatises (or "parts") that cover a very large range of topics including the existence and nature of God, the notion of creation, the nature and abilities of angels, human nature and its powers, the concept of human happiness, the characteristics of human action, the goal of human living, human virtues and vices, the life and work of Christ, and the meaning and significance of the Christian sacraments.[12]

Aquinas's early biographers seem relatively uninterested in sorting out the details of his career from around 1256. But we can safely suppose that he vacated his teaching position at Paris before 1260, that he lived and taught for a time at Orvieto in Italy, that in 1265 he was assigned to establish a Dominican house of studies in Rome, and that by 1269 he was again teaching in Paris. In Orvieto he composed his *Catena aurea* (*Golden Chain*), a commentary on the four Gospels made up of quotations from the church fathers.

He also wrote an edition of a liturgy for the newly created feast of Corpus Christi and a commentary on the Book of Job. In Rome, as well as beginning the *Summa theologiae*, he worked on his Disputed Questions *De potentia* (*On the Power of God*); his theological synthesis known as the *Compendium theologiae* (*Compendium of Theology*); his political treatise, *De regno* (*On Kingship*); and a commentary on Aristotle's *De anima* (*On the Soul*). Having returned to Paris in or around 1268, he continued with the *Summa theologiae*. He also produced the Disputed Questions *De virtutibus* (*On Virtues*), *De aeternitate mundi* (*On the Eternity of the World*, a discussion of the question "Did the world have a beginning?"), and *De unitate intellectus* (*On the Unity of the Intellect*, a critique of Averroes on the nature of mind). He also began commentaries on the Gospels of Matthew and John, and commentaries on Aristotle's *Physics*, *Nicomachean Ethics*, and *Metaphysics*.

In 1272 Aquinas was assigned to establish yet another Dominican study house. He chose to do so in Naples, where he still continued to write and teach—forging on with the *Summa theologiae* (now into its third part) and probably lecturing on St. Paul's Letter to the Romans and the Book of Psalms. In December 1273, however, he abandoned his usual routine and wrote nothing else. He was evidently a sick man, though we do not know what, precisely, ailed him. Late in 1273 he was instructed to attend the Second Council of Lyons, but he became gravely ill en route. He died in the Cistercian Abbey of Fossanova on the 7th of March 1274.

III

Can we quickly summarize the thinking of Aquinas? In the early twentieth century this was often presented in a number of textbooks chiefly designed for seminarians, handbooks suggesting that Aquinas has a quickly reportable system to offer. And it is still not uncommon to find people who contend that Thomism, as his thinking is sometimes called, can be easily articulated in a series of key propositions (something like the articles of the Apostles' Creed). But Aquinas is not easily paraphrased. And given what the word "Thomism" has come to mean in many circles, it is probably fair to say that Aquinas was not a Thomist. Original, brilliant, and much more sophisticated than many of his disciples, he was someone whose writings show an active mind at work, a mind concerned to explore, as well as to look for, definitive answers, a mind also prepared to acknowledge the limits of human reason. It is impossible to guess what he would say in detail on matters about which he wrote were he alive today. But anyone reading him seriously can hardly suppose that he would be anything other than horrified at the suggestion that he was offering something rightly describable as a "system."

With that said, however, it is not impossible to give some indication of arguments and conclusions which surface in the writings of Aquinas. And to start with, it is helpful to note that his readers will never properly get his measure unless they recognize that, as he puts it, "the beginning and end of all things" is God.[13] Aquinas's thinking is first and foremost theistic. This is evident even from such texts as *De principiis naturae* and his commentaries on Aristotle, in which he seems to be primarily concerned with matters that present-day readers can also find discussed in works by authors with no belief in God. In saying so, I do not mean to suggest that Aquinas, as Russell claimed, was nothing but an apologist determined to dream up "reasons" in support of Roman Catholicism. And it should not be assumed that when Aquinas uses the word "God" he takes it to mean the same as do many who say that they believe in God. The point to grasp is that Aquinas had certain views about what he called "God," views which are never too far in the background throughout his writings. He thought, for example, that we can know that it is true to proclaim that God exists. He did not think that we can know what God's existence amounts to. But he thought that "God exists" (*Deus est*), considered as an asserted proposition, is something which can be supported without any reliance on religious authority.

Why so? St. Anselm of Canterbury (1033–1109) and Descartes argued that the existence of God can be proved on the basis of the concept of God. In their view, "God does not exist" is demonstrably self-contradictory because of what "God" means. Others have said that God is a direct object of human experience (as people might be thought to be to each other). But Aquinas takes a different line. He finds no demonstrable contradiction in the proposition "God does not exist." He also claims that "the awareness that God exists is not implanted in us by nature in any specific way."[14] Aquinas's consistently held conclusion is that we can know that God exists only by inference from the world as encountered by means of our senses. In his view, which might be usefully compared with the writings of classical empiricist philosophers such as John Locke (1632–1704) and David Hume (1711–76): "The knowledge that is natural to us has its source in the senses and extends just so far as it can be led by sensible things . . . We arrive at a knowledge of God by way of creatures."[15] Aquinas does not think that those who believe in God's existence are necessarily unreasonable in doing so if they cannot produce sound inferential arguments for their position. Somewhat like Wittgenstein, he holds that there is nothing "to stop someone accepting on faith some truth which that person cannot demonstrate, even if that truth in itself is such that demonstration could make it evident."[16] But, so he holds, an explicit knowledge that God exists can only be arrived at indirectly. To be more precise, his view is that we can know that God exists only by a process of causal reasoning. "Any effect of a cause," he says, demonstrates that that cause exists, in cases where the effect is better known to us, since effects are dependent upon causes, and can only occur if the causes already exist. From effects evident to us, therefore, we can demonstrate what is not evident to us, namely that God exists."[17]

How does Aquinas think that we can do this? In his famous "Five Ways" (ST I, 2,3) he offers a series of much discussed arguments each of which concludes that there is indeed a God. Each of them begins by drawing attention to what Aquinas takes to be some general feature of things known to us on the basis of experience. They then suggest that none of these features can be accounted for in ordinary mundane terms, that we must move to a level of explanation which transcends any with which we are familiar. According to the First Way, the occurrence of change in the universe ultimately implies an unchanged changer who is not part of the universe. According to the Second Way, causal dependency in the universe must ultimately derive from a first cause who is not causally dependent, as, so Aquinas argues in the Third Way, must all things subject to generation and perishing. Elsewhere in the text of the Five Ways, Aquinas maintains that the goodness and perfection in the things of our experience must proceed from what is wholly good and wholly perfect. He also argues that the world provides evidence of intelligent agency bringing it about that certain things act in a regular or goal-directed way. In other words, according to the Five Ways, questions we can raise with respect to what we discover in day-to-day life raise further questions whose answers can only be thought of as lying beyond what we encounter.

Though they effectively introduce and have recourse to it, the Five Ways do not really highlight the heart of Aquinas's philosophy of God, which lies in his claim that everything other than God owes to God its existence and all that is real in it for as long as it exists. According to Aquinas, apart from God there are only creatures. And although creatures *have* being, God, says Aquinas, *is* Being (or "Subsistent Being Itself" [*Ipsum Esse Subsistens*]). Having asked whether *Qui Est* ("The One Who Is") is the most appropriate name for God, Aquinas replies that it is since, among other reasons, "it does not signify any particular form, but rather existence itself (*sed ipsum esse*)." "Since the existence of God is his essence," says Aquinas, "and since this is true of nothing else . . . it is clear that this name is especially appropriate to God."[18] This conclusion of Aquinas has given rise to a huge amount of controversy. Writers in the Thomist tradition have praised it in glowing terms. According, for instance, to Father W. Norris Clarke S.J., "The crown of the entire Thomistic vision of the universe is the notion of God as infinitely perfect pure Plenitude of Existence, ultimate Source and Goal of all other being."[19] According to the great medievalist Étienne Gilson, the notion to which Clarke refers constitutes the true genius and originality of Aquinas and makes him a genuine existentialist.[20] Others, however, have taken a different line. In the view of Anthony Kenny, for instance, Aquinas's teaching about God as *ipsum esse subsistens* can be described as "sophistry and illusion."[21] According to C. J. F. Williams, it is thoroughly undermined by the work of Gottlob Frege (1848–1925).[22]

Which party is right in this dispute? Critics of Aquinas on the topic of God and being commonly suggest that Aquinas takes "being" or "existence" to be the name of a property or attribute with which God is to be identified. But though his language sometimes suggests otherwise, it is not Aquinas's view that being is a property or attribute. Hence, for example, he holds that to say "Socrates exists" (*Socrates est*) is not to attribute a characteristic to Socrates but, rather, to say what Socrates is essentially (a human being, as Aquinas would argue). "No entity without identity," observed W. V. Quine (1908–2000). Or, as Aquinas puts it, existence is given by form (*forma est essendi principium*).[23] Aristotle held that there is no such class of things as things which simply *are*. Aquinas's view is that there is nothing we can intelligibly characterize simply by saying that it is. And, so he holds, to say that something like Socrates has being (*esse*) is to register the fact that "Socrates" is a genuine person and not the name of a fictional character. We can, he thinks, certainly speak of Socrates as having being (*esse*). But to do so, he argues, is not to note what Socrates is like (as we would if we said something like "Socrates has pneumonia"). Rather, it is to register the fact that we can make true statements about a human being called "Socrates." For Aquinas, Socrates *has being* if we can truly say things like "Socrates is a man," "Socrates is snub nosed," "Socrates is a clever thinker," and so on (as we cannot say, for example, with respect to Oliver Twist). As Herbert McCabe puts it, in Aquinas's view: "It is not simply in our capacity to use signs, our ability, for example, to understand words, but in our actual use of them to say what is the case that we have need of and lay hold of the *esse* of things. It is only by analogy that we can speak of the 'concept' of *esse*; we do not have a concept of existence as we have a concept of greenness or prevarication or polar bears."[24]

In that case, however, what does Aquinas mean when speaking of God as the cause of the being (*esse*) of things and of God as *Ipsum Esse Subsistens*? Perhaps the best way to come to understand him is to recognize that, for him, it makes sense to ask, "Why is there anything at all?" or "Why is there something rather than nothing?" Confronted by things, we naturally ask causal questions. Confronted by Fred, we might naturally ask who his parents were. Confronted by a species of animal, we might naturally ask how this came about. According to Aquinas, however, such inquiries should lead us to a deeper level of questioning. For he thinks it proper to ask, not "What in the world produced this?" but "What produced everything?" At the end of his *Tractatus Logico-Philosophicus*, Wittgenstein remarks: "Not *how* the world is, is the mystical, but *that* it is."[25] For Wittgenstein, *how the world is* is a scientific matter with scientific answers. But, he insists, even when the scientific answers are in, we are still left with the *thatness* of the world, the fact *that* it is. As Wittgenstein himself puts it: "We feel that even if *all possible* scientific questions be answered, the problems of life have still not been touched at all."[26] And Aquinas is of the same mind even though his understanding of the world in not that of Wittgenstein's *Tratatus*. We can, Aquinas thinks, explore the world and develop a *scientific* account of what things in it are and how they came to be there. But he also thinks that we are then left with a decidedly *nonscientific* question. His view is that, as well as asking, "What *in the world or universe* accounts for this, that, or the other?" we can also ask, "How come *any* world or universe at all?" or "How come the whole familiar (scientific or day to day) business of asking and answering 'How come?'?"

It is here that Aquinas thinks in terms of God as the source of the being of things (the Creator) and as *Ipsum Esse Subsistens*. For him, the question "How come any universe?" is a serious causal one to which there must be an answer. And he gives the name "God" to whatever the answer is (since those who believed in God of whom he was aware [orthodox Jews, Muslims, and Christians] took God to be the cause of the existence of the universe [the Creator]). Since Aquinas thinks that God makes the universe to be, he reasons that God can be nothing in it and therefore nothing definable and characterizable as things within it are. If God is the Creator, Aquinas reasons in his Commentary on Aristotle's *Peri Hermeneias*, then God must be "outside the realm of existents, as a cause from which pours forth everything that exists in all its variant forms" (*extra ordinem entium existens, velut causa quaedam profundens totum ens et omnes eius differentias*).[27]

In other words, Aquinas thinks that it makes sense to deny that God, like a creature, *has* being. Rather, so he suggests, we might speak of God as Being Itself. His meaning is not that God is an is-ing kind of thing. His point is essentially a negative one. Since the claim that God is *Ipsum Esse Subsistens* seems to be telling us what God is, one might expect Aquinas to defend it in an account of God's properties or attributes. But that is not what he does. We cannot, he argues, know what God is. We must content ourselves with considering "the ways in which God does not exist, rather than the ways in which he does."[28] And it is here that his talk of God as *Ipsum Esse Subsistens* comes in. It is part of an account of ways in which God does not exist. Its chief purpose is to deny that God is a creature. As some authors would say, it is an exercise in negative theology.

IV

Aquinas's approach to the question of God's nature often seems to be anything but negative. He argues that God is, for instance, good, omnipotent, omniscient, and eternal.[29] Yet his readers should be warned to watch for the extent to which his writings show him to be someone who believed that God defies our conceptual equipment and is therefore seriously unknowable to living human beings such as you and me. On the other hand, however, Aquinas had little doubt that creatures such as you and I are objects which philosophers might well try to get their minds around to good effect. At one level, he took people to be almost as mysterious as God since he thought of them as created for a goal which exceeds our understanding. At another level, however, he thought of them as identifiable objects to be studied and reflected upon. So he had positive views about what it is to be human, views which he expressed with no special appeal to the teachings of theologians or to any other religious authority.

He thought, for example, that people are essentially physical animals who also have a nonphysical side to them. According to authors such as Plato (c. 428–c. 348 B.C.) and Descartes, people are very much not this: they are essentially nonmaterial intellectual things which are contingently linked, yoked, or attached to what is bodily. And in the philosophy of many contemporaries, they are nothing but material objects in motion. For Aquinas, however, people are something in between: neither wholly immaterial nor purely material. According to him, they are physical things which also function at a nonphysical level. Or, as he often observes, they are creatures with a certain kind of *soul*. Following Aristotle, Aquinas takes it that anything alive has a soul (or is *animate* as opposed to *inanimate*). "Inquiry into the nature of the soul," he says, "presupposes an understanding of the soul as the root principle of life in living things within our experience."[30] But what kind of soul does Aquinas take the human creature to have? What, in his view, is present in the kind of life had by people?

To begin with, he argues, people are things with a bodily life. In particular, he stresses, they are sensing things. Like dogs and cats, they can interpret the world by sight, taste, smell, and so on. According to Aquinas, however, people are also things which can know or understand. And it is this fact, he thinks, which renders them more than simply physical. For he takes sensation and understanding to be radically and significantly different. According to Aquinas, sensations are particular physical occurrences going on in particular physical organisms. And for this reason he takes them to be what we might call the ultimate in private property. He does not, of course, deny that two people can share a sensation in that, for instance, you and I can both feel heat when sitting before a fire. But, so he thinks, the occurrence of the sensation of heat in me is different from its occurrence in you—just as my breathing is *my* breathing and not *your* breathing. Aquinas views sensations as local or confined, as, so to speak, "trapped" in the bodies of those who have them. Echoing Aristotle, however, he also maintains that people enjoy more than sensations. For, on his account, people can have knowledge, which he takes to be universal and unconfined—the ultimate in public property. And it is as knowers, Aquinas thinks, that people are more than merely bodies in motion. For, he holds, though I cannot have your very own sensations, I can have the very same thoughts as you, from which it follows, he concludes, that knowing is not a physical process since physical processes are events which occur in and to different individuals.

One way of putting all this is to say that meanings, for Aquinas (as for Wittgenstein), can never be particular physical objects. His view of understanding is that it should never be confused with encountering a thing at the sensory level and should never be identified with any individual physical process. Aquinas thinks that we cannot understand material individuals. We can confront them at a sensory level, but that, he argues, is different from understanding them. On his acount, understanding is expressible in judgments or statements, and it can be shared by human beings (though not with other animals) in a way that sensations cannot. And, so Aquinas argues, since statements can be either true or false, knowledge or understanding can lead people to recognize alternatives. To understand a statement, Aquinas thinks, is also to understand its negation. It is to be able to view the world as containing possibilities, as conceivably being other than it is in fact now. And, for this reason, Aquinas also holds that with the ability to understand comes the ability to *act* and not simply to *react*. Why? Because, he thinks, action involves more than being affected by external stimuli and responding accordingly. It depends on understanding how things are and how they could be. And it consists in seeking that they should be one way as opposed to some other way.

According to Aquinas, nonhuman animals can also be said to seek. For he thinks that they have tendencies to behave in accordance with their natures, that they have "appetites."[31] We speak of water naturally "seeking" its own level, and Aquinas, in a similar way, speaks of animals "seeking" to be what they naturally are and to have what they naturally need. Left to themselves, he thinks, they just are what they are by nature. They may be interfered with and may, therefore, become thwarted or defective. And how they behave in particular circumstances may be impossible for us to predict with a high degree of accuracy. According to Aquinas, however, in the absence of interference, they simply realize their natures. They "seek" to be themselves. But not, Aquinas holds, in a conscious sense. Their seeking is not based on knowing how things might be and moving accordingly. It is not a matter of planning that a possibly attainable end should come to pass. It is a combination of instinct affected by circumstances. It is a product of complex and given structures. It is lived out rather than chosen. And, so Aquinas thinks, it therefore falls short of action—or, at any rate, of what he takes to be genuine human action. For, in his view, action is irreducibly and consciously end directed, and it depends on understanding since it is only by understanding the world that we can consciously seek to affect it. Aquinas does not want to say that we cannot act unless we have a complete understanding of the world and of how things are within it. Indeed, he thinks, we often act in ignorance. But he also holds that we cannot truly act without some conception of how things are and of how they might be. And it is thus that he views human action as end or goal directed (i.e., intentional). In Aquinas's view, human action differs from the behavior of nonhuman animals since it is done for reasons. It always invites the question "With a view to what are you doing that?"

V

For Aquinas, then, acting persons intend (aim at) what attracts them. But what is going on as they act in specific circumstances? Aquinas's answer is that they live out or engage in examples of what he calls "practical reasoning." On his account, human action is always a reasonable business since it always involves seeking what one takes (even if mistakenly) to be somehow desirable. And, in this sense, he conceives of it as always conforming to a certain pattern of reasonableness comparable to what is involved when we reason not about what to do (practical reasoning) but about what is the case (theoretical reasoning). We may, Aquinas thinks, reason to the *truth* of some matter. We might work out how things *are*. But we can also, he says, reason as to *what is to be done*. We might work out *how to behave*. And this, he thinks, is what we are doing as we settle down to action in practice.

On Aquinas's account, essential to human action is what he calls "choice" or "decision" (*electio*). Or, to put it another way, Aquinas takes human action as a *doing in the light of alternatives*.[32] In saying so, however, he does not mean that action is something which *follows* choice or decision—as if acting people *first* make choices or decisions and *then* act on them. For Aquinas, actual human actions are human choices or decisions, and to describe them is to state how we have chosen or decided (what our choices or decisions have amounted to). Yet Aquinas does not think that our actions come out of the blue, as it were. According to him, particular choices or decisions reflect the way in which people think. They also reflect the character of the people in question. Or, as Aquinas puts it, choice (*electio*) springs from *deliberation* (*consilium*), and both choice and deliberation arise from *dispositions* of various kinds.

When he refers to deliberation (*consilium*), Aquinas has in mind a reasoning process having to do with how to obtain what we want. Action, he thinks, starts with desire for something one finds attractive (something one takes to be good). But how is that something to be achieved? Here, he says, reason comes in as suggesting the recipe for success. Before choosing what to do (before actually acting), we may have to consider how best to get what we are looking for at the outset.[33] We may be clear as to what we want to achieve. But we might have to think about how to achieve it. Or, as Aquinas puts it:

> The field of practice is attended with much uncertainty, for our acts are engaged with contingent individual cases, which offer no fixed and certain points because they are so variable. The reason does not pronounce a verdict in matters doubtful and open to question without having conducted an investigation. Such an inquiry is necessary before coming to a decision on what is to be chosen; it is called deliberation.[34]

The end to be achieved is not, one should notice, the business of what Aquinas means by deliberation. He does not conceive of this as helping us to determine what we want or should want. In his view, we deliberate in the light of desire. We do not desire in the light of deliberation. For Aquinas, deliberation presupposes goals, ends, or intentions.[35] But not all courses of action lead to the same goal. And some courses of action can be better at getting us what we want than others. According to Aquinas, therefore, deliberation has to do with means. It is a way of helping our will to have its full rein. It is rational reflection on how to obtain what we want.[36]

Yet what about our wants? How does Aquinas see these as entering into the occurrence of genuine human actions? This is where the notion of dispositions comes in. For, to put it as simply as possible, Aquinas views the wants reflected in particular human actions as deriving from what we are (or from what we have become), considered not just as doing this or that but as being people *of a certain kind*—people who find it desirable to act in certain ways, people with particular tastes, likes, and dislikes. His conclusion is that concrete actions reflect our characters or settled personalities. He thinks that there are patterns of action to which we tend as individuals, and that our tendencies can be affected or influenced by our past and by choices we make. We do not act in a historical vacuum. We act on the basis of dispositions.

What I am calling a "disposition" Aquinas calls a *habitus*,[37] and though *habitus* can be translated "habit," it is better rendered by "disposition."[38] That is because Aquinas's *habitus* is not a "habit" in the modern sense. When we speak today of people having a habit, we normally imply that they would find it hard *not* to act in certain ways. So, we speak of someone having the habit of smoking. A habit, for us, is a kind of addiction. For Aquinas, however, a *habitus* puts one's activity more under one's control than it might otherwise be. In this sense, to have a *habitus* is to be *disposed to* some activity or other—not because one tends to that activity on every possible occasion, but because one finds it natural, readily coped with, an obvious activity to engage in, and so on. In Aquinas's thinking, to be fluent in a foreign language would be to have a *habitus*. Someone who possesses it may refrain from displaying it for one reason or another. But when speaking the language, such a person will do so easily and with a proficiency which many lack entirely. Or, again, people who are naturally or instinctively generous would, for Aquinas, have a *habitus*. They would be generous without effort. There would be little or no question of "going against the grain." As Anthony Kenny explains, a *habitus* for Aquinas is "half-way between a capacity and an action, between pure potentiality and full actuality."[39] Suppose you say that you can speak French. Your statement could be true even though you are not speaking French. But it will not be true just because it is possible for you to speak French in some abstract sense. "I can speak French" does not entail that I am speaking French at the time the statement is made. On the other hand, however, it entails more than the suggestion that it is logically possible for me to speak French. It entails that I have a genuine ability which not everyone has. In this sense, "I can speak French" ascribes to me an ability or skill which endures over time and can, as things are, be exercised in actual definite bits of behavior. In the thinking of Aquinas, it ascribes to me a *habitus* or disposition.

We may put it by saying that, in Aquinas's view, people can acquire settled ways of acting. And, for him, this means that they can acquire a settled range of aims, tastes, or wants which play a vital role when it comes to concrete decisions. For, he holds, these express our wants—even insofar as they spring from deliberation. In choosing, so he thinks, we aim for what attracts us and we ignore or avoid what does not. And we pay attention to what attracts us even as we consider how to obtain what we want—since how we choose to achieve our purposes depends on what we are prepared to take seriously and on what we are prepared to disregard.[40] Or, as Aquinas frequently explains, human actions reflect the virtues and vices of people. For, on his account, virtues and vices are dispositions to act in certain ways—the difference between them being that virtues help us to act well as human beings while vices help us to act badly.[41] Hence, for example, with an eye on what he calls the virtue of temperateness (the disposition to act so as not to be overcome by certain, mostly physical, desires), Aquinas writes:

Since sinful and virtuous acts are done by choice, and choice is the desire for something about which one has deliberated beforehand, and deliberation is an inquiry, there needs to be a quasi-syllogistic deduction regarding every virtuous or sinful act. And yet a temperate person syllogizes in one way, an intemperate person in another way, and a continent person in one way, an incontinent person in another way. For only the judgment of reason moves the temperate person. And so the temperate person employs a syllogism with three propositions and deduces like this: no fornication should be committed; this act would be fornication; therefore, I should not do it. And the intemperate person completely follows his desires, and so even such a person employs a syllogism with three propositions and quasi-deduces like this: everything pleasurable should be enjoyed; this act would be pleasurable; therefore, I should do it. But both the continent person and the incontinent person are moved in two ways: indeed by reason to avoid sin, and by concupiscence to commit it. And the judgment of reason prevails in the case of the continent person, while the movement of concupiscence prevails in the case of the incontinent person. And so both employ a syllogism with four propositions but reach contrary conclusions. For the continent person syllogizes as follows. No sin should be committed. And although the judgment of reason proposes this, the movement of concupiscence causes the person to reflect that everything pleasurable should be pursued. But because the judgment of reason prevails in the person, the person subsumes under the first proposition and draws a conclusion as follows: no sin should be committed; this is a sin; therefore, this should not be done. And the incontinent person, in whom the movement of concupiscence prevails, subsumes under the second proposition and draws a conclusion as follows: everything pleasurable should be pursued; this is pleasurable; therefore, this should be pursued. And properly speaking, such a person is one who sins out of weakness. And so it is evident that such a person, although knowing regarding the universal, nonetheless does not know regarding the particular, since the person subsumes according to concupiscence and not according to reason.[42]

Aquinas is not here asserting that people go through a complicated piece of reasoning every time they decide to act. His point is that the intellectual structure of decisions (their "logic" if you like) can be exhibited in a rational form. And, in making the point, he is anxious to stress that the ways in which we act can be profoundly affected by the characters we have developed—whether virtuous or vicious.[43]

VI

In that case, however, what becomes of human freedom? If, as Aquinas thinks, our behavior can be strongly affected by our character, can we ever really choose to act as we do? Or are we the victims of something beyond our control? Writers on Aquinas sometimes say that his answer to these questions is that people can choose to act as they do, and that people are not always the victims of what is beyond their control, since people have *free will*. But that is not quite right. What Aquinas believes in is not "free will" but "free choice."

When Aquinas attributes freedom to people, he frequently says that they have what he calls *liberum arbitrium*. Though translators of Aquinas often render this phrase by the English expression "free will," its significance is different.[44] Why? Because the thesis that people have free will is commonly taken to mean that freedom is something which belongs *only* to the will, that it is, if you like, the prerogative of will or a peculiar property of it. And Aquinas does not share this assumption. For, as we have seen, he believes that will and understanding are intimately commingled when it comes to human action. On his account, intellect and will are at no point separated in the exercise of practical reason. There is no act of practical intelligence which is not also one of will, and vice versa.

Yet Aquinas is prepared to ask whether or not the choices people make on the basis of what they think and are attracted to can be genuinely attributed to *them* and are not, in fact, the action of something else working in them in a way which renders them nonresponsible for what they do. And this is the question he has in mind when, for example, he asks in the *De malo* (*On Evil*), "Do human beings have free choice in their acts or do they choose necessarily?" and when he asks, in other works, "Do people have *liberum arbitrium?*"[45]

The operative word in the question "Do human beings have free choice in their acts or do they choose necessarily?" is "necessarily." In this context, it means something like "inevitably" or "unavoidably." If you pour acid on a human hand, the skin will immediately corrode. And it will do so inevitably, unavoidably, or, as we might say, necessarily. If you drop a ton weight on a mouse, the mouse will swiftly become an ex-mouse. And it will do so inevitably, unavoidably, or, as we might say, necessarily. But what about the actions of people? Are these what they are inevitably, unavoidably, or necessarily? Is everything we do to be thought of as coming to pass as skin reacts to acid and as mice get squashed by weights? Aquinas's answer is "No." But why?

To begin with, he has theological reasons. For, as he says in various places, Scripture teaches that people have freedom. In the Book of Ecclesiastes, we read: "God from the beginning constituted and left human beings in the hands of their own deliberation." Aquinas takes this passage as ascribing to people the freedom to decide.[46] He thinks that if people lacked such freedom, there could be nothing we could recognize as moral philosophy. Just as various natural sciences rest on the assumption that things undergo change, so, in Aquinas's view, thinking about morality rests on the assumption that people act with freedom. Or, as he puts it in the *Summa theologiae*: "Man is free to make decisions. Otherwise, counsels, precepts, prohibitions, rewards, and punishment would all be pointless."[47] If you believe that there is no change, then you cannot consistently be a physicist or a research chemist. By the same token, Aquinas suggests, you cannot seriously engage in ethical thinking if you deny the reality of human freedom.

But Aquinas's most developed defense of human freedom is neither biblical nor *ad hominem*. It springs from his conviction that human actions are done for reasons and that they cannot therefore be assimilated to processes which come about inevitably, unavoidably, or necessarily. Why not? Because, he says, it belongs to the very nature of reason to deliberate with an eye on alternatives. Some of the changes which things undergo happen, Aquinas thinks, because things are doing what they cannot avoid doing in the circumstances. But, he insists, this is not the case when people act for reasons. Why not? Basically, so he argues, because acting for reasons means thinking, and because reasons for action can never compel assent.

Here, once again, it is important to note how, in Aquinas's view, human animals differ from nonhuman ones. In fact, he thinks that they have a great deal in common, for he takes both to be living things with the ability to undergo sensations. He also takes both to have various inbuilt desires, tendencies, or instincts which greatly affect their behavior. According to Aquinas, however, people can understand how things are and respond (rather than merely react) to them on this basis. They do not just behave. They can describe what is around them, and they can behave as they do for reasons which are different from what might be mentioned when accounting for the behavior of nonhuman animals. One might well speak of the reason why the cat chased the mouse. But "reason" here has nothing to do with framed intentions. There may be reasons why the cat chased the mouse. But they are not the cat's reasons. In Aquinas's opinion, however, human action is precisely a matter of things acting with reasons of their own. He also thinks that with the ability to act with reasons of one's own comes an understanding of the world under many different descriptions. As Aquinas sees it, the ability to understand the world under many different descriptions is why people have the ability to act with reasons of their own.

It might help here if we focus on the notion of interpreting the world. In Aquinas's view, this is something which both human and nonhuman animals do. For both of them have senses in terms of which the world becomes significant for them. According to Aquinas, however, people can interpret the world not just as *sensed* but also as *understood*. So they can speak about it. They can, for instance, not just *feel* wetness. They can *talk* about it raining. And they can ask what rain is and why it is raining now though it was not raining yesterday. On Aquinas's account, people can interpret the world by *describing* it. And, he thinks, this opens out for them possibilities of interpretation which are just not available to nonhuman animals. As Aquinas sees it, to be aware of things not just in terms of their sensible appearance but also under a description is also to be aware of things under an *indefinite* number of descriptions.

Suppose that I and a mouse smell a piece of cheese. On Aquinas's account, the cheese is significant for the mouse and, all things being equal, it will be drawn to it. According to Aquinas, however, I can perceive the cheese as more than something that is to be eaten without thinking. I can see it as somebody else's cheese or as bad for me if I want to lose weight or as what I promised to give up for Lent or as more expensive than I can decently afford, and so on. Aquinas reasons that my ability to think of the cheese in these ways is the root of my human freedom. For, he argues, there is a big difference between how we might think of something like a piece of cheese and how we inevitably think about certain other matters.

Consider the way in which we think when reasoning as follows:

If all human beings are mortal
and all Australians are human beings,
then all Australians are mortal.

Here we cannot but accept the conclusion given the premises supplied. And no additional information can leave us with any alternative but to accept it. We accept the conclusion of necessity.

But now consider this argument:

I want to get to Paris.
If I catch this flight, it will get me to Paris.
so I should catch this flight.

Might additional information leave me unable but to conclude that I should catch the flight? Well hardly. What about "If I catch this flight, I shall be boarding an airplane with terrorists on it"? If I consider the flight under that description, then I will not conclude that I should catch it. Aquinas thinks that, when reflecting on the world, we can always view it under different descriptions. So he also thinks that we can engage with it, not because we are forced to think about it in only one way, but because we are able to think about it in different ways. And we can act accordingly. Or, as Anthony Kenny helpfully explains:

> If the will is a rational appetite, an ability to have reasons for acting and to act for reasons, then the nature of the will must depend on the nature of practical reasoning. In practical reasoning the relationship between premises and conclusion is not as tight or as easy to regiment as that between premises and conclusion in theoretical reasoning. When we look at a piece of practical reasoning—reasoning about what to do—we often appear to find, where the analogy of theoretical reasoning would lead us to expect necessitation, merely contingent and defeasible connections between one step and another. Aquinas believed that the peculiar contingency of practical reasoning was an essential feature of the human will as we know it . . . He states this contingency as being the fundamental ground of human freedom.[48]

For Aquinas, people have freedom of choice since, unlike nonhuman animals, they can interpret the world in different ways (under different descriptions) and act in the light of the ways in which they interpret it. In this sense, he thinks, their actions are governed by reasons which are fully their own.[49] As we have seen, his view is that we are drawn to what we take to be good. But, so he also thinks, we are not compelled to act in any particular way simply because of our tastes. On his account, we aim for what we want in a world in which we (as thinkers) can recognize different things as likely to satisfy us in different ways. And on this basis we deliberate with an eye on means and ends. And, so he concludes, we cannot but agree that the choices we make are not necessary in the way that the scorching of skin is a necessary consequence of acid being poured on it or that the eating of a piece of cheese might be inevitable for a mouse. Our choices, he thinks, are actions which flow from what we, as individuals, are. They reflect our desires and our view of things.[50] And they might have been otherwise. In place of a particular repertoire of particular instincts, people, Aquinas thinks, have a general capacity to reason. And since particular matters like what to do in this or that situation are not subject to conclusive argument, people, he reasons, are not determined to any one course.

Yet Aquinas does not think that our actions come about as wholly uncaused. Some philosophers have argued that people can be free only if their actions have absolutely no cause outside themselves. But this is not Aquinas's view. For, he argues, though people can act freely, it must still be the case that their actions are caused by God. Aquinas finds it unthinkable that any created event, including whatever we take to be there when human choosing occurs, should come to pass without God making it to be.

Why? Because of what we have already seen him teaching about God as the creator of things. For him, God is the cause of the existence of everything, the reason there is something rather than nothing, the source of *esse*. And since Aquinas takes human free actions to be perfectly real, he concludes that they must, like anything else, be caused to exist by God. Or, as he writes in the *De potentia* (*On the Power of God*): "We must unequivocally concede that God is at work in all activity, whether of nature or of will." According to Aquinas, God "causes everything's activity inasmuch as he gives the power to act, maintains it in existence, applies it to its activity, and inasmuch as it is by his power that every other power acts."[51]

One may, of course, say that if my actions are ultimately caused by God, then I do not act freely at all. Aquinas, however, would reply that my actions are free if nothing in the world is acting on me so as to make me perform them, not if God is not acting in me. His position is that "to be free means not to be under the influence of some other *creature*, it is to be independent of other *bits of the universe*; it is not and could not mean to be independent of God."[52] For him, God does not interfere with created free agents by pushing them into action in a way that infringes their freedom. He does not act *on* them (as Aquinas thinks created things do when they cause others to act as determined by them). He makes them to be what they are—freely acting agents. And, with these points in mind, Aquinas argues that human freedom is not something to be thought of as threatened by God's causality. On the contrary: his position is that we are free, not *in spite of* God, but *because of* God.[53] Or, as he writes in his commentary on Aristotle's *Peri Hermeneias*:

God's will is to be thought of as existing outside the realm of existents, as a cause from which pours forth everything that exists in all its variant forms. Now *what can be* and *what must be* are variants of being, so that it is from God's will itself that things derive whether they must be or may or may not be and the distinction of the two according to the nature of their immediate causes. For he prepares causes that must cause for those effects that he wills must be, and causes that might cause but might fail to cause for some effects that he wills might or might not be. And it is because of the nature of their causes that some effects are said to be effects that must be and others effects that need not be, although all depend on God's will as primary cause, a cause which transcends this distinction between *must* and *might not*. But the same cannot be said of human will or of any other cause, since every other cause exists within the realm of *must* and *might not*. So of every other cause it must be said either that it can fail to cause, or that its effect must be and cannot not be; God's will however cannot fail, and yet not all his effects must be, but some can be or not be.[54]

In terms of this account, God is not to be thought of as an external agent able to interfere with human freedom by acting on it coercively from outside. God is to be thought of as the cause of all that is real, as both free created agents and nonfree created agents exist and operate. Or, as Aquinas writes in the *Summa theologiae*:

Free decision spells self-determination because man by his free decision moves himself into action. Freedom does not require that a thing is its own first cause, just as in order to be the cause of something else a thing does not have to be its first cause. God is the first cause on which both natural and free agents depend. And just as his initiative does not prevent natural causes from being natural, so it does not prevent voluntary action from being voluntary but rather makes it be precisely this. For God works in each according to its nature.[55]

Commenting on this passage, Anthony Kenny describes it as teaching that "self-determination is . . . compatible with divine determination," so that Aquinas "appears to believe that freedom is compatible with some sorts of determinism."[56] But this is a very misleading way of representing Aquinas since he strongly denies that God should be understood as what would normally be thought to be a determining agent. Normally, such an agent is taken to be something in the world which acts on something else so as to render the second thing's behavior or processes inevitable. According to Aquinas, however, God does not act *on* things. He makes things *to be* (from nothing). When seeking to understand what Aquinas says about God and human freedom, one must, as so often when reading Aquinas, keep firmly in mind how strongly he wishes to distinguish between God, the Creator, and creatures.

VII

For Aquinas, then, right reflection on human agency turns out to have a theological dimension. And the same, he thinks, goes for right reflection on other matters. In that case, however, how is Aquinas to be characterized as an author? Is he primarily a theologian? Is he a philosopher who sometimes incorporated theological teachings into his writings? Is he some kind of hybrid philosopher-theologian? A number of Aquinas's readers have taken these questions very seriously. And the result has been a range of often conflicting portraits. According to some people, Aquinas is a theologian through and through. He is definitely not a philosopher. We have already noted Bertrand Russell's presentation of this conclusion, but it has also been echoed by people in sympathy with Aquinas, as Russell was not. For example, according to Mark Jordan, Aquinas "chose not to write philosophy."[57] For others, however, Aquinas is very much a philosopher and ought, indeed, to be thought of as one of the greatest. We have already seen Anthony Kenny suggesting as much. And he has recently found support from Norman Kretzmann. Focusing on the *Summa contra Gentiles*, Kretzmann finds Aquinas to be someone willing to approach theological topics "from the bottom up," that is, with serious regard to austerely philosophical questions and arguments.[58] For Kretzmann, the *Summa contra Gentiles* might be aptly named the *Summa philosophica*.

What should be said with reference to this debate? To begin with, it should be firmly stressed that it would be utterly wrong to hold that Aquinas was no theologian. After all, he functioned as a master of theology. And theological concerns are paramount in many of his writings. This is evidently true when it comes to his biblical commentaries. But it is also true in the case of other works. For example, the first topic raised in the *Summa theologiae* is what Aquinas calls *sacred teaching*. And he clearly wishes to stress both that this is his chief concern in the discussions which follow and that it comprises the revealed content of Christian faith, understood as truth which cannot be arrived at by merely philosophical argument. One sometimes encounters the idea that Christian doctrine is rational in the sense that it is grounded on philosophical demonstrations which any thinking person ought to accept. But this is not Aquinas's view. He thinks that rational arguments in defense of Christian doctrine cannot claim to be probative. Christian doctrine has to be taught by God.[59] Hence the need for sacred *teaching*.[60]

Another fact to be reckoned with in this connection is that Aquinas's first teaching job was that of *baccalaureus biblicus*, a position which required him to study and expound the Bible. The same demand was laid upon him when he became *magister in sacra pagina*. For Aquinas, as for the other professors at Paris in his day, the Bible was the word of God and, therefore, something in the light of which other teaching was to be judged.[61] And he thought that it is here that *sacra doctrina* is to be found. For him, *sacra doctrina* and *sacra scriptura* can be used interchangeably.[62] In his view, access to revelation is given in the words of canonical Scripture, and especially in the teaching of Christ contained there. Christ, he says, is "the first and chief teacher of the faith" (*fidei primus et principalis Doctor*) and, being God, knows divine truth without benefit of revelation. With him come the prophets and apostles (including the evangelists). And from all of them, and from nothing else, comes the matter of revelation. *Sacra doctrina* (the chief concern of the *Summa theologiae*) is, for Aquinas, the content of Scripture. It is also the content of the Christian creeds since, in his view, these basically amount to a restatement of what is in Scripture—a pocket Bible, so to speak. The Old and New Testaments need to be studied with care, Aquinas argues, since "the truth of faith is contained in Holy Writ diffusely, under various modes of expression, and sometimes obscurely, so that, in order to gather the truth of faith from Holy Writ, one needs long study and practice."[63] The creeds are needed to make the truth of faith quickly accessible to everyone. But they add nothing to what is already contained in Scripture. They merely summarize or highlight with a view to the needs of those who hear them.[64] Teachings such as this clearly mark Aquinas out as a theologian. And the case for calling him such becomes stronger when we note the ease with which Aquinas can move from what we might call philosophical positions to others which evidently go beyond them.

Take, for instance, the way in which his account and evaluation of human behavior proceed. As we have seen, according to Aquinas, one can give a sensible account of how people come to act as they do with no particular theological commitment. He also thinks that, even from a nontheological perspective, one can give some account of the difference between acting well and acting badly—the difference between succeeding as a human being (being a good human being) and failing as such (being a bad human being). Or, as we may put it, he thinks that it is possible to offer a sound philosophical account of human action. He also thinks it possible to give good philosophical reasons for acting in some ways rather than in others. So he can say that though "there is a true bliss located after this life," it is also true that "a certain imitation of bliss is possible in this life if human beings perfect themselves in the goods firstly of contemplative and secondly of practical reason" and that "this is the happiness Aristotle discusses in his *Ethics* without either advocating or rejecting another bliss after this life."[65] Yet, Aquinas takes God to be the ultimate (even if unrecognized) object of human desire. His approach to human conduct is infected by this conviction. For it leads him to see human actions as having more than what we might call a merely human significance. It leads him to see them as significant before God and as affecting our standing as God's creatures.

More precisely, it leads him to see human actions as being in or out of tune with what he calls "Eternal Law." According to Aquinas, "Law is nothing but a dictate of practical reason issued by a sovereign who governs a complete community."[66] He adds, "The whole community of the universe is governed by God's mind."[67] "Through his wisdom," says Aquinas, "God is the founder of the universe of things, and . . . in relation to them he is like an artist with regard to the things he makes. . . . And so, as being the principle through which the universe is created, divine wisdom means art, or exemplar, or idea, and likewise it also means law, as moving all things to their due ends. Accordingly the Eternal Law is nothing other than the exemplar of divine wisdom as directing the motions and actions of everything."[68]

In Aquinas's view, God and the Eternal Law are one and the same reality.[69] On his account, therefore, human actions must ultimately be viewed as conforming, or as failing to conform, with the goodness that God is essentially. On Aquinas's account, God, who is perfectly good, is the standard by which creatures can be thought of as good or as failing to be good. So, when people succeed or fail in goodness, they succeed or fail with respect to God. Insofar as they succeed, then, Aquinas thinks, they reflect the goodness that is God. Insofar as they fail, they stray from this goodness. Or, as Aquinas says, they sin. Drawing on St. Augustine of Hippo, he defines sin as "nothing else than to neglect eternal things, and to seek after temporal things." All human wickedness, he adds, "consists in making means of ends and ends of means."[70]

In other words, Aquinas takes bad human actions to be actions the nature of which can only be properly grasped if we see them as leaving us short of what God is all about. As he says in the *Summa theologiae*:

A human act is human because it is voluntary. . . . A human act is evil because it does not meet the standard for human behavior. Standards are nothing other than rules. The human will is subject to a twofold rule: one is proximate and on his own level, that is, human reason; the other is the first rule beyond man's own level, that is, the eternal law which is the mind of God.[71]

On this account, there is no conflict between rational human action and action which conforms to the goodness that is God. But the former is seen as an instance of the latter—the idea being that sound moral philosophy is, in the end, also sound from the viewpoint of theology.

In fact, Aquinas never called himself a philosopher. In his writings, "philosophers" always fall short of the true and proper "wisdom" to be found in the Christian revelation. Be that as it may, there is also a case for calling him a philosopher, as long as we bear in mind points such as those noted above. Though his chief preoccupations were manifestly theological, Aquinas frequently turns to them in ways that are philosophical in a fairly straightforward sense. If a philosopher is someone whose literary output is the work of one who is not, first and foremost, a Christian believer, and if a philosopher writes with only little or no religious commitment, then Aquinas is certainly not a philosopher. But one might also think of philosophers as people prepared to try to think clearly while not invoking religious doctrines as premises in arguments. And on that understanding, Aquinas counts as a philosopher. Hence he can robustly defend the powers of what he calls "natural reason" and can write about logic, the world of nature, human cognition, human action, metaphysics, ethics, and other topics without employing theological premises.[72] Hence he can also write commentaries on philosophical texts by non-Christians which respect them on their own terms: as attempts to understand how things are or ought to be without recourse to theological authorities. Religious authors can write in very different ways. They can proceed with no sense of what a rigorous argument looks like. Or they can write on the assumption that there are really no serious philosophical questions to be asked either about the meaning of their religious beliefs or about the grounds on which they are held. They can also suppose that nonreligious thinkers have little to offer, and they can avoid discussing some of the questions which have most preoccupied philosophers. Aquinas does not write in any of these ways. Even his most explicitly theological works display high standards of argumentative rigor. They are also full of probing and intelligent questions concerning both the significance and truth of religious claims and the credibility of competing claims.

VIII

The following essays explore some of these questions and the answers which Aquinas gave to them. The first, by James A. Weisheipl, situates Aquinas against the background of Aristotle and indicates how some of his teachings fed into Aquinas's philosophy of nature. The three subsequent essays expound and discuss what Aquinas has to say on three topics to which he frequently turns with little or no recourse to theological premises. For want of a better label, you might think of these essays as devoted to some of Aquinas's "basic metaphysics." In "Matter and Actuality in Aquinas," Christopher Hughes examines Aquinas's claim that matter is somehow both potential and actual. In the following essay, Hermann Weidemann aims to disentangle the various ways in which Aquinas uses the verb "to be." In "The Realism of Aquinas," Sandra Edwards critically examines what Aquinas has to say on a topic which has busied philosophers since at least the time of Plato: the so-called problem of universals. In doing so, she makes some interesting and unusual comparisons between Aquinas and John Duns Scotus (c. 1266–1308).

Essays 1 to 4 have little of detail to offer concerning Aquinas on the topic of God's existence and nature. As we have seen, however, this was something which greatly concerned him, as did the question of the scope and limits of human reason when it comes to things divine. So this is the subject matter of Essays 5 to 8. In the first of these, Rudi A. te Velde offers a careful analysis of the *Summa contra Gentiles* that is designed to estimate how Aquinas, in this work at least, stands on what we might call the relationship between philosophy and theology. In essay 6, Scott MacDonald tries accurately to reconstruct the logic of one of Aquinas's earliest and most controversial arguments for God's existence. This argument, in the *De ente et essentia*, has been subject to various readings, so MacDonald confines himself to the task of patiently seeking to show what it actually amounts to. He does not try to evaluate it. In essay 7, however, John F. Wippel combines both interpretation and evaluation as he turns to the *Summa theologiae*'s Five Ways. In doing so, he aims to correct some misreadings of them. He also draws attention to some of their strengths and weaknesses. Since, as Aquinas himself notes in his Introduction to *Summa theologiae* I,3, the claim that God exists naturally raises the question "What is God?", essay 8 follows up on Wippel's discussion with an attempt by me to say what Aquinas is driving at in his answer to this question. My suggestion is that he offers an account of God which can be read as both positive and negative, though more negative than positive when it comes to intelligible content.

Essays 9 to 11 may be thought of as studies in Aquinas's account of what it is to be human. In "Intentionality: Aquinas and Wittgenstein," Anthony Kenny turns to what he calls Aquinas's account "of the harmony between world and thought." Central to this is the claim that "forms" exist "intentionally" in the mind. Kenny considers what this claim might mean and whether it has merit. He also tries to relate it to the thinking of authors other than Aquinas. In essay 10, Gyula Klima critically expounds Aquinas's view of the human soul. According to Klima, Aquinas's position constitutes a successful way of avoiding some starkly contrasting accounts of what we are. As we have seen, in talking about people Aquinas insists on their ability to choose. This aspect of his teaching is the focus of essay 11, in which Eleonore Stump seeks to show how Aquinas's view of human freedom emerges from his account of human understanding and will. She also considers how it should be characterized in the light of some other accounts of human agency.

Aquinas took people to be free individuals able to seek what is good and to avoid what is bad. But how does he think about goodness and badness in general? And what consequences does he draw concerning goodness and badness in human behavior? Both of these questions are at issue in essay 12, by Eleonore Stump and Norman Kretzmann, who discuss Aquinas's criteria for the evaluation of actions together with his teaching that "being" and "goodness" are "the same in reference, differing only in sense." In his treatment of human action, Aquinas, like Aristotle, is very much preoccupied with the fact that people live together (that they are political animals). So essay 13, by Paul E. Sigmund, is devoted to what Aquinas has to say about law and politics. One will never understand him on these topics, however, unless one takes account of what he calls *prudentia*, which he speaks of as holding "special place in the enumeration of the virtues."[73] Though *prudentia* is normally, and quite reasonably, rendered into English as "prudence," in essay 14 Herbert McCabe explains why we might take Aquinas's use of the word to signify something like what Jane Austen called "good sense." In explaining himself, McCabe offers an analysis of Aquinas's understanding of conscience, moral responsibility, and practical reasoning in general. Since Aquinas's own discussion of these matters draws heavily on his view of what he calls the "passions of the soul," Peter King's essay (on Aquinas and the passions) is a fitting concluding chapter with which to round things off.

But there cannot really be any "rounding off" when it comes to a volume such as the present one. Aquinas was an abnormally energetic author with wide ranging intellectual interests. No volume of essays can hope to cover his pursuit of them all in the way that it deserves to be. My hope is that the present volume will help readers to find their way around some of Aquinas's major ideas and to be encouraged to explore them further.

Notes

1. Bertrand Russell, *A History of Western Philosophy* (New York: Simon and Schuster, 1945), p. 463.

2. *Philosophy* 65 (1990), p. 116.

3. Anthony Kenny, ed., *Aquinas: A Collection of Critical Essays* (Notre Dame, Ind: University of Notre Dame Press), p. 1.

4. Hence, for example, Aquinas is the focus of one of Cambridge University Press's distinguished series of *Companions* to major philosophers: see Norman Kretzmann and Eleonore Stump, eds., *The Cambridge Companion to Aquinas* (Cambridge: Cambridge University Press, 1993). Note also that two major journals have recently devoted whole numbers to the thinking of Aquinas. See *The Monist* 80 (1997) and *Revue Internationale de Philosophie* 52, no. 2 (1998).

5. The attempts in question are (1) Jean-Pierre Torrell, *Saint Thomas Aquinas: The Person and His Work* (Washington, D.C., Catholic University of America Press, 1996); (2) Simon Tugwell ed., *Albert and Thomas: Selected Writings* (New York and London: Paulist Press, 1988), pp. 201–67, and (3) James A. Weisheipl, *Friar Thomas D'Aquino* (Oxford: Basil Blackwell, 1974; republished with Corrigenda and Addenda, Washington, D.C.: Catholic University of America Press, 1983).

6. The University of Naples, founded by Frederick II, was a somewhat unusual

place when Aquinas arrived there. Unlike other major centers of learning in Europe, its origins were secular, not ecclesiastical. It was the first university established by civil charter. Cosmopolitan in character, it gave free rein to the study of thinkers such as Aristotle, many of whose works were banned in the University of Paris in 1215. Early accounts of Aquinas's life mention two people in particular under whom he worked at Naples. Of one, a certain "Master Martin," we know nothing. But research has recently uncovered some information concerning the other, known as "Master Peter of Ireland." See Michael Bertram Crowe, "Peter of Ireland: Aquinas's Teacher of the ARTES LIBERALES," in *Arts liberaux et philosophie au Moyen Age* (Montreal: Institut d'Etudes Médiérales; Paris: Librairie Philosophique J. Vrin, 1969).

7. Readers of Aquinas should not underestimate the fact that he was a Dominican. His writings regularly reflect the spirit of the Dominican Order. For an indication of Dominican thinking in its first phase, see Simon Tugwell, *Early Dominicans* (New York: Paulist Press, 1982).

8. Dionysius the Areopagite wrote four major works which circulated from around the sixth century: *The Divine Names, The Mystical Theology, The Celestial Hierarchy,* and *The Ecclesiastical Hierarchy.* But we do not actually know who he was. In the New Testament we are told that when St. Paul preached at Athens "some men joined him and believed, among them Dionysius the Areopagite," and he was long thought to be this person. But we now know that his writings must have been completed well after the New Testament period (hence the "Pseudo" in "Pseudo-Dionysius"). A great deal of what is often called "Western mysticism" is deeply indebted to him. He was an influence, for instance, on the author of the text known as *The Cloud of Unknowing.* For introductions to Dionysius, see Andrew Louth, *Denys the Areopagite* (London: Geoffrey Chapman, 1989) and Paul Rorem, *Pseudo-Dionysius: A Commentary on the Texts and an Introduction to Their Influence* (New York and Oxford: Oxford University Press, 1993). Also see "Albert and the Dionysian Tradition," in *Albert and Thomas,* ed. Tugwell. The relation between Dionysius and Aquinas is explored in Fran O'Rourke, *Pseudo-Dionysius and the Metaphysics of Aquinas* (Leiden: E. J. Brill, 1992), though O'Rourke, perhaps, makes them seem to be more in agreement than they actually are.

9. For the relationship between Albert and Thomas, see James A. Weisheipl, *Thomas D'Aquino and Albert His Teacher* (Toronto: Pontifical Institute of Medieval Studies, 1980).

10. Lombard's *Sentences* was written around the end of the 1140s. The work was intended as an aid to the study of Scripture and the Fathers. By the time of Aquinas it was in use as an official university textbook for students of theology. And it remained so for a long time afterward. At present, the best study of Lombard is Marcia L. Colish, *Peter Lombard,* 2 vols. (Leiden: E. J. Brill, 1994).

11. *Summa contra Gentiles* (sometimes abbreviated as SG) I, 9,4.

12. The "parts" of the *Summa theologiae* (which is sometimes abbreviated as ST) are known as the *Prima pars* (often abbreviated as I or as Ia), the *Secunda pars* (itself divided into sections called the *Prima secundae* [often abbreviated as II.I or 2a1ae] and the *Secunda secundae* [often abbreviated as II.II or 2a2ae]), and the *Tertia pars* (often abbreviated as III or 3a). Each of these units breaks down

into segments called "Questions." These consist of a series of "Articles," which raise detailed problems bearing on the topic of the Question to which they belong. Each Article typically consists of "Objections" and "Replies" together with what is usually referred to as the *corpus* (body) of the Article. In the Objections Aquinas typically raises some of the strongest arguments he knows *against* the position he wants to defend. In the *corpus* he presents his own arguments for this position. In the Replies he tries to explain why the objections he has cited *do not* count against it.

13. Introduction to ST I, 2. In what follows, quotations from the *Summa Theologiae* came from the Blackfriars edition (London and New York, 1964–1980).

14. ST I, 2,1.

15. ST I, 12,12; I, 88,3.

16. ST I, 2,2 ad 1. For Wittgenstein, see *On Certainty*, (edited by G. E. M. Anscombe and G. H. von Wright (Oxford: Basil Blackwell, 1974). See also G. E. M. Anscombe, "What Is It to Believe Someone?" in *Rationality and Religious Belief*, ed. C. F. Delaney (Notre Dame, Ind.: University of Notre Dame Press, 1979).

17. ST I, 2,2.

18. ST I, 13,11.

19. Norris Clarke *Explorations in Metaphysics* (Notre Dame, Ind.: University of Notre Dame Press, 1995), p. 24.

20. Cf. Étienne Gilson, *The Christian Philosophy of St. Thomas Aquinas* (London: Victor Gollanz, 1961), introduction and chaps. 3 and 4.

21. Anthony Kenny, *Aquinas* (Oxford: Oxford University Press, 1980), p. 60.

22. C. J. F. Williams, "Being," in *A Companion to the Philosophy of Religion*, ed. P. Quinn and C. Taliaferro (Oxford: Basil Blackwell, 1997), chap. 27.

23. ST I, 76, 2.

24. Herbert McCabe, "The Logic of Mysticism," in Martin Warner (ed.), *Religion and Philosophy*, ed. Martin Warner (Cambridge: Cambridge University Press, 1992), p. 45.

25. Ludwig Wittgenstein, *Tractatus Logico-Philosophicus*, trans. D. F. Pears and B. F. McGuinness (London: Routledge and Kegan Paul, 1961), 6.44.

26. Ibid., 6.52.

27. Book 1, lectio 14. Cf. ST I, 13,8.

28. See the introduction to *ST* Ia,3.

29. See ST I, 5; I, 25; I, 14; I, 10.

30. ST I, 75,1.

31. Aquinas also ascribes natural tendencies or appetites to nonorganic things and to creatures (e.g., angels) who are wholly immaterial. And he ascribes them to people considered as merely physical organisms.

32. So he denies that nonhuman animals exercise choice as they respond to external stimuli. See ST II.I, 13,2. Choice, for Aquinas, can only belong to beings who can consciously opt for one way of proceeding rather than another in the light of reason.

33. I say "we may have to consider" since Aquinas does not think that action always proceeds from a process of inquiry or reasoning. He thinks that it proceeds in this way when we are initially uncertain as to how to get what we

want. Where such uncertainty is lacking, then so is deliberation. See ST II.I, 14,4.

34. ST II.I, 14,1.

35. ST II.I, 14,2.

36. Of course, Aquinas does not mean that deliberation cannot lead us to want to act in ways which we might not have thought about before deliberating. So he can speak of it as involving advice from others (see ST II.I, 14,3). His point, however, is that the purpose of deliberation is to work out effective ways of getting what we want to start with.

37. There is an extended treatment of *habitus* in ST II.I, 49–54.

38. For a defense of this translation, see the introduction to volume 22 of the Blackfriars edition of the *Summa theologiae*.

39. Ibid., p. xxi.

40. According to Aquinas we think of what we are attracted to thinking of, and we are attracted to what we think of—which is not to be confused with believing what we want to believe. Aquinas's point is that decisions to act depend on the fact that we pay attention to what we want to attend to and that we are attracted to what we present to ourselves as good.

41. Notice, therefore, that Aquinas, unlike some moralists, does not think of and evaluate human actions simply with respect to whether or not they count as obeying or disobeying rules. He is concerned with human action as something to which education is relevant. He is concerned with the acquiring of character which enables people instinctively to act well.

42. *De malo* III, 9 ad 7. For a detailed discussion of temperance by Aquinas, see ST II.II, 141–54.

43. For Aquinas on virtues in general, see *ST* III, 55–67. Philosophers sometimes ask how people can do what they know to be bad, a topic that Aquinas touches on in *De malo* III, 9. Some thinkers have held that we do what we know to be bad out of ignorance. Others have held that we do what we know to be bad because our actions spring from will, not knowledge, so that we can know what is good but fail to aim for it. For Aquinas, however, the will is our being attracted by the good as it appears to our minds. So, though he concedes that bad actions sometimes spring from ignorance, he also thinks that will depends on understanding and that understanding depends on will. He therefore argues that we do what we know to be bad because of a sidelining of reason through weakness of temperateness or through strength of uncontrolled passion. For this reason, his account of what is sometimes called "weakness of will" depends on his notion of a *habitus*. We can do what we know to be wrong because we have become the sort of people who instinctively act in certain ways. And he thinks, that we can be held responsible for ending up like this.

44. Aquinas uses no Latin expression which corresponds exactly to the English "free will." He speaks of will (*voluntas*) but not of free will (*libera voluntas*) or freedom of the will (*libertas voluntatis*).

45. For Aquinas discussing *liberum arbitrium*, see Question XXIV of the *De veritate* and ST I, 83.

46. This is Aquinas's biblical "proof text" in *De malo* VI. He also invokes it in *ST* I, 83, 1.

47. *ST* I, 83,1.

48. Anthony Kenny, *Aquinas on Mind* (London and New York: Routledge, 1993), pp. 76–77.

49. One might suggest that our thinking is identical with processes in our brains over which we have no control. And one might therefore suggest that our actions have irreducibly physical causes over which we have no control. For Aquinas, however, thinking cannot be identified with any physical process. On his account, we depend on our bodies in order to interpret the world. Indeed, he thinks, all our knowledge depends on the ways in which we function as bodily things. But, he suggests, our interpreting the world cannot be identified with a particular physical process. If it were, he thinks, then meanings would be the same as physical objects, which, in his view, they are not.

50. Aquinas, I should stress, does not deny that people may often behave without exercising freedom of choice. For he takes them to be part of a material world in which all sorts of things, with reasons of their own, can interfere with people's ability to act. As he indicates in the *De malo*, however, he does not conclude that behaving under the influence of something else automatically exonerates people from responsibility. We would normally agree that drivers under the influence of alcohol might well not have chosen to kill those knocked down by their cars. But we would normally regard them as responsible for what they brought about if we thought that they chose to drive while drunk. In the same way, Aquinas thinks that responsibility can be ascribed to people when they bring things about even if they do not directly intend to do so.

51. *De potentia* III, 7. I quote from Timothy McDermott, ed., *Aquinas: Selected Philosophical Writings* (Oxford and New York: Oxford University Press, 1993), pp. 299 ff.

52. I am quoting here from Herbert McCabe, *God Matters* (London; Geoffrey Chapman, 1987), p. 14.

53. For a recent defense of a similar line of reasoning, see William E. Mann, "God's Freedom, Human Freedom, and God's Responsibility for Sin," in *Divine and Human Action*, ed. Thomas V. Morris (Ithaca: Cornell University Press, 1988). See also Brian Davies, "The Problem of Evil," in *Philosophy of Religion: A Guide to the Subject*, ed. Brian Davies (London: Oxford University Press, 1998).

54. *Commentary on Aristotle's "De interpretatione,"* Book I, Lectio 14. I quote from McDermott, *Aquinas: Selected Philosophical Writings*, pp. 282–83. Cf. *De malo* XV, 7 ad 15.

55. *ST* I, 83,1 ad 3.

56. Kenny *Aquinas on Mind*, p. 77.

57. Mark Jordan, "Theology and Philosophy," in *The Cambridge Companion to Aquinas*, p. 233. Other authors stressing the theological character of Aquinas's writings include Étienne Gilson, Armand Maurer, and Anton Pegis. For Gilson's position, see John F. Wippel, "Étienne Gilson and Christian Philosophy," in *Metaphysical Themes in Thomas Aquinas*, by John F. Wippel (Washington, D.C.: Catholic University of America Press, 1984). For Maurer, see *Saint Thomas Aquinas, Faith, Reason, and Theology: Questions I–IV of His Commentary on the "De Trinitate" of Boethius*, trans. Armand Maurer (Toronto: Pontifical Institute of Medieval Stud-

ies, 1987). For Pegis, see Anton Pegis, "*Sub Ratione Dei:* A Reply to Professor Anderson," *New Scholasticism* 39 (1965).

58. See Norman Kretzmann, *The Metaphysics of Theism* (Oxford: Clarendon Press, 1997), chap. 1. For a more recent argument that Aquinas is truly to be deemed a serious philosopher, see James C. Doig, *Aquinas's Philosophical Commentary on the "Ethics": A Historical Perspective* (Dordrecht: Kluwer Academic Publishers, 2001).

59. Aquinas allows that one can cite reasons which might be held to carry *some* weight with respect to truths of faith. But for him they are no more than pointers or ways of drawing attention to what coheres with truths of faith. "Arguments from human reason cannot avail to prove what must be received on faith" (ST I, 8). If *sacra doctrina* contains human reasoning, says Aquinas, that is "to make clear other things that are put forward in this teaching" and to provide "extrinsic and probable arguments" (ibid.)

60. A strong case has been made for thinking of the *Summa theologiae* as a textbook for Dominican friars in formation, which would clearly render it primarily a theological work. See Leonard E. Boyle, *The Setting of the "Summa theologiae"* (Toronto: Pontifical Institute of Medieval Studies, 1982).

61. Aquinas calls God the author of Scripture (*auctor sacrae scripturae est Deus*: I, 1,10). For Aquinas and Scripture, see J. van der Ploeg, "The Place of Holy Scripture in the Theology of St. Thomas," *Thomist* 10 (1947); Per Erik Person, *Sacra Doctrina: Reason and Revelation in Aquinas* (Oxford: Basil Blackwell, 1970); Wilhelmus G. B. M. Valkenberg, *Words of the Living God: Place and Function of Holy Scripture in the Theology of St. Thomas Aquinas* (Leuven: Peeters, 2000).

62. See ST I, 1,1; I, 1,8; I, 1,9.

63. ST II.II, 1,9.

64. Ibid.

65. *Commentary on the "Sentences" of Peter Lombard*, Book 4, Distinction 49, Question 1, Article 1. I quote from McDermott, *Aquinas: Selected Philosophical Writings*, pp. 325–26.

66. ST I, 91,1.

67. Ibid.

68. *ST* II.I, 93,1.

69. According to Aquinas, God cannot be thought of as an individual with properties really distinct from himself. We speak of God as if he were just this, and Aquinas thinks that it is proper that we should do so (ST, I 13,1). However, he argues in various places, properties which we truly attribute to God (e.g., knowledge, power, goodness, or whatever) are not distinct realities in God, as they are in us. Nor are they distinct from the subject God is. As we may put it, Aquinas's view is that there is, in reality, no real difference between *who* God is and *what* God is. This is part of what is commonly referred to as Aquinas's "doctrine of divine simplicity" (which also holds that God's nature is *esse*, that God is *Ipsum Esse Subsistens*), and it has been subject to much philosophical and theological criticism. For an exposition of it, see Brian Davies, *The Thought of Thomas Aquinas* (Oxford: Clarendon Press, 1992), chap. 3. For defenses of it, see Brian Davies, "Aquinas and the Doctrine of Divine Simplicity," in *Language, Meaning, and God*, ed. Brian Davies (London: Geoffrey Chapman, 1987); and

Eleonore Stump and Norman Kretzmann, "Absolute Simplicity," *Faith and Philosophy* 2 (1985). For a recent book which aims to defend the notion of divine simplicity, see Barry Miller, *A Most Unlikely God* (Notre Dame, Ind.: University of Notre Dame Press, 1996). For a book which offers a full-scale attack on the notion, see Christopher Hughes, *On a Complex Theory of a Simple God* (Ithaca: Cornell University Press, 1980).

70. ST II.I, 71,6.
71. Ibid.
72. For Aquinas on natural reason, and its limits, see SG I, 4 and SG I, 8.
73. ST II.II, 47, 5.

I

The Commentary of St. Thomas
on the *De caelo* of Aristotle

The "commentary" or *Sententia de caelo et mundo* of St. Thomas is a work of great maturity and profundity. It is one of Thomas's last writings, and it reveals a breadth of scholarship and achievement wanting, for the most part, in his earlier Aristotelian commentaries, such as those on the *Ethics, Physics, De anima,* and early parts of the *Metaphysics*; but it comes to grips with profound problems of Aristotelian philosophy inherent in the conflicting views of Greek and Arab commentators. I. T. Eschmann rightly noted that "it represents the high water-mark of St. Thomas's expository skill."[1] In long, subtle digressions, Thomas discusses and evaluates the views of other commentators reported by Simplicius, as well as the views of Simplicius himself, who is a primary source in this commentary. As in earlier commentaries, Thomas was also concerned with the teaching of Averroes, which deeply influenced the masters in arts at Paris in the late 1260s and throughout the 1270s. The excessive adoption of Averroes by masters in arts resulted in the condemnation of thirteen Averroist theses on December 10, 1270, by the bishop of Paris, Etienne Tempier, and in the more sweeping condemnation by the same bishop on March 7, 1277. Simplicius and Averroes are in fact the two basic sources for Thomas's commentary on *De caelo*.

Thomas did not comment on *De caelo* until he had the full text in hand, together with the commentary of Simplicius. Although there were a number of translations of Aristotle's *De caelo* available from the Arabic, Thomas insisted on having a good translation from the Greek corrected by his friend and confrère William of Moerbeke. Wherever translations existed from the Greek, Moerbeke did not translate anew but rather revised specific readings of words and phrases according to a Greek exemplar. The first translation of *De caelo* from the Greek was made by Robert Grosseteste, the bishop of Lincoln, between 1247 and 1253, the date of his death. Grosseteste's translation went only as far as Book III, c. 1, 299a11; but he also translated the corre-

37

sponding commentary of Simplicius. We do not know how much influence this translation had, for it has not yet been found intact in any manuscript. Moerbeke, it would seem, used the Grosseteste translation for his own revision of Books I and II, before proceeding with an original translation of Books III and IV, together with the full commentary of Simplicius. Moerbeke completed his revision and translation on June 15, 1271, at Viterbo, where the papal court of Pope Gregory X resided. Within a relatively short time, Moerbeke's translation of *De caelo* became the "common," or "vulgate," text used in the schools as part of the *Corpus recentior* of Aristotle's writings.

Moerbeke's translation was not the only one available to Latin scholastics. In fact, they had five versions in whole or in part from which to study the thought of Aristotle's *De caelo*:

1. A *summary* in sixteen chapters by Avicenna as the "second book" of the *libri naturales*, translated from the Arabic, probably by Dominic Gundissalinus and John Avendehut around 1150.
   Incipit: "Collectiones exposicionum ab antiquis Graecis in libro Aristotilis qui dicitur liber celi et mundi. . . . Differentia inter corpus et quamlibet aliam magnitudinem hec est . . ."
   Remarks: Undoubtedly this summary was included in the general condemnation of Aristotle's works in 1210 ("nec commenta") and in 1215 ("nec summe de eisdem") because it taught the eternity of the world. It exists in several MSS, and a much-emended text was published at Venice in 1508.
2. *De caelo veteris translationis*, translated from the Arabic by Gerard of Cremona (d. 1187).
   Incipit: "Summa cognicionis nature et scientie ipsam demons-trantis . . ."
   Remarks: This version was the common one used in the schools before being replaced by the new version of Moerbeke. Without doubt this version is the one intended by the statutes of the arts faculty in Paris, March 19, 1255 (*Chart. U.P.*, I, 277–79, n. 246). Albertus Magnus used this version for his own commentary, and it is printed in the new edition of Albert's works, *Opera Omnia*, V (Cologne, 1971).
3. *De caelo cum commentario magno Averrois*, translated from the Arabic by Michael'Scot, ca. 1231–35.
   Incipit: "Maxima cognicio nature et scientia demonstrans ipsam . . ."
   Remarks: This version was frequently published with the commentary of Averroes, e.g., the italic type in the Venice edition of 1574. Michael Scot dedicated this work to Stephen de Pruvino, who with two other masters was commissioned by Pope Gregory IX in 1231 to examine Aris-

totle's writings on natural philosophy and to report on their contents (*Chart. U.P.*, I, 143–44, n. 87; see note 2 by Denifle, ibid., p. 144).

4. *De caelo translationis Lincolniensis*, incomplete, covers Books I–III, 1, 299a11 ("huc usque d. R." MS Vat. lat. 2088), translated from the Greek together with the corresponding commentary of Simplicius by Robert Grosseteste in England between 1247 and 1253. Cf. *Aristoteles Latinus*, I, 53.

Incipit: uncertain because "no complete MS of Grosseteste's translation has yet been identified" (S. H. Thomson, *The Writings of Robert Grosseteste* [Cambridge, 1940], p. 66).

Remarks: D. J. Allan has shown that Book II of this version is to be found in full in Oxford, Balliol Coll. MS 99; see "Mediaeval Versions of Aristotle, *De caelo*, and of the Com. of Simplicius," *Mediaeval and Renaissance Studies* 2 (1950), 82–120. D. A. Callus remarks that "the *De caelo*, left incomplete, was his [Grosseteste's] last work" (*Robert Grosseteste* [Oxford, 1955], p. 67).

5. *De caelo novae translationis*, I–II revised, III–IV translated from the Greek by William Moerbeke with the commentary of Simplicius, completed in Viterbo, June 15, 1271.

Incipit: "De natura scientia ferre plurima videtur circa corpora et magnitudines et horum existens passiones et motus . . ."

Remarks: This new version, the common text used in the schools in the late thirteenth century, replacing the translation of Gerard of Cremona, was the base text used by St. Thomas for his commentary on *De caelo*; the commentary of Simplicius was thoroughly exploited in Thomas's work on the heavens, and he had partially used it earlier, without sufficient comprehension, in his commentary on the *Metaphysics*, Book XII (Lambda). A contaminated form of this version is generally printed with the works of Thomas; it was also published at Venice in bold Roman type with the commentary of Averroes (*De caelo*, 1574). The Moerbeke version of Aristotle's *De caelo*, with the full commentary of Simplicius, was published in Venice by Heronymus Scotus in 1548.

Aristotle's treatise *De caelo* was written in four books after completion of the *Physics*, as is proved by the numerous cross-references Aristotle himself makes to the *Physics* (e.g., *De caelo* 270a18; 273a13; 275b18; 305a21; 311a13, etc.). All Arab and Latin commentators refer to *De caelo* as the "second book" of natural philosophy, and Thomas notes that it is the first treatise after the *Physics*.[2] In the first two books, Aristotle discusses the constitution and simple movements of the universe as a whole; in the third and fourth books, he discusses the simple motions of the sublunar elements. In Thomas's view, the first two books discuss "bodies which move with circular motion," whereas the last two discuss "bodies which move with rectilinear motion."[3]

Thomas did not comment on all four books, but stopped abruptly at III, 3, 302b9 (III, lect. 8, n. 9), as all of Thomas's bibliographers acknowledge. The so-called official catalogue drawn up by Reginald of Piperno for the canonization process lists the work as "super libros de Caelo tres."[4] Nicholas Trevet lists it as "caeli et mundi, primum, secundum et tertium."[5] Tolomeo of Lucca simply notes that the commentary is not complete: "De caelo et De generatione, sed non complevit."[6] Bernard Gui lists the work as "super tres libros de caelo et mundo."[7] The second Prague catalogue lists it as "glosas super 3 libros celi et mundi."[8] After Tolomeo of Lucca noted that De caelo and De generatione were left incomplete, he stated that "these books were completed by master Peter of Alvernia [Auvergne], his most faithful disciple, master in theology and a great philosopher, later bishop of Clermont." Grabmann notes that at least two MSS (Paris, Bibl. Mazarine 3484 and Oxford, Balliol College 321) explicitly state at the end of the composite commentary: "In hoc completur expositio magistri Petri de Alvenia in tertium et quartum Caeli et Mundi Aristotelis, ubi praeventus morte venerabilis vir frater Thomas de Aquino omisit."[9] At the commentary on III, 3, 302b9, in Vatican MS Vat. lat. 2181, fol. 111v, the scribe wrote: "Usque huc frater Thomas. Incipit magister Petrus de Alvenia usque in finem quarti celi et mundi." There can be no doubt that the authentic commentary of Thomas breaks off in chapter 3 at the words "Itaque palam et quod sunt elementa, et propter quid sunt" (302b) in the version of Moerbeke.

One basic question is, why did Thomas not finish his commentary? All the traditional sources say that he was prevented by death. I. T. Eschmann, however, claims that the commentary is not "unfinished": "Whether it is an unfinished work, as is commonly asserted, seems doubtful."[10] He gives no arguments in support of this view, but he says, "The beginning of Aquinas's exposition of De generatione et corruptione gives us to understand that he [Thomas] knew no more Aristotelian text of De caelo than [that] which he explained." A study of the text, however, renders such a view most implausible.

Thomas certainly knew two versions of the complete text translated from the Arabic; in earlier works, such as Summa theologiae I, Thomas knew and referred to all four books in these versions. The question is whether Thomas had more text of the Moerbeke version than that which he commented upon. Moerbeke, as we know, translated Books III and IV directly from the Greek, and Thomas obviously knew this translation, for he commented on III, 1–3, well beyond the version of Robert Grosseteste, and well into the versions from the Arabic. Therefore Thomas had at least chapters 1–3 in the version of Moerbeke. The force of this argument will become clear when the Latin versions of *De caelo* are published in the *Aristoteles Latinus*.

Further, in the commentary itself, Thomas indicates that he knew the existence of the part not commented upon by him: e.g., at III, lect. 2, n. 1: "in quarto libro ibi *De gravi autem et levi*" (= IV, 1, 307b29); and at III, lect. 3, n. 2: "Partim autem inferius in hoc eodem libro" (= III, 5). These references seem to indicate the portion of the Moerbeke text not commented upon by Thomas.

Also, the opening passage of *De generatione* does not sustain Eschmann's argument. The passage reads:

> First he [Aristotle] expresses what he principally intends; and this contin-
> ues to the end of the book *De caelo*, where he says: *De gravi quidem igitur*
> *et levi determinandum sit hoc modo*. And there then follows: *De generatione*
> *autem et corruptione natura generatorum et corruptorum*, that is, of those
> things which naturally are generated and corrupted.

In this passage, the first lemma is the concluding sentence of *De caelo*, and the second lemma is the opening sentence of *De generatione*. Without further study, it is difficult to say what version of *De generatione* Thomas had in mind, but it was probably that of Moerbeke. The important point is that Thomas had at hand the concluding sentence of Book IV of *De caelo*, and there is no reason why Thomas could not have completed his commentary on *De caelo* had he lived. The traditional view that Thomas's commentary on *De caelo* is "unfinished" must stand. He was undoubtedly unable to finish the work when he was unexpectedly afflicted by a stroke or breakdown on December 6, 1273. Scribes, unaware of what happened to Thomas on December 6, would naturally think that he was prevented by death—"praeventus morte."

From what has been said, it is clear that Thomas's *Sententia de caelo et mundo* must be dated late in his life. It was composed after Moerbeke finished his translation of the text and of the commentary by Simplicius on June 15, 1271. Thomas obtained this translation while he was still in Paris (January 1269 to spring 1272), as is confirmed by the letter of the Parisian faculty of arts sent to the general chapter of the Order of Preachers meeting in Lyons in 1274 after the death of Thomas. In the letter, dated May 3, the faculty of arts asked for four favors, the third of which was a request for the books that Thomas himself had promised to send them:

> And permit us also to mention the commentary of Simplicius on the *De*
> *caelo et mundo*, and an exposition of Plato's *Timaeus*, and a work entitled

De aquarum conductibus et ingeniis erigendis; for these books in particular he himself promised would be sent to us.[11]

Moerbeke's translation arrived in Paris while Thomas was commenting on Book Lambda (XII) of the *Metaphysics* in 1271, for in certain passages Thomas made use of Simplicius's commentary. Whether or not Thomas's commentary on *De caelo* was begun in Paris and continued in Naples cannot yet be determined. The masters in arts of Paris in their second petition asked the Dominican chapter to send them "some writings of a philosophical nature, begun by him [Thomas] at Paris, left unfinished at his departure, but completed, we have reason to think, in the place to which he was transferred."[12] Thomas could have begun his commentary on *De caelo* at Paris after June 1271 and continued it in Naples, where he was assigned in September 1272; or he could have begun it in Naples. What is certain is that Thomas took Moerbeke's text with him to Naples.

At Naples, William of Tocco saw Thomas writing his commentary on Aristotle's *De generatione et corruptione*, which he believed to have been Thomas's "last work in philosophy."[13] It is unfinished, ending abruptly in I, 5, 322a33 (I, lect. 17), and exists in only four manuscripts; it was unknown to the Parisian stationers even as late as 1304. When Thomas wrote his commentary on *De generatione* I, lect. 7, n. 1, he used the phrase "as we have made clear [*manifestavimus*] in VIII *Physic.* and in I *De caelo*," thus signifying that at least the first book of *De caelo* was completed before *De generatione* I, lect. 7, which was written in Naples. Therefore Thomas must have written his commentary on *De caelo* between June 1271 (Paris) and December 6, 1273 (Naples). It is accordingly one of Thomas's last works in philosophy, and one of considerable maturity and reflection. The influence of Simplicius is clear on almost every page; it seems to have aroused Thomas's critical acumen to the utmost. It can be considered the profoundest of all his commentaries on Aristotle. It has no equal. Even Albert's scholarly commentary on the *De caelo* fades in comparison with Thomas's. For this we have to thank the genius of Thomas and the stimulus of Simplicius, the celebrated sixth-century Greek commentator on Aristotle.

In this brief study it is impossible to do justice to Thomas's commentary. But perhaps certain highlights can be pointed out for further study.

The Subject Matter of *De caelo*

Every scholastic introduction to a new book to be discussed examines first the location of this book in the ensemble of the whole science, and its unique and proper subject matter distinct from other treatises. All of Aristotle's *libri naturales* were universally thought to belong to the unique science of the philosophy of nature. The unique character of natural science, or the philosophy of nature, is derived from the manner of defining concepts in that science, as Thomas shows in his *In Boethium De Trinitate,* q. 5, aa. 1–2. Every concept in the philosophy of nature, no matter how analogous it may be, is defined in terms of sensate matter, *materia sensibilis.* These definitions leave out of consideration, or abstract from, individual matter. That is to say, the natural philosopher is primarily concerned not with individual instances of his encounter with nature but rather with the species, or common nature, as such. In reality, the species (or common nature) does not exist as such outside the mind; there are only individual instances. But those species and common natures do exist as individuals. Individuals, as such, come into being and pass away, and there can be no speculative science of such individuals, except history. Therefore the philosopher who wishes to study nature must abstract the universal elements of his concern from the individual instances of his experience and experimentation. This kind of abstraction was called "total abstraction" (*abstractio totalis*) by the scholastics, for it temporarily leaves out of consideration the "parts" or existent individuals of which the species, or common nature, can be predicated. Without individual instances existing in nature, the natural philosopher could never comprehend the universal whole; but the truth he seeks must be formulated in terms of universal definitions, statements, laws, and hypotheses. Whatever is retained necessarily involves *materia sensibilis,* i.e., definitions formulated in terms of what can be sensed by touch, sight, sound, taste, and smell, as well as magnitude and number. All such tangible characteristics are needed to define concepts and laws in natural philosophy. Thus if the natural philosopher wants to talk about gravitation, he does not limit his concern to the free-fall of this particular body at this particular instant of history but formulates statements and laws about all heavy bodies in various circumstances that are of universal validity.

The kind of abstraction used in natural science can be grasped more easily by comparing its subject to that of the mathematical sciences. Mathematics, to get anywhere, must leave out of consideration all aspects that are properly sensible, like apples and pears, and consider only the quantitative "form," namely, number and magnitude, which are "common sensibles." Every degree of mathematical abstraction retains a quantitative "form"; this abstraction is called, in scholastic language inherited from the Arabs, *abstractio formalis,* or *abstractio partis,* because a part of reality, namely, sensible matter, is left out of consideration. This kind of abstracting a formal part from the whole is legitimate, as Aristotle says, and does not result in any falsity,[14] because the mathematician does not assert that such a separation really exists in nature. If the mathematician asserted that "surfaces and volumes, lines and points" exist in nature as separated from sensible matter, he would be in error.[15] Nevertheless, a certain kind of matter is still retained in mathematical abstraction; it is called *materia intelligibilis*, because mathematical entities can be imagined distinctly by the mind, so that we can speak of parallel lines, variously plotted points, different kinds of circles, and the like. Intelligible matter allows for infinite multiplicity in mathematical reasoning. Like individual matter in sensible objects, intelligible matter is the principle of individuality in mathematics. On a more superficial level, one must also admit that the mathematician leaves out of consideration the individual instances of an imagined quantity; for this reason, some of the later scholastics maintained that total abstraction is common to all the speculative sciences. This is no more than a consequence of intellectual behavior, which cannot know the individual as such but must deal with the intelligible, which is universal.

Consequently, all the concepts and statements in natural philosophy are in terms of sensible matter in general, so that an animal is defined in terms of "blood and bone," and not "this blood and these bones."

In a science as vast as natural philosophy, there must be an orderly procedure whereby one progresses from the most general to the particular. The general principle of all human study is that the mind must proceed from the more common and general aspects, better known to us, to the more special and particular aspects, less known to us but better knowable in themselves. Consequently, the study of natural science should progress from the general aspects considered in the *Physics* to the more detailed considerations of the other *libri naturales*. The eight books of the *Physics* are an overall consideration of problems basic to the study of nature itself, that is, of the concept of nature as the principle of motion and rest in all natural things, and include a consideration of all the physical aspects of motion, such as causality, place, time, space, kinds of motion, continuity, and the necessity of a first mover of the universe. After such general considerations of nature and motion, required for an understanding of the whole of natural science, the philosopher should progress to a consideration of the particular species of motions and natures. This scientific progression is explained simply by St. Thomas when he says:

Scientific knowledge which is possessed of things only in general is not a complete science in its ultimate actuality but stands midway between pure potentiality and ultimate fulfillment. . . . Hence it is clear that the fullness of scientific knowledge requires that it not remain simply in generalities but proceed even to its species.[16]

In his commentary on the *Physics*, one of Thomas's earliest commentaries on Aristotle, he describes the contents of the *libri naturales* subsequent to the

Physics.[17] *De caelo* analyzes natural bodies as mobile according to local motion, "which is the first species of motion." *De generatione* analyzes motion toward form and the basic changes in elementary bodies precisely as mutable in general. The *Meteororum* discusses specific types of transmutation in nature. The pseudo-Aristotelian book *De mineralibus* discusses inanimate mobile bodies whose motions are composite, while the motion of composite animate bodies is discussed in the book *De anima* and in books subsequent to it.

In the prooemium to *De caelo*, therefore, Thomas again follows the general pedagogical method of proceeding from the general to the particular.[18] Aspects common to all of nature are seen as treated in the *Physics.* Thus "what remains in the other books of natural science is to apply these common aspects to their proper subjects." In this application, the more simple and general are discussed before the complex and specific. In this view, Book I of *De caelo* considers the entire corporeal universe prior to considering its parts; Book II considers simple bodies prior to the mixed; and Books III and IV consider elemental bodies prior to the complex and compound bodies. Since one aspect common to all the books of *De caelo* is body, "the first topic of discussion in the very beginning of this book is body, to which must be applied all that was set forth about motion in the *Physics.*"

Aristotle's *De caelo* is a complicated treatise in four books, and it is difficult to find the unifying thread. But commentators and scholastics had a penchant for discovering unity before proceeding to dissect it. Even though the *De caelo* discusses "bodies" throughout, this fact does not sufficiently identify the precise subject matter of the four books. Even though "the first topic of discussion in the very beginning of this book is body, to which must be applied all that was set forth about motion in the *Physics,*" this topic does not sufficiently unify the treatise, since there are many kinds of bodies in the heavens and on the earth.

The title, *De caelo*, can be understood in three senses. It can refer to (1) the outermost sphere that moves with diurnal motion; (2) all the heavenly bodies that move circularly; or (3) the entire universe. According to Simplicius in his prooemium, Alexander of Aphrodisias "believed that the subject primarily treated therein is the universe." Alexander assumed that Aristotle restricted himself to discussing general characteristics of the heaven and the earth—its eternity, finiteness, uniqueness, and the like. However, Iamblichus and Syrianus, according to Simplicius, thought the term "heaven" to apply to the heavenly bodies that move circularly. Iamblichus maintained that other bodies in the universe are discussed in *De caelo* "consequentially, insofar as they are contained by the heavens and influenced by them," whereas Syrianus held that other bodies are discussed "incidentally [*per accidens*] insofar as a knowledge of other bodies is assumed in order to explain what is being said of the heavens." But one might object that the consideration of elementary bodies and their motions cannot be called "incidental," or *per accidens*. The heavens and the four elements are simple bodies; and after Aristotle discusses the heavenly bodies in Book II, he proceeds to discuss the four terrestrial elements of earth, water, fire, and air as a principal consideration in Books III and IV. "The Philosopher is not wont to assign a principal part in some science to things that are brought up only incidentally."[19]

Therefore Simplicius argued that the subject matter of *De caelo* has to be "simple bodies," and since among all simple bodies the heavens predominate, it is reasonable to entitle the whole book *De caelo*.[20] If Aristotle had in fact intended to talk about the universe as such, Aristotle would have had to discuss all the parts of the world, even plants and animals, as Plato does in the *Timaeus*.

But Thomas argues against Simplicius, saying that if Aristotle were talking only about simple bodies, he would have had to discuss everything pertaining to simple bodies. In fact, Aristotle discusses only one aspect, that of their being light and heavy, leaving out of discussion their qualitative aspects, such as their being cold or hot, reserving this for the subsequent book *De generatione*.

Thomas prefers to follow the view of Alexander in saying that the subject of this book is the universe itself, and that simple bodies are discussed insofar as they are parts of the universe. Parts of the universe constitute the whole insofar as they have a determined position (*situs*) in the whole. That is, the heavenly bodies and the four terrestrial elements primarily and *per se* have a determined position by reason of their basic motions, which are simple. Since it is a question of position, Aristotle discusses the terrestrial elements not in terms of hot and cold, dry and moist, and so forth, but only in terms of their lightness and heaviness, which determine their position in the whole. For this reason, continues St. Thomas, there is no need to discuss other parts of the universe, such as stones, plants, and animals, according to their proper natures, but only insofar as their movements are dominated by heavy and light elements, which constitute them in their being. This proper, or specific, consideration of such compound bodies belongs to other books of the *libri naturales*.

Thomas goes on to conclude that this view agrees with what is usually said among the Latins, that "this book discusses mobile body with respect to position, or place, which motion indeed is common to all parts of the universe."[21] Among the "Latins" Thomas certainly included himself and Albertus Magnus. In his earlier work on the *Physics*, Thomas specifies the subject matter of *De caelo* as being "mobile [body] according to local motion, which is the first species of motion."[22] In his paraphrase of *De caelo*, Albert, writing around 1251, says, "There is a single science about those mobile bodies, not because here we discuss them precisely as moved by different natures, but rather precisely as they have a singular potentiality in general and a singular act, which is local motion."[23]

Later Thomists, with only partial justification, classified the *libri naturales* according to their generic motions. Thus the books of the *Physics* were said to discuss motion in general, while *De caelo* considers bodies in simple local motion, *De generatione* considers alterations leading to substantial changes, and *De anima* and its subsequent books consider augmentation of animals. Such mental gymnastics are oversimplifications of the contents of the Aristotelian books as understood by Albert and Thomas. It is true enough, however, that *De caelo* is concerned with simple bodies that move with local motion. It is not concerned with the local motion of animals precisely as living beings who are the cause of their own voluntary motions, for this subject is discussed in *De motibus animalium*; rather it is concerned with their rectilinear motion resulting from the predominance of certain elements, as when an animal loses balance and falls to the ground or when a bird in flight is shot down.

Thus, in Thomas's view, *De caelo et mundo* is concerned with the universe and the place of simple bodies in it. The place of these bodies in the universe is determined by their local motion, namely, the motion of celestial bodies circularly and the motion of the elements upward and downward, depending on their natural heaviness and lightness. Whatever is scientifically determined in *De caelo* is to be applied to other books in the *libri naturales*.

Celestial Motions

For Thomas, there are two basically distinct sciences that study the movements of the heavenly bodies: natural science, meaning the philosophy of nature, and astronomy. Both of these sciences have a common subject matter, the motions of the heavens. But the principles used in studying these motions are formally different. That is, natural philosophy uses the principles of nature outlined in the eight books of the *Physics*, with "nature" (φύσις) regarded as an active or passive principle of specific activity. Nature as an active principle is the innate form of the body that spontaneously and dynamically determines both the motion and the goal, unless some other body impedes its natural activity. Nature as a passive principle is the innate receptivity of the matter for actions performed on it by natural agencies. These principles will be discussed again shortly. For the present it is sufficient to see that natural philosophy discusses the physical and natural motions of the heavens from the viewpoint of "nature" (φύσις). It is also concerned with natural magnitudes, distances, velocity, and natural causes of those movements seen in the heavens in terms of nature, sensible matter, and motion.

Astronomy, on the other hand, is a science radically dependent on mathematical principles, such as those proved in geometry and in the highest branches of mathematics. Since both natural science and astronomy deal with the same celestial phenomena, they are said to share in the same material object (*obiectum materiale*). But since they differ profoundly and radically in their medium of demonstration, they constitute two separate and distinct sciences, each having its own identity and validity by reason of its formal object, its *ratio formalis obiecti*.[24]

The distinction between natural science and astronomy does not mean that they are mutually exclusive. On the contrary, they are of mutual interest and concern. The conclusions of the one can provoke the other to further inquiry and possible corroboration, as in the earth's sphericity, center of movement, the meaning of time, and so forth. Both approaches are useful and even necessary. Both construct hypotheses to account for the phenomena perceived by sense. However, the hypotheses postulated by the naturalist involve natural causes and natural mathematical devices to account for the phenomena, even if those devices cannot be verified in nature.

The basic problem faced by early astronomers was the obvious irregularity of planetary motion. These planets, or "wandering stars," sometimes seem to move faster, sometimes slower; sometimes they seem to be stationary, and at other times they seem to move backward with a retrograde motion.[25] Not only is such irregularity unbecoming in celestial motions, thought to be the domain of the gods, but it is impossible to study these motions scientifically without some reference to rational regularity. According to Simplicius:

> Eudoxus of Cnidos was the first Greek to concern himself with hypotheses of this sort, Plato having, as Sosigenes says, set it as a problem to all earnest students of this subject to find what are the uniform and ordered movements by the assumption of which the phenomena in relation to the movements of the planets can be saved.[26]

Eudoxus started with the assumption that all planetary movements must be regular and homocentric, i.e., having the same center around which to revolve, namely, the center of the earth. For Eudoxus the phenomena of celestial movements could be saved by postulating a number of regular spheres for each planet, each rotating around different axes at different speeds. For him each of the planets, including the sun and moon, has three basic motions: first, in respect to the sphere of the fixed stars moving from east to west; second, in respect to the middle of the zodiac through which the planets move; and third, in respect to the breadth or longitude of the zodiac.[27] All told, Eudoxus postulated twenty-seven spheres and motions to account for the phenomena rationally.[28]

Callippus, a younger contemporary of Eudoxus, postulated a far greater number of spheres, amounting to fifty-five in all (or forty-seven, if one did not postulate the additional eight for the rotation of the sun and moon).[29] Aristotle himself could not decide on the exact number of spheres (and consequently movers) needed "to save the appearances." In fact, Aristotle was not particularly concerned about the exact number of movers and decided to leave this question open "to more powerful thinkers."[30] For Aristotle the important issue was that celestial bodies cannot move themselves but must be moved by something else that is not physical.

Aristotle and the astronomers of his day assumed that all celestial motion had to be regular, circular, and homocentric. Pedestrian observation indicates that the earth and its center are the stationary point around which all the celestial bodies rotate. But this simplistic explanation involves many difficulties and does not account for all the phenomena. Because of these difficulties, "Hipparchus and Ptolemy hit upon eccentric and epicyclic motions to save what appears to the senses concerning celestial motions."[31] It is impossible, as all scholastics realized, that Aristotle and Ptolemy should be both right in the domain of a single science. While Aristotle's natural philosophy made sense, it did not account for all the data accumulated by astronomers. And while Ptolemy's astronomy accounted for all the phenomena, it assumed such mathematical devices as eccentrics and epicycles that could not be physically true. For Thomas, such an escape is not a demonstration but a kind of supposition, that is, a hypothesis.[32] But even if Ptolemy's supposition were true in nature, continues Thomas, "nevertheless all the celestial bodies would be moved around the center of the earth in its diurnal motion, which is the motion of the outermost sphere rotating the whole [universe] and all things within it."[33]

The status of astronomical hypotheses, such as epicycles and eccentrics, was of particular interest to Thomas, because they could not be verified physically; but their assumption in astronomy did account for the known motion of the planets within the sphere of the fixed stars. Thomas's views are clear:

It is not necessary that the various suppositions (i.e., hypotheses) which they [the astronomers] hit upon be true. For although these suppositions save the appearances, we are nevertheless not forced to say that these suppositions are true, because perhaps there is some other way men have not yet discovered by which the appearance of things may be saved concerning the stars.[34]

This same view was also expressed by Thomas some six years earlier in his *Summa theologiae*:

There are two kinds of argument put forward to prove something. The first goes to the root of the matter and fully demonstrates some point; for instance, in natural philosophy there is a conclusive argument to prove that celestial movements are of constant speed. The other kind does not prove a point conclusively but shows that its acceptance fits in with the observed effects; for instance, an astronomical argument about eccentric and epicyclic motions is put forward on the ground that by this hypothesis one can show how celestial movements appear as they do to observation. Such an argument is not fully conclusive, since an explanation might be possible even on another hypothesis.[35]

In other words, the hypotheses of astronomy are significant in that they may account for all the phenomena without forcing the mind to acknowledge their physical certainty. As in the case of the movement of the earth, the appearances could be saved by holding either that the earth is stationary and the heavens are moving about it, or that the heavens are stationary and the earth is moving within the heavens, or that both the earth and the heavens are moving.[36]

In the first part of Aristotle's *De caelo* there are two main issues: the nature of celestial bodies, and the nature of celestial motion. From the nature of the motion, one can argue to the nature of the body—but not vice versa. The celestial body is said to be incorruptible, different from terrestrial bodies, eternal, and perfect, and its motion is said to be uniform, regular, and circular. The celestial body was said to be incorruptible because no corruption or even alteration had been seen to occur in the heavens despite long centuries of observation by astronomers. Had Aristotle noted the sunspots observed by Galileo, he undoubtedly would have acknowledged corruption, or at least alteration, in the sun. But the fact was that neither Aristotle nor any of the ancient astronomers ever observed any change in celestial bodies. From this it follows that the matter in celestial bodies must be different from terrestrial matter, for on earth, matter is the root of corruptibility. Hence celestial matter was designated as the "fifth element," different from the prime matter of earth and having no "privation" for change. Further, if there is no "privation" in celestial matter, it must be "perfect," since in it there is nothing wanting. Furthermore, it follows that celestial bodies and the whole universe must be eternal, for there can be no "before" before time and motion, as Aristotle proved in the *Physics* and assumed in *De caelo*. Thomas knew perfectly well that Aristotle maintained the eternity of the universe. But on this point, Thomas argued that there is no conclusive argument one way or the other with regard to the eternity or temporality of the universe. The only basic issue for Thomas was that the universe had to be created by God either in time or in eternity.[37]

Similarly, the only kind of motion observed in the heavens is local motion that is perpetual, never tending to rest but ever flowing. While observation shows that planetary motion is irregular, this irregularity cannot be understood except in terms of regularity that is thought not to be. In other words, all irregularity must be defined in terms of regularity. The same is true of uniformity in velocity, for there can be no difform motion except in relation to that which is uniform. That is to say, there can be no denial of uniformity and regularity except in terms of uniformity and regularity. But the only local motion that can be uniform and regular is circular motion. All motions on earth (1) come to rest in some finality achieved and (2) tend to accelerate as they approach the term of motion. Celestial motions are not like that, for it needs be that they continue forever in a state of uniform velocity. Consequently, the task of the ancient astronomer was to determine the exact number of uniform circular motions needed to account for the irregularity of planetary motion.

The important issue for Thomas, as for Aristotle, was the cause of celestial motion, i.e., the efficient cause responsible for all the motions needed in the heavens to account for the phenomena. There were many observers in antiquity and in the Middle Ages who maintained that it is the very nature of a spherical body to rotate with uniform circular motion. This was the view of Plato and Copernicus; but others, including Aristotle and Thomas, insisted on the radical difference between celestial and terrestrial motions. Terrestrial motions are of two kinds: natural and violent. All natural motion comes about from some internal principle that determines the body to act in a certain kind of way, while violent motion must be explained by some external force acting upon the body, the body itself contributing nothing to it.[38] Violence, like chance, happens only rarely and unpredictably, and it cannot be said that the regularity of the heavens is due to violence or chance. While violent action can be seen on earth, Aristotle totally excludes it from celestial motions. Natural motions, on the other hand, are of two kinds: animate and inanimate. Animate motions are those produced by living bodies, whose "soul" is the efficient cause of movement through its various parts. Inanimate motions are those emanating from an internal active or passive principle, but not through efficient causality. That is to say, the soul of living things is the efficient cause, the *motor*, of animate motions, whereas the "nature" of inanimate things moves spontaneously and dynamically toward a specific kind of motion and finality by the active principle within the inanimate body, provided that these motions are not impeded by some obstacle. The formal nature of a nonliving body is not a *motor*; it is not an efficient cause of its own motion. The true efficient cause of such spontaneous natural activity is the "generator" of the body in the first place; it is the generator who produced the natural form. Once the form is generated by a distinct agency, the body immediately, spontaneously, and dynamically (*subito* and *statim*) manifests all its natural accidents, motions, and finality.[39] Once the natural body is generated, there is no need to look for another *motor* or efficient cause to account for its natural motions.

Celestial motions, for Aristotle, cannot be explained by the nature of the physical sphere, as Plato would have it. For Aristotle, the celestial body has no intrinsic formal principle causing it to move spontaneously in circular rotation. Nevertheless, these regular, uniform, and eternal motions are "natural" and partake of the divine. Therefore, for Aristotle, celestial bodies are animated by a soul, which is the *motor*, the efficient cause of celestial movement.[40] Thus for Aristotle, each sphere was animated by a special soul, which was the formal cause, as well as the efficient cause, of celestial motion. The number of souls (or divinities) depended on the number of motions required to explain celestial motions. Aristotle, adopting the view of Callippus, postulated fifty-two or forty-seven. Each soul of the sphere was itself a substance separate from matter, and hence these souls were called separate substances. For Thomas it did not make much difference (*nec multum refert*) whether the sphere was moved by a soul inherent in the body or by a distinct substance, separate from matter, moving the sphere through its efficient causality.[41] What was clear to him was that a heavenly body had to be moved by something distinct from itself, and that this mover had to be a substance separate from matter. One could, therefore, conclude that each celestial sphere moves itself by reason of its animate form, so that the ultimate soul of the first sphere was the first mover of the universe. Thomas, of course, preferred to think of these separate substances not as souls animating celestial bodies but as separate efficient causes, like an "angel" moving the body.[42]

Since, for Aristotle, there can be only one universe, the mover of the outermost sphere has to be unique and supreme, for all other motions depend upon it. This ultimate mover, it would seem, was the unmoved mover. At least this is the view many recent historians take in explaining the views of Aristotle. It would seem from Aristotle's discussion in *Metaphysics* XII, however, that the ultimate unmoved mover is a separate substance for whose sake the first mover acts, a substance which is subsistent thinking thought.[43] Already in Thomas's day there were some who maintained that God was (according to Aristotle) only the final cause of all; there were also others who maintained that Aristotle's God is only a *causa movendi* and not a *causa essendi*. Rejecting these views, Thomas says, "It should be noted that Aristotle here [*De caelo* I, 4, 271b33] posits God to be maker [i.e., the efficient cause] of the celestial bodies, and not just a cause after the manner of an end, as some have said."[44] In other words, each celestial sphere has a separate substance, either animating it or pushing it, but beyond the first "soul," the *anima mundi*, there is the creator and final cause of all, whom Aristotle, according to Thomas, calls God, who creates as well as moves the entire universe. "And so it is evident that although Aristotle postulated the eternity of the world, he did not for this reason deny that God is the *causa essendi* of the universe, as some would have it, claiming that God is only a *causa movendi*."[45]

The Earth and Terrestrial Motions

Apparently in antiquity there were some who thought that the earth is flat. Aristotle mentions Anaximenes, Anaxagoras, and Democritus as giving "the flatness of the earth as the cause of its immobility."[46] To those who thought the earth flat, one might add the Jews, for whom the firmament was like an inverted bowl or upper hemisphere. No one in the age of Columbus had reason to think that the earth is flat or that if one came to the "edge" of it, one would fall off. This might have been the popular opinion of some unlearned men, but it was never the view of philosophers and scientists. Even those who postulated a cosmic fire, the sun, as the center of the universe, like the Pythagoreans, maintained that the earth is a sphere or globe which moves with uniform motion around the sun. The sphericity of the earth is most readily seen in an eclipse of the moon, when the earth comes between the sun, the source of light, and the moon, upon which the shadow of the earth is cast. Aristotle frequently referred to the free-fall of heavy bodies as proof of the earth's sphericity: no matter how distant the points of experiment are, heavy bodies always fall perpendicular to the earth as its center, and not parallel to each other. One could also argue, as many ancients did, from the experience of watching ships come into port: at first only the uppermost part of the mast is visible before the whole ship is seen.

The real problem in antiquity, and in the Middle Ages too, was in determining the center of the universe; or, to put the question in another way: Is the earth at rest or in motion? Heraclitus, Aristarchus of Samos, and the Pythagoreans maintained that the earth revolves around the sun, or cosmic fire, which is the center of the universe. Aristotle and the great majority of thinkers opted for the experience of sense, in which the earth is stable and the heavens revolve. If the universe is finite and revolving, then its center, whatever it may be, must be immobile. The center of any revolving sphere is immobile. As far as calculations are concerned, it makes little difference whether the earth is mobile or immobile, but it makes a great deal of difference to the natural philosopher, who wants to know what things really are in their nature. In antiquity, Anaximander, Anaxagoras, Democritus, Empedocles, Platonists, and Aristotelians opted for a stable earth around which all the heavens revolve.[47] If the center of the universe is taken to be the center of the spherical earth, then it necessarily follows that the center of the earth is immobile. If that be granted, it also follows that "up" and "down" are absolute terms, so that if a piece of terrestrial earth were to be put where the moon now is, that earth would tend to move toward the center where the earth now is. Aristotle defines the terms "up" and "down" in terms of the local motion of bodies toward the center of the universe (earth) or away from it. Thus bodies are called "heavy" if they tend toward the center of the earth, and "light" if they tend away from the center and toward the celestial bodies.

Both Aristotle and Thomas considered the earth to be a "sphere of no great size."[48] Relying on the mathematicians of his day, Aristotle gave the earth's circumference as 400,000 Greek stades. Thomas calculated this as 50,000 Roman miles, since for him a Greek stade is one-eighth of a Roman mile. Hence the universe, Aristotle contends, is "of no great size." Thomas, however, notes that

according to the more careful measurements of present-day astronomers, the earth's circumference is much less, i.e., 20,400 miles as Al-Fragani says; or 180,000 stades as Simplicius says, which is roughly the same, since 20,000 is one-eighth of 160,000.[49]

In explaining what Aristotle meant by "no great size," Thomas notes that astronomers of his day hold that the sun is 170 times greater in size than the earth. Today we hold that the sun's radius is 109 times greater than the earth's equatorial radius.

The method used by Thomas's sources, which he carefully explained, is based on the terrestrial length compared to one degree of difference in the heavens:

Astronomers were able to calculate this [distance] by considering how much space of earth makes for a difference of one degree in the heavens; and they found that it was 500 stades according to Simplicius, or 56 and ⅔ miles according to Al-Fragani. Hence, multiplying this number by 360, which is the number of degrees in the heavens, they found the size of the earth's circumference.[50]

According to the calculations of modern scientists, Aristotle's estimate is twice too large, and Simplicius's and Thomas's figure not large enough; for Aristotle's measurements came to approximately 46,000 miles, and Al-Fragani's and Simplicius's come to about 20,500, whereas a rough modern calculation is 24,900 miles at the equatorial circumference. It would seem that Thomas learned the method of calculating the size of the earth from

Simplicius or from Albert the Great, who claims to be following Alcemenon (whoever he was) and Ptolemy.[51] Albert's commentary was written some twenty years earlier than Thomas's.

In Books III and IV, Aristotle considers the position of heavy and light bodies, but Thomas commented only as far as III, c. 3, 302b9 (lect. 8). In this brief space there are two important points to consider.

First, Thomas carefully identifies the first mover of the universe in the order of natural movers. This first mover, being made up of "soul" and "heavenly body," moves itself and in its motion moves everything in the heavens. This first mover is comparable to Plato's mover who first initiates the movement of elements into a structured universe. Such a "first mover," which moves itself in the perpetual movement of the first sphere, "should not be understood as the absolutely first, because this latter is absolutely immobile [*omnino immobile*], as proved in Phys. VIII and in Metaph. XII." Rather, such a mover is "the *primum movens* in the category of natural movers, which moves itself, as composed of a *motor* and a *motum*, as proved in Phys. VIII, 5 (lect. 10)."[52] In this passage, Thomas admits that the first physical mover could, if one wished to hold it, be considered a self-mover, i.e., a composite of a celestial body and an immaterial, immortal soul, as Aristotle seems to suggest. But Thomas insists both here and elsewhere that beyond such a self-mover there is another reality, whom we call God. It would seem that this passage in the commentary on *De caelo*, written at the height of his intellectual powers, agrees satisfactorily with the position advanced when Thomas was a young master in theology composing the first book of the *Summa contra gentiles*, in which he discussed various proofs for the existence of God.[53] In the earlier *Summa*, Thomas had argued to the existence of a first mover who is not moved by anything outside itself. But, he suggests, since such a mover is not necessarily totally unmoved, Aristotle argues further, saying that this idea can be understood in one of two ways: either totally unmoved, in which case it is God, or self-moved, in which case there must be a first mover beyond, who is in no way moved, not even *per accidens*, and this mover we call God. For Thomas, movers of the spheres were not souls but angels who move the bodies in the order of efficient causality. Beyond the highest angel who moves the outermost sphere, there is another reality who is the efficient and final cause of all. This reality he calls God, the Christian God. Never once did Thomas doubt that Aristotle had demonstrated the existence of the one, true God.

The second point Thomas discusses at some length in his commentary on the third book of *De caelo* pertains to gravitational motion. For Aristotle, natural bodies have a natural motion which belongs *per se* to that body. Bodies which naturally move with rectilinear motion have "gravity" and "levity," the latter being a term awkward to translate. Nature, as defined by Aristotle, is a principle (ἀρχή) of motion and rest in those things in which it resides *per se*.[54] Bodies, therefore, are called "natural" which have such a nature and such a natural motion. But all natural rectilinear motion is either up or down, i.e., either heavy or light. Therefore all natural bodies on earth have a natural rectilinear motion. But all rectilinear motion is either up or down. Therefore all natural bodies on earth move either up or down.[55] Among the four simple bodies on earth, namely, earth, water, air, and fire, only two can be said to move absolutely up or absolutely down, namely, earth and fire. Earth is said to move down absolutely because it always tends to fall below water, while fire always tends to move beyond air. Water and air are said to be *relatively* heavy or light because water moves downward in relation to air, but upward in relation to earth, while air moves up in relation to water, but down in relation to fire. Statements such as these are to be understood only in a broad and relative sense, for nature often shows mountains to be higher than lakes, and air higher than fire. Whatever small validity Aristotle's theory of the elements has today, the natural movement of all simple bodies must be seen strictly in a relative context, as I have tried to show elsewhere.[56]

The important point is that a heavy body, for example, has within it a formal, active, dynamic principle whereby it moves downward *secundum principium activum sive formale*. This principle is "nature" as *form*. But all bodies have "nature" also as *matter*, which is an intrinsic passive principle for being acted upon by other natural bodies; this is "nature" *secundum principium passivum, receptivum sive materiale*. This concept of "nature" (φύσις) as an intrinsic active or passive principle is essential to all of Aristotle's philosophy; without an understanding of it, nothing can be correctly understood in any branch of his teaching, least of all in natural philosophy.

The concept of "nature" as an intrinsic principle, both active and passive, distinguishes natural motion from violent ones. Violent motion is one forced upon the body from without; that is, the source of that motion lies in another body, and the body being forced reacts contrary to its nature. "An unnatural movement presupposes a natural movement which it contravenes."[57] Thus violence presupposes nature, as the motion of a heavy body upward presupposes its natural tendency downward. Following Aristotle, Thomas explains the movement of projectiles after they have left the hand of a thrower in terms of the medium which has the means of carrying the projectile against its nature.[58] Thus the Aristotelian explanation of violent motion requires that there be a medium, such as water or air, to allow the possibility of violent motion; in this case, the medium is a necessity, not just a convenience *ad bene esse*.[59]

But Averroes claimed that the medium is absolutely necessary not only for violent motion but for natural motion as well.[60] As Thomas points out, Averroes gives two basic arguments for the need of resistance in natural motion.[61] The first argument is drawn from the need for an efficient cause of all natural movement. The *motor separatus*, or efficient cause, of all heavy and light bodies is the generator, which, in giving the form, gives as a consequence all the natural motions that derive from that form, just as it gives all natural accidents which flow from that form; and so the generator causes natural motion by means of that form. Natural motion, however, ought to follow immediately from its *motor*, its efficient cause. But since natural motion follows immediately not from its efficient cause (the generator) but from the substantial form, it would seem that the substantial form is the proper *motor coniunctus*, the immediate cause of natural motion. And so it would seem, according to Averroes, that heavy and light bodies—in a certain sense—move themselves: of course, not *per se*, for things that move themselves properly (*per se*) have to be divided into "mover" and "moved," which division cannot be properly found in heavy and light bodies, which are divided only into form and matter, the latter of which is not, strictly speaking, "moved." Hence it remains that a heavy or light body moves itself *per accidens*, i.e., much as a sailor moves a ship through whose movement he himself is moved. Similarly, both the light and the heavy body, through their substantial forms, move the air, upon whose motion the heavy and the light body are moved. Hence, Averroes concludes that air is indispensable for natural motion.

The second argument Averroes gives is in his commentary on *Phys.* IV, text. comm. 71, where he says that there must be some kind of resistance between the mover and the moved. But there is no resistance between the matter of a heavy or a light body and their substantial form, which is the principle of their motion. Therefore it is necessary that there be resistance from the medium, which is air or water. Therefore Averroes concludes that air is indispensable for natural motion.

Thomas notes that both of these arguments are based on the same error.[62] Averroes believed that the substantial form of the heavy or light body is an active principle of motion after the manner of a *motor*, or efficient cause of motion, in such a way that there would have to be some resistance to the form's inclination, and also that the motion does not immediately proceed from the generator who produced the form in the first place. Thomas insists that this assumption is altogether false: *hoc est omnino falsum*. For Thomas, the substantial form of heavy and light bodies is a principle of motion not as an agent, a *motor coniunctus*, but as a principle, or source, by which (*quo*) the mover causes motion; it is like color, which is the principle by which we see. In all natural inanimate motion the substantial form is no more than an instrument *by which* the agent acts.

Thomas explicitly says that "the motion of heavy and light bodies does not derive from the generator by means of any other moving source." That is, there is no need to look for any resistance beyond what already obtained between generator and generated, agent and patient. Consequently, natural motions do not need a medium in which to move, whereas violent motions do. Whatever moves naturally already has everything it needs to move; it has an innate source, or power, of moving. In short, it has "nature" as an active formal principle, which is not an efficient cause. So there is absolutely no need to look for any other efficient cause to impel such bodies when they move naturally; there is no need to postulate a *motor coniunctus*; there is no need to look for any other efficient cause of motion distinct from the generator which produced the natural form in a given body. The case of violent motion is different, for in violent motions the source of movement is always outside the body being moved, impelling the projectile along. Thomas is explicit here and elsewhere: natural motion is possible even in a void, or vacuum; natural motions do not need the resistance of a medium.

The commentary on Aristotle's *De caelo* by St. Thomas Aquinas is a valuable source for his mature thought on the basic principles of natural philosophy. There is no evidence of a change of teaching, but there is ample evidence to show that we have here a deeper understanding of the basic elements of his philosophy of nature.

Notes

1. "A Catalogue of St. Thomas's Works: Bibliographical Notes," in É. Gilson, *The Christian Philosophy of St. Thomas Aquinas* (New York, 1956), item 31, p. 402.

2. Thomas, *In I De caelo*, prooem., n. 3.

3. Thomas, *In III De caelo*, lect. 1, n. 1.

4. P. Mandonnet, *Des Écrits Authentiques de S. Thomas D'Aquin*, ed. 2 revue et corrigée (Fribourg, 1910), p. 31.

5. Ibid., p. 49.

6. Ibid., p. 61.

7. Ibid., p. 69.

8. M. Grabmann, *Die Werke des hl. Thomas von Aquin*, 3d ed. (Münster Westf., 1949), p. 97.

9. Ibid., p. 276.

10. Eschmann, "Catalogue," item 31, p. 402.

11. A. Birkenmajer, "Vermischte Untersuchungen," *Beiträge z. Gesch. d. Phil. d. MA.*, Bd, XX, H. 5, pp. 6ff.

12. Ibid.

13. "Processus Canonizationis S. Thomae Aquinatis, Neapoli," n. 58, *S. Thomae Aquinatis Vitae Fontes Praecipuae*, ed. A. Ferrua (Alba, 1968), p. 287.

14. Aristotle, *Phys.* II, 2, 193b34.

15. Ibid., 193b24.

16. Thomas, *In I Meteorol*, lect. 1, n. 1.

17. Thomas, *In I Phys.*, lect. 1, n. 4.

18. Thomas, *In I De caelo*, lect. 1, n. 3.

19. Ibid., prooem., n. 4.

20. Simplicius, op. cit., prooem., fol. 2rb.

21. Thomas, *In I De caelo*, prooem., n. 5.

22. Thomas, *In I Phys.*, lect. 1, n. 4.

23. Albert, *I De caelo*, tr. 1, c. 1, ed. cit., 1, 60–63.

24. Thomas, *Sum. theol.* II-II, q. 1, a. 1.

25. Thomas, *In II De caelo*, lect. 17, n. 2.

26. Simplicius, *In II De caelo*, 12, comm. 43, fol. 74r-v.

27. Artist., *Metaph.* XII, 8, 1073b18–31.

28. Cf. T. L. Heath, *Aristarchus of Samos* (Oxford, 1913), pp. 195–96.

29. Arist., *Metaph.* XII, 8, 1073b31–1074a14.

30. Ibid., 1074a16.

31. Thomas, *In I De caelo*, lect. 3, n. 7.

32. Ibid.

33. Ibid.

34. Thomas, *In II De caelo*, lect. 17, n. 2.

35. Thomas, *Sum. theol.* I, q. 32, a. 1, ad 2.

36. Thomas, *In II De caelo*, lect. 11, n. 2.

37. Ibid., lect. 1, nn. 2–3; I, lect. 22, n. 1; *Sum. theol.* I, q. 46, a. 1; *De aeternitate mundi*.

38. Arist., *Eth. Nic.* III, 1, 1110a1–3.

39. Thomas, *In III De caelo*, lect. 7, nn. 5–8; James A. Weisheipl, *Nature and Motion in the Middle Ages* (Washington, D.C., 1985), chap. 1.

40. See Weisheipl, *Nature and Motion*, chap. 7.

41. Thomas, *In II De caelo*, lect. 3, n. 3.

42. Ibid.

43. Arist., *Metaph.* XII, 7, 1072b25–29.

44. Thomas, *In I De caelo*, lect. 8, n. 14; cf. *In VI Metaph.*, lect. 1, n. 1164; *In VIII Phys.*, lect. 3, n. 6.

45. Thomas, *In VIII Phys.*, lect. 3, n. 6.

46. Arist., *De caelo* II, 13, 294b14–15.

47. Thomas, *In II De caelo*, lect. 20, n. 3.

48. Ibid., lect. 28, n. 3; Arist., *De caelo* II, 14, 298a7–8.

49. Thomas, *In II De caelo*, lect. 28, n. 4.

50. See Simplicius, *Comm. in libros De caelo* II, comm. 67.

51. Albert, *De caelo*, Lib. 2, tr. 4, cap. 11, ed. Cologne 1971, V/1, p. 201, lines 26–63.

52. Thomas, *In III De caelo*, lect. 6, n. 2.

53. *Sum. cont. gent.* I, c. 13.

54. Arist., *Phys.* II, 1, 192b21–23.

55. Thomas, *In III De caelo*, lect. 7, n. 2.

56. J. A. Weisheipl, "Space and Gravitation," *The New Scholasticism* 29 (1955), 175–223.

57. Arist., *De caelo* III, 2, 300a24–25.

58. Thomas, *In III De caelo*, lect. 7, nn. 5–6.
59. Ibid., n. 6.
60. Averroes, *De caelo* III, comm. 28.
61. Thomas, *In III De caelo*, lect. 7, n. 8.
62. Ibid., n. 9.

2

Matter and Actuality
in Aquinas

I

Aquinas often describes matter as a being in potentiality (*ens in potentia*) or as a being that is or exists in potentiality (*est in potentia*).[1] He also often describes matter as a being in potentiality alone, or as a being that exists only in potentiality. For example, at *Summa Theologiae*, Ia, 76, 1, *responsio*, he writes:

> Form is actuality and matter is a being in potentiality alone (*ens in potentia tantum*).

And at *De Spiritualibus Creaturis, un.*, 1, *ad* 8um, he says:

> Matter can not properly be said to exist except in potentiality. (*Materia non proprie dici quod est, cum non sit nisi in potentia.*)[2]

Matter, as a being in potentiality, but not actuality, contrasts with the subject or individual substance, which is a being in actuality. The contrast is clearly drawn in Aquinas' discussion of change at *Summa Theologiae*, Ia, 45, 2, *ad* 2um:

> It is essential to change that something which is the same be different now from the way it was before. Sometimes it is the same being in actuality (*ens actu*) which is different now from the way it was before, as in the case of qualitative, quantitative, and locational change; sometimes it is the same being in potentiality alone (*ens in potentia tantum*), as happens in substantial change, the subject of which is matter.

In both substantial and accidental change, we have the same subject before and after the change. In the case of accidental change, that subject—the individual substance—is a being in actuality; in the case of substantial change, that subject—matter—is a being in potentiality alone. Here, as elsewhere, Aquinas seems to mean by "in potentiality alone", "in potentiality but not in actuality".

For Aquinas, matter is not actually, but only potentially, a being. At the same time, though, substantial form makes matter actually exist, or gives matter actual existence:

> Form's coming to matter makes matter actually exist (*Forma adveniens materiae facit ipsam esse in actu: De Spiritualibus Creaturis, un., 1, responsio*).

Form gives actual existence (*esse actuale*) to matter (*Summa Theologiae*, Ia, 29, 2, *ad* 5um).[3] If form makes matter actually exist, then—it would seem—matter must actually exist (since nothing can fail to do what something makes it do). Indeed, although Aquinas does not say *sic et simpliciter* that matter is actual, he does say in many places that matter is actual through form:

> Matter is a being in actuality (*ens actu*) through form. (*Summa Theologiae*, Ia, 50, 5, *responsio*.)
> Matter has actual existence (*esse in actu*) through substantial form. (*Summa Theologiae*, Ia, 76, 6, *responsio*.)[4]

If matter is actual through form, then—it would appear—matter is actual. ("Matter is actual through form" seems equivalent to "Matter is actual on account of having form", and P on account of Q entails P.)

How can Aquinas (consistently) maintain both that matter is a being in potentiality alone, and that matter is a being in actuality? Two possibilities immediately suggest themselves. Perhaps the matter that exists only potentially is a different sort of matter from the matter that is form-actuated, and actual. Or perhaps the matter that exists only potentially, and exists actually, is potential and actual at different times.

As we shall see, the first suggestion is on the right track. But it faces the following problem: in a number of places, Aquinas describes matter as both potential and form-actuated in the very same sentence. For instance, at *De Spiritualibus Creaturis, un., 1, ad* 5um, he writes

> Matter is a being in potentiality, and becomes a being in actuality through the coming of form.

In a similar vein, in his commentary on Aristotle's *Metaphysics* (Book IX, L 8, C 1860), he tells us that

> Matter is in potentiality until it receives a form . . . then it exists in actuality.

Both of these passages seem to imply that the same matter that is a being in potentiality alone before the acquisition of a form, is a being in actuality after its acquisition. The same goes for *Summa Theologiae*, Ia, 75, 6, *responsio*:

> Matter acquires actual existence (*esse in actu*) according as it acquires form.

These considerations appear to favor the second suggestion, according to which (for Aquinas) the same matter that exists in potentiality at one time, exists in actuality at another. The difficulty is that, on Aquinas' account, there is not, and could not be matter that is not 'perfected' by some substantial form or other.[5] Moreover, for Aquinas, any substantial form is as fit as any other to make something an actual being, or make something exist in actuality.[6] So if matter exists in actuality when it is actuated by (some) substantial form, then matter always exists in actuality (and never exists only in potentiality). To put the point another way, if matter acquires actual existence according as it acquires substantial form, then matter has always had and will always have actual existence. If matter is never without (substantial) form, and (substantial) form as such actuates, we may say—as Aquinas does—that matter does not *of itself* exist in actuality, or *of itself* participate in actual existence.[7] At least, we may say that if "existing of itself" means "existing by itself". But, as we have seen, Aquinas wants to say, not just that matter doesn't exist in actuality by or of itself, but also that matter doesn't exist in actuality (full stop).

In sum, the texts give us some reason to worry about the consistency of Aquinas' views on the actuality of matter. In what follows, I shall argue that there is room for an interpretation on which those views are consistent. To make room, we will need to see that when Aquinas says that matter is a being in potentiality, but not in actuality, what he means by "being", and by "potentiality" is rather different from what we are likely to mean by those terms.

II

At *De Spiritualibus Creaturis*, un., 1, *ad* 8um, Aquinas writes that matter cannot properly be called *quod est*, because it *est* only in potentiality. Given that *est* is used here without a predicative complement, it is natural to translate it as "exist". If we do that, we shall conclude that Aquinas is saying that matter cannot properly be said to exist, since it exists only in potentiality. The difficulty is that this last claim sounds like the claim that there isn't any matter, though there could (yet) be some. And it is clear that, for Aquinas, matter does not have the status of an as yet unactualized *possibile*, like the statue I might make from a bit of marble, or the third child we might have. After all, Aquinas holds that matter has been around since the creation of the world (cf. *Summa Theologiae*, Ia, 66, 1).

This difficulty stems from the fact that we are wont to regard "exists" as what David Lewis calls a "blanket term"—that is, a term that applies to anything (real) at all. The same goes for "being" used as a noun. Aquinas, however, does not think of *est* or *ens* as (univocal) blanket terms. Instead he thinks of those terms as having a variety of increasingly narrow and increasingly proper senses. Thus at *De Ente et Essentia*, 1, he writes that *ens* has two senses. In one sense (like "object" for the Meinongian) it covers anything about which we can form an affirmative proposition, including things that do not exist *in rerum natura*, but only in the mind.[8] In another, narrower sense, the term *ens* covers only things that have real existence, and is divided by the categories.[9] (It is this intermediate sense of *ens* that is probably closest to the way we understand the English terms "being" and "entity.") In a still narrower sense, Aquinas avers, *ens* covers individual substances, but not (received) forms:

> Only substances are properly and truly called beings (*entia*); an accident does not have being (*esse*), though something is on its account. For this reason we say that an accident is of a being (*entis*) rather than a being (*ens*), and the same goes for all other non-subsistent forms. (*Summa Theologiae*, Ia, 90, 2, *responsio*.)

In the narrowest—and for Aquinas the most proper—sense, an *ens* is something that exists, but does not exist either as a form or a part of anything else that exists *per se*.

Given that an *ens* is a thing that *est*, it is not surprising that, for Aquinas, *esse* is ambiguous in just the way *ens* is. In its broadest sense, *esse* may be attributed to any *ens* in the broadest sense, and thus to things having no real existence (*Quodlibetum* 9, 2, 2, *responsio*). In a narrower sense, *esse* may be attributed to all and only real things (the ones falling under the categories). In its narrowest and most proper sense, *esse* may be attributed only to things that *exist per se*, and neither to received forms or *esse* nor to things like hands and feet, which, as Aquinas puts it, "exist not in themselves but in a whole":[10]

Esse is attributed only to a substance which subsists *per se*: everything which does not subsist *per se* but in another and with another, whether it is an accident, or a substantial form, or any part, does not have *esse* as though it truly were. (*Quodlibetum* 9, 2, 2, *responsio*.)

In its narrowest sense—and in the sense in which it is most often used by Aquinas—*esse* means "existence as a complete individual being" (just as, in its narrowest sense, *ens* means "complete individual being").

Why "complete individual being" rather than "complete individual substance"? Aquinas often makes it sound as if *esse* in the strictest sense may be attributed only to individual substances (e.g., in the passage just cited), but he holds that in the sacrament of the Eucharist, "floating" accidents (anchored in no individual substance) have *esse* in the strictest sense, and are, like (finite) individual substances, composed of *esse* and *quod est* (*Summa Theologiae*, IIIa, 77, 1, *ad* 1um).

Given Aquinas' views on the de-inherence of accidents in the sacrament of the Eucharist, we might suppose that having *esse* in the narrowest sense is just existing (in the blanket sense), and being neither a part of, nor a property of, anything else. But *esse* so defined will not cover all and only those things Aquinas thinks *esse* most strictly construed covers, if stones are parts of the houses or heaps made out of them. After all, Aquinas would not say that the stones in a heap or a house lack *esse* most narrowly construed, inasmuch as they are parts of something else. The way *esse* gets attributed to a house and its stones is, Aquinas thinks, quite different from the way *esse* gets attributed to, say, an animal and its organs. In the latter case, it is only the whole (the animal) that has (strict) *esse*; in the former case it is only the parts (the stones) that do. For Aquinas, neither a heap nor a house has a substantial form of its own (*Summa Theologiae*, IIIa, 2, 1, *responsio*), and having a substantial form of one's own is a precondition for having *esse* strictly construed (*De Principiis Naturae*, 1).

Now Aquinas does not seem averse to thinking of stones as parts of heaps or houses (see again *Summa Theologiae*, IIIa, 2, 1, where he offers stone houses and heaps of stones as examples of a one constituted from a many). So, whatever *Quodlibetum*, 9 might suggest, it seems that, for Aquinas, what disqualifies a thing from having *esse* strictly construed is not being a part of something else, but being a part of something else that has *esse* strictly construed (equivalently, being a part of something else that is one *simpliciter*, and not just one *secundum quid*).

If this is so, we cannot define *esse* in the strictest sense in terms of the blanket concept of existence, and the concepts of part and property. In fact, I don't know any way to define *esse* strictly construed in terms of concepts I have a full grasp of. *Esse* so construed applies to Aristotelian first substances (and to accidents miraculously transformed into non-inherent individuals), but this doesn't pin down the intension of *esse* until the intension of "first substance" is pinned down. Though it is clear enough that such things as men, trees, and stones belong to the intension of "first substance", I am unclear as to where the boundaries of that intension lie. Consider the case of certain undersea sponge-like creatures made up of cells that are neither highly specialized, nor highly organized. Should we say (would Aquinas want to say) such beings are individual substances, and have *esse*, unlike the cells they are made of? Or should we say (would Aquinas want to say) that the cells are substances, and have *esse*, unlike the *unum secundum quid* they constitute? I don't know. Living beings are according to Aquinas first substances *par excellence*, but I doubt Aquinas countenanced the possibility of one living thing's being part of another. If he had, perhaps he would not have held that one first substance is never part of another.[11]

Setting these questions aside, we can now see why Aquinas would want to deny that matter is actually an *ens*, and deny that it actually has *esse*. Matter is not a complete individual substance, but only a part of a part of a substance—that is, a part of an essence which, together with predicamental accidents and *esse*, constitutes an individual substance. As Aquinas puts it at *Summa Contra Gentiles*, II, 54:

> Matter is a part of a substance . . . and *esse* is attributed not to the matter but to the whole.

So, as long as the strictest and most proper senses of *ens* and *esse* are in play, matter isn't actually an *ens*, and doesn't actually have *esse*.

III

Though this makes it easier to see why matter isn't a being in actuality (*ens actu*) and doesn't exist in actuality, it doesn't help us see how matter could be a being in potentiality, or exist in potentiality. If matter is by nature an incomplete being—*incompletissimum inter omnia entia*, as Aquinas puts it at *De Spiritualibus Creaturis, un., 1, responsio*—and if only complete beings are *entia*, how could matter be even potentially an *ens*? It is no good objecting that matter is the right sort of thing to be an *ens* in the less strict senses of the term; in those senses, matter is actually, and not just potentially, an *ens*.

It might be thought that these worries arise from a failure to properly unpack the phrase *ens in potentia tantum*. If matter is a being in potentiality, towards what is it in potentiality? Form(s):

Matter, considered as such, is in potentiality towards form. Considered in itself... matter is in potentiality towards the forms of all those things of which it is common matter. Through any one form, however, it is in act only with respect to that form. So it remains in potentiality towards all the other forms. (*Summa Theologiae*, Ia, 66, 2, *responsio*.)

If an *ens in potentia tantum* is something that is only potentially an *ens*, we encounter the difficulty that matter is actually an *ens* in the laxer senses, and (apparently) not even potentially an *ens* in the strictest sense. There is no problem, though, if when Aquinas says matter is an *ens in potentia tantum*, he means that matter is (actually) a being (in a laxer sense) in potentiality in a certain way—*viz.*, in potentiality towards having every sort of (sublunary) substantial form except the one it actually has.

In fact, though, Aquinas describes matter not just as in potentiality towards substantial form, but also as in potentiality towards substantial *esse* (*De Principiis Naturae*, 1). Substantial *esse* is the *esse* ascribed to substances—that is, *esse* in the strictest sense. Inasmuch as Aquinas holds that matter is in potentiality towards (some) *esse* strictly construed, it seems he must hold matter is in potentiality towards being (some) *ens* strictly construed. In fact, Aquinas says explicitly at both *De Principiis Naturae*, 1, and his Commentary on the *Metaphysics*, IX, L 7, C 1848, that when a man is generated, some matter which was potentially a man (*potentia homo*) becomes actually a man (*actu homo*).[12] Given that a man is an *ens* in the strict sense, whatever is in potentiality towards being a man is in potentiality towards being (some) *ens* in the strict sense. Once again, we seem driven to conclude that, for Aquinas, matter isn't just something potentially having the form of a certain *ens*, but is also potentially a certain *ens*.

Aquinas' just cited remarks on generation raise a further problem. With Aristotle, and (he takes it) against the pre-socratics, Aquinas insists that the generation of a man is generation *simpliciter* (generation in an unqualified sense), and not generation *secundum quid* (that is, alteration).[13] When something comes to be a man, it comes to be (full stop). But how can it be true that in generation a man comes to be, if it is also true that in generation, something already there—some matter—comes to be a man? Aquinas thinks there is no incompatibility here, in as much as, when a man comes to be, nothing actual comes to be a man (cf. *De Spiritualibus Creaturis*, un., 3, responsio, where Aquinas says that Aristotle refuted pre-socratic arguments against generation and corruption *simpliciter* by affirming that matter exists, not actually, but only potentially). It is not clear, though, how the non-actuality of matter solves the difficulty in question. After all, Aquinas admits that in at least one sense of "existent", "existent" is a blanket term, applying to all real beings, whether complete or incomplete. Moreover, he is clearly committed to the view that in the process that terminates in something's being a man, something pre-existent *in the blanket sense*—a bit of matter—becomes a man. Why isn't this enough to rule out that the process terminates in a man's coming to be? How can it be true at one and the same time both that a pre-existent X becomes a Y, and that a Y comes to be *simpliciter*?

It can be true both that a pre-existent X becomes Y, and that Y comes to be (*simpliciter*), as long as, in becoming Y, X becomes something else. For instance, it can be true both that day becomes night, and that night comes to be (*simpliciter*), because when day becomes night, day becomes something else. Also, suppose that you start with some iron, and add chromium and nickel to it (in the right proportions). Then the iron you start with becomes—or if you prefer, turns into or is turned into—steel; and when iron becomes or is turned into steel, steel comes to be (*simpliciter*).

Just as the addition of chromium and nickel to iron makes a bit of iron steel, for Aquinas the "addition"—that is, the advent—of a human form makes a bit of matter become (turns that matter into) a man. Not that that bit of matter ever is a man.[14] A bit of matter is, as we have seen, only part of the man it is turned into, in the way that (we might say) iron is only part of the steel it is turned into, or—to vary the analogy—a bit of flour is only a (nearly maximal) part of the enriched flour it turns into when vitamins are added to it. (Enriched flour is not, on the most natural way of understanding the term, pure flour adjoining some enrichers, but flour-plus-enrichers: an industrial buyer who ordered 10 tons of enriched flour would expect to get 10 tons of flour-plus-vitamins, rather than 10 tons of flour with several pounds of vitamins mixed in.)

So, just because matter is one thing, and the substance matter becomes is something else, Aquinas can consistently maintain both that matter becomes substance, and that (material) substances come to be (*simpliciter*); that (ungenerated) matter becomes the thing generated when it is brought to actuality by form. (See the Commentary on the *Metaphysics*, VII, L 6, C 1412.)

If this is right, and if a bit of matter is potentially a man, the potentiality of some matter to be a man is of a different sort from, say, the potentiality of a man to be pale. Something potentially pale has the potentiality to *be* pale; something that is potentially a man has the potentiality to *become* or *turn into* a man. In his discussion of what he calls potentialities towards accidental *esse*, and potentialities towards substantial *esse* at *De Principiis Naturae*, 1, Aquinas does not distinguish potentialities-to-be from potentialities-to-become in those terms: while the potentialities are clearly distinguished in terms of their having as their object different kinds of *esse*, they are not explicitly distinguished in terms of their being different kinds of potentialities (that is, in terms of their being potentialities in different senses). But if some matter's potentiality to be a man is a straightforward potentiality-to-be, then *contra* Aquinas, 'man' is a phase sortal for a bit of matter, and what we ordinarily think of as generation in an unqualified sense is just alteration.

If on the other hand the potentiality at issue is a potentiality-to-become, and the strict sense of *ens* is in play, then a bit of matter can be potentially, but not actually, an *ens*. I suggest that Aquinas has in mind a potentiality-to-become, and *ens* in the strict sense, when he says that matter is an *ens in potentia*, and becomes an actual being (*fit ens actu*) through the advent of form (*De Spiritualibus Creaturis, un., I, ad 5um*). More generally, I think that Aquinas' claim that matter is an *ens in potentia tantum* is best understood as the claim that matter isn't an *ens* but could become (or be turned into) one. Similarly, his claim that matter *est in potentia tantum* is best understood as the claim that matter is not the sort of thing that can actually have *esse*, but only the sort of thing that could become, or be turned into, something that actually does.

It might be objected here that since every bit of matter there is has already been "turned into" a complete being, matter will after all be actually, and not just potentially, a complete being. But this presupposes that matter actually is what it has been turned into, which is not true. When some iron has been turned into steel, it does not become true that that iron is steel. When some matter has been turned into a man, it does not become true that that matter is a man. So Aquinas can say that matter isn't actually a complete being, even if it can be and has been turned into one; and that matter is potentially a being, in that it is (always) true of (a bit of sublunary) matter that it could yet be turned into this or that sort of complete being.[15]

IV

As we have seen, Aquinas says both that

(1) Matter *de se* has *esse incompletum*.

and

(2) Matter has *esse completum* through form.[16]

There is no problem about why Aquinas asserts (1); matter by itself—matter not "enriched" by the addition of form—lacks complete *esse*. But there is still the problem we started with about how Aquinas can consistently assert (2), given that, by his lights, matter doesn't have *esse completum*. If matter doesn't actually have *esse completum*, how can matter have it *per formam*?

The answer seems to be that the matter that doesn't have *esse completum* is different from the matter that has *esse completum* through form. At *De Principiis Naturae*, 2, Aquinas draws a distinction between two types of sublunary matter:

> Some matter has form as a component, like the bronze that is the matter of a statue: the bronze itself is composed of matter and form. Bronze is accordingly not called prime matter, since it has form. [Only] that matter which is construed without any form or privation, but is subject to form and privation, is called prime matter, inasmuch as there is no other matter prior to it.

Because the bronze of the statue is hylomorphically complete, it has *esse completum*. So, where *esse* is *esse completum*, it can be true both that

(a) The (prime) matter of the bronze does not have *esse*.

and that

(b) The (form-including) matter of the statue has *esse* through its (brazen) substantial form.

Another sort of matter that has composition of (prime) matter and form is flesh:

> If we consider, some flesh . . . according to what is formal in it, in this sense, the flesh always remains . . . but if we consider the flesh according to its matter, then it does not remain, but is gradually destroyed and renewed. (*Summa Theologiae*, Ia, 119, 1, ad 2um.)

Similarly, the human body that is the matter of a human being is itself partly composed of form. Like flesh, the body undergoes compositional change, which only form-including matter can do. Also, if the human body were prime matter, it would be ingenerable and incorruptible; but the body goes out of existence at death. (Of course, a dead body may remain after death; but for Aquinas a dead body [or corpse] is not a human body in the strict sense: see, e.g., *Summa Theologiae*, IIIa, 25, 6, ad 3um, and *De Spiritualibus Creaturis*, un., 9, ad 3um.)

It can accordingly be true both that

(c) The (prime) matter of this flesh (or of this body) does not have *esse*.

and

(d) The (form-including) matter of this man (this man's body) has *esse* through its form (this man's soul). (See *De Spiritualibus Creaturis*, 4, responsio: *Totum corpus et omnes eius partes habent esse substantialem et specificum per formam*.)

Moral: Aquinas can consistently assert both (1) and (2), because (1) is about 'thin' or prime matter, and (2) is about 'thick' or form-including matter. (I use the phrase 'form-including matter', rather than 'informed matter', because 'informed matter' is ambiguous. On one way of understanding the phrase, informed matter is matter-plus-form, just as enriched flour is flour-plus-vitamins. On another way of understanding the phrase, informed matter is [pure] matter that stands in the in-union-with relation to some form. So although "prime matter" unambiguously means thin or pure matter, "informed matter" does not unambiguously mean thick or form-including matter; it could be taken to mean either thick matter or thin matter.)

V

The distinction between thick and thin matter enables us to reconcile apparently conflicting Thomistic claims about matter and *esse*. Once the distinction is drawn, however, it is natural to ask how a bit of thick matter is related to the individual substance it constitutes, and the essence thereof. By way of conclusion, I shall indicate why this question seems to me to raise some problems about the internal coherence of Aquinas' hylomorphic account of the nature of material substances.

What is the relation between a bronze statue and its thick matter (the bronze it is made of)? We might suppose that the bronze statue is an individual substance distinct from the (brazen) thick matter it was made from, but Aquinas would not see things this way. If he did, he would say that a statue comes to be *simpliciter* when some bronze takes on the shape of the statue—and this he clearly denies at *De Principiis Naturae*, 1. Where artefacts are concerned, he holds, there aren't two distinct items—the individual substance and its thick matter—because "in artefacts, the matter alone is the substance" (Commentary on the *Metaphysics*, IX, L 3, C 1719).

Is the relation between a man and his thick matter (his flesh and bones, his body) also identity? Aquinas seems to think not:

> A body is a part of a man. (*Summa Theologiae*, Ia, 76, 1, *responsio*.)

> Sometimes from things joined together a third thing results, as . . . a man is composed of soul and body. (*Quodlibetum*, 2, 2, 1.)

Both of these citations seem to say that a body is not the whole of a man, and the second seems to say that a soul is not a part of a body. (Given that Wimbledon is a part of London, how could it be true that from the joining of Wimbledon and London, a third thing results?) Now, as we have seen, a human body is a bit of thick matter. As such, it must be partly composed of a substantial form. If the substantial form that is the human soul is not a part of the body, then the body must be partly composed of a substantial form different from the soul. This entails that one man is (partially) constituted by two different substantial forms—one intrinsic to his thick matter and one extrinsic to (though presumably joined to) that matter. This last conclusion, of course, is unacceptable to Aquinas. If the body has a substantial form of its own, distinct from the soul, Aquinas insists, then the soul is an accidental form.[17]

It might be thought that this is a problem for Aquinas' hylomorphic account of human beings in particular, but not for his hylormorphic account of material substances in general. What it shows—it might be said—is that if Aquinas wants to think of the body as thick matter, and of the soul as a substantial form, then he should think of the soul as a part of the body, and of the body as the same as the man—in just the way he does think of the brazen form as part of the bronze, and the bronze as the same as the bronze statue.

But why does Aquinas think of the soul and the body as proper parts of a man? Is it just because he is influenced by a conception of body and soul incompatible with a thoroughly hylomorphic account of them? I don't think so. I think he holds that body and soul are proper parts of a man because he holds that body is to soul as matter is to form,[18] and that

(3) For any material substance, there is exactly one bit of matter, and exactly one substantial form, such that
    (i) The substance is essentially constituted by that bit of matter and that form.
    (ii) Both the matter and the form (at least partially) constitute the (individual) essence of that substance.

(iii) Neither the matter nor the form (taken individually) wholly constitute the (individual) essence of that substance.

and

(iv) The matter and the form jointly wholly constitute the (individual) essence of that substance.[19]

Now, whether or not body is to soul as matter is to form, (3) will be
incompatible with the doctrine of the unicity of substantial form, given
that—as Aquinas agrees—some substances do not have their thin matter
essentially. Let s be any such substance. No matter-form pair whose matter
is thin will satisfy (C) for s, since, we are supposing, there is no bit of thin
matter that substance s is essentially constituted by (so condition (i) is not
met). So if any matter-form pair satisfies (C) for s, it will consist of a bit of
thick or form-including matter m, and a form f. If m is a bit of thick matter,
it must have some (substantial) form as a part, but that form may or may
not be the (substantial) form f. Suppose it is. Then m and f jointly wholly
constitute the essence of substance s if and only if m wholly constitutes the
essence of s. (Compare: Socrates and his hand jointly wholly constitute a
thing if and only if Socrates wholly constitutes that thing.) So if m has f as
its formal part, the pair <m, f> fails to satisfy (C) for s, because either m
wholly constitutes the essence of s, in which case condition (iii) is not met,
or m only partially constitutes the essence of s, in which case condition (iv)
is not met. The only way that the thick matter m and the form f can jointly
wholly constitute the essence of s, even though neither m nor f (taken
individually) wholly constitutes the essence of s, is if the substantial form f
is distinct from the substantial form that partially constitutes m—in which
case the unicity of substantial form goes by the board, inasmuch as some
material substance will be partially constituted of two different substantial
forms (one that makes its (thick) matter the kind of thick matter it is, and
one that makes it the kind of material substance it is).

In sum: given that Aquinas thinks that there is exactly one substantial form
in a substance, it seems he cannot consistently hold that for each individual
substance, there is some bit of individual matter that only partially constitutes
the (individual) essence of that substance. The only sorts of matter there are
are thick matter and thin matter (since every bit of matter is either partly
composed of substantial form or not partly composed of substantial form).
No bit of thin matter even partially constitutes the essence of a (compositionally changeable) material substance;[20] some bit of thick matter wholly
constitutes the essence of that substance.

Perhaps I am mistaken in thinking that Aquinas accepts (3). Even if this is so, there is still some interest in the claim that Aquinas is committed to the idea that the thick matter that individuates a material thing wholly constitutes its essence. If he is so committed, his version of hylomorphism is rather different from what we might have expected it to be.

It is plausible that, even if a particular mountain is essentially constituted by a bit of rock, there is more to that mountain's essence than just being constituted by that bit of rock. After all, if the bit of rock constituting, say, Monte Grande somehow melted down into an enormous puddle of molten rock, Monte Grande would cease to exist—because it had lost its shape (or its solidity), not because it had "lost its stuff". *Being Monte Grande*, it seems, is not just *being made of this rock*, but *being made of this rock and having (more or less) this shape*.

So if we think of Monte Grande's essence hylomorphically, we might naturally think of it as constituted by some thick matter (the rock) and a form. That form might be thought of (less plausibly) as just the shape of Monte Grande, or (more plausibly) as a form the possession of which entailed having (more or less) the shape of Monte Grande. The point is that we need *something* (formal) to complete Monte Grande's essence, inasmuch as the continued existence of Monte Grande's thick matter is not sufficient for the continued existence of Monte Grande.

We have already seen that Aquinas rejects a "thick matter plus form" account of the essence of statues and other artefacts. It now appears that he would have to reject such an account for mountains and other *naturalia* as well. Again, if an essence has some thick matter in it, there's no room left there for a shape or any other additional form.

It seems to follow that the only things that have (a particular bit of a particular kind of) matter *per essentiam* are the bits of matter themselves. One might have thought hylomorphism, with its recognition of a non-material essential principle, was just the sort of view that could accommodate the possibility of a material object's being essentially made of this bit of this kind of stuff (e.g., this flesh) without just being that bit of stuff. But the doctrine of the unicity of substantial form appears to foreclose this possibility. For better or for worse, the hylomorphist who (like Aquinas) accepts the unicity of substantial form seems committed to the view that only bits of stuff have their stuff essentially.[21]

Notes

1. See, for example, *Summa Theologiae*, Ia, 3, 2, and 3, 8; *Summa Contra Gentiles*, I, 17 and II, 16; and *De Spiritualibus Creaturis*, un., I, *ad* 5um.

2. See also *Summa Theologiae*, Ia, 76, 7, *ad* 3um; and *De Principiis Naturae*, 4.

3. Elsewhere Aquinas says that form makes matter exist *simpliciter*, or gives *esse simpliciter* to matter (see *Summa Theologiae*, Ia, 77, 6, *responsio*, and the dis-

puted question *De Anima, un., 9, responsio.* As we shall see, *esse simpliciter* is *esse actuale.*

4. Cf. also *De Principiis Naturae,* 4; *De Ente et Essentia,* 6; and *Quodlibetum,* 3, 1.

5. See *Quodlibetum,* 3, 1, 1: *De Principiis Naturae,* 2; *De Spiritualibus Creaturis, un.,* 1, *responsio,* etc.

6. Cf. *De Anima, un., 9, responsio: Est autem proprium formae substantialis quod det materiae esse simpliciter.*

7. See *De Principiis Naturae,* 2: *Materia] per se numquam potest esse;* and *De Spiritualibus Creaturis, un.,* 1, *responsio: Materia non per se participat esse.* [My emphasis.]

8. *Sciendum est igitur quod ens per se dupliciter dicitur: uno modo quod dividitur per decem genera, alio modo quod significat propositionum veritatem. Horum autem differentia est quod secundo modo potest dici ens omne id de quo affirmativa propositio formari potest, etiam si illud in re nihil ponat. (De Ente et Essentia,* 1.)

9. I don't know how to reconcile Aquinas view that real being is divided by the categories with his view that *esse,* though an accident in the broad sense of being extra-essential, is not a predicamental accident.

10. The phrase is taken from *De Unione Verbi Incarnati, un.,* 2, *responsio.*

11. See the Commentary on the *Metaphysics,* VII, L 13, C 1590–1, where Aquinas says that substances are not composed of other (actual) substances.

12. "If we take this man who is now actually a man, before him in time there was some matter that was potentially a man . . . what is potentially a man becomes actually a man as a result of the man generating him, who is a being in actuality." (Commentary on the *Metaphysics,* IX, L 7, C 1848.)

13. See, for example, *De Spiritualibus Creaturis, un.,* 3, *responsio;* and *Summa Theologiae,* Ia, 76, 4, *responsio.*

14. *Haec est vera: hoc materiatum est homo, non autem haec: materia est homo* (from the Commentary on the *Metaphysics,* VII, L 2, C 1289).

15. It is not infrequently suggested that the Aristotelian conception of (prime) matter as a being only in potentiality is a logically muddled one, resting on a failure to appreciate certain conceptual truths about potentiality and actuality. For example, in an appendix to his commentary on Aristotle's *De Generatione et Corruptione,* C. J. F. Williams writes:

> What is actually the case just is the case. This frequently forgotten fact
> about actuality . . . should prevent us from saying such things as 'It is all
> things in potentiality, but nothing in actuality'. What is actually nothing, is
> nothing. If prime matter is nothing in actuality, there is no such thing.
> What there is is a real confusion in Aristotle's thinking, a notion of prime
> matter which is internally incoherent and to which nothing therefore corre-
> sponds.

Whether or not this criticism is fair to Aristotle, I don't think it could be directed at Aquinas' conception of matter. Whatever his description of matter as "pure potentiality" might suggest, Aquinas does not (incoherently) deny that matter is actually something—in Williams' sense—the blanket sense—of "some-thing". Nor does he deny that matter actually has properties: he holds that, for example, (every bit of) matter always has the property of being in union with some substantial form. Aquinas does (coherently) deny that matter is some thing, where "thing" means *ens completum*.

16. See *De Principiis Naturae*, 1: *Materia . . . de se habet esse incompletum*; and *De Principiis Naturae*, 4: *Materia non habet esse completum nisi per formam*.

17. For a very clear statement of the doctrine of the unicity of substantial form, see *Summa Theologiae*, Ia, 76, 4, where Aquinas says that for one thing there is but one (substantial) form, and that "it is by the soul that the body is a body".

18. See, for example, *Summa Theologiae*, Ia, 76, 1, responsio: *Necesse est dicere quod intellectus sit humani corporis forma*. See also *Quodlibetum*, 11, 6, un.: *Illud autem est essentiale cuiuslibet individui quod est ratione ipsius, sicut cuilibet rei materiali sunt essentialia materia et forma . . . prineipia essentialia hominis sunt] anima et corpus*.

19. See *Quodlibetum*, 11, 6, un.*, where Aquinas argues for the numerical identity of a man's risen body with his ante-mortem body:

> In order that a thing be numerically identical, the identity of its essential principles is required . . . What is essential to any individual is what belongs to its nature, as form and matter are essential to a material being . . . Therefore if the essential principles remain, so too does the individual (*remanentibus principiis essentialibus, ipsum individuum remanet idem*).

A bit of matter and a form are the essential principles of a material substance: their continued existence is individually necessary and jointly sufficient for the continued existence of that substance. (So, Aquinas goes on to say in the passage from which the above citation is taken, the body and the soul are the essential principles whose continued existence is individually necessary and jointly sufficient for the continued existence of a man.) I find it difficult to believe that Aquinas would put things this way if he thought that either the bit of matter or the form whose continued existence was necessary for the continued existence of the individual *wholly* constituted the essence of that individual, and hence just was the essence of that individual. It would be very odd to describe the essence of a thing as one of its two essential principles. Other passages indicating that Aquinas thinks of (individual) matter and (individual) form as partial constituents of an (individual) essence include *De Ente et Essentia*, 2, and *Summa Theologiae*, Ia, 75, 4, and 119, 1.

20. Of course, if some thick matter partially or wholly constitutes an individual essence at a time, and some thin matter partially constitutes that thick matter at that time, there is a sense in which the thin matter partially constitutes that individual essence at that time. But thin matter does not even partially constitute the essence of a (compositionally changeable) material substance, in the sense that thin matter cannot be numbered among the *principia essentialia* whose continued existence is individually necessary and jointly sufficient for the continued existence of that substance.

21. In writing this essay, I have benefited from many *buoni consigli patavini*, especially from Mario Mignucci. Many thanks also to Norman Kretzmann, for his comments and suggestions on an earlier version of this essay.

3

The Logic of Being in Thomas Aquinas

Being acquainted with the familiar distinction between the "is" of existence, the "is" of predication, and the "is" of identity, which Hintikka has labeled "the Frege trichotomy" (pp. 433f), a modern student of Thomas Aquinas's doctrine of being cannot fail to realize that this distinction, though it seems not to have been ignored by Aquinas, is overshadowed in his writings by another distinction between two semantically different uses of the verb "be", which he borrows from Aristotle. My aim in this paper is, first, to examine how the two distinctions are related to one another; secondly, to show that Aquinas, though drawing these distinctions, does not commit himself to the assumption that the verb "be" is genuinely ambiguous[1] and, finally, to elucidate how Aquinas avoids such a commitment.

Since it is an ontological and to a certain extent even a theological rather than a logical point of view from which Aquinas approaches the problem of the semantically different uses of the verb "be", what he has to say concerning the logic of being is split up into a lot of scattered remarks, mainly the by-product of metaphysical reflections, from the larger context of which they have to be gathered and put together like the pieces of a jigsaw puzzle. In view of this, not a few of the moves I shall make in my following attempt to trace a coherent picture of Aquinas's logical treatment of the verb "be" will be little more than conjectural.

I

The distinction which plays the predominant role in Aquinas's theory of being is twofold rather than threefold and has indeed been called "a fundamental ontological dichotomy in Thomas Aquinas's thought". In accordance with this dichotomy, for which he invokes the authority of Aristotle (*Metaph.*

Δ 7, 1017 a 22–35),[2] we have to distinguish between the use we make of the verb "be" to express the being of something which falls under one of the ten categories (i.e. the being of something which is either a substance, e.g. a man, or an accidental property, e.g. the white colour of a man), on the one hand, and the use we make of the verb "be" to express the truth (i.e. the being the case) of a true proposition,[3] on the other hand:

> Philosophus, in V *Metaphys*. [. . .], ostendit quod ens multipliciter dicitur. Uno enim modo dicitur ens quod per decem genera dividitur: et sic ens significat aliquid in natura existens, sive sit substantia, ut homo, sive accidens, ut color. Alio modo dicitur ens, quod significat veritatem propositionis. . . . (*In II Sent*. dist. 34, q. 1, a. 1, c)[4]

Used in the first way, we are told by Aquinas, the verb "be" refers "to the act of a being thing insofar as it is being, i.e. to that by which something is called actually being in reality" (*esse dicitur actus entis in quantum est ens, idest quo denominatur aliquid ens actu in rerum natura: Quodl*. IX, q. 2, a. 2[3], c), e.g. to the act of living which is the being of whatever is alive (*In I Sent*. dist. 33. q. 1, a. 1, ad 1). Understood in this sense the term "being thing" (*ens*) applies to "something naturally existing, be it a substance, like a man, or an accidental property, like a colour" (*In II Sent*. dist. 34, q. 1, a. 1, c). Used in the second way, however, the verb "be" serves to answer the question whether there is (*an est*) such and such a thing (ibid; cf. *S.th*. I, q. 48, a. 2, ad 2; *De malo* q. 1, a. 1, ad 19). The distinction between the two uses of the verb "be" so far considered thus amounts to distinguishing between two different existential uses of this verb, which we may, following Peter Geach, call its use in an *actuality* sense and its use in a *there-is* sense, respectively.[5]

Whereas an entity A falling under one of the ten categories in virtue of its having an essence can be said to be in the sense that A actually exists as well as in the sense that there is such a thing as A, an entity A which lacks an essence, because it is rather a privation of some being than a being in itself, can be said to be only in the latter sense. Sentences of the form "A is" (i.e. "A exists"), where "A", to judge from the examples chosen by Aquinas, is a placeholder for concrete or abstract general terms, like "(a) man" or "(a) colour", and for concrete or abstract singular terms, like "Socrates" or "blindness", can thus be put to two different uses. In analysing the second use Aquinas comes close to the modern analysis of existence statements in terms of the existential quantifier. What we convey by saying that blindness exists, to take one of Aquinas's favourite examples, is, according to him, nothing but the fact that it is true to say that something is blind (*Dicitur enim, quod caecitas est secundo modo, ex eo quod vera est propositio, qua dicitur aliquid esse caecum: In V Metaph*. lect. 9, no. 896; cf. *De pot*. q. 7, a. 2, ad 1).

Being the privation of sight, blindness is not being in the sense that it actually exists, however, because—unlike an animal that happens to be blind—it has no essence which could be actualized in reality. Since Socrates, for example, has such an essence (or nature), to say that Socrates exists (*"Socrates est"*) is either to say, on the one hand, that he actually exists (or is alive) as the human being that he essentially is, or to say, on the other hand, that there is such a person as Socrates (cf. *In V Metaph.* lect. 9, no. 896).[6]

Of these two uses of the verb "be" the latter is regarded by Aquinas as the more comprehensive; for whatever can be said to be in the sense that it exists as a substantial thing or as an accidental property of such a thing can also be said to be in the sense that its existence can be truly affirmed, but not the other way round. The existence of blindness, for example, can be truly affirmed by saying that there is blindness (*caecitas est*); but nonetheless blindness is not to be found among the entities which belong to the furniture of our actual world, because it is rather a lack of actuality than something actually existing (cf. *In II Sent.* dist. 34, q. 1, a. 1, c).

His distinction between these two existential uses of the verb "be" aside, Aquinas is well aware of the difference between the "is" of predication and the "is" of identity, as witness a couple of texts in which he distinguishes between something's being predicated of something "in the way of an identity" (*per modum identitatis*: *S.th.* I, q. 39, a. 5, ad 4) and something's being predicated of something "in the manner in which a universal thing is predicated of a particular one" (*sicut universale de particulari*: ibid.). A predication of the latter kind, which in contradistinction to the so-called *praedicatio per identitatem* (*S.th.* I, q. 39, a. 6, ad 2; *In III Sent.* dist. 7, q. 1, a. 1, c) he also calls (*praedicatio*) *per denominationem sive informationem* (*In III Sent.* dist. 5, expos. textus), is for Aquinas a predication "more properly" so called (*magis propria praedicatio*: ibid.).[7]

Concerning predications properly so called, Aquinas draws a distinction between substantial and accidental predications, which embraces the distinction between the two existential uses of the verb "be" already mentioned, in that this verb, according to whether it is used in its *actuality* sense or in its *there-is* sense, either functions as a *substantial* predicate, which corresponds to the question "What is . . . ?" (*quid est?*), or as an *accidental* one, corresponding to the question "Is there such a thing as . . . ?" (*an est?*) (cf. *In II Sent.* dist. 34, q. 1, a. 1, c; *In V Metaph.* lect. 9, no. 896; *De malo* q. 1, a. 1, ad 19).

Aquinas's view that to use the verb "be" in its actuality sense and, hence, existentially is to use it as a predicate which corresponds to the question of what a given thing is might seem rather odd. It is explained by the fact that, to Aquinas's mind, it is only in accordance with a thing's essence or nature that actual being (or existence) belongs to a thing; for the actual being of a thing is nothing but the actuality of that thing's essence (*actus essentiae: In I*

Sent. dist. 33, q. 1, a. 1, ad 1). Despite this intimate connection between a thing's having an essence and its being actually existent, which accounts for Aquinas's tendency to assimilate the use of the verb "be" in its *actuality* sense with its use as a *substantial* predicate, there is a difference between the essence of a thing and its actual existence, which is the actuality of its essence. This difference is taken into account by Aquinas when, instead of drawing his standard twofold distinction between the use we make of the verb "be" to refer to "the essence of a thing or (to) its act of being", on the one hand, and the use we make of it to refer to "the truth of a proposition", on the other hand (*De pot.* q. 7, a. 2, ad 1), he occasionally contrasts being as being true with being as being what a thing is (i.e. with the nature or essence of a thing), on the one hand, and with being as being actually existent (i.e. with the actuality of a thing's essence), on the other hand:

> ... esse dicitur tripliciter. Uno modo dicitur esse ipsa quidditas vel natura rei [...]. Alio modo dicitur esse ipse actus essentiae [...]. Tertio modo dicitur esse quod significat veritatem compositionis in propositionibus, secundum quod 'est' dicitur copula. (*In I Sent.* dist. 33, q. 1, a. 1, ad 1)

As regards Aquinas's doctrine that in answering the question whether there is such and such a thing we are using the verb "be" as an accidental predicate which signifies the truth of a proposition, it is not self-explanatory either, especially since it is this use of the verb "be" that is taken by Aquinas to be its copulative one ibid.; cf. *In III Sent.* dist. 6, q. 2, a. 2, c; *In V Metaph.* lect. 9, no. 896; *S.th.* I, q. 48, a. 2, ad 2). For a modern reader who has become accustomed to distinguishing the copulative use of "is" and its use in the there-is sense as its respective predicative and existential uses from its so-called veridical use[8] such a doctrine looks highly implausible. Some comments on the view taken by Aquinas are therefore in order.

From Aquinas's point of view it is by "signifying a propositional combination, additionally invented by the (human) soul in the act of linking a predicate to a subject" (*significat compositionem propositionis, quam anima adinvenit coniungens praedicatum subiecto: S.th.* I, q. 3, a. 4, ad 2) that the copula signifies the truth of the sentences in which it occurs (*significat veritatem propositionis: S.th.* I, q. 48, a. 2, ad 2). That is to say that in its copulative use the verb "be" signifies that a predicate is said to be true of a subject or, more accurately, that a predicate-term is said to be true of what a subject-term stands for.[9] What Aquinas is obviously trying to say in this account of the copula is that, used in a simple sentence of the form "*S* is *P*" to make a statement, the copulative "is" performs not only the predicative function of establishing a "propositional combination"[10] between the predicate-expression "*P*" and the subject-expression "*S*" (where "*S*" stands proxy for general terms, like "[a] man",[11] as well as for singular ones, like "Socrates"), but also the assertive function of indicating the speaker's commitment to the truth of what is expressed by the propositional combination of "S" and "P". In other words, when used to make the statement that S is P, the copula serves not only as a propositional link between "S" and "P", but also as an expression for the truth-claim which, whether it is warranted or not, i.e., whether the sentence "S is P" is true or not, we are making to the effect that "P" is true of what "S" refers to whenever we assert that S is P.

As for Aquinas's doctrine that it is by means of the copulative "is" that the question whether there is such and such a thing is answered (cf. *S.th.* I, q. 48, a. 2, ad 2), which seems to result from a confusion between the predicative and the existential uses of the verb "be", it is accounted for by the fact that existence statements of the form "There is F-ness" or "F-ness exists" (e.g. "Blindness exists") are analysed by Aquinas in terms of the corresponding predicative statements of the form "Something is F", in which the "is" functions as copula. When we assert the existence of a privation (e.g. the existence of blindness, which is the privation of sight), "our intellect links that privation", we are told by Aquinas, "to a subject as being something like a form (thereof)" (*intellectus componit privationem cum subiecto, sicut formam quamdam: In II Sent.* dist. 37, q. 1, a. 2, ad 3). This analysis can be expanded in a straightforward way to the effect that any predicative statement of the form "S is P" can be viewed as the copulative counterpart of an existence statement of the form "There is such a thing as S (that is) P", to which it is equivalent.

That Aquinas indeed assumes such an equivalence to obtain is suggested, for example, by his account of what it is for something coincidentally to be. What is called "coincidentally being" (*ens secundum* [or *per*] *accidens*) is so called, Aquinas says in his Commentary on Aristotle's *Metaphysics* (*In V Metaph.* lect. 9, no. 885), "on account of a comparison of an accident (i.e. an accidental property) to a substance; and this comparison is signified by the verb 'is', when (a sentence like) 'a man is white' is uttered; whence this whole thing (called) a white man is (something which is) coincidentally being":

ens secundum accidens prout hic sumitur, oportet accipi per comparationem accidentis ad substantiam. Quae quidem comparatio significatur hoc verbo 'est' cum dicitur 'homo est albus'. Unde hoc totum, homo [est][12] albus, est ens per accidens ibid.

This account seems to rest on the assumption that the predicative statement that a man is white is equivalent to the existence statement that there is such a thing as a white man (or, in other words, such a thing as a man who is white).

The relation between the so-called "Frege trichotomy" and what has been called Aquinas's "fundamental ontological dichotomy" may be depicted by the following diagram:

"is" of to be	existence	predication (properly so called)	(predication of) identity
in act	actuality sense	substantial	substantial (?)
true	there-is sense	accidental	accidental (?)

II

In the preceding section it was shown that Aquinas's dichotomy between being as *actually* being (or being *in act*) and being as being *true* is related to the familiar Frege trichotomy between the "is" of existence, the "is" of predication, and the "is" of identity in such a way that each member of the former division may be subdivided in accordance with the latter one, to the effect that the verb "be" can be put to two different existential as well as to two different predicative uses (presumably including what Aquinas calls predications *"per modum identitatis"* [*S.th.* 1, q. 39, a. 5, ad 4]).

Does Aquinas, when distinguishing between different uses of the verb "be", ever imply that this verb is genuinely ambiguous? The passages of his writings so far considered favour a negative answer to this question, which, as a matter of fact, is expressly given by Aquinas in his Commentary on Aristotle's *Peri hermeneias* (*De Interpretatione*). Commenting on the passage in which Aristotle says that "by itself" the word "being" is "nothing" (Ch. 3, 16b 23f), Aquinas rejects Alexander of Aphrodisias' explanation according to which the word "being" is said to be "nothing" because it is "said equivocally of the ten categories": . . . *scilicet ipsum ens, de quo dicit quod nihil est (ut Alexander exponit), quia ens aequivoce dicitur de decem praedicamentis (In I Peri herm.* lect. 5, no. 70 [19]). "This explanation", Aquinas says, "does not seem to be appropriate, for in the first place, 'being' is not, strictly speaking, said equivocally, but according to the prior and posterior; whence, said absolutely, it is understood of that of which it is said primarily":[13]

haec expositio non videtur conveniens, tum quia ens non dicitur proprie aequivoce, sed secundum prius et posterius; unde simpliciter dictum intelligitur de eo, quod per prius dicitur ibid.

At first sight the passage just quoted might suggest that Aquinas's rejection of the view that the word "being" is used, strictly speaking, in an equivocal or ambiguous way is meant by him to be confined to the use we make of the verb "be" to express the actual existence of what falls under one or the other of the ten categories. That this is by no means the case, however, is shown by the fact, already pointed out, that on both sides of his dichotomy Aquinas tends to assimilate the existential and the predicative uses of the verb "be" by attributing to it, on the one hand, the role of a substantial predicate when it is used in its *actuality* sense and, on the other hand, the role of an accidental predicate when it is used in its *there-is* sense. In addition, Aquinas assimilates the predicative use which, according to him, is made of the verb "be" even in a statement of identity with the predicative use of this verb properly so called in the following way:

In every true affirmative statement the predicate(-term) and the subject (-term) must in some way signify what is really the same but conceptually different. That this is so is clear in the case of statements whose predicate is an accidental one as well as in the case of those whose predicate is a substantial one. For it is obvious that (the terms) 'man' and 'white' (e.g.) are the same as regards the subject-thing (they signify), but different with regard to the (respective) concept (under which they signify it); for the concept of (a) man is a different concept from that of (a) white (object). Similar considerations apply when I utter (the sentence) '(A) man is an animal'; for the very same thing which is a man is truly an animal, because in one and the same subject-thing there is to be found both a sensitive nature, on account of which it is called an animal, and a rational nature, on account of which it is called a man. Hence in this case, too, predicate and subject are the same as regards the subject-thing (they signify), but different with regard to the (respective) concept (under which they signify it).
    Even with statements in which the same thing is predicated of itself, this is in some way the case, insofar as our intellect treats what it assigns to the subject(-position) as being on the side of a subject-thing, whereas what it assigns to the predicate(-position) is treated by it as belonging to the nature of a form existing in a subject-thing, in accordance with the saying that predicates are taken formally and subjects materially.
    While it is the plurality of predicate and subject which answers to the

conceptual difference, it is the (propositional) combination (of subject and predicate) by means of which our intellect signifies the real identity (*S.th.* I, q. 13, a. 12, c).[14]

The Latin text runs as follows:

in qualibet propositione affirmativa vera oportet quod praedicatum et su-biectum significent idem secundum rem aliquo modo, et diversum secun-dum rationem. Et hoc patet tam in propositionibus quae sunt de praedi-cato accidentali quam in illis quae sunt de praedicato substantiali.
Manifestum est enim quod 'homo' et 'albus' sunt idem subiecto et differ-unt ratione; alia enim est ratio hominis et alia ratio albi. Et similiter cum dico 'homo est animal'; illud enim ipsum quod est homo vere animal est; in eodem enim supposito est et natura sensibilis, a qua dicitur animal, et rationalis, a qua dicitur homo; unde hie etiam praedicatum et subiectum sunt idem supposito, sed diversa ratione.
Sed et in propositionibus in quibus idem praedicatur de se ipso, hoc aliquo modo invenitur, inquantum intellectus id quod ponit ex parte su-biecti trahit ad partem suppositi, quod vero ponit ex parte praedicati tra-hit ad naturam formae in supposito existentis, secundum quod dicitur quod praedicata tenentur formaliter, et subiecta materialiter.
Huic vero diversitati quae est secundum rationem, respondet pluralitas praedicati et subiecti; identitatem vero rei significat intellectus per ipsam compositionem.[15]

According to this text, there is a close affinity between predicative statements properly so called and statements of identity to the effect that, on the one hand, a *predicative* statement involves what has been called an "identity factor in predication"[16] insofar as it states the *identity* of what its subject-term stands for with what its predicate-term is true of, whereas, on the other hand, a statement of *identity* exhibits a *predicative* feature in that the identity it states is expressed as the *inherence* of a form (or property) in a thing being subjected to it.[17] That is to say—to make explicit what Aquinas seems to be implying— that, just as the predicative statement that Socrates is white states the in-herence in Socrates of the property of whiteness as the identity of Socrates with something white,[18] the identity statement that Socrates is Socrates states the identity of Socrates with himself as the inherence in Socrates of the property of being Socrates.[19]

If Aquinas does not regard the verb "be" to be genuinely ambiguous as far as the so-called Frege trichotomy of the different uses of "is" into the "is" of existence, the "is" of predication, and the "is" of identity is concerned, does he not assume a genuine ambiguity to obtain at least with respect to his own dichotomy of the different uses of "is" into the "is" as applied to what falls under one of the ten categories, on the one hand, and the "is" as applied to a true proposition, on the other hand?

That he in fact does so is suggested by his saying that Avicenna (= Ibn Sīnā) "has been deceived by the equivocation of being (i.e. of the verb 'be')" (*deceptus est ex aequivocatione entis; In X Metaph.* lect. 3, no. 1982), which is equivocal, according to Aquinas, in that "the 'is' which signifies a propositional combination is an accidental predicate", whereas "the 'is' which is divided by the ten categories (i.e. which has its meaning specified by the kind of entity whose being it affirms) signifies the very natures of the ten genera" (ibid.).

That the phrase *"aequivoctio entis"*, as it is used here by Aquinas, is not to be understood in the sense of a genuine ambiguity of the verb "be", however, but rather in the sense of a "multiplicity of applications"[20] of this verb, is attested by the comparison which Aquinas makes between the two members of his "fundamental ontological dichotomy"[21] in several passages of his writings.

Since this comparison throws some light on the reason why in sticking to the dichotomy at issue Aquinas does not commit himself to the view that with respect to it the verb "be" is genuinely ambiguous, it is worth entering into its details. This will be the task for the next section.

III

Of the two modes of being that the verb "be" can be used to signify, namely being as being actually existent under one of the ten categories and being as being true, "the second is comparable to the first", we are told by Aquinas, "as an effect is to its cause; for it is from a thing's being in reality that the propositional truth and falsity follows which our intellect signifies by means of the word 'is' insofar as it is (used as) a verbal copula":

> ... iste secundus modus comparatur ad primum sicut effectus ad causam. Ex hoc enim quod aliquid in rerum natura est, sequitur veritas et falsitas in propositione, quam intellectus significat per hoc verbum 'est' prout est verbalis copula. (*In V Metaph.* lect. 9, no. 896)

The same point is made in Aquinas's Commentary on the *Sentences* of Peter Lombard, where we read that "as signifying the truth of a propositional combination, in which respect (the word) 'is' is called the copula, being is to be found in the combining and dividing intellect (i.e. in the intellect forming affirmative and negative propositions) as the completion of truth, but founded upon the being of the thing (thought of), which is the act of (that thing's) essence":

> Tertio modo dicitur esse quod significat veritatem compositionis in propositionibus, secundum quod 'est' dicitur copula; et secundum hoc est in intellectu componente et dividente quantum ad veri[22] complementum, sed fundatur in esse rei, quod est actus essentiae. (*In I Sent.* dist. 33, q. 1, a. 1, ad 1)

What prevents Aquinas's ontological dichotomy from reflecting a genuine ambiguity of the verb "be" is, according to the passage just quoted, the fact that being as actually existing (or falling under one of the ten categories), on the one hand, and being as being true (or being the case), on the other hand, are two modes of being of which the latter depends on the former in such a way that the truth of what we say is effected by and founded upon the actual existence of what we talk about.

As an attempt to account for the non-ambiguity of the verb "be" the passage to be considered next deserves especial attention. Commenting on Aristotle's statement, made in *Peri herm. (De int.)* 3, 16b 24, that the word "being" (that is to say, the verb "is") "co-signifies some (propositional) combination" (or "composition"), Aquinas remarks that, according to Aristotle, it does so because

> it does not signify such a composition principally but consequently. It primarily signifies that which is perceived by our intellect in the mode of actuality absolutely; for 'is', said simply, signifies to be in act, and therefore signifies in the mode of a verb. However, the actuality which the verb 'is' principally signifies is the actuality of every form or act commonly, whether substantial or accidental. Hence, when we wish to signify that any form or act actually is in some subject, we signify it by means of the verb 'is' [. . .]; and for this reason the verb 'is' consequently signifies a (propositional) composition. (*In I Peri herm.* lect. 5, no. 73[22])[23]

The Latin text runs as follows:[24]

> Ideo autem dicit [Aristoteles] quod hoc verbum 'est' consignificat compositionem, quia non eam principaliter significat, sed ex consequenti; significat enim primo illud quod cadit in intellectu per modum actualitatis absolute; nam 'est', simpliciter dictum, significat in actu esse; et ideo significat per modum verbi. Quia vero actualitas, quam principaliter significat hoc verbum 'est', est communiter actualitas omnis formae[25] vel actus substan-

tialis vel accidentalis, inde est quod cum volumus significare quamcumque
formam vel actum actualiter inesse alicui subiecto, significamus illud per
hoc verbum 'est' [. . .]. Et ideo ex consequenti hoc verbum 'est' significat
compositionem.

Far from being an interpretation which could be said to reveal the proper
sense in which Aristotle himself intended his saying that the word "be(ing)"
co-signifies (i.e. additionally signifies) some (propositional) combination to
be understood[26] the text just quoted is nevertheless peculiarly enlightening
with regard to Aquinas's own view of the relation between being in the
absolute sense of actually being (or being actually existent) and being in the
copulative sense of something's being true of something else. In addition to
what we have already been informed of, namely the fact that being in the
latter sense depends on being in the former sense as an effect depends on
its cause, the passage under consideration gives us the reason why it is by
means of one and the same word (namely the verb "be") that these two
distinct senses can be expressed.

For Aquinas, the *actuality* sense of the verb "be" seems to be, as it were,
its "focal meaning" (to borrow G.E.L. Owen's happy term),[27] i.e. its primary
sense, by reference to which it is secondarily and derivatively used in whatever other sense it may have. If a given use or sense of a word can be shown
to be derivative, "if it can be explained how the word in question comes to
have the sense that it has by reference to another sense which is for that
reason primary",[28] Aquinas's account of the relation between the use we
make of the verb "be" in its *actuality* sense and the use we make of it in its
copulative sense can surely be said to be an account of the derivability of the
latter sense from the former and, hence, an account of the fact that the verb
"be" is not genuinely ambiguous.

Since to use the verb "be" as copula (i.e. as a sign of propositional combination) is for him "to signify that a (certain) form or act actually is in some
subject" (*significare . . . formam vel actum actualiter inesse alicui subiecto*), Aquinas is indeed able to explain the fact that the verb "be" can be put to this
copulative use by reference to the absolute use we make of it to signify that
something is actually existent—be it a substance, the actual existence of
which is the actuality of the substantial form it has (or, for that matter, the
actuality of the substantial act it performs, e.g. the actuality of the act of
living performed by an animal; cf. *In I Sent.* dist. 33, q. 1, a. 1, ad 1), or an
accidental property, the actual existence of which is the actuality of the accidental form (or act) it identically is (e.g. the actuality of the form of whiteness or of the act of running).

IV

A final comment on Aquinas's treatment of the verb "be", which will serve to round out the picture, may conveniently be added to what has been said so far. It must be noticed, to begin with, that, according to Aquinas, the mode of being signified by the copulative "is" does not belong to the reality of our world, but only to the proposition-forming activity of our intellectual soul: As opposed to the mode of being which is "the act of a being thing insofar as it is being" (*actus entis in quantum est ens: Quodl.* IX, q. 2, a. 2 [3], c), the copulative being (*esse . . . secundum quod est copula verbalis:* ibid.) is not to be found in *rerum natura*, but only *in actu animae componentis et dividentis* (ibid; cf. *In* III *Sent.* dist. 6, q. 2, a. 2, c: "*hoc esse non est in re, sed in mente quae coniungit subiectum cum praedicato*").

Since to be in the copulative sense of something's being something is, for Aquinas, to be true in the sense of its being the case (or a fact) that something is something, his view that the copulative being is, as it were, only an intellectual being, "additionally invented by the (human) soul in the act of linking a predicate to a subject" (*S.th.* I, q. 3, a. 4, ad 2), commits him to excluding what we would call facts from his ontology, reserving to them, in a sense which reminds one of Frege's dictum that "a fact is a thought that is true",[29] the peculiar status of true thoughts; or so it seems.

That it is only substances and their substantial forms, on the one hand, and accidental properties of substances, on the other, that Aquinas is willing to admit into his ontology is obvious from his assumption that only things having an essence or a form, which makes them fall under one of the ten categories, can be said actually to be (cf. *Quodl.* IX, q. 2, a. 2[3], c; *In* II *Sent.* dist. 37, q. 1, a. 2, ad 3), because the actual existence of anything is nothing but the actuality of its essence (cf. *In* I *Sent.* dist. 33, q. 1, a. 1, ad 1) or its form (cf. *In* I *Peri herm.* lect. 5, no. 73[22]).

As for Aquinas's view that facts, as opposed to particular things and their properties, are not real entities but mental ones to which something in reality corresponds, witness the account he gives of St Augustine's definition of truth in terms of his ontological dichotomy in *De ver.*, q. 1, a. 1. The definition in question, according to which "the true is that which is" (*verum est id quod est*), we are told by Aquinas, can be accounted for either by saying that "it defines truth (only) insofar as it has a foundation in reality, and not insofar as it belongs to the complete notion of truth that reality corresponds to (the way it is conceived of by our) intellect", or by saying that, when the true is defined as that which is, "the word 'is' is not (to be) taken in the sense in which it signifies the act of being, but in the sense in which it indicates that our intellect is establishing a (propositional) combination, i.e. in the sense in which it signifies that a proposition(-al content) is being affirmed; the meaning of (the words) 'the true is that which is' would then be that (truth obtains) when something which is (the case) is said to be (the case)":

> ... dicendum quod diffinitio illa Augustini datur de veritate secundum quod habet fundamentum in re et non secundum id quod ratio veri completur in adaequatione rei ad intellectum.—Vel dicendum quod cum dicitur verum est id quod est, li est non accipitur ibi secundum quod siguificat actum essendi sed secundum quod est nota intellectus componentis, prout scilicet affirmationem propositionis significat, ut sit sensus: verum est id quod est, id est cum dicitur esse de aliquo quod est. (ibid. ad 1; cf. *De ver.* q. 1, a. 10, ad 1; *In I Sent.* dist. 19, q. 5, a. 1, ad 1)

What Aquinas seems to be contrasting here is, on the one hand, the sense in which the expression "something which is" means "something which actually exists" and, on the other hand, the sense in which it means "something which is the case". This is confirmed by his reply to the objection that from St Augustine's definition of truth it seems to follow that nothing is false, because this definition implies that the false is that which is not (*De ver.* q. 1, a. 10, obj. 1). After having repeated that in defining the true as that which is, the definition at issue "does not perfectly express the notion of truth but, as it were, materially only, save insofar as (the verb) 'be' signifies that a proposition(-al content) is being affirmed, so that we might say that true is what is said or thought to be such as it is in reality":

> ista diffinitio 'verum est id quod est' non perfecte exprimit rationem veritatis sed quasi materialiter tantum, nisi secundum quod li esse significat affirmationem propositionis, ut scilicet dicatur id esse verum quod sic esse dicitur vel intelligitur ut in rebus est (ibid. ad 1),

he points out that "in this way we might also say that false is what is not, i.e. what is not such as it is said or thought (to be); and this is to be found in reality":

> et sic etiam falsum dicatur quod non est, id est quod non est ut dicitur vel intelligitur: et hoc in rebus inveniri potest. (ibid.)

According to this account, the false is not to be identified with anything that does not actually exist, but with something said or thought to be the case without really being the case or, in short, with something that is not the case.

Aquinas's concluding remark that "this is to be found in reality" does not refer, of course, to that which is false in the sense that it is not such as it is said or thought to be, i.e. to that which is not the case; for what is not the case is, by the very fact of its not being the case, excluded from reality. What the remark in question must be taken to refer to is rather the fact that something is not such as it is said or thought to be, i.e. the fact that something which is said or thought to be the case is not really the case, which "is to be found in reality" (*in rebus inveniri potest*) insofar (and only insofar) as reality does not correspond to what is said or thought to be the case.

That does not mean, however, that what in fact *is* the case when reality *does* correspond to what is said or thought to be the case is itself something to be found in reality; for it is nothing but a propositional content (or a thought), nowhere to be found but in our intellect truly affirming it, whereas in reality there are only substances and accidental properties thereof, whose actual existence is that which corresponds or fails to correspond to what is said or thought to be the case. This at least is the view which Aquinas seems to have adopted, as witness his statement, already quoted above, that "as signifying the truth of a propositional combination, in which respect (the word) 'is' is called the copula, being is to be found in the combining and dividing intellect as the completion of truth,[30] but founded upon the being of the thing (thought of), which is the act of (that thing's) essence" (*In I Sent.* dist. 33, q. 1, a. 1, ad 1).[31]

If we have succeeded in putting together the scattered pieces of our jigsaw puzzle to form a correct picture of the position held by Aquinas with regard to the logic of being, we may note two interesting features of this position. For one thing, it enables Aquinas to subscribe to a correspondence theory of truth which is far from being trivial; for the way in which he tries to establish a connection between the two fundamental modes of being and the two corresponding uses of the verb "be" which we have seen him distinguishing throughout his work seems to have forced upon him the view that what makes a predicative statement of the form "*S* is *P*" true is not simply the fact (or its being the case) that *S* is *P*, but rather the actual existence of the property signified by "*P*" as a (substantial or accidental) property of the subject-thing referred to by "*S*".

That this is indeed a position which Aquinas would be prepared to defend is suggested by his saying, in a text already quoted above, that it is "a comparison of an accident(-al property) to a substance which the verb 'is' signifies when (a sentence like) 'a man is white' is uttered": "*Quae quidem comparatio (accidentis ad substantiam scil.) significatur hoc verbo 'est' cum dicitur 'homo est albus'* " (*In V Metaph.* lect. 9, no. 885). Another piece of evidence is the above-cited passage from Aquinas's Commentary on Aristotle's *Peri hermeneias* in which the copulative "is" is described as "signifying that a (certain) form or act actually is in some subject" (lib. I, lect. 5, no. 73[22]).

In view of Aquinas's thesis that the copulative "is" signifies the truth of the sentence in which it occurs (cf. *S.th.* I, q. 48, a. 2, ad 2; *In III Sent.* dist. 6, q. 2, a. 2, c) the two passages just quoted strongly support the assumption that, according to Aquinas, the sentence "a man is white" signifies—as the condition of its truth and, thus, as the condition of its being the case (or its being a fact) that a man is white—that whiteness is actually existent as a property inherent in a man.

This brings us to a second point, which is closely related to the first. When Aquinas declares, on the one hand, that it is a "propositional combination, additionally invented by our (intellectual) soul" (*compositio propositionis, quam anima adinvenit: S.th.* I, q. 3, a. 4, ad 2; cf. *In II Sent.* dist. 34, q. 1, a. 1, c), and, on the other hand, that it is "the actual being in some subject(-thing) of a (certain) form or act" (*formam vel actum actualiter inesse alicui subiecto: In I Peri herm.* lect. 5, no. 73 [22]) which the copulative "is" signifies, he seems to have in mind something like a distinction between a word's signifying something to the effect that it expresses a sense and its signifying something to the effect that it has a reference. In the light of such a distinction, which is crucial in cases in which, instead of a form actually existing in reality, a privation of some actual being (e.g. blindness) is combined with a subject-thing by means of the word "is" (cf. *In II Sent.* dist. 37, q. 1, a. 2, ad 3), it must be noticed, as regards the passage quoted from Aquinas's Commentary on *Peri hermeneias*, that, though it is the copulative *sense* or *meaning* of the verb "be" which he intends to explain there by reference to the sense in which "to be" means "to be in act", what he does in fact explain by reference to this actuality sense of the verb "be" seems not to be, strictly speaking, what the copulative "is" *means*, but rather what it *refers to*, namely a certain form's actually being in something subjected to it.

What may have helped Aquinas in this way to blur the distinction between meaning (or sense) and reference, which he is elsewhere, following Aristotle, careful enough to observe (cf. *In I Peri herm.* lect. 2, no. 15[5]: ". . . *necesse fuit Aristoteli dicere quod voces significant intellectus conceptiones immediate et eis mediantibus res*"), is the fact that in drawing his distinctions concerning the different uses of the verb *"esse"* ("to be") he is making prominent use of the verb *"significare"* ("to signify"), which is, as it were, neutral with respect to the sense/reference distinction.[32]

Notes

1. By saying that a word is *ambiguous*, I mean that it has several distinct senses and can thus be put to semantically different uses; by saying that a word is ambiguous but *not genuinely so*, I mean that its different senses are in some way or other systematically connected, for instance in such a way that "a number of secondary senses depend upon a single primary one" D. W. Hamlyn, 'Focal

Meaning,' *Proceedings of the Aristotelian Society* 78 (1977/78) p. 6). B. Miller's distinction between "casually ambiguous" and "systematically ambiguous" expressions (Barry Miller, 'In Defence of the Predicate "Exits" '; *Mind* 84 (1975), p. 346).

2. The question to what extent Aquinas's account of this dichotomy is faithful to the position held by Aristotle himself is not easy to answer. In the present paper it will simply be disregarded. For Aquinas's Commentary on Aristotle's *Metaphysics* cf. Doig (1972), together with the critical review by Georg Wieland, *Archiv für Geschichte der Philosophie* 57 (1975), 73–78.

3. It must be noticed that it is, in general, a declarative sentence, and not the propositional content thereof, that Aquinas uses the term "propositio" to refer to. 4 Cf. *De ente et essentia*, Ch. 1, *De pot.* q. 7, a. 2, ad 1, and the other passages listed by Veres (1970, pp. 92–97).

5. Cf. Geach (1969): "Existence in the sense of actuality (*Wirklichkeit*) is several times over emphatically distinguished in Frege's works from the existence expressed by 'there is a so-and-so' (*es gibt ein*—). Indeed, he says that neglect of this distinction is about the grossest fallacy possible—a confusion between concepts of different level" (p. 65). Cf. ibid, Ch. 4 ('Form and Existence', pp. 42–64), where Geach is discussing "what Aquinas meant by his term esse, or *actus essendi*, 'act of existing' " (p. 42). For an attempt to defend Geach's view on the different senses of "exists", which has been criticized by Dummett (1973, pp. 386f), see Miller (1975).

6. Cf. Hermann Weidemann, ' "Socrates est"/"There is no such thing as Pegasus" ': Zur Logik Singulärer Existenz Aussagen nach Thomas von Aquin und N. Van Orman Quine', *Philosophisches Jahrbuch* 86 (1979).

7. Cf. Herbert McCabe, *Summa Theologogiae*, Vol. 3 (Eyre and Spottiswoode, London, 1964), p. 770.

8. Cf. Khan (1973), Ch. VII: 'The Veridical Use' (pp. 331–370).

9. Like Aristotle before him, Aquinas seems to have muddled together what Geach calls "two sorts of truth", namely "the truth of propositions, and the truth of predications" (1972, p. 15).

10. For this term cf. Strawson (1974, pp. 20–22). "A truth-or-falsity-yielding combination we call a propositional combination" (p. 21).

11. If in a sentence of the form "*S* is *P*" a general term functions as subject-term, the sentence in question is traditionally called an "indefinite proposition" (cf. *In I Peri herm.* lect. 11, no. 150[8]). Since its general subject-term is not explicitly quantified, such a sentence, e.g. "(A) man is white" (*homo est albus*: ibid.), can be treated as logically equivalent either to a particular proposition ("Some *S* is *P*") or to a universal one ("Every *S* is *P*").

12. The "est" of the Marietti edition which I have enclosed in square brackets should be deleted ; cf.no. 894: ". . . hoc totum, quod est homo albus, est ens secundum accidens, ut dictum est".

13. Oesterle's translation (1962, p. 51), slightly modified.

14. My translation (for different ones cf. McCabe (1964, p. 95), Malcolm (1979, p. 394).

15. Cf. *S.th.* I, q. 85, a. 5, ad 3: ". . . compositio autem intellectus est signum identitatis eorum quae componuntur. Non enim intellectus sic componit, ut dicat quod homo est albedo; sed dicit quod homo est albus, idest habens albedinem;

idem autem est subiecto quod est homo, et quod est habens albedinem". For the context of this quotation see note 17 below.

16. Veatch (1974, p. 419). Similarly, Malcolm speaks of an "identity aspect of predication" (1979, p. 394 and passim. Referring to *S.th.* I, q. 13, a. 12, c, and I, q. 85, a. 5, ad 3, Veatch launches a heavy attack on Geach to the effect that "Geach in his reference to both of these passages never gives his readers any intimation that they both contain unequivocal assertions as to the presence of an identity factor in affirmative predication" (Veatch, 1974, p. 418). In the face of such criticism it must be acknowledged that in the original version of his paper "Subject and Predicate" (1950), apparently unknown to Veatch, Geach had commented on the latter of the two passages in question as follows (with an additional reference to *S.th.* I, q. 39, a. 5, ad 5): "As regards the truth-conditions of an affirmative predication (*compositio*), he [Aquinas] rejects the view that subject and predicate stand for two different objects, which we assert to be somehow combined; on the contrary, the truth of the predication requires a certain identity of reference. Thus, if the predicate 'white' is to be truly attached to the subject 'man' or 'Socrates', there must be an identity of reference holding between 'man', or 'Socrates', and 'thing that has whiteness' ('*quod est habens albedinem*'); the two names must be *idem subiecto*. Notice that what is here in question is the reference of a *descriptive name*, not of a predicate; Aquinas does not hold, indeed he expressly denies, that predicates like 'white' stand for objects (*supponunt*). His theory is that if the predicate 'white' is truly attached to a subject, then the corresponding descriptive name 'thing that has whiteness' must somehow agree in reference with the subject" (p. 478; cf. Malcolm, 1979, pp. 395f).

Unfortunately this comment, which would have rendered Veatch's criticism almost pointless, is absent from the rather different version, referred to by Veatch, in which "Subject and Predicate" has been incorporated into Geach's book *Reference and Generality* (1968, pp. 22–46; 1980, pp. 49–72).

17. Leaving aside the controversy between Geach and Veatch, which it is not my present concern to settle, I should like to point out the following problem, which seems to have gone unnoticed by both authors: The text of *S.th.* I, q. 13, a. 12, c, suggests that to account for the truth-conditions of a sentence of the form "S is P" in terms of the identity of what the subject-expression "S" stands for with what the predicate-expression "P" is true of is to answer the question of what the sentence refers to in reality, and that to account for the conditions of its truth in terms of the inherence of the form of P-ness in what "S" stands for is to describe the sense expressed by the sentence, i.e. the mode of conceiving the real identity it refers to; the text of *S.th* I, q. 85, a. 5, ad 3, suggests, however, that it is just the other way round. For the passage quoted from this text in Note 15 above is embedded in the following context: "Invenitur autem duplex compositio in re materiali. Prima quidem formae ad materiam; et huic respondet compositio intellectus qua totum universale de sua parte praedicatur [. . .]. Secunda vero compositio est accidentis ad subiectum; et huic reali compositioni respondent compositio intellectus secundum quam praedicatur accidens de subiecto, ut cum dicitur 'homo est albus'.—Tamen differt compositio intellectus a compositione rei; nam ea quae componuntur in re sunt diversa; compositio autem intellectus est signum identitatis eorum quae componuntur" (ibid.). Ac-

cording to this account, it is the combination of the accidental property of whiteness with a man that corresponds to the (true) sentence "(A) man is white" in reality, whereas the identity of a man with something that is white (or has whiteness) seems to be what the sentence in question expresses as the sense in which it is to be understood: "... et secundum hanc identitatis rationem intellectus noster unum componit alteri praedicando," ibid.). Other texts relevant to the problem of reconciling the apparently different accounts given in *S.th* I, q. 13, a. 12, c, and in *S.th.* I, q. 85, a. 5, ad 3, are *S.th.* I, q. 16, a. 2, c, *S.th.* III, q. 16, a. 7, ad 4, *In VI Metaph.* lect. 4, no. 1241, *In IX Metaph.* lect. 11, no. 1898.

18. If a predicate-term like "white" is combined not with a singular subject-term like "Socrates" but with a general one like "man", a word which, like "some" or "every", specifies "the *kind* of identity of reference" (Geach, 1950, p. 478; cf. p. 479) required for the truth of the resulting sentence must be added or understood from the context (see note 11 above).

19. Cf. Geach (1950, pp. 476f).

20. Jaakko Hintikka, 'Aristotle and the Ambiguity of Ambiguity', in J. Hintikka, *Time and Necessity* (Oxford University Press, Oxford, 1973), p. 6, together with the critical review by Dorothea Frede, *Philosophische Rundschau* 22 (1976), 237–242.

21. Cf. Veres (1970).

22. I have conjectured *"veri"* instead of the *"sui"* of Mandonnet's edition, which does not make good sense. My conjecture is based on Aquinas's remark, immediately following the quoted passage, "sicut supra de veritate dictum est", which refers back to dist. 19, q. 5, a. 1, ad 1: "Vel potest dici, quod definitiones istae dantur de vero non secundum completam sui rationem, sed secundum illud quod fundatur in re". Other pieces of evidence are *In II Sent.* dist. 37, q. 1, a. 2, ad. 1 ("ver dupliciter potest considerari. Vel secundum quod fundatur in re [...]. Vel secundum quod completur operatione animae compositionem formantis") and *De ver.* q. 1, a. 1, ad 1 ("... secundum id quod ratio veri completur in adaequatione rei ad intellectum").

23. Oesterle's translation (1962, p. 53), slightly modified.

24. For a detailed analysis of this text cf. Albert Zimmermann, "Ipsum enim ('est') nihil est" (Aristoteles Periherm. I, c. 3). Thomas von Aquin über die Bedeutung der 'Kopula', *Miscellanea Mediavalia 8* (Walter de Gruyter, Berlin/New York, 1971).

25. I have deleted the comma after "formae" in the Leonine and Marietti editions, because it is misleading. As the clause "cum volumus significare quamcumque formam vel actum actualiter inesse alicui subiecto" shows, the words "actualitas omnis formae[,] vel actus substantialis vel accidentalis" are not to be taken in the sense of "actuality of every form, be it a substantial or an accidental act" ("Wirklichkeit jeder Form, sowohl eines substanzialen wie auch eines akzidentellen Aktes": Zimmermann, 1971, p. 292), but in the sense of "actuality of every substantial or accidental form or act" (in Oesterle's translation "or act" is missing).

26. Cf. Weidemann (1982).

27. For a critical account of the idea of "focal meaning" cf. Hamlyn (1977/78).

28. Hamlyn (1977/78, p. 5). Although Hamlyn states this condition as a nec-

essary one ("It will be possible to show the use or sense to be derivative *only* if . . .": ibid., my italics), he obviously assumes that it is also sufficient; cf. p. 6: "Thus the example satisfies the condition that a sense is derivative from another when an explanation of its derivability is in principle forthcoming. Without that it would have been a case of straight ambiguity".

29. "Eine Tatsache ist ein Gedanke, der wahr ist": Gottlob Frege, "Der Gedanke: Eine logische Untersuchung", *Beitr. zur Philos. des deutschen Idealismus* I (1918/19), 58–77; reprinted in *Gottlob Frege: Logische Untersuchungen*, herausgegeben und eingeleitet von G. Patzig (Vandenhoeck & Ruprecht, Göttingen, 1966), pp. 30–53 (quotation, p. 50). For an English translation cf. *Gottlob Frege: Logical Investigations*, ed. with a preface by P. T. Geach, transl. by P. T. Geach and R. H. Stoothoff (Basil Blackwell, Oxford, 1977), quotation, p. 25.

30. See note 22 above.

31. Cf. Aquinas's statement that "this man committing a sin (i.e. the fact that this man commits a sin) is a kind of mental entity insofar as it is called true": "hoc quod est istum peccare est quoddam ens rationis prout verum dicitur" (*In* II *Sent.* dist. 37, q. 1, a. 2, ad 1). Cf. also *In* VI *Metaph.* lect. 4, no. 1241:". . . compositio et divisio, in quibus est verum et falsum; est in mente, et non in rebus [. . .]. Et ideo illud, quod est ita ens sicut verum in tali compositione consistens, est alterum ab his quae proprie sunt entia, quae sunt res extra animam, quarum unaquaeque est aut quod quid est, idest substantia, aut quale, aut quantum, aut aliquod incomplexum, quod mens copuiat dividit."

32. For helpful comments I am grateful to Gregg Beasley.

4

∿

The Realism of Aquinas

In his book *On Universals*, Nicholas Wolterstorff examines Aquinas' theory of universals and concludes that it suffers from "a crucial and incurable ambiguity, or incoherence." Wolterstorff charges Aquinas with denying that there is anything two distinct things have in common while maintaining that forms or natures may be the forms or natures of several distinct things. Aquinas' resolution of the apparent contradiction is said to consist of the assertion that forms or natures exist outside the mind only as individualized in singulars and exist as universals only when they are abstracted from such things by some intellect. Universals are then concepts abstracted from distinct singulars which are similar but not identical. But in that case, Wolterstorff shows, it is not one nature which is abstracted but several and so-called universal concepts cease to have any foundation in reality.[1]

The purpose of this paper is to re-examine Aquinas' theory of universals in order to assess the force of Wolterstorff's criticisms of it. In the course of the re-examination I look at the different ways in which Aquinas describes natures, the ambiguity of terms such as 'universal' and 'similar' in his writings, and employ his often ignored theory of identity and distinction to show finally that, contra Wolterstorff, Aquinas does maintain that numerically distinct individuals of a kind share a nature and can thus be said to be identical with one another in a certain sense. Aquinas turns out to be almost as strong a realist as Duns Scotus.

I. Natures as Such

According to Aquinas, the nature of a thing is its essence or quiddity, that which makes the thing the sort of thing it is. It is also said to be that through which a thing is intelligible, and is thus identified with the formal aspects of a thing for only what is formal is intelligible.[2] But matter is not entirely omitted from the nature of a thing, and Aquinas discusses two ways in which it can be included.[3] A nature taken abstractly is signified by a term like 'humanity' and consists of both substantial form and common or undesignated matter, e.g. flesh and bones which are common to the whole species of men, though it prescinds from designated matter, e.g. *these* flesh and *these* bones by which this individual is distinguished from all others. A nature taken in this way is called the form of the whole, being more than the substantial form although still only a part of the individual. It is that whereby Socrates, for example, is a man, but it omits other aspects of Socrates the individual, e.g. his accidents, existence, designated matter. In contrast a nature taken concretely does not omit these individuating conditions but contains them implicitly. It can thus be predicated of individuals as in 'Socrates is a man,' 'Fido is a dog,' as natures abstractly taken cannot, for we cannot truly say 'Socrates is humanity' or 'Fido is caninity.'[4] When we say 'Socrates is a man' we are saying that Socrates has humanity and something else besides though this additional part is left unspecified.

A nature can also be considered in several other ways in terms of its relation (or lack of relations) to existence. First, a nature can be considered as it exists in individuals outside the mind, and it exists thus as individualized, as the nature of Socrates or the nature of Plato, etc. Second, it can be considered as it exists in created intellects which understand it, and in this way it abstracts from all individuating conditions because it is the nature of human understanding to grasp only the general aspects of things. Since there are distinct created intellects with distinct acts of understanding, the nature can be said to have different acts of existence in the different intellects understanding it. Third, a nature can be considered absolutely according to its intelligible structure (*ratio*) alone, in abstraction from any individuating conditions and from any kind of existence be it real or intentional. Of the nature as absolutely considered (hereafter simply called the nature as such), Aquinas says, "nothing is true of it except what is attributed to it as such. . . . For example, *rational and animal* are attributed to a man as a man, and others which fall in its definition. Indeed *white* or *black* or whatever is not part of the intelligible structure of *humanity* is not attributed to a man as a man."[5] Fourth, a nature can be considered in relation to its existence in the divine intellect as an idea. In *Quodlibet* VIII Aquinas notes some of the connections among these four ways of considering natures:

> . . . That which is prior is always the reason for what is posterior, and when the posterior is removed, the prior remains but not conversely. Thence it is that what is attributed to a nature according to an absolute

consideration is the reason for its being attributed to some nature according to the existence which it has in a singular, and not conversely. For Socrates is rational because man is rational, and not conversely. So if Socrates and Plato did not exist, rationality, would still be attributable to human nature. Likewise, the divine intellect is the reason for the nature absolutely considered and for the nature in singulars. And the nature absolutely considered and in singulars is the reason for the human understanding and in some way the measure of it.[6]

These connections will be further examined below.

Both existence in individuals and existence in a created intellect are said by Aquinas to be accidental to a nature as such. There is nothing about humanity, for example, which requires its existing in Socrates or in Plato or in any individual at all. And there is nothing about it which requires its existing in any created intellect, for there may well be natures comprehended by no such intellect. The nature as such is the nature in itself alone as intelligible structure only. It contains only what necessarily pertains to that structure, i.e. what is reflected in any definition of it. When such a nature does exist, however, Aquinas maintains that it exists either in individuals or in an intellect because in itself it has no existence.

Natures as such are what the human intellect grasps in its first operation, the apprehension of indivisibles, by abstracting these natures from the individuating conditions with which they are found both in extramental things and in the phantasms of these derived from the senses. Thus the intellect receives absolute forms or natures, according to Aquinas.[7] And the absolute form or nature as such as it exists in individuals, and the absolute form or nature as it exists in the knowing intellect, are identical in a sense. That is, they are identical not with respect to existence but with respect to intelligible structure. For Aquinas maintains that knowledge is a con-formity: "Anything is known as its form is in the knower" and "The understood in act is the intellect in act, inasmuch as a likeness of the thing understood is the form of the intellect."[8] Once we abstract from existence there is simply no difference between the form or nature of the object known and the form or nature received by the intellect. The nature or form as such is then the link between the world and the intellect in Aquinas' epistemological realism, and he can refer both to the concept of a nature and to the nature in the object indifferently as a *ratio* or intelligible structure.[9]

Although the nature as such taken concretely is predicable of individuals, the nature itself has essentially neither unity nor multiplicity, neither community nor individuality.[10] It cannot be essentially common to many things or wherever it is found there will be community and we could as truly reason, for example, 'Socrates is a man, therefore Socrates is common to many' as we can 'Socrates is a man, therefore Socrates is an animal.' Nor can it be essentially individual, for if it were the nature of Socrates it could not then be the nature of any other individual. (It cannot be essentially not in Socrates either or Socrates would never have that nature.) It cannot be essentially many or it would never be one when it is the essence of an individual, and it cannot be essentially one or it could never be multiplied and so several individuals would have numerically the same essence.

There must, however, be a sense in which the nature as such is one in itself, for it is distinct from other natures. Aquinas himself acknowledges this unity.[11] Humanity is not caninity, what it is to be human is not what it is to be a dog (and this would be the case even if the two natures had the same instances or if they had none). But to say that a nature as such is one nature distinct from all others is not to say that it is one nature of and in individuals or created intellects. The unity and plurality denied it by Aquinas are unity and plurality in relation to things external and accidental to it. The nature as such as absolute, is not essentially related to anything outside it. If the nature as such has unity, however, must it not also have some being? Aquinas, like most medievals, maintains that being and unity are convertible—whatever is is one, and what is one is in some way. In his commentary on Aristotle's *Posterior Analytics* he remarks that incorruptibles are beings more than corruptible things are and, since the intelligible structure or nature as such is incorruptible and individuals are not, the former is more a being than are the latter. But this is not true, he says, with regard to natural subsistence, for in that area individuals have more being.[12] What kind of being is he talking about then, if it is not existence in individual things? It is certainly not intentional existence in created intellects. Intelligible structures, we are told, are eternal and incorruptible only in the divine mind.[13] But the nature as such is not to be confused or identified with God's idea of it. In *Quodlibet*, VIII, 9.1, a.1, Aquinas clearly distinguishes the two—the nature as such is secondary, the nature as existing in the divine intellect is primary. And he mentions Pseudo-Dionysius' reference to natures as such as "gifts of God, which are exhibited by creatures, both universally and particularly considered, such as beauty *per se*, life *per se*, . . . i.e. the very nature of life." Natures as such he says are eternal in the sense that they would still have the properties essential to them even if all creatures ceased to exist; in contrast with divine ideas, he calls them created natures. Yet created existence is either in individual things or in intellects.

Without existence, a nature is nothing: "Not only existence, but the quiddity itself is said to be created, because before it has existence it is nothing, except perhaps in the creating intellect where it is not a creature but the creative essence."[14] Natures as such do not then populate an obscure realm of Aviccunian possibles prior to receiving existence. According to John Wippel, "Before the actual creation of a given entity, . . . and before the actual creation of the universe, its divine idea is the maximum degree of reality, enjoyed by any possible entity, whether or not it will eventually come into actual existence."[15] Divine ideas are ways in which the divine essence is imitable. There is no separate existence for natures as such, no being apart from the divine mind on which they depend and in which they are eternal, or from creatures which imitate the divine essence, or from intellects which know the creatures and their natures. They are not separate Platonic Forms. Natures as such are rather the common ground of reality and intelligibility, eternal and immutable, knowable by God and creatures alike, capable of creation but of a different order from the created things which participate in them. We must not be misled by Aquinas' use of terms like 'abstraction' and 'consideration' into thinking that natures as such, because intelligible, are somehow dependent for being on our knowing processes. Nor must we be misled by his talk of being and unity into regarding them as Platonic Forms somehow existing in separation from God and creatures. A created thing is said to be true—true through its nature—because it is in its intelligible structure a likeness of the divine mind. Similarly, a created intellect is true when there is a conformity or likeness between its concept of a thing and the thing itself. The basis for the conformity in each case is the nature itself, the intelligible structure which takes on various kinds of existence while remaining yet one and the same and true in itself.[16]

There is another reason for thinking that the nature as such has its own unity. Aquinas holds that there is a real distinction between any individual and the nature it has.[17] Socrates is not humanity, nor is he his humanity. But to say that this distinction is real is not to say that it is a distinction between things really separable from each other. Socrates in separation from his nature would not be Socrates, and natures have no real existence apart from the individuals which have them. Yet his nature is independent of Socrates in the sense that it does not have to exist in this individual. No individual is part of its intelligible structure. And the intelligible structure of an individual as individual (and not as a member of some species) contains more than its nature. Rather, the distinction is real in the sense that it is discovered but not manufactured by the mind. It is a distinction consistent with a real numerical identity of its terms—Socrates and his humanity are one individual substance. It the nature were really identical with the individual in any sense but this, the nature could be found only in this individual. Since "those are distinct one of which is not the other," there must be some sense in which the nature has unity apart from the numerical unity of the individual.[18]

II

Despite Aquinas' reference to natures as such as "natures absolutely considered," I have argued that for him they are objective. What then are their relations to universals? Are natures as such universals or are they the objective foundations of universals?

Properly speaking, Aquinas says, universals are not the natures of things, for universals are "one in and about many," "common to many," "predicable of many."[19] Natures as such have been denied both unity and plurality, community and individuality, in relation to things external to them. (And of course a nature which is mind-independent cannot be predicable at all for predication is one of the operations of the intellect.) It is rather that natures must be rendered universal by the intellect after it has abstracted them from the individuating conditions with which they exist in things. Aquinas says that, as abstracted, *man* "has a uniform relation to all individuals which are outside the soul according as it is a likeness of all of them and brings all into cognition insofar as they are men."[20] The intellect must recognize this relation of likeness and attribute to the intelligible structure or *ratio* it has abstracted an intention of universality.[21] The *ratio* man then becomes a species because it is recognized to be equally a likeness of several individuals of the same sort; *animal* becomes a genus because it is recognized to be a likeness of individuals differing in species, and so on. Aquinas is clear that, apart from such activity of the intellect, there is no universality in the nature as such: "The intention of universality cannot be attributed to a common nature except according to the existence which it has in an intellect, for thus only is it one about many, according as it is understood apart from the principles by which one is divided into many."[22]

What foundation do universals have in reality? Is there something one and the same in numerically distinct individuals of the same sort? Or are individuals of the same sort merely similar? Modern commentators like Wolterstorff often interpret Aquinas as answering the second question negatively and the third affirmatively. But while there is some support for this view in Aquinas' works, he is less than clear on the subject. Even in the same part of the same work we can find him making apparently opposing remarks like the following:

Every form existing in a singular supposit through which it is individuated is common to many either really or at least conceptually. . . . [23]

The unity or community of human nature, however, is not real but only according to the consideration [of an intellect].[24]

We have seen that, while not essentially common to many, a nature is capable of belonging to many things, even if in fact it is received only in one individual. For Aquinas, the form of the sun was accidentally received by just one thing although there was no reason, he thought, why there could not be many suns. But we are faced with the following difficulty: forms or natures exist in things only as individuated—in the case of material things, a nature belongs to this or that material individual. Socrates's humanity is here, Plato's is there. How then can the nature humanity be common to many numerically distinct individuals? And if it isn't common, how are they of the same sort? Are they merely similar and the intellect, ignoring their numerical distinctness based on matter, forms one and the same concept which is a likeness of both equally? In that case the only common factor is the concept. Is there just particularism coupled with concept nominalism in Aquinas or is there true realism based on some identity among things?

One of the difficulties in trying to sort out Aquinas' position is that many of the terms he uses are ambiguous, and deliberately so. This is the result of what Allan Wolter has called "the isomorphism between thought and reality" which runs through most medieval philosophies.[25] It comes out most forcefully in Aquinas' definition of truth as adequation or conformity of knower and known object.[26] The form or nature of the known is in a way the same as the form or nature in the knower, albeit with a different sort of existence. It is important that for Aquinas "To know things through their likenesses existing in the knower is to know them in themselves or in their own natures."[27] It is thus legitimate, given this isomorphism, to use a term which applies primarily to a concept of the intellect to the thing known through this concept, or conversely. (This is not true where the isomorphism breaks down—some concepts do not have real correlates.) We have seen how there is a dual use of 'ratio' or 'intelligible structure' for Aquinas. 'Universal' is another term subject to different uses. Properly speaking, it signifies a second intention, a mental construction or relation, and is so used frequently by Aquinas. But we also find him calling universals "natures common to many" when two numerically distinct things agree in a nature or accident; sometimes universal natures are said to be "apprehended in particulars" or to be "one and the same in all singulars" or to be "present in many."[28] And when he says in De Spiritualibus Creaturis that "the universal does not have unity because it is understood by me and you, for to be understood by me and you is accidental to the universal," he seems also to be using 'universal' to signify a nature in things rather than a second intention.[29] His use of the term 'species' is similar. Working the other direction, 'nature' and 'form' primarily signify nonmental realities but are occasionally used to signify their mental correlates for both terms can mean 'intelligible structure'. To add to the difficulties, key terms like 'likeness' ('similitudo') 'unity', and 'identity', are subject to multiple interpretations, for there are different types of likeness, unity, and identity for Aquinas. 'Likeness' can signify ordinary resemblance, or unity in quality, or agreement in any sort of form (and in this last sense it is really a kind of identity).[30] Both identity and unity come in real and rational types. Frequently used terms like 'common' and 'agreement' (*'convenientia'*) are also troublesome. 'Common' can mean either 'being present in many things at the same time' or 'being predicable of them'.[31] 'Agreement' seems often to be synonymous with 'unity'.

It is only with such multiple meanings in mind that we can begin to attempt an interpretation of a passage like the following:

> If someone seeks the definition of something, he must attend to those things which are similar to it and also to those which are different from it. . . . It is first necessary to consider about similar things something the same found in all of them, e.g. something the same may be found in all men who agree in being rational. . . . And so it must be considered until some *one common* intelligible structure is arrived at, for this will be the definition of the thing. If indeed such consideration does not lead to one common intelligible structure,. . . . clearly that whose definition is sought will not be *one according to essence* but many. . . . (my italics)[32]

Such a passage could lend support to either a similarity or an identity interpretation of Aquinas. But it must be remembered that 'similar' can mean unity in form or nature. And references to unity and identity dominate this passage—unity and sameness of form in distinct things, unity and community of intelligible structure, unity of essence, unity of definition. Given the isomorphism between thought and reality accepted by Aquinas, if there are universal concepts which are likenesses of real things we should expect to find him asserting that there is some unity in things providing the basis for such concepts. It is my contention that this is just what we do find—unity at the level of intelligible structures or natures as such. Such unity is required by Aquinas' view of human knowledge, particularly science. Among all intelligent beings there is a community of simple concepts or *rationes*, even though the linguistic terms which signify these differ among men.[33] (This includes God, who knows all things according to their proper intelligible structures.) The knowledge shared by teacher and pupil, for example, is one and the same.[34] But such intelligible structures are not numerically identical among individuals of a kind so they must have another sort of identity. The particular type of knowledge called science is knowledge of absolute natures and what necessarily and universally pertains to them.[35] Because these natures are likenesses of the ideas in the divine intellect the intelligible world is one and the same, eternal and changeless, whatever the being knowing that world and whatever the means by which it knows. A theory of universals based on mere similarities among things could not provide the basis for such a community of knowledge, for resemblances are notoriously perceiver-relative, i.e. two things that appear similar to me may not so appear to another person. As things are known and created by God so can they be known by his creatures according to their capacities. Human knowledge is solidly founded upon the way things are.

Why then has Aquinas been so often interpreted as having held a similarity theory of universals? One reason seems to be a lack of complete understanding of his language. He does say that universals exist only in the soul, but 'universal' here means second intention, a purely mental construction; he also says that universals exist in things, in a derivative sense. The above-cited isomorphism and the linguistic ambiguities that result are too often ignored by interpreters, as is the unusual use of 'similar'. Then too there are Aquinas' remarks like the following: "All singular men are not one man outside the mind";[36] "Socrates is similar to Plato in humanity, but not as though there were numerically one humanity existing in the two";[37] "in diverse singulars there is not numerically one nature which could be called the species; the intellect apprehends as one that in which all the singulars agree, and so in the apprehension of the intellect a species, which really is diverse in diverse individuals, is made indivisible";[38] "The humanity which is understood exists only in this or in that man."[39] But as we shall see, numerical identity or unity is not the only sort. In passages like these, Aquinas takes pains to avoid imputations of Platonism as he understands it—the belief that there are numerically distinct Forms like man-in-himself, or man in general, existing in separation from singulars.[40] But he does agree with the Platonists that if there were such natures existing apart from individuating matter each would be numerically one.[41] However, natures as such do exist in things as individualized, yet they are somehow one and the same in distinct individuals. This brings us to another cause for misinterpretation of Aquinas, a lack of understanding of his full theory of identity and distinction.

III. Identity and Distinction

Aquinas makes use of two basic sorts of identity or unity, and hence two basic sorts of nonidentity (distinction) and multiplicity. Unity he defines simply as undividedness: Every being is one or undivided and on that unity is grounded its existence.[42] Identity is a type of unity, undividedness in substance, and can be either real or rational (from 'ratio'—often misleadingly translated as 'mental' or 'conceptual'):

... Identity is a unity or union, either because those that are said to be the same are many according to being yet the same insofar as they agree in some one respect, or because they are one according to being but the intellect uses this unity as many in order to understand a relation. ...

This is the case when something is said to be the same as itself. ... It is otherwise, however, when some two are said to be the same either in genus or in species.[43]

These two types of identity correspond roughly to two types of unity, unity *simpliciter* and unity *secundum quid*. Those which are one according to being would be one *simpliciter* and many *secundum quid*; those "divided according to essence and undivided rationally" would be many *simpliciter* and one *secundum quid*, e.g. what are numerically many and specifically one.[44] Aquinas frequently uses the terms 'one' and 'identical' interchangeably.

Real identity (or unity *simpliciter*) is numerical identity (or unity) in a subject. Real distinction, on the other hand, is not always a distinction between two things or subjects. Aquinas sometimes implies that various principles within one thing, although not really separable from each other, are really distinct. Cases in point are the distinction between a thing's matter and its form, between its substance and an accident of it, between its specific essence and its existence. Such distinctions within a thing are also said to be rational, however, on the grounds that the intelligible structure of one principle or form is not identical with that of the other. Thus the distinction between a thing's substance and an accident of it is called both real and rational.[45] Here again the real and the rational are not two mutually exclusive domains. The real-rational division is not then the same as the real-mental division. Rational distinctions may be real distinctions in the sense that they can obtain independently of any intellect's consideration of them. They may also at times be mental constructions, as when an intellect considers one and the same thing in two distinct ways when there is no corresponding distinction of forms or principles within the thing.

Aquinas treats rational identity in several different ways. Two really distinct things of the same kind have the same intelligible structure and are said to be rationally identical.[46] There is also said to be a rational identity where there is just one thing considered under intelligible aspects either wholly or partly the same, e.g. *man* and *rational animal*, or *man* and *animal*.[47] In this case the *rationes* themselves are the terms of the identity relation. Finally, there is a kind of rational identity between the form in an extramentally existing object and the form of that object as it exists in a knower.

As the passage cited in the first paragraph of this section indicates, identity and unity are relativized by Aquinas in the sense that two relata can be identical or one in one way while being distinct or many in another. Such relativization is found in his discussion of true affirmative propositions, for example. These, he says, signify both a real identity and a rational distinction of what subject and predicate terms signify.[48] When we truly assert 'Socrates is white', 'white' signifies an accidental form really inhering in the subject Socrates—they comprise a thing numerically one—yet 'white' does not mean the same as 'Socrates' for the intelligible structure *white* is not the same as the intelligible structure *Socrates*. But there is another type of relativization which is of more interest to us in this discussion of Aquinas' theory of universals. Rational identity is said by Aquinas to be compatible with a real distinction of relata. Things which are numerically distinct can, we have been told, be one or the same in *ratio*, e.g. in species or in genus.

Since Aquinas countenances such relativizations of identity and distinction, it may be well to digress briefly and try to determine with exactly what notion of identity he is working. Contemporary philosophers who adopt some kind of relativized version of identity usually make appropriate changes in such principles as Leibniz's Law, (x) (y) [(x=y)⊃ (Fx≡Fy)], and the transitivity of identity.[49] Did Aquinas accept these basic principles, and if so, how did he propose to modify them to fit his theory? The first question can be answered in the affirmative for he cites the principle, "What are the same are so related to each other that what is predicated of one is also predicated of the other."[50] Transitivity is also acknowledged in many places in his works.[51] There is also a principle of Distinction: What are distinct are such that something is truly predicated of one and not the other, (x) (y) [x≠y)⊃ (∂F) (Fx & ~ FY) v (Fy & ~ Fx))].[52] Aquinas sees, of course, that Leibniz's Law and transitivity can obtain only where x and y are both really and rationally identical.[53] Where there is a real identity with a rational distinction between relata, or a rational identity with a real distinction, the distinction takes precedence. That is, all distinctions, whether compatible with some identity or not, are governed by the Principle of Distinction. Aquinas does not fully develop a set of restrictions for Leibniz's Law and transitivity though he alludes to them in *De Fallaciis*:

[With regard to identicals], sometimes what is true of one may be concluded to be true of the other, namely when something is predicated of one according as [*secundum quod*] it is the same as the other; . . . If indeed it is predicated of one insofar as it is divided from the other it will not be predicated of the other; if, however, insofar as it is not diverse from the other, it will be predicated of the other also. If *white* is predicated of *animal* insofar as it is the same as *man*, it is necessary that it be predictable of *man*; if, however of *animal* insofar as it is divided from *man*, it is not necessary that it be predicated of *man*, and if it is concluded to be so predicated there will be a fallacy of accident.[54]

What he seems to be saying is that from the truth of 'x is identical with y' and 'Fx' we cannot automatically infer the truth of 'Fy' using Leibniz's Law. We can do so only where x and y are both really and rationally identical. But the passage is difficult, and understanding it requires some familiarity with what Aquinas has to say about reduplicative terms and their logical roles—in Latin terms such as *secundum quod, inquantum, ut* (equivalent to our *qua* and translated here as 'as' or 'according as').

Propositions with reduplicative terms are discussed by Aquinas in connection with the two natures of Christ:

> It must be said that that which in some proposition is reduplicated with this 'insofar as' is that through which the predicate is predicated of the subject. So it is necessary that in some way it be the same as the subject and in some way with the predicate, as the middle term in an affirmative syllogism is related to the predicate as to that which follows it through itself [*per se*]. For nothing is predicated of something according as it is an animal unless it is predicated of animal *per se* according to some manner of *per se* predication. However, it is related to the subject as that which is in some way included in the subject.[55]

Aquinas goes on to say that what is predicated of the subject can be related to it as its substance (either the individual itself or its nature), as one of its four causes, or as one of its accidents. The truth conditions for a reduplicative proposition of the form 'x insofar as it is F is G' seem then to be as follows:

1. 'x is F' must be a true proposition. That is, F and x must be the same in some way or, in the formal mode, 'F' must be predicable of x in some way.
2. 'x is G' must be a true proposition, for similar reasons.
3. 'F is G' must be a necessarily true proposition. To paraphrase Aquinas, "Nothing is predicated of x according as it is F unless it is predicated of F per se or necessarily." For 'G' to be predicated of F necessarily, G must be part of the intelligible structure of F as in the example he gives.

Returning to the example in the passage from *De Fallaciis*, 'An animal insofar as it is a man is white' is true just in case 'An animal is a man' and 'An animal is white' are both true, and 'A man is white' is necessarily true.

This treatment of reduplicative propositions can be applied to our case of rational identity and real distinction to block some applications of Leibniz's

Law. Rational identity is identity in some respect only, intelligible structure. Nonetheless, 'Socrates is a man' and 'Plato is a man' are both true, and there is identity of a sort. We can truly assert such propositions then as 'Socrates as a man is identical with Plato as a man,' the reduplicative term signifying that intelligible structure in terms of which there is identity of the other two terms. Nonetheless this is true also: 'Socrates as an individual is distinct from Plato as an individual' and reflects the real distinction of Socrates and Plato. The Principle of Distinction applies without qualification, so there are then things that can be truly predicated of Socrates and not Plato, *qua* individuals. Since Socrates and Plato are identical insofar as they are men and since Socrates's being a man entails his being an animal, the same will be true of Plato and we can assert truly 'Plato is an animal'. "What is true of one may be concluded to be true of the other . . . when something is predicated of one *insofar as* it is the same as the other" (my italics). By means of the reduplicative proposition, we can apply Leibniz's Law in limited fashion. If x as F is G, and y is also F, y can be concluded to be G as well; *being G* is predicated of x *insofar as* it is F—that respect with which x and y are identical. It can also be predicated of y truly. Whatever is true of one of two relata which are rationally identical insofar as it has a certain intelligible character will be true of the other relatum insofar as it has this same intelligible character. Rational identity then is true identity, but at a certain level only. A revised version of Leibniz's Law might read: If x is F and y is F (i.e. x and y are rationally identical insofar as they are F), then if 'F is G' is necessarily true and if 'x as F is G' is true, then 'y as F is G' is also true. (Something similar could be worked out for cases of real identity and rational distinction of relata though I have not tried to do that here.)

Nothing about Aquinas' treatment of rational identity above warrants our concluding that if two relata are rationally identical they must necessarily be really identical also (they may, but need not be). Real individuals are for Aquinas different sorts of things from intelligible characters or *rationes* which may be had by individuals; to confuse the two is to make a category mistake. Two individuals exist at different places at the same time. This says nothing against the possibility of their being identical in some intelligible character for intelligible characters (natures as such) are not the sorts of things that are bound to spatial and temporal existence (except through the individuals which have them). This man exists here and now; *man* then exists here and now but is not precluded from existing there now also. To assume otherwise is, as Moore said, to assume "that there is no distinction between the sense in which two concrete things can be said to be 'locally separate', and that in which two characters can be said to be so."[56] Aquinas does not make this assumption.

IV

In the preceding sections I have attempted to show what the nature as such is for Aquinas, and how it is distinct from both individuals which have natures and from intellects which understand them. The nature as such has no existence of its own; it is an intelligible structure or character but not by that fact simply a mental construction. The nature as such is objective, eternal, immutable, a creation of God and a reflection of the divine essence. It is also the subject of science and demonstration and the foundation of our knowledge of universals, though the nature as such is not itself a universal. One and the same nature as such can exist in many numerically distinct individuals and in each case its real existence is tied down to the individuating conditions of that existence. Yet the nature as such in this thing can be truly identical with the nature as such in that distinct thing. The nature as such can also be released from these individuating conditions which are anyway not essential to it when it is understood by some intellect: to the nature as understood can be attached an intention of universality so that it is related to many distinct individuals although it is not essential to it to be so related.

Of this theory, Nicholas Wolterstorff has said, "This theory, ingenious as it is, suffers from a crucial and incurable ambiguity, or incoherence."[57] That it does suffer from ambiguity has been amply shown. Is it also incoherent? Wolterstorff supports his conclusion as follows:

1. Human nature is the nature of Socrates, and human nature is the nature of Plato.
2. If human nature is the nature of Socrates and also the nature of Plato, then the nature of Socrates is identical with the nature of Plato.
3. On the other hand, if "the nature of Socrates" and "the nature of Plato" refer to different things then neither of these phrases can be used to stand for that nature which is supposedly the nature of both. Then it is false that it is the human nature of Plato, and false that it is the nature of both.

According to Wolterstorff, Aquinas denies the truth of 2 and must thereby accept 3. When it comes to abstraction then, he must hold that two natures or forms, which are similar but not identical, have been abstracted from Socrates and Plato, and "not one distinct thing, human nature." If that is so, Wolterstorff concludes that we do not have a universal concept even in the intellect but rather two concepts whose differences we ignore. "The activity of attending to one thing and ignoring the different accidental traits which may have accrued to it, must not be confused with the activity of attending to two similar things and ignoring their differences".[58] Wolterstorff's criticism is to the point only if Aquinas holds a resemblance theory of universals.

In the light of what has been shown in the preceding sections, I do not think that it can be maintained that Aquinas denied number 2. There is too much evidence to the contrary. It is true, however, that he maintained that natures or forms exist only in individuals or intellects, and that in the former they exist under individualizing conditions of designated matter. The intellect receives one and the same nature, *ratio*, in understanding Socrates and in understanding Plato. But designated matter is unknowable, cannot be received by the intellect, so there is no way for an intellect to consider it and ignore it. If the intelligible structure of a thing must be understood as unindividuated, there is no way for the intellect to take in the individuating conditions and ignore them. In fact, any intelligible character of an individual is really distinct from that individual and understandable apart from it.

Points 1–3 above are expressed by Wolterstorff, not Aquinas. Were Aquinas confronted with them, he would have to say the following: Human nature is indeed the nature of Socrates (i.e. the specific nature)—Socrates is human, he is intelligible primarily as a human, he is human because he has the substantial form (rational soul) of a human in the appropriate sort of animal body. Plato too is human. Both of them have human nature, though human nature is only a part of each of them. This human nature in each exists under individuating conditions provided by designated matter and its accidents. So 1 and 2 must be conceded. In order to assert 3, we must shift from talking about the specific natures of things to talking about their individual natures. If 'the nature of Socrates' refers not to human nature but to the individual nature, i.e. human nature with all its individuating conditions, then 'the nature of Socrates' and 'the nature of Plato' do not refer to the same thing—these expressions refer to the individuals themselves as individuals. Socrates is not Plato, what it is to be Socrates is not what it is to be Plato. But that does not mean what it is to be human is different in each of them. Forms are individualized, for on its substantial form follows the existence of a thing. The form of this is then distinct from the form of that because it is received in different matter. Remove the material distinction and there is no difference of form. The form as intelligible structure remains one and the same, however, despite the individuating conditions. (It is perhaps the ambiguity of 'form' that is Aquinas' most serious problem—forms as bearers of existence must be individuated; forms as intelligible structures, natures as such, need not be.) We have two distinct individuals, each with its own substantial form, each a numerically distinct instantiation of a specific nature as such, yet one in intelligibility, and subject to the same defining formulas and scientific explanations.

In some ways, Aquinas' theory could stand some tightening up. The ambiguities are frustrating and often misleading. The status of the nature as such is left unclear—it seems to be a being but it can't be; it seems to have its own unity but it can't because then it would have to have its own being. Duns Scotus can perhaps be seen as offering a solution to some of the difficulties that remain unresolved in Aquinas. Scotus gives the nature as such its own unity across individuals, a unity which is real but less than numerical for it is not an individual in itself, and its own diminished existence. The distinction between nature and individual is clarified into a formal distinction between the nature as such and the principle of individuality, the haecceity of a thing. The nature is contracted to a haecceity, and both are unitively contained within one individual existence. If Aquinas is indeed a realist as I have tried to show, the difference between these two major medieval philosophers is not so great as has frequently been maintained.

Notes

1. Nicholas Wolterstorff, *On Universals: An Essay in Ontology* (Chicago, 1970), p. 146. Similar interpretations are offered by Peter Geach, *Three Philosophers* (Oxford, 1963), p. 84; F. C. Copleston, *Aquinas* (Baltimore, 1963), p. 91; James F. Ross in his Introduction to Suarez, *On Formal and Universal Unity* (Milwaukee, 1964), p. 13. David Armstrong thinks Aquinas' theory may be a kind of particularism coupled with concept nominalism: see his *Universals and Scientific Realism* (Cambridge, 1978), 1: 87.

2. On form as essence, see St. Thomas Aquinas, *In V Meta.*, 2, n. 764; VII, 11, n. 1531 and 13, n. 1567; *Summa Theol.*, III, 3, 2 ad 3; *Sum. cont. Gent.* IV, 36; *Comp. Theol.*, I, c. 10; *De Ente et Essentia*, c. 1. Nature is essence generally, although in a way accidents have natures also since they are forms, e.g. natures like what it is to be white or square, etc. Most of what is said about, natures as such below will apply to these as well, and Aquinas sometimes uses accidental natures as his own examples.

3. St. Thomas Aquinas, *De Ente et Essentia*, c. 3; *In Boetii de Hebdomadibus Expositio*, I, 2. See also *De Pot.* IX, 1.

4. See *De Ente et Essentia*, c. 3; also *Sum. cont. Gent.*, I, 21; *De Pot.*, IX; 1; *In VII Meta.*, 11, n. 1521; *Comp. Theol.*, c. 154.

5. ". . . Nihil est verum de ea nisi quod convenit sibi secundum quod lmiusmodi. . . . Verbi gratia homini, in co quod est homo, convenit rationale et animal et alia quae in eius definitione cadunt; album vero vel nigrum, vel quidquid huiusmodi quod non est de ratione humanitatis, non convenit homini in eo quod *est* homo." *De Ente et Essentia*, c. 4, ed. C. Boyer (Rome, 1970), pp. 29–30.

6. "In his ergo illud quod est prius, semper est ratio posterioris; et remoto posteriori remanet prius, non autem e converso; et inde est quod hoc quod competit naturae secundum absolutam considerationem, est ratio quaro competat naturae alicui secundum esse quod habet in singulari, et non e converso. Ideo enim Socrates est rationalis, quia homo est rationalis, et non e converso;

unde dato quod Socrates et Plato non essent, adhue humanae naturae ration-alitas, competeret. Similiter etiam intellectus divinus, est ratio naturae absolute consideratae, et in singularibus; et ipsa natura absolute considerata et in singu-laribus est ratio *intellectus humani*. et quodammodo mensura ipsius." *Quodl.* VIII, I, I, ed. R. Spiazzi (Marietti, 1956), p. 159.

7. *Summa Theol.*, I, 75, 5, esp. ad 1, and 85, 1.

8. Sic autem cognoscitur unumquodque, sicut forma eius est in cognoscente. *Summa Theol.*, I, 75, 5, Blackfriars ed. (New York, 1964–1000) II: 22. See also *De Ver.*, II, 6. The second quote, ". . . intellectum in actu est intellectus in actu, inquantum similitudo rei intellectae est forma intellectus. . . ." is from *Summa Theol.*, I, 85, 2 ad 1; see also 17, 3; 88, 1 ad 2; and *In VI Meta.*, 4, n. 1234.

9. On *ratio*, see *I Sent.*, d.2, q.1, a.3; *De Pot.*, VII, 6, and I, 2 ad 10; *Summa Theol.*, I, 13, 1 and 4; *Sum. cont. Gent.* I, 53.

10. *De Ente et Essentia*, c.4, Boyer ed., p. 31.

11. See *In I Post. Anal.*, lectio 37.

12. Ibid.

13. *Summa Theol.*, I, 16, 7 ad 1.

14. ". . . Non solum esse, sed ipsa quidditas creari dicitur: quia antequam esse habeat, nihil est, nisi forte in intellectu creantis, ubi non est creatura, sed creatrix essentia." *De Pot.*, III, 5 ad 2, in *Quaestiones Disputatae*, ed. P. Bazzi et al. (Marietti, 1965), p. 49.

15. John Wippel, "The Reality of Nonexisting Possibles according to Thomas Aquinas, Henry of Ghent, and Godfrey of Fontaines," *Review of Metaphysics* 34 (1981), p. 733.

16. In *I Poster. Anal.*, lect. 37. Also *Summa Theol.*, I, 16, 3.

17. *I Sent.*, d.5, q.1, a.1; *Summa Theol*, III, 2, 2; *In III De Anima*, 8, nos. 705 and 706. In some passages he merely says they differ, but the difference is clearly contrasted with a merely conceptual distinction in God, e.g. *Summa Theol.*, I, 3, 3; *I Seat.*, d.34, q.1, a.1; *Quodl.*, II, 2, 2; *Sum. cont. Cont.*, IV, 81; *In VII Meta.*, 11, n. 521.

18. "Sed in ratione distinctionis est negastio: distincta enim sunt quorum unum non est aliud." *Bum. cont. Gent.*, I, 71, *Opera Omnia*, Leonine ed. (Rome: Vatican Polyglot Press, 1882–), 13:206.

19. See, for example, *In I Post. Ana.*, lect. 19; *In II De Animo*, 12, n. 386; *In VII Meta.*, 13, nos. 1571 and 1572; *In Peri Herm.*, I, 10.

20. ". . . Et ideo habet rationem uniformem ad omnia individua quae sunt extra animam, prout aequaliter est similitudo omnium et inducens in cogniti-onem omnium, inquantum sunt homines." *De Ente et Essentia c.* 4, ed. Boyer, p. 31.

21. *De Pot.*, VII, 6.

22. ". . . Naturae communi non potest attribui intentio universalitatis nisi se-cundum esse quod habet in intellectu: sic enim solum est unum de multis, prout intelligitur praeter principia, quibus unum in multa dividitur; . . ." *In II De Anima*, 12, n. 380, ed. M. Pirotta (Turin and Rome: Marietti, 1925), p. 98.

23. ". . . Omnis forma in supposito singulari existens, per quod individuatur, commuuis est muitis, vel secundum rem vel secundum rationem *saltem:* . . ." *Summa Theol., I*, 13, 9, Blackfriars ed., 3:82.

24. "Unitas autem sive communitas humanae naturae non est secundum rem, sed solum secundum considerationem: . . ." Ibid., 39, 4 ad 3, p. 278.

25. Allan Wolter, "The Realism of Scotus," *Journal of Philosophy* 59 (November, 1962), p. 727.

26. *Summa. Theol.*, I, 75, 5, and 85, 2; *De Ver.*, VI; *In II De Anima*, 13, n. 789.

27. ". . . Cognoscere res per earum similitudines in cognoscente existentes, est cognoscere ens in seipsis, seu in propriis naturis: . . ." *Summa Theol.*, I, 12, 9, Blackfriars ed., 3:32. See also *De Unit. Intellectus*, V, n. 256, and *Summa Theol.*, I, 14, 0 ad 1.

28. For the ambiguity of 'universal' see such passages as *Summa Theol.*, I, 85, 3; *Sum. cont. Gent.*, I, 65, and II, 52; *De Spirit, Creat.*, 10 ad 14; *In VII Meta.*, 13, nos. 1572–1574; *In II De Anima*, 12, n. 378; *In Peri Horm.*, I, 10; *In II Post. Anal.*, n. 16 and n. 20; *De Unit. Intellectus* V, n. 257; *Comp. Theol*, c. 14; *II Sent.*, d.3, q.1, a.2 ad 3.

29. ". . . Universale non ex ea parte habet unitatem, qua est a me et a te intellectum; intelligi enim a me et a te accidit universali." *De Spirit. Creat.* 10 ad 14, ed. Leo W. Keeler (Rome: Universitas Gregoriana, 1959), p. 134.

30. *De Ver.*, II, 3 ad 9, and 5 ad 5 and 7, and VIII, 8; *Summa Theol.*, I, 4, 3.

31. *De Ver.*, VII, 6 ad 7.

32. ". . . Si aliquis inquirit definitionem allcuius rei, oportet quod attendat ad ea quae sunt similia illi, et etiam ad ea quae sunt differentia ab illa re. . . . primo oportet circa similia considerare quid idem in omnibus inveniatur; puta quid idem inveniatur in omnibus hominibus, qui omnes conveniunt in hoc quod est esse rationale. . . . Et ita est considerandum quousque perveniatur ad aliquam unam rationem communem. Haec enim erit definitio rei. Si vero talis consideratio non inducat in unam rationem communem, . . . manifestum erit quod illud cuius definitio quaeritur, non erit unum secundum essentiam, sed plura: . . ." *In II Post. Anal.*, lect 16, Leonine ed. 1184, n. 553.

33. *In Peri Herm.*, I, 2.

34. *De Unit. Intellectus* V, n. 258.

35. *Summa Theol.*, I, 16, 7 ad I and 2; *In Boeth. de Trin.*, V, 2 ad 4; *De Ver.*, II, 4 ad 2.

36. ". . . Omnes homines singulares non sunt unus homo extra animam, . . ." *In Peri Herm.* I, 10, Leonine ed. 1:48.

37. ". . . Socrates est similis Platoni in humanitate, non quasi una humanitate numero in utroque existente." *In II Post. Anal.*, 20, n. 11, Leonine ed., 1.

38. "Non enim in diversis singularibus est aliqua natura una numero quae possit dici species. Sed intellectus apprehendit ut unum id in quo omnia inferiora conveniunt. Et sic in apprehensione intellectus, species fit indivisibilis quae realiter est diversa in diversis individuis." *In X Meta.*, 1, n. 1930, ed. Cathala (Turin and Rome: Marietti, 1964), p. 402.

39. "Humanitas quae intelligitur non est nisi in hoc vel in illo homine; . . ." *Summa Theol.*, I, 85, 2 ad 2, Blackfriars ed. 12:62.

40. *In VII Meta.*, 14, n. 1593, and 13, n. 1571; *In I Post Anal.*, 37.

41. *Comp. Theol.*, I. c. 15; *Summa Theol.*, I, 50, 4; *Sum. cont. Gent.*, II. 52, for example.

42. *Summa Theol.*, I, 11, 1.

43. ". . . Identitas est unitas vel unio; aut ex eo illa quae dicuntur idem, sunt

plura secundum esse, et tamen dicuntur idem in quantum in aliquo uno conveniunt. Aut quia sunt unum secundum esse, sed intellectus utitur eo ut pluribus ad hoc quod relationem intelligat. . . . Sicut cum dicitur aliquid esse idem sibiipsi. . . . Secus autem est, quando aliqua duo dicuntur esse idem vel genere vel specie." *In V Meta.*, 11, n. 912, ed. Cathlan, p. 245.

44. ". . . Divisum secundum essentiam, et indivisum secundum rationem, . . ." *Summa Theol.*, I, 11, 1 and 2, Blackfriars ed. 2:158.

45. On matter and form, see *Summa Theol.*, I, 75, 6; 85, 5 ad 3; *In VIII Meta.*, 1, n. 1687; *De Spirit. Creat.*, a.1 ad 6; *De Ente et Essentia*, c. 5; *In II De Anima*, 1, n. 215. On substance and accident, see *De Spirit. Creat.*, n.3; *In VII Meta.*, 2, n. 1291; *In V*, 2, n. 548; *IV*, 7, n. 622; *Summa Theol.*, I, 13, 12; *De Ver.*, III, 2 ad 3. On essence and existence, see *Sum. cont. Gient.*, II, 52; *De Pot.*, VII, 2 ad 5; *Summa Theol.*, I, 54, 3.

46. *In V Meta.*, 11, n. 912, and 8, n. 877; *Summa Theol.*, I, 11, 1 ad 2, and 28, 1 ad 2; *De Div. Nom.*, XI, n. 911; *De Ente et Essentia*, c. 5.

47. *De Fallaciis*, c. 12: *In III De Anima*, 7, n. 781; *In III Phys.*, 5, n. 318.

48. *Summa Theol.*, I, 13, 12.

49. For some of the attempts, see David Wiggins, *Identity and Spatio-temporal Continuity* (Oxford, 1967).

50. "Quaecumque sunt idem, ita se habent, quod quidquid praedicatur de uno, praedicatur et de alio." *Summa Theol.*, I, 40, 1, 3a, Blackfriars ed. 7:140. See also *De Fallaciis*, c. 12, n. 678; *In III Phys.*, 5, n. 318; *De Pot.*, VIII, 2 ad 10.

51. *Summa Theol.*, I, 28, 3; *In Boetii de Hebdomadibus Expositio* I, 4, n. 60; *In I Post. Anal.*, 43.

52. *Sum. cont. Gent.*, IV, 14.

53. *De Pot.*, VIII, 2 ad 10; *In III Phys.*, 5, n. 318; *De Fallaciis*, c. 12, n. 678.

54. "Contingit autem quandoque ut quod est verum de uno, concludatur esse verum de altero, scilicet quando aliquid attribuitur uni secundum quod est idem alteri; . . . Si vero attribuitur uni secundum quod est ab altero divisum, non inerit alteri; si autem ut non diversum ab altero, erit et alterius: sicut si album attribuatur animali inquantum est idem homini, oportet quod conveniat homini, si autem animali ut est divisum ab homine, non oportet quod conveniat homini, et si concludatur inesse, erit fallacia *accidentis*, . . ." *De Fallaciis*, c. 12, n. 670, in *Opusoula Philosophica*, ed, R. Spiazzi (Turn and Rome: Marietti, 1954), p. 234.

55. "Dicendum quod id quod in aliqua propositione reduplicatur cum hoc quod dico, *secundum quod*, est illud per quod praedicatum convenit subjecto. Unde oportet quod aliquo modo sit idem cum subjecto et aliquo modo idem cum praedicato. Sicut medius terminus in syllogismo affirmativo *ad praedicatum quidem* habet comparationem sicut ad id quod per se, consequitur ipsum—nihil enim convenit alicui secundum quod est animal, nisi illud animali per se conveniat secundum quemcumque modum *dicendi per se*—*ad subjectum* autem comparatur sicut id quod aliquo modo includitur in subjecto." *Scriptum super Libros Senteniarum*, III, d.10, q.1, a.1, ed. Mandonnet and Moos (Paris, 1947), 3:331.

56. G. E. Moore, "Are the Characteristics of Particular Things Particular or Universal?" *Philosophical Papers* (New York, 1962), p. 20.

57. Wolterstorff, op. cit., p. 146.

58. Ibid., p. 148.

5

Natural Reason in the *Summa contra Gentiles*

A distinctive feature of Aquinas's *Summa contra Gentiles* is the central role the author assigns to natural reason in his project of manifesting the truth of Christian faith. Reason is supposed to give a rational account of the truth of what faith professes about God, to arrive at a *veritas demonstrativa*, which will be shown to accord with the Christian religion. It is mainly because of this emphatic and what seems to be a rather presumptuous role of natural reason that the work has occasioned so much discussion and, consequently, diversity of opinion among the interpreters of Aquinas's thought. Is the *Contra Gentiles*, insofar as reason is the leading principle of the investigation, to be regarded as a kind of 'philosophical' *summa*, as it was sometimes labeled in the past? The objection immediately arises that the fourth book explicitly deals with those truths of faith which are above reason. And further, on account of its declared subject-matter—the truth of the Catholic faith—it seems unmistakably a theological work or, more exactly, a work in which the truth of Christian faith is expounded and defended. Those who stress the theological character of the work, a work written from the point of view of faith, usually refer to what seems to be the original title: "On the Truth of the Catholic Faith against the Errors of the Infidels."[1]

The riddle of the *Contra Gentiles* goes deeper than the question of whether it is intended primarily as a theological or as a philosophical work, based on reason as a common human faculty for truth. As Pegis notes in his introduction to the English translation, the work has posed two main problems for its interpreters.[2] One concerns the purpose and nature of the work with reference to the historical situation that occasioned it. What position does it take in the historical encounter of the Latin West with the Greco-Islamic philosophical conception of the world? The second problem, according to Pegis, concerns the internal organization of the *Contra Gentiles*. How are its four books related to one another? What is its main point of view or idea that inspires the work as a whole?

The commonly accepted view takes the *Contra Gentiles* foremost as a work of Christian apologetics intending to give a rational defense of faith against the Greco-Islamic philosophical picture of the world. According to Pegis, the work is part of the Christian reaction against Islamic intellectual culture, especially against Islamic Aristotelianism. And Chenu, in his well-known *Introduction*, regards it as an "apologetic theology," a defense of the whole body of Christian thought against the Greco-Islamic scientific conception of the world.[3] Weisheipl agrees with this view: the author of this work must be seen primarily as an apologist whose aim is to convince the learned Muslims and Jews in Spain of the truth of the Christian faith and to combat their erroneous opinions.[4]

The apologetic view of the *Contra Gentiles* can draw support from an old tradition according to which Thomas was asked by Raymond of Peñafort, the former master general of the Dominican Order, to compose a work "against the errors of unbelievers" as an aid in conversion. This story, the source of which is a chronicle written by the Dominican Peter Marsilio in 1313, links the work with the training of Dominican missionaries for an apostolate among the learned Muslims and Jews in Islamic Spain, who were thoroughly versed in Aristotelian philosophy. In spite of its imaginative charm this testimony seems to be no more than a piece of hagiographic invention.[5] As Jordan remarks, the *Contra Gentiles* would be an odd missionary manual by the Dominican standards of the thirteenth century. Contrary to the ideals of Dominican missionary activity, its author shows very little familiarity with the religious beliefs and languages of his adversaries. Chenu too qualifies the missionary and even apologetic intention of the *Contra Gentiles*. It is clear, he says, that the work exceeds by far the requirements of a simple missionary manual. It is above all a work devoted to the contemplation of the truth ("une oeuvre de contemplation de la vérité").[6]

According to Corbin, in his voluminous book on the development of Aquinas's theological thought, the *Contra Gentiles* must be seen as a strictly theological work, a work written for Christian believers about the truth of their Catholic faith. It is Aquinas's "second comprehensive theological discourse," a second *summa* in which Aquinas resumes and modifies the project of his first *summa*, the *Scriptum*, in the light of the results of his methodological investigation in the commentary on Boethius's *De trinitate*.[7] Therefore Aquinas's intention to combat the errors of the unbelievers is not to be taken as motivated by any practical or apologetic urgency; it is but a secondary means of manifesting more effectively the brightness of truth by contrasting it with the darkness of falsehood.[8]

Corbin's analysis of Aquinas's methodological reflection on the problem of the autonomy of theology versus philosophical thought is impressive and very subtle. His fundamental assumption is that the three main works about Christian doctrine mark the different phases on the road of Aquinas's theological development. Compared to the *Summa theologiae*, Aquinas's final solution to the problem of the inner unity of theology as science of faith, the theological concept of the *Contra Gentiles* still shows an inner ambivalence on account of its division of the truth of faith into a part accessible to reason and a part not accessible. This inner rupture in its structure indicates that the philosophical part is not yet adequately integrated in the theological synthesis.

Within the scope of this essay we cannot fully do justice to Corbin's complicated thesis. One can wonder, however, to what extent the *Contra Gentiles* is comparable with the *Summa theologiae* in the light of Aquinas's search for a satisfying conception of theology. The suggestion that Aquinas, writing the earlier work, was seeking to solve a problem he finally succeeded in solving when he wrote the later one cannot claim any support from what he explicitly declares to be his intention in the *Contra Gentiles*. I see no reason why the *Contra Gentiles* should not be approached as a work in its own right, with an intention different from the *Summa theologiae* and an intelligible structure adapted to that intention. So it is not at all evident to me that the *Contra Gentiles* must be regarded as 'theological' in the same sense as the *Summa theologiae* is explicitly meant to be a theological *summa*, nor as a *summa* in the sense of a comprehensive work dealing with the whole of Christian doctrine.

The *Contra Gentiles* is a work in which the author intends to manifest the truth of the Catholic faith. In order to proceed in a disciplined and responsible way, so Aquinas remarks in the beginning of 1.3, it is essential to determine by which method this truth can be manifested. Faced with the truth of the things faith professes about God, we are asked to consider how the truth of God is accessible to our intellect. This reflection leads to a *duplex modus veritatis* (1.3), a twofold mode of truth in the things we profess about God. Some truths that "we" (the Christian community) profess about God exceed the grasp of reason, as for example that he is one and three. Other things we believe to be true about God can be known by natural reason, namely things, such as God's existence and his unity, that have been proved demonstratively by the philosophers, guided by the light of natural reason. The division of the *Contra Gentiles* is based on this twofold mode of truth. In the first three books natural reason is the leading principle of the inquiry into the truth. Here reason investigates the truth about God and the universe as perceived and confirmed by faith. In the fourth book, however, Aquinas goes on to discuss the truth of those elements of Christian doctrine which are outside reason's natural competence. Aquinas's program of manifesting the truth of what is professed by faith requires an acute sense of the nature and limits of the human capacity for knowing the truth. Reason has to be persuaded to make truth in itself not dependent on its own power of understanding but rather to correct itself and its forms of thought in order to understand, without any presumption to comprehend, the higher intelligibility of faith. It is characteristic of the *Contra Gentiles* that natural reason, in its search for truth, is constantly reminded of its human point of departure. The work is not only, in the first three books, an investigation of truth by means of reason. It is also, throughout the whole work, an investigation of reason itself in relation to the truth. Reason is that which investigates and is itself investigated. I take this double role of reason as one of the most distinctive features of the *Contra Gentiles*. Aside from the idea of "truth in itself," natural reason is the main character in it.

In what follows I would like to focus on the role natural reason plays in the *Contra Gentiles* and especially on the way Aquinas tries to enlighten reason and to confront it with its human and creaturely condition. In order to do this I will concentrate on Aquinas's discussion of the relationship between faith and reason in the introductory chapters and in the prologue of book 4. But first questions about the author's intention and audience have to be considered.

The Office Of Those Who Are Wise

The *Contra Gentiles* is, strictly speaking, neither a theological nor a philosophical work. Although its subject matter may be rightly characterized as theological and its method to a certain extent as philosophical, both categories are nevertheless unsuitable for describing its proper point of view. For Aquinas, to argue theologically means to argue from premises given by revelation. Theology is *scientia fidei*, an argumentative and discursive exposition of the doctrine of faith, in which reason fulfills an instrumental role, particularly with regard to the so-called *"praeambula fidei."* The preambles include what can be naturally known about God, those things the truth of which is required and presupposed by faith, for instance that God exists, that God is one, immaterial, and so on. The position of reason in the *Contra Gentiles* is different from the one it occupies in the *"praeambula."* This expression does not even occur. Aquinas does make a distinction between truths about God which can be known by natural reason and truths which exceed the power of reason. Yet this distinction is based on the scope of natural reason and is formulated without any reference to revelation.

The possibility of determining the scope of natural reason with respect to the divine truth requires a standpoint that leaves room for a critical assessment of reason's competence in divine matters. This standpoint appears to be that of the wise. It is Aquinas's declared intention to assume the task of someone wise (*officium sapientis*). With this "office," Aquinas creates something new, an intellectual point of view that is formally different from theology as well as philosophy.

In 1.1 ("Quid sit officium sapientis"), Aquinas describes the task of those who are wise. On the basis of a few well-chosen references and formulas he sketches in an ingenious way the intellectual perspective of the wise. The fundamental idea is introduced right in the beginning with the motto, taken from one of the wisdom books: "My mouth shall meditate truth, and my lips shall hate impiety" (Proverbs 8:7). These words, from the mouth of a personified Wisdom, suggest a twofold office for someone wise, namely, to meditate and speak forth divine truth and to refute opposed error. Someone wise is first and foremost interested in the question of truth—and not of any truth, just the truth of the first principle. As it belongs to those who are wise to consider the truth claimed by human opinions and beliefs, so it belongs to them to refute any opposing falsehood, that is, the opinions that wrongly claim to be true.

The office of the wise is introduced without any reference to faith and faith's claim to truth. The point of view of the wise concerns the truth and nothing but the truth. It is only in 1.2 that Aquinas connects the "truth" with how the Christian tradition concretely perceives the truth. The *officium* as he intends to pursue it is formulated as follows: to make known the truth that the Catholic faith professes and to set aside the errors that are opposed to it.

The leading point of view in the *Contra Gentiles* can be circumscribed as the sapiential interest in the truth of what Christians confess about God. The *sapiens* is defined as one who considers human beliefs and opinions about the meaning of the universe in the light of their 'truth value'. Significantly, Aquinas does not use the expression "Catholic truth," as he does in the prologue of the *Summa* (where he calls himself a doctor of Catholic truth). The one who is wise does not expound a sacred doctrine; he does not consider the meaning reality has in the light of divine revelation. He is particularly concerned with the truth that the Catholic faith *professes*.[9] His starting point lies at the human level of how people think of the truth and what they profess to be the truth, however much authorized by a divine revelation. The *sapiens* does not proceed from the truth itself as revealed in Scripture. He examines human opinions and beliefs, even if they are based on revelation, in the light of the truth. He argues, collects arguments, and most of all he examines arguments in the light of the truth, since his expertise permits him to discriminate and to judge the arguments pro and contra. It is especially important to emphasize this human point of departure. Only at the level of faith as a human articulation and a religious embodiment of a revealed truth is it possible to confront the claims of faith with alternative claims made by those outside the Christian community, and to investigate faith's truth by means of human reason.

To be wise is to consider things in the light of truth. This truth is what Aquinas calls the "truth of the universe," the final end to which all things are ordered. This end is the ultimate meaning of reality, especially of human life. In 1.2 it becomes clear that the "truth of the universe" has been given a normative and substantial expression in the *fides catholica*. This, at least, is what Aquinas believes, and it is from this point of view that he assumes his office. The term "officium" refers to a public task.[10] Someone who holds an 'officium' is charged with a task or duty directed to others, for the benefit of the community he lives in. For Aquinas, this community is the Christian community of believers (*fideles*), which is based on the truth-consensus of faith.

Aquinas's way of speaking about truth may sound rather pretentious to our ears. If he assumes that the Catholic faith, by divine guarantee, is the expression of the truth, so that each deviation from this faith is necessarily a deviation from the truth, what can he do, acting as one who is wise, but simply repeat and reconfirm the traditional formulas of faith? Or does Aquinas, as a wise man, pretend to have a privileged access to the truth itself? Is the wise person someone who *knows* the truth? I do not think Aquinas would put it in this way. Someone wise is not in full possession of wisdom, but one whose task it is to make known, in whatever way, the truth as professed and claimed by the Catholic faith. In other words, Aquinas proposes to show, to his fellow believers, that the Catholic *claim* to truth can in fact be understood and self-consciously affirmed, against the numerous alternative claims, as a reasonable claim to *truth*. Aquinas does not pretend to have an immediate access to truth itself, by transcending the human point of view from which any rational investigation of truth proceeds.[11] The beliefs and opinions of people about the "truth of the universe" are open to a critical evaluation and assessment, not by an appeal to an intuition of truth, but by examining those opinions in the light of the logical basis—for example natural reason or an authoritative expression given to it (the writings of Aristotle!)—on which people actually base their claims. Neither reason nor faith provides an immediate access to the truth. Every hold on truth and every expression given to it in human discourse is mediated by the world of sense-experience to which our intellect is naturally directed.

Aquinas's point of departure is the "truth of the universe" as formulated, reflected on, preached, and experienced in the faith of the Christian community. There exists a Catholic consensus about truth based on Scripture and tradition. Yet this consensus of the community of believers is never a totally undisputed and unrivalled possession of truth. The Christian community in the thirteenth century saw its own convictions and beliefs confronted with other claims to truth, which by their very existence called the claim of faith into question. These are the *errores infidelium*, the more or less persuasive claims to truth that are contrary to the Catholic consensus. Out of respect for the truth these errors are to be taken with all seriousness. They are not simply to be disregarded as evidence of malice or stupidity. It belongs to the task of those who are wise to discuss these alternative claims, to analyze how it came about that reason falsely convinced itself of their truth, and to set them aside as unjustified and untrue. This is their office, their service for the benefit of the Christian community of believers, which is now able to appropriate self-consciously the truth it confesses over against the erroneous claims of others.

It seems to me that Aquinas's immediate aim is not to prove the validity of the Catholic claim before others (*infideles*). His office is not one of missionary activity aiming at conversion. On the contrary, the office is needed because of the threatening effect the various errors have on the Christian consciousness of truth. Natural reason, according to its historical reality in Greco-Islamic philosophy, calls the Christian perception of truth into question. In this sense, the *Contra Gentiles* seems to me comparable to Maimonides' *Guide of the Perplexed*.[12] The *Guide* is meant for the educated Jew who experiences difficulties in reconciling the traditional faith and law as the basis for Jewish life with the Aristotelian philosophical view of the world. Maimonides' intention is to show that the law may be understood by the way of truth (*per viam veritatis*); his aim is to show the intellectual Jew a way of reading and appreciating the spiritual truth of Scripture behind its anthropomorphic and symbolic appearance, which causes so many perplexities. Both the *Guide* and the *Contra Gentiles* are addressed to a community of believers living in a determinate historical constellation. In both communities the sayings of Scripture have a normative force for the spiritual and moral life of believers. Both Maimonides and Aquinas are engaged in interpreting the sayings of Scripture, not in the sense of biblical exegesis, but in an exegesis that aims at a rational appreciation of the deeper truth of Scripture. At the end of each chapter of the *Contra Gentiles* a passage from Scripture is given to confirm the truth found by reason. It confirms that the truth of reason is not set aside by the higher intelligibility of Scripture, which is founded in the divine truth itself.

Reason and the Existence of 'Others'

The *officium* of the wise is not as such necessarily committed to reason as the way of giving the truth of faith a rational expression. Aquinas introduces natural reason in answer to the existence of 'others', outside the Christian community, who do not accept the authority of Scripture and whose counterclaims, therefore, cannot be refuted successfully on the basis of Scripture. One of the problems Aquinas sees himself confronted with is that some people, "such as Mohammedans and pagans," do not have a holy book in common with Christians (*nobiscum*) on the basis of which disputes in matters of truth can be settled. Therefore, he concludes, in order to deal with the errors of these 'others', we must have recourse (*recurrere*) to natural reason, since all are forced to give their assent to reason. Reason is a kind of common ground and provides Aquinas with a common language that enables him to discuss the truth in a way compelling to the opponent of faith.

Aquinas clearly opts for natural reason by way of *strategy* in order to deal with erroneous opinions of non-Christians, not because reason is thought to be superior. In fact, natural reason is even deficient (*deficiens*) in respect to "divine matters." But the fact that some hold opinions, based on rational thought, that are contrary to Christian faith is a motive for Aquinas to descend to the common ground of reason and to speak the same language; the language of a philosophical discourse on the "truth of the universe." This strategy leads to the general program of the *Contra Gentiles*, formulated as follows: "while we are investigating some truth, we shall also show what errors are set aside by it; and we shall likewise show how the demonstrative truth (*veritas demonstrativa*) is in accordance with the Christian religion."[13]

In the *Contra Gentiles*, at least in the first three books, Aquinas enters by way of strategy into the discourse of reason and employs the language of the *philosophi*. This appears even from the choice of arguments and the use of a specific philosophical vocabulary. For instance, the treatment of the divine essence in book 1 relies heavily on the metaphysics of Avicenna. Without mentioning his name Aquinas borrows several arguments from Avicenna. He even speaks about God's simplicity in terms of *"necesse esse,"* which is particularly striking as this formula is completely absent in the *Summa theologiae*.[14] Apparently, the investigation of the truth of what faith professes by means of reason is not a process of inventing new arguments without any precedent but more one of appropriating and reformulating the available arguments of the philosophers whose writings give witness to what reason can investigate with respect to the truth of God.

Another typical example of the language of natural reason in the *Contra Gentiles* is the word *'felicitas'*, a term used in the Latin translation of Aristotle's *Ethics*. *'Felicitas'* refers to natural human happiness, the ultimate human perfection that can be reached in virtue of natural powers. This natural happiness, as conceived by the philosophers, consists in contemplating the truth as perfectly as possible within the limits of earthly life.[15] *'Beatitudo'*, on the other hand, is a typical word of faith. It refers to the Christian view of happiness as something that consists in the vision of God which is expected to come in a future life by divine grace. So when Aquinas comes to speak about the necessity of grace for human perfection (3.147, "Quod homo indiget divino auxilio ad beatitudinem consequendam"), he uses 'beatitudo'.[16] Aquinas is fully aware of a distinctive language and vocabulary of the *philosophi* as opposed to the language of Christian faith. He writes here from a point of view that never loses sight of this distinction.

It is part of the strategic motivation that Aquinas does not surrender completely to natural reason. Reason does not play the role of judge, standing above the claims of believers and unbelievers. Reason is in fact claimed by one of the parties, the one in which the errors against the Christian faith are to be found. Aquinas's acceptance of reason goes together with the recognition that on numerous issues the claims of reason, as embodied in the opinions of philosophers, conflict with the Catholic consensus about truth. His intention is to show that in the erroneous opinions reason is in fact entangled in error and has arrived at conclusions that are incorrectly derived from the basic principles by which reason proceeds in its understanding of truth. The investigation by means of reason is at the same time an investigation of reason itself according to its concrete embodiment in the philosophical doctrines with which Aquinas was acquainted.

Who, then, are these 'others', the *infideles*? And in what sense can Aquinas be said to address himself to them? In his book about Aquinas's conception of theology, Patfoort argues that the *Contra Gentiles* is a comprehensive teaching of Christian doctrine to be read by believers in order that they may explain and defend the truth of faith to non-Christians. The work should be seen as a presentation of Christian doctrine for the purpose of an ecumenical debate ("*une tentative d'oecuménisme*") between Christians and the learned Muslims and Jews in Spain.[17] Patfoort sees evidence for the missionary intention in Aquinas's use of the phrase "to convince the adversary" (1.9). Here Aquinas explains how he proposes to proceed. First, he intends to treat those truths of faith which are within reason's competence. With respect to this kind of divine truth, he will bring forward both demonstrative and probable arguments, "by which our adversary may become convinced." Then, in book 4, those truths will be dealt with which exceed the power of reason, in which case we ought not to try to convince the adversary by arguments but only to answer his arguments and objections against the truth.

Are these words to be understood in the sense that Aquinas intends to provide a collection of arguments for his fellow-believers in order that they may effectively persuade the unbeliever of the truth of the Christian faith? Is to convince the same as to convert by rational means? Patfoort takes '*convincere*' in the subjective sense of persuasion. He is not much impressed by the difficulty with which Gauthier confronted him, namely, that in medieval Latin 'convincere' does not yet have the modern meaning of "persuading someone to believe that something is true or false."[18] In its medieval use, 'convincere' should be taken in a more objective sense as referring to the outcome of a logical process of argument that is compelling for all the participants in the dispute, regardless of whether some of them feel subjectively convinced. According to the rules of a scholastic disputation the opponent is forced to give his assent when the conclusion is shown to follow logically from premises on which both partners agree. *Convincere* does not appeal to the will, as does rhetorical persuasion, but to the intellect. By the logical force of the argument the intellect is compelled to give its assent.[19]

Therefore I cannot agree with the view put forward by Jordan either.[20] According to him, the division into two types of truth has "a rhetorical motivation" and separates two "possibilities for effective persuasion." As based on the distinction between the realm in which reason can be persuaded by demonstration and one in which reason can be addressed but not conclusively persuaded, Aquinas's program is formulated "in terms of a rhetorical or pedagogical efficacy." However, contrary to Patfoort, Jordan does not think Aquinas's intention is to convince directly the prospective convert, but to show rather to believers how an adversary *could* be convinced. "As it teaches believers how to persuade, the *Contra Gentiles* must also persuade believers to become habituated in the whole of Christian wisdom."[21]

It seems to me misleading to read in the use of *convincere* an intention of rhetorical persuasion. The twofold mode of truth is primarily a logical division, a division of the truth claims of faith into one part that can be demonstratively made known as true in the light of natural reason and another, the truth of which cannot be made known in the light of reason. Reason derives its force and capacity for truth from first and self-evident principles, which are constitutive for our human, sense-mediated mode of knowing the truth. So by the logical force of its principles the human intellect knows the truth of those things that fall under the senses. What transcends the domain of sense-experience can be known only in so far as its knowledge is implied in the very intelligibility of sensible things. Through the rational procedure of demonstration, therefore, one can never conceptually grasp the truth of God himself. The light of reason cannot make the truth of God as such present to our intellect. Only in this sense might rational arguments have a persuasive force for the believer, since reason does not contribute to the inner truth and certainty of faith—the truth of which is founded in God's knowledge of himself (*prima veritas*)—but only to the way the truth of faith can be appropriated within the domain of human experience and understanding.[22]

One cannot conclude from the phrase "to convince an adversary" that the *Contra Gentiles* is meant to support a historical debate of Christian missionaries with Islamic and Jewish intellectuals. It seems very unlikely that in Aquinas's mind the 'adversaries' stood for a historically definable group of people. He was much more interested in the content of the errors, in the fact that they represent actual possibilities of rational thought, which can produce in the mind of people false conceptions of God (and thus of a false god). The list of errors is not restricted to contemporary thought. The errors are attributed to the ancient natural philosophers, to the "Platonists," to Avicenna and Averroes (they are not in all respects trustworthy guides in interpreting Aristotle), to heretics like Origen and the Manichees, but most of all simply to "quidam," to anonymous teachers who hold a more or less reasonable opinion, based on philosophical principles, that conflicts with the truth of Christian faith. They are all formally *adversarii* so far as they hold an opinion that objectively calls into question the truth as confessed by the Christian community (*"quae de Deo confitemur"*). So a manifestation of the truth of faith would only be successful if the opposed error is shown to be an error. When the opponent bases his claim on reason, the only way to combat this erroneous claim is by means of reason, by showing with rational arguments that in the light of truth reason must correct itself.

Reason, however, is not simply a timeless, *a priori* logical basis for deciding conflicting truth claims in history. Natural reason itself is a historical entity in the sense that the masters of the medieval university learned what natural reason is and should be from reading and assimilating the writings of Aristotle, Avicenna, and others. This means that natural reason was not neutral in respect to the truth. Reason was connected with a philosophically elaborated picture of the "truth of the universe." The great theological debates of the thirteenth century were all about elements of this picture that were felt to be contrary to the traditional Christian view, such as the eternity of the world, the unity of the intellect, and the nature of human happiness. In the process of assimilating the Aristotelian corpus the medievals were confronted with claims of reason that they could not accept. Aquinas's strategy is to discuss and combat the claims in the light of reason's own criteria and rules learned from the *philosophi* themselves. Insofar as faith requires not only confession but also reflection and understanding in order to be a human faith, Aquinas shows the believer how 'philosophical' reason can be assimilated if only reason is brought to correct its errors and false pretensions and becomes aware of its human point of view in relation to the truth of faith.

The investigation of reason as embodied in philosophical thought is especially directed at those issues which are typical of the rationalistic spirit of Greco-Islamic philosophy. The work includes themes such as cosmological determinism versus the Christian perception of human morality (arguments against fate, against a determining influence of the stars on the human acts of will and intellect), Islamic necessitarianism versus God's freedom in creation (*non per necessitatem naturae sed per voluntatem*) and the certainty of God's providence without this imposing necessity on the course of things. Another point of interest is Aquinas's concern to reconcile the absolute simplicity of God's essence with his knowing and willing many things. These are just a few examples to illustrate which philosophical ideas are envisaged and denounced by Aquinas in the *Contra Gentiles* and how he seeks to purify reason from its necessitarianism in order to integrate rational thought in his exposition of the Christian perception of the "truth of the universe."

The Twofold Condition of Natural Reason: The Human Condition of Reason

A crucial question preliminary to the project of the *Contra Gentiles* asks to what extent reason can be integrated in the Christian perception of truth without its character as a faith-based relation to the truth being dissolved. Can reason be convinced of the reasonableness, even of the necessity, of holding something in faith? This question as to whether it is fitting (with regard to what in human nature is rational) to hold a truth in faith is dealt with in 1.4–5 according to the twofold division of truth. With respect to both types of truth an apparently very reasonable objection can be made. First, an inspired doctrine proposed to human beings for belief would seem rather useless (*frustra*) within the realm of what naturally can be known about God, since reason can handle it sufficiently by itself. Second, human beings should not be asked to believe what their reason cannot investigate. The divine Wisdom has endowed human nature with reason, which should be sufficient for it to attain the knowledge of God required for its perfection. In both objections natural human reason claims to be self-sufficient in matters of truth, even with the help of an argument based on divine providence.

A reason that cannot tolerate our being asked to hold something on faith represents a veritable Trojan horse for the Christian community. If reason were justified in its claim to autonomy, the only way Christianity could affirm its faith would be by rejecting reason, by excluding rational reflection based on philosophy. Aquinas chooses not to go along that way. It is his conviction that natural reason can be integrated in the Christian consciousness of truth, but not unless reason gives up its claim to autonomy and acknowledges its human condition in knowing the truth. Not reason as such, but the presumption of reason to have an absolute hold on truth prevents a reasonable understanding of the truth of faith. So the issue is not a defense of the 'reasonableness' of Christian faith before reason. Aquinas's objective is to confront natural reason with its own condition, to make reason aware of its limitations in order to prevent reason from unreflectively imposing its own limits on the search for truth. We need more truth than our reason can grasp.

According to Aquinas, three awkward consequences would follow if the truth about God that can be known naturally were left solely as a matter of inquiry for human reason. These consequences all concern the *human* condition of reason. Reason is embodied in human life, is a part of the human being, which does not coincide with its reason. First, the exercise of reason depends on external conditions that are not equal for all human beings. Some people do not have the physical disposition required for a rational inquiry into the truth. Not everyone is naturally gifted with intellectual powers sufficient to pursue the highest level of knowledge. Others are prevented from contemplating the truth in matters divine by the necessities of daily life. Not everyone has the leisure for contemplative inquiry, which is required for arriving at the highest peak of human knowledge. Finally, there are some who are cut off by indolence (*pigritia*), that is, human inertia. For in order to arrive at knowledge of God, a knowledge of many things must already be possessed. The whole of philosophy has to be learned to prepare oneself for the highest philosophical discipline of metaphysics, which deals with divine things. It has to be recognized that not everyone wishes to carry out such a great intellectual labor for the mere love of knowledge.

The second reason why it would be inconvenient to make the knowledge of God dependent solely on natural reason concerns the condition of reason itself. As a part of human life reason requires a great deal of training and education. The process of education takes time. In order to grasp the truth by means of rational inquiry, reason needs a long training—not only the reason of the individual, passing from turbulent and foolish youth to the ripeness and wisdom of old age, but also reason in its historical development. The history of philosophy bears witness to the slow development of philosophical reason towards a more profound and metaphysical view of the nature of reality. As Aquinas remarks in *Summa theologiae* 1.44.2, "the ancient philosophers gradually, and as it were step by step, advanced in the knowledge of truth." Only after a long time and with great difficulty is the human intellect made capable of thinking from a metaphysical perspective about the truth of God.

The third awkward consequence concerns the *results* of human reasoning. Rational investigation does not lead infallibly to true results. Owing to the weakness of the power of judgment and to the admixture of sense-images, reason's true conclusions will be mixed with errors. Even if some conclusions are demonstratively proven, not all people are sufficiently versed in logic to be able to judge the power of demonstration and to discern valid demonstrations from probable or sophistical arguments. Certitude is not only a matter of logically correct reasoning, but most of all of human appreciation and assessment of the logical conclusiveness of an argument. "That is why it was necessary that the unshakeable certitude and pure truth concerning divine things should be presented to men by way of faith."[23]

The message of *Contra Gentiles* 1.4 is that reason is a human capacity, embedded in concrete human life, and that therefore it is not convenient to make the human perception of the "truth of the universe" dependent solely on the inquiry of reason. So from the point of view of the human condition of reason, the factual claim of Christianity to have a divinely inspired doctrine does make sense and should not be condemned as unintelligible.

The Creaturely Condition of the Reason

It is not immediately evident why we should believe something on the authority of divine revelation, the truth of which cannot be examined by reason because it is said to be above reason. What could be the meaning of this 'above' for human reason? Why is the truth of faith called 'supra-rational' and not simply irrational, outside the categories of reason? Only when reason realizes its creaturely condition in knowing the truth can it acknowledge something beyond its power as having nevertheless the character of truth. The revelation of something that exceeds the power of reason has the beneficial effect of confronting reason with its creaturely condition, of making reason aware that truth as such is not defined by its own rational comprehension of truth.

The central issue of *Contra Gentiles* 1.5 is the limitedness of natural reason in relation to the truth. In the first argument Aquinas's point is that reason may not impose its own limits on human desire. We are directed to a higher good than human fragility can experience in the present life. The human mind must be "called to something higher than our reason" (*"evocari in aliquid altius quam ratio nostra"*) in order that we learn to direct our desire to a higher end than reason can experience.

The second argument put forward by Aquinas is a most interesting and difficult one to understand. His point is that reason should think correctly about God. Since God's substance surpasses the natural knowledge of which human beings are capable, reason is persuaded to think about God as something that exceeds its conceptions. By the very fact that some things about God are proposed to human beings for belief, reason becomes aware of its limits in relation to the truth of God. It is brought to think about God as being above everything that reason can think. So the very fact that some truths are revealed that go beyond reason makes reason reflect on its limits and correct its view of God—not in the sense that revelation provides reason with new information, but in the sense that reason comes to a new understanding of what it means to have a conception about God at all. Confronted with the supra-rational claim of faith reason acquires a Socratic insight into how its conceptual knowledge is related to God's truth. Reason knows God to be beyond its knowledge of God (*sciat se Deum nescire*).[24]

The next argument also concerns the limits of reason. Some, so Aquinas says, have such a presumptuous opinion of their own rational ability that they deem themselves able to measure the nature of everything. It is the presumption that the capacity of reason imposes its own measure on the truth itself. Especially in book 4 the presumption of reason is a recurring motif. According to Aquinas, this presumption arises from a misunderstanding of reason with respect to its own capacity for truth. Reason thinks itself to be the source of truth. From this rationalistic presumption the human mind might be freed by a perspective on truth that surpasses reason.

In the last argument Aquinas turns against those who, out of falsely conceived humility, argue that human beings should restrict themselves to earthly matters and leave the divine matters to God alone. Once again, reason should not restrict the human quest for truth to its own capacity. Aquinas cites with approval the remark of Aristotle: "man should draw himself towards what is immortal and divine as much as he can." There is more truth to be known than human reason can handle.

Can Reason Recognize Itself In Faith's Intelligibility?

If reason, aware of its own condition, cannot and may not reject a faith-based claim for truth, then the next question arises whether the believer's holding something in faith really corresponds to an objective truth. Is it not just foolishness to place one's faith in the truth of "wonderful stories"[25] that are beyond human experience? It is clear that reason does not have access to the logical ground on which the truth of faith is based. But does faith have its own reasons or is it just 'wishful thinking'? Aquinas counts as legitimate reason's concern that people should not frivolously believe what they have heard.

The question of levity in 1.6 does not, as one might think at first sight, concern the credibility of faith, as if to justify the believer's act of faith. Aquinas is not so much interested in the typical modern question, "Is it rational to give assent to what is proposed to me for belief?" It is not a matter of the subjective evidence on the part of the believer, but of whether the subjective belief that something is true corresponds to an objective truth. Only when faith is related to an objective truth, not essentially different from the truth of reason (see 1.7), can reason be expected to investigate the truth claims of faith and to refute objections against it. Even when faith is said to be above reason, it cannot lack truth, without which it would be foolish to believe, nor have a different kind of truth, which would contradict human reason. So the question posed by Aquinas in 1.6–7 is preliminary to his project in the *Contra Gentiles*: How can reason recognize itself in the truth of faith?

His answer comes down to the simple observation that in the history of the Christian religion human reason has apparently recognized itself in the proclaimed faith. It is very unlikely that the Christian faith should be based on fables invented for credulous people. The divine origin and the truthfulness of the Christian message have been confirmed, not only by way of miracles but also, more convincingly, by the inspiration given to human minds, "so that simple and untutored persons come to possess the highest wisdom and the readiest eloquence."[26] Aquinas's point is that the wisdom of the apostles, which was not esoteric but public and therefore open for human reason to assess its character as wisdom, cannot be explained in a purely human way (e.g., by education). Further, by the arguments of this inspired wisdom many people, both simple and learned, became convinced and converted to Christian faith. They were not persuaded by the force of arms or by the promise of pleasure; even in the midst of the tyranny of persecutors they chose to join the Christian movement. Could it be by any other motive than the force of truth? Christian faith preaches values that are contrary to the 'natural' human inclination to the visible and material world. So evidently it was not 'worldly' motives that led so many people to accept the truth of faith. On the contrary, people were asked to give up the pleasures of the flesh and the things of the world in order to set their hopes on something invisible. Evidently they were willing to do so, not because they were all stupid or misled, but because they recognized the inner truth and felt convinced by it.

Still the possibility exists that faith has a different kind of truth, a different 'logic' than that of rational thought. We are told that the truths of faith surpass the human intellect. But what if they simply contradict the logic of our rational minds? According to Aquinas, the exercise of human reason is made possible by some basic principles, the truth of which is known naturally. Those principles cannot be thought to be false since they are constitutive of rational thought and human understanding of truth. Now if the truth claimed by the Christian faith were opposed to a truth of reason, we could not accept them both as true, since our rational nature makes this impossible. We would have to give up our nature if we were asked to accept contrary opinions as true.

This kind of conflict, however, is quite improbable, since it would mean a conflict in God himself. As a created faculty human reason is related to the truth according to principles that are not established by reason itself, but by the transcendent source of all truth. Only when we realize that natural reason is not an independent source of truth will it become clear that in principle there cannot be a conflict between the claims of reason and the truth of faith. It is impossible for faith to have a 'logic' of its own, a logic that would be irrational to the eyes of reason. Even if reason cannot demonstrate fully the truth of what faith professes, it still can appreciate its higher intelligibility by reflecting on the traces and likenesses of the divine mystery within the sensible world. When reason gives up its presumption to be the measure of the truth, it can pursue its quest for truth beyond the limits of rational demonstration. The mystery of God is not a mystery because it defeats the attempts of reason to understand, but because its truth attracts reason beyond its comprehension.

The Threefold Knowledge About God

With the transition to book 4, the critical point in the plan of the *Contra Gentiles* has arrived. Now the method of investigating the truth of what faith confesses by means of reason does not suffice any more. In book 4 Aquinas intends to deal with those elements of faith's confession about God which are beyond human experience, beyond what natural reason can investigate. Faith professes the mystery of God as the "truth of the universe" according to three parts: first, the confession that God is one and three; second, the mystery of the incarnation of God's son; and third, the resurrection of human bodies together with the everlasting happiness of human souls. Human experience can offer no evidence for these claims. What now can be the task of reason? Must it be silenced before the supra-rational truth of faith?

The transition to the supra-rational truths of faith gives Aquinas cause to assume the *duplex modus* from the beginning in order to clarify the epistemological basis of this division in truth with respect to our intellect. What faith professes about God can be verified in the light of reason only to a certain extent. Why is this? Because it is connatural to the human intellect to derive its knowledge from sensible things. Departing from sensible things, it cannot arrive through itself at a proper concept of God's essence. Only by reflecting on the intelligible order that reason perceives in the sensible world is it led to some knowledge of God as the first principle and cause of all being. Since the way human reason follows in its search for truth clearly does not suffice to manifest the whole truth of what faith professes, there must be a different way by which the truth of faith *supra rationem* comes down to us. Aquinas has thus far left the nature of this second "way" in the dark. At the beginning of book 4, he must make clear what the proper logical foundation of this supra-rational truth is and how this truth is given to us.

In the prologue of book 4, Aquinas describes two ways given to human beings for attaining some knowledge of God. The first way is through creation (*via per creaturas*), the second through revelation (*via per revelationem*). Both ways are forms of mediation. Each effects a mediate union between the knower and the known, the human intellect and the divine substance. For both ways the divine truth (*veritas divina*) is but mediately present to the human intellect. The intellect is related to God through articulated claims, the truth of which it does not know in the light of God's own truth. The two ways correspond to reason and faith as the two 'logical' forms under which divine truth can become present in human discourse. It becomes present not perfectly, but only in an anticipatory and still 'darkened' way. In the case of the way *per creaturas*, the medium is the hierarchical order of natures in the world, the result from God's providential plan. This medium not only presents an imperfect likeness of God's essence, it is known adequately by the human intellect only with great difficulty. Human beings can reach only a faint knowledge of God by pursuing the way upward in creation with reason. As the perfect knowledge of God is the end of human existing, and since human beings, as creatures, cannot remain idle, a second way to God through revelation accords perfectly with the divine goodness. "In order that man might have a firmer knowledge of Him, God revealed certain things about Himself that transcend the human intellect."[27] The insufficiency of natural reason with respect to the perfect knowledge of God is one motive for God's descending through revelation to human knowledge.

Even the knowledge handed down to us through revelation remains imperfect, however, since the way of revelation too is 'mediated' by our sense-bound susceptibility. What comes to us by revelation is received according to the mode of our nature. Revelation is not a voice from heaven. It does not produce an immediate encounter between human beings and God. God's revelation, according to Aquinas, comes to us within the visible world in the form of speech (*per modum locutionis*). God's word is made known through the speaking of prophets and apostles, through preaching that aims to instill faith in those listening. Faith comes from hearing. The truth of the revealed message does not appear to be seen; it has to be believed (*non videnda sed credenda*).

There is a certain order in God's revelation, well suited to human needs and capacities: The biblical history of revelation shows a pedagogical structure of increasing disclosure on God's part. Humanity advances slowly, gropingly, towards understanding of God. The way of revelation does not end in faith. Human beings seek to see what they believe. The biblical revelation points forwards to a future in which they will be freed from their earthly condition and raised up to see the truth now only revealed.

Although the way of revelation is consummated in an immediate knowledge of God, so long as we live on earth the knowledge of faith cannot completely satisfy our desire to see God. Aquinas gives two reasons why revealed knowledge fails to satisfy in comparison to the full knowledge enjoyed by those who see God. First, only a part of the divine mystery has been revealed in Scripture. Second, this partial truth has come to us "under certain likenesses and darknesses of words" (*"sub quibusdam similitudinibus et obscuritatibus verborum"*). In the obscure sayings of Scripture, the divine mystery is hidden by veils (*"velaminibus occultata"*), so that only the *studiosi* may grasp the hidden sense behind the surface, the sense that is unaffected by the mockery of the incredulous.

By describing the way of revelation in contrast to the natural knowledge of God, on the one hand, and the eschatological vision of God, on the other hand, Aquinas has now set forth the hermeneutical and methodological principles for the procedure of book 4. In dealing with truths of faith revealed by God, one must take the sayings of Scripture as principles. On the basis of them, one must try one's best to understand the true sense of what is taught obscurely in Scripture. One must also defend it against the attempts of the unbelievers to make it seem ridiculous (*"a laceratione infidelium defendendo"*). One should not presume to understand the things of faith perfectly—in other words, to prove their truth by reducing them to principles evident in the light of reason. On the contrary, these truths must be proved by the authority of Scripture. The truth of what faith professes has its logical basis in the *prima veritas*, the divine truth as known by God himself.[28] The claims of faith can only be proved from the authoritative expression of the *prima veritas* in Scripture. Nevertheless, it remains to show that the truth of faith is not opposed to natural reason, so that the Christian faith may be defended "against the attacks of the unbelievers" (*"ab impugnatione infidelium"*).

Natural reason still has its part to play in book 4. Reason will appear once again in the encounter with the 'others'. It is not that the truth of faith as such has to be ascertained by reason, but rather that some, using reason, have conceived opinions that set up obstacles—may still set up obstacles—to the process of human understanding and the expression of the revealed truth. In this respect the "attacks of the unbelievers" are thought to be dangerous by Aquinas, even when they are not intended as attacks but as corrections of faith-formulas in the light of what some take to be truth. These arguments are "attacks" so far as they attempt to show that the Christian claim to truth cannot be substantiated. The Christian theologian, acting in the office of the wise, cannot simply put these attacks aside. After all, they appeal to the natural human respect for and obligation to truth. They are dangerous, because wrong ideas about God may cause believers to direct their lives to the wrong end.

For example, with respect to the "generation" in God of the eternal Son, certain teachers "presumed to measure this mystery by their own comprehension of it and conceived various and vain opinions about it."[29] In the views of heretics like Arius and Sabellius, reason has apparently taken offense at the truth of faith and so has distorted the mystery by measuring it with its own logic. In these attacks, reason presumes to correct faith in the light of what it thinks to be the truth without reflecting critically on its own relation to the truth. To defend the Catholic faith against these heretical opinions, Aquinas will show that faith, as articulated and confessed by the Christian Church, is not impossible in the light of reason.

What does it mean to show that the truth of faith is not impossible in the light of reason? At first sight it would seem that Aquinas intends to defend the Catholic faith by refuting reason's various objections. Reason has to be silenced, since these truths of faith are said to be outside reason's competence. It seems no wonder, then, that reason turns into a heretical reason when it tries to understand the mystery of faith. But in fact the point of Aquinas's discussion of Arius and Sabellius is rather to argue that reason, faced with the mystery of faith, need not agree either to keep silent or to become heretical. In the long development of Catholic orthodoxy, heretical reason has been defeated successfully by the truth of faith—not silenced by the political mechanism of ecclesiastical power. The development of Christian doctrine shows that human reason can correct itself as it tries to understand and to articulate the mystery of God hinted at in the obscurities of Scripture.

Catholic orthodoxy is the result of a learning in which the heretical views of Arius and Sabellius played an important part. The heretics found it quite contrary to rational truth to accept a "generation" in God. As Aquinas remarks, human reason, proceeding from the properties of creatures, experiences difficulties in a great variety of ways in this secret of divine generation.[30] It was because reason imposed its own categories on the divine mystery, without correcting these categories in the light of Scripture, that Sabellius and Arius were led to two opposed errors, the one denying the personal distinction between the Father and the Son, the other denying the full divinity of the Son. The Catholic faith, keeping to the middle road,[31] holds with Arius against Sabellius that the Father is distinct in person from the Son, but with Sabellius against Arius that Christ is true and natural God, the same in nature as the Father, although not the same in person. Only the Catholic Church, taught by the texts of Scripture[32] to correct the opposed errors of Arius and Sabellius, confesses a true "generation" in God. The fact that the Catholic faith is the middle road is a sign of its truth. "For, as the Philosopher says, even falsehoods give witness to the truth, for falsehoods stand apart not only from the truth but from one another."[33] The opposed views of Arius and Sabellius condemned one another as false; the partial truth in each is saved in the whole truth of the Catholic confession. The development of Christian doctrine displays a proper rationality so far as human reason, confronted with its initial onesidedness, is led by truth itself to correct and transcend its categories in order to express the higher intelligibility of faith.

What has to be pushed back is the presumption of reason, its uncritical and unreflective attitude to the truth, and not reason as such. Reason has to learn, by reflecting on the origin of its categories in sensible reality, that the truth of faith is not impossible. Aquinas's use here of a double negation is very striking. At the end of the chapter in which he sums up the various difficulties and impossibilities reason experiences with "generation" in God, he concludes that since truth is strong in itself and cannot be overcome by any attack, his intention must be to show that the truth of faith cannot be overcome by reason ("*ratione superari non possit*").[34] This is a characteristic and illuminating remark. The next chapter (4.11), in which he carries out this intention, is most remarkable for its speculative depth and vision. Here reason learns that its own difficulties concerning divine "generation" can be overcome when it is brought to acknowledge that the hierarchical structure of the universe discloses a logic of perfection and unity that, at its very summit, admits plurality and distinction. The idea of a hierarchy is used to teach reason that its conceptual framework is derived from and adapted to a level of being that shows in itself a dynamic, self-transcending character. By the very force of truth, reason is compelled to give up its objections. It has now come to understand that these difficulties are not taken from the nature of truth itself but from the way reason conceives truths, "proceeding from the properties of sensible things." The development of the Catholic expression of the truth of faith was at the same time reason's way of learning of rational reflection and self-correction. In it human reason is led to acknowledge that it does not establish by itself the conditions under which it knows the truth. It comes to see that truth is not constituted by its categories. It grasps, in other words, that it is a created faculty.[35]

Notes

1. In early manuscripts of the work the title used is "Liber de veritate catholicae fidei contra errores infidelium." See the Leonine edition of the *Contra Gentiles* in *Opera omnia iussu impensaque Leonis XIII. P. M. edita* (Rome, 1882–), 13: xiib, and the references in Mark D. Jordan, "The Protreptic Structure of the 'Summa contra Gentiles'," *The Thomist* 50 (1986): 173–209, at p. 182, n. 31. It seems

likely that this long and awkward title has been abbreviated into "summa contra gentiles."

2. *Summa contra Gentiles*, trans. Anton C. Pegis et alii (Notre Dame, Ind.: University of Notre Dame Press, 1975), General Introduction, p. 20.

3. Chenu, *Introduction à l'étude de saint Thomas d'Aquin*, 3rd ed. (Montréal: Institut d'études médiévales, and Paris: J. Vrin, 1974), p. 250.

4. James A. Weisheipl, *Friar Thomas d'Aquino: His Life, Thought, and Work*, rev. ed. (Washington: Catholic University of America Press, 1983), p. 133.

5. See Michel Corbin's critical analysis of the story about Raymond de Peñafort in *Le chemin de la théologie chez Thomas d'Aquin* (Paris: Beauchesne, 1974) and also the extensive discussion in Jordan, "Protreptic Structure," pp. 174–182. Jordan concludes that the circumstantial evidence does not really help us to understand the *Contra Gentiles*.

6. Chenu, *Introduction*, p. 253.

7. Corbin, *Chemin de la théologie*, p. 630.

8. Corbin, *Chemin de la théologie*, p. 509. René-Antoine Gauthier takes the same view in his "Introduction historique" to *Thomas d'Aquin, Somme contre les Gentils* I, trans. R. Bernier and M. Corvez (Paris: Lethielleux, 1961) 1:87: "si dans ce propos l'erreur a sa place, ce n'est pas dans le mesure où elle est professée par des hommes, c'est dans la mesure où par son contraste elle rend plus lumineuse la vérité."

9. '*Profitetur*' means to speak forward, to declare openly that something is true. See also 1.9: "veritatis, quam fides profitetur et ratio investigat." In citing or quoting from the *Summa contra Gentiles*, I use the edition of Ceslaus Pera, Petrus Marc, and Petrus Caramello (Turin: Marietti and Paris: Lethiellux, 1961–1967).

10. An *officium*, Aquinas explains in *Summa theol.* 2–2.183.3 ad 2, implies that one carries out an activity that is related to others ("actus qui referuntur ad alios"). For instance both a doctor and a judge hold an *officium*. Aquinas refers to Isidore's *Etymologiae* 6.19 (PL 82:252). Isidore there explains '*officium*' etymologically as doing things that are not offensive to anyone, but beneficial for all ("officium est ut quisque illa agat quae nulli officiant, id est noceant, sed prosint omnibus"). The relation to others as a part of the office is mentioned by Aquinas explicitly in *Summa contra Gentiles* 1.1 ("aliis disserere").

11. Recall the remark in *Summa contra Gentiles* 3.48 (Pera no. 2258): "Non igitur homines in cognitione veritatis sic se habent quasi in ultima fine existentes."

12. See Jordan, "Protteptic Structure," p. 196, who points to some interesting similarities and some dissimilarities between the *Guide* and the *Contra Gentiles*.

13. *Summa contra Gentiles* 1.2: "Simul autem veritatem aliquam investigantes ostendemus, qui errores per eam excludantur; et quomodo demonstrativa veritas fidei christianae religionis concordet."

14. See *Summa contra Gentiles* 1.15, 1.16, 1.18, 1.19 and particularly 1.22, on the identity of essence and *esse* in God. This last chapter, as Weisheipl remarked, is almost a paraphrase of Avicenna's *Metaphysica* 8.4 (*Friar Thomas d'Aquino*, p. 133).

15. See *Summa theol.* 1.62.1: "Una (ultima perfectio) quidem, quam potest assequi virtute suae naturae: et haec quodammodo beatitudo vel felicitas dicitur."

16. Earlier, in 3.25 (Pera no. 2068), Aquinas mentions in one passage both

"beatitudo" and *"felicitas."* The first is connected with a text from Matthew 5:8: "Blessed (*beati*) are the pure in heart, for they will see God"; the second, with Aristotle's *Ethics.* From 3.25 on, Aquinas uses the term *"felicitas"* almost exclusively, except, for instance, in 3.62 (Pera no. 2376), where *"beatitudo"* is used in connection with an erroneous opinion of Origen, who in spite of his being a heretic still belongs to the Christian tradition.

17. Albert Patfoort, *Thomas d'Aquin: Les clés d'une théologie* (Paris: FAC-éditions, 1983), p. 105: "Bref la *Summa contra Gentiles* serait une école de présentation aux infidèles de la foi chrétienne, une tentative d'oecuménisme, avant la lettre, entre chrétiens et infidèles."

18. Patfoort, *Thomas d'Aquin,* p. 114, n. 19.

19. See, for example, *Scriptum super Sent.* 3.24.2.2a arg. 4, ed. Pierre Mandonnet and M. F. Moos (Paris: Lethielleux, 1929–1947), no. 40: "omnis probatio convincens intellectum ad assentiendum facit scientiam"; *Summa theol.* 1–2.51.3 co (*Opera omnia* [Leonine] 6.328b): "una propositio per se nota convincit intellectum ad assentiendum firmiter conclusioni"; and 2–2.4.1 co (8:44a): "per auctoritatem divinam intellectus convincitur ad assentiendum his quae sunt fidei." These texts, which are cited by Patfoort (*Thomas d'Aquin,* p. 117) to underline his 'subjective' view of *convincere,* clearly favor the 'objective' sense. As it is the self-evident proposition which logically founds the truth of the conclusion, and which in virtue of this logical foundation compels the intellect, so it is the authority of God, revealing himself in Holy Scripture, which *is* the logical ground for us to give our assent to the truth of faith.

20. See Jordan, "Protreptic Structure," pp. 173–209.

21. Jordan, "Protreptic Structure," p. 190.

22. It is against this background that the great number of arguments, so characteristic for the *Contra Gentiles,* must be understood. By the fact that for each articulated aspect of the divine truth the reader is given a series of diverse arguments, taken from the writings of the philosophers and the Christian doctors, he becomes aware that no argument as such is capable of conceptualizing adequately the intended truth itself, but is a more or less convincing way of leading the human intellect to a rational understanding of the truth of faith. In each chapter the truth under discussion is not defined by the logical conclusiveness of any singular argument.

23. *Summa contra Gentiles* 1.4: "Et ideo oportuit, per viam fidei, fixa certitudine, ipsam veritatem de rebus divinis hominibus exhiberi."

24. This is an Anselmian motif, as in *Proslogion* 15, in *Opera omnia,* ed. Franciscus Salesius Schmitt (Edinburgh: Thomas Nelson & Sons, 1946–1961), 1: 112: "Ergo, Domine, non solum es quo maius cogitari nequit, sed es quiddam maius quam cogitari possit." See also Thomas Aquinas, *Quaestiones disputatae De potentia* 7.5 ad 14, ed. Paulus M. Pession in *Quaestiones disputatae II,* 10th ed. (Turin and Rome: Marietti, 1965), p. 60b: "illud est ultimum cognitionis humanae de Deo quod sciat se Deum nescire, inquantum cognoscit, illud quod Deus est, omne ipsum quod de eo intelligimus, excedere."

25. *Summa contra Gentiles* 1.6 (Pera no. 35): "quasi *doctas fabulas secuti,* ut II Petri (I,16) dicitur."

26. *Summa contra Gentiles* 1.6 (Pera no. 37): "et, quod est mirabilius, humana-

rum mentium inspiratione, ut idiotae et simplices, dono Spiritus sancti repleti, summam sapientiam et facundiam in instanti consequerentur."

27. *Summa contra Gentiles* 4.1 (Pera no. 3341): "ut firmior esset hominis de Deo cognitio, quaedam de seipso hominibus revelavit, quae intellectum humanum excedunt."

28. As Aquinas notes in 4.1 (Pera no. 3345), the angels and the other beatified know the divine mysteries in the First Truth, that is the perfect knowledge by which the divine truth is seen in itself. The imperfect knowledge of faith is derived from this perfect knowledge.

29. *Summa contra Gentiles* 4.4 (Pera no. 3358): "Hulus autem doctrinae veritatem quidam perversi homines suo sensu metiri praesumentes, de praemissis vanas et varias opiniones conceperunt."

30. *Summa contra Gentiles* 4.10 (Pera no. 3446): "humana ratio, ex creaturarum proprietatibus procedens, multiplicem in hoc secreto divinae generationis patitur difficultatem."

31. Summa contra Gentiles 4.7 (Pera no. 3426): "Fides ergo catholica, media via incedens."

32. See Summa contra Gentiles 4.7 (Pera no. 3424): "Ex praemissis igitur et consimilibus sacra Scripturae documentis Ecclesia catholica docta."

33. Summa contra Gentiles 4.7 (Pera no. 3426): "Ex quo etiam indicium veritatis catholicae sumi potest; nam vero, ut Philosophus dicit, etiam falsa testantur; falsa vero non solum a veris, sed etiam ab invicem distant."

34. Summa contra Gentiles 4.10 (Pera no. 3460): "Haec igitur et similia sunt ex quibus aliqui, divinorum mysteria propria ratione metiri volentes, divinam generationem impugnare nituntur. Sed, quia veritas in seipsa fortis est et nulla impugnatione convellitur, oportet intendere ad ostendendum quod veritas fidei ratione superari non possit." The idea of an objective truth, which excludes by its force every falsehood, still requires the rational labor of refuting and dissolving the arguments which are brought forward against the truth of faith. However powerful by itself, truth can only become effective within the realm of human life through the medium of reason. That is why the work of "dissolving" (*dissolvere*) the arguments which form an obstacle to the acceptance of the truth is so important to Aquinas.

35. I would like to acknowledge a generous grant from the Niels Stensen Foundation, which made possible the research that resulted in this essay.

6

⚶

The *Esse/Essentia* Argument in Aquinas's *De ente et essentia*

⚶ Despite all of the attention which has been paid to the issues which Aquinas raises in an important argument in Chapter 4 of *De ente et essentia*[1] (I shall call it the *Esse/Essentia* [E/E] Argument), no one has offered a detailed account of exactly what the argument *is*.[2] There have been discussions of its general character, of the interpretation of certain of its segments and conclusions, and of the argument's place in the broad context of Aquinas's thought. It seems to me, however, that one must be clear about the precise structure of the argument before one can address these more general questions. In Section 1, therefore, I shall set out the E/E Argument in detail and discuss some misconstruals of the argument's structure. On the basis of the exegetical work done in Section 1, I shall sketch in Section 2 an interpretation of the E/E Argument paying special attention to its status as an argument for the real distinction between *esse* and essence. I shall then consider briefly in Section 3 one interpretation of the argument which differs from mine.

1.1

At the beginning of Chapter 4 Aquinas rejects the view that separate substances are composed of matter and form.[3] Insofar as they do not exhibit the composition of matter and form, separate substances are simple. The view that separate substances are in some sense simple, however, is open to two possible objections. First, it might be objected that if separate substances are simple, they are like God, which is impossible. Second, it might be pointed out that Aquinas himself has claimed that individuation is dependent on matter.[4] If separate substances do not have matter, then it will be impossible to individuate them. Aquinas devotes the remainder of the chapter to meeting these two objections. His tasks, then, are to show that, although separate substances lack the composition of matter and form, they are not (like God) simple in every way and are not pure actuality,⁵ and that, although they have no matter, they may still be individuated. The first task is the one Aquinas undertakes in the passage with which I am concerned.

Aquinas makes clear what the argument is supposed to establish by stating the conclusion at the outset. He says that although separate substances are form alone without matter, "nevertheless, they are not simple in every way nor are they pure actuality but they are permeated by potentiality" (lines 2–3). The argument proceeds to establish that they are not simple in every way (lines 26–28) and that they are a mixture of potentiality and actuality (lines 49–51).

I believe that the following schema accurately represents Aquinas's E/E Argument:⁶

(E/E1) Whatever belongs to a thing and is not part of its essence either
    (a) comes from without and effects a composition with the essence or [4–6]
    (b) itself constitutes the entire essence. [11–12]
(E/E2) No essence can be understood without its parts. [6–7]
(E/E3) Every essence [except the Divine essence] can be understood without anything being understood about its *esse*. [7–8]
∴(E/E4) A thing's *esse* is not part of its essence.
(E/E5) Suppose that there is something [call it X] which is *esse* alone, so that it is *esse* itself subsisting. [19–20]
(E/E6) Pluralization occurs in one of only three ways:
    (i) by the addition of some differentia,
    (ii) by a form being received in different matters, or
    (iii) by one thing being absolute and another being received in something. [12–19]
(E/E7) Anything which is *esse* alone cannot receive the addition of a differentia. [20–22]
∴(E/E8) X cannot be more than one in virtue of (6i).
(E/E9) Anything which is *esse* alone cannot receive different matters. [22–24]
∴(E/E10) X cannot be more than one in virtue of (6ii).
∴(E/E11) If there is anything which is its own *esse*, there is at most one such thing.⁷ [24–25]
∴(E/E12) For any other thing besides this one, its *esse* is other than its essence. [25–26]
(E/E13) Intelligences are entities which are other than this one.⁸

∴(E/E14) There is *esse* besides essence in intelligences. [26–28]

(E/E15) Everything which belongs to something either

    (a) is caused by the principles of its nature or

    (b) comes to it from some extrinsic principle. [29–32]

(E/E16) A thing's *esse* cannot be caused by the thing's essence [i.e., a thing's *esse* is not accounted for by (15a)], because it is impossible that a thing produce itself in *esse*. [32–35]

∴(E/E17) It must be that every thing such that its *esse* is other than its essence has *esse* from another [i.e., a thing's *esse* is accounted for by (15b)]. [35–36]

(E/E18) One cannot go to infinity in efficient causes. [40–41]

∴(E/E19) There is something which is the cause of *esse* for all things in virtue of the fact that it is *esse* alone. [37–40]

(E/E20) Everything which receives something from another is in potentiality with respect to what is received, and what is received is the actuality of the thing. [45–46]

∴(E/E21) All things [other than God] are in potentiality with respect to *esse* which they receive from God.]

∴(E/E22) Potentiality and actuality are found in intelligences. [49–50]

In Sections 1.2–1.4 below I shall take up three features of this schema which might appear to be problematic.

1.2

Some justification is necessary for the fact that premiss (E/E1), and consequently steps (E/E1)–(E/E4), of the schema depart from Aquinas's actual text. Aquinas actually begins with the following claim: "For whatever is not of the concept of an essence or quiddity comes from without and effects a composition with the essence . . ." (lines 4–6). I make two additions to this text, however, to form premiss (E/E1) of the reconstruction. First I have expanded Aquinas's "whatever" to "whatever belongs to a thing," and second, I have added a claim which Aquinas makes later in the text (at lines 11–12) to his initial claim to make premiss (E/E1) a disjunction. I shall discuss my reasons for making the first addition in this section and my reasons for making the second in the next.

Substituting "whatever belongs to a thing" for Aquinas's simple "whatever" amounts to nothing more, I think, than making explicit what he perhaps justifiably, leaves implicit. Strictly speaking, the claim that whatever is not of the concept of an essence comes from without and effects a composition with the essence is false. There are plenty of things which are not part of the concept of an essence which do not come from without and effect a composition with it—viz., things which have nothing whatsoever to do with the thing in question. Squareness is something which is not part of the essence of a human being, but neither does it come from without and effect a composition with the essence of a human being. Squareness does not belong to human beings at all. So the general principle is not absolutely general, and the unqualified "whatever" needs to be qualified if the claim is to be true.

No one would want to press this objection against Aquinas, however because it is clear that he means by "whatever" something like "whatever belongs to a thing."[9] Anything which belongs to a thing or is true of a thing in actuality might plausibly be said either to be a part of the thing's essence or to be extrinsic to the essence but combined with it in the actual thing. My first addition to Aquinas's actual text, then, I take to be a mere filling out of what is implicit.

1.3

I make premiss (E/E1) of the argument a disjunction by adding what Aquinas says in lines 11–12 to his introductory general principle because I think doing so displays most perspicuously the underlying logical structure of the E/E Argument. There is, I think, a difference between the rhetorical presentation of the argument in the text and its actual logical structure. My schema attempts to lay bare the logical structure while adhering as closely as possible to the actual text of *De ente* 4.

As the text stands, Aquinas begins the argument with a general principle: Whatever belongs to a thing and is not part of the concept of its essence comes from without and effects a composition with it. As the argument develops, however, it becomes apparent that the general principle is too strong and requires qualification. Aquinas himself points it out. After drawing the apparent conclusion: "Therefore it is clear that *esse* is other than essence or quiddity" (lines 10–11), Aquinas immediately adds the qualification: "unless perhaps there is something whose quiddity is its very *esse*" (lines 11–12). Aquinas notices that he is not entitled to the straightforward conclusion that *esse* is other than essence because there is a possibility which he has not yet dealt with—viz., that *esse* is the very essence of the thing. The general principle, then, is too strong because it restricts the possibilities to two when there are in fact three. It claims that *esse* must be either part of the essence or other than the essence. Aquinas recognizes that in fact it could be part of the essence, other than the essence, *or* identical with the essence. Having started with a major premiss which is too strong, Aquinas qualifies his conclusion: "Therefore it is clear that *esse* is other than essence or quiddity, unless perhaps there is something whose quiddity is its very *esse*." The logical structure of the argument is displayed most straightforwardly if the qualification is incorporated into the general principle rather than added to the conclusion.

The following schema represents what I take to be the underlying logical structure (ULS) of the E/E Argument:

(ULS1) There are three ways to account for a thing's *esse:* either
    (a) its *esse* is part of its essence or
    (b) its *esse* comes to its essence from without, effecting a composition with it, or
    (c) its *esse* is itself the entire essence of the thing.
(ULS2) It is not the case that (a).
(ULS3) If it is the case that (c), then it is so for at most one thing.
∴(ULS4) For all other things it must be the case that (b).

(E/E1) corresponds to (ULS1), (E/E2)–(E/E4) correspond to (ULS2), (E/E5)–(E/E11) correspond to (ULS3), and the conclusion (E/E12) corresponds to the conclusion (ULS4).

Some commentators have identified the first portion of the E/E Argument (lines 3–11) as the *Intellectus Essentiae* (IE) Argument because it appears to derive a distinction between *esse* and essence from considerations about the concept or notion of an essence (*intellectus essentiae*).[10] The IE Argument runs as follows:

(IE1) Whatever is not part of an essence is other than the essence.
(IE2) *Esse* is not part of any essence.
∴ (IE3) *Esse* is other than any essence.[11]

If my remarks about the underlying logical structure of Aquinas's argument are right, then the IE Argument is not to be found in *De ente* 4.

In fact, for Aquinas, the IE Argument is unsound as it stands. (IE1) is false because, as Aquinas points out, it is too strong. There is another possibility— the possibility that *esse* and essence are identical—which (IE1) does not account for. Aquinas does take account of this third possibility in the E/E Argument. He draws the unqualified conclusion that *esse* is other than essence only much later in the argument [lines 25–26; (E/E12)]. The IE Argument is not to be found in the E/E Argument, and the structure of Aquinas's argument is represented more accurately by (ULS1)–(ULS4).

It might appear puzzling that Aquinas draws the conclusion (E/E11) without treating the case mentioned in (E/E6iii). Aquinas appears to suggest that there are three ways in which pluralization can occur: (i) by addition of some differentia, (ii) by a form being received in different matters, or (iii) by one thing being absolute and another being received in something. He rejects (i) and (ii) as impossible accounts of the plurality of things whose essences are *esse* itself but he never takes up (iii). Commentators usually account for the gap in the argument by pointing out that (E/E6iii) is obviously an unacceptable account of plurality among things whose essences are *esse* itself.[12] But to account for the lack of an explicit treatment of this by supposing that Aquinas thought it too obvious to mention would overlook a strategy of argumentation common in Aquinas's writings.

The third account of pluralization which Aquinas offers involves one thing's being considered as absolute and another as received in something— Aquinas offers the example of a separated heat and a heat received in something—and it is obviously true that that will not do as an account of pluralization among things whose essences are *esse* itself. To argue for this way of pluralizing would be to admit that there is actually only one thing which is *esse* itself, namely, *esse* considered as absolute.[13] It is important to note, however, that it is this third account of pluralization which Aquinas intends to use to account for the plurality of *esse* in all existing things. There is only one thing, *esse* itself, which is absolute, and *esse* is received in other things as in effects from a cause. Aquinas, therefore, does not reject this third account explicitly even though it is unacceptable in the immediate context because he intends to return to it and to accept it in a slightly different context later in the argument. The way of pluralizing described in (E/E6iii) is in fact the way of pluralizing which provides the conclusion for the whole argument. The conclusion is that there is one thing which is *esse* itself and that all other things receive their *esse* from it: "It is clear, therefore, that an intelligence is form and *esse* and that it has *esse* from the first being which is *esse* alone . . ." (lines 41–43).

The strategy which Aquinas uses here (and elsewhere),[14] then, is to provide among the disjuncts of a disjunctive premiss the account which will turn out to be the correct one or the important one for the positive purposes of the argument. In considering each disjunct, Aquinas passes over the relevant one in order to return to it later in the final resolution of the argument or discussion. The conclusion explicitly picks up the loose end left dangling earlier and completes the argument neatly. Aquinas's failure to deal with the third account of pluralization does not represent a lacuna in need of explanation but is, in fact, a deliberate strategy which links pieces of the argument together.

2

So far I have been concerned merely with laying out Aquinas's argument as precisely as possible. I wish now to offer some interpretative remarks about the nature of the E/E Argument and its conclusions. I think that some of my conclusions in Section 1 above about the structure of the argument will be useful in determining substantive issues regarding its interpretation.

2.1

One might be led by the rhetorical presentation of the argument to the view that the E/E Argument begins with concepts alone entirely abstracted from the real world. From Aquinas's opening words: "For whatever is not of the concept of an essence . . . ," it looks as though we are to begin by noticing that we have certain concepts—concepts of essences—and by undertaking an inspection of their contents. It appears that we are to begin by looking for the concept of *esse* among the contents of our concepts of certain essences.

I think that such a view of the starting point of the E/E Argument is mistaken. There is no doubt that noticing that we have certain concepts of essences and inspecting their contents are involved as a *part* of the argument, but these conceptual activities are not *the starting point* of the argument. Seeing that the argument does not begin in the conceptual realm will be crucial for understanding the nature of the argument.

The argument begins, I have suggested, with the following general principle:

(E/E1) Whatever belongs to a thing and is not part of its essence either comes from without and effects a composition with the essence or itself constitutes the entire essence.

The principle does not, it seems to me, start us off solely with concepts or their contents but with an observation about "whatever belongs to a thing," i.e., about characteristics of things.[15] The principle enumerates the different ways in which some characteristic which belongs to a thing can be related to the essence of the thing to which it belongs. If F belongs to x, the principle claims, then there are a limited number of ways to account for F's belonging to x.

Now, since the principle with which the E/E Argument starts is an observation about any characteristic, F, belonging to a thing, x, it is clear that the principle can have application only to cases in which the particular F in question does in fact belong to the particular x in question. In order for the general principle expressed in (E/E1) to get the argument off the ground, therefore, it must be assumed that the particular case to which the principle will be applied is one in which F does in fact belong to x. If the particular value of F at issue in the argument does not belong to the individual, x, in question, then premiss (E/E1) is a non-starter. So any argument which begins with (E/E1) must assume the knowledge that the particular value of F at issue does belong to the individual, x. The starting point of the E/E Argument is the general principle together with the knowledge that the particular F belongs to the particular x.

What does this assumed knowledge that the particular F belongs to the particular x amount to? For certain values of F and x, values for which F is an essential characteristic of a particular species and x is the species or nature, e.g., when "rationality" or "ability to rise from its own ashes" is taken for F and "human being" or "phoenix" is taken for x, such assumed knowledge need not involve anything empirical. We can know that rationality belongs to a human being or the ability to rise from its own ashes to a phoenix without appeal to observations about the real world. But for all other values of F only observations about the real world can tell us that F belongs to x. If the argument assumes the knowledge that F belongs to x, and if the particular F in question is not an essential characteristic of the x in question, then the argument must assume some empirical knowledge.

Of course the particular case to which Aquinas wants to apply the general principle, and the particular case for which the need for assumed empirical knowledge is clearest, is the case of *esse*. In order for the principle to do any work and in order for the argument to get off the ground at all, Aquinas must assume the knowledge that *esse* in fact belongs to things; that is, that some things exist. Without the assumption that some things exist Aquinas's use of the general principle makes no sense and the argument never gets started. The starting point of the E/E Argument, therefore, is the general principle expressed in (E/E1) together with the assumption that the principle is applicable to the case of *esse*; the starting point, that is to say, is the general principle together with the knowledge that some things exist.

Once it is seen that (E/E1) is the general principle moving the E/E Argument the overall strategy of the argument becomes clear. If we know that things exist, and if (E/E1) is true, then, in order to discover *how esse* is related to the essences of things, we need only consider in turn each of the possibilities suggested by (E/E1). If we can show that two of the possibilities cannot explain how the *esse* of things is related to their essences, then we know that the remaining one must offer the correct account. This is the procedure Aquinas in fact follows; it is outlined in the schema ULS in Section 1.3 above.

The three possible ways to account for the fact that a thing exists, it will be recalled, are the following:

(a) A thing's *esse* is part of its essence.
(b) A thing's *esse* comes to its essence from without and effects a composition with it.
(c) A thing's *esse* is itself the entire essence of the thing.[16]

The sub-argument which disposes of (a) occurs at (E/E2)–(E/E4). It is this particular sub-argument which appears first in the actual presentation of the argument in the text of Chapter 4 and it is the portion of the argument which involves inspecting the contents of our concepts of essences. It is the portion of the argument which shows that *esse* is not an essential character-istic of any of the things (other than God) to which it belongs. Aquinas believes that we are able to grasp the essences of things intellectually in concepts which are indeterminate with respect to *esse*, and so purely con-ceptual considerations are sufficient to rule out (a). These purely conceptual considerations form only a sub-argument, however, within a larger strategy the aim of which is the analysis of existing things.

(E/E5)–(E/E11) is the sub-argument which disposes of (c) as a general account of the relation between a thing's *esse* and its essence. The existence of at most one thing can be accounted for by (c), and all other existing things must be handled by some other account.

The only remaining possibility of the three (presumably exhaustive) pos-sibilities is (b): A thing's *esse* comes from without and effects a composition with the thing's essence. Hence, the main conclusion follows immediately at (E/E12): For any other thing besides this one, its *esse* is other than its essence. The argument immediately generated by the general principle to-gether with the assumption that some things exist is complete. We have assumed that some things exist and we have eliminated all but one possible account of how a thing's *esse* might be related to its essence. If *esse is* related to a thing's essence, and only one possible account of that relation remains, then the thing's *esse* and essence must be related in that way.

2.3

The question which has occupied commentators is whether or not the conclusion (E/E12) is to be taken as claiming that there is a *real* distinction between *esse* and essence or *esse* and thing. I think that there are two considerations which show that (E/E12) must be taken as the claim that there is a real distinction between *esse* and essence.

I have already laid out the first consideration. It is that the general principle which determines the structure and strategy of the argument is a principle having to do with the relation between *esse* and the essence *of an existing thing*. Things exist, which is to say that *esse* is a characteristic belonging to things, and the general principle is a claim about the ways that such a characteristic can be related to the essences of the things to which it belongs. When all the possible relations have been considered, the result must be a conclusion about the relation of *esse* to essence in existing things, i.e., in reality.

The second consideration which shows that (E/E12) claims a real distinction is the following. As we have seen, Aquinas offers the E/E Argument in order to show that intelligences are neither simple in every way nor pure actuality. From (E/E12) Aquinas immediately derives the conclusion which establishes the first disjunct of that negative disjunction, i.e., the conclusion that intelligences are not simple in every way. The conclusion is: (E/E14) There is *esse* besides essence in intelligences. I can see no other way to read this conclusion than as claiming a real distinction between *esse* and essence *in intelligences*. There is no way that (E/E14) can show that intelligences are not simple in every way unless it is the claim that there is a *real* distinction in intelligences. If (E/E14) must be read as claiming a real distinction, and if (E/E14) follows from (E/E12), then (E/E12) must also be read as claiming a real distinction.

(E/E15)–(E/E22) take care of the second disjunct of the negative disjunction, i.e., they show that intelligences are not pure actuality. At (E/E12) the conclusion that *esse* and essence are really distinct is left in its negative form: *esse* and essence are not the same; *esse* is other than essence. (E/E12) does not tell us *how* they are related in things which actually exist even though it tells us that they are not identical in those things. More argument is needed to show precisely what this otherness-relation comes to. The argument from (E/E15)–(E/E22) provides the positive characterization of the distinction. *Esse* and essence are related as actuality and potentiality, and so actuality and potentiality are found in intelligences. Intelligences, therefore, are not pure actuality. The argument is complete, and Aquinas has achieved his purpose of showing that his rejection of universal hylomorphism earlier in Chapter 4 does not commit him to the view that intelligences are simple in every way and pure actuality.

3

I wish in the last section to take up very briefly one interpretation of the E/E Argument in *De ente* 4 which differs from mine. Joseph Owens has maintained that Aquinas cannot have established a real distinction between *esse* and essence as early in the argument as (E/E12). As Owens sees it, the real distinction is not established until much later, at (E/E19).[17]

It is Owens's view that there is a certain feature of Aquinas's epistemology which is relevant to the interpretation of the E/E Argument as an argument for the real distinction. Aquinas believes that essences and the fact that certain things exist are known through different activities of the understanding. Essences are known through the first activity of the understanding, simple apprehension, since essences are the proper objects of the understanding. The fact that something exists, on the other hand, is known through the second activity of the understanding, judgment.[18]

According to Owens, it is a consequence of this epistemological position that merely recognizing that our concept of *esse* and our concept of an essence are different concepts does not entail that *esse* and essence are different in reality. It is possible that they are identical in reality despite the fact that the understanding, in virtue of the fact that it knows them in two different ways, forms different concepts of them. Since the concept of *esse* is not known originally through apprehension but is derived from what is originally known through judgment, it cannot provide the basis for an inference to conclusions about *esse* in reality. Aquinas, then, as evidenced by his rejection of the ontological argument, could not allow that an argument which begins with the concept of *esse* can arrive at a conclusion about the real distinction between *esse* and essence.[19]

Owens argues that it is Aquinas's view that, although our derivative concept of *esse* is not sufficient to ground an inference to conclusions about *esse* in reality, the concept of *esse* which we have as a result of understanding that God exists—i.e., that there is a nature which is *esse* itself existing in the real world—is sufficient to ground such an inference. Once we have a concept of *esse* which corresponds to a real nature, God, we are in a position to see that *esse* cannot be identical with any other essence. Hence, *esse* must be really distinct from essence. Aquinas can draw this conclusion, according to Owens, only after proving the existence of God.[20]

Now, if the E/E Argument in *De ente* 4 begins solely with considerations having to do with the concept of *esse* and concepts of essences, then Aquinas's epistemological views and the restrictions they place on arguments for the real distinction will be relevant for the interpretation of the argument. Owens does think that the E/E Argument starts in the conceptual realm alone.[21] He interprets the beginning of the E/E Argument this way, I think, because he identifies the first stage of the argument as the IE Argument,[22] and the IE Argument seems clearly to be concerned solely with concepts and their contents. From this view of the starting point of the argument and from the epistemological considerations he adduces, Owens concludes that Aquinas cannot have established a real distinction between *esse* and essence prior to the point at which the E/E Argument is carried beyond the conceptual realm in which it began. The crucial shift from conceptual to existential realm, in Owens's view, occurs at (E/E16). About the portion of the argument represented in (E/E15)–(E/E19) Owens says:

> The demonstration is not a dialectical process. It does not consist in an elaboration of concepts. Rather, it is thrown out of the order of formal causality into the order of efficient causality. . . . It is concerned rather with the actuality in the thing that is known originally not through a concept but through judgment.[23]

Since, according to Owens, the E/E Argument prior to (E/E15) is an elaboration of concepts, there can be no conclusion prior to (E/E15) which claims that there is a real distinction. A real distinction is not established until the existence of God has been proved; that is, not until (E/E19).

I do not wish to discuss whether Owens is right in attributing to Aquinas this epistemological position and its consequences or whether they are views to which Aquinas ought to have committed himself. What I do wish to challenge is Owens's view that Aquinas's epistemological views are relevant for interpreting the E/E Argument.

I have argued, in the first place, that the E/E Argument beginning at (E/E 1) is not merely an elaboration of concepts. The only portion of the argument which could be called an elaboration of concepts is (E/E2)–(E/E4) which is an argument subordinated to the general strategy. The E/E Argument does not begin with the IE Argument (the IE Argument does not occur in *De ente* 4) and it does not begin solely in the conceptual realm. The general principle which gets the argument started assumes that some things exist, and so the entire E/E Argument from the first premiss on is concerned with *esse* in things which, according to Aquinas, is known originally through judgment. The whole of the argument, then, is concerned with things in reality, and no shift from the order of formal to the order of efficient causality occurs later in the argument. If the E/E Argument does not begin solely in the conceptual realm, then Aquinas's view about the impossibility of arguing from a concept of *esse* to the conditions of *esse* in reality are irrelevant for interpreting the E/E Argument and have no bearing on whether or not (E/E12) establishes a real distinction.

In the second place, I have argued that Aquinas's strategy is not to deduce conclusions about *esse* from a concept of *esse* and a concept of essence. His strategy is to pin down the way in which an existing thing's *esse* is related to the thing's essence. The strategy assumes that we have knowledge of the fact that things exist, and a general principle tells us what the possibilities are. The relations the argument considers are relations between the *esse* and essence in real things. If the strategy of the argument does not proceed to (E/E12) from considerations about the concept of *esse*, then Owens's worries that we cannot have a concept of *esse* from which we can draw conclusions about the relation of *esse* to essences until we know that *esse* is a real nature are unfounded with regard to the E/E Argument.

It seems to me, then, that taking the considerations which Owens introduces to be relevant to the interpretation of the E/E Argument is the result of a confusion about the structure and nature of the argument. If I am right about the structure and nature of the argument, then Owens's considerations do nothing to show that (E/E12) cannot be the conclusion that *esse* and essence are really distinct.

If one has still other, more general philosophical or historical reasons for wanting to deny that Aquinas could have established a real distinction by means of the sort of argument I have attributed to him, two straightforward options are open. One might claim that Aquinas's views in *De ente et essentia* are inconsistent with his later, more mature views, or one might reject the E/E Argument as unsound. I should think that the general principle (E/E1) is the place to begin a critique of the argument. But I shall pursue neither of these suggestions. My purpose has been to show how the argument which Aquinas presents in *De ente* 4 must be interpreted if careful attention is paid to the actual structure of the argument.[24]

Appendix: St. Thomas Aquinas, *De ente et essentia*, Chapter 4 (376.90–377.154)

1 Therefore, although substances of this sort are forms alone without matter, nevertheless they are not simple in every way nor are they pure

actuality but they are permeated by potentiality. This is clear in the following way. For whatever is not of the concept of an essence or
5 quiddity comes from without and effects a composition with the essence, because no essence can be understood without those things which are parts of the essence. But every essence or quiddity can be understood without anything being understood about its *esse*—for I can understand what a man or phoenix is and nevertheless not know whether
10 it has *esse* in reality. Therefore it is clear that *esse* is other than essence or quiddity, unless perhaps there is something whose quiddity is its very *esse*. And this thing can only be one and first because it is impossible that something be pluralized except by the addition of some differentia— as the nature of a genus is multiplied into species—or by a form being
15 received in different matters—as the nature of a species is multiplied into different individuals—or by one thing being absolute and another being received in something—for example, if there were a separated heat, it would, by its very separation, be other than heat which is not separated. But if one supposes that there is something which is *esse*
20 alone so that it is *esse* itself subsisting, this *esse* would not receive the addition of a differentia because then it would no longer be *esse* alone but *esse* and some form besides it. And even less could it receive the addition of matter because then it would be not subsisting but material *esse*. Thus what is left is that such a thing which is its *esse* can be only
25 one. Thus it must be that for any other thing besides it its *esse* is other than its quiddity or nature or form. Thus it must be that in intelligences there is *esse* besides form, and so it has been said that an intelligence is form and *esse*.

But everything which belongs to something either is caused by the
30 principles of its nature—as the ability to laugh in man—or comes to it from some extrinsic principle—as light in the air from the influence of the sun. But it cannot be that *esse* itself is caused by the very form or quiddity of the thing (I mean as by an efficient cause) because then something would be the cause of itself and something would produce
35 itself in *esse*, which is impossible. Therefore it must be that every such thing the *esse* of which is other than its nature has *esse* from another. And because everything which is through another is reduced to that which is through itself as to a first cause, it must be that there is something which is the cause of *esse* for all things in virtue of the fact that it is
40 *esse* alone, otherwise one would go to infinity in causes since everything which is not *esse* alone has a cause of its *esse*, as has been said. It is clear, therefore, that an intelligence is form and *esse* and that it has *esse*

from the first being which is *esse* alone, and this is the first cause which is God.

45 But everything which receives something from another is in potentially with respect to that, and that which is received in it is its actuality. Therefore it must be that the quiddity itself or the form which is the intelligence is in potentiality with respect to *esse*, which it receives from God, and that *esse* is received in the manner of actuality. And so potenti-

50 ality and actuality are found in intelligences, not form and matter, however, except equivocally.*

Notes

1. *De ente et essentia*, Leonine edition, vol. 43. The text I shall be discussing is 376.90–377.154 in the Leonine edition. I have provided a translation of the text in an appendix. Quotations will be from this translation, and I will give the line numbers from the translation immediately following the quotation.

2. For a bibliography of the literature on *De ente* 4 see John F. Wippel, "Aquinas's Route to the Real Distinction," *Thomist* 43 (1979): 279, n. 1.

3. "Separate substance" is Aquinas's designation for an entity which is immaterial, i.e., separated from matter. At the beginning of Chapter 4 Aquinas indicates that there are three types of separate substances: souls, intelligences—by which he means angels and the movers of the heavenly bodies—and the first cause. In the course of the argument he takes intelligences alone as representative of separate substances generally. The view of universal hylomorphism, the view Aquinas is criticizing in the present chapter, is that all substances contain matter and form. The designation "separate substance" would not, therefore, be acceptable to someone holding universal hylomorphism.

4. In Chapter 2, 373.254–73.

5. Strictly speaking, if an entity is not absolutely simple, then it follows that it is not pure actuality. All that Aquinas has to do to show that intelligences are not pure actuality is to show that they are not absolutely simple. His argument, however, is more complex. He treats the issue of pure actuality in some detail and separately from the issue of absolute simplicity. He does this, I think, for two reasons. First, focusing on the issue of pure actuality allows him to show that the *esse*-essence relation is a species of the actuality-potentiality relation (see 2.3 below). Second, he wants to direct our attention to the potentiality-actuality distinction because it is the basis on which he will resolve the problem of individuation for separate substances. The resolution of that problem follows immediately after the E/E Argument (377.167ff.).

6. The aim of the schema is to present Aquinas's argument in a logically rigorous way. To achieve that aim I have standardized terminology—e.g., I have used "essence" throughout although Aquinas's text sometimes uses *quiditas* instead of *essentia*, and I have paraphrased or slightly altered the text where doing so makes the formal presentation of the argument more perspicuous.

7. In Section 1.4 below I shall discuss Aquinas's failure to take up (E/E6iii) before drawing this conclusion.

8. Aquinas is using intelligences as representative of separate substances generally; see n. 3.

9. I am not altogether happy with my choice of the verb "belongs" here. I am following Aquinas's usage at line 29 where the Latin term is *conuenit*. "Belongs" suggests the relation which a property bears to its subject, and so suggests that the thing to which the property or whatever other thing belongs has existence independently of that which belongs to it. Although the general principle is intended to cover the property-subject relation it is meant to be broader and to cover, among other cases, the *esse*-thing relation. *Esse*, of course, does not belong to something which exists independently of it. I shall go on using the term "belongs" intending it to include but not to be restricted to the property-subject relation.

10. Joseph Owens, "Quiddity and Real Distinction in St. Thomas Aquinas," *Mediaeval Studies* 27 (1965): 5; Leo Sweeney, "Existence/Essence in St. Thomas Aquinas's Early Writings," *Proceedings of the American Catholic Philosophical Association* 54 (1963): 105ff.; Wippel, "Aquinas's Route," 282.

11. Sweeney characterizes the argument slightly differently, "Existence/Essence," 106.

12. For example, Wippel, "Aquinas's Route," 288–89; Joseph Bobik, *Aquinas on Being and Essence* (Notre Dame, 1965), 171.

13. Bobik offers this explanation of the lacuna, ibid.

14. See, for example, Aquinas's use of the same strategy in his *In Boetii De hebdomadibus*, Marietti edition, M. Calcaterra, O.P., ed. (Rome, 1954), Lectio II, Section 24 (396–97). There Aquinas indicates that there are three different kinds of participation. The claim that *id quod est* participates in *esse* is properly understood in only one of the three ways. Aquinas eliminates the first two possibilities and leaves the third until much later in the treatise when he reaches the final resolution of the problem, where the third alternative turns out to be the right one. In the *De hebdomadibus* commentary Aquinas is more explicit about the strategy he is using. He indicates to the reader that he is leaving the third alternative aside for the moment: "Praetermisso autem hoc tertio modo participandi, impossibile est quod secundum duos primos modos ipsum esse participet aliquid" (397). For another example see *Commentum in librum I Sententiarum*, Dist. 8, Q. 1, A. 2, Solutio.

15. It is difficult to find terminology that is not too suggestive of "property." I take "characteristic" here to be more general than "property." See n. 9 above.

16. It is necessary for the completeness of the argument that these three possibilities be taken as exhaustive.

17. Joseph Owens, "Quiddity," 1–22; "Stages and Distinction in *De ente*: A Rejoinder," *Thomist* 45 (1981), 99–123.

18. For a brief account of this feature of Aquinas's epistemology see Owens, "Stages," 106–7.

19. Ibid., 117–21.

20. Owens, "Quiddity," 17–19; Owens, "Stages," 108–10.

21. His argument on page 16, Owens, "Quiddity," implies that he takes the argument up to my (E/E15) to be "an elaboration of concepts."

22. Owens, "Quiddity," 5ff.

23. Ibid., 16.

24. I am very grateful to John Boler, Norman Kretzmann, and Eleonore Stump for comments on earlier versions of this paper and to Norman Kretzmann for the many hours he spent discussing this material with me.

*. Huiusmodi ergo substantie, quamuis sine forme tantum sine materia, non tamen in eis est omnimoda simplicitas nec sunt actus purus, sed habent permixtionem potentie; et hoc sic patet. Quicquid enim non est de intellectu essentie uel quiditatis, hoc est adueniens extra et faciens compositionem cum essentia, quia nulla essentia sine hiis que sunt partes essentie intelligi potest. Omnis autem essentia uel quiditas potest intelligi sine hoc quod aliquid intelligatur de esse suo: possum enim intelligere quid est homo uel fenix et tamen ignorare an esse habeat in rerum natura; ergo patet quod esse est aliud ab essentia uel quiditate. Nisi forte sit aliqua res cuius quiditas sit ipsum suum esse, et hec res non potest esse nisi una et prima: quia impossibile est ut fiat plurificatio alicuius nisi pet additionem alicuius differentie, sicut multiplicatur natura generis in species; uel pet hoc quod forma recipitur in diuersis materiis, sicut multiplicatur natura speciei in diuersis indiuiduis; uel per hoc quod unum est absolutum et aliud in aliquo receptum, sicut si esset quidam calor separatus esset alius a calore non separato ex ipsa sua separatione. Si autem ponatur aliqua res que sit esse tantum ita ut ipsum esse sit subsistens, hoc esse non recipiet additionem differentie, quia iam non esset esse tantum sed esse et preter hoc forma aliqua; et mulio minus reciperet additionem materie, quia iam esset esse non subsistens sed materiale. Vnde relinquitur quod talis res que sit suum esse non potest esse nisi una; unde oportet quod in qualibet alia re preter eam aliud sit esse suum et aliud quiditas uel natura seu forma sua; unde oportet quod in intelligentiis sit esse preter forman, et ideo dictum est quod intelligentia est forma et esse.

Omme autem quod conuenit alicui uel est causatum ex principiis nature sue, sicut risibile in homine; uel aduenit ab aliquo principio extrinseco, sicut lumen in acre ex influentia solis. Non autem potest esse quod ipsum esse sit causatum ab ipsa forma uel quiditate rei, dico sicut a causa efficiente, quia sic aliqua res esset sui ipsius causa et aliqua res se ipsam in esse produceret: quod est impossibile. Ergo oportet quod omnis talis res cuius esse est aliud quam natura sua habeat esse ab alio. Et quia omne quod est per aliud reducitur ad id quod est per se sicut ad causam primam, oportet quod sit aliqua res que sit causa essendi omnibus rebus eo quod ipsa est esse tantum; alias iretur in infinitum in causis, cum omnis res que non est esse tantum habeat causam sui esse, ut dictum est. Patet ergo quod intelligentia est forma et esse, et quod esse habet a primo ente quod est esse tantum, et hoc est causa prima que Deus est.

Omne autem quod recipit aliquid ab alio est in potentia respectu illius, et hoc quod receptum est in eo est actus eius; ergo oportet quod ipsa quiditas uel forma que est intelligentia sit in potentia respectu esse quod a Deo recipit, et illud esse receptum est per modum actus. Et ita inuenitut potentia et actus in intelligentiis, non tamen forma et materia nisi equiuoce.

7

∾✿∾

The Five Ways

As anyone with even a casual acquaintance with Aquinas's writings is aware, it is in the *Summa theologiae* (ST) I, q. 2, a. 3 that he presents his best-known formulation of argumentation for God's existence. A number of the arguments from his earlier writings foreshadow most, if not all, of the "five ways" of the *Summa theologiae*. These points of similarity notwithstanding, Thomas gives a personal and particular touch to each of the five ways themselves. Because of the relatively later date of this treatment (ca. 1266–1268), because of the apparently wider readership at which the *Summa theologiae* is aimed, and because of the comprehensive way in which the five ways are fitted together, these arguments for God's existence have received more attention from Thomas's students than any of his other efforts to establish this point.[1]

At the same time, it should be remembered that the amount of space accorded to each of the five ways is relatively brief and that in certain instances, at least, familiarity with some of Thomas's most fundamental metaphysical options is presupposed by them.[2] Finally, the question has often been raised concerning whether the five ways are intended by Thomas to form one developing argument for God's existence, or five distinct and more or less independent arguments. To put this in other terms, how are these five proofs intended to fit together? Before making any attempt to answer this question, however, it will first be necessary for us to consider each of them in turn.

Question 2 of the First Part of the *Summa theologiae* is addressed to this issue: Does God exist?[3] In a. 1 Thomas again rejects any claim that God's existence is self-evident (*per se notum*) to us, even though he continues to hold that the proposition "God exists" is self-evident in itself. Its predicate is identical with its subject since God's essence is his act of being (*esse*). Because we do not know of God what he is, that he exists is not known to us *per se* but needs to be demonstrated by means of things which are better known to us, i.e., his effects. Thomas's denial that God's existence is self-evident to us also leads him to reject the Anselmian argument for God's existence.[4]

In a. 2 Thomas distinguishes between a demonstration which moves from knowledge of a cause to knowledge of its effect, that is, demonstration of the reasoned fact (*propter quid* demonstration), and demonstration which moves from knowledge of an effect to knowledge of its cause and is called demonstration of the fact (demonstration *quia*). This second kind of demonstration rests upon the fact that an effect depends upon its cause. If the effect is given, its cause must preexist. It is by means of this kind of demonstration that God's existence can be established.[5]

In replying to the second objection in this same a. 2, Thomas makes an interesting comment. According to the objection, the middle term in a demonstration is a thing's quiddity. But when it comes to God we cannot know what he is but only what he is not. Therefore we cannot demonstrate that God exists. In his response Thomas notes that when a demonstration moves from our knowledge of an effect to knowledge of its cause, we must put the effect in the place of the definition of the cause if we are to prove that the cause exists. This is especially true when we are dealing with God. In order to prove that something exists we need only use as a middle term a nominal definition of that which is to be demonstrated, not a real (or quidditative) definition. This follows, continues Thomas, because the question "What is it?" comes after the question "Is it?" But we apply names to God from what we discover in his effects. Therefore, in demonstrating his existence from an effect we may use as a middle term that which the name God signifies, that is, some purely nominal definition. Curiously, in each of the five ways, Thomas does not explicitly carry out this step for us, but leaves it for the reader to supply.[6]

1. The First Way

With this we come to a. 3: "Whether God exists." Thomas begins the corpus of this article by writing that God's existence can be proved in five ways. The first and more evident (*manifestior*) way is that which is based on motion (*motus*). It is certain and evident to the senses that some things in this world are moved (*moveri*). (I shall translate this verb passively rather than intransitively.) But whatever is moved is moved by something else. In support of this claim, Thomas argues that nothing is moved except insofar as it is in potency to that to which it is moved. But something moves insofar as it is in actuality, since to move is nothing else but to reduce something from potency to act. And something can be reduced from potency to act only by some being in actuality. To illustrate this point Thomas notes that it is something which is actually hot (such as fire) which renders that which is only potentially hot (such as wood) actually hot and thereby moves and alters it. (This example is significant, for it indicates that if the argument starts from the fact of observable motion, motion itself is being taken more broadly than local motion; at the very least it also includes alteration.) Thomas now argues that it is not possible for the same thing to be in act and in potency at the same time and in the same respect but only in different respects. Thus what is actually hot cannot at the same time be potentially hot (with respect to the same degree of heat, we should understand), but it is at that time potentially cold. Therefore, it is not possible for something to be mover and to be moved in the same respect by one and the same motion, or for it to move itself (in this strict sense). Therefore, everything which is moved must be moved by something else.[7]

Thomas next turns to the second major part of the argument based on motion. If that by which something is moved is itself moved, this second mover must itself be moved by something else, and so on. But one cannot regress to infinity in moved movers. If there were no first mover, there would be no other mover, since second movers do not move unless they are moved by a first mover. Thus a stick does not move unless it is moved by a hand. Therefore we must arrive at some first mover which is moved by nothing whatsoever, and this everyone understands to be God.[8]

Keeping the two arguments from motion in *Summa contra Gentiles* (SCG) I, c. 13 in mind, we are in position to make some comments about the argument from motion in ST I, q. 2, a. 3. First of all, as we have just noted in passing, the point of departure for the argument as it is presented here now seems to be broader.[9] Motion as it is used here is not restricted to instances of local motion but, as the text explicitly indicates, is taken broadly enough so as to apply to alteration as well. Given this, one wonders whether we may apply it to any kind of motion and perhaps even to changes which are not classified by Thomas as motions in the strict sense, e.g., generation and corruption.

It should be noted that in commenting on *Physics* III, Thomas writes that in working out his definition of motion (*motus*) there Aristotle uses this term broadly so as to apply it to change (*mutatio*). Motion, therefore (meaning thereby change), is the act of that which exists in potency insofar as it is in potency. In that context Thomas speaks of motion in terms of quantity, in terms of quality, and in terms of place, as well as in terms of substance (generation and corruption).[10] In commenting on *Physics* V, Thomas follows Aristotle in dividing change (*mutatio*) into three species—generation, corruption, and motion. (Again he remarks that in Bk III Aristotle had taken the term "motion" broadly so as to apply it to all the kinds of change.) In Bk V, however, he finds Aristotle using the term "motion" more strictly so as to apply it to only one of these three species. When motion is taken in this restricted sense it may in turn be divided into motion in quality (alteration), motion in quantity (increase or decrease), and motion in place (local motion). Substantial change (whether generation or corruption) is not motion taken strictly; it is only change (*mutatio*).[11]

To return to Thomas's first way, therefore, we would seem to be justified in regarding motion taken strictly in any of its three kinds as a possible starting point for the argument, i.e., alteration, local motion, and increase or decrease in quantity. If Thomas is using the term broadly so as to equate it with change, we could even use substantial change as a possible point of departure for the first way. In fact he will explicitly appeal to generation and corruption in developing his third way.

Given all of this, I am inclined to limit motion as it appears as the starting point of the first way to some form of motion taken strictly, but to suggest that in the course of justifying the principle of motion—whatever is moved is moved by something else—Thomas uses motion broadly enough to apply to any reduction from potentiality to actuality. If this is correct, it will mean that in the second part of the argument, where he considers a possible regress to infinity, he intends to eliminate any kind of moved mover or changed changer or any series of the same as an adequate explanation for the observable motion or motions with which his argument began. He seems to have allowed for a similar broader understanding of motion at a certain stage in his second argument from motion in SCG I, c. 13, and perhaps also at one point in his first argument. Nonetheless, the starting point for both of those arguments appears to be motion taken strictly and, to be specific, local motion. Perhaps it is because the first way in the *Summa theologiae* begins with readily observable phenomena—local motion and alteration—that Thomas describes it as the "more manifest" way.[12]

Moreover, in his effort to justify the principle that whatever is moved is moved by something else, Thomas does not mention the first two long and involved physical approaches he had used in SCG I, c. 13. He simply builds his argument on the difference between potentiality and actuality, and develops this reasoning more fully than he had done in SCG I, c. 13. If this reasoning as it appears in the *Summa contra Gentiles* already points to a broader and more metaphysical way of justifying the principle of motion, the same holds for the present context. And if Thomas's attempt to justify this principle is valid, it should apply to any reduction from potentiality to actuality or to any kind of change, not merely to motion taken in the strict sense.[13]

Almost as a matter of definition Thomas explains that something is moved only insofar as it is in potency to that toward which it is moved. In other words, that which is moved must be capable of being moved. But something moves only insofar as it is in actuality. Thomas does not mean to suggest by this that something must be or have formally that which it communicates to something else through motion. It must either be or have such formally, or else possess that characteristic virtually; this is to say, it must have the power to produce its effect. It is only with this qualification in mind that one can say of Thomas's reasoning that he means thereby that one cannot give that which one does not have (either formally or virtually).[14]

Central to Thomas's argument is the claim that something cannot be in act and in potency at the same time and in the same respect, but only in different respects. For instance, that which is actually hot cannot at the same time be potentially hot (that is, it cannot lack the same degree of heat it actually possesses); but at the same time it is potentially cold since it is capable of being cooled. This is an important part of Thomas's argument since he concludes from this that it is not possible for something to be a mover and to be moved in one and the same respect by one and the same motion, or for it to move itself (in this strict sense).[15] And if this is granted, Thomas can conclude that if something is moved, that is, if it is reduced from potentiality to actuality, this can only be because it is moved by something else. If Thomas's reasoning is valid, this principle should apply, as we have already remarked, not only to the three species of motion taken strictly, but also to change, that is, to every genuine reduction from potentiality to actuality.[16]

In the second part of the argument Thomas considers and rejects as unsatisfactory appeal to a regress to infinity in moved movers. He does so along lines which are by now familiar to us. If there is no first mover, i.e., no mover that is not moved by anything, there will be no other; for a second mover does not move except insofar as it is moved by a first mover. As before, I take this to mean not that there could not be an unending regress of moved movers but as arguing that such is irrelevant: unless there is a first mover, a mover that is not moved by anything, no other motion will be possible.[17]

Thomas's first way has generated a considerable amount of discussion in the secondary literature.[18] Many of the objections raised against the argument have to do with its claim that whatever is moved is moved by something else. Already within Thomas's century there were those who denied that this applies to all cases. Exceptions should be made, it was argued, and first and foremost for spiritual activities such as human volition. Not long after Thomas's death Henry of Ghent maintained that a freely acting agent can reduce itself from a state of not acting to acting or, as he would eventually put it, from virtual act to formal act.[19] In addition, objections were at times raised at the physical level, having to do with projectile motion, the fall of heavy bodies, and the rise of those that are light (according to the Aristotelian theory of natural place). Thus a Duns Scotus would sharply restrict the application of this motion-principle even at the purely physical level.[20] And more recently, of course, it has often been urged that the principle is rendered invalid by Newtonian physics and the principle of inertia.[21]

While detailed discussion of these points would require far more attention than space will permit here, a few remarks may be made about each of them. So far as Thomas is concerned, the principle does apply universally. Whenever we are dealing with a reduction from potentiality to actuality, appeal must be made to some distinct moving principle to account for this. If our acts of volition involve any such transition from potentiality to actuality, the same will hold for them.

In the *Summa theologiae* I–II, q. 9, Thomas spells out some of his views concerning this. In a. 1 he is seeking to determine whether the will is moved by the intellect. He notes that something needs to be moved by something else insofar as it stands in potency to different things. He then distinguishes two ways in which a power of the soul can be in potency to different things: (1) simply with respect to acting or not acting (the exercise of an act); and (2) with respect to the particular kind of act, i.e., doing this or doing that (the order of specification). In the first case the focus is on a subject which sometimes acts and sometimes does not. In the second case the focus is on the object which serves to specify that act itself. In the order of exercise the will moves the other powers of the soul, including the intellect, to act. As Thomas puts it, we use the other powers of the soul when we will to do so. But he also recalls that since every agent acts for the sake of an end, the principle (the final cause) of the motion which is efficiently caused by the agent derives from the end (a particular good which falls under the object of the will, the good in general). But in the order of specification or determination of the act, the intellect moves the will by presenting a suitable object to it in the manner of a formal principle.[22]

Prior to this treatment in ST I–II, q. 9 (and the parallel discussion in *De malo*, q. 6), Thomas had identified the kind of causality exercised by the intellect with respect to the will as final rather than as formal. Under that assumption, which is not Thomas's position in these two works dating ca. 1270–1271, it would still be true that neither the intellect nor the will would move and be moved under the same aspect and in the same respect. The will would move the intellect as an efficient cause and would be moved by it in the order of final causality. Even so, in our present text where he refers to the causality exercised on the will by the object as presented by the intellect as formal causality, he is still satisfied that he has not violated the motion-principle. Indeed, in a. 3 of this same q. 9 he explicitly asks whether the will moves itself. In responding he explains that the will moves itself in this sense that, because it wills an end; it moves itself to will the means to that end. This does not mean, he points out in replying to objection I, that the will moves and is moved in the same respect. It rather means that insofar as the will wills an end, it reduces itself from potency with respect to the means to that end so as to will them in actuality.[23]

As Thomas explains in a. 4, insofar as the will is moved by its object, it is moved by something external. (This, of course, is in the order of specification or determination and not in the order of efficient causality.) But, he continues, insofar as the will is moved to exercise its act of willing, we must also hold that it is moved by some external principle. That which is at times an agent in act and at times an agent in potency must be moved to act by some mover. Such is true of the will. As Thomas has indicated, the will can move itself to will the means to a given end. But this in turn presupposes an appropriate act on the part of the intellect, i.e., taking counsel. And the act of taking counsel on the part of the intellect presupposes still another act of the will which moves it to so act. Since we cannot regress to infinity by tracing one act of the will back to an act of the intellect and that back to another act of the will etc., Thomas concludes that the will proceeds to its first motion from an impulse (instinctus) given it by some external mover, and finds support for this in Aristotle's *Eudemian Ethics*.[24]

In his Disputed Questions *De malo*, q. 6, Thomas develops much of this same thinking. Here, too, he introduces the distinction between a change or motion which has to do with exercising the act of a power, and that which has to do with its specification. In dealing with the exercise of the act of the will, he observes that just as the will moves other powers, so does it move itself. He maintains that it does not follow from this that the will is in act and potency at the same time and in the same respect. Rather the will moves itself by moving the intellect to take counsel. Again he maintains that the act of choice on the part of the will presupposes an act of counsel on the part of the intellect, and that this in turn presupposes a prior act by the will. To avoid falling into an infinite regress, Thomas again concludes that the will is moved to its first motion by something external or exterior to it. He goes on to tell us more about this externally caused impulse which first moves the will to act. This impulse cannot be provided by a heavenly body, since the will is grounded in reason (the intellect), which is not a corporeal power. He concludes, therefore, developing a remark made by Aristotle in his *De bona fortuna* (really taken from Bk VII of the *Eudemian Ethics* as he indicates in ST I–II, q. 9), that what first moves the will and the intellect must be something above them both, i.e., God. Since God moves all things in accord with their nature as movable beings—for instance, light things upward and heavy things downward—so does he move the will in accord with its condition or nature, that is to say, not in necessary fashion but as undetermined or freely.[25]

In order to place this within its broader metaphysical context we should recall that for Thomas created agents, including those that act freely, are second causes. God alone is the first cause. Nonetheless, such created agents are true causes. In the case of a human agent, Thomas has acknowledged that it can move itself in the qualified way already mentioned—by willing the means to a given end. But like all created agents, such a freely acting agent is not the first cause of its operations, including intellection and volition. As Thomas points out in q. 3, a. 7 of his *De potentia*, God may be said to cause the actions performed by created agents in four different ways: (1) by giving to a created agent the power by means of which it acts; (2) by continuously sustaining (conserving) this created power in being; (3) by moving or applying the created operative power to its activity; (4) by serving as principal cause of that of which the created agent is an instrumental cause.[26] With respect to point 4 it should be noted that at times Thomas uses the language of first cause and second cause rather than that of principal cause and instrument to express this relationship between God and other agents.[27]

In the *Summa theologiae* I, q. 105, a. 5, Thomas makes this same point in slightly different fashion. God works in the activities performed by created agents: (1) by serving as the final cause of such agents; (2) by acting as an efficient cause of their operations inasmuch as second causes act by reason of the first cause which moves them to act; (3) by giving to created agents the forms which are their principles of operation and by keeping these in being. As I have indicated elsewhere, we might combine into one the third and fourth ways mentioned in the text from the *De potentia*, as Thomas himself seems to do, and view this as equivalent to the second way of the text from ST I, q. 105.[28] It is this particular form of divine causality that is of greatest interest to us here, because it shows that Thomas honors the motion principle in all cases of creaturely agency.

It is also important to note Thomas's view that if God serves as an efficient cause of creaturely operations, including human volition, he does so as the first cause. Created agents are true causes, and even true principal causes, of their appropriate operations. Moreover, although this is not our primary concern at the moment, Thomas insists that this divine causality or divine motion with respect to free human operations does not detract from their freedom. Essential to Thomas's position is the point we have just seen above—that God, the first cause, moves created agents to act in accord with their natures. If he moves natural agents to act in accord with their natures, that is, necessarily, he moves free agents to act in accord with their nature, that is, freely.[29]

My reason for introducing this discussion here is not to examine Thomas's defense of human freedom but to show that in his eyes even free human activity does not violate his conviction that whatever is moved is moved by something else. At the same time, I would not recommend that one take human volition as a point of departure for Thomas's argument from motion for God's existence. This does not seem to be the kind of starting point he has in mind for his "more manifest" way, since some philosophical effort will be required to show that motion by something else is involved in volition. Moreover, the full appreciation of Thomas's views concerning the interrelationship between divine causal activity (as the first moving cause) and free human activity presupposes that one has already demonstrated God's existence and identified him as a creating, a conserving, and the first moving cause. Only then will Thomas be in position to proceed in the other direction, as it were, and view things from the standpoint of God as the First Mover.[30]

For more detailed explanation and discussion of Thomas's application of the principle of motion to purely physical motions such as those already mentioned, the reader may consult a series of studies by J. Weisheipl. If we may quickly summarize his findings, in the case of what Thomas regarded as natural motions, i.e., the fall of a heavy body or the rising of a light body, he holds that the motion of such bodies is caused by something else, that is, by the generating agent of the bodies in question. This, therefore, and not the bodies themselves, is to be regarded as the efficient cause of such motions. As for violent motions, in many instances Thomas would regard it as evident that what is moved is moved by something else—for instance, that a stick is moved by a hand, or that a heavy object is lifted upwards by someone or something in opposition to its natural tendency to fall. In the more difficult case of projectile motion, where the apparent mover is no longer in direct contact with the object which has been thrown or hurled, Thomas still thinks that his principle applies. With Aristotle he accounts for such motion by holding that what serves as a medium—air, for instance—has now been given the power to move the projectile. Even so, such a communicated power is not to be regarded as the principal cause of the motion, but only as an instrument of the true efficient cause—the one who originally threw or hurled the object.[31]

Well and good, one may counter, but with the rise of Newtonian physics and the principle of inertia, and for that matter, already with Galileo's explanation of the motion of a body along an idealized frictionless plane, Thomas's principle of motion has been rendered invalid. And if it fails to apply in this case, one cannot claim universal validity for it or use it with any confidence in a proof for God's existence. For that matter, Aristotle's distinction between natural and violent motion also seems to have been rendered obsolete.[32]

Without attempting to enter into a full discussion of these particular questions from the standpoint of the philosophy of science or the philosophy of nature, I would recall the following points. First of all, if Thomas's explanation of natural motion is correctly understood, it does not imply that a distinct moving cause must be constantly conjoined with a body which it moves naturally. While one will hardly wish today to defend the view that light bodies tend to go up, etc., one may hold that it is because of their natures that bodies tend to behave in certain ways, for instance, to fall. If with Newton one wishes to account for this by appealing to a force exercised by another and distinct body, Thomas's general principle will not necessarily be violated. Our falling body will still be moved by something else. But as he sees things, it is the generating principle of the falling body which is the efficient cause of its tendency to fall and therefore of its actual downward motion unless it is prevented from falling by some obstacle.[33]

As for Thomas's acceptance of Aristotle's explanation of projectile motion, not too many thinkers today will be inclined to endorse their view that some moving power is communicated to the air or to some surrounding medium and that this accounts for the continuing motion of the object in question. But today's defender of Thomas's general principle of motion may still insist on searching for some efficient cause to account for the continuing motion of such a projectile, the principle of inertia notwithstanding. This point seems to have been partially recognized by Newton himself, in that he (and Descartes) acknowledged that the principle of inertia would not explain the origin of motion in the universe.[34]

For instance, one might concede a great deal to the Newtonian theory and regard motion as a state, like rest. Then one would simply appeal to an extrinsic force, and therefore to some extrinsic mover, to account for any change in the state of rest or of uniform motion enjoyed by a given body.[35] As for the body's possession of its state (rest or motion), one would again trace this back to the generating principle which produced the body with a nature such that it will remain at rest or in motion until it is acted on by some external force. I should emphasize the point, however, that this is not the way in which Thomas and Aristotle actually accounted for projectile motion.

Or one might grant considerably less to the Newtonian theory of inertia as a philosophical explanation and insist that, in spite of its ability to offer a satisfactory physico-mathematical description of uniform motion, it leaves the philosophical search for causes unanswered.[36] In attempting to offer such an explanation one might, with certain later medieval thinkers (including some Thomists, though not Thomas himself), appeal to a theory of impetus. According to this account a transitory power would be given to the moving body by the original hurler or thrower of a given projectile. This power would continue to enable the body to move after it was no longer in direct contact with the hurler, and would serve as an instrumental cause for the motion of the projectile. The original hurler would be the principal efficient cause of the motion. Some students of Aquinas—including Weisheipl—regard this explanation as in accord with Thomas's principles, even though it is not the view Thomas himself defended.[37]

Finally, various writers have argued that the principle of inertia itself has never been demonstrated.[38] This is a controversy into which I am not prepared to enter. But if this claim should prove to be correct, there would be little reason for Aquinas's students today to jettison what he regarded as a demonstrated philosophical principle—that whatever is moved is moved by another—because of seeming difficulties in reconciling it with an unproved principle of Newtonian physics and mechanics. This will be especially so for those who accept Thomas's more metaphysical justification of his principle of motion, that is, the one based on the distinction between potentiality and actuality and ultimately, therefore, on the distinction between being and nonbeing. In sum, strategies such as these are available in dealing with such alleged counterexamples for one who accepts the motion principle on philosophical and metaphysical grounds. Moreover, as at least one writer has proposed, one might, unlike Thomas, simply exclude local motion as a starting point for the argument and use another example such as alteration.[39]

This final remark brings me back to an issue already touched on: Is Thomas's first way physical or metaphysical in nature? Or to put this in different terms: Does this argument for God's existence fall under the science of being as being or under the science that studies being as mobile? As we have now seen, the argument takes as its starting point a fact that is central to physics (philosophy of nature), i.e., motion. To that extent one might argue that it is intended by Thomas to fall within the scope of physics. Moreover, it borrows heavily from Aristotle's *Physics*, especially as it is presented in the two versions in SCGI, c. 13. Nonetheless, its most convincing effort to establish that whatever is moved is moved by something else rests on a broader (and metaphysical) point, the distinction between act and potency and the impossibility that any being might be in act and potency at the same time and in the same respect. This impossibility is by no means restricted to mobile being, but applies to the full range of being as being (the subject of metaphysics). And this justification is the only one offered for the principle of motion in the first way of the *Summa theologiae*.

Again, in presenting what appears to be primarily a physical argument from motion in SCG I, c. 13 (his second argument), Thomas has been forced to consider the possibility of a self-mover for the first heavenly sphere which is itself moved by something else in some other way, that is, in the order of desire. If such a self-mover exists, it will still be subject to his principle of motion and will depend on the unmoved mover in the order of final causality. At this point one has the impression that even this argument in SCG I, c. 13, is passing over from physics to metaphysics.

Hence my view is that the first way as it appears in ST I, q. 2, a. 3 starts from a physical fact, but that if it is to reach the absolutely unmoved mover or God, it must pass beyond this and beyond a limited and physical application of the principle of motion to a wider application that will apply to any reduction of a being from not acting to acting. In other words, the argument becomes metaphysical in its justification and application of the motion principle, and only then can it succeed in arriving at God. This means that, in its refutation of an infinite regress of moved movers as an alternative explanation, the argument concludes to a source of motion that is not itself moved in any way whatsoever and, therefore, is not reduced from potency to act in any way.

Still another way of approaching this would be to suggest that Thomas is really interested in the existence of motion from the outset and must ultimately conclude to the existence of a being that is pure actuality in order to account for the existence of the motion with which it begins. Therefore the argument would be metaphysical from beginning to end, since it would reason from the caused character of the existence of motion to an uncaused cause of the same.[40]

I would prefer to recast this suggested interpretation so that the argument would reason from the efficiently caused character of moved or changing being (rather than from the existence of motion). However, my greatest difficulty with this suggestion is historical. The argument would no longer be Thomas's first way as this appears in the text of ST I, q. 2, a. 3.

Before moving on to Thomas's second way, I should mention some additional questions about the first way which the presentation in ST I, q. 2, a. 3 seems to leave unanswered. First of all, is the argument based exclusively on motion as caused in the order of efficient (or moving) causality, or does it ultimately shift to the order of final causality? This issue can be raised both because of the apparent difference between Aristotle's procedure in *Physics* VII and VIII, on the one hand, and in *Metaphysics* XII, on the other, and because of Thomas's reference in SCG I, c. 13 to the possibility of reaching a self-moving first mover which would still be moved by something else in the order of desire and hence, we may conclude, as its final cause. In the text of the first way in ST I, q. 2, a. 3, however, there is no explicit reference to motion in the order of desire or to final causality. Moreover, the example mentioned at the very end of the argument—a stick which does not move unless it is moved by a hand—would make one think only in terms of efficient causality. Hence it is in that way that I prefer to read the argument.[41]

A second question may be raised, having to do with the concluding remark to the effect that all recognize this first unmoved mover as God. Has Thomas succeeded in establishing the point that there is only one such being at this point in his reasoning? If so, why does he argue explicitly for divine unicity (uniqueness) in ST I, q. 11, a. 3? Thomistic interpreters remain divided on this issue, but many recognize the fact that it is only in q. 11 that Thomas explicitly establishes divine unicity.[42] This procedure at least suggests that Thomas himself may have recognized that the claim that his unmoved mover is God needs to be supported and completed by additional argumentation.

In fact, at this point in Thomas's reasoning, one would not yet know whether the first mover is intelligent, or personal, or infinitely perfect, etc. So it is that Thomas will eventually develop each of these points in due course, along with others, in discussing the divine names. And there is, of course, the additional fact that Thomas is not content to offer only an argument from motion or a first way in ST I, q. 2, a. 3. All of this would seem to support the view that Thomas himself was aware that his demonstration of God's existence was not yet completed at the end of his first way.

At the same time, we should bear in mind Thomas's opening remark before he begins in question 3 and the following to take up the divine names or attributes. Once we have recognized that a given thing exists, it remains for us to determine how it exists in order that we may know of it what it is. But since we cannot know what God is but only what he is not, we must now consider the ways in which he is not. It is in the course of doing this, according to Thomas's own plan, that he establishes God's simplicity, and then his perfection, infinity, immutability, and unity. Throughout this discussion Thomas takes it as given that he has already (in his five ways) proved that God exists. With this lingering question still in mind,[43] therefore, we shall now turn to Thomas's presentation of his second argument for God's existence in ST I, q. 2, a. 3.

2. The Second Way

As Thomas himself tells us, this argument is based on efficient causality. Again it takes as its point of departure something that is given to us in the world of sensible things—the fact that there is an order of efficient causes. By this Thomas means that we find that certain things efficiently cause other things, and that they depend on prior causes in order to do so. He immediately reasons that nothing can be the efficient cause of itself, for then it would be prior to itself, and this is impossible. If we may supply the reasoning that is implied, his point is that for something to cause itself efficiently, it would have to exist in order to cause (itself), and yet would not exist, insofar as it was being caused. From this he expects us to conclude that since we do experience causes that are caused, because they cannot cause themselves they must be caused by something else.[44]

If this is granted, the possibility of a series of efficient causes which are themselves caused by something else must be faced. Thomas argues that one cannot regress to infinity in ordered efficient causes. As he explains, in such an ordered series of efficient causes, the first member is the cause of the intermediary, and that in turn is the cause of the last member in the series whether there is only one intermediary cause or whether there are many. But if there were no first among efficient causes there would be no intermediary causes and therefore no last cause; for if one takes away a cause, one also eliminates the effect. In an infinite series of caused efficient causes, there will be no first efficient cause. Hence there will be no intermediary causes and no last effect. This is enough for Thomas to reject a regress to infinity as a viable alternative to a first efficient cause.[45]

While the terms in which this argument is cast differ from those for the first way, much of the same basic structure reappears. Again one begins with a fact which, for Aquinas, is based on undeniable data offered through sense experience: among the things we experience through the senses, some are causes of others, and some of these causes are ordered, that is, subordinated to others in the exercise of their causality. This confidence on Thomas's part is undoubtedly owing to his Aristotelianism, his own realistic theory of knowledge, and the high degree of credibility which he assigns to what we today often refer to as "common sense." Although he does not spell out particular examples for us in this argument, he would undoubtedly include substantial changes (generation and corruption of substances) as well as various instances of motion taken strictly which we have discussed above in connection with the first way, i.e., alteration, local motion, increase and decrease.[46]

For those who would prefer a more metaphysically grounded illustration of efficient causality at work, I would suggest an approach based on the efficiently caused character of any being in which essence and act of being (esse) differ as, for instance, Thomas has developed this in c. 4 of his De ente et essentia.[47] However, I hasten to add that this is not the kind of efficient causality that is immediately given to us in sense experience. In adopting such a procedure, therefore, one would now have changed the point of departure for Thomas's second way.

As I have already indicated, Thomas reasons that nothing can be its own efficient cause. Given this, by implication he is also holding that whatever is efficiently caused must be so caused by something else. This is the version of efficient causality which is at work in Thomas's second way and, as in the first way, though more briefly this time, Thomas again offers a particular justification for this within the argument itself. In other words, he does not simply assume the principle of causality as an axiom which he might apply in each and every case. For that matter, we have already seen him proceeding in similar fashion in c. 4 of the *De ente*. There too he had judged it necessary to show that a being in which essence and *esse* differ is efficiently caused.[48]

With this we may turn to the second general step in his argument—the rejection of an infinite regress of caused causes as a viable alternative to the existence of a first cause. In reasoning which recalls that which we have already seen, Thomas makes it clear that he is dealing with what we may call essentially ordered causes (*lit.* ordered causes), that is, the case where the causal activity by a prior member of the series is required here and now for the exercise of causal activity by all subsequent members in that same series. Thomas had allowed and would continue to allow for the philosophical possibility of an infinite series of causes which are related to one another only *per accidens*, e.g., of fathers generating sons or of a carpenter replacing one hammer with another *ad infinitum*. Once again, as I read the argument, he is not concerned here with refuting the very possibility of a beginningless series of essentially ordered caused causes, but with showing that such a series is meaningless and has no explanatory power unless one also admits that there is an uncaused cause. It is in this sense that I take his usage of the term "first."[49]

As in the first way, Thomas quickly concludes to the existence of some "first efficient cause," i.e., some uncaused cause, which is named God by everyone.[50] Once more we may raise the issue of divine unicity or uniqueness: Does this argument, simply taken in itself, prove that there is only one Uncaused Cause (God)? Might it not lead to the conclusion that there are as many first causes as there are different series or at least different kinds of series of ordered caused causes? And does the argument manage to show that the first cause whose existence it establishes is intelligent, personal, all perfect, infinite, etc.? Thomas's second way tells us no more about these issues than does his first way, it would seem, although it does make it clear that in his mind the first unmoved mover of the first way and the first efficient cause of the second way are identical and also that this being exercises efficient causality.

Before leaving the second way it may be helpful for us to compare it more fully with the argumentation for God's existence presented in c. 4 of the *De ente*. Both have in common the fact that they are based on efficient causality. Both must take into account a possible objection having to do with a regress to infinity in caused causes. But the argument in the *De ente* begins at the level of beings in which essence and *esse* are not identical, and therefore at an explicitly metaphysical level. The second way begins with instances of causal activity which are evident to the senses, and ultimately concludes that there must be a first uncaused cause to account for such causal activity.

If, as I have suggested, the issue of divine uniqueness seems to be left unexamined by the second way, such is not true of the argument in *De ente*, c. 4. Because that argument begins with the essence-*esse* distinction, it focuses on one instance of efficient causation, that of *esse* itself. It reasons to the existence of an uncaused cause of *esse* and therefore an uncaused being which is itself pure *esse*. This insight seems much closer to what the metaphysician seeks in attempting to understand something about God. Moreover, this argument anticipates our concern about divine unicity, since it has reasoned from the impossibility of there being more than one being in which essence and *esse* are identical. Because there can at most be one such being, essence and *esse* differ in all other beings. Such beings therefore are caused in terms of their very being. This conclusion in its turn enables Thomas to show that there is in fact only one being in which essence and *esse* are identical. From all of these perspectives, therefore, the procedure in the *De ente* seems to be more satisfying to the metaphysician.[51]

But if all of this is so, why did Thomas not simply repeat the argumentation from the *De ente* as his second way in ST I, q. 2, a. 3? Perhaps, we may surmise, because of its highly metaphysical character he viewed the argument of *De ente*, c. 4 as more difficult for beginning students to grasp in its essentials. He may have realized that not all of his contemporaries, including many beginning students of theology, either understood or shared his views on the relationship between essence and *esse*. And he may not have wished to make his argumentation for God's existence dependent upon such a subtle metaphysical conclusion.

3. The Third Way

With this we come to the third of Thomas's five ways, the argument based, to use his terminology, on the possible and the necessary. We find, Thomas begins, that certain things are possibles, i.e., they have the possibility of existing and not existing. His evidence for this claim is the fact that certain things are generated and corrupted and therefore can exist and not exist. But it is impossible, Thomas continues, for all things which exist to be of this kind; for that which has the possibility of not existing at some time does not exist. If, therefore, all things are capable of not existing, at some time (*aliquando*) there was nothing in reality. But if this were so, even now there would be nothing; for what does not exist does not begin to exist except through something else that exists. Given all of this, Thomas concludes that not all beings are possible beings; there must be some necessary being.[52]

At this point today's reader might assume that Thomas's argument has reached its conclusion. But if we bear in mind the distinction between possible beings and caused necessary beings which appears in his argument in SCG I, c. 15, we will not be surprised to find him adding a second and important step to the third way.[53] Every necessary being either depends on something else for its necessity or it does not. But it is not possible to proceed to infinity in necessary beings which depend upon something else for their necessity—just as, Thomas reminds us, he has already shown with respect to efficient causes (see the second way). Therefore there must be some being which is necessary of itself and which does not depend upon another cause for its necessity. This is the being which is the cause of the necessity present in other things, and it is referred to by everyone as God.[54]

Few other texts in Aquinas have occasioned so much controversy among interpreters as the first phase of this argument.[55] In an effort to understand Thomas's procedure here, we shall review the various steps in that phase and single out certain contested points. Once more Thomas takes as his point of departure something which we may derive from sense experience, that is, our awareness that certain beings are possible beings. As he uses the term "possible" here he means that they have the possibility of existing or not existing. As we see him doing in SCG I, c. 15, here again he closely associates possible beings with their capacity to be generated and corrupted. This, in fact, is the empirical evidence with which the argument begins. Because certain things which we experience are subject to generation and corruption, we may conclude that they are possible beings, not necessary beings. As Thomas sees things, such beings are composed of matter and form. It is this composition which renders them liable to corruption; and because of such composition, they naturally come into being by being generated. However, strictly speaking, Thomas need not assume at this point in his argument that such beings are composed of matter and form. The fact that they come into being through generation and cease to be through corruption is enough for him to make the point that they are possible beings.[56]

It is with the very next sentence that the difficulties in interpreting this argument begin: "It is impossible for all things which exist to be such [i.e., possibles], because what has the possibility of not existing at some time (quandoque) does not exist." Immediately one wonders how the expression "at some time" (quandoque) is to be taken: Does Thomas mean to say thereby that what is possible has been nonexistent at some time in the past, or that it will be nonexistent at some time in the future? Each reading continues to have its defenders.[57] Before attempting to answer this question, we should also note the following sentence: "If therefore all things have the possibility of not existing, at some time *(aliquando)* there was nothing in reality." From this Thomas concludes that if this were so, even now there would be nothing.[58] The fact that in the last-quoted sentence there is a reference to the past ("at some time there was nothing") strongly suggests that Thomas would have us interpret the previous sentence in the same sense. What he is asserting, therefore, is that if all things are possibles (capable of existing and of not existing), at some point in the past all things would have been nonexistent. Therefore at that point in the past there would have been nothing whatsoever and consequently there would be nothing now. Since this final supposition is contrary to fact, so is the assumption from which it follows, that is, that all things are possibles.[59]

If we take the argument this way, the question remains: How can Thomas move from the first disputed statement to the second one without being guilty of the fallacy of composition or a quantifier shift? It is one thing for him to say that what has the possibility of not existing did not exist at some time in the past. This statement makes sense if we emphasize the point that any such being—a possible—comes into existence by being generated, that is to say, after it has not existed. Unless we wish to suggest that some such being may have been produced from eternity by being created and thereby already also concede the existence of an eternal creative principle, it seems that we must grant Thomas's claim: if something has been generated, its existence was preceded by its nonexistence.[60]

But what of Thomas's next statement? If all things are possibles (capable of existing and not existing), at some point in the past nothing would have existed. This statement goes considerably farther than the previous one. If we suppose that every individual being is a possible and therefore has not existed at some point in the past, how does it follow from this that the totality of existing things will all have been nonexistent at the same point in the past? While some have defended Thomas against the charge of committing the fallacy of composition or a quantifier shift in this step, it is difficult to regard such defenses of his reasoning as successful.[61]

To expand upon this for a moment, suppose that we grant that every possible being—every being which comes into existence by generation—exists only after it has been nonexistent. Well and good, we may comment, but this admission hardly leads to the conclusion that the totality of possible beings will all have been nonexistent simultaneously at some point in the past. Why not rather suggest that one possible being has come into being after another, and that after another, extending backwards into a beginningless past? Under this supposition, some possible being or beings will have existed at any given point in time, although no single possible being will have existed from eternity. While Thomas himself does grant the philosophical possibility of an eternally created world, he does so ultimately only under the assumption that there is also an eternal creative cause. While this is true, he cannot assume the existence of such a being at this point in the third way.

One might appeal to some other form of reasoning at this step in order to show that the explanation just proposed will not of itself be enough to account for the existence of any given possible being, whether or not one posits a beginningless series of possible beings extending back into the past. Therefore, we must grant the existence of a being that is not a possible but which is necessary if we are to account for the generation of any and all possible beings.[62] This, however, would be to introduce into the third way a different kind of reasoning, based on causality, a kind which we have already seen in the first and second ways in connection with a proposed regress to infinity in moved movers or in ordered caused causes, and a kind which will reappear in the second phase of the third way itself (as applied to caused necessary beings). While such an interpretation is defensible from the metaphysical standpoint, it would entail a substantial addition to Thomas's text and a serious recasting of the first part of the third way. So true is this that one might then doubt that one was still dealing with Thomas's third way, for the temporal references in the first part would now lose their importance.[63]

In order to understand more fully Thomas's procedure in this third way, a number of recent commentators have concentrated on various possible historical sources for this argument. Aristotle, Avicenna, and Moses Maimonides have all been proposed, and not without reason. Nonetheless, careful comparison of these with the text of Thomas's third way shows that while he must have been influenced by some of them, especially by Aristotle and Maimonides, in penning his version of the argument, he has developed it in his own way.[64] In short, recourse to such earlier sources will not rescue the argument from this crucial weakness in its first stage. Why Thomas himself did not regard this as a serious flaw in his argument is something I have been unable to determine.

As for the remainder of the first phase of the argument, its conclusion follows naturally enough. If we concede that at some point in the past nothing whatsoever existed, there would be nothing now; for what does not exist cannot begin to exist except by reason of something which exists. While Kenny has expressed some reservations about this claim, and while David Hume rejected all attempts to demonstrate it, Thomas had no doubt about it: if something begins to exist, it must be brought into existence by something else which exists.[65] He had already argued for this in somewhat different terms in accounting for the origins of motion in his first way, and in terms of efficient causation in his second way. And he had made the same point with respect to existence itself in c. 4 of his *De ente*.[66]

To repeat his reasoning in my own terms, if something begins to exist after it has not existed, this can only be owing to itself, or to nothing whatsoever, or to something else, i.e., a cause. To say that a thing is the efficient cause of its own existence is to imply that it is and yet is not at the same time and in the same respect; for it must be if it is to communicate existence (to itself) or to act as a cause, and it must not be if its existence is to be caused efficiently. To suggest that it owes its existence to nothing whatsoever is to hold that there is no explanation for its existence. Since it is not self-existent (which follows from the fact that it did not always exist but began to be), to hold that there is no explanation for its present existence is to render that existence unintelligible. For Thomas, at least, this is to fly in the face of common sense and to reject the intelligibility of being. Hence, as he sees things, only the third alternative remains. If something begins to exist after it has not existed, it must be brought into existence by something else.[67]

In the second part of the argument a line of reasoning reappears which occurs in SCG I, c. 15. If one grants that a necessary being does exist (to account for the coming into existence of the possible beings with which the argument began), such a being may or may not depend upon something else for its necessity (and, we may assume, for its existence). But one cannot regress to infinity in caused necessary beings (literally: "in necessary beings whose necessity is caused"), just as one cannot do so with efficient causes, as has been proved (see the second way). Therefore there must be an uncaused necessary being, which causes the necessity of the others, and which everyone calls God.[68]

This second phase of the argument is much less controversial and is, in my opinion, sound. Whether or not it succeeds in establishing the point that there is only one uncaused necessary being is, of course, another matter, and much of what we have said above about the conclusions of the first and second ways continues to apply. Additional reflection will be required to show that there is only one first and totally uncaused necessary being if we are to justify the claim that this being is God. One could, of course, reason that at this point in the argument Thomas is discussing beings that depend upon something else not only for their necessity but for their very existence. If so, one could then reason that their cause is an uncaused source of *esse* and therefore uncaused *esse* in and of itself. Even so, the argument will remain incomplete until it has been shown that there can only be one such being. One might do this by adopting Thomas's procedure in q. 11, or by introducing reasoning similar to that which he has presented in the *De ente*, c. 4.[69]

In sum, the first phase of the third way strikes me as being open to serious criticisms along the lines already pointed out. In this phase it is considerably less convincing than the argumentation from SCG I, c. 15. Why Thomas introduced this particular step into his argument in ST I, q. 2, a. 3 continues to be a matter for speculation.[70] In my opinion, no completely satisfying explanation has been forthcoming. By introducing this first step he has, of course, established the third way clearly enough as a different kind of argument from either the first or second way. But one could say the same of the much less troublesome argument offered in SCG I, c. 15. There, too, he incorporates into his argumentation the distinction between possible beings, caused necessary beings, and an uncaused necessary being and there, too, he begins with possible beings and then moves on to consider caused necessary beings in order to reason to the existence of an uncaused necessary being.

4. The Fourth Way

Thomas's fourth way is based on the varying degrees of perfection we find among beings. It immediately strikes the reader as being much more Platonic and Neoplatonic in inspiration than any of the other ways, even though in presenting it Thomas twice refers to a passage from Aristotle's *Metaphysics*. Foreshadowings of this kind of approach appear in his Commentary on I *Sentences* and in *Summa contra Gentiles* I, c. 13.[71] As he develops this argument in the *Summa theologiae*, among things we find something that is more and less good, more and less true, more and less noble, and so too with respect to other perfections of this kind. But the more and less are said of different things insofar as they approach in diverse fashion something which is (such) to a maximum degree. (To illustrate this Thomas cites the example of heat: that is hotter which more closely approaches something which is hot to the maximum degree.) Therefore there is something which is truest and best and noblest and hence which is also being to the maximum degree. In support of this conclusion Thomas observes that those things which are true to the maximum degree also enjoy being to the maximum degree, and cites Bk II of the *Metaphysics*.[72] He is evidently basing this on the convertible character of being and of ontological truth, a point which he had developed more fully elsewhere, especially in *De veritate*, q. 1, a. 1.[73] With this the first part of his argument comes to an end; but rather than regard his task as completed, Thomas introduces a second stage.

In this second stage he reasons that what is said to be supremely such in a given genus is the cause of all other things which are present in that genus. (In illustration he returns to the example of fire: being hot to the maximum degree, fire is the cause of heat in all other things, as Aristotle maintains in the *Metaphysics*.) Therefore, Thomas concludes, there is something which is the cause of being *(esse)* for all other beings, as well as of their goodness and every other perfection. And this we call God.[74]

In the first stage of this argument Thomas again appeals to the world as we experience it, and goes on to apply a general principle to the same. As for the world as we experience it, we note that certain things are more and less good, true, noble, etc. By referring to things as more and less good, Thomas must have in mind their ontological goodness, that is to say, their goodness of being. In *De veritate*, q. 1, a. 1 he had singled out goodness, along with truth and unity, as characteristics which are found wherever being itself is realized and which are convertible with being. Consequently, along with thing *(res)* and something *(aliquid)*, which he also regards as coextensive with being, these are often referred to as transcendental properties of being.[75] To say that something enjoys goodness of being is to indicate that it is an object of appetite. And to say that one thing enjoys greater ontological goodness than another is to imply that it is a more desirable object in itself. Given Thomas's hierarchical view of the universe and his conviction that ontological goodness and being are really convertible, we can understand why he would view an animal as enjoying greater ontological goodness than a mere stone. The animal is endowed with life and with the power of sensation, whereas the stone is not. At the same time, an animal lacks the power of understanding which a human being enjoys and is therefore less good, ontologically speaking, than a human being.[76]

In referring to things as more and less true Thomas is thinking of truth of being or ontological truth, not of truth as it exists in the intellect (logical truth). He has in mind that quality present in any being in virtue of which it can be grasped by intellect or, to put it in other terms, the intelligibility of being. Since such truth or intelligibility is found wherever being is realized, Thomas also regards being and truth as convertible with one another. To say that one thing enjoys greater truth (of being) than another is to make the point that, viewed in itself, it is more intelligible than the other. And this in turn follows from the fact that its degree of being is greater than that present in the other. In the world as we experience it, there do seem to be varying degrees of intelligibility, or of ontological truth. Thus according to Thomas's thinking a substantial form is more intelligible than its corresponding prime matter; the essence of a human being is more intelligible than that of a rock. In sum, corresponding to the hierarchy of being is a hierarchy of ontological truth, or of intrinsic intelligibility of being.[77]

In referring to certain things as more and less noble than others, Thomas has created something of a problem for his readers. Does he intend to single out another characteristic, distinct from ontological goodness and ontological truth? If so, what does he have in mind? It is difficult to answer this question with any degree of certainty. R. Garrigou-Lagrange takes nobility as synonymous with perfection, and this suggestion may well be correct. For instance, in SCG I, c. 28 Thomas describes as universally perfect that to which no excellence *(nobilitas)* of any kind is lacking. He also indicates that a thing's excellence *(nobilitas)* follows upon its mode of being *(esse)*. Accordingly, I would suggest that by this term Thomas wants to signify the varying degrees of pure ontological perfection or excellence we discover in the different beings we experience in the world about us. Just as some share more fully in ontological goodness and truth than do others, so too they may be regarded as being more perfect or more excellent, ontologically speaking, than others. Excellence *(nobilitas)* should not be regarded as a distinct transcendental.[78]

This in turn leads to another question: Does Thomas wish to restrict the starting point of the fourth way to gradation in transcendental perfections such as truth and goodness? (Interestingly enough, he does not mention ontological unity.) Or does he wish to include what we might call pure but not transcendental perfections such as life, knowledge, will, etc.? While not found wherever being is realized, such perfections also admit of degrees and, when freed from all limitation, may be applied analogically even to God, or so Thomas will maintain.[79] These perfections have the advantage of being readily recognizable in varying degrees in the world about us. But since Thomas has not explicitly singled them out in presenting the fourth way, it will be better for us not to base his argument upon them. For then one might wonder whether the general principle to which he appeals is also intended to apply to them as well as to strictly transcendental perfections. Here, therefore, I shall restrict the argument to transcendental perfections such as goodness and truth.

As Thomas expresses this principle in his text, the more and less are said of different things insofar as they approach in diverse fashion something which is such to the maximum degree. As some writers have pointed out, the example to which Thomas turns hardly proves his point. It is unnecessary for us to assume that something enjoys a maximum degree of heat in order to be aware that one kettle is hotter than another. Nonetheless, since this is only an example drawn from an outmoded medieval physics, we need not regard it as central to Thomas's argument.[80] But we may still ask: How does Thomas justify this general principle? Is it immediately evident that the more and less are said of different things only insofar as they approach something which is such to a maximum degree? Even if we restrict this principle to transcendental perfections such as those named by Thomas—goodness, truth (and nobility)—it is difficult to see how he can move so quickly from our recognition of greater and lesser degrees of these perfections to the existence of something which is such perfection to the maximum degree.

In attempting to justify this step in the argument, some commentators have maintained that it should not be interpreted as resting solely on exemplar causality. Instead, they suggest, there is an implicit appeal to efficient causality in this first stage. That which possesses goodness or truth or nobility in only a greater and lesser degree must receive such perfections from some distinct efficient cause. Therefore, one may conclude to the existence of an uncaused cause of goodness, truth, and nobility, which itself is such perfection of its essence. Confirmation for this interpretation may be sought by referring to the second stage in Thomas's text. There he reasons that what is supremely such in a given genus is the cause of everything else which belongs to that genus.[81]

Any such effort, however, runs counter to the literal text of the fourth way, or so it seems to me. The first stage of the argument concludes to the existence of something which is truest and best and noblest and hence being to the maximum degree. The final point—that it is also being to the maximum degree—is based on the convertibility of ontological truth and being, and is supported by an appeal to Aristotle's *Metaphysics*, as we have noted. But until this point in the argument no reference has been made to efficient causality. It is only in the second step, after the existence of a maximum has been established, that Thomas attempts to show that this maximum is also the cause of being, goodness, etc., for all other things.[82] Hence there seems to be no justification in Thomas's text for the claim that his proof for the existence of a maximum rests on or presupposes reasoning from efficient causation. It follows, therefore, that if we wish to present the argument as it appears in his text, it can only be based on extrinsic formal causality, i.e., on exemplar causality.

But if this argument for the existence of a maximum is free from any reference to efficient causation, is it valid? This question is more difficult to decide. Thomas makes earlier appeals in his texts to similar argumentation. In his Commentary on I *Sentences*, d. 3, he offers two arguments based on eminence. The first is taken from eminence insofar as this applies to being. The good and the better are so named in comparison to that which is the best. Since among substances a body is good and a created spirit still better, there must be some best from which the goodness present in body and spirit derives. But, Thomas offers no justification in that context for the general claim that where there is a good and a better, there must be a best.[83]

The second argument based on eminence focuses on human knowing. If we find things which are more and less beautiful, we can recognize them as such only by reason of their proximity to something which is the very principle of beauty. From this general cognitive principle Thomas quickly concludes to the existence of something from which bodies (which are beautiful) and spirits (which are more beautiful) derive their beauty. Once again, however, in the immediate context he offers no justification either for this general cognitive principle or for the ontological conclusion he draws from it.[84] While this cognitive principle makes perfect sense within an Augustinian account of human knowing, it is difficult to see how it can be granted within the terms of Thomas's own theory of knowledge and his conviction that our knowledge begins with and must in some way be derived from sense experience.[85]

Still another seeming anticipation of the fourth way is offered within this same discussion from Thomas's Commentary on I *Sentences*, an argument which Thomas describes as taken from the Dionysian way of negation (*remotionis*). Beyond everything which is imperfect there must be something which is perfect and admits of no imperfection whatsoever. Thomas goes on to apply this to bodies and then to things which are incorporeal and changeable. Beyond all of these there must be something which is completely immobile and perfect, or God.[86] Once again, however, Thomas does not see fit to justify his operative principle—that beyond that which is imperfect there must be something which is completely and totally perfect. While antecedents may be cited for such reasoning from within the Christian Neoplatonic tradition (see, for instance, Boethius's *Consolation of Philosophy* and Anselm's *Monologium*), one wonders how Thomas can justify such a claim within his own metaphysical perspective.[87]

When we return to another foreshadowing of the fourth way in *Summa contra Gentiles* I, c. 13, our perplexity remains. There Thomas reasons that if we recognize one thing as truer than another, this can only be because it comes closer to that which is true without qualification and to the maximum degree. From this he quickly draws the conclusion that there must be something which is being to the maximum degree. While this final point follows from the convertibility of ontological truth (truth of being) and of being itself, the general working principle on which the argument rests remains without justification—that the more and the less in the order of truth (and being) enables one to conclude immediately to the existence of something which is true to the maximum degree.[88]

As we return to the fourth way of the *Summa theologiae*, we wonder whether Thomas regards this general principle as self-evident. One writer has suggested that perhaps his powers of penetration were such that he immediately saw that varying degrees of transcendental perfection require a subsisting maximum to account for their imperfect realizations in the beings we experience. Within a Platonic and Neoplatonic framework, the self-evidence of such a claim might be more readily granted. But within Thomas's distinctive metaphysical approach, even though a considerable Platonic and Neoplatonic influence must be recognized, today's reader of his text may protest: the principle in question is not self-evident to him or her.[89]

One way of supplying the missing justification is to appeal to Thomas's metaphysics of participation and to regard the fourth way as an argument based on participation. This seems to be the approach adopted by C. Fabro. As he points out, there is another and later version of such an argument in Thomas's *Lectura* on St. John's Gospel, dating ca. 1270–1272.[90] As Thomas presents this argument, it is based on the nobility (*dignitas*) of God and is the way of the "Platonists." At the same time, it is clear from the context that Thomas accepts this argument as his own. Everything which is (such) by participation is reduced to something which is such of its essence as to something first and supreme. (Thus all things which participate in fire are reduced to fire which is such of its essence.) But since all things which exist participate in *esse* and are beings through participation, there must be something at the summit of all things which is *esse* of its essence in that its essence is its *esse*. This is God, the most sufficient and noblest and most perfect cause of all *esse*, from whom all things which exist participate in *esse*.[91]

This is an interesting approach and it rests on a principle frequently employed by Thomas in other contexts. That which participates in something must be traced back to something which is that perfection of its essence. Hence, that which exists by participating in *esse* must be traced back to something which is the act of being (*esse*) of its very essence.[92] Because this argument explicitly invokes participation and deals with it in the order of *esse*, it is more satisfying from a metaphysical standpoint than that offered in *Summa theologiae* I, q. 2, a. 3.

At the same time, we may ask whether this kind of argumentation can be justified without some implicit or explicit appeal to efficient causality. In fact, some such appeal seems to be involved at two levels within the argument. First of all, without stating this explicitly, the argument assumes that if something participates in a given characteristic, and especially in *esse*, it does not possess that characteristic of its essence or of itself. This follows from Thomas's general description of participation in his Commentary on the *De Hebdomadibu*[93] Moreover, in various contexts he states that a participated characteristic is present in a participating subject only insofar as it is efficiently caused therein. This will follow so long as one is dealing with real or ontological participation, not-merely with the logical participation of a less extended concept in one that is more extended, for instance, participation of a species in a genus.[94]

But what of participation of beings in *esse*? Thomas is convinced that this is a case of real participation. At times he reasons from the participated character of *esse* in particular entities to real distinction and composition therein of essence and *esse*.[95] In order to strengthen the claim that a participated being is efficiently caused, one might reason as follows. Because a participated being's essence differs from its *esse*, its *esse* must be received from without, i.e., it must be efficiently caused. As Thomas develops this in

Summa theologiae I, q. 3, a. 4, whatever is present in a thing in addition to its essence must be caused in that thing either by the principles of its essence (as is true of a proper accident), or else by something external (as heat is caused in water by fire). If the *esse* of a thing is distinct from that thing's essence, the same will apply. It must be caused either by the essential principles of that thing or by something external. But since a given thing cannot be the efficient cause of its own *esse*, the *esse* of any such thing cannot be caused by its intrinsic and essential principles. Therefore, its *esse* must be caused by something else.[96]

The argument from participation for God's existence also seems to rest on efficient causality at a second level. One must justify the claim that what exists by participation is to be traced back or reduced to that which exists of its essence. In order to do this, one should again consider and eliminate as a viable alternative to the unparticipated source appeal to a series of beings which would simply participate in other and higher participating beings and these in still others *ad infinitum*. It is true that in the first stage of the fourth way of the *Summa theologiae* Thomas does not explicitly bring out either of these points, i.e., the proof that beings which participate in *esse* are efficiently caused, or the consideration of an infinite regress of participating beings. Nor does he bring out the second point in the argument in his *Lectura*. It seems to me, however, that this should be done if one is to view the fourth way as an argument based on participation and if one wishes to justify that argument within Thomas's metaphysics.[97]

In doing this, however, I must acknowledge that we will have reinterpreted the fourth way seriously, and even in its substance. It will no longer be based solely on exemplar causality in its first stage, as its text indicates that it was originally intended to be. It will now be equivalent to the argument offered in the *Lectura* on St. John's Gospel. But unless some such reinterpretation or substitution is introduced, it seems unlikely that the argument's first stage can be regarded as successful in its attempt to prove that a maximum actually exists.[98]

In discussions of the fourth way reference is sometimes made to Thomas's slightly earlier argumentation in *De potentia*, q. 3, a. 5. There he is attempting to show that nothing that exists apart from God is uncreated. He offers three arguments to make this point. The first may be regarded as an argument for God's existence. The remaining two, attributed by Thomas respectively to Aristotle and to Avicenna, are less clearly so. They seem to take God's existence as already established and concentrate on showing that all beings other than God receive their *esse* from him. In these latter two arguments the theme of participation is explicitly introduced.[99]

The first argument runs as follows. If one single characteristic is common to many things, it must be caused in each of them by a single cause. This common feature cannot belong to each of the different individuals by reason of that which is proper to it as an individual; for each individual, by reason of that which it is in itself, is distinct from the others, and diversity in causes results in diverse effects. But since *esse* is common to all things and since each, when considered in itself, is distinct from the others, Thomas concludes that the *esse* realized in each must be given to it by some one cause. And this, Thomas comments, seems to be Plato's argument, since he held that before every multitude there must be some kind of unity.[100]

There is some disagreement among commentators concerning whether or not this is an argument based on participation. While Fabro concedes that the term "participation" does not appear in it, he seems to think that the notion is present therein.[101] Since the argument begins with the fact that *esse* is common to all existing things, we may, it seems to me, regard the argument as resting on the participation by the many in the perfection of *esse*. On the other hand, Van Steenberghen, while granting the argument's validity, contends that it does not start from participation but that it is based on the ontological similarity which obtains between finite beings.[102] To me this is simply another way in which Thomas makes the point that different beings merely participate in *esse (commune)*, and that no one of them is identical with it. In any event, it is another form of argumentation based on efficient causality. By reasoning that the common perfection (*esse*) cannot be accounted for in the many which share in it by an appeal to that which is proper to and distinctive of each, Thomas is in effect showing that *esse* is efficiently caused in each of them.[103] Hence this argument can hardly be regarded as one that is based on degrees of perfection, or as an equivalent of the fourth way, although it can easily be substituted for the first stage of that argument.

As for the second stage of the argument as it stands in *Summa theologiae* I, q. 2, a. 3, the point of this step is to prove that once we have established the existence of a maximum, we may also show that it is the efficient cause of the being, goodness, and other perfection present in other things. This part of the argument is much less troublesome than the first stage, or so it appears to me.[104] But it presupposes that one has already established the existence of the maximum in the argument's first stage, or else, as I have suggested, that one has substituted an argument based on participation in that stage to reach an unparticipated source. Enough has been said about this to enable us to move on now to the last of the five ways.

5. The Fifth Way

Thomas introduces this argument by noting that it is based on the way things are governed (*ex gubernatione rerum*). We see that certain things which lack knowledge, that is to say, natural bodies, act for the sake of an end. In support of this claim Thomas reasons that it follows from the fact that they always or at least usually (*frequentius*) act in the same way in order to attain that which is best. This shows that they reach their respective end(s) not by chance but by intention. But "things which lack cognition do not tend to an end unless they are directed [to it] by some knowing and intelligent being, as an arrow is directed [to its target] by an archer." Therefore, there is some intelligent being by which all natural things are ordered to their end, and this we call God.[105]

While the fifth way is sometimes confused with an argument based on order and design and the need for a supreme designer, Thomas's text makes it clear that he really has in mind an argument based on final causality in nature. Hence it bears much greater resemblance to the argument for divine providence in *De veritate*, q. 5, a. 2 than to the argument from design of *Summa contra Gentiles* 1, c. 13.[106]

Like the other five ways, this argument begins with something which Thomas regards as evident to us from the world of everyday experience. Natural bodies, that is to say, things which are equipped with their own natures but lack the power of cognition, act for the sake of an end. Thomas knows that it is one thing for us to be aware that natural bodies act, for instance, that a heavy body tends to fall or a hot body to rise; but it is something else for us to conclude that such bodies act for an end.[107] Immediately, therefore, two possible objections come to mind. Perhaps the action of natural bodies can be accounted for merely by appealing to efficient causal activity. Or perhaps their seeming action for an end is not to be credited to the influence of any final cause but only to chance.

As regards the first objection, Thomas had learned from Aristotle about two ancient schools of thought which left no place for final causality. Some admitted of nothing but material causes; others defended the existence of efficient causes but still saw no need for final causes. Against such views Thomas had always defended the need for final causes, along with efficient, formal and material causes, in accounting for operations in nature such as generation.[108]

For instance, in his youthful *De principiis naturae*, c. 3, he had reasoned that while matter, form, and privation may be regarded as principles of generation, they are not sufficient of themselves to explain this process. Something which is in potency cannot reduce itself to act. Therefore an agent is required to account for this, for instance, to reduce copper from being a statue only potentially to being such in actuality by educing the form of that statue from potentiality to actuality. The form of the statue cannot do this, since it does not actually exist until the statue itself is produced. Hence in addition to matter and form there must be some efficient or moving or agent cause. But as Aristotle states in *Metaphysics* II, what acts does so only by tending toward something. Therefore, there must also be a fourth cause or principle—that which is intended by the agent. This we call the end.[109]

In developing this final point, Thomas comments that if both natural agents and voluntary agents tend toward an end (*intendit finem*), it does not follow from this that every agent knows its end or deliberates about it. Agents whose actions are not determined, i.e., voluntary agents, must know the end if they are to determine their action to one thing rather than another. But the actions of natural agents are determined and, therefore, they need not choose means to their end. Indeed, they cannot do so, we may add. Thomas takes an example from Avicenna to show that one who plays a cithara need not deliberate about every pluck of the strings. If this were required, it would result in untimely delays and would destroy the beauty of the music. But it is surely more evident that voluntary agents deliberate than that purely natural agents do. Therefore and a fortiori, Thomas concludes that natural agents need not deliberate and that nonetheless they tend to their ends. For such an agent to tend to its end is nothing else than for it to have a natural inclination to that end, as Thomas goes on to explain.[110]

Especially important in this discussion for our immediate purpose is Thomas's claim that an agent can act only by tending toward something, i.e., an end. This applies not only to voluntary agents but to those which are determined by their natures to act in given ways. As Thomas argues in another early text (*In II Sent.*, d. 25, q. 1, a. 1), nothing acts except insofar as it is in act. Therefore every agent must be determined to one or other alternative. That which is equally open to different alternatives is, in a certain way, in potency to both, and nothing will follow from it unless it is determined to one or the other. But if an agent is to be determined to a given action, this can only be through some act of knowing which presents the end for that action.[111]

Thomas speaks in much the same vein in his considerably later *Summa theologiae* I-II, q. 1, a. 2, while supporting his contention that every agent acts for an end. First among the causes is the final cause. Matter does not receive a form unless it is moved by an agent, since nothing can reduce itself from potency to act. An agent does not move except by tending to an end (*ex intentione finis*). To prove this he reasons that if an agent were not determined to a given effect it would not produce this effect rather than any other one. Therefore, in order for it to produce a given effect, it must be determined to something which serves as its end. In sum, Thomas's view is that unless we recognize the need for an end to influence an agent in its action, we will be unable to account for the fact that the agent produces a determined effect or, indeed, that it acts at all.[112]

To return to the text of the fifth way, suppose one grants to Thomas that the actions of natural bodies cannot be fully accounted for merely by appealing to efficient causal activity. The second objection remains. Perhaps such behavior on the part of natural bodies is owing to chance. Against this suggestion he replies briefly in the fifth way by citing the fact that natural things act always or at least usually in the same way in order to attain that which is best. In other words, mere chance cannot account for a regularly repeated pattern of behavior on the part of natural entities, and especially not when this activity achieves that which is best. Thomas had already made this same point and developed it somewhat more fully in his *De veritate*, q. 5, a. 2.[113]

Moreover, we should note that Thomas, following Aristotle, does not regard chance as a being or as a cause *per se* but only *per accidens*. Chance is simply our way of referring to a situation in which independently operating causes intersect or collide without any of the particular agents foreseeing that this will happen. Yet each of these agents has its particular end. An illustration is offered by Boethius. A farmer discovers buried treasure while plowing a field. Both the farmer and the one who originally buried the treasure operated for their respective particular ends, and neither intended for the farmer to discover the treasure. Because this intersection of their independently intended actions was not foreseen by either, we refer to the discovery as a chance event.[114]

If one accepts this explanation of chance events, mere chance can hardly account for the regular and beneficial activity of natural agents, whether we regard that activity as beneficial only for the agents themselves, or also for nature taken as a whole.[115] Moreover, far from excluding the influence of ends upon agents, such an account really presupposes it. If we may emphasize this point, each particular agent acts for its particular end.

This is why Thomas eliminates in his fifth way any explanation based on chance. He is convinced that particular actions cannot be rendered intelligible unless one recognizes the influence of an end upon an agent. Because of this he goes on to argue that things which lack knowledge do not tend to an end except insofar as they are directed to it by some knowing and intelligent being as, for example, an arrow is directed to its target by an archer.[116]

He says the same both in his Commentary on Bk II of the *Sentences* (d. 25, q. 1, a. 1) and in q. 1, a. 2 of the *Prima secundae*. If we may fill in his reasoning a bit, his point is this. An agent does not act in a given way unless it is influenced by an end. Noncognitive agents cannot explicitly know their ends. Hence the only way of accounting for the ability of an end to influence such an agent is to appeal to an inclination which is impressed upon that agent by some intelligent being. Such an intelligent being can, of course, have in mind the end of the noncognitive agent's action.[117] This is why

Thomas writes in the text from the *Prima secundae* that agents which lack reason tend to an end through a natural inclination so as to be moved, as it were, by something else and not by themselves. Because they do not grasp the end of their action as such, they do not order themselves to that end; they are ordered to it by something else.[118]

Finally, Thomas's reference in the fifth way and in ST I–II, q. 1, a. 2 to an arrow which tends to its determined target because it is so directed by an archer might raise another question for the reader.[119] Does Thomas think that the inclination of purely natural agents to their respective ends is simply impressed on them in passing fashion, as it were, by some other intelligent being? Or does he rather have in mind a permanent inclination which is part of their very being?

The example of the archer and the arrow might lead one to believe that Thomas has in mind only the first alternative. And this would perhaps be enough for him to argue from finality in nature, though it might not be sufficient for him to show that there is only one intelligence which is responsible for such finality.

It is clear, however, from other texts that he really defends the second alternative. For instance, in the text from *In II Sent.*, d. 25, q. 1, a. 1, he had observed that the actions of natural entities are not in vain; such entities are ordered to their actions by an intellect which "constitutes" such natures. From this he goes on to conclude that the whole of nature is, in a certain fashion, the work of intelligence.[120] And on other occasions he refers to a natural body's inclination to behave in a certain way and to tend to a certain end as its natural appetite. Moreover, as he explains in ST I, q. 5, a. 5, a thing's inclination to an action follows upon its form.[121] We conclude, therefore, that what ultimately causes the form of a natural agent is also responsible for that agent's inclination to its given end. Thomas says as much in *De veritate*, q. 25, a. 1.[122]

If one grants the validity of Thomas's reasoning up until this point, other questions may be raised about the fifth way. First of all, if he has shown that there is some intelligent being by whom all natural things are ordered to their end(s) and which we call God, can he show that there is only one such being? In other words, it seems once more that the question of the uniqueness of this supreme being must still be faced. Secondly, if such an intelligent being orders natural things to their appropriate end or ends by imposing a natural inclination upon them, is this not to say that this intelligence is also their efficient cause? If so, it would seem that the ultimate source of finality in the universe must be identified with the supreme efficient cause of all such beings. Thirdly and finally, this brings up the issue of the unity of the five ways themselves: Are they viewed by Thomas as five distinct arguments, each of which leads to God's existence? Or are they rather thought of as different steps in one longer and more involved argumentation for this conclusion?

6. The Uniqueness of God

In taking up the first of these questions we return to a broader issue which may be raised about each of the five ways. Do Thomas's arguments really succeed in showing that there is only one first and unmoved mover, or first efficient cause, or uncaused necessary being, or absolute maximum or, in the case of the fifth way, one supreme intelligence which is responsible for the fact that all natural agents act for an end? Or do they leave open the possibility that there might be more than one of at least some of these—for instance, more than one unmoved mover or uncaused cause? Moreover, does his argumentation show that the unmoved mover is identical with the uncaused cause, the absolutely necessary being, the supremely perfect being, and the supreme intelligence?

One may doubt whether any of these arguments, as they stand in the text of *Summa theologiae* I, q. 2, a. 3, fully establishes divine uniqueness, i.e., that there is one God and only one God. Our doubt concerning this is strengthened by the fact that in ST I, q. 11, a. 3, Thomas explicitly addresses himself to this issue. It might have been less confusing for the reader if Thomas had clearly indicated in the course of presenting the various five ways that he would eventually complete them by establishing divine uniqueness.[123] Be that as it may, it remains for us now to turn to his discussion of this in q. 11, and then to certain other works where he also explicitly takes up this issue.

Question 11 is addressed to the topic of divine unity. Articles 1, 2, and 4 deal with the issue of unity taken in the sense of ontological unity or the transcendental one, i.e., the undividedness of being from itself. For Thomas, since this characteristic of being is found wherever being itself is realized, it must also be present in God. But it is only in a. 3 that the question of divine uniqueness—the claim that there is only one God—is taken up explicitly.[124]

In a. 3 Thomas offers three arguments to show that there is only one God. The first of these is based on God's simplicity. That by reason of which an individual is this individual cannot be communicated to many. For example, that by reason of which Socrates is man can be communicated to many; but that by reason of which he is this man cannot be so communicated. Otherwise, just as there cannot be many Socrateses, so too there could not be many men. Because God is identical with his very nature, that by reason of which he is God and that by reason of which he is this God are one and the same. Therefore there cannot be many Gods.[125]

In order to do justice to this argumentation, one should turn back to earlier articles in the *Summa theologiae* on which it is based, that is to say, to Thomas's efforts to show that God is simple and in particular that God is identical with his nature. Thomas had devoted the whole of q. 3 to divine simplicity. As we have remarked above, he had introduced q. 3 by noting that this discussion is part of his effort to show how God is not. In this particular case he does so by arguing that all composition is to be denied of God.[126]

Thus in the opening articles of q. 3 Thomas shows first that God is not a body (a. 1); secondly that there is no matter-form composition in him (a. 2); and then in a. 3 that there is no composition in God of quiddity or essence or nature, on the one hand, and the subject which subsists *(suppositum)*, on the other—or, as Thomas also puts it, that God is identical with his essence or nature.[127]

Thomas develops the last-mentioned point by drawing upon his theory of the individuation of material substances and his views on the relationship between nature and the subsisting subject (supposit). In things composed of matter and form, essence or nature differs from the subject which exists (supposit). This is because essence or nature includes in itself only those things which fall within the definition of the species (as humanity includes only that which falls under the definition of human being). But individual matter and the accidents which serve to individuate it are not included within the definition of the species. For instance, this flesh and these bones and the accidents which designate this matter are not included within humanity, though they do fall under that which this human being is. Hence a human being, meaning this human being, and humanity are not completely identical; humanity is signified as a formal part of a human being. A human being (this subsisting subject) includes something which humanity considered in itself does not.[128]

In things which are not composed of matter and form and which are not rendered individuals by individual matter, forms are individuated of themselves. Hence these forms are subsisting subjects (supposits). Given this, in such beings there is no (real) distinction between nature and the subsisting subject (supposit). Therefore, since God is not composed of matter and form, concludes Thomas, it follows that God is identical with his deity, his life, and whatever else may be predicated of him. In other words, God, taken as a subsisting subject, is identical with his essence or nature.[129] If one grants this, it will of course follow that there can only be one God; for that by which deity is deity is identical with that by which deity is God.

One point remains to be examined in this argumentation. This is the assertion that in God there can be no composition of matter and form. Thomas had considered this in a. 2. In brief he had rejected matter-form composition in God: (1) because God as pure actuality excludes matter which is potentiality; (2) because every composite of matter and form is perfected by its form and is good through its form and, therefore, good only by participation, something which cannot be said of God, the first and best being; (3) because every agent acts through its form. Hence that which is the first and *per se* agent must be form primarily and *per se*. Because God is the first efficient cause, such is true of him. Being form of his essence, therefore, God is not composed of matter and form. In sum, these arguments against matter-form composition in God follow from the conclusions of the first way, i.e., that God is pure act (argument one); the second way, that God is the first efficient cause (argument three); and presumably the fourth way, that God is the first and best being (argument two).[130]

To return now to Thomas's defense of divine uniqueness in q. 11, a. 3, there he builds a second argument upon the infinity of divine perfection. He notes that he has already shown that God includes within himself the total perfection of being. If there were many Gods, they would have to differ from one another. Therefore something would have to belong to one which did not belong to another. If this were a privation, the God to whom it belonged would not be perfect. And if it were a perfection, that perfection would be lacking to the other God(s). Therefore there cannot be many Gods.[131]

In order to appreciate this argument we shall again have to turn back to earlier articles in the *Summa* on which it is based. Before doing this, we should mention Thomas's third argument for divine uniqueness in q. 11, a. 3. This argument appeals to the unity of the world, a unity which is manifested by the fact that different things in the world are ordered to and subordinated to one another. But if things which differ are united to form one order, they must be so united by some ordering principle. Many things are better reduced to a single order by one ordering principle than by many; for one thing is a *per se* cause of that which is one, whereas many things do not cause that which is one except *per accidens*. Since that which is first is most perfect and is such *per se* and not merely *per accidens*, the first principle which reduces the different things in the world to a single order must be one rather than many. This is God.[132]

This argument is not quite so metaphysical as the previous two and, in my judgment, not so convincing within the context of Thomas's metaphysics. It has more of an empirical base, i.e., the order we discover in the universe. If one grants that such a universal order is present, the validity of the argument rests both upon our discovery of that order and upon our inability to account for it in any other way except by appealing to one supreme ordering principle. It reminds one of an argument for God's existence based on order and design. And it strikes me as being more of an argument from fittingness than a convincing demonstration.

With this we may return to the background for the most interesting of these three arguments for divine uniqueness, the second one, which is based on the impossibility of there being more than one infinitely perfect being. Presupposed by this argument, of course, is the claim that God is infinitely perfect or, as Thomas also puts it, that God includes within himself the total perfection of being.[133]

In q. 4, a. 1 Thomas had built his case for divine perfection upon his previously established conclusion that God is the first efficient cause and presumably, therefore, on the conclusion of the second way. The first efficient cause, Thomas reasons, must be most perfect. Just as matter insofar as it is matter is in potency, so too, an agent insofar as it is an agent is in act. Therefore the first active principle, i.e., the first efficient cause, must be in act to the maximum degree, and therefore perfect to the maximum degree. In support of this final point Thomas reasons that something is said to be perfect insofar as it is in act; by the perfect we mean that to which nothing of its appropriate perfection is lacking.[134]

In replying to objection 3 Thomas develops this final point. The objection points out that Thomas has already argued that God's essence is identical with his *esse* (see q. 3, a. 4). But *esse* seems to be most imperfect, since it is most universal *(communissimum)* and admits of additions. In reply Thomas counters that *esse* itself is the most perfect of all; for it is related to all things as their act. And nothing enjoys actuality except insofar as it exists. Therefore *esse* itself is the actuality of all things, including forms themselves. Hence it is related to other things not as that which receives is related to that which is received, but rather as that which is received to that which receives it. When one speaks of the *esse* of a human being or of a horse, Thomas goes on to explain, *esse* is taken as that which is formal and received. Against the objection, therefore, he maintains that *esse* is the most perfect of all. If God is self-subsisting *esse*, we can easily see why Thomas regards God as perfect.[135]

If Thomas has connected perfection with actuality in the corpus of this article, in replying to objection 3 he has now just as clearly grounded actuality and therefore perfection in *esse*. As he uses the term *esse* in this discussion, he has in mind the intrinsic act of being *(actus essendi)*. It is this which is the most perfect of all, which accounts for the fact that things exist, and which is related to a creature's essence as that which is formal and received. To repeat a point just made, if God is self-subsisting *esse*, he must be self-subsisting perfection.

In q. 4, a. 2, Thomas goes on to show that the perfections of all other things are present in God, either formally or virtually, we should add. As Thomas explains, this means that God is universally perfect in the sense that no excellence of any kind is lacking to him. He offers two arguments to establish this. The first is based on the fact that whatever degree of perfection is present in an effect must be found in its efficient cause, either in the same way if we are dealing with causes and effects of the same kind (univocal causes, as Thomas sometimes describes them), or in more eminent fashion if the cause differs in kind from and is more perfect than the effect (equivocal causes, in Thomas's terminology). In proof he reasons that it is evident that an effect preexists virtually in its efficient cause. This is simply to say that the agent has the power to produce the effect. But this is for an effect to preexist not in less perfect fashion but in a more perfect way. An agent insofar as it is an agent is perfect. Because God is the first efficient cause, the perfections of all things must preexist in him in preeminent fashion.[136]

In his second argument to show that the perfections of all things are in God, Thomas recalls his earlier proof that God is self-subsisting *esse*. It follows from this that God must contain the full perfection of being within himself. For instance, if there could be such a thing as subsisting heat, nothing of the perfection of heat could be lacking to it. Because God is subsisting being *(esse)* itself, nothing of the perfection of being can be lacking to him. Given this, it follows that the perfections of all things belong to God; for the perfections of all things pertain to the perfection of being. Thomas supports this final point by reminding us once again that things are perfect insofar as they enjoy the act of being *(esse)* in some fashion.[137]

Since Thomas has explicitly referred back to his earlier proof that God is identical with his act of being *(esse)*, it will be useful now for us to turn to his discussion of this in q. 3, a. 4. In order to establish this, Thomas offers three arguments.[138] First of all, as we have already seen above in discussing a way of strengthening the fourth way, he reasons that whatever is present in a given thing in addition to its essence must be caused either by the principles of that thing's essence (as is true of proper accidents, such as the ability to laugh in a human being), or else by some external principle. Therefore, if the act of being *(esse)* of a thing differs from its essence, its act of being must be caused either by some external principle or else by that thing's essential principles. But it is not possible for a thing's act of being to be caused merely by its essential principles, since nothing can be the cause of its own act of being *(esse)*, if indeed its act of being is caused. Therefore, if the act of being of a given thing differs from its essence, its act of being *(esse)* must be caused by something else. But in his second way Thomas has already shown that God is the first efficient cause and, therefore, that his act of being is not caused. From this it follows simply by denying the consequent that essence and act of being do not differ in God.[139]

As a second argument Thomas reasons that God must be identical with his act of being *(esse)* because *esse* is the actuality of every form or nature. For instance, goodness or humanity is not said to be realized in actuality except insofar as it exists. Hence an act of being *(esse)* must be related to an essence which differs from it as act to potency. Since there can be no (passive) potentiality in God, in him essence and act of being *(esse)* do not differ. We may presume that the point that there is no potentiality in God follows for Thomas from the conclusion of the first way and also, as he indicates in q. 3, a. 1, from the fact that God is the first being.[140]

As a third argument for the identity of God with his act of being, Thomas reasons that if something merely has *esse* but is not identical with its *esse*, it is a being only by participation. If God were not identical with his act of being *(esse)*, he would be a being only by participation. He would not be the first being.[141] It is for these three reasons, therefore, that Thomas holds that essence and act of being *(esse)* are identical in God and as a consequence, that God is subsisting *esse*.

Finally, since Thomas has built his second major argument for divine uniqueness upon the infinity of divine perfection, we may ask how he establishes the infinity of God. Although Thomas develops this point on many occasions in his writings, in the *Summa theologiae* I his explicit discussion appears in q. 7, a. 1. There he distinguishes between the kind of infinity which may be ascribed to matter, and the kind attributed to form. Matter is said to be infinite (we might substitute the term "indefinite") in the sense that it can receive many forms. Because it is determined and perfected by the form it receives, the infinity assigned to matter falls on the side of imperfection. The infinity which Thomas ascribes to form is a mark of perfection. It refers to the fact that form, insofar as it is form, is common to many and is not perfected by the matter which receives it. Rather it is limited thereby in that its fullness is contracted by the matter that receives it.[142]

Thomas next recalls that the act of being *(esse)* is the most formal of all. He has shown that the divine act of being is not received by anything else and that God is identical with his act of being *(esse)*. From this he now draws the conclusion that God is infinite and perfect. In other words, in this argument Thomas appeals to his understanding of *esse* as that which is most formal and actual and by implication to his axiom that unreceived act (in this case, the act of being) is unlimited. Because God's *esse* is unreceived by anything else, it is unlimited. Therefore God himself is infinite and perfect.[143]

If we may briefly summarize this somewhat complicated background for Thomas's second argument for the uniqueness of God, it rests upon the following points. According to q. 3, a. 4, God is identical with his act of being. According to q. 4, a. 1, as the first efficient cause God must be in act to the maximum degree and, therefore, perfect to the maximum degree. Hence, according to q. 4, a. 2 the perfections of all other things must be present in God either formally or virtually. Finally, according to q. 7, a. 1, because the divine act of being is not received and therefore limited by anything else and because God is identical with his act of being, God's act of being is unlimited or infinite. Therefore God is infinite. Given all of this, in q. 11, a. 3 Thomas can reason that because God includes within himself the total perfection of being and because there cannot be many infinitely perfect beings, there cannot be many Gods. Therefore there is only one God.

At this juncture it may be helpful for us to consider some arguments for divine uniqueness which Thomas offers in other contexts. There is a long discussion of this in the SCG I, c. 42. Since not all of the arguments offered there are equally convincing and since they are quite numerous, here I shall single out one which strikes me as being of considerable interest. This, the second argument offered there, reminds one of a principle used again by Thomas in his second argument in ST I, q. 11, a. 3. The argument in SCG I, c. 42 is based on divine perfection. Thomas begins by recalling that he has already shown that God is totally perfect. Therefore, if there were many Gods, there would have to be many beings which are completely and totally perfect. But this is impossible. For if no perfection is lacking to any one of them, and if no imperfection is found in any of them, there will be no way in which they can be distinguished from one another. Therefore there cannot be many such beings.[144] Again we see Thomas accepting as proved the point that God is totally perfect, and reasoning that two completely perfect beings could not be distinguished from one another and therefore cannot exist.

Since Thomas introduces this particular argument by recalling that he has already shown that God is completely perfect, we may now turn briefly to his discussion of divine perfection in SCG I, c. 28. There he offers a series of arguments to make his point. He begins by observing that God, who is identical with his act of being *(esse)*, is a perfect being in every way or, to translate literally, universally perfect. As Thomas explains, this means that no excellence *(nobilitas)* of any kind can be lacking to God.[145]

In his first full argument for divine perfection, Thomas reasons that a thing's excellence belongs to it in accord with its act of being *(esse)*. For instance, no excellence would be present in a man by reason of his wisdom unless it were through wisdom that he *is* indeed wise. Thus a thing's excellence is in accord with the way (mode) in which it enjoys *esse*. If a thing's *esse* is restricted to some greater or lesser specific mode of excellence, that thing is accordingly said to be more or less excellent. And if there is something to which the total power of being *(virtus essendi)* belongs, no excellence which can pertain to any thing can be lacking to it. But a thing which is identical with its act of being *(esse)* enjoys the act of being according to the total power of being. (Thomas illustrates this by calling upon one of his favorite examples. If there were a subsisting whiteness, nothing of the power of whiteness would be lacking to it because of any deficiency on the part of a receiving subject. In other words, precisely because it was a subsisting whiteness, it would not be received by any distinct subject and could not be limited thereby.) But, as Thomas reminds us, he has already shown above (in c. 22) that God is identical with his act of being. Therefore God possesses *esse* according to the total power of being *(esse)* itself. Consequently, no possible excellence can be lacking to God.[146]

Thomas builds another argument for divine perfection upon his previously established conclusion that God is pure actuality (see c. 16). But that which is in potency in no way whatsoever and which is pure actuality must be most perfect; for a thing is perfect insofar as it is in act. As pure actuality, therefore, God is most perfect.[147]

With respect to Thomas's explicit argumentation for divine uniqueness in SCG I, c. 42, we should note that he does not yet assume there that God is infinite. In fact he will take up divine infinity in the immediately following chapter 43. In this respect, therefore, his procedure in the *Summa contra Gentiles* differs from that which he would later follow in the *Summa theologiae.* Having already established divine infinity in ST I, q. 7, he can there justifiably rest part of his argumentation for divine uniqueness upon divine infinity when he takes this up in q. 11.

Nonetheless, within a very different context in the *Summa contra Gentiles,* that is, in Bk II, c. 52, Thomas does offer an interesting argument for divine unicity which is based upon divine infinity. There Thomas is attempting to show that in created intellectual substances *esse* (the act of being) and "that which is" (essence) differ. His first three arguments attempt to show that there can only be one being which is identical with its act of being and, therefore, that in all others essence and act of being *(esse)* differ.[148]

According to the third argument, it is impossible for there to be two completely infinite instances of the act of being *(esse).* This follows because completely infinite *esse* embraces the total perfection of being. If such infinity were present in two different things, there would be no way in which one could be distinguished from the other. But subsisting *esse* must be infinite, since it is not limited by any receiving principle. Therefore it is impossible for there to be any other case of subsisting existence *(esse)* apart from the first being.[149]

This argument ultimately rests on a by now familiar central axiom of Thomas's metaphysics: unreceived *esse* is unlimited. Thomas joins this with the point that there would be no way in which completely unlimited or infinite instances of *esse* could be differentiated from one another. At the same time, this argument's location within this particular chapter of the *Summa contra Gentiles* reminds us that other arguments offered there and elsewhere by Aquinas to show that there can only be one instance of self-subsisting *esse* may also be regarded as arguments for divine uniqueness.[150]

We shall conclude our consideration of Thomas's argumentation for divine uniqueness by turning to his presentation in the *Compendium theologiae* I, c. 15 (ca. 1265–1267), which probably precedes the discussion in ST I, q. 11 by a year or so. There he offers two major metaphysical arguments. The first reminds us of his first argument in ST I, q. 11, a. 3. That whereby a common essence is rendered individual cannot be communicated to many. Thus, while there can be many human beings, it is not possible for this individual human being to be more than one. If an essence is individuated of itself and not by reason of anything else, it cannot belong to many subjects. But the divine essence is individuated of itself, since in God there is no distinction between his essence and the subject which exists (essentia et quod est). In support of this Thomas harks back to his proof in c. 10 that God is identical with his essence. Therefore there can only be one God.[151]

The second argument in c. 15 is still more interesting. Thomas now maintains that there are two ways in which a form may be multiplied: either by reason of differences (as when a generic form is so divided), or by being received in different subjects. But if there is a form which cannot be multiplied in the first way, i.e., through differences, and which does not exist in a distinct subject, it cannot be multiplied at all. For instance, writes Thomas as he appeals again to his familiar example, if whiteness could subsist apart from any receiving subject, it could only be one. But the divine essence is identical with the divine act of being (esse), as Thomas has shown in c. 11. Therefore, since the divine-esse is, as it were, a form that subsists in itself, it can only be one.[152]

Notwithstanding the fact that Thomas had offered argumentation for God's existence in c. 3 of the Compendium and additional argumentation to show that he is unmovable, eternal, and necessary of himself (cc. 4–6), he has judged it necessary to devote a separate treatment in c. 15 to show that God is unique. This parallels his procedure in SCG I and in ST I, and also confirms our judgment that he realized that without this additional argumentation his proof that God exists would not be complete. At the same time, as we have remarked before, this additional step was not necessary in his presentation in De ente, c. 4, because there his proof that there could at most be one subsisting esse is a necessary step in his argument for distinction between essence and act of being in everything else and also, therefore, for his metaphysical argument for God's existence.

Having now considered a number of Thomas's explicit arguments for divine uniqueness, we may ask whether they are also sufficient to show that the one uncaused efficient cause of all other being must itself be identified with the ultimate source of finality in the universe. (It can more easily be granted that the unmoved mover, the being that is necessary per se, and even the maximum being of the fourth way may be identified with the first efficient cause of the second way.) Thomas clearly intends this. Thus he has identified as one and the same God the first efficient cause and the ultimate source of finality in the universe, i.e., the intelligent being which is responsible for the presence of finality in purely natural agents. But has he proved this point?[153]

That this is not an idle question is suggested by his earlier recognition in *Summa contra Gentiles* I, c. 13 that if by arguing from motion one arrives at a mover which is responsible for the motion in the universe, one may still ask whether that mover acts for an end beyond itself. As the reader will recall, Thomas there reasoned that one must ultimately conclude to the existence of an unmoved mover which does not move for the sake of an end beyond itself. In that context he seems to have combined an argument based on efficient causation of motion with one grounded on the need for an unmoved mover in the absolute sense—that is, one that does not depend upon anything other than itself even in the order of final causality.[154]

Within the context of the fifth way and its parallels, however, Thomas's procedure is different. Here he reasons to the existence of some intelligent being in order to account for the fact that noncognitive agents act for an end. If this end is to influence them in their activity and if by definition they themselves are incapable of knowing such an end, it must preexist in cognitive fashion in some intelligence which efficiently causes such natures and imposes upon them their inclinations to their respective ends.[155] In other words, this intelligent being is also the first efficient cause of such natures. And if Thomas has successfully shown that there can be only one first un-caused efficient cause of all other things and that this being is intelligent, it will follow that there is also one supreme intelligent source responsible for the finality of natural agents precisely because the two are one and the same.[156]

Thomas offers explicit argumentation to show that God is intelligent. It will suffice here to mention ST I, q. 14, a. 1. There he reasons that the immateriality of a thing determines if and to what extent it is capable of knowing. This follows from his (and Aristotle's) view that a thing is capable of knowing to the extent that it can grasp the form of some other thing in immaterial fashion. Because God is supremely immaterial, as Thomas has argued above in q. 7, a. 1, he now concludes that God is capable of knowing to the maximum degree.[157]

Moreover, as Thomas explains in replying to the first objection in q. 14, a. 1, perfections as realized in creatures are attributed to God in more perfect fashion. Therefore, when a name taken from a perfection found in a creature is assigned to God, we must negate of it all that follows from the imperfect manner in which it is realized in the creature.[158] We may presume, therefore, that Thomas would permit us to argue in this fashion as well for the presence of intelligence in God. Underlying this reasoning is Thomas's conviction that there is some kind of similarity, in spite of great diversity, between an effect and its first cause.[159]

7. The Unity of the Five Ways

In concluding this discussion of Thomas's five ways, I would like to return to the third issue already mentioned at the end of Section 5: Does Thomas regard the five ways as five distinct arguments for God's existence, or rather as five different versions or perhaps steps of one and the same argument? From our examination of each of them, the answer to this should now be clear. It is true that there is considerable similarity between the five ways, in that each begins with some datum based on sense experience and each, by reasoning from effect to cause, concludes to the existence of a first and uncaused cause in order to account for the effect that served as the starting point. Nonetheless, because each way begins with a different starting point and because reasoning from effect to cause is applied in different ways in each of them, each should be regarded as a distinct argument. If one grants this, however, a related question remains: Has Thomas presented the five ways in accord with some systematic organizing principle and, if so, does he regard them as the only valid ways in which God's existence can be demonstrated? There is considerable diversity of opinion among Thomistic interpreters concerning these two questions.[160]

One approach, developed by A.-R. Motte among others, holds that the grouping of the five ways is first and foremost empirical (i.e., historical) in origin. It results from Thomas's reflection upon and usage of the different historical sources he had available. He drew upon various approaches in the previous philosophical and Christian tradition which he found most suitable for his purposes. He never claimed that the five ways can be reduced to a single logical scheme or that they are the only valid ways of proving God's existence.[161]

Others have tried to reduce the five ways to a single logical scheme and/or to claim that in Thomas's mind they exclude other possible ways in which one can reason to God's existence.[162] Our examination in *The Metaphysical Thought of Thomas Aquinas* of other forms of arguments for God's existence in Thomas's texts, including that offered in *De ente*, c. 4, to cite one of the most important, should make it unnecessary for us to devote more attention to the last-mentioned claim. The fact that he developed other arguments in other texts does not support the claim that he regarded the five ways as the only valid ways of proving God's existence. Nor do we have any textual evidence from the *Summa theologiae* or elsewhere to suggest that he later rejected those other approaches.

As for the former suggestion, that the five ways can be reduced to some single logical scheme, some have attempted to reduce all five of them in some way to the four causes.[163] Such attempts strike me as being forced.

First of all, there is the obvious point that there are five ways but only four supreme kinds of causes. Moreover, as just mentioned above, it is clear that all of the five ways in some way reason from an effect, presumably one that is given to us in the world of sense experience, to an uncaused cause of the same. Common to the first three ways is an appeal to some form of efficient causation, whether in the order of motion (the first way), or in the order of caused causes (the second way), or in the order of beings subject to generation and corruption and then of beings which are not subject to generation and corruption but which are still caused (the third way). The fourth way stands out because of its different point of departure—varying degrees of perfection in the observable universe. While its first stage seems to rely exclusively on formal exemplar causality, I have suggested above that if this argument is to be regarded as valid, the participated and therefore efficiently caused character of beings which enjoy limited degrees of perfection must also be introduced in that stage. Thomas himself does not explicitly do this in the argument's first stage, but he does introduce efficient causality in its second stage. As we have also seen, the fifth way is based on final causality in purely natural entities, a phenomenon which in Thomas's judgment points to the existence of a first intelligence which efficiently causes such agents together with their inclinations to act for ends. Finally, efforts to reduce the five ways to the four causes all founder, at least in my judgment, when they attempt to reduce one or another argument to the order of material causality.

In dealing with this issue it is enough for us to acknowledge these points along with our recognition of the fact that Thomas sees fit to complete these arguments in various ways in his discussion of the divine attributes. To impose upon the five ways some overriding logical plan which would account for their supposed interlocking symmetry is to go far beyond Thomas's text, and to risk distorting his thought. And as I have already indicated, to regard the five ways as excluding in Thomas's mind all other possible ways of arguing for God's existence runs counter to his procedure in other passages. Some, H. J. Johnson, for instance, have emphasized the point that in ST I, q. 2, a. 3 Thomas explicitly states that it can be proved in five ways that God exists.[164] To me this does not indicate that Thomas therefore regarded the number five as exhaustive and/or that he must have had in mind a systematic organizing plan such as the four causes in making this selection. I would simply note that his text does not state that God's existence can be proved in *only* five ways.

On a more positive note, however, I would conclude by observing that each of the five ways does contribute something to our understanding of God, although the different perspectives which they offer do not, of course, point to any real distinctions within God himself. From our standpoint, however, to recognize God as the unmoved mover, the uncaused cause, the absolutely necessary being, the maximumly perfect being, and the source of finality within the universe enriches our effort to arrive at some fuller understanding of him. And this, together with the historical sources which were available to Thomas, his critical evaluation of their philosophical power, and his customary method of offering more than one argument for a given conclusion, should suffice to explain why he offered more than one way in ST I, q. 2, a. 3, and, for that matter, more than one argument for God's existence elsewhere in his writings.

Notes

1. On Thomas's intention to write the *Summa* for beginners (in theology) see John F. Wippel, *The Metaphysical Thought of Thomas Aquinas* (Washington, D.C., 2000), Ch. X, n. 50, and the references there to Boyle, Torrell, and O'Meara. Also see James A. Weisheipl, *Friar Thomas D'Aquino* (Washington, D.C., 1983), pp. 218–19; M.-D. Chenu, *Introduction à l'étude de saint Thomas d'Aquin*, 2d ed. (Montréal-Paris, 1954), pp. 255–58. Weisheipl also observes that while Thomas managed to carry out his purpose of addressing beginning students in theology in the first part of his work, the second and third parts "are far from being a simple introduction" (pp. 222–23).

2. Some of this background is provided in Chapter 11 of my *The Metaphysical Thought of Thomas Aquinas*. It is good to bear in mind that Thomas himself sets his five ways within the background of his own philosophy and metaphysics. This in turns suggests that it is a highly questionable procedure simply to extract the five ways from their broader setting within Thomistic metaphysics and to expect them to, as it were, "stand on their own."

3. "Circa essentiam vero divinam, primo considerandum est an Deus sit . . ." (Leon. 4.27).

4. See Leon. 4.27–28, and the text cited in my *Metaphysical Thought of Thomas Aquinas*, Ch. X, n. 32. For his rejection of the Anselmian argumentation see ad 2 (p. 28).

5. Leon. 4.30. Note in particular: "Ex quolibet autem effectu potest demonstrari propriam causam eius esse . . . : quia, cum effectus dependeant a causa, posito effectu necesse est causam praeexistere. Unde Deum esse, secundum quod non est per se notum quoad nos, demonstrabile est per effectus nobis notos."

6. Leon. 4.30. If we may anticipate the first way for the sake of illustration, it begins with an effect, the fact that things are moved. By using the principle that whatever is moved is moved by something else, and by eliminating appeal to an infinite regress of moved movers as an adequate explanation, it concludes to the existence of a first and unmoved mover, or God. Here the effect—motion (the fact that things are moved)—serves as the middle term in the argument as Thomas presents it. However, in order for the argument to conclude explicitly to God's existence we must supply another syllogism such as this as suggested by Van Steenberghen: By the term "God" one means a being which is the First Mover of all motions which occur in this world. But such a first Mover exists.

Therefore God exists (*Le Problème de l'existence de Dieu dans les écrits de S. Thomas D'Aquino* (Louvain-La-Neuve, 1980), pp. 171–72; cf. p. 164). This syllogism uses a nominal definition, "First Mover," as one would expect from Thomas's reply to objection 2. But it is not this nominal definition which serves as a middle term in the first way as Thomas actually presents it, but rather an observable effect, i.e., that things are moved. Thomas's first way is really directed to establishing the minor of our supplied syllogism.

7. "Prima autem et manifestior via est, quae sumitur ex parte motus. Certum est enim, et sensu constat, aliqua moveri in hoc mundo. Omne autem quod movetur, ab alio movetur. Nihil enim movetur, nisi secundum quod est in potentia ad illud ad quod movetur: movet autem aliquid secundum quod est actu. Movere enim nihil aliud est quam educere aliquid de potentia in actum: de potentia autem non potest aliquid reduci in actum, nisi per aliquod ens in actu: sicut calidum in actu, ut ignis, facit lignum, quod est calidum in potentia, esse actu calidum, et per hoc movet et alterat ipsum. Non autem est possibile ut idem sit simul in actu et potentia secundum idem, sed solem secundum diversa: quod enim est calidum in actu, non potest simul esse calidum in potentia, sed est simul frigidum in potentia. Impossibile est ergo quod, secundum idem et eodem motu [for: *modo*], aliquid sit movens et motum, vel quod moveat seipsum. Omne ergo quod movetur, oporter ab alio moveri" (Leon. 4.31). Along with Van Steenberghen (op. cit., p. 167); Anthony Kenny, *The Five Ways* 7, n. I; and *Summa Theologiae*. Vol. 2: Existence and Nature of God (New York-London, 1964), (London, 1969), p. 12, I have substituted *motu for modo* in this text. However retention of the reading *modo* will not change the argument.

8. "Si ergo id a quo movetur, moveatur, oportet et ipsum ab alio moveri; et illud ab alio. Hic autem non est procedere in infinitum: quia sic non esset aliquod primum movens; et per consequens nec aliquod aliud movens, quia moventia secunda non movent nisi per hoc quod sunt mota a primo movente, sicut baculus non movet nisi per hoc quod est motus a manu. Ergo necesse est devenire ad aliquod primum movens, quod a nullo movetur: et hoc omnes intelligunt Deum" (Leon, 4.31).

9. For the texts from (SCG) I, c. 13, see Leonine edition pp. 10–11 (cited in my *Metaphysical Thought of Thomas Aquinas*, Ch. XI, n. 40 [for the first argument from motion]), and p. 12 (for the second argument).

10. *In III Phys.*, lect. 2, pp. 144–45, nn. 285–286. Note in particular: "Unde convenientissime Philosophus definit motum, dicens quod motus est *entelechia*, idest *actus existentis in potentia secundum quod buiusmodi*" (n. 285); "Accipit enim hic motum communiter pro mutatione, non autem stricte secundum quod dividitur contra generationem et corruptionem, ut dicetur in quinto" (n. 286).

11. *In V Phys.*, lect. 2, p. 322, n. 649: "Ubi considerandum est quod Aristoteles supra in tettio ubi motum definivit, accepit nomen *motus* secundum quod est commune omnibus speciebus mutationis. Et hoc modo accipit hic nomen *mutationis: motum* autem accipit magis stricte, pro quadam mutationis specie." See lect. 3, n. 661 (there are only three species of *motus*), n. 662 (there is no *motus* in the genus substance because motion taken strictly is between contraries, and there is no contrariety in the genus substance); lect. 4 (on the three kinds of *motus* taken strictly).

12. See my discussion in *The Metaphysical Thought of Thomas Aquinas*, Ch. XI, n. 54, and the texts quoted in n. 58 (from the first argument in SCG I, c. 13, and its third way of justifying the claim that whatever is moved is moved by something else); n. 76 (from the second argument in SCG I, c. 13, and its attempt to show that a perpetual self-mover of the outermost heavenly sphere, as apparently proposed by Aristotle, must still be moved in the order of final causality by a completely unmoved mover or God).

13. See *The Metaphysical Thought of Thomas Aquinas*, Ch. XI, nn. 58 and 59 and the corresponding part of my text.

14. See ibid., Ch. XI, n. 59. Cf. Scott MacDonald, "Aquinas's Parasitic Cosmological Argument," *Medieval Philosophy and Theology* I (1991), pp. 133–35.

15. As Thomas puts it: something cannot be reduced from potentiality to actuality except by some being in actuality (*ens in actu*). Insofar as a thing is in potency to a given act, it is not yet that act. See n. 7 above.

16. Some, Van Steenberghen for instance, would take *moveri* more broadly so as to apply to *motus* in the strict sense and to generation and corruption, i.e., to change in all its forms, and apparently even at the beginning of the argument. See *Le problème*, pp. 169–70.

17. See my discussion of this with reference to SCG I, c. 13 in my *Metaphysical Thought of Thomas Aquinas*, Ch. XI, nn. 62–64. Also see W. L. Rowe, *The Cosmological Argument* (Princeton, 1975), pp. 18–19, 32–38, where he reformulates and attempts to salvage what he regards as Thomas's question-begging formulation in the first and second ways. On the relation between God, the ultimate principal cause, and other causes see the interesting remarks by Gilson in his "Prolégomènes à la *prima via*," AHDLMA 30 (1964), pp. 64–65. In reading this one should bear in mind the two ways in which Thomas uses the notion of instrument. See my *Metaphysical Thought of Thomas Aquinas*, Ch. XI, n. 65.

18. See Van Steenberghen, *Le problème*, p. 180, n. 28. Others will be cited below.

19. For Henry see his Quodlibet 9, q. 5 ("Utrum voluntas moveat se ipsam"), R. Macken, ed. (Leuven, 1983), pp. 99–139; Quodlibet 10, q. 9, R. Macken, ed. (Leuven, 1981), pp. 220–55 ("Utrum subiectum per se possit esse causa sifficiens sui accidentis"). These date from Easter (i.e., during Lent) and Christmas (i.e., during Advent) of 1286. See Macken's edition of Henry's Quodlibet I (Leuven-Leiden, 1979), p. xvii. Henry seems to have developed his theory of virtual vs. formal willing in Quodlibet 10, or by that time. For discussion of Henry's views see Macken, "La volonté humaine, faculté plus élevée que l'intelligence selon Henri de Gand," in: *Rescherches de Théologie ancienne et médiévale* 42 (1975), pp. 5–51; "Heintich von Gent im Gespräch mit seinen Zeitgenossen über die menschiche Freiheit," in: *Franziskanische Studien* 59 (1977), pp. 125–82, especially pp. 141–58; R. Effler, *John Duns Scotus and the Principle "Omne quod movetur ab alio movetur,"* pp. 15, 64–66; Wippel, *The Metaphysical Thought of Godfrey of Fontaines*, pp. 180–81, 190–91.

20. See Effler, op. cit., pp. 16–17, and throughout the rest of his study. It should be noted, however, that with Duns Scotus, Effler interprets the subject of the principle of motion to mean "everything which is in motion" rather than "whatever is moved." See pp. 33–35. This, of course, runs counter to Thomas's understanding of the principle as I read him.

21. For a helpful survey see J. Weisheipl, "Galileo and the Principle of Inertia," Ch. III of his *Nature and Motion in the Middle Ages* (Washington DC., 1985), pp. 49–63. In particular Weisheipl considers the views of William Whewell, Ernst Mach, Pierre Duhem, Alexandre Koyré, Anneliese Maier, and Stillman Drake. Each of these thinkers also assigns a greater or lesser role (considerably lesser according to Koyré) to Galileo in discovering the principle of inertia. As Weisheipl sums up his survey: ". . . all of these historians are unanimous in seeing a radical incompatibility between Aristotle's demand for causes of motion and Galileo's (and modern science's) rejection of efficient causes. From the philosophical point of view perhaps Anneliese Maier's statement of the problem is typical: "Aristotle's principle 'Everything that is moved, is moved by another' had to be rejected to allow for the modern principle of inertia" (pp. 62–63).

22. Art. 1 is directed to this question: "Utrum voluntas moveatur ab intellectu." See Leon. 6.74–75. From this discussion note in particular: "Motio autem ipsius subjecti est ex agente aliquo. . . . Et ideo ex hac parte voluntas movet alias potentias animae ad suos actus. . . . Sed objectum movet, determinando actum, ad modum principii formalis. . . . Et ideo isto modo motionis intellectus movet voluntatem, sicut praesentans ei obiectum suum." Also see ad 3: ". . . dicendum quod voluntas movet intellectum quantum ad exercitium actus . . . Sed quantum ad determinationem actus, quae est ex parte obiecti, intellectus movet voluntatem. . . . Et sic patet quod non est idem movens et motum secundum idem." On Thomas's distinction between the exercise and the specification of an act see D. Gallagher, "Free Choice and Free Judgment in Thomas Aquinas," *Archiv für Geschichte der Philosophie* 76 (1994), pp. 262–70.

23. On the development in Thomas's thinking on the causality exercised by the intellect and its object on the will, see O. Lottin, *Psychologie et morale aux XIIIe siècles* (Louvain-Gembloux, 1942), pp. 226–43 (on earlier writings), 252–62. For additional references concerning this see Gallagher, "Free Choice," p. 250, n. 10. Torrell dates ST I–II in 1271 and *De malo*, q. 6 around 1270. Whether one can establish the chronological priority of either of these sources over the other on the grounds of internal evidence is doubtful, in my judgment, although some have attempted this. See Gallagher, p. 261, n. 40 for references. For our purposes the teaching of these two sources is the same, but different from earlier discussions in *De veritate*, SCG, and ST I. ST I–II, q. 9, a. 3 is explicitly directed to this question: "Utrum voluntas moveat seipsam." In developing his answer Thomas draws an analogy between the will and the intellect. In knowing principles the intellect can reduce itself from potency to act as regards its knowledge of conclusions that follow from those principles. In like fashion the will, in that it wills an end, moves itself to will the means to that end. See his reply to objection 1: ". . . dicendum quod voluntas non secundum idem movet et movetur. Unde nec secundum idem est in actu et in potentia, Sed inquantum actu vult finem, reducit se de potentia in actum respectu eorum quae sunt ad finem, ut scilicet actu ea velit" (Leon. 4.78).

24. Leon. 6.78–79. Note in particular: "Sed eo modo quo movetur quantum ad exercitium actus, adhuc necesse est ponere voluntatem ab aliquo principio exteriori moveri. Omne enim quod quandoque est agens in actu et quandoque

in potentia, indiget moveri ab aliquo movente. Manifestum est autem quod voluntas incipit velle aliquid, cum hoc prius non vellet. Necesse est ergo quod ab aliquo moveatur ad volendum. . . . Unde necesse est ponere quod in primum motum voluntatis voluntas prodeat ex instinctu alicuius exterioris moventis, ut Aristoteles concludit in quodam capitulo *Ethicae Eudemicae*." For Aristotle see *Eudemian Ethics*, Bk VII, c. 14 (1248a 25–32). Also see Thomas, ibid., ad I, ad 3.

25. See *Quaestiones disputatae De malo*, q. 6 (Leon. 23.148:308–149:415). Note in particular: "Sed cum voluntas non semper voluerit consiliari, necesse est quod ab aliquo moveatur ad hoc quod velit consiliari; et si quidem a se ipsa, necesse est iterum quod motum voluntatis praecedat consilium et consilium praecedat actus voluntatis; et cum hoc in infinitum procedere non possit, necesse est ponere quod quantum ad primum motum voluntatis moveatur voluntas cuiuscumque non semper actu volentis ab aliquo exteriori, cuius instinctu voluntas velle incipiat." After concluding that it is God who first moves the will and intellect, Thomas comments: "Qui cum omnia moveat secundum rationem mobilium, ut levia sirsum et gravia deorsum, etiam voluntatem movet secundum eius conditionem, non ex necessitate sed ut indeterminate se habentem ad multa" (p. 149:410–415). Also see ad 3 for this final point (p. 150:498–511).

26. Thomas introduces this particular part of his discussion by observing that God does not operate in natural things in such fashion that the natural thing itself would do nothing. In order to explain just how it is that God operates in the operations performed either by a natural agent or by a created will, he then introduces the fourfold way indicated in our text. See ed. cit., pp. 57–58. In summing this up again at the end of the corpus of this same article, he makes it clear that he is applying this fourfold way in which God is the cause of created agents to volitions as well: ". . . sequetur quod ipse in quolibet operante immediate operetur, non exclusa operatione voluntatis et naturae" (p. 58).

27. Cf. the text from ST I, q. 105, a. 5, cited in n. 28. Cf. *De veritate*, q. 24, a. I, ad 5, cited in my *Metaphysical Thought of Thomas Aquinas*, Ch. XI, n. 65.

28. See ST I, q. 105, a. 5 (Leon. 5.4/6). Cf. ad 3. Here Thomas is developing his answer to the question: "Utrum Deus operetur in omni operante." See my *Metaphysical Themes in Thomas Aquinas* (Washington, D.C., 1984) p. 260. Also see my remark there in n. 56 about Thomas's views concerning God as the proper cause of *esse*.

29. For other texts on this correlation between created agents and God see, for instance, SCG III, c. 70 (ed. cit., p. 306). This does not mean that one part of the effect is caused by God and another by the created agent, but rather that the entire effect is to be assigned to God (as principal cause) and to the created natural agent (as an instrument). For additional texts where Thomas applies this to freely acting created agents, see SCG I, c. 68 (p. 64); SCG III, cc. 88, 89 (pp. 331–32). Note that Thomas concludes his discussion in c. 89 by appealing to the text from the *Eudemian Ethics* VII, c. 14. For texts where Thomas attempts to reconcile this theory of divine agency with human freedom see, for instance, *De potentia*, q. 3, a. 7, ad 13; ad 14 (ed. cit., p. 59); ST I, q. 19, a. 8, and ad 3 (Leon. 4.244); ST I, q. 83, a. 1, ad 3 (Leon. 5.307); ST I–II, q. 10, a. 4, and ad 1 (Leon.

6.89); *De malo*, q. 6 (as cited above in n. 25). For discussion see my *Metaphysical Themes*, pp. 258–63.

30. R. Garrigou-Lagrange seems to be of another opinion concerning this. In his *God: His Existence and His Nature*, Vol. 1, p. 268, after presenting Thomas's proof from motion, he comments: "This proof from motion may be exemplified in another way by considering motions of the spiritual order, as St. Thomas has done in the article of his *Summa* entitled, 'Whether the Will is Moved by any External Principle?' (Ia IIae, q. 9, a. 4)." However, Thomas does not present this kind of motion in that context as the starting point for his proof for God's existence. On the other hand, Garrigou-Language makes some interesting points in his discussion of objections to the argument from motion (see pp. 270–87), although his treatment is not primarily historical.

31. Especially helpful with reference to this is Weisheipl's "The Principle *Omne quod movetur*," in his *Nature and Motion* Ch IV, pp. 75–97. Also see there Ch II ("Natural and Compulsory Movement"); Ch V ("The Specter of *motor coniunctus* in Medieval Physics"). For Thomas's views on the generating principle as the moving principle or cause of the natural motions of physical bodies see pp. 90–93. Among the various passages he cites from Thomas note: *In VIII Phys.*, lect, 8 (Maggiòlo ed.), p. 542, n. 1036 (an excellent summarizing passage on which also see my *Metaphysical Thought of Thomas Aquinas*, Ch. XI, n. 57); *In II Phys.*, lect. 1, p. 74, n. 144 (for fuller discussion see Weisheipl, p. 19, n. 78); *De potentia*, q. 3, a. 7 (ed. cit., p. 57). For an interesting critique of Weisheipl's interpretation of Thomas's explanation of the natural motions of physical bodies see D. B. Twetten, "Back to Nature in Aquinas," *Medieval Philosophy and Theology* 5 (1996), pp. 205–43. On Thomas's acceptance of Aristotle's account of the motion of projectiles see Weisheipl, *Nature and Motion*, p. 31, n. 30; pp. 64–66. For Thomas see *In VIII Phys.*, lect. 22, pp. 621–22, nn. 1161–1163; *In III De caelo*, lect. 7, p. 305, n. 591. For another succinct summarizing text see *De potentia*, q. 3, a. 11 (ed. cit., p. 75).

32. See n. 21 above.

33. In connection with this Kenny comments that to explain the fall of such a body by the gravitational pull of the earth (with Newton) "would seem to be more favourable to Aristotle's principle than his own mechanics are" (*The Five Ways*, p. 16, n. 1). However, this seeming support from Newtonian mechanics for the Aristotelian-Thomistic principle proves to be a mixed blessing, as Kenny also points out: "For the gravitational attraction of two bodies is mutual, whereas the Aristotelian relation of 'moving' must be an asymmetrical one if it is to lead to an unmoved mover" (p. 30). Hence it seems better, if one would defend Thomas's principle of motion, to interpret it in the case of falling bodies as he did by applying it to the generating principle and by regarding this as the mover. For another succinct exposition of Thomas's theory as applied to natural and violent motion see A. Moreno, "The Law of Inertia and the Principle *Quidquid Movetur ab Alio Movetur*," *The Thomist* 38 (1974), pp. 316–25.

34. See Newton, *Optics*, Bk III, Part I (in Great Books of the Western World, Vol. 34, p. 540): "By this principle [*vis inertiae*] alone there never could have been any motion in the world. Some other principle was necessary for putting bodies into motion; and now they are in motion, some other principle is necessary for

conserving the motion." Cited by William Wallace, "Newtonian Antinomies against the *Prima Via*," *The Thomist* 19 (1956), p. 185; and by Kenny, *The Five Ways*, p. 28. For Descartes see his *Principles of Philosophy*, II, 36: "As far as the general (and first) cause is concerned, it seems obvious to me that this is none other than God Himself, who, (being all-powerful) in the beginning created matter with both movement and rest; and now maintains in the sum total of matter, by his normal participation, the same quantity of motion and rest as He placed in it at that time" (trans. and notes by V. Rodger Miller and R. P. Miller [Dordrecht-Boston-London, 1983], p. 58). In the immediately following context, Descartes argues for this from God's immutability and constancy. See II, 37 for his "first law of nature": "that each thing, as far as is in its power, always remains in the same state; and that consequently, when it is once moved, it always continues to move" (p. 59). See II, 38 for his application of this to projectile motion (pp. 59–60). By seeking for some causal explanation for the continuation of such motion, today's defender of the Thomistic principle will be asking for a cause to account for more than the beginning of that motion.

35. For such a suggestion see J. Maritain, *Approaches to God* (London, 1955), pp. 24–27. Maritain reasons that if we do take the principle of inertia as established and if hypothetically we grant "it a meaning beyond the mere empiriological analysis of phenomena," it will be enough to take it as indicating that "Every body which undergoes a change *in regard to its state of rest of motion* changes under the action of another thing" (p. 26). For him this will suffice to preserve Thomas's principle that whatever is moved is moved by something else.

36. See Wallace, "Newtonian Antinomies against the *Prima Via*," pp. 173–86, especially p. 180.

37. See Weisheipl, *Nature and Motion*, pp. 31–33 (though it was first developed by the Franciscan Francis de Marchia, and then by Jean Buridan, presumably working independently, Thomists such as Capreolus and Domingo de Soto claimed that the impetus theory of motion was also Thomas's position); pp. 66–69, 95–96.

38. See Weisheipl, op. cit., pp. 36–42, 48, 49, 269; Moreno, "The Law of Inertia," pp. 307–13; Wallace, "Newtonian Antinomies against the *Prima Via*," pp. 178–80. Also cf. Kenny's presentation and discussion of what he describes as the "counter-attack with Mach" (op. cit., pp. 29–31).

39. Cf. E. Gilson, *Elements of Christian Philosophy* (Garden City, New York, 1960), p. 63: "To be both in act and in potency in the same respect would amount to being and not being in the same respect and at the same time." For an effort to free Thomas's argument from motion from an outmoded physical theory see MacDonald, "Aquinas's Parasitic Argument," pp. 135–38, where he overcomes projectile motion as a counterexample to the motion principle by restricting motion as used in the argument to alteration and increase and decrease in quantity. While this approach is philosophically defensible, it may grant more than is necessary to the alleged counterexample.

40. See Owens, "Immobility and Existence for Aquinas," in *St. Thomas Aquinas on the Existence of God* (Albany, 1980), pp. 219–20; "The Conclusion of the *Prima Via*," in ibid., pp. 148, 158–60, 166–68. Cf. Ch. XI, n. 79 above. Also see the

discussion concerning this occasioned by T. Kondoleon's review of Knasas's *The Preface to Thomistic Metaphysics* in his "The Start of Metaphysics," *The Thomist* 58 (1994), pp. 121–30; followed by Knasas, "Thomistic Existentialism and the Proofs *Ex Motu at Contra Gentiles* I, c. 13," *The Thomist* 59 (1995), pp. 591–615; and Kondoleon, "The Argument from Motion and the Argument for Angels: A Reply to John F. X. Knasas," *The Thomist* 62 (1998), pp. 269–90. Knasas defends and develops Owens's position on this. For a review and critique both of what he calls the "Physical" and the "Existential" readings of the first way see D. B. Twetten's "Clearing a Way for Aquinas: How the Proof from Motion Concludes to God," in *Proceedings of the American Catholic Philosophical Association* 70 (1996), pp. 260–64. See pp. 267–71 for his proposed "Metaphysical" reading, which in various respects is close to what I am proposing here.

41. See n. 8 above.

42. For discussion and reference to others such as Cajetan, S. Vanni Rovighi, Garrigou-Lagrange, and M. Cocci, see Van Steenberghen, *Le problème*, pp. 178–80. Also see MacDonald, "Aquinas's Parasitic Argument," pp. 146–55, who is struck by the fact that the first way establishes the existence of an unmoved mover, but not an immovable mover. To achieve this he believes it must be completed by other ways, such as the third and the fifth.

43. For Thomas see ST I, q. 3: "Cognito de aliquo an sit, inquirendum restat quomodo sit, ut sciatur de eo quid sit. Sed quia de Deo scire non possumus quid sit, sed quid non sit, non possumus considerate de Deo quomodo sit, sed potius quomodo non sit. Primo ergo considerandum est quomodo non sit; secundo, quomodo a nobis cognoscatur; tertio, quomodo nominetur" (Leon. 4.35). The lingering question is this: At this point in ST I, that is, after completing his five ways, does Thomas think that he has already demonstrated that only one God exists?

44. "Secunda via est ex ratione causae efficientis. Invenimus enim in istis sensibilibus esse ordinem causarum efficientium: nec tamen invenitur, nec est possibile, quod aliquid sit causa efficiens sui ipsius; quia sic esset prius seipso, quod est impossibile" (Leon. 4.31).

45. "Non autem est possibile quod in causis efficientibus procedatur in infinitum. Quia in omnibus causis efficientibus ordinatis, primum est causa medii, et medium est causa ultimi, sive media sint plura sive unum tantum: remota autem causa, removetur effectus: ergo, si non fuerit primum in causis efficientibus, non erit ultimum nec medium. Sed si procedatur in inifitum in causis efficientibus, non erit prima causa efficiens: et sic non erit nec effectus ultimus, nec causae efficientes mediae; quod patet esse falsum. Ergo est necesse ponere aliquam causam efficientem primam: quam omnes Deum nominant" (Leon 4.31).

46. See nn. 10, II above for references. Cf. Van Steenberghen, op. cit., p. 185.

47. For discussion of this see my *Metaphysical Thought of Thomas Aquinas*, Ch. XI, Section 2.

48. In the second way, however, from the very beginning of the argument the focus is on causes that are caused rather than on effects (as in *De ente*, c. 4) or on things that are *moved* (as in the first way). In those two arguments Thomas subsequently shifts the focus to caused causes or to moved movers when he deals with the issue of an infinite regress.

49. See the remarks in my *Metaphysical Thought of Thomas Aquinas*, Ch. XI, Section 2 (*De ente*, c. 4); Ch. XI, Section 4 (first argument, from motion, second and third arguments, against infinite regress); and Ch. XII, Section 1 (first way).

50. See the final part of the text as quoted above in n. 45.

51. In this discussion I am assuming that my way of interpreting the general procedure in c. 4 of the *De ente* is correct. See my *Metaphysical Thought of Thomas Aquinas*, Ch. V, Section 1.

52. "Tertia via est sumpta ex possibili et necessario: quae talis est. Invenimus enim in rebus quaedam quae sunt possibilia esse et non esse: cum quaedum inveniantur generari et corrumpi, et per consequens possibilia esse et non esse. Impossible est autem omnia quae sunt, talia [omit: semper] esse: quia quod possibile est non esse, quandoque non est. Si igitur omnia sunt possibilia non esse, aliquando nihil fuit in rebus. Sed si hoc est [Van Steenberghen: esset] verum, etiam nunc nihil esset: quia quod non est, non incipit esse nisi per aliquid quod est; si igitur nihil fuit ens, impossibile fuit quod aliquid inciperet esse, et sic modo nihil esset: quod patet esse falsum. Non ergo omnia entia sunt possibilia: sed oportet aliquid esse necessarium in rebus" (Leon. 4.31). On the omission of *semper* from the text in accord with the majority of manuscripts see Van Steenberghen, *Le problème*, pp. 188–89; T. O'Brien, *Metaphysics and the Existence of God*, (Washington, D.C., 1960), pp. 226–27, n. 83; J. F. K. Knasas, "Making Sense of the *Tertia Via*," *New Scholasticism* 54 (1980), pp. 488–89; Kenny, *The Five Ways*, p. 55. With Van Steenberghen and O'Brien, I think it should be omitted. So, too, did Godfrey of Fontaines, if one may judge from the *abbreviatio* of the third way which he himself transcribed in the margin of a manuscript in his personal library, Paris, Bibl. Nat. 15.819, fol. 226r; "Impossibile est enim omnia possibilia esse, quia quod possibile est non esse, quandoque non est."

53. See my *Metaphysical Thought of Thomas Aquinas*, Ch. XI, nn. 96, 97.

54. "Omne autem necessarium vel habet causam suae necessitatis aliunde, vel non habet. Non est autem possibile quod procedatur in infinitum in necessariis quae habent causam suae necessitatis, sicut nec in causis efficientibus, ut probatum est. Ergo necesse est ponere aliquid quod sit per se necessarium, non habens causam necessitatis aliunde, sed quod est causa necessitatis aliis: quod omnes dicunt Deum" (Leon. 4.31).

55. For references to many of these see J. Owens, "*Quandoque* and *Aliquando* in Aquinas's *Tertia Via*," pp. 447–75; Kansas, "Making Sense of the *Tertia Via*," pp. 476–511; Van Steenberghen, *Le problème*, p. 205, n. 37. Cf. my *Metaphysical Thought of Thomas Aquinas*, Ch. XI, nn. 101, 102, 104. See T. K. Connolly, "The Basis of the Third Proof for the Existence of God," *The Thomist* 17 (1954), pp. 281–349, especially pp. 281–99, for a survey of much of the earlier literature concerning this.

56. On this see T. Miyakawa, "The Value and the Meaning of the 'Tertia Via' of St. Thomas Aquinas," *Aquinas* 6 (1963), pp. 250–51.

57. Though I have already cited the troublesome text above in n. 52, I will repeat the two troublesome sentences here and in n. 58. The first one reads: "Impossibile est autem omnia quae sunt, talia esse: quia quod possibile est non esse, quandoque non est." For some who hold that Thomas means to say that such a possible will be nonexistent at some point of time in the future see U.

Degl'Innocenti, "La validità della 'terza via'," *Doctor Communis* 7 (1954), pp. 41–70, especially 51–56; Kenny, *The Five Ways*, pp. 57–58; Gilson, *The Christian Philosophy of St. Thomas Aquinas* (New York: 1956) p. 69. For some who take Thomas as wishing to say that any such possible being must have been nonexistent before it began to exist and who therefore see his statement as referring to the past see L. Chambat, "La 'Tertia Via' dans saint Thomas et Aristote," *Revue thomiste*, n. s. 10 (1927), pp. 334–38, especially 335; J. Bobik, "The First Part of the Third Way," Owens: *New Scholasticism* 54 (1980), pp. 142–60, esp. 144–45; J. Owens, "*Quandoque* and *Aliquando* in Aquinas' *Tertia Via*" Bobik: *Philosophical Studies* 17 (1968), pp. 457–59; Van Steenberghen, *Le problème*, pp. 192–98. Still others give a nontemporal reading to *quandoque* and *aliquando* (see the following sentence in Thomas's text), meaning thereby that his purpose is rather to show that any possible being, if left to its own devices, would be incapable of existing and therefore nonexistent. See, for instance, H. Holstein, "L'origine aristotélicienne de la 'tertia via' de saint Thomas," *Revue philosophique de Louvain* 48 (1950), pp. 366–67; Knasas, "Making Sense of the *Tertia Via*," pp. 486–89.

58. "Si igitur omnia sunt possibilia non esse, aliquando nihil fuit in rebus" (as cited in n. 52 above).

59. For some who would read the argument this way see Bobik, Owens, and Van Steenberghen as cited above in n. 57.

60. This point is brought out effectively by Bobik in his "The First Part of the Third Way," pp. 157–58. If a possible as Thomas here uses it is "a thing such by its nature that its non-existence both *precedes* and *follows* its existence," it is the period of preceding nonexistence which is essential for this step in the third way. Here the expression *quandoque* cannot mean "after," since the proof uses as its point of departure actually existing things which are capable of existing and not existing. "By elimination, therefore, 'quandoque' must mean *before*." Also see Owens, "*Quandoque* and *Aliquando* in Aquinas' *Tertia Via*," pp. 457–58, 472–73, n. 38.

61. See, for instance, Owens, "*Quandoque* and *Aliquando*," especially pp. 461–64, and p. 463, n. 26, for a defense and for references to other recent discussions of this. Also see L. Dewan, "The Distinctiveness of St. Thomas' 'Third Way'," *Dialogue* 19 (1980), 201–18.

62. Owens appeals to the Aristotelian procedure in *Metaphysics* XII, c. 6, according to which eternal motion and time are not destructible and presuppose the existence of separate substances. "The suicidal supposition that all things are possibles excludes *ipso facto* any eternal succession" (p. 461). "In the Aristotelian series no series can go backward eternally, if all things are possibles" (p. 462). In his effort to defend the argument against the charge of a quantifier shift, he contends that the argument does not reason that because "*each* possible was non-existent at one time, therefore all things if possibles were together non-existent at one time." Rather it reasons that "universal possibility ('all have the possibility for non-existence') entails universal non-existence" (p. 464). But how is this point demonstrated? Owens argues that to propose an infinite regress in time of possible beings would presume granting the reality of something necessary. In order to establish this, however, he is introducing a different kind of reasoning which in fact leads him to view this reasoning as essentially the same

as that in SCG I, c. 15 (see pp. 464–66). In my judgment, however, this reasoning is missing from the text of the third way.

63. In fact, the reformulation is so pronounced that the third way will no longer be the third way of ST I, q. 2, a. 3. Moreover, unlike Owens (pp. 465–66), I do not regard the third way as it stands in ST I, q. 2, a. 3 as essentially the same argument as that presented in SCG I, c. 15. The presence of the temporal references in the first part of the third way and their absence from the first part of the argument in SCG I, c. 15 indicate an essential distinction between the two. For additional discussion of this difficulty with the third way, i.e., an apparent quantifier shift as he describes it, see Kenny, *The Five Ways*, pp. 63–65. While I have differed with Kenny's view that *quando* should be taken as referring to some time in the future rather than to the past, his criticisms of the passage now under consideration must be taken seriously. For some others who reject the validity of this step in Thomas's procedure see Bobik, "The First Part of the Third Way," pp. 158–59; T. Pater, "The Question of the Validity of the *Tertia Via*," in Vol. 2 of *Studies in Philosophy and the History of Philosophy* (Washington, D.C., 1963), pp. 137–77 (for an extended critique of both of the difficult statements in the argument in light of the defenses offered by Connolly and Del'Innocenti). On the other hand, D. O'Donoghue seems to be oblivious to this difficulty. See his "An Analysis of the *Tertia Via* of St. Thomas," *The Irish Theological Quarterly* 20 (1953), pp. 129–52.

64. For a brief résumé of earlier twentieth-century scholarship concerning Aquinas's sources for his third way see Knasas, "Making Sense of the *Tertia Via*," pp. 477–80. For some who would see Maimonides as the major source see P. Gény, "À propos des preuves thomistes de l'existence de Dieu," *Revue de philosophie* 24 (1931), pp. 575–601, esp. 586–87; Gilson, *Le thomisme*, 6th ed. (Paris, 1965), pp. 79–81, apparently agreeing with C. Baeumker that here Thomas follows Maimonides step by step. For Baeumker see his *Witelo, Ein Philosoph und Naturforscher des XIII. Jahrhunderts* (Beiträge zur Geschichte der Philosophie des Mittelalters, III–2 [Münster, 1908]), p. 338. For Maimonides see *The Guide of the Perplexed*, S. Pines, trans. (Chicago, 1963), Bk II, c. 1, pp. 247–48; *Dux seu Director dubitantium aut perplexorum*, Bk II, c. 2, fol. 40v. While there are similarities between Maimonides' presentation of this argument and that found in Aquinas, there are also significant differences between the two versions. Hence other writers have rightly concluded that Thomas's argument is not reducible to that of Maimonides. See, for instance, Chambat, "La 'Tertia Via'," pp. 334, 338; Holstein, "L'origine aristotélicienne de la 'tertia via'," p. 361. Some have singled out Aristotle's *De caelo*, I, c. 12 as Thomas's source. See Connolly, "The Basis of the Third Proof," pp. 312–49, with special emphasis on Thomas's procedure in his Commentary on *De caelo* I (*lectiones* 22–29); O'Donoghue, "An Analysis of the *Tertia Via* of St. Thomas," pp. 129–51 (*De caelo* along with some other Aristotelian texts). For criticism of this effort to interpret the third way by means of Thomas's Commentary on *De caelo* I see Knasas, "Making Sense of the *Tertia Via*," pp. 480–89. Still others single out *Metaphysics* XII, c. 6. See Chambat, pp. 335–38; Holstein, pp. 361–67; Knasas, p. 489. Yet, the parallelism is by no means perfect. Hence it seems best to acknowledge that while Aristotle is surely a source, Thomas is not simply repeating either his text or that of Maimonides (or Avicenna). See

Owens, "*Quandoque* and *Aliquando*," p. 469; and n. 31 on Avicenna. In his "The Distinctiveness of St. Thomas' 'Third Way'," p. 213, n. 5, Dewan has proposed a text from Albert the Great's Commentary on the *Metaphysics* as another possible source for Thomas. See *Metaphysica* II.2 (Cologne, ed., 16.2, p. 482:40–71). While this is possible, the similarities between Thomas's text and Albert's can just as likely be traced back to their common sources, especially Aristotle and Maimonides.

65. For Kenny see *The Five Ways*, p. 67, and his discussion of Hume's critique in his *Treatise*. For the latter see *A Treatise of Human Nature*, L. A. Selby-Bigge, ed.; 2nd rev. edition by P. H. Nidditch (Oxford, 1978), Bk I, Pt. III, Section 3 (pp. 78–80).

66. See my *Metaphysical Thought of Thomas Aquinas*, Chapter XI, nn. 17, 18. Cf. n. 19.

67. In the argumentation in *De ente*, c. 4 Thomas has already established real distinction of essence and *esse* in the beings with which he is concerned. In the third way he does not presuppose this point. For Thomas's own version of the first step in SCG I, c. 15, see Ch. XI, Section 4, n. 95.

68. See the text as cited above in n. 54.

69. As will be seen below in Section 6, Thomas's procedure in q. II indicates that he was fully aware of this.

70. For a listing of various suggested explanations of this and for discussion see Van Steenberghen, *Le problème*, pp. 203–5.

71. See my *Metaphysical Thought of Thomas Aquinas*, Ch. XI, Section I and Section 4 (n. 87).

72. "Quarta via sumitur ex gradibus qui in rebus inveniuntur. Invenitur enim in rebus aliquid magis et minus bonum, et verum, et nobile: et sic de aliis huiusmodi. Sed *magis et minus* dicuntur de diversis secundum quod appropinquant diversimode ad aliquid quod maxime est: sicut magis calidum est, quod magis approximant maxime calido. Est igitur aliquid quod est verissimum, et optimum, et nobilissimum, et per consequens maxime ens: nam quae sunt maxime vera, sunt maxime entia, ut dicitur II *Metaphy*." (Leon. 4.32). I have followed a suggestion by Van Steenberghen by assuming that the term *tale* is to be understood after *maxime est* in the third sentence. The logic of the argument demands this ("But more and less are said of different things insofar as they approach in different fashion something which is [such: inserted] to a maximum degree"). See *Le problème*, p. 213. For the text from Aristotle see his *Metaphysics* II, c. I (993b 30–31). Fabro notes that both here and in the reference to Aristotle's *Metaphysics* in the second stage of the argument Thomas has in mind this same general passage from *Metaphysics* II (see 9936 25–31); but in the earlier version which appears in SCG I, c. 13, Thomas had referred not only to this text in Aristotle but to another from *Metaphysics* IV, c. 4 (1008b 31–1009a 2). For Fabro see his "Sviluppo, significato e valore della 'IV Via'," *Doctor Communis* 7 (1954), p. 78; cf. p. 75, n. 5. In citing Aristotle's *Metaphysics* (993b 30–31) Thomas has converted the references to *vera* and *entia*, but legitimately so in light of the convertibility of ontological truth and being.

73. Leon. 22.1.5:161–6:200. Cf. Thomas's reply to objection 4: ". . . dicendum quod verum est dispositio entis non quasi addens aliquam naturam nec quasi

exprimens aliquem specialem modum entis sed aliquid quod generaliter invenitur in omni ente, quod tamen nomine entis non exprimitur . . ." (p. 7:229–234). Cf. ad 6. Cf., my *Metaphysical Thought of Thomas Aquinas*, Aertsen, *Medieval Philosophy and the Transcendentals* (Aertsen: Leiden-New York-Cologne, 1996), c. 6 (pp. 243–89); Wippel, "Truth in Thomas Aquinas," *Review of Metaphysics* 43 (1989), pp. 307–21.

74. "Quod autem dicitur maxime tale in aliquo genere, est causa omnium quae sunt illius generis: sicut ignis, qui est maxime calidus, est causa omnium calidorum, ut in codem libro dicitur. Ergo est aliquid quod omnibus entibus est causa esse, et bonitatis, et cuiuslibet perfectionis: et hoc dicimus Deum" (Leon. 4.32). For Aristotle see n. 72 above.

75. On Thomas's derivation of the transcendentals see my *Metaphysical Thought of Thomas Aquinas*, Ch. VI, Section 5. Goodness expresses the agreement of being with the appetitive power of the soul in that the good is that which all things desire (Leon. 22.1.5:156–159). On the transcendental character of goodness also see ST I, q. 5, a. 1 (*bonum* and *ens* are the same in reality though they differ according to reason); a. 2 (in terms of its intelligible content being [ens] is prior to goodness); a. 3 (every being insofar as it is being is good). On this final point also see Thomas's *In De Hebdomadibus*, lect. 3 (Leon. 50.275:40–277:143); lect. 4 (pp. 279:III–280:160). Cf. Thomas's *De malo*, q. 1, a. 1 (Leon. 23.5–6) and a. 2 (pp. 10:130–11:195); *De veritate*, q. 21, a. 1 (Leon, 22.3.592:89–594:244); a. 2 (p. 596: 61–96). The whole of q. 21 is highly recommended to the reader. Also see Aertsen, *Medieval Philosophy and the Transcendentals*, c. 7, esp. pp. 299–319.

76. For discussion of Thomas's hierarchical view of the universe of created being see, for instance, Gilson, *The Christian Philosophy of St. Thomas Aquinas*, Part Two (London, 1961), pp. 147–248; J. de Finance, *Être et agir* (de Finance: 2nd ed. Rome, 1960), pp. 314–55; J. Legrand, *L'univers et l'homme dans la philosophie de saint Thomas*, Vol. I (Brussels, 1946); J. H. Wright, *The Order of the Universe in the Theology of St. Thomas Aquinas* (Rome, 1957); O. Blanchette, *The Perfection of the Universe according to Aquinas* (University Park, Pa., 1992).

77. On the convertibility of truth and being see *De veritate*, q. 1, a. 1 and ad 4 (cited in n. 73 above). Also see his reply to objection 5: ". . . concludit Philosophus quod idem est ordo alicui rei in esse et veritate, ita scilicet quod ubi invenitur quod est maxime ens, est maxime verum" (Leon. 22.1.7:242–245). For Aristotle see *Metaphysics* II, c. 1 (cited in n. 72 above). Here Thomas has not converted *ens* and *verum*. He distinguishes truth as it exists in the intellect (what we may refer to as "logical" truth) from truth of being ("ontological" truth). In addition to *De veritate*, q. 1, a. 1, see a. 2 (Leon. 22.1.9); *In I Sent.*, d. 19, q. 5, a. 1 (note in particular: ". . . verum per prius dicitur de veritate intellectus, et de enuntiatione dicitur inquantum est signum illius veritatis; de re autem dicitur, inquantum est causa . . ." [Mandonnet ed., Vol. 1, p. 486]); SCG I, c. 60; ST I, q. 16, a. 2. See a. 3 and ad 1 on the convertible character of *verum* and *ens*. For fuller discussion see J. Vande Wiele, "Le problème de la vérité ontologique dans la philosophie de saint Thomas," *Revue philosophique de Louvain* 52 (1954), pp. 521–71, esp. 545–54; F. Ruello, *La notion de vérité chez Saint Albert le Grand et Saint Thomas d'Aquin de 1243 à 1254* (Louvain-Paris, 1969), pp. 179–227 (on *In I Sent.*, d. 19, q. 5. a. 1); Aertsen and Wippel as cited above in n. 73.

78. For brief discussions of this see Garrigou-Lagrange, *God: His Existence and His Nature*, Vol. 1, p. 306; Van Steenberghen, *Le problème*, pp. 209, 216. For SCG I, c. 28, see ed. cit., p. 29 ("Et dico universaliter"). Note that in this context Thomas also applies *nobilitas* to wisdom. While granting this, for the sake of simplicity I will restrict it within the context of the fourth way to transcendental perfections. Also see Wagner, *Die philosophischen Implikate* (S. Th. I, 2, 3c), pp. 95–97. He considers and rightly rejects identifying the *nobile* with the beautiful.

79. See Thomas's discussion of God's *scientia, vita, et voluntas* in ST I, qq. 14, 15, 18, and 19.

80. See Fabro, "Sviluppo, significato e valore," (Leiden, 1989), Full title is: *Die philosophischen Implikate der "Quarta Via." Eine Untersuchung zum Vierten Gottesbeneis bei Thomas von Aquin* (S.Th. I, 2, 3c) pp. 101–2; Van Steenberghen, *Le problème*, pp. 215–16. As Van Steenberghen points out, for Aristotle and his medieval followers, fire is hot of its essence and to the maximum degree. While they regarded the sun as the cause of heat in earthly things, they did not regard it as hot in itself (see n. 20, where he corrects Fabro on this detail). For fuller discussion see Wagner, *Die philosophischen Implikate*, pp. 115–21. While he concludes that this example would have been illuminating for Thomas's contemporaries who shared his world-view, Wagner denies that the controlling principle of the first part of the fourth way rests upon the example for its justification (p. 120).

81. For Thomas's text see n. 74 above. See M. Corvez, "La quatrième voie vers l'existence de Dieu selon saint Thomas," in *Quinque sunt viae*, L. J. Elders, ed. (Vatican City, 1980), pp. 75–83, esp. pp. 77–78 (he reasons from diversity of beings in the world to the distinction of essence and existence in such beings, and from this to their efficiently caused character); Garrigou-Lagrange, *God: His Existence and His Nature*, Vol. 1, pp. 301–17. Cf. Wagner, op. cit., pp. 18–25 (on Garrigou-Lagrange's approach). For a helpful summary of some other recent approaches see J. Bobik, "Aquinas's Fourth Way and the Approximating Relation," *The Thomist* 51 (1987), pp. 17–36.

82. For the text see n. 74 above. For others who agree that in its first stage the argument is based solely on exemplar causality and is intended by Thomas to establish the existence of a really existing Maximum (or God) see L. Charlier, "Les cinq voies de saint Thomas," pp. 181–227, especially pp. 208–11; Van Steenberghen, *Le problème*, p. 211; A. Little, *The Platonic Heritage of Thomism* (Dublin, 1949) pp. 62–68, 80, and c. VII (passim); Bobik "Aquinas's Fourth Way," pp. 33–36 (along with other authors cited in this article). Cf. J.-P. Planty-Bonjour, "Die Struktur des Gottesbeweises aus den Seinsstufen," *Philosophisches Jahrbuch* 69 (1962), pp. 282–97, who rather sees the entire proof as resting solely on what he calls the principle of participation through formal hierarchy, without relying on efficient causality. For discussion see Wagner, *Die philosophischen Implikate*, pp. 29–37.

83. For this text see my *Metaphysical Thought of Thomas Aquinas*, Ch. XI, n. 10.

84. See ibid., n. 11.

85. According to Augustine, if I am to recognize any number, or the laws of number, this can only be because the notion of number is already "impressed" on my mind. So too, if I am to recognize immutable truths such as that all men

desire happiness or seek to be wise, these notions too must in some way already be impressed on my mind, presumably through divine illumination. See his *De libero arbitrio*, Bk II, c. 8, 20, 79–23, 92; c. 9, 26, 102–103 (CCSL Vol. 29, pp. 250–52, 254).

86. For the text see my *Metaphysical Thought of Thomas Aquinas*, Ch. XI, n. 8.

87. For Boethius see his *Consolation of Philosophy*, Bk III, pr. 10. ed. cit., p. 274:9–15: "Omne enim quod inperfectum esse dicitur, id inminutione perfecti imperfectum esse perhibetur. Quo fit, ut si in quolibet genere imperfectum quid esse videatur, in eo perfectum quoque aliquid esse necesse sit. Etenim perfectione sublata, unde illud quod inperfectum perhibetur exstiterit ne fingi quidem potest." For Anselm see his *Monologium*, cc. 1, 4 (Schmitt ed., Vol. I, pp. 14–15, 17–18).

88. Ed. cit., p. 14. For this text see Ch. XI, of my *Metaphysical Thought of Thomas Aquinas*, n. 87 and my discussion there.

89. See Little, *The Platonic Heritage of Thomism*, p. 100: "But though St. Thomas obviously considers that his statement needs no proof, philosophers of lower but yet good intelligence do not find the statement in the sense just explained self-evident. . . ." Also see Van Steenberghen, *Le problème*, who notes that Thomas presents the principle as immediately evident or as *per se notum*; he does not demonstrate it. See pp. 209–10. Cf. Maritain, *Approaches to God*, pp. 40–43.

90. "Sviluppo, significato e valore," pp. 81 (for the text); 82 (on the privileged character of this presentation); 89–102 (interpretation of the argument). On the date see, Jean-Pierre Torrell, *Saint Thomas Aquinas: The Person and His Work* (Washington, D.C., 1996), p. 339.

91. See *Lectura super evangelium Johannis*, Busa ed., Vol. 6, p. 227: "Quidam autem venerunt in cognitionem dei ex dignitate ipsius dei: et isti fuerunt platonici. Consideraverunt enim quod omne illud quod est secundum participationem, reducitur ad aliquid quod sit illud per suam essentiam, sicut ad primum et ad summum; sicut omnia ignita per participationem reducuntur ad ignem, qui est per essentiam suam talis. Cum ergo omnia quae sunt, participent esse, et sint per participationem entia, necesse est esse aliquid in cacumine omnium rerum, quod sit ipsum ipsum esse per suam essentiam, idest quod sua essentia sit suum esse: et hoc est deus, qui est sufficientissima, et dignissima, et perfectissima causa totius esse, a quo omnia quae sunt, participant esse." Note that this is one of four ways (*modi*) in which Thomas here remarks that the ancient philosophers came to knowledge of God. For all four see Fabro, "Sviluppo, significato et valore," pp. 79–82.

92. For some other texts see, for instance, ST I, q. 44, a. 1: "Si enim aliquid invenitur in aliquo per participationem, necesse est quod causetur in ipso ab eo cui essentialiter convenit; sicut ferrum fit ignitum ab igne." Cf. the reply to obj. I: ". . . quia ex hoc quod aliquid per participationem est ens, sequitur quod sit causatum ab alio. Unde huiusmodi ens non potest esse, quin sit causatum . . ." (Leon. 4.455). See *De substantiis separatis*, c. 3, where Thomas is attempting to bring out points of agreement between Plato and Aristotle. After referring to Plato's theory of participation he comments: ". . . omne autem participans aliquid accipit id quod participat ab eo a quo participat, et quantum ad hoc id a quo participat est causa ipsius: sicut aër habet lumen participatum a sole, quae est causa illuminationis ipsius" (Leon. 40.D46:11–15). Also see *Compendium theo-*

logiae, c. 68: ". . . omne quod habet aliquid per participationem reducitur in id quod habet illud per essentiam sicut in principium et causam, sicut ferrum ignitum participat igneitatem ab eo quod est ignis per essentiam suam" (Leon. 42.103:18–22). Cf. c. 123: "Item, ea quae sunt per participationem reducuntur in id quod est per essentiam sicut in causam: omnia enim ignita suae ignitionis ignem causam habent aliquo modo" (Leon. 42.127:27–30). Cf. Wagner, *Die philosophischen Implikate*, pp. 103–5.

93. See my *Metaphysical Thought of Thomas Aquinas*, Ch., IV, n. 7 for the "definition" of participation offered by Thomas in his Commentary on the *De Hebdomadibus*: when something receives in particular fashion that which belongs to another in universal (total) fashion, it is said to participate in it. See n. 8 there for the third kind of participation—that whereby an effect participates in its cause. It is under this third kind, as we have seen, that participation of beings in *esse* is to be placed.

94. See the texts cited in n. 92 above on the connection between being participated and (efficiently) caused. Also see *Metaphysical Thought of Thomas Aquinas*, Ch. V, Section 4, for texts where Thomas reasons directly from the participated character of *esse* in particular beings to real distinction and composition of essence and *esse* therein. A merely conceptual distinction between essence and act of being will not suffice to account for the fact that given beings really do participate in *esse*. See, for instance, the text from Quodilbert 2, q. 2, a. 1, cited in *Metaphysical Thought of Thomas Aquinas*, Ch. V, n. 98. This is why he can reason from the participated character of such beings to the composition of essence and *esse* within them, and thus to their being efficiently caused.

95. See *Metaphysical Thought of Thomas Aquinas*, Ch. V, Section 4.

96. Leon. 4.42. Note in particular: "Si igitur ipsum esse rei sit aliud ab eius essentia, necesse est quod esse illius rei vel sit causatum ab aliquo exteriori, vel a principiis essentialibus eiusdem rei. Impossibile est autem quod esse sit causatum tantum ex principiis essentialibus rei: quia nulla res sufficit quod sit sibi causa essendi, si habeat esse causatum. Oportet ergo quod illud cuius esse est aliud ab essentia sua, habeat esse causatum ab alio." Since this cannot be said of God, Thomas concludes that in him essence and act of being cannot differ.

97. The question may be raised concerning whether he regarded these points as necessary but as implied by his texts, or whether he did not even regard them as essential for an argument based on participation. While this is difficult to determine on purely historical grounds, they seem to me to be necessary for such an argument on philosophical grounds.

98. On the other hand, if one grants that this stage succeeds in establishing the existence of a maximum in the order of ontological truth, goodness, and nobility, one should also grant its inference that a maximum exists in the order of being.

99. For this text see ed. cit., p. 49. Fabro seems to regard all three arguments as proofs for God's existence. See his "Sviluppo, significato et valore," pp. 75–78. On these texts also see Van Steenberghen, *Le problème*, pp. 140–43, who regards only the first as an argument for God's existence.

100. Ed. cit., p. 49. Note especially: "Oporret enim, si aliquid unum communiter in plutibus invenitur, quod ab aliqua una causa in illis causetut; non enim

potest esse quod illud commune utrique ex se ipso conveniat, cum utrumque, secundum quod ipsum est, ab altero distinguatur; et diversitas causarum divetsos effectus producit."

101. "Sviluppo, nificato et valore" p. 77.

102. *Le problème*, p. 221. Cf. p. 140.

103. Van Steenberghen also regards this as a way of showing that *esse* is efficiently caused in finite beings by an infinite being. See *Le problème*, p. 221, n. 1.

104. For the text, see n. 74 above. This part of the proof hardly seems to be crucial if one appeals to efficient causality (or to participation) in the argument's first stage, although it will still serve to complete the overall argumentation.

105. "Quinta via sumitur ex gubernatione rerum. Videmus enim quod aliqua quae cognitione carent, scilicet corpora naturalia, operantur propter finem: quod apparet ex hoc quod semper aut frequentius eodem modo operantur, ut consequantur id quod est optimum; unde patet quod non a casu, sed ex intentione perveniunt ad finem. Ea autem quae non habent cognitionem, non tendunt in finem nisi directa ab aliquo cognoscente et intelligente, sicut sagitta a sagittante. Ergo est aliquid intelligens, a quo omnes res naturales ordinantur ad finem: et hoc dicimus Deum" (Leon: 4.32).

106. For these see *The Metaphysical Thought of Thomas Aquinas*, Ch. XI, Section 3 (and nn. 33, 34); Section 4 (n. 90), and my discussion there.

107. That Thomas is aware of this distinction is indicated by the fact that he immediately offers some argumentation to show that natural bodies act for an end, i.e., the fact that they always or at least more frequently act in the same way in order to obtain that which is best.

108. See Leon. 22.1.143:141–148 (cited in my *Metaphysical Thought of Thomas Aquinas*, Ch. XI, n. 31).

109. Leon. 43.41:120–42:19. For Aristotle see *Metaphysics* II, c. 2 (994b 13–16).

110. Leon. 43.42:19–41. For Avicenna see his *Sufficientia*, I, c. 14, fol. 22rb.

111. See Mandonnet ed., Vol. 2, p. 645 (where Thomas is defending the presence of free will in God). Note from his response: "Determinatio autem agentis ad aliquam actionem, oportet quod sit ab aliqua cognitione praestituente finem illi actioni."

112. Leon. 6.9. Note Thomas's comment regarding this determination to an end: "Haec autem determinatio, sicut in rationali natura fit per rationalem appetitum, qui dicitur voluntas; et in aliis fit per inclinationem naturalem, quae dicitur appetitus naturalis." For discussion see J. Maritain, *A Preface to Metaphysics* (New York, 1948), pp. 124ff.; C. A. Hart, *Thomistic Metaphysics: An Inquiry into the Act of Existing* (Englewood Cliffs, N.J., 1959), pp. 65–66, 298; G. Klubertanz, "St. Thomas' Treatment of the Axiom, *Omne Agens Agit Propter Finem*," in *An Etienne Gilson Tribute*, C. J. O'Neil, ed. (Milwaukee, 1959), pp. 104–5. For this same kind of argumentation also see SCG III, c. 2, where it appears within a series of arguments intended to show that "omne agens in agendo intendit aliquem finem." Some of these are, in fact, rather aimed at showing that one cannot regress to infinity in actions. For criticism of a number of them see Kenny, *The Five Ways*, pp. 98–103. Curiously, however, Kenny omits the argument just mentioned which is, in my judgment, the most effective one offered there or elsewhere by Thomas. As it runs in the *Summa contra Gentiles*: "Item. Si agens non tenderet

ad aliquem effectum determinatum, omnes effectus essent ei indifferentes. Quod autem indifferenter se habet ad multa, non magis unum eorum operator quam aliud: unde a contingente ad utrumque non sequitur aliquis effectus nisi per aliquid determinetur ad unum. Impossibile igitur esset quod ageret. Omne igitur agens tendit ad aliquem determinatum effectum, quod dicitur finis eius" (ed. cit., p. 228).

113. See *The Metaphysical Thought of Thomas Aquinas*, Ch. XI, nn.30, 31. For similar reasoning see SCG III, c. 3, where Thomas presents a series of arguments to show that "omne agens agit propter bonum." See the third argument beginning with "Adhuc." Note especially: "Videmus autem in operibus naturae accidete vel semper vel frequentius quod melius est. . . . Si igitur hoc evenit praeter intentionem naturalis agentis, hoc erit a casu vel fortuna. Sed hoc est impossibile: nam ca quae accidunt semper vel frequenter, non sunt casualia neque fortuita, sed quae accidunt in paucioribus . . . Naturale igitur agens intendit ad id quod melius est . . ." (ed. cit., 229).

114. For Aristotle see *Physics* II, c. 5, passim. For Boethius see his *Consolation of Philosophy*, Bk V, pr. I. Note in particular his definition of chance: "Licet igitur definite casum esse inopinarum ex confluentibus causis in his quae ob aliquid geruntur eventum" (*The Theological Tractates . . . The Consolation of Philosophy*, ed. cit., pp. 386–88).

115. See Thomas's Commentary on Aristotle's discussion of chance in the *Physics*, especially *In II Phys.* lect. 8, pp. 105–6, nn. 214–215. The text of the fifth way seems to leave the last point mentioned in my text unclear: Is Thomas there holding that natural agents act so as to reach that which is best for themselves, or that which is best for the whole of nature? The first alternative would be enough to support his claim that since such agents act to attain that which is best for them always or at least in the greater number of cases, such action cannot be owing to chance. The second alternative seems to be suggested by Thomas's conclusion from the fifth way that there is one intelligent being by which all natural things are ordered to their end. Hence it seems that Thomas would defend both alternatives and that they are not mutually exclusive. Cf. Van Steenberghen, *Le problème*, p. 231. But this again raises the question whether this argument succeeds in proving that there is *one* supreme intelligence.

116. For the text see above, n. 105.

117. For the text from *In II Sent.*, d. 25, q. 1, a. 1, see Mandonnet ed., Vol. 2, p. 645 (cf. n. 111 above). Note: ". . . nec aliquod agens finem sibi praestituere potest nisi rationem finis cognoscat et ordinem ejus quod est ad finem ipsum, quod solum in habentibus intellectum est. . . ."

118. See n. 112 above for ST I–II, q. 1, a. 2. The text continues: "Illa vero quae ratione carent, tendunt in finem per naturalem inclinationem, quasi ab alio mota, non autem a seipsis: cum non cognoscant rationem finis, et ideo nihil in finem ordinare possunt, sed solum in finem ab alio ordinantur" (Leon. 6.9). For a fuller discussion of natural appetite, sensitive appetite, and rational appetite (will) see *De veritate*, q. 25, a. 1. In describing natural appetite Thomas comments: ". . . nihil enim est aliud appetitus naturalis quam quaedam inclinatio rei et ordo ad aliquam rem sibi convenientem, sicut lapidis ad locum deorsum" (Leon. 22.3.729: 131–136).

119. For the text from ST I–II, q. 1, a. 2, see Leon. 6.9.

120. Mandonnet ed., Vol. 2, p. 645.

121. "Ad formam autem consequitur inclinatio ad finem, aut ad actionem, aut aliquid huiusmodi: quia unumquodque, inquantum est actu, agit, et tendit in id quod sibi convenit secundum suam formam" (Leon. 4.63).

122. See Leon, 22.3.729:141–144: "Sed haec apprehensio praeexigitur in instituente naturam, qui unicuique naturae dedit inclinationem propriam sibi convenientem."

123. According to Van Steenberghen, none of the five ways, with the exception of the fourth, establishes the uniqueness of God. And as he sees things, the fourth way is invalid as it is presented in ST I, q. 2. a. 3. See Le problème, pp. 235–36, 297. However, if one recasts the fourth way as I have proposed above in order to defend its validity, one may still raise the issue of divine unicity at its conclusion.

124. In a. 1 Thomas asks whether unity adds anything to being. As he explains, unity does not add any real thing to being but only the negation of division of being from itself; because of this it follows that unity is convertible with being. In a. 2 he distinguishes the way in which numerical unity is opposed to numerical multiplicity from the way in which unity of being is opposed to multitude. In a. 4, while showing that God is supremely one *(maxime unus)*, he concentrates on ontological unity rather than on divine uniqueness. God is supremely one because he is supremely undivided from himself; this follows from the fact that he is perfectly simple. On the transcendental one see Aertsen, *Medieval Philosophy and the Transcendentals*, pp. 201–42.

125. Leon. 4.111. Note in particular: "Manifestum est enim quod illud unde aliquod singulare est *hoc aliquid*, nullo modo est multis communicabile . . . Hoc autem convenit Deo: nam ipse Deus est sua natura, ut supra ostensum est. Secundum igitur idem est Deus, et hic Deus. Impossibile est igitur esse plures Deos."

126. Leon. 4.35. Cf. n. 43 in our text above.

127. See Thomas's general introduction to q. 3: "Tertio: utrum sit in eo compositio quidditatis, sive essentiae, vel naturae, et subiecti" (p. 35). In a. 3 itself Thomas begins his response this way: "Respondeo dicendum quod Deus est idem quod sua essentia vel natura" (p. 39).

128. ST I, q. 3, a. 3 (Leon. 4.39–40). Note in particular: ". . . sciendum est, quod in rebus compositis ex materia et forma, necesse est quod different natura vel essentia et suppositum. . . . unde id quod est homo, habet in se aliquid quod non habet humanitas." For fuller discussion of the relationship between nature and supposit see my *Metaphysical Thought of Thomas Aquinas*, 15 Ch. VIII, Section 1.

129. Leon. 4.40.

130. ST I, q. 3, a. 2 (Leon. 4.37–38).

131. Leon. 4.111. Note especially: "Secundo vero, ex infinitate eius perfectionis. Ostensum est enim supra quod Deus comprehendit in se totam perfectionem essendi. Si ergo essent plures dii, oporteret eos differre. Aliquid ergo conveniret uni, quod non alteri."

132. Ibid.

133. See n. 131 above.

134. Leon. 4.50. Note: "Deus autem ponitur primum principium, non materiale, sed in genere causae efficientis: et hoc oportet esse perfectissimum. . . . Secundum hoc enim dicitur aliquid esse perfectum, secundum quod est actu: nam perfectum dicitur, cui nihil deest secundum modum suae perfectionis."

135. Ibid. ". . . ipsum esse est perfectissimum omnium: comparatur enim ad omnia ut actus. Nihil enim habet actualitatem, nisi inquantum est: unde ipsum esse est actualitas omnium rerum, et etiam ipsarum formarum."

136. Leon. 4.51–52. Note that if Thomas holds that an effect preexists in a more perfect efficient cause in more perfect fashion, such is not true of the way an effect preexists in the potency of its material cause. There it preexists more imperfectly.

137. Leon. 4.52. Note: "Omnium autem perfectiones pertinent ad perfectionem essendi: secundum hoc enim aliqua perfecta sunt, quod aliquo modo esse habent. Unde sequitur quod nullius rei perfectio Deo desit."

138. As Thomas introduces his reply: "Respondeo dicendum quod Deus non solum est sua essentia, ut ostensum est, sed etiam suum esse" (Leon. 4.42).

139. Ibid. See n. 96 above.

140. Leon. 4.42. In q. 3, a. 1 see corpus, arg. 2 (Leon. 4.35–36).

141. Leon. 4.42.

142. Leon. 4.72. Cf. Ch. IX above, nn. 41, 42, 43, 44, 48 on form or act as limited by matter as a potency that receives it, and the application of the axiom that unreceived act is unlimited to the issue of divine infinity.

143. Leon. 4.72. Note: "Cum igitur esse divinum non sit esse receptum in aliquo, sed ipse sit suum esse subsistens . . . ; manifestum est quod ipse Deus sit infinitus et perfectus." Central to this argument is the assumption that unreceived *esse* is unlimited. Thomas often appeals to this axiom in order to establish divine infinity. See, for instance, In I Sent., d. 8, q. 2, a. 1 (Mandonnet ed., Vol. I, p. 202); In I Sent., d. 43, q. 1 a. 1 (p. 1003); SCG I, c. 43 (ed. cit., p. 41); SCG II, c. 52 (for which see n. 149 below); Compendium theologiae, c. 18 (Leon. 42.88:7–8).

144. Ed. cit., p. 38 ("Praeterea"). Kretzmann rejects this argument on the grounds that it implicitly assumes "that every characteristic must count either as a perfection or as an imperfection," which strikes him as false. I assume he envisions the possibility of a distinguishing characeric in one all-perfect being which would distinguish it from another without itself being a perfection or an imperfection. For Thomas, however, to the extent that such a characteristic is actual (there could be no passive potentiality in an all-perfect being), it must be a perfection. And if it is a privation or negation of something positive present in another all-perfect being; it would have to be counted as a lack of perfection in the first all-perfect being, i.e., an imperfection. For Kretzmann see *The Metaphysics of Theism* (Oxford, 1997), p. 160. For his presentation and defense of another more extensive argument for God's uniqueness in c. 42 based on Thomas's earlier conclusion that God is a necessary being *per se*, see pp. 161–65.

145. ". . . Deus tamen, qui non est aliud quam suum esse, est universaliter ens perfectum. Et dico universaliter perfectum, cui non deest alicuius generis nobilitas" (ed. cit., 29).

146. Ed. cit., pp. 29–30, cited in my *Metaphysical Thought of Thomas Aquinas*, Ch. V, n. 109. See my comments in Ch. V, Section 5 on Thomas's references to a "power of being" in this text and elsewhere. On this particular text also see Kretzmann, op. cit., pp. 133–38.

147. Ed. cit., p. 30: "Amplius. Unumquodque perfectum est inquantum est actu; imperfectum autem secundum quod est potentia cum privatione actus. Id igitur quod nullo modo est in potentia sed est actus purus, oportet perfectissimum esse."

148. Ed. cit., p. 145. For discussion of the first three arguments see my *Metaphysical Thought of Thomas Aquinas*, Ch. V, Section 2, and nn. 51–54.

149. Ed. cit., p. 145: ". . . esse enim quod omnino est infinitum, omnem perfectionem essendi comprehendit; et sic, si de duobus talis adesset infinitas, non inveniretur quo unum ab altero differret."

150. For a number of these see *The Metaphysical Thought of Thomas Aquinas*, Ch. V, Section 2.

151. Note that this argument is preceded by another less persuasive one which reasons that if the term "god" is applied equivocally, to say "there are many gods" will not be to the point. If it is applied univocally, the many gods would have to agree in genus or in species. But he has shown that God cannot be a genus or species (Leon. 42.87:1–10). For the argument analyzed in our text see p. 87:11–21. Cf. n. 125 above for ST I, q. 11, a. 3.

152. Leon. 42.87:22–35. In *De ente*, c. 4. Thomas had also mentioned reception of a form in matter as another possible way of multiplying specific forms in individuals, and rejected this as not applicable to subsisting *esse*. See Leon. 43: 376:105–377:121.

153. Indeed, the conclusion established by each of the five ways he has identified with God. Compare the conclusion of the second way (and of the first and third, for that matter) with the conclusion of the fifth way.

154. See my *Metaphysical Thought of Thomas Aquinas*, Ch. XI, n. 76 for the text and discussion of the same.

155. Cf. *In II Sent.*, d. 25, q. 1, a. 1 (Mandonnet ed., Vol. 2, p. 645); *De veritate*, q. 25, a. 1 (Leon. 22.3.729:141–44), cited above in n. 122.

156. I am assuming here that for Thomas the ultimate efficient cause of a finite nature is the cause both of its essence and its act of being *(esse)*. See, for instance, *De potentia*, q. 3, a. 5, ad 2 (ed. cit., p. 49).

157. Leon. 4.166. For more on Thomas's view that knowledge involves possessing the form of a thing in immaterial fashion see ST I, q. 84, aa. 1–2.

158. Leon. 4.166–67.

159. See ST I, q. 13, a. 5: "Et sic, quidquid dicitur de Deo et creaturis, dicitur secundum quod est aliquis ordo creaturae ad Deum, ut ad principium et causam, in qua praeexistunt excellenter omnes rerum perfectiones" (Leon. 4.147).

160. For a helpful review of a number of these competing interpretations, see Van Steenberghen, *Le problème*, pp. 238–41.

161. See his "A propos des 'Cinq voies'," *Revue des sciences philosophiques et théologiques* 27 (1938), pp. 577–82. To support his case Motte cites the dependency of the five ways as they are presented in the *Summa theologiae* upon Thomas's argumentation in SCG I, cc. 13 and 15, and the explicit references in SCG to

historical sources, that is, to the arguments by which philosophers and *doctores Catholici* have proved that God exists (SCG I, c. 13, ed. cit., p. 10). Thomas there goes on to offer two detailed arguments based on motion, each of which he assigns to Aristotle, another argument taken from Aristotle's *Metaphysics* II (to refute appeal to an infinite regress of efficient causes), one taken from both *Metaphysics* II and IV (based on degrees of truth), and one explicitly assigned to John Damascene (the argument from the way things are governed). One of the arguments offered for divine eternity in SCG I, c. 15 strongly foreshadows the third way. However, Motte (pp. 579–80) does not bring out sufficiently the differences between the argument from divine governance in SCG I, c. 13 and the fifth way, and between the argument based on possible and necessary being of SCG I, c. 15 and the third way. See p. 580 for his still sound conclusion that no systematic idea or scheme predetermined either the organization or the number of the five ways.

162. L. Charlier rejects the first effort (to reduce the five ways to a single proof; though they complement one another, each is a distinct proof), but supports the second claim (Thomas thought that all other valid proofs could be reduced to the five ways). See his "Les cinq voies de saint Thomas," pp. 189–90. In addition to Motte's critique of efforts to reduce the five ways to complementary aspects of a single proof (p. 577), see Van Steenberghen, *Le problème*, pp. 238–41 (especially for his résumé and critique of more recent efforts to reduce the five ways to a single organizing principle or scheme). Owens comments: "The impression that the five ways are the only ones recognized by Aquinas, and that all other variations have to be reduced in one way or another to their forms, stems from the Neoscholastic manuals." See his "Aquinas and the Five Ways," in *St Thomas Aquinas on the Existence of God*, p. 257, n. 1.

163. See, for instance, L. Elders, "Justification des 'cinq voies'," *Revue thomiste* 61 (1961), pp. 207–25 (most surprising is his attempt to base the first way on material causality); H. Johnson, "Why Five Ways? A Thesis and Some Alternatives," in *Actes du quatrième congrès international de philosophie médiévale* (Montreal, 1969), pp. 1143–54, especially pp. 1143–45 (who would base the third way on material causality). For Elders's more recent thought concerning this see his "Les cinq voies et leur place dans la philosophie de saint Thomas," in *Quinque sunt viae*, L. J. Elders, ed., Studi tomistici 9 (Vatican City, 1980), pp. 133–46. Here he continues to reduce the five ways to the four kinds of causality, again basing the first way on material causality and basing the third way on a fifth kind of causality, God's communication of *esse* to other things (pp. 138–39). See p. 141 (for his critique of efforts by A. Kenny to link the third way to material causality); p. 145 (for his conclusion that because of the close bond between the five ways and the kinds of causality, a new proof for God's existence which would differ fundamentally from the five ways is not possible). Now also see his *The Philosophical Theology of St. Thomas Aquinas* (Leiden, 1990), pp. 85–88. For Kenny see *The Five Ways*, pp. 35–37. Also see Maritain, *Approaches to God*, pp. 18–19, for the view that because the various ways start from different facts based on experience, they are specifically distinct proofs. Also see M. F. Johnson, "Why Five Ways?" in *Proceedings of the American Catholic Philosophical Association* 65 (1991), pp. 107–21, who, unsuccessfully, in my opinion, proposes still another organizing principle

for the first four ways based on Aristotle's discussion of actuality and potentiality in *Metaphysics* IX, while the fifth way would attain to God as the source of directed motion. He rightly regards the five ways as formally distinct proofs (pp. 110, 115). For an earlier attempt to find a key to the organization of the first four ways in Aristotle's discussion of actuality and potentiality in *Metaphysics* IX see L. Dewan, "The Number and Order of St. Thomas's Five Ways," *Downside Review* 92 (1974), pp. 1–18.

164. H. J. Johnson, op. cit., p. 1151.

8

⌘

Aquinas on What God Is Not

Thomas Aquinas was very concerned with the question "What is God?". And he thought that he had answers to this question. God, he says, is the beginning and end of all things, the Creator of a world which depends on him for its existence.[1] Among other things, Aquinas also holds that God is alive, perfect, good, eternal, omnipresent, omnipotent, and omniscient, that God is three persons sharing one nature, and that God became a human being so that humans might share in the life of God.[2] Yet in the writings of Aquinas we also find him holding that God is deeply mysterious. "The divine substance", he says, "surpasses every form that our intellect reaches. Thus we are unable to apprehend it by knowing what it is".[3] God, he maintains, "is greater than all we can say, greater than all we can know; and not merely does he transcend our language and our knowledge, but he is beyond the comprehension of every mind whatsoever, even of angelic minds, and beyond the being of every substance".[4] According to Aquinas: "The most perfect [state] to which we can attain in this life in our knowledge of God is that he transcends all that can be conceived by us, and that the naming of God through remotion (*per remotionem*) is most proper . . . The primary mode of naming God is through the negation of all things, since he is beyond all, and whatever is signified by any name whatsoever is less than that which God is".[5]

What does Aquinas mean when saying that we can speak truly of God even though we do not know what God is? One thing to stress is that when he denies that we know what God is he clearly does not intend to suggest that we can claim no knowledge of God at all. His meaning is that God is not an object in our universe with respect to which we can have what we would nowadays call a "scientific understanding". According to Aquinas, we know what something is (*quid est*) when we can single it out as part of the material world and define it. More precisely, we know what something is when we can locate it in terms of genus and species.[6] In saying that we cannot know what God is, therefore, he is chiefly denying that God belongs to a natural class and that God can be defined on this basis. Were he writing in English today he would not be saying "We do not know anything about God" or "We lack any knowledge of God".[7]

On the other hand, however, he does think that the nature of God defies our powers of understanding. He often says that an explicit human knowledge of God has to be derived from a process of inference making use of premises concerning the world as grasped by sensory experience. For Aquinas, we know God as accounting for or bringing about ourselves and our world. And this knowledge is limited. God, for Aquinas, transcends our attempts to picture or describe. So he thinks, for example, that it is equally appropriate to talk of God both in concrete terms and in abstract terms. In Aquinas's view, we cannot think of God as something with a nature shared by others. We cannot think of God as one of a class in a world of things. On Aquinas's account, God and God's nature are not, for us, distinguishable.[8] And hence, so he argues, while it makes sense to say such things as that "God is good" or "God is wise", it makes equal sense to say "God is goodness" or "God is wisdom". According to Aquinas, God is also the same as his existence. He is "subsistent existence" (*ipsum esse subsistens*).[9] Or, as Aquinas often puts it, God is entirely simple.

In effect, Aquinas's view is that the very logic of our language cannot capture God. We normally talk about, and understand, things by singling them out as subjects of statements and by saying what properties they have. Thus, for example, we say that Mary is tall and thin, or that the dog in the kitchen is black and weighs twenty pounds. For Aquinas, however, though we are forced to talk of God in a similar way because of the way our language works—though we are forced to say things like "God is good" or "God is wise"—that manner of putting things is also misleading. For, as Aquinas sees it, God is not something to be distinguished from what is ascribed to him. Mary might be good and Mary might be wise. But Mary is not goodness or wisdom. But, says Aquinas, having said that God is good or that God is wise, we must also allow that God cannot be distinguished from what is ascribable to him. So God is goodness, and God is wisdom, and the being of God is not something different from God himself.

When saying this kind of thing, Aquinas does not mean, as some have seemed to think, that statements like "God is good" and "God is wise" are synonymous.[10] But, so he thinks, what makes them true is the reality of God (i.e. God), which, so he says, is not to be thought of as something distinct from what can be affirmed of it. According to Aquinas, we can distinguish between what a word like "goodness" means and what is actually there in something that we call "good".[11] So there is a sense in which he thinks that we know what we are saying when we say, for example, that God is good. But he does not think that God is something we can single out and understand so as seriously to be able to say that we know what it is—even though he thinks that we can say, for example, "God is good". His conclusion, therefore, is that, though we can understand the meaning of the word "good" when saying that God is good, we cannot understand what God is. And he wants to say the same when it comes to anything which we might wish to affirm of God. We cannot know what any perfection ascribable to God is like as it exists in him. We can know what it is like for something to be a good human being or a good computer or a good meal. But God, says Aquinas, is not a good such-and-such. He is no kind of such-and-such. And he cannot be thought of as a perfect such-and-such regardless of the perfection in question.

In that case, however, can we know anything at all of God? People sometimes approach Aquinas on this question by focusing on what they call his "doctrine of analogy". They mean that Aquinas has something rightly called a "doctrine of analogy" which he viewed as a device for working out what we can know about God. And, though this idea has been rejected by some readers of Aquinas, it is not without merit.[12] For Aquinas certainly holds that we can make statements concerning God which we can know to be true. And in defending this position he invokes the notion of analogy. Take, for example, the first five articles of the famous Question 13 of the *Summa Theologiae*. Here Aquinas defends the following theses: (1) We can use words to talk of God; (2) Some of the words we use state what God is in himself; (3) We significantly speak of God while saying different things about him; and (4) We can apply certain words to God and to creatures analogously—i.e. neither univocally nor purely equivocally. Theses 1–3 are clearly intended by Aquinas as leading to 4, which he develops by providing what looks like a rule of thumb for speaking of God in a true and literal way. "Whatever is said both of God and creatures", Aquinas explains, "is said in virtue of the order that creatures have to God as to their source and cause in which all the perfections of things pre-exist transcendently". What does this mean? Article 3 of Ia,13 provides a clue: "God is known from the perfections that flow from him and are to be found in creatures yet which exist in him in a transcendent way". Aquinas thinks of effects as showing forth the nature of their cause.[13] An effect, for Aquinas, is somehow like its cause. So his view is that from God's effects we can know what God is since God is their cause. And that gives us what I just referred to as what looks like a "rule of thumb" offered by Aquinas for speaking truly of God. First take your creature. Then assume that it is like God since God is its Creator. Then speak accordingly of God.

This rule of thumb, however, might easily be used to defend what Aquinas would manifestly deny. Cats have fur. And God is the creator of cats. Does it follow that God is furry? Aquinas denies that God is anything material, and, since fur is pretty corporeal, we can expect him to deny that God is furry.[14] Yet he would not, I think, say that his "rule of thumb", as I call it, must therefore be simply abandoned. For it comes from him with a qualification.

An effect, for Aquinas, always resembles its cause.[15] But this, he thinks, need not mean that it looks like its cause or that it resembles it by being exactly like it.[16] Aquinas's idea is that a cause expresses itself in its effects and is therefore knowable from its effects. Suppose I stagger around and speak incoherently. You might wonder why I am doing this. Suppose you learn that I have just drunk a large amount of alcohol. You will say: "Oh, I see. Of course that explains it". But why? Aquinas would say that it is not at all surprising that the alcohol made me act as I did, because that is what alcohol characteristically does when drunk in large quantities by human beings. His line is that alcohol is something the effects of which show it forth. So he will say that my drunken state resembles alcohol since it shows forth the power of alcohol as it takes place in me. I cannot, when drunk, be described as looking like alcohol. But, so Aquinas thinks, I, when drunk, certainly exemplify what alcohol is when it works on me. In this sense, so he holds, I resemble it. When I am drunk, so Aquinas would say, I am alcohol in action. Alcohol being itself in me. Or, as Aquinas puts it: "What an agent does reflects what it is" (*omne agens agit sibi simile*).[17] Cashed with reference to God as Creator, this means that God shows himself in all of his effects even though we cannot say that, for example, God is furry. Just as alcohol can show itself in me without being inebriated, so, for Aquinas, God shows himself in his effects without being furry. And this is why we might agree with those who say that Aquinas has a doctrine of analogy which we can use as a rule of thumb for saying what we know about God. The rule would be: "All of God's creatures show us what God is—somehow".

But how, for Aquinas, does the world give us knowledge of God as its cause? How does he think of his "rule" as helping us to a knowledge of God? Some have argued that this question is best answered in largely negative terms. In *Aquinas, God and Action*, for instance, David Burrell suggests that Aquinas is out to lay down "the universal (or logical) principles governing discourse about divine things rather than establishing a doctrine of God". Insofar as Aquinas has a doctrine of God, says Burrell, "it is a dreadfully austere one".[18] But other readers of Aquinas have not found him offering quite the austerity proposed by Burrell. Why not? Largely because of what Aquinas says about analogy. He maintains that one can use certain words of God and creatures in an analogical sense. And he seems to think that this fact allows us to speak of God in a literal way. Like 'univocal' and 'equivocal', 'analogical', for Aquinas, signifies a literal way of talking. 'New York is a city' and 'Paris is a city' give us univocal uses of 'city'; but both statements are literally true. 'Baseball players use bats' and 'Bats have wings' give us equivocal uses of 'bat'. But both statements here are also literally true. And, according to Aquinas, 'I have a good computer' and 'God is good' give us analogical uses of 'good' in two literally true statements. And, with this fact in mind, it is wrong, so some have stressed, to think of Aquinas along the lines suggested by authors like Burrell. If Aquinas holds that we can speak of God literally, then, so they reason, Aquinas has a positive doctrine of God.[19]

Yet how should we view analogy as it is invoked by Aquinas when talking of God? Commenting on the view that discourse concerning God is 'analogical', P. T. Geach observes: "It would be better to say that it turns out to be analogical: what happens, on Aquinas's view, is that we first call God 'wise'; then discover that 'the wisdom of God' is a designation of God himself, whereas the like does not hold of any other being whom we rightly call 'wise'; and thus reflecting upon this, we see that 'wise' cannot be applied to God in the same way as to other beings"[20] And Geach here is right. In the *Summa Theologiae* (as elsewhere) Aquinas only mentions analogy after he has explained why God must be spoken of in certain specific ways. Ia,13 follows a set of Questions in which Aquinas argues for the truth of a number of positive assertions concerning God. And most of Ia,13 looks as though it can be read as a general account of what Aquinas has been doing since Ia,1. To understand texts like Ia,13, then, we need to consider what has led up to them. And if we do that we shall see that Aquinas has a characteristic way of arriving at the sort of thing he says in texts like Ia,13.

He begins by trying to reject certain arguments for the conclusion that God exists. Is God's existence something one can deny only by failing to pay attention to a basic and undeniable deliverance of the intellect? Is there not a direct and explicit awareness of God present in all who care to reflect at all? Might "God exists" be as obviously true as the denial of what is clearly logically contradictory? Aquinas discusses such questions in a number of places, and his answer is always "No".[21] We can know that God exists, he thinks. But only by virtue of a certain kind of argument—an argument from effect to cause. In Aquinas's view, we do not have an understanding of what God is. So we cannot reason to God on the basis of any such understanding. But we can start with things of which we do have some understanding. From these, Aquinas thinks, we can argue to God as their cause.

Suppose, for example, that someone develops certain physical symptoms. We wonder what accounts for them. But we do not know that anything we understand (virus X, Y, or Z, for instance) has been around to account for them. In that case, we presume that the symptoms have a cause, and we do our best to construct an account of what this cause might be like. Here we are saying: "Given this, then there must be something which accounts for it. Now let us try to understand what this something must be like". According to Aquinas, we are saying just this when offering viable arguments for God's existence. In his view, any such argument must be one which starts with things of which we do have some knowledge and it must reason to God as less known but as accounting for them—as in the case of the famous "Five Ways".[22] Each "Way" begins with what, unlike God's nature, is clear to us. And they reason to a not-so-clear cause of this. They "do not presuppose any view of the nature of God, they simply begin with philosophical puzzles arising from features that we understand and take us to what we do not understand".[23] Or, as Aquinas himself writes: "When we argue from effect to cause, the effect must take the place of a definition of the cause in the proof that the cause exists; and especially so when the cause is God. For when proving anything to exist the central link is not what the thing is— we cannot even ask what it is until we know that it exists".[24]

Yet Aquinas does, in a sense, ask "What is God?". And he does, in a sense, have answers to the question. If we know that Fred is coughing up blood we assume that, as we often vaguely put it, something is causing this. Let us suppose that we cannot put our finger on the culprit or culprits. Most of us would then find ourselves saying that we shall have to settle for doing our best to talk about the offender or offenders in a roundabout kind of way. And that is how Aquinas proceeds as he develops what might be called his philosophical account of God's nature. In the interlude between Ia,2 and Ia,3 he writes: "Having recognized that a certain thing exists, we have still to investigate the way in which it exists, that we may come to understand what it is that exists". And much of the *Summa Theologiae* following that remark, and much that Aquinas writes in other works, can be read as an effort on his part to say what we are talking about when we say that God exists. The remark itself is immediately followed by another which seems to pull in a different direction. For, says Aquinas, "we cannot know what God is, but only what he is not" and must therefore "consider the ways in which God does not exist, rather than the ways in which he does". But we need to see what that statement means in the light of what Aquinas says generally.

One way of reading it would leave us taking Aquinas as holding that we can only say that God is not this, not that, not the other . . . *ad infinitum*. But that is clearly not his position if it is taken to mean that we can make no true affirmative predications concerning God. When Aquinas in the *Summa Theologiae* says that we must consider the ways in which God does not exist he goes on to offer a series of discussions designed to do just that. Ia,3 (*de Dei simplicate*) tells us what kinds of composition (*compositio*) cannot be attributed to God. Ia,7 and Ia,9 tell us that God is limitless and unchangeable, i.e. *not* limited and *not* changeable. In Ia,4 and in Ia,11 Aquinas, in an apparently positive vein, argues that God is perfect and that God is one (*unus*). But here again he is telling us what God is not. As Geach observes: "A moment's thought shows that there is no such perfection as perfection: we cannot sensibly predicate 'perfect' unless we have in mind a perfect A, where 'A' stands in for a general term with some definite content".[25] And Aquinas does not suggest otherwise. God, he argues, is perfect not as having a particular perfection but as being wholly actual. As for "God is one", says Aquinas, the meaning is that God is not subject to multiplication, that there cannot be several God.[26] Yet Aquinas clearly holds that we can make true affirmative predications concerning God. And he explicitly denies that when we do so we are only saying what God is not. "Some", he writes, "have said that sentences like 'God is good', although they sound like affirmations, are in fact used to deny something of God rather than to assert anything".[27] But he rejects that position.[28]

So Aquinas thinks that "God is alive" has positive content, and he thinks the same of other assertions about God, ones which, in his view, we can know to be true.[29] And, though Aquinas continually stresses our ignorance when it comes to God, he also writes so as to suggest that he wants to shy away from the suggestion that we cannot know that certain statements with God as subject are true. Why so? Partly it is because he follows the Bible and the teaching of the Church, both of which provided him with apparently positive statements concerning God. But Aquinas also gives reasons for supposing that some positive statements about God are ones we can defend without appeal to Scripture and Church authority. Take, for example, "God is good". Why say that? Well, so Aquinas replies, it is a natural thing to say since the good is what is desirable and since God is the cause of the existence of everything other than himself and must therefore have in him all that things tend to in being good and in seeking their good.[30] Or again, what about "God is omnipresent" and "God is eternal"? Aquinas defends the first statement by arguing that since God makes all places, he is in them all as making them to be.[31] The second statement is defensible, he argues, since anything eternal is wholly unchangeable and since God must be that if he is the source of the world of change.[32] Here, as in many other arguments he offers, Aquinas is holding that there are reasons for saying that God really is thus and so. Insofar as the reasons lead to their conclusions, he thinks, we have grounds for making various positive statements concerning God. In this sense, so he holds, we know what God is, and in this sense he employs what I have called his "rule of thumb". Affirmative predications concerning God are, in his view, wrung from us by argument.[33] Critics of belief in God have sometimes asked theists to prove in the abstract that statements about God are "coherent" or "meaningful" before ever considering why we might want to say that God is whatever we say that he is. And some theists have seemed to accept that proof like this ought to be supplied.[34] But a proof that **p** is true is proof that **p** is possibly true since it is proof that p is actually true. And much of Aquinas's thinking on the sense it makes to say "God is F", "God is G", etc. is inseparable from the reasons he thinks we have to speak in this way. And when Aquinas says that we can speak positively of God he intends us to understand that we can sometimes speak literally and not just figuratively. As we can see from texts like Ia,1,9, Aquinas certainly thinks that we can speak of God figuratively, that most Christian discourse will be figurative, and that speaking figuratively need not mean speaking falsely. But figurative statements about God can always, in his view, be rightly denied. I may say that God is a mighty fortress, but I may, Aquinas thinks, sensibly deny this by adding that God is not made of stone. Yet, so Aquinas also thinks, there are many things to be said of God which just cannot be sensibly and with reason denied. Hence, for example, it is, in his view, always false to say that it is not the case that God is good, omnipresent, and eternal. And, so Aquinas also thinks, statements like "God is good", "God is omnipresent", and "God is eternal" are wrung from us by argument, though they also come with the authority of Scripture and the Church.

But Aquinas also holds that other less positive things we need to say about God are equally wrung from us by argument. And here we return to what, in his view, cannot be said about God. God is nothing material. God is not an instance of a kind. God cannot be thought of as distinct from his "attributes" and his existence. God is entirely simple or non-composite. If Aquinas believes that there are reasons for saying that God is positively thus and so, he also maintains there are reasons for denying certain things about God. And all of his thinking here, together with what we have now seen concerning his general approach to knowledge of God, is clearly presupposed when he comes to write texts like Ia,13. Indeed, they form part of the argument of such texts. Ia,13,1 asks whether we can use any words to refer to God. Aquinas's reply notes that we can know of God through God's effects, but must also remember that God is simple. Ia,13,2 asks whether any of the words we use of God express something of what God is. Aquinas's answer to this question appeals to the fact that what we can know of God is derived from our knowledge that God is the cause of creatures. It then adds that, since God is the transcendent cause of all creatures, creatures fail to represent him adequately so that words like "good", when based on the goodness experienced in creatures and applied to God, signify "imperfectly".

Aquinas's use of the notion of analogy brings together all of these aspects of his teaching. We are not, he says, always equivocating when we apply certain terms to God and to creatures. We can argue for God's existence and we can argue for statements of the form "God is F". Here we use words which we apply when first talking of creatures, and we could not manage to do that if our use of the words as applied to God and creatures were purely equivocal.[35] On the other hand, so Aquinas also wants to say, "it is impossible to predicate anything univocally of God and creatures" since God, unlike creatures, is wholly simple. "Every effect that falls short of what is typical of the power of its cause", Aquinas argues, "represents it inadequately, for it is not the same kind of thing as the cause. Thus what exists simply and in a unified way in the cause will be divided up and take various different forms in such effects". And, so Aquinas adds, "the perfections which in creatures are many and various pre-exist in God as one".[36]

It has been argued that Aquinas cannot really mean what he says when he denies that a word can be applied to God and to a creature univocally since he clearly believes that God really is, for example, good, and since he does not think that calling God good is saying something entirely different from what is being said when calling a creature good.[37] And there is value in this suggestion if we construe "univocal" as meaning "not equivocal". There is value in the suggestion too if we draw a certain distinction between "meaning" and "sense". The word "good" does not "mean" something different when we refer to good beef, good spin-dryers, and good neighbours. We do not have special words meaning "good as beef", "good as a spin-dryer", and "good as a neighbour". One word serves for all. But we are not saying the same of all the things which we call "good" since, as we might say, we use the word with different senses—meaning that we put it to varying uses. And with this point in mind, and with an eye on Aquinas, we might suggest that "the whole point of analogical predication is that the meaning remains the same (univocal) but the *sense* is different"[38] But we must also bear in mind that Aquinas wants to deny that God belongs to any natural class. On his account, "God is F" and "Creature X is F" are not attributing F-ness to each as F-ness may be attributed to each members of any natural class.

For Aquinas, God transcends the world of natural things, and attributes ascribed to him are not just present in him somewhat differently from the way in which they are present in creatures said to have them. For, on Aquinas's account, God, strictly speaking, does not have attributes. Simple and indistinguishable from his "attributes", God, for Aquinas, has whatever it takes to bring it about that there are creatures with whatever attributes they have.[39] In his commentary on Aristotle's *Peri Hermeneias* he refers to God's will (not to be distinguished from God) as "existing outside the realm of existents, as a cause from which pours forth everything that exists in all its variant forms" (*extra ordinem entium existens, velut causa quaedam profundens totum ens et omnes eius differentias*)".[40] In terms of this picture, God is not a substance with attributes distinguishable from itself and shareable, in different degrees, with other things.[41] God is the cause of all such substances. Since Aquinas thinks that these have their existence from God, and since he thinks that causes somehow contain their effects, he concludes that there is a likeness of creatures to God and that this can serve to justify much that we say of God. But this likeness, for Aquinas, is not that between members of a natural kind or even between members of different natural kinds.[42]

For this reason, Herbert McCabe is correct to note that "for St Thomas, when we speak of God we do not know what we are talking about. We are simply taking language from the familiar context in which we understand it and using it to point beyond what we understand into the mystery that surrounds us and sustains the world we do partially understand".[43] For this reason also, Alexander Broadie is right to note that, although Aquinas denies that we can speak of God only by negations, and although he cites Maimonides as a major exponent of the thesis he is rejecting, there is still a striking similarity between the thinking of Aquinas and Maimonides when it comes to the "names of God".[44] Both insist that we do justice to God by denying that God is what creatures are. Aquinas looks for more than negative assertions concerning God.[45] But Maimonides concedes that terms implying imperfection cannot be fittingly used of God. So, on his view, not just anything said of God is acceptable. In his commentary on Book 1 of Peter Lombard's *Sentences* (Distinction 2,1,3), Aquinas, interestingly, tries to reconcile Maimonides (speaking negatively of God) and Dionysius and St Anselm (speaking positively of God). "It is clear", he suggests, "that neither view contradicts what the other wants to say, since the first people do not say that God is lacking in any mode of perfection, and the second do not say that there are in God any qualities or non-subsistent things".

At this point it might help if we focus on Aquinas's teaching that God is the source of the fact that things have being—or, as Aquinas puts it in Latin, that God is the source of the *esse* of things. As Aquinas often uses it, the word *esse* is best translated as if it were a kind of noun, literally as "the to be". Normally, though, when Aquinas uses *esse* in this sense, translators report him as talking about "being", which is also a perfectly respectable way of translating him. But we should not suppose that Aquinas thinks of *esse* as if it were an individual of some kind (as Mary is an individual woman, or Paul an individual man). Nor does Aquinas think that *esse* is a distinguishing property or quality of anything—like redness or being short-sighted. *Esse*, for Aquinas, is no independently existing thing. Nor is it anything that can enter into a description of what a thing is (in the language of Aquinas, it is not the name of a "form"). Yet it is, so he thinks, something very much to be reckoned with.

To try to understand what Aquinas is driving at here, we can start by noting that there is a difference between knowing what something is and knowing whether or not the thing actually exists. By this I mean that we can know what something is if we know the meaning of a word—the word "cat", say. But understanding the meaning of "cat" is different from knowing that there are any cats. You can see this if we change the example and talk, instead, about knowing what a unicorn is. We will not be puzzled if we read a story which features unicorns. We will not say, "But the word 'unicorn' does not mean anything; 'unicorn' is a piece of gibberish". On the other hand, however, we will not suppose that there are any unicorns.

Now suppose that something actually turns up in the world which fits with what we mean when we use the word "unicorn". In that case, we can study it. And as a result of doing this, we might come to a deeper sense of what a unicorn is. We might develop a science of unicorns, just as we have developed a science of cats. We might come to know what a unicorn is in a way that goes beyond being able to make sense of stories with the word "unicorn" in them. We might come to know what a unicorn is in a way that goes beyond knowing the meaning of a word.[46]

Aquinas would put all this by saying that we might come to distinguish between *what* a thing is and *whether or not it is*. He would also say that, if a thing is, it has *esse*. Once again, I stress that Aquinas does not think of *esse* as a property or quality of anything. On his account, if a unicorn turned up so that we could produce a science of unicorns (an account of what unicorns are), we would not end up saying that as well as being like horses, say, they have *in addition* the characteristic of *esse*. But Aquinas does want to insist that genuine, breathing unicorns (genuine subjects of scientific investigation) would be different from what we might call "the meanings of words"—as when we observe that we can understand what "unicorn" means without believing that there are any unicorns. Or, as Aquinas would say, genuine, breathing unicorns would have *esse*—just as cats do.

But now suppose we ask how it comes about that there are cats. There are such things as cats. But how come that there are cats?

When we ask "How come?", the objects of our concern are fairly specifiable for the most part. We may, for example, wonder how it comes to be that some local phenomenon obtains. Why are there mountains to the east of Paris? Why is there a cat called Thor, who belongs to a Jesuit priest in New York (as there is) and who is called Thor since, according to his owner, he is "simply divine"?

Sometimes, however, the range of our inquiry may be wider. Someone might explain why there are mountains to the east of Paris. But we might then wonder why there should be *any mountains*, whether east of Paris or anywhere else. And we might wonder how there come to be *any cats*, whether in New York or anywhere else.

And if these questions are answered we might deepen the range of our inquiry. Mountains and cats are there for reasons to be documented and explored by physicists, geologists, chemists, astronomers, and so on. They will tell us how it comes to be, not that this and that individual is there, but why things of certain kinds are there. And in telling us this they will be invoking levels of explanation which run deeper and deeper.

In doing so, however, they will always presume a background of things, a world or universe in the light of which explanation is possible. The mountains east of Paris are explicable on geological and other grounds. Cats are explicable in genetic and other terms. And, if we ask why geology is possible and why genetics is possible, we shall again be looking for things of a kind behaving in certain ways.

But we might further deepen the level of our inquiry. For we might ask, not "What in the world accounts for this, that, or the other?", but "Why any world at all?". How come the whole familiar business of asking and answering "How come?".

The point to stress now is that this, for Aquinas, is a crucial question. For him, the question "How come any universe?" is a serious one to which there must be an answer. And he gives the name "God" to whatever the answer is. God, for Aquinas, is the reason why there is any universe at all. God, he says, is the source of the *esse* (and of the *essentia*) of things—the fact that they are more than the meanings of words.

Now (and this is what the last few paragraphs have been leading up to), Aquinas's views on *esse*, among other views he had, lead him to his conclusion that we cannot know what God is. How so? The answer Aquinas gives is that in speaking of whatever accounts for the fact that things have *esse* we must be careful not to attribute to it anything which cannot be true of whatever it is that accounts for there being any universe at all. For example, says Aquinas, we cannot suppose that God is part of the world of space and time. Nor can we suppose that God is subject to the limitations and changes which affect things spatial and temporal. So it will be nonsense to speak of God as literally being *here* as opposed to *there*, or as literally being *now* as opposed to *then*. And it will be nonsense to speak of God as something passing through successive states. And it will be even more nonsense to think of God as changing because other things have an effect on him. So it will be wrong to say that things in the world can modify God somehow. It will be wrong to say that they can, for instance, cause God to know things or cause God to undergo emotions. It will also, says Aquinas, be wrong to say that God has a character in any sense we can understand. Or, to put it another way, it will be wrong to assert that God is an individual—in the familiar sense of "individual" where to call something an individual is to think of it as a member of a class of which there could be more than one member, as something with a nature shared by others but different from that of things sharing natures of another kind. According to Aquinas, to conceive of God as the reason why there is any universe at all is to conceive of God as the source of diversity and therefore as the source of there being classes with different members, classes containing things with characteristic activities and effects. In Aquinas's view, therefore, God cannot be thought of as something with a character which is shown by what it typically produces (as, say, alcohol can be thought of as a substance with a character which is shown by what it typically produces). If God is what accounts for there being any universe, then God accounts for there being anything we can single out as having a nature distinct from other things: God accounts for everything we can understand. But, so Aquinas thinks, something which accounts for everything we can understand cannot be thought of as having a character which is indicated by what it typically produces. Alcohol has a character shown by what it typically produces. But to see that this is so is also to be aware that it produces *these* effects and not *those*. Given his views about God as source of *esse* however, Aquinas wants to say that God does not produces *these* effects and not *those*. God produces *esse*—the condition of us being able to describe things as truly being like *this* or like *that*.

In short, and as I mentioned earlier, Aquinas thinks that we cannot know what God is because we cannot have a science of whatever it is that accounts for there being any universe at all. "How come any universe at all?" is clearly not a scientific question. For it is asking how come that science itself is possible. And its answer cannot be anything which a scientist could investigate or analyze. Scientific questions concern objects or events which are part of the material universe. And answers to these questions refer us to other things of the same kind, to more objects or events which are part of the material universe. But the universe is not an object or event within itself. And whatever accounts for there being a universe cannot be this either. And that is what Aquinas wants to say. In asking how there comes to be any universe, we are raising what he would call the question of creation (because the notion that the universe is created is the notion that it is made to be). And, so he insists, to say that something is created is not to locate it in historical terms or in terms of things having effects within the universe (in terms, so we might say, of *transformers*). According to Aquinas, to call something created is to speak of it as derived, not because it has come from something equally derived, and not because it has come to be because something has been transformed. For Aquinas, to call something created is to speak of it as derived because its existence as such is derived. To view the universe as created, he thinks, is not to place it in a context of scientific causes. It is to see that there is a question to ask after science has done all the work it can possibly do. According to Aquinas, there is a puzzle concerning the fact that there is anything there to be identified and spoken about and explained in terms of scientific or transforming causes.

For this reason, and in spite of the way in which he thinks that we can speak truly and literally of God, authors like David Burrell have reason on their side as they tell us what Aquinas thinks of God. There is a serious austerity in his thinking and one can see why it might be said that he has no doctrine of God. One might even say that Aquinas may be called an "agnostic". He is not, of course, an agnostic in the usual, modern sense of the word. We normally think of an agnostic as someone who typically says something like "We do not know, and the universe is a mysterious riddle". And that is not quite what Aquinas wants to say. But he certainly wants to say something with a highly agnostic ring to it.

The late Victor White O.P. once tried to put what Aquinas wants to say in this form: "We do not know what the answer is, but we do know that there is a mystery behind it all which we do not know. And if there were not, there would not even be a riddle. This Unknown we call *God*. And if there were no God, there would be no universe to be mysterious, and nobody to be mystified".[47] A problem with this way of representing Aquinas's thinking is that it seems to make him say (in modern everyday English) that God is wholly unknown and that we really have no idea at all what "God" means. And that is not quite his line. But his final position on our knowledge of God is decidedly agnostic, and White's paraphrase is, perhaps, more helpful than misleading in the long run. What Aquinas thinks about God may be compared with what we find at the end of Wittgenstein's *Tractatus Logico-Philosophicus*.[48] Here we read: "Not *how* the world is, is the mystical, but *that* it is".[49] For Wittgenstein, *how the world is* is a scientific matter with scientific answers. But, so he insists, even when the scientific answers are in, we are still left with the *thatness* of the world, the fact *that* it is. As Wittgenstein himself puts it: "We feel that even if *all possible* scientific questions be answered, the problems of life have still not been touched at all".[50] Aquinas seems to be saying something similar when he speaks of *esse* and creation. Unlike Wittgenstein, however, Aquinas sets himself to probe and to try to talk about the mystical. In a serious sense he does have a doctrine of God and his position is optimistic. But it is also highly modest.[51]

Notes

1. *Summa Theologiae*, Ia, Introduction to Q.2. Cf. Ia,1,3 ad 1; Ia,93,4 ad 1; Ia,45,1; *De Potentia*, VII,9.

2. Cf. *Summa Theologiae*, Ia,18; Ia,4; Ia,6; Ia,10; Ia,8; Ia,25; Ia,14; Ia,29; 2a2ae, 23,2 ad I; 2a2ae,24,2.

3. *Summa Contra Gentiles*, I,14.

4. Commentary on Dionysius's *Divine Names*, I,iii,77.

5. Commentary on Dionysius's *Divine Names*, I,iii,83–4.

6. Cf. Commentary on Peter Lombard's *Sentences*, I, d.37, q.3, a.3; *Sent.*, I, d.43, q.I. a.I; *Sent.*, IV d.7, q.I. a.3.

7. Cf. G.E.M. Anscombe and P. T. Geach, *Three Philosophers* (Oxford, 1961), p. 117. Cf. also John F. Wippel, *Metaphysical Themes in Thomas Aquinas* (Washington, 1984), pp. 239 f.

8. Cf. *Summa Theologiae*, Ia,3,3.

9. Cf. *Summa Theologiae*, Ia,3,3; *Summa Contra Gentiles*, I,22; *De Potentia*, VII,2.

10. Cf. *Summa Theologiae*, Ia,13,4 and *Summa Contra Gentiles*, I,35.

11. Aquinas understands what Frege would have called the distinction between "sense" and "reference". Cf. Gottlob Frege, *Collected Papers on Mathematics, Logic and Philosophy*, ed. Brian McGuiness (Oxford, 1984), pp. 157 ff. Cf. also Gerard J. Hughes, "Aquinas and the Limits of Agnosticism", in Gerard J. Hughes (ed.), *The Philosophical Assessment of Theology* (Tunbridge and Georgetown, 1987), pp. 42 ff.

12. For someone playing down the idea that Aquinas had a theory of analogy which he thought of as able to furnish us with knowledge of God, see Herbert McCabe O.P., Appendix 4 to Volume 3 of the Blackfriars edition of the *Summa Theologiae* (London and New York, 1964). According to McCabe, "too much has been made of St Thomas's alleged teaching on analogy. For him, analogy is not a way of getting to know about God, nor is it a theory of the structure of the universe, it is a comment on our use of certain words" (p. 106).

13. Cf. *Summa Contra Gentiles*, I,29; I,49; II,16; II,21; II,46; III,21; *Summa Theologiae*, Ia,6,1; 91,2; 105,1 ad 1.

14. Cf. *Summa Theologiae*, Ia,3,1.

15. Aquinas distinguishes different senses of "cause". Here I am concerned with what he has in mind when speaking of what he calls an "efficient cause". But we have to remember that, for Aquinas, God is more than an efficient cause.

16. Cf. *Summa Contra Gentiles*, I,29.

17. The thesis is repeated in many places by Aquinas. For some examples see *Summa Contra Gentiles*, I,29; I,73; II,6; II,20. Aquinas's thinking here can be traced at least as far back as Aristotle. Cf. *Metaphysics*, 12.4. 1070b30 ff. It is helpfully expounded by Timothy McDermott in *St Thomas Aquinas, "Summa Theologiae". A Concise Translation* (London, 1989), pp. xxxiii–xxxiv.

18. David Burrell, *Aquinas, God and Action* (London and Henley, 1979), pp. 21 and 13. Cf. A. D. Sertillanges, *Les Grandes Thèses de la Philosophie Thomiste* (Paris, 1928), Ch. 3.

19. Cf. Patrick Sherry, "Analogy Today", *Philosophy* 51 (1976).

20. Anscombe and Geach, op. cit., pp. 122 f.

21. Cf. *Summa Theologiae*, Ia,2,1; *Summa Contra Gentiles*, I,10–11; *De Veritate*, X,12.

22. *Summa Theologiae*, Ia,2,3.

23. Herbert McCabe, "The Logic of Mysticism—I", in Martin Warner (ed.), *Religion and Philosophy* (Cambridge, 1992), p. 48.

24. *Summa Theologiae*, Ia,2,2 ad 2.

25. P. T. Geach, "The Meaning of 'God'—II", in Warner, op. cit., p. 86.

26. Cf. *Summa Contra Gentiles*, I,42.

27. *Summa Theologiae*, Ia,13,2.

28. *Summa Theologiae*, Ia,13,2.

29. Having noted that Aquinas says that we must settle for knowing what God is not rather than what he is, Ralph McInerny reasonably observes that "this conviction scarcely reduces him to silence" and that one "might even find in the *Summa* a matter-of-factness in discussing things divine that seems presumptuous". See Ralph McInerny, *Being and Predication* (Washington, D.C., 1986), p. 272.

30. Cf. *Summa Theologiae*, Ia,6,1; *Summa Contra Gentiles*, I,13.

31. Cf. *Summa Theologiae*, Ia,8.

32. Cf. *Summa Theologiae*, Ia,10,2; *Summa Contra Gentiles*, I,99.

33. For an essay exploring this line of thinking see C.J.F. Williams, "Existence and the Meaning of the Word 'God'", *The Downside Review* LXXVII (1958).

34. Cf. Richard Swinburne, *The Coherence of Theism* (Oxford, 1977).

35. Cf. *Summa Theologiae*, Ia,13,5.

36. *Summa Theologiae*, Ia,13,5.

37. Cf. Swinburne, op. cit., Ch. 4. Cf. also Sherry, op. cit.

38. Cyril Barrett, "The Logic of Mysticism—II", in Warner, op. cit., p. 66.

39. For a helpful critique of the view that talk about God and creatures as Aquinas thinks of God is sensibly construed as univocal, see Hughes, op. cit.

40. Book 1, lectio 14. Cf. *Summa Theologiae*, Ia,13,8 ad 2.

41. Cf. *Summa Contra Gentiles*, I,25 and 26; *Summa Theologiae*, Ia,3,5.

42. Hence Aquinas argues that perfections "attributable" to God and creatures belong primarily to God and only secondarily to creatures. Cf. *Summa Theologiae*, Ia,13,3.

43. McCabe, "The Logic of Mysticism—", p. 58.

44. Alexander Broadie, "Maimonides and Aquinas on the Names of God", *Religious Studies* 23 (1987). Broadie usefully develops his reading of Maimonides and notes strong parallels between Aquinas and Maimonides in "Maimonides on the Great Tautology: Exodus 3,14", *Scottish Journal of Theology* 47 (1994).

45. *Summa Theologiae*, Ia,13,2.

46. Cf. Aquinas's Commentary on Aristotle's *Posterior Analytics* (*Comm. in II, Post Anal.*, Cap. VII, Lect. 6): "Si non sit aliqua res cuius essentiam definitio significet nihil differt definitio a ratione exponente significationem alicuius nominis". That is: "If there is nothing to have its essence signified by a definition, then the definition is no different from the explanation of the meaning of a term".

47. Victor White O.P., *God the Unknown* (London, 1956), pp. 18 f.

48. Ludwig Wittgenstein, *Tractatus Logico-Philosophicus*, trans. C. K. Ogden (London, 1933). Cf. "Wittgenstein's Lecture on Ethics", *The Philosophical Review* LXXIV (1965).

49. *Tractatus*, 6.44.

50. *Tractatus*, 6.52.

51. For helpful comments on drafts of this paper I am indebted to Victor Austin, Alexander Broadie, Avery Dulles S.J., Denis Geraghty O.P., Norman Kretzmann, Herbert McCabe O.P., Timothy McDermott, James Sadowsky S.J., and Sara Penella.

9

Ñо

Intentionality

Aquinas and Wittgenstein

In part I, section V of the *Philosophical Grammar* Wittgenstein sets himself a problem.

> That's *him* (this picture represents *him*)—that contains the whole problem
> of representation.
>
> What is the criterion, how is it to be verified, that this picture is the
> portrait of that object, i.e. that it is *meant* to represent it? It is not similar-
> ity that makes the picture a portrait (it might be a striking resemblance of
> one person, and yet be a portrait of someone else it resembles less). . . .
>
> When I remember my friend and see him 'in my mind's eye', what is
> the connection between the memory image and its subject? The likeness
> between them?
>
> . . . Here we have the old problem . . . the problem of the harmony be-
> tween world and thought. (*PG*, p. 102)

In this essay I will say something about Wittgenstein's answer to his own
question, his account of the harmony between world and thought. But
mainly I will discuss an older solution to this old problem, to the question
what makes a picture of X a picture *of* X, what makes an image of X an
image *of* X, what makes a thought about X be *about* X?

One of the most elaborate and also one of the most puzzling accounts
of the harmony between the world and thought is Aquinas' doctrine of
the immaterial intentional existence of forms in the mind. According to
Aquinas, when I think of redness, what makes my thought be a thought
of redness is the form of redness. When I think of a horse, similarly, it is
the form of horse which makes the thought be a thought of a horse and
not of a cow. What makes the thought of a horse the thought of a horse
is the same thing as makes a real horse a horse: namely, the form of

243

horse. The form exists, individualized and enmattered, in the real horse; it exists, immaterial and universal, in my mind. In the one case it has *esse naturale*, existence in nature; in the mind it has a different kind of existence, *esse intentionale*.

What are we to make of this strange doctrine? The first question that arises is: what is a form? One of the most illuminating accounts of Aquinas' doctrine of forms is given by Geach in his paper 'Form and existence'.[1] This contains a useful comparison between Frege's theory of functions and Aquinas' theory of forms. Just as Frege regarded a predicate, such as ' . . . is a horse', as standing for a particular kind of function, namely a concept, so Aquinas held that a general term such as 'horse' standing in predicate position referred to a form. The form referred to by the predicate that occurs in the sentence 'Socrates is wise' may be referred to also by the phrase 'the wisdom of Socrates'; but this latter expression must not be construed as 'wisdom, which belongs to Socrates', just as 'the square root of 4' does not mean 'the square root, which belongs to 4'. 'The wisdom of Socrates' in Geach's terminology refers to an *individualized* form; the expression which indicates the generic form, the form strictly so called, is not 'wisdom' nor 'the wisdom of Socrates' but 'the wisdom of . . . ' (Cf. *Summa Theologiae*, Ia, 3, 2 ad 4; Ia, 50, 2). 'Wisdom' *tout court* means nothing in heaven or earth; wisdom is always *wisdom of*; as Aquinas puts it, it is of something (*entis*) rather than itself something (*ens*). Against Plato's doctrine that the form signified by a general term is 'one over against many', Aquinas insisted that the question 'one or many' is itself only intelligible if we ask it in relation to a general term that signifies a form or nature.

Geach admits that the account he gives of individualized forms does not accord in all respects with Aquinas' language; but it is a most interesting analysis in its own right, whether or not it is to be found in its worked out form in Aquinas' writings. Geach treats Aquinas as Aquinas treated Aristotle—improving his insights, tactfully masking his confusions, charitably resolving his ambiguities. This may exasperate historians, but it is the philosophically rewarding way to read a classic text. But in some cases Geach benignly interprets Aquinas in a way which fathers on him interpretations which fall foul of what Aquinas says explicitly elsewhere. This is the case, as I shall later try to show, when Aquinas' doctrine of form is expounded by Geach in the context of intentional existence.

Another author who has contributed greatly to the exposition of Aquinas' theory of intentionality in recent years is the Canadian Jesuit Bernard Lonergan. In his book *Verbum*,[2] Lonergan links the doctrine of intentionality with the Aristotelian theorem of the identity in act of knower and known. In the *De Anima* we are told, as Lonergan summarizes, that

the one operation, sensation, is effected by the sensible object and received in the sensitive potency; as from the object it is action; as in the
subject, it is passion; thus, sounding is the action of the object and
hearing the passion of the subject, and so by the theorem of identity,
sounding and hearing are not two realities but one and the same.
(p. 147)

Because of differences between Greek and English vocabulary, Aristotle's
point is easier to illustrate with an example such as taste. A piece of sugar,
something which can be tasted, is a sensible object; my ability to taste is a
sensitive potency; the operation of the sense of taste upon the sensible object
is the same thing as the action of the sensible object upon my sense; that is
to say, the sugar's tasting sweet to me is one and the same event as my
tasting the sweetness of the sugar. The sugar is actually sweet, but until put
into the mouth is only potentially tasting sweet: the scholastic jargon for this
was to say that the sugar, outside the mouth, was sweet 'in first act' but not
'in second act'. It is the second actuality, sweetness in second act, which is
at one and the same time the sugar's tasting sweet and the tasting of the
sweetness of the sugar. (Something like black coffee, which can be made
sweet if you put sugar into it, is not sweet either in first act or second act,
but only in potentiality.)

Aquinas adopted this Aristotelian theorem, and frequently states it in its
Latin version: *sensibile in actu est sensus in actu*. But he also emphasizes the
corresponding doctrine about thought as well as the theorem about sensation. Not only is the actualization of a sensible object the same thing as the
actualization of the sense-faculty; so too the actualization of an object of
thought is the same thing as the actualization of the capacity for thinking.
Intelligibile in actu est intellectus in actu.

The meaning of the slogan, however, according to Lonergan, has under-
gone a change. The meaning is not the original Aristotelian identity in second
act, but rather assimilation at the level of ideas, or, as they are called by
Aquinas, *species*. Knowing, according to Lonergan, is essentially a matter of
assimilation: like is known by like.

Its grounds in Aristotelian theory are reached easily: as the thing is the
thing it is in virtue of its form or species, so too a thought is the ontological reality it is in virtue of its own form or species; so further, unless
the form of the thing and the form of the thought were similar, there
would be no ground for affirming that the thought was a thought of the
things. (p. 148)

The similarity must be a similarity not at the level of matter, but of form: it must be an immaterial assimilation.

> The senses are receptive of sensible forms without the matter natural to those forms, much as wax is receptive of the gold of which the seal is made. In human intellect immaterial assimilation reaches its fulness in immaterial reception: not only is the matter of the agent not transferred to the recipient, as the gold of the seal is not transferred to the wax; not only is the form of the agent not reproduced in matter natural to it, as in sensation; but the form of the agent object is received in a strictly immaterial potency, the possible intellect. (p. 149)

'Possible intellect' is a transliteration of the Latin '*intellectus possibilis*', which is Aquinas' term for the intellect in its role as storehouse of thoughts and ideas. 'Receptive intellect' might be a more illuminating English term for it. This intellect, Lonergan tells us, summarizing Aquinas,

> . . . is not the form of any organ; it has no other nature but ability to receive; it stands to all intelligible forms as prime matter stands to all sensible forms; and precisely because it is in act none of the things to be known, it offers no subjective resistance to objective knowing.

The substance of Lonergan's account of intentionality, then, is as follows. If A is to know X, then the form of A's knowing must be similar to the form of X which is known, but it must also be different. It must be similar in essence, if X is to be known; but it must be different in mode, if A is to be a knower and not merely the known.

> Modal difference of form results from difference in recipients: the form of colour exists naturally in the wall, but intentionally in the eye, because wall and eye are different kinds of recipient; similarly angels have a natural existence on their own but an intentional existence in the intellects of other angels. (p. 151)

Intentional existence and immaterial existence are not the same thing. A pattern exists, naturally and materially, in a coloured object; it exists, intentionally and materially, in the eye or, according to Aquinas, in the lucid medium. Gabriel is a form which exists immaterially and naturally in its own right; it exists immaterially and intentionally in Raphael's thought of Gabriel. The characteristic of intellectual thought, whether of men or angels, is that it is the existence of form in a mode which is both intentional and immaterial.

I leave Aquinas' account of angelic understanding to those who are better acquainted than I with angels; I want to consider his thesis as a thesis about human thought. According to Lonergan's interpretation, the theory is essentially that the form of X when X is thought of is similar to the form existing in an object which is really X. But on Geach's interpretation the doctrine of intentionality should not be treated as a doctrine of the similarity of forms, but as a doctrine of the identity of forms. Geach puts the matter thus:

> What makes a sensation or thought of an X to be *of an X* is that it is an individual occurrence of that very form or nature which occurs in an X— it is thus that our mind 'reaches right up to the reality'; what makes it to be a *sensation* or *thought* of an X rather than an actual X or an actual X-ness is that X-ness here occurs in the special way called *esse intentionale*, and not in the 'ordinary' way called *esse naturale*.

So for Geach we have not just similarity but identity of forms. To be sure, my thought of a horse and the form of that horse grazing in the field are two *occurrences* of the form; but they are two occurrences of the *same* form, every bit as much as two occurrences of the form of horse in two horses grazing side by side.

Which is the correct interpretation of Aquinas, Lonergan's or Geach's? In my view, neither interpreter has the matter wholly right, and a third interpretation is possible which is both a more accurate account of Aquinas and a more plausible account of the nature of intentionality.

Lonergan is not successful in establishing that there is a shift of meaning between the two slogans *sensibile in actu est sensus in actu* and *intelligibile in actu est intellectus in actu*. Geach is right that the same theorem of identity is being enunciated both in the case of sensation and of understanding. Aquinas is committed to the identity of the objects of thought and the activity of the thinker just as he is to the identity of the activity of a sense-object and the activity of the sense-faculty. But there is no doubt that the doctrine about thought is more difficult to understand than the doctrine about sensation, and it is not surprising that Lonergan should attempt to adulterate it.

In stating the theorem with regard to the senses earlier I said that a piece of sugar was a sensible object. This is not strictly correct: it is the piece of sugar *qua* sweet ('*dulce*', 'the sweet') which is the sensible object; it is the sweetness of the sugar whose actuality is identical with the taster's tasting, not the sugar itself. In the case of a secondary quality such as sweetness, it is easy enough to accept the theorem of identity in second act. We can understand that the secondary quality in act is one and the same as the activity of the appropriate sense; the sweetness of X just is the ability of X to taste sweet. (It is related, of course, to various chemical properties and constituents of X; but that relation, unlike the relation to the activity of tasting sweet, is a contingent one.) But suppose that I think of the redness of X: can it be said that the redness of X just is the ability that X has to be thought of as red? Surely not: so how can the doctrine of identity in act apply to thought as well as to sensation?

To see how, we must recall that for Aquinas the real object of all human knowledge is form. The senses perceive the accidental forms of objects that are appropriate to each modality: with our eyes we see the colours and shapes of objects; with our noses we perceive their smells; colours, shapes, and smells are accidental forms or accidents, as opposed to substantial forms, the forms which locate things in their appropriate species. The accidental forms which are perceived by the senses are individual forms—it is the colour of *this rose* that I see and even the most powerful nose cannot take in the smell of the universal *sulphur*. Substantial form, on the other hand, is grasped not by the senses but by the intellect: the proper object of the human intellect is the nature of form of material things. Material things are composed of matter and form, and the individuality of a parcel of matter is not something that can be grasped by the intellect. The intellect can grasp what makes Socrates a man but not what makes him Socrates; it can grasp his form but not his matter; or rather, more strictly, it grasps his nature by grasping the form plus the fact that the form must be embodied in some matter or other of the right kind. But because it is matter which is the principle of individuation, the form which is grasped by the intellect is universal, unlike the individual accidental forms which are the objects of sense-perception.

This feature is neglected in Geach's presentation of the theory that the form of the thought is the same as the form of the object of thought. Geach argues that we must make a real distinction between form and existence: in the case of each individualized form there is a distinction between the form and its *esse*. But Aquinas' doctrine of intentionality does not provide grounds for such a distinction, contrary to what Geach says. It is no part of Aquinas' doctrine that there is one same individualized form of horse which occurs in a particular horse, say Eclipse, with *esse naturale* and occurs also in my mind with *esse intentionale*. What we have are two different individualizations of the same form, not two different existences of the same individualized form. The form, in the mind, is individuated by its thinker.

Geach writes:

When Plato thinks of redness, what exists in Plato is not a certain *relation* to redness or red things, but *is* redness, is an individual occurrence of the very same form of which another individual occurrence is the redness of this rose.

There is an equivocation in the sense of 'individual occurrence' here. The occurrence of redness in a particular rose is an individual occurrence because it is an occurrence of redness in a particular rose: it is the redness of *this rose*. The occurrence of redness when Plato thinks of redness is not individual by being the thought of the redness of any particular thing, but by being a thought thought by a particular thinker, namely Plato. It was a constant doctrine of Aquinas that thought, as such, is not directly of individual things at all, neither of individual forms like the redness of Socrates nor of individual substances like Socrates himself (e.g. *S. Th.*, Ia, 86, 1). When I think of Socrates there is no form of Socrateity having intentional existence in my mind; unlike Duns Scotus, who believed in individual essence, *haecceitas*, Aquinas would have denied that there was any such form. According to Aquinas, when I think of Socrates there is in my mind only the universal form of humanity; I can use this form to think of Socrates only by placing it within a context of sensory imagery (*phantasmata*). The individual humanity of Socrates has *esse naturale* in Socrates but it does not have *esse intentionale* in my mind or in anyone's mind; the universal, humanity, has *esse intentionale* in my mind, but it does not have *esse naturale* in Socrates or in any human being. In neither case do we have one same individualized form with two different modes of *esse*. So the doctrine of intentionality is not, as Geach represents it, a doctrine of two modes of existence of the same individualized form. For in thought there are no individualized forms, only universals.

An accurate account of Aquinas' theory of intentionality has to give full weight to his thesis that there is no intellectual knowledge of individuals. Aquinas wrote:

> Plato thought that the forms of natural things existed apart without matter and were therefore thinkable; because what makes something actually thinkable (*actu intelligibile*) is its being non-material. These he called ideas. Corporeal matter, he thought, takes the form it does by sharing in these, so that individuals by this sharing belong in their natural kinds or types; and it is by sharing in them that our understanding takes the forms that it does of knowledge of the different kinds and types. But Aristotle did not think that the forms of natural things existed independently of matter, and forms existing in matter are not actually thinkable. (*S. Th.*, Ia, 19, 3)

Forms existing in matter, Aquinas says, are only thinkable in the same way as colours are visible in the dark. Colours are perceptible by the sense of sight; but in the dark colours are only perceptible potentially, they are not actually perceptible. The sense of vision is only actuated—a man only sees the colours—when light is present to render them actually perceptible. Similarly, Aquinas says, the things in the physical world are only potentially thinkable or intelligible. An animal with the same senses as ours perceives and deals with the same material objects as we do; but he cannot have intellectual thoughts about them—he cannot, for instance, have a scientific understanding of their nature. To explain our ability to do so we have to postulate a species-specific capacity for abstract thought: what Aquinas calls the agent intellect, the *intellectus agens* which he contrasts with the receptive intellect or *intellectus possibilis*. We, because we can abstract ideas from the material conditions of the natural world, are able not just to perceive but to think about and understand the world.

Does this mean that Aquinas is an idealist? Does he mean that we never really know or understand the world itself, but only our own immaterial, abstract, universal ideas? Aquinas was not a representative idealist: he explicitly rejected the thesis that the intellect can know nothing but its own ideas. But Aquinas' thesis does mean that he is anti-realist in one of the many senses of that term. And, though he did not think that we can know nothing but our own ideas, he rejected equally the idea that our knowledge of material objects could be something which was purely intellectual. In this, I believe, his instinct was sound, if we identify 'intellectual' with 'linguistic'.

When I think of a particular human being, there will be, if I know her well, very many descriptions I can give in language to identify the person I mean. But unless I bring in reference to particular times and places there may be no description I can give which would not in theory be satisfiable by a human being other than the one I mean; I cannot individuate simply by describing her appearance, her qualities. Only perhaps by pointing, or taking you to see her, can I make clear which person I mean; and pointing and vision go beyond pure intellectual, linguistic, thought.

Similarly, Aquinas thought, if I bring in spatiotemporal individuating references I have left the realm of intellectual thought: from the point of view of a pure spirit there would be no such framework.

Our intellect cannot have direct and primary knowledge of individual material objects. The reason is that the principle of individuation of material objects is individual matter; and our intellect understands by abstracting ideas from such matter. But what is abstracted from individual matter is universal. So our intellect is not directly capable of knowing anything which is not universal. (*S. Th.*, Ia, 86, 1)

It is by linking universal intellectual ideas with sensory experience that we know individuals and are capable of forming singular propositions such as 'Socrates is a man'.

If Plato was wrong, as Aquinas thought he was, then there is not, outside the mind, any such thing as human nature as such; there is only the human nature of individual human beings like Jack and Jill. But, because the humanity of individuals is form embedded in matter, it is not something which can, as such, be the object of intellectual thought. In Aquinas' terminology, an individual's humanity is 'intelligible' (because a form) but not 'actually intelligible' (because existing in matter). It is the agent intellect which, on the basis of our experience of individual human beings, creates the intellectual object, humanity as such. This, then, is the sense in which Aquinas, though not an idealist, is anti-realist. The ideas are not intermediate entities which represent the world: they are modifications of our intellect consisting in the acquired ability to think certain thoughts. But the universals which the ideas are ideas of are themselves things which have no existence outside the mind, as universals. Their only existence is their ability to occur in thoughts. Thus the actuality of the universal thoughts is one and the same thing as the actuality of the capacity for intellectual thought. *Intelligibile in actu est intellectus in actu.*

Putting Aquinas' doctrine in modern terms, we might say that our thoughts have the sense they have because of the universal forms in which we think; they have the reference they have to individuals because of the sensory context in which they occur. In *Philosophical Investigations*, II, xi, Wittgenstein wrote:

> 'At that word we both thought of him.' Let us assume that each of us said the same words to himself—and how can it mean MORE than that?— but wouldn't even those words be only a *germ*? They must surely belong to a language and to a context, in order really to be the expression of the thought *of* that man.
>
> If God had looked into our minds he would not have been able to see there whom we were speaking of. (PI, p. 217)

If by 'mind' we mean 'intellect' Aquinas would have agreed. To see my reference to an individual, God would have to look outside the intellect to the *phantasmata*.

It is not altogether clear what Aquinas means by *phantasmata*: I have been translating his references to them by vague and benign phrases such as 'reference to a context of sense and imagination'. I believe that in Aquinas' dicta about phantasms there is combined a correct and important insight about the relation between the intellect on the one hand and the imagination and senses on the other, with a confused theory about the nature of the imagination and the character of mental imagery.

Aquinas often states that phantasms are necessary not only for the acquisition of concepts but also for their exercise. In this life at least, it is impossible for us to think any thought except by attending to phantasms. We can see this, he says, if we reflect that injury to the brain can impede thought, and if we remember that we all conjure up images when we are doing our best to understand something. However dubious these arguments may be, it does seem to be true that there must be some exercise of sense or imagination, some application to a sensory context, if we are to be able to pin down someone's habitual knowledge or beliefs to an exercise on a particular occasion. He need not recite to himself his belief in his imagination, or see its content in his mind's eye perhaps; but at least something in his sensory experience or conscious behaviour must occur for it to be possible to latch the thought on to a date and time.

Attention to phantasms is, according to Aquinas, necessary for any thought, even of the most abstract and universal kind. But a special type of relationship to phantasms (*reflexio supra phantasmata*) is needed if the thought is to be a thought concerning individuals rather than universals. In a manner which remains mysterious, Aquinas seems to have thought that only the appropriate accompanying mental imagery would differentiate a thought about Socrates from a thought about Plato or about any other human being. Even if this is so, it seems that the same questions about individuation could arise about the mental imagery as arise about the thought, unless we relate the imagery in some way to a transaction in the world outside the imagination. This brings us back to Wittgenstein's question from which we began: what makes an image of X an image of X? Wittgenstein's own answer to his problem goes as follows:

> How can I know that someone means [a] picture as a portrait of N?—
> Well, perhaps he says so or writes it underneath.
>
> What is the connection between the portrait of N and N himself? Perhaps that the name written underneath is the name used to address him. . . .
>
> The image of him is an unpainted portrait.
>
> In the case of the image too, I have to write his name under the picture to make it the image of him. (PG, p. 102)

Aquinas' theory of the imagination is in some sense naive and unsatisfactory: he calls the imagination an inner sense and his picture of how it operates is modelled far too closely on the operation of the senses. He seems to have thought that an inner sense differed from an outer sense principally in having an organ and an object inside the body (in the brain) rather than outside. Wittgenstein and others have shown how misleading this picture of the imagination is. If we are to accept Aquinas' view that it is *phantasmata* which give references to individuals, we have to fill out his account with the kind of considerations which Wittgenstein adduces.

While Aquinas' account of the imagination seems unacceptable, he has a clear grasp of the relationship between the intellect and the imagination when thought takes place in mental images or in subvocal speech. In such cases it is not the imagery that gives content to the intellectual thought, or meaning to the words which express the thought. It is the intellect that gives meaning to the imagery—whether imagined words or pictures or mental images—by using it in a certain way. In the book of our thoughts it is the intellect that provides the text; the mental images are illustrations. (Cf. PI, I,§663.)

We can sum up Aquinas' doctrine of intentionality thus. Both sense-perception and the acquisition of intellectual information and matters of the reception of forms in a more or less immaterial manner by a human being. In both perception and in thought a form exists intentionally. When I see the redness of the setting sun, redness exists intentionally in my vision; when I think of the roundness of the earth, roundness exists in my intellect. In each case the form exists without the matter to which it is joined in reality: the sun itself does not enter into my eye, nor does the earth, with all its mass, move into my intellect.

> A sensory form exists in one manner in the thing which is outside the
> soul, and in another manner in the sense itself, which receives the form
> of sensible objects without their matter—the colour of gold, for instance,
> without the gold. (S. Th., Ia, 84, 1c)

But intentional existence is not, as such, completely immaterial existence. The form in the eye lacks the matter of gold but not the matter of the eye; it is an individualized form, not a universal. And according to Aquinas the redness exists intentionally not only in the eye but in the lucid medium through which I see it.

But matters are different with the forms of thought. In the intellect there is no matter for the forms to inform. The receptive intellect indeed has no other nature than its ability to be informed by forms existing intentionally; if it had, it would be incapable of understanding whatever shared its nature, as coloured spectacles prevent one from distinguishing white light from light of their own colour (Ia, 75, 2; 87, 1). The occurrence of concepts and thoughts in the intellect is not a case of the modification of any matter: there is no moulding of mysterious mental material. If the intellect were composed of matter and form, the forms of things would be received into it in all their concrete individuality, so that it would known only the singular, as the senses do, which receive forms of things in a physical organ (Ia, 75, 5).

Aquinas' doctrine of the intentional existence of forms remains one of the most interesting contributions ever made to the philosophical problem of the nature of thought. Suppose that I think of a phoenix. There seem to be two things which make this thought the thought it is: first, that it is a thought of a phoenix and not of a cow or of a goat; secondly, that it is my thought and not your thought or Julius Caesar's. These seem to be the two essential properties of any thought: to have a content and to have a possessor. Of course, thoughts may have other properties too—e.g. they may be profound or childish, exciting or depressing, and so on—but the two things essential to any thoughts seem to be that they should be somebody's thoughts and that they should be thoughts of something. Any theory of the nature of thought must give an account of both these features.

Theories of thought propounded at different times emphasize different members of this pair of features. From the time of Descartes until comparatively recently the problem 'What makes my thoughts my thoughts' has comparatively rarely struck philosophers as problematic at all; but many have sought to give a solution to the problem of the relation of a thought to what it is a thought of. Does a thought become a thought of X by being like X? Or is the relationship between thought and its object some other relationship? How can it be a relationship at all, since we can have thoughts of what does not exist, like my thought of a phoenix, and there is nothing in such a case for my thought to be related to. Moreover, even if we could agree on the relationship—say resemblance—and concentrate on the cases where there are things to be related to—say horses—there is still the problem: what *has* the relationship. A statue of a horse is a piece of stone or bronze, resembling, with greater or less success, a real horse; but in the mind there is nothing corresponding to the stone or the bronze to bear the resemblance. Aquinas' answer, that what makes the thought of a horse the thought of a horse is not any resemblance but an occurrence of the same thing which makes a horse a horse, makes easier the question concerning the content of the thought; but it makes more striking the question: what makes A's thought of a horse A's thought? There is nothing in the content of a thought that makes it one person's thought rather than another's. Innumerable people beside myself believe that two and two make four: when I believe this what makes the belief *my* belief?

The question was a very lively one in Aquinas' time and the subject of much controversy between Latin and Arab interpreters of Aristotle. Aquinas insisted, against the Averroists, that such a thought is my thought and not the thought of any world-soul or supra-individual agent intellect. But to the question what makes them *my* thoughts his only answer is the connection between the intellectual content of the thought and the mental images in which it is embodied. It is because these mental images are the products of my body that the intellectual thought is my thought. This answer seems unsatisfactory for many reasons. Wittgenstein, who reawoke philosophers to the importance of the question of individuating the possessor of a thought, was surely better inspired when he urges us to look at the expression of a thought to supply the criteria for individuating its possessor. Aquinas has nothing of value to offer in the search for such criteria: his significance for the modern reader here is that he alerts one to the existence of the problem.

But, if we make allowances for this lacuna in Aquinas' theory, can we say that in other respects the thesis of intentionality can be regarded as a sound philosophical account of the nature of thought?

The theorem that the activity of a sensible property is identical with the activity of a sense-faculty seems to be strictly true only of secondary qualities like taste and colour; it is only of these that we can say that their only actualization, the only exercise of their powers, is the actualization of sense-faculties. A primary quality, like heaviness, can be actualized not only be causing a feeling of heaviness in a lifter, but in other ways such as by falling and exerting pressure on inanimate objects.

But the intellectual equivalent of the theorem of identity in second act still seems defensible as a formulation of a particular kind of anti-realism. The actuality of the object of thought is the actuality of the power of thinking. That is to say, on the one hand, the intellect just is the capacity for, the locus of, intellectual thought; it has no structure or matter; it is just the capacity for thought. (Or, if we say it has a structure, all that this can mean is that it is a capacity which can be stratified, hierarchically, into other abilities and powers.) On the other hand, the object of intellectual thought, redness as such, is something which has no existence outside thought. Or so we must say unless we are prepared to embrace the Platonism which Aquinas rejected.

Of course, material objects are not to be identified with universals. They are objects which are thinkable in potency: their thinkability, their intelligibility, is their capacity to be brought under the universal concepts of the intellect's creation.

It is a commonplace to distinguish between two concepts of concept, of *Begriff*. There is an objective one, associated with Frege (a *Begriff* as something 'out there', mind-independent, the reference of a predicate), and a subjective one, associated with Wittgenstein (a concept as, e.g., the learnt mastery of a word in a language).

If Aquinas is right, the two kinds of *Begriff* are facets of the same item. The redness of *this* has existence outside thought; it has its own history and causal interactions; but redness as such has no existence outside thought. Redness as such is not something I think *of,* as I think of Napoleon; it is something, rather, which I think when I think of redness without thinking of the redness of any particular object. The thinkability of the redness of *this* is its ability to be abstracted by the human abstractive power, the species-specific ability to master language, the *intellectus agens.*

I have attempted to combine Aquinas' theory of intentional existence with the *prima facie* very different account of intentionality sketched by Wittgenstein. The resulting theory, if I am right, has the merit that it enables one to avoid the realist idealism of Platonism without falling into the conceptualist idealism of many anti-realists, past and present.

Notes

1. P. T. Geach, 'Form and Existence', *Proceedings of the Aristotelian Society,* 1954–5, pp. 250–76.
2. Bernard Lonergan, *Verbum* (Notre Dame Press, 1967).

10

⚬𝒩⚬

Man = Body + Soul

Aquinas's Arithmetic of Human Nature

For philosophers who find both a dualistic and a purely materialistic account of the human soul unacceptable, the Aristotelian-Thomistic conception of the soul as the substantial form of the living body may appear to be an intriguing alternative. However, even if one is not afraid of the prospect of committing oneself to an apparently "obsolete" metaphysics, developing such a commitment may not look to be a wise move after all, since upon closer inspection the doctrine may seem to be frustratingly obscure, if not directly self-contradictory.

In what follows I first present what may seem to be a fundamental problem of Aquinas's conception. Second, I will provide the solution that emerges from some crucial distinctions made by Aquinas in this context. The subsequent analysis of these distinctions will show how they fit into the larger context of Aquinas's general metaphysical, mereological and logical considerations, providing further clues as to how these considerations fit together in Aquinas's thought. In the concluding section I will argue that with the proper understanding of these conceptual connections, despite possible appearances to the contrary, Aquinas's conception does indeed offer a viable alternative to the modern dilemma of dualism vs. materialism.

1. The Problem

In his book *Aquinas on Mind*, Anthony Kenny calls our attention to the problem as follows:

If we identify the human soul with Aristotelian substantial form, it is natural to identify the human body with prime matter. But body and soul are not at all the same pair of items as matter and form. This is a point on which Aquinas himself insists: the human soul is related to the human body not as form to matter, but as form to subject (S 1–2,50,1). A human being is not something that has a body; it is a body, a living body of a particular kind. The dead body of a human being is not a human body any longer—or indeed any other kind of body, but rather, as it decomposes, an amalgam of many bodies. Human bodies, like any other material objects, are composed of matter and form; and it is the form of the human *body*, not the form of the matter of the human body, that is the human soul.[1]

Despite the fact that one might object to the way in which Kenny poses the problem—unfortunately, the rather sloppily presented contrast between matter and subject is not quite supported by the passage he refers to, and Aquinas himself would not contrast the two in the way in which Kenny intends this contrast[2]—there *is* a genuine problem here.

For Aquinas does indeed say *both* that a human being *is* a human body, namely, a rational, sensitive, living body, *and* that a human being *consists of* a soul and a body. But these two claims are apparently incompatible. For according to the latter claim the body is an integral part[3] of the whole human being consisting of body and soul. But then the whole human being cannot be this body, for no integral part can be the same as the whole of which it is only a part.

Furthermore, if the human soul is the substantial form of the human body, then, since what a substantial form informs is the Aristotelian prime matter according to Aquinas, it seems that the human body has to be prime matter.[4] However, the human body cannot be prime matter, since prime matter in itself cannot exist in actuality, whereas the human body obviously does exist in actuality.[5]

To be sure, at this point one might easily retort that the human body does exist in actuality precisely because it is actually informed by the soul. So the human body *is* prime matter *actually informed by the soul*.[6]

However, this quick riposte will not do. For if we were to identify the human body with *the matter* that the soul informs *in the context of the claim that a human being is composed of body and soul*, then we would also have to admit that the human body in this composition is that component which persists through a substantial change, such as death, since prime matter *in the composition of a material substance* is precisely that part which is the permanent subject of a substantial change, when it loses one substantial form and takes on another.[7] But the human body does not persist through death, for when it ceases to be informed by the soul it ceases to be, since the dead body of the human being is not a human body, except equivocally, according to Aquinas. So the human body cannot be prime matter, which is the immediate and persistent subject of the substantial form of the body.

On the other hand, given Aquinas's theory of the unity of substantial forms, it seems that it cannot be anything else either. For according to this theory, a substantial form cannot have anything else as its subject but prime matter, since otherwise it would have to inform something that would already exist in actuality. But this is impossible, for something that exists in actuality already has its own substantial form, so it cannot take on any other form as its substantial form.[8]

In fact, Aquinas's doctrine of the unity of substantial forms involves even further strange consequences in this regard. For according to this doctrine, the form on account of which a man is a body, his corporeity, is the same as that on account of which he is an animal, his animality, and this, in turn, is the same as that on account of which he is a human, his humanity. But Aquinas also argues that a man's humanity or quiddity is what he calls the "form of the whole" [forma totius], as opposed to the "form of the part" [forma partis], which he identifies as the soul, and that the form of the whole differs from the form of the part because the form of the whole contains both matter and form.[9] So the form of the whole, the quiddity of man, contains the soul as its part, so it obviously cannot be the same as the soul. But if it is not the same as the soul, and yet it is a form of the human being, and it is clearly not an accidental form, then it seems that we have at least two substantial forms here, one of which is a part of the other, and which, besides the form of the part, also contains matter! At this point, perhaps, our confusion has reached its peak, so it is about time we set about clarifying the basic concepts involved in these considerations.

2. The Solution

The question, then, is this: exactly how are we to understand Aquinas's claim that a human being essentially consists of body and soul, given his other claim that the soul is the one and only substantial form of the body?

To answer this question first we have to consider Aquinas's distinction, which he takes over from Avicenna, between several senses of the term 'body'.[10] In his *De Ente et Essentia* he writes as follows:

The name 'body' can be taken in several senses. For a body (1), insofar as it is in the genus of substance, is said to be a body (1) because it has such a nature that three dimensions can be designated in it, but the three designated dimensions themselves are the body (2) which is in the genus of quantity. But it happens that something that has some perfection also has a further perfection, as is obvious in the case of man, who has a sensitive nature, and beyond that also an intellective one. Likewise, to the perfection of having such a form that in the thing three dimensions can be designated another perfection can be added, such as life, or something like that. The name 'body' (3), therefore, can signify something which has a form from which there follows the designability of three dimensions with precision, namely, so that from that form no further perfection would follow, but if something is added, then it is beyond the signification of 'body' (3) in this sense. And in this sense the body (3) will be an integral and material part of an animal, for in this way the soul will be beyond the signification of the name 'body' (3), and it will be superadded to the body itself, so that the animal will be constituted from these two, namely, from the soul and the body (3), as its parts. But the name 'body' (1) can also be taken so that it should signify some thing which has a form on account of which three dimensions can be designated in it, whatever that form may be, whether it may give rise to some further perfection or not. And in this sense 'body' (1) will be a genus of 'animal', for an animal contains nothing which is not contained implicitly in a body (1). For the soul is not a form other than that on account of which in that thing three dimensions can be designated; and so when it was said that a body (1) is that which has such a form that three dimensions can be designated in it, it was understood so that whatever that form might be, whether animality or stoneness, or whatever else. And thus the form of animal is implicitly contained in the form of body (1), insofar as body (1) is its genus.[11]

To understand this passage correctly, we have to recall that according to Aquinas concrete common names *signify* the forms or natures of things, however, they do not *refer to*, or, using the medieval technical term, *supposit for* [*supponit pro*], these forms in virtue of their signification, but rather to the things themselves that have these forms in actuality. What we can use to refer to a form itself is the abstract name corresponding to the concrete name.[12] But then, if it turns out that we use a name in different senses, that is, with various significations, this means that the same name in its different senses signifies different forms in the same thing, and thus, in the corresponding different senses, the corresponding abstract term will refer to those different forms. For example, if someone is a bachelor both in the sense of holding a bachelor's degree and in the sense of being unmarried, then his bachelorhood in the first sense is certainly not the same as his bachelorhood in the second sense, which is clearly shown by the fact that if, he gets married he loses the latter, but not the former. In fact, this example also shows that the *forms signified* [*formae significatae*] by concrete terms and referred to by their abstract counterparts do not even have to be *forms* in the strict metaphysical sense of being some determinations of some real, whether substantial or accidental, act of being of their supposita.[13] For, obviously, the *forms signified* by the term 'bachelor' in both senses are some beings of reason: in the first sense the *form signified* is a relation of reason connecting the bachelor in question to some academic institution and its regulations, while in the second sense it is the privation of a relation of reason connecting him to his spouse, insofar as these relations are recognized by the relevant members of society.[14]

In the same way, while the term 'body', insofar as it is the genus of all bodies, signifies the substantial form of all bodies, referred to by the term 'corporeity' in the first sense, the same term in the sense in which it is in the genus of quantity signifies an accidental form of the same bodies, namely, their corporeity in the second sense, that is, their dimensions extending them in space.[15] But it is neither the first, nor the second sense of the term 'body' distinguished by Aquinas that is relevant to the claim that a human being, or indeed, any living being, is composed of body and soul. For the sense of the term 'body' relevant here, as Aquinas characterizes it, is clearly the sense in which a lifeless body, say a stone, is said to be a body, with the strict implication of lacking life. But since no living body can be a body in this sense, the corporeity of a living body in this sense is obviously not the substantial form of a living body. So while the forms signified by the term 'body' in the first and the third senses distinguished by Aquinas coincide in lifeless bodies, since in these bodies the term in both of these senses signifies their substantial form, the negative implication of the third sense of the same term, which it does not have in the first sense, prevents it from signifying the substantial form of living beings in this sense; therefore, in this sense it cannot refer to the whole living being, but only to a part of it.

So with this distinction at hand we can give an acceptable answer to the question of how Aquinas can claim *both* that a human being *is* a body *and* that he or she *has* a body, as his or her integral part. For a human being *is* a body in the first sense, while it *has* a body in the third of the three senses distinguished here, and thus no inconsistency is involved in these two claims.

However, this solution still does not answer the further doubts raised above. For it is still not clear how the corporeity signified in a human being by the term 'body' in its first sense is related to the corporeity signified in the same human being by the same term in its third sense, and how these are related to the soul of the same human being.

Before going into the details of this issue, however, we should recall the simple truth that there is more than one way to slice a cake. That is to say, the division of any integral whole into its integral parts will always depend on how we distinguish the parts in the whole.

Nevertheless, we must also keep in mind that the apparent arbitrariness involved in distinguishing the parts of something according to *our* criteria does not make these parts "unreal". For example, if we take the hapless Socrates and distinguish his left and right or upper and lower parts, in this process we get parts no less real than by distinguishing his members or organs, the only difference being that while in the former cases we distinguished his parts on the basis of their spatial orientation, in the latter we distinguished them on the basis of their function. To be sure, we may find some divisions to be *more natural* than others, in that they better "cut at the joints" of some whole. But that has rather to do with the relative unity of the parts in constituting the absolute unity of the whole, or *vice versa*, than with the reality or non-reality of the parts.[16] As St. Thomas reminds us:

> ... nothing prevents some things from being many in some respect and being one in another. Indeed, all sorts of things that are many are one in some respect, as Dionysius says in the last chapter of *On Divine Names*. But we have to be aware of the difference that some things are many absolutely, and one in some respect, while the case is the reverse with others. Now something is said to be one in the same way as it is said to be a being. But a being absolutely speaking is a substance, while a being in some respect is an accident, or even [only] a being of reason. So whatever is one in substance, is one absolutely speaking, yet many in some respect. For example, a whole in the genus of substance, composed of its several integral or essential parts, is one absolutely speaking, for the whole is a being and a substance absolutely speaking, while the parts are beings and substances in the whole. Those things, however, which are diverse in substance, and one by accident, are diverse absolutely speaking, and one in some respect, as many humans are one people, or many stones are one heap; and this is the unity of composition or order. Likewise, many individuals that are one in genus or species are many absolutely speaking, and one with respect to something, for to be one in genus or species is to be one with respect to reason. [For example,] in the genus of natural things, some whole is composed from matter and form, as man from body and soul, who is one natural being, although he has a multitude of parts ... [17]

So, although it is up to us to assign *our* criteria of distinguishing the integral parts making up some integral whole, which is, again, marked off *by us* as being the whole constituted by those parts, there will nevertheless be some absolute standard according to which the mereological constitution of the whole is not dependent on us, namely, the ontological status of the parts so distinguished and of the whole thus marked off. That is to say, even if we are absolutely free to regard a heap of stones as one, and an individual stone as a part of this one, nevertheless it is obvious that the unity of the individual stones is not of the same kind as the unity of the heap. For the heap is not a being in the same sense as the stones are, since precisely in that sense in which a stone is *one being* the heap is *not one being*, but rather it is *several beings*. Again, we are absolutely free to regard one half of one of these stones as one part of this one stone and the other half as the other part of the same stone, yet, it is clear that the unity of each of its halves is not the same as the unity of the stone, for in the sense in which one half of it is one being, the stone is not one being, but two beings, whereas in the sense in which the stone is one being, its halves are not even beings at all. For the stone is actually a being in its own right, while neither of its halves is actually a being in its own right; it only *can be* a being in its own right *if* the stone is actually cut into those two halves. But as the stone is actually undivided, it is one substance actually, while its two halves are two substances only potentially.[18] And since only that thing is one entity in the absolute, unqualified sense which is a being in the absolute, unqualified sense, and only what is actually a substance is a being in the absolute, unqualified sense, only the stone is actually one in the absolute, unqualified sense. And so, despite the fact that we could distinguish in the stone two halves, and we can say that it is made up of those two halves, this will not make the stone into two beings or two entities.

Furthermore, when we divide a stone into two parts, we can do so in a number of different ways, since obviously such a division need not result in two equal halves:

So clearly, if we divide it into two halves, or into one third and two thirds, or one quarter and three quarters, we are able to mark out these parts even before actually dividing it, on the basis of how much of the quantity of the whole we conceive of as belonging to the one part, and how much as belonging to the other. But then, in a similar manner, we can distinguish in the same thing not only parts of its quantity on this basis, but also any sorts of other parts, on the basis of how much of whatever we conceive in the thing we conceive as belonging to the one part and how much as belonging to the other.

Now, what does all this mean concerning the composition of man from body and soul? First of all, it is clear that the term 'body' in the first sense, in which it is the genus of all bodies, since it is predicable of a whole human being and not only of some part of him or her, signifies the unique substantial form of any human being, and so what it signifies in human beings, their corporeity, coincides with their rational soul.[19] In this sense, therefore, we do not distinguish the body from the soul as a part from another part, but as the whole from one of its parts.[20] But this part of this whole, namely, the soul, is not distinguished from the other parts on the basis of dividing the quantity of this whole. Rather, the distinction is made on the basis of the different perfections, indicating the different modes of existence that we conceive in this whole namely, the spatio-temporal, material mode of existence which this body has in common with all bodies, as opposed to the mode of existence which enables this body to perform several sorts of vital functions, that is, life, which it has in common with all living beings. But once we have distinguished these two modes of existence, namely, material, spatio-temporal existence on the one hand, and life on the other, we can obviously use different names, or the same names in different senses, to signify the substantial forms on account of which a thing has one of these modes of existence, or the other, or both in its own unique act of substantial being. So if we distinguish corporeity as that substantial form on account of which whatever has it exists in a material, spatio-temporal manner, whether the thing in question is alive or not, then the corporeity thus distinguished will clearly coincide in all living bodies with their soul, conceived as that substantial form on account of which whatever has this form is alive, whether it is a body or not. Therefore, in this non-exclusive sense, both the corporeity thus conceived and the soul thus conceived are nothing but the form of the whole, that is, the essence or quiddity of a living body. But if we conceive of corporeity as that on account of which whatever has it exists in a spatio-temporal manner, but is *not* alive, the corporeity thus conceived cannot coincide with the substantial form of a living body, so this conception of corporeity can mark out only some part of the essence of a living body. Also, if we conceive of the soul as that on account of which whatever has it is alive but is not a body, the concept of soul thus conceived can mark out only some part of a living body, in which both material existence and life are united in its single act of substantial existence, its spatio-temporal, material life.

Of course, spatio-temporality and life in themselves are not incompatible, which is shown by the manifest existence of living bodies. However, they do not entail each other either, as is shown by the manifest existence of lifeless bodies as well as by the at least conceivable existence of living immaterial substances. Therefore, it should come as no surprise that we can form both the non-exclusive and the exclusive concepts of those substantial forms on account of which any substance has either life or spatio-temporality or both. Accordingly, the concepts of 'body' and 'soul' in the relevant non-exclusive and exclusive senses can indeed be properly characterized by the following entailments and denials of entailments, just as St. Thomas suggested:

1. x is a body$_1$ $\rightarrow$ x is spatio-temporal
2. $\sim$ (x is a body$_1$ $\rightarrow$ x is not alive)
3. x is a body$_2$ $\rightarrow$ x is spatio-temporal & x is not alive
4. y is a soul$_1$ $\rightarrow$ (x has y $\rightarrow$ x is alive)
5. $\sim$ (y is a soul$_1$ $\rightarrow$ (x has y $\rightarrow$ x is not spatio-temporal))
6. y is a soul$_2$ $\rightarrow$ (x has y $\rightarrow$ x is alive & x is not spatio-temporal)

Therefore, the essence of a living body, which can be referred to as a corporeity, in the first, non-exclusive sense, has to consist of a corporeity in the second, exclusive sense, and of a soul also in the second, exclusive sense, as its integral parts:

7. corporeity$_1$ (of a living body$_1$) = corporeity$_2$ (of the same living body$_1$) + soul$_2$ (of the same living body$_1$)

By contrast, the corporeity of a non-living body will be the same essence in both senses:

8. corporeity$_1$ (of a non-living body$_1$) = corporeity$_2$ (of the same non-living body$_1$),

But then a *living body*$_1$ will have to consist of a body$_2$ and a soul$_2$:

9. living body$_1$ = soul$_2$ (of the same living body$_1$) + body$_2$ (of the same living body$_1$)

In fact, this is precisely how Cajetan interprets St. Thomas's above-quoted remarks in his commentary on the *De Ente et Essentia*:

As of now, it seems to me that it must be said that man is composed from soul and body, and is a third thing not only as composed from two things, but also as from two parts which are a whole in reality. I take body not in so far as it is the genus, but in so far as it signifies a part, and take soul in its exclusive meaning, as defined in II *de Anima*. Thus viewed, body means a composite of matter and a corporeal perfection taken exclusively. Soul means the perfection of life exclusively.

I prove my thesis thus. Body differs really from soul, and not as a whole differs from a part; therefore it differs as a part from a part. The added point is proved: the whole includes, at least confusedly, the part, but the body viewed in this way excludes the soul. Thus the body is included in the definition of the soul as a subject supporting the soul, as St. Thomas says there. The first proposition is evident in itself and conceded by all. The consequence draws its force from an adequate division. For if the soul and the body differ really, the body must differ really from the soul as a whole from the part or as a part from a part. Man, therefore, is composed from body and soul as from parts that are really distinct, which was our thesis.[21]

3. Man = Body$_2$ + Soul$_2$

So far, so good, one might say, but can all this "word-magic" solve *the genuine philosophical problem* of body and mind? For even if by using these "rubber-band" concepts of body and soul one may save the consistency of what Aquinas says in various contexts, making them comprise more in one context and less in another, body and soul are still claimed to be really distinct parts of a human being in the above-described exclusive senses of these terms. But then, if the body and the soul are really distinct entities, with one belonging to the spatio-temporal physical world and the other belonging to some alleged spiritual realm, then we immediately seem to face here the problem of "mysterious" interaction vs. causal closure, all too familiar from the woes of Cartesian dualism.

To this, we have first to reply that since a philosophical problem is some conceptual conflict, or rather a bundle of conceptual conflicts within a broad conceptual framework, there is no such thing as "the genuine philosophical problem" of anything apart from the conceptual framework that gives rise to it. So, if we find that despite superficial appearances to the contrary St. Thomas's concept of body and soul are sufficiently different from the concepts figuring in the modern problem of body and mind, we may well find that in his conceptual framework the familiar problem, or rather the familiar bundle of problems, need not and does not arise at all. Indeed, what lies at the bottom of all the familiar problems is the assumption that body and soul are two distinct entities of radically different natures, having entirely distinct causal powers rooted in these distinct natures, on account of which they are accessible by us for observation in radically different ways.

If we understand it properly, however, we can easily realize that the real distinction of body and soul in the Thomistic-Aristotelian framework means nothing like this. In the first place, that body and soul, in the exclusive senses of these terms, are distinct parts of the same entity does not mean that they are distinct entities in the sense in which subsistent entities are distinct from one another. As St. Thomas often repeats, *unum convertitur cum ente:* there is one entity, absolutely speaking, whenever there is a being having one act of existence, even if the being in question is composed of several parts. But body and soul, as distinguished in the exclusive senses of these terms, have the same unique act of substantial existence, namely, the life of a living body; therefore, body and soul are one being, one entity, absolutely speaking, not two entities. Since causal powers and the corresponding actions belong to the beings which perform those actions by means of those powers, if the body and the soul are one being, then no question of their *inter-action* can arise on the basis of their distinct causal powers rooted in their radically distinct natures. For this question can properly be raised only concerning distinct beings each having a substantial act of being of its own, founding their distinct causal powers and the corresponding actions.[22]

However, at this point it may seem that by laying so much emphasis on their substantial unity this position does not leave any room for the *real distinction* of body and soul, or indeed, for a non-materialistic conception of the soul. For if soul and body are one entity, namely, a living body, having all their powers and actions in common in the whole they constitute, then their distinction is apparently a merely conceptual one: the concepts of body and soul provide us merely with different aspects for considering the same, essentially material entity.

But this objection is based on a radical misunderstanding of what it means for essential parts of the same entity to be distinct from one another, and yet to constitute the same one entity. For even if, for example, Socrates is an ensouled body, a unitary substance with one act of substantial being, his essential parts, his body and soul in the exclusive senses of these terms, are strictly distinct parts in the unitary whole insofar as the one part is that which accounts for one distinct sort of perfections of the whole Socrates, namely, spatio-temporality and whatever that entails; whereas the other part is that which accounts for another sort of perfections, namely, human life, and whatever that entails. But since these are obviously distinct perfections, whose distinction is given regardless of the intellect's consideration, the parts of the whole accounting for these perfections, each for its own sort, have to be parts that are really distinct, again, regardless of the intellect's consideration.

Nevertheless, while we maintain their real distinction in this way, we also have to realize that body and soul can be distinct *only* as distinct parts of the same substantially one whole. Indeed, they cannot possibly be distinct in the same way as the whole they constitute is distinct from other wholes of the same kind. For the whole they constitute is a complete substance, which therefore is a complete being in the primary, unqualified sense of the term 'being', having its own unique substantial act of existence. But then, no part of this one whole can have the same act of being in the same way, for otherwise they would not be parts in the whole, but whole beings in the same unqualified sense of the term as the original whole. Therefore, the essential parts of the whole, since they are essential, share the same act of being as the whole; nevertheless, since they are parts, they can have this existence only in the sense in which a part in a whole can. As St. Thomas says:

> ... existence [esse] is said to be the act of a being [ens] insofar as being, that is, that by which something is denominated a being in the nature of things. And being in this sense is attributed only to the things themselves which are contained in the ten categories, whence 'being' [ens] predicated on account of such [an act of] existence [esse] is divided by ten categories. But this [act of] existence [esse] is attributed to something in two senses. In one sense as to *that which* [quod] properly and truly has being, or exists. And thus it is attributed only to a *per se* subsisting substance; whence that which truly exists is said to be a substance in bk. 1. of the *Physics*. All those [things], however, which do not subsist *per se*, but in others and with others, *whether they are accidents or substantial forms or any sorts of parts*, do not have existence [esse] so that they themselves would truly exist, but existence [esse] is attributed to them in another sense, namely, as to something *by which* [quo] something exists; as whiteness is said to exist, not that it itself would subsist in itself, but because it is by [this whiteness] that something has it that it is white . . .[23]

What this means, then, is that in line with St. Thomas's general conception of the analogy of being, the whole and its essential parts, while they are denominated beings on account of the same substantial act of existence, they are not denominated beings in the same sense. For the whole substance is denominated a being in the primary, unqualified sense of being, in the sense in which only a complete, self-subsistent entity can be called a being, existing on its own. The essential parts of this being, namely, its matter and substantial form, however, can be called beings only in some derivative sense of the term. For the form can be called a being only in a secondary sense, because, insofar as it is a form, it can be said to exist only in a secondary sense. And this is so because for a form to exist in this secondary sense is nothing but for it to inform that which exists in the primary sense, namely, the primary substance. But this is just another way of saying that for the form to exist is nothing but for the thing to exist, or to have existence, *in respect of the form*, which makes it clear that the sense in which existence is attributed to the form is obtained by adding some qualification to the sense in which existence is attributed to the substance which is said to exist in the primary, unqualified sense. Obviously, similar considerations apply to the body, in the exclusive sense of the term, insofar as it is the other essential part of a living being.

But then, if we recognize the analogical character of the predication of the notion of being with respect to the whole and with respect to its essential parts, it should come as no surprise that body and soul in the exclusive senses of these terms are said to be one being, in the primary sense of the term, yet they can be said to be two beings in the derivative sense in which distinct parts of a whole can be said to be beings. But since having power and action can attach properly only to a being in the primary sense, the problem of interaction between body and soul still cannot arise, for both the actions and the corresponding powers will still belong only to the unified whole, and not to either of the parts. This has to be the case, at least, unless there is some action which can properly be said to belong only to one of them, in which case that part will also have to be regarded as a being not only in the sense in a which a part is a being, but also in the sense in which the whole is.

But this is precisely the point Aquinas makes with respect to the unique case of the human soul in his proof for its immortality:

We have to say that the human soul is entirely incorruptible. For a clear understanding of which we should consider that what per se belongs to something cannot be removed from it, just as from a man it cannot be removed that he is an animal, nor from a number that it is either even or odd. It is clear, however, that being per se belongs to form, for everything has being in virtue of its proper form; whence being can in no way be separated from form. Therefore, things composed of matter and form are corrupted by losing the form to which being per se belongs. But the form itself cannot be corrupted per se, but it is corrupted *per accidens*, insofar as the composite thing that exists by the form loses its being, provided the form is such that it is not *a thing that has being*, but it is only that *by which* the composite thing has being. If, therefore, there is a form which is *a thing that has being*, then it is necessary for that form to be incorruptible. For being is not separated from *something that has being*, except by its form getting separated from it; therefore, *if that which has be-*

ing is the form itself, then it is impossible that being should be separated from it. It is manifest, however, that the principle by which a man understands is *a form that has being* in itself, and [that it does not have this being] only *as that by which* something [else] exists. For understanding, as the Philosopher proves in bk. 3. of the *De Anima*, is not an act performed by some bodily organ.[24]

Now, clearly, if understanding is the act of the intellective soul alone (which is a claim to be established by a separate argument, but that need not concern us here),[25] then this means that the soul has some action and the corresponding power, which only a subsistent being has. But then, if the soul is a subsistent entity, this means that it is a being not only in the derivative sense in which a substantial form is a being, but also in the unqualified sense in which a subsistent entity is a being.

As we could see in the foregoing considerations, body and soul are one being in the absolute, unqualified sense, not two beings united in some mysterious interaction with one another. Nevertheless, despite the fact that this one being, the whole human being, is a material substance, if Aquinas's claim that understanding is the act of the soul alone is true, then the form of this being has some act of its own which denominates the whole only through this part to which alone it can belong.[26] But then, since this form has an activity of its own, it is a form which has the being of the whole not only in the sense in which any other form insofar as a form has being, but also in the same sense in which the whole has it. Therefore, it could be destroyed also only in the sense in which the whole is destroyed, namely, by losing its substantial form, but since it is a form, that is precisely the sense in which it cannot be destroyed. Hence, it is incorruptible. But then, if we really understand how these claims fit together, we can clearly see that Saint Thomas's conception does indeed manage to steer its way safely between the Scylla of dualism and the Charybdis of materialism.

Notes

1. Anthony Kenny, *Aquinas on Mind* (London and New York: Routledge, 1993), 28.

2. For Aquinas the contrast between (prime) matter and subject in the strict sense is the contrast between that which is informed by a substantial form and that which is informed by an accidental form. See c. 1. of his *De Principiis Naturae*. However, apparently, Kenny rather intends to distinguish here between what in another place Aquinas calls *subiectum informe* and *subiectum formatum*; cf. text quoted in n. 6. But this is not the issue in the text referred to by Kenny.

3. Cf. in *Meta* lb. 5, lc. 21, n. 1099. For detailed discussion of the notions of integral part and whole, as opposed to other kinds of parts and wholes distin-

guished by medieval philosophers, see Desmond Paul Henry, *Medieval Mereology* (Amsterdam-Philadelphia: B.R. Gruener, 1991); for a discussion of Aquinas's views in particular see especially pp. 218–328. However, in general, for the purposes of the present discussion the concept of integral part can be defined as follows: a is an integral part of A if and only if a ≠ A and there is some b such that a + b = A. For example, a slice of a cake is an integral part of it, since the slice is not the cake, yet there is something, namely, the rest of the cake, such that the slice and the rest together are the cake. (Here, if someone has worries concerning the possible situation in which the slice is actually cut out, and thus the separated part and the rest do not make up the original cake, we can take 'the rest' to include not only the remaining quantitative part, but also its continuity with the slice. Cf. what St. Thomas says about the issue in *Meta* lb. 5. lc. 21. esp. nn. 1104–1108.) Likewise, the tone C is an integral part of the chord C major, for the tone is not the chord, yet there is something, namely, the tones E and G together, such that the tone C and the tones E and G together are the chord C major, that is, C + E + G = C major. As these examples show, the '+' symbol in the above definition is used as a collective nominal conjunction, which is in fact the general logical notion that has the familiar arithmetical operation only as its special case, as restricted to numerals. However, in general, if 'a' and 'b' are any two names, then 'a + b' is another name, the name of the integral whole having a and b as its integral parts, and the truth of 'P(a + b)' does not imply either 'Pa' or 'Pb'. For example, while two and three are five, neither two nor three are five, and even if Plato and Socrates are men, neither of them is men, although, of course, each of them is a man, etc.

4. "... the essence of the rational soul is immediately united to the body, as form to matter, or shape to a piece of wax, as is said in bk. 2 of *On the Soul*. We should know, therefore, that agreement can be considered in two ways: either with respect to the properties of nature, and in this way the soul and the body are very different, or with respect to the proportion of potency to act, and in this way the soul and the body maximally agree. And this agreement is required in order that something be united with something else as its form, for otherwise an accident would not be united to its subject, or form to matter." 2SN d. 1, q. 2, a. 4, ad 3-um.

5. "... the Philosopher in bk. 2 of *On the Soul* says that the soul is the act of the organic physical body. Therefore, that which is compared to the soul as matter to act is already an organic physical body, which cannot exist except by means of some form by which it is established in the genus of body. The body, therefore, has its own being besides the being of the soul." QDA a. 1, obj. 5

6. "To the fifteenth objection we should reply that in the definitions of forms sometimes the subject is placed as uninformed [*subiectum ut informe*], as when we say: motion is the act of something existing in potency. Sometimes, however, we place there the subject [already] informed [*subiectum formatum*], as when we say: motion is the action of something mobile, or: light is the act of something shining. And this is how we say that the soul is the act of the organic physical body, for it is the soul that makes it an organic physical body, just as light makes something shine." QDA a. 1, ad 15-um.

7. Cf. *De Princ.* c. 1.

8. Cf. *QDA* a. 9. In. corp.; *STI* q. 76, aa. 6, 7; *2SN* d. 1, q. 2, a. 4; *SCG* lb. 2, c. 71; etc.

9. *4SN* d. 44, q. 1, a. 1, ad 2-um; *SCG* 4, 81; *QDL* 2, q. 2, a. 2; in *Meta* lb. 7, lc. 9.

10. Cf. *1SN* d. 25, q. 1, a. 1, ad 2-um; *SCG* lb. 4, c. 81.

11. *EE* c. 2. In the translation I marked each occurrence of the term 'body', indicating in each particular case in which of the three senses distinguished here the term is being used.

12. To be sure, there are concrete terms which refer to the forms they signify, but they do so not on account of their signification but on account of the simplicity of the thing they signify. Cf. *3SN* d. 11, q. 1, a. 4; *1SN* d. 33, q. 1, a. 2, ad 2. For further details on Aquinas's semantic theory, see Gyula Klima, "The Semantic Principles Underlying Saint Thomas Aquinas's Metaphysics of Being," *Medieval Philosophy and Theology* 5 (1996).

13. As St. Thomas wrote: ". . . we should say that that from which something is denominated does not always have to be a form as far as the nature of the thing is concerned, but it is enough if it is signified in the manner of a form, grammatically speaking. For a man is denominated from his action or clothing and the like, which in reality are not forms." QDP q.7, a.10, ad.8

14. Concerning the semantic role and ontological status of beings of reason in Aquinas, see Gyula Klima, "The Changing Role of *Entia Rationis* in Medieval Philosophy: A Comparative Study with a Reconstruction," *Synthese*, 96(1993), 25–59.

15. "A mathematical body is said to be a body considered only according to its quantitative dimensions, and this is the body in the genus of quantity." 25N d.30, q.2, a.2.

16. Cf. here what Aristotle and Thomas say about the different kinds of unity in *Meta* lb. 5. lc. 7 and 8. See also Gyula Klima, "Aquinas on One and Many," *Documente Studi sulla Tradizione Filosofica Medievale*, 11(2000), 195–215.

17. *STI*–2 q. 17, a. 4.

18. Cf. e.g. in *Meta* lb. S, lc 21, n. 1102; in *Meta* lb. 7, lc 16, nn. 1632–1633.

19. Cf.: "For the soul is not a form other than that on account of which in that thing one could designate three dimensions, and so, when we said that a body is something that has such a form, we understood any form whatsoever, whether animality or stone-ness or any other." *EE* c. 2.

20. Cf. text quoted in n. 6.

21. Thomas de Vio Cajetan, *Commentary on Being and Essence*, tr. L. H. Kendzierski and F. C. Wade, S.J. (Milwaukee, Wis.: Marquette University Press, 1964)

22. "Nothing can operate on its own (per se), except what subsists. For only a being in act can operate; therefore, everything is operating in the way in which it is. And this is the reason we do not say that heat heats, but (we say that) the hot thing does." *STI* q. 75, a. 2.

23. *QDL* 9. q. 2, a. 2, in corp.

24. *QDA* a. 14, co.

25. Since in this context we are only concerned with what it means to say that the soul is both a form and a subsistent substance, and not with proving its truth, we should only consider under what conditions it would be true. To

be sure, I also think Aquinas's argument for the claim that understanding is the act of the intellect alone can indeed be shown to work, but the proof of this claim is a different issue, to be dealt with in another paper.

26. And this is why we can truly say that a man understands, and not only that a human soul understands, despite the fact that the act of understanding is an act inherent only in the soul, and not in the body-soul composite. Cf.:". . . the operations of parts are attributed to the whole on account of the parts. For we say that a man sees with his eyes and hits with his hand, but in a different way than [we say that] a hot thing heats with its heat, for heat does not heat at all, properly speaking. Therefore, one can say that the soul understands, just as the eye sees, but it would be more appropriate to say that a man understands with his soul." *ST1* q. 75, a. 2, ad 2-um. Cf. also *De Unitate Intellectus*, c. 3, n. 69. For a thorough discussion of Aquinas's general rule concerning the proper denomination of a whole by some property of its part see Gyula Klima, "Libellus pro Sapiente: A Criticism of Allan Bäck's Argument against St. Thomas Aquinas's Theory of the Incarnation," *The New Scholasticism*, 58(1984), 207–219.

II

Aquinas's Account of Freedom

Intellect and Will

It is difficult to develop a comprehensive and satisfactory account of Aquinas's views of the nature of human freedom.

For one thing, contemporary discussions of free will tend to belong to an older, non-Thomistic tradition of thought about the topic. In this tradition, human freedom is a property of just one component of human mental faculties, namely, the will; and freedom consists in an agent's ability to will autonomously in general and independently of the intellect in particular. The influence of this tradition persists in contemporary discussion, both for libertarians and for their opponents, with the result that Aquinas's account tends to be interpreted by its lights. Consequently, the lineaments of his theory are obscured. For Aquinas, freedom with regard to willing is a property primarily of a human being, not of some particular component of a human being. Furthermore, the will is not independent of the intellect. On the contrary, the dynamic interactions of intellect and will yield freedom as an emergent property or a systems-level feature.

Another reason why interpreting Aquinas's account is difficult is that he gives a complicated analysis of the several acts of will he takes to be associated with a free bodily action. Scholars sometimes pick out a subset of these acts or even just one of them as if for Aquinas freedom of the will were lodged in that sort of act of will alone. So, for example, it is sometimes said that Aquinas has a particularly full treatment of free will in *De malo* q.6 because in that text he discusses at length *liberum arbitrium*.[1] But there is something anachronistic about trying to identify *liberum arbitrium* with free will in our sense;[2] volitions characterized by *liberum arbitrium* are associated for Aquinas with only one sort of voluntary act, namely, the sort he calls *electio*. *De malo* q.6 is therefore not about freedom of the will as a whole but only about one of the acts of will, namely, *electio*, in which such freedom is exemplified. (In order to avoid confusion, I will leave both 'liberum *arbitrium'* and *'electio'* untranslated and let their meanings emerge from a consideration of Aquinas's views.)

For these reasons, to understand Aquinas's account of human freedom, I will focus on his account of the nature of intellect and will, the interactions between them, and the emergence of freedom from their interaction. With that background, I will look in detail at Aquinas's theory of freedom, in particular at his views of human ability to do otherwise and the relation of that ability to freedom. Finally, I will consider what answer can be given to a taxonomic question: Is Aquinas's theory a compatibilist account, as is sometimes claimed, or is it a libertarian theory; and if it is a libertarian theory, what species of libertarianism is it?

Because of his views of divine grace and its effect on the will, we cannot be entirely clear about Aquinas's theory of freedom without also understanding his account of grace.[3] But this is a large subject, which needs a careful treatment of its own. Furthermore, it is Aquinas's firm conviction, reiterated in many passages, that God moves the will only in accord with its nature, and not against it. According to Aquinas himself, then, his account of grace should not alter the conclusions we reach about his theory of the nature of the will, independently considered. This essay will therefore consider Aquinas's account of the will apart from his views of grace.

1. Intellect and Will

Contemporary philosophers tend to operate with a conception of the will as the mind's steering-wheel, neutral in its own right but able to direct other parts of the person. Aquinas's conception is different. He takes the will to be not a neutral faculty but a bent or inclination. The will, he says in the *Summa theologiae* (hereafter ST), is a hunger, an appetite, for goodness.[4] By 'goodness' in this connection Aquinas means goodness in general, not this or that specific good thing; that is, the will is an inclination for what is good, where the phrase 'what is good' is used attributively and not referentially.

By itself the will makes no determinations of goodness; apprehending or judging things as good is the business of the intellect. The intellect presents to the will as good certain things or actions under certain descriptions in particular circumstances, and the will wills them because it is an appetite for the good and they are presented to it as good. For this reason the intellect is said to move the will not as an efficient cause but as a final cause, because its presenting something as good moves the will as an end moves an appetite.[5] This is one reason for calling the will a 'moved mover' (as Aquinas notes that Aristotle does), because, in moving what is under its control, the will is moved by an object intellectively apprehended as good, or an "intellectively cognized appetible,"[6] as Aquinas puts it.

Understood in this way, the will can be seen as part of a larger scheme. Because all things are created by a good God who wills what is good for his creatures, all things are created with an inclination of their own to the good, but of very different sorts. Some, like plants or even inanimate things, have a built-in inclination to the good apart from any cognition of the good. Aquinas sometimes calls this inclination a natural appetite. (The sort of thing he has in mind is exemplified by plants naturally turning toward sunlight.) Higher up the ladder of being are animals of certain sorts which are naturally inclined to the good but with some (sensory) cognition.[7] They can cognize particular goods, although they lack the ability to reflect on them or to think of them as good. Inclination dependent on limited cognition of this sort Aquinas calls 'sensory appetite'. Higher still are human beings, whose inclination to the good is dependent on intellect, which allows them not only to cognize particular goods but to think about them reflectively as good. This inclination is rational appetite, and it is what Aquinas takes the will to be.[8] So close is the association between intellect and will for Aquinas that he often speaks of the will as being in the intellect,[9] and he thinks that anything which has intellect must also have will.[10]

Understood as rational appetite, the will is the primary mover of all the powers of the soul (including itself) except the nutritive powers,[11] and it is also the efficient cause of motion of the body. Most important for our purposes, the will exercises some degree of efficient causality over the intellect. In some circumstances, it can command the intellect directly to adopt or to reject a particular belief.[12] It can also move the intellect by directing it to attend to some things and to neglect others,[13] or even to stop thinking about something altogether. So, for example, while you are reading a magazine, you come across an advertisement asking for money for children, with an emotionally powerful picture of a starving child. Your intellect recognizes that if you look at the ad for very long, you are likely to succumb to its emotional force. Intellect sees the goodness of contributing to the charity, but it also recognizes that if you give money to this charity, you won't have it for the new computer you have been coveting. Your desire for the new computer is strong and influences intellect to rank saving money for the computer as best for you now. In consequence of the finding on intellect's part, and with this influence from the passions, will directs intellect to stop thinking about the charity, and (after a further interaction of intellect and will) you turn the page of your magazine.

As this example shows, in addition to control over intellect by will, the passions—sorrow, fury, fear, greed, etc.—can also influence the intellect, because in the grip of such a passion, something will seem good to a person which might not seem good to her otherwise.[14] The intellect, however, typically isn't compelled by the passions in any way;[15] it can resist them, for example, by being aware of the passion and correcting for its effects on judgment, as one does when one leaves a letter written in anger until the next morning rather than mailing it right away. Furthermore, the passions are themselves theoretically subject to the will. In other animals, Aquinas says, motion follows directly from the sensitive appetite's positive or negative reaction. In human beings, however, the sensitive appetite awaits the act of the will, which is the superior appetite. The lower appetite, Aquinas thinks, isn't by itself sufficient to cause movement in other powers unless the higher appetite, the will, permits that movement.[16] That is why, for example, human beings can go on hunger strikes and stay on them to the point of starvation.

I raise the subject of the relation of the passions to intellect and will, however, only to put it to one side. Although Aquinas has many interesting things to say about the moral psychology of the passions, his account of the intellect and will and the freedom that emerges from their interaction is more than enough for our focus here. I will therefore introduce the passions into the discussion only when it is necessary to do so in order to understand what Aquinas has to say about intellect and will.

Just as the will can affect the intellect in various ways, so the intellect can move the will (as a final, not an efficient, cause) in more than one way. The will can be moved to will as distinct from not willing—the "exercise" of its act; or it can be moved to will this rather than that particular thing—the "specification" of its act.[17]

There is nothing in this life that invariably and ineluctably moves every human will to the exercise of its act, because it is always in a person's power to refuse to think of the thing at issue.[18] Since will wills something only in case intellect presents it as some sort of good, the fact that will can command intellect to stop thinking about something means that will can, indirectly, turn itself off, at least with regard to a particular action or issue. This is only a limited ability on the part of the will, however, since the apprehensions of the intellect can occur without any preceding act of will and so in some cases may force the issue back on the agent's attention. That is why, for example, the prisoner who wants not to think about what is happening next door where other prisoners are being tortured will find that their screams make him recur to what he wants to stop thinking about.[19]

As far as the specification of its act is concerned, there is no object, other than happiness in this life and God in the next, which by its nature necessarily moves every human will to want *that*.[20] Because God has created the will as a hunger for the good, every human will by nature desires the good. And whatever is good to such a degree and in such a way that a person cannot help but see it as good, the will of that person wills by natural necessity. One's own happiness is of this sort,[21] and so a person necessarily wills happiness.[22] But even things which have a necessary connection to happiness aren't willed necessarily unless the willer is cognizant of their necessary connection to happiness.[23] Except for happiness, and things so obviously connected with it that their connection is overwhelming and indubitable, it is not the case that every human will is in general determined to one thing because of its relation to the intellect. On Aquinas's account, the will wills only what the intellect presents at that time as good under some description. Acts of will, then, are for something apprehended or cognized as good at a particular time in particular circumstances, as distinct from something which is good considered unconditionally or abstractly. Besides happiness and the vision of God, all other things are such that they can in principle be considered good under some descriptions and not good under others, so that there is nothing about them which must constrain the will of any agent always to want them. So, for example, the further acquisition of money can be considered good under some descriptions in some circumstances—e.g., the means of sending the children to school—and not good under others—e.g., wages from an immoral and disgusting job.

Finally, the will can move itself in more than one way. It can move itself indirectly by commanding intellect to stop thinking about something, as we've just seen. It can also move itself indirectly because in virtue of willing a certain end it moves itself to will the means to that end. That is, the will wills a certain means because it wills a particular end and because intellect presents that means as best for attaining that end.

But a more direct control over itself is possible for the will, too. All the higher powers of the soul, Aquinas holds, are able to act on themselves.[24] So, for example, intellect is able to cognize itself.[25] By the same token, the will can will to will.[26] In fact, Aquinas confronts a problem that has troubled some contemporary hierarchical accounts of the will, namely, that there may be an infinite regress of higher-order willings. I can will that I will something, and I can also will that I will that I will something, and so on, apparently *ad infinitum*. But in such an apparently infinite series, the will is not actually taking ever-higher orders of volition as its object. At some point, Aquinas thinks,[27] the apparently higher-order volitions collapse, and the object of the will is just whatever action was at issue at the beginning of the series of volitions.

If intellect does present something to the will as good, then, because the will is an appetite for the good, the will wills it—unless will directs intellect to reconsider, to direct its attention to something else, or to stop considering the matter at hand. Will's doing such things, of course, is a result of intellect's presenting such actions on the part of the will as good, and that act of intellect may itself be a result of previous acts on the part of the will directing the attention of the intellect. On Aquinas's view, every act of willing is preceded by some apprehension on the part of the intellect, but not every apprehension on the part of the intellect need be preceded by an act of will.[28]

It is apparent, then, that on Aquinas's account, the will is part of a dynamic feedback system composed primarily of the will and the intellect, but also including the passions. The interaction between will and intellect is so close and the acts of the two powers so intertwined that Aquinas often finds it difficult to draw the line between them. So, for example, he says that

> ... it happens sometimes that there is an act of the will in which something of the [preceding] act of reason remains ... and, *vice versa*, there is [sometimes] an act of reason in which something of the [preceding] act of will remains.[29]

That is why it sometimes looks as if, for Aquinas, will engages in acts of apprehension and intellect engages in acts of willing.

If we remember this part of Aquinas's account, and also take seriously his identification of the will as a hunger or appetite, we will be less likely to identify the will on his account as nothing more than a toggle switch with three positions: accept, reject, and off. Aquinas's account of the will is more complicated than such an identification implies. Because it is an appetite, the will can have dispositions, so that it can be more or less readily inclined to want something; it can will something with more or less strength.[30] It can give specific commands to body parts. And under the pull of the passions, for example, it can influence what intellect presents to it as good by selectively directing the attention of the intellect.

For this reason, too, although Aquinas's account of the will assigns a large role to intellect, he isn't committed to seeing immoral actions simply as instances of mistakes in deliberation, since intellect's deliberations are in many cases dependent on the will's influence. In cases of incontinence, where the intellect seems to be representing something as good which the will isn't willing, Aquinas would say that the intellect, influenced by the will, is in fact being moved by opposed desires to represent the thing in question as both good (under one description) and not good (under a different description), so that the intellect is double-minded.[31] In the last analysis, what the intellect of the incontinent person represents as the best alternative in *these* circumstances at *this* time isn't what the agent takes to be good considered unconditionally or in the abstract.

Cases of incontinence illustrate the further complicating fact that intellect need not present one simple, unified result to will. Sometimes an agent is entirely of one mind about something, and what intellect presents to will is one unified message that a particular thing is good. But what is no doubt also often the case is that an agent's intellect is not entirely unified. The doctor has recommended x-raying the agent's head to check for a sinus infection. On the one hand, the agent's intellect may recognize, the doctor is an expert in her field, and her advice for that reason should be followed. On the other hand, the intellect may be aware that even low-level x-rays are carcinogenic, and the intellect may wonder whether the doctor's ordering the x-ray reflects her concern to avoid malpractice law-suits rather than her own view about what is necessary for the health of her patient.

Furthermore, the influence of the passions may also complicate the case. It might be that a patient's intellect supposes some medical tests are in fact medically required, but his passions might recoil strongly from the tests. In that case, his aversion may influence the intellect to give a divided verdict: on the one hand, it would be good to undergo the tests because they are important for health; on the other hand, it would be bad to undergo the tests because they are painful or disgusting. In such cases, there may be considerable interaction among intellect, will, and passions, until, in consequence of such iterated interaction, one side or another of the divided intellect becomes strong enough to override the other. This is a process familiar enough to anyone who has had to talk himself into doing something he originally feared or disliked.

2. The Relation of Freedom to Intellect and Will

One of the perplexing things about the preceding analysis of the relation of intellect to will is that it isn't immediately apparent in what sense the will is free.

It is helpful in this connection to notice that Aquinas recognizes a distinction between freedom of action and freedom of willing.[32] He acknowledges, for example, that we can lose our freedom of action while retaining our freedom with regard to willing. Even when the will itself is not compelled or coerced in any way, he says, the members of the body can be impeded by some external cause so that they don't follow the command of the will.[33] While an agent might still be free with regard to his willing in such a case, he wouldn't be free with regard to his actions, which in the case envisaged are at least in part under some control other than his own. In order for an agent to have freedom of action, then, it isn't sufficient that his will be free in its willing of that action. It must also be the case that there is no external impediment to the action of the relevant body parts and that those parts are themselves functioning normally.

Consequently, freedom of action is not a property of just one component of a human being. Rather, it is a property of a whole system, comprised at least of the will and the members of the body. It emerges when the will is freely commanding a certain sort of movement and when the relevant bodily parts are functioning normally and are not kept by any cause external to the agent from being under the will's control.

It is helpful to see this feature of freedom of action, because it points us in the right direction for Aquinas's account of free will: for Aquinas, freedom with regard to willing is also a feature of a whole system.

In explaining what constitutes a distinctly human action, Aquinas puts the point this way. What differentiates human beings from non-rational animals is that a human being is master of his acts, in virtue of having intellect and will. Consequently, no freedom with regard to willing remains for a person who, through madness, for example, has lost the use of his intellectual faculties.[34] Aquinas makes the same point another way by saying that the root of freedom is in the will as subject but in the reason as the cause.[35] That is, the property of freedom inheres in the will, which is the subject for the property, but it does so because of the intellect; will's relations to and interactions with the intellect are the source of the freedom in the will. Freedom with regard to willing, then, is not a characteristic either of the will or of the intellect alone.[36] Like freedom of action, freedom with regard to willing emerges from the functioning of a system, in this case the system comprised of intellect and will.

Furthermore, Aquinas says that an agent is master of his acts or has his acts in his own power insofar as they are voluntary, and that it is a person's voluntary acts which make him subject to praise or blame.[37] But, in his view, whatever is voluntary requires an act of the intellect as well as an act of the will.[38] Seconding a view of Damascene's, Aquinas calls a voluntary act "an act that is a rational operation."[39] In fact, Aquinas holds that because the will has the relation it has to the intellect, all the acts of the will are voluntary, whether they are simple acts of will (such as willing an end) or are commands to some other power which the will controls (such as willing to move one's arm).[40] Finally, in Aquinas's view, anything that takes away an agent's use of her intellectual faculties also takes away the voluntariness of her action.[41]

A voluntary act is thus a special case of being moved by an intrinsic principle.[42] Whatever is moved by an intrinsic principle in such a way that it acts for an end which it cognizes as an end has within itself the principle of its action. Some creatures act with a limited cognition of the end for which they are acting, so that their acts are voluntary but in a limited sort of way. The acts of young children and some animals are voluntary in this way. Normal adult human beings can have a full cognition of their ends, and so they can have complete voluntariness with regard to their acts.[43]

By the same token, and perhaps as a consequence of the same thought about the voluntary, Aquinas thinks that anything external to the agent which acted coercively on the agent's will would thereby destroy voluntariness. That the voluntary movement of the will be from an extrinsic principle, Aquinas says, is impossible.[44] This is not an empirical claim but a conceptual one. For something to be an act of will, it has to stem from an intrinsic source, in particular the will as informed by the intellect. So, Aquinas says,

> an act of the will is nothing other than an inclination which proceeds
> from an interior cognizing principle. . . . but what is compelled or violent
> is from an extrinsic principle.[45]

If something extrinsic to the agent were to act on the will with efficient causation, then the tie of the will to the intellect, from which acts of will get their voluntary character, would be broken, and so the act of the will wouldn't be voluntary—or to put it more nearly as Aquinas seems to think of it, in such a case it wouldn't be a real act of the will at all.

We might wonder here why Aquinas wouldn't grant that an act of will could be voluntary even if it were caused by an extrinsic principle, provided that the extrinsic principle produced its effects by operating directly on the agent's intellect and only thereby, indirectly, on the agent's will. Aquinas considers something like this question himself when he asks whether Satan could bring it about that a human being sin.[46] Aquinas subscribes to the demon-possession theory of mental illness, so he supposes that Satan can causally determine a human intellect (to one degree or another) by possessing it. But this is to destroy it as a human intellect; an insane person has lost his reason. At any rate, if some external agent S has taken over entirely the intellect of some human H, then the intellect that is operative in that human person is S's and not H's. In that case, what the will operative in H wills might be voluntary, but it would count as S's will, not H's, since the intellect that informs the willing is S's. In this case, there can be an extrinsic principle S which operates on the intellect of some other agent H, but the operation of the extrinsic principle won't give us an act of will that can count as H's.

On the other hand, if we were to imagine Satan (or the evil neurosurgeon) invading H's intellect only partially, for example, by producing a thought or a train of thoughts, H's intellect will then examine that thought or set of thoughts and evaluate it, retaining or rejecting it according as it seems right to H to do so. In that case, however, the voluntary acts of will which may result will stem from the reflections of H's intellect, not S's. Here again, then, we will not have a case in which a voluntary act of will on H's part is causally determined by an extrinsic principle S, operating through H's intellect.

So, worries about grace aside, it should by now be clear that Aquinas is not a compatibilist. The causal chain resulting in any voluntary act on an agent's part has to originate in the system of the agent's own intellect and will. If it originates in some cause external to the agent which acts with efficient causation on the agent's will, what results will not be an act of will at all. And if it takes over the agent's intellect which in turn determines the content of the agent's will, what results will not be an act of *the agent's* will. So while extrinsic principles may influence human volition, as, for example, we sometimes do when we persuade one another by arguments, causes external to an agent cannot effect a voluntary act of will on that agent's part, either directly or indirectly.

If Aquinas isn't a compatibilist, what sort of incompatibilist is he? It seems clear that he must be a libertarian. And yet, although the outlines of Aquinas's theory of human freedom are now somewhat clearer, it still isn't obvious in what sense the will—or the system of will and intellect—is supposed to be free. No doubt, part of what gives rise to this perplexity is the presupposition, common enough in discussions of free will, that libertarian free will includes or even just consists in the ability to do otherwise.[47] But in what sense is it possible for the will, or the will-and-intellect, to do otherwise on Aquinas's view?

3. *Liberum arbitrium* and the Ability to Do Otherwise

Aquinas's account of a person's ability to will otherwise typically occurs in connection with his discussion of *liberum arbitrium*, and it is because of what Aquinas says about this that he is supposed by many scholars to see human freedom just as a function of the will's ability to do otherwise.

It is true that Aquinas makes a strong connection between *liberum arbitrium* and the ability to do otherwise. In fact, although 'liberum arbitrium' means 'free judgment', Aquinas sometimes sounds as if *liberum arbitrium* is just the power of the *will* to do otherwise than it does. For example, he says, "whoever has *liberum arbitrium* has it in his power to will or not to will, to do or not to do."[48]

Nonetheless, it is a mistake to suppose that 'liberum arbitrium' is Aquinas's term for the freedom of the will in general. In fact, he explicitly associates *liberum arbitrium* with only one of the acts of will needed to produce a bodily movement in a free human action, namely, the act of will which is *electio*. So, for example, he says, "*liberum arbitrium* is that in accordance with which we have *electio*."[49] And in another place he says,

> with regard to intellective appetite, will and *liberum arbitrium*—which is nothing but the power of *electio*—are related just as intellect and reason are related with regard to intellective cognition. . . . Now the act of *electio* is to desire something for the sake of obtaining something else, so that, strictly speaking, it has to do with means to an end. . . . Therefore, it is clear that will is related to the power of *electio*—that is, to *liberum arbitrium*—just as intellect is related to reason.[50]

Elsewhere he associates the act of *liberum arbitrium* just with the selection of a means to an end,[51] which is *electio*.

So although, on Aquinas's account, *liberum arbitrium* involves being able to do otherwise, it is not identical to freedom of the will in general but instead picks out just the power of the will manifested in the act Aquinas calls *electio*.

Now *electio* is the will's assenting to the means which the intellect has apprehended as best for the end wanted by the willer.[52] It is therefore a very specific sort of act of will. Furthermore, not every free action has an act of *electio* in the series of acts of will and intellect producing such an action. When the intellect finds only *one* acceptable means to an end, then the act of *electio* collapses into the act of consent[53]—an act of will which is *not* associated with *liberum arbitrium*—precisely because there aren't alternatives available for intellect and will to rank-order.[54]

In addition, even understood narrowly as confined to the power of the will producing *electio*, *liberum arbitrium* isn't a property of the will alone. It can be understood as a property of the will only insofar as the will itself is understood to be the *rational* appetite and to have a close tie to the intellect. In some places Aquinas speaks of *liberum arbitrium* as if it were in fact a power of both the will and the intellect. When he is asking whether God has *liberum arbitrium*, one of the objections he raises begins with the uncontested remark that "*liberum arbitrium* is a faculty of reason and of will."[55] Elsewhere he says,

> *liberum arbitrium* should be considered on the basis of *electio*. But both the cognitive power and the appetitive power contribute something to *electio*. From the cognitive power we need counsel, by which we determine what is to be preferred to what, and from the appetitive power we need the desire to accept what counsel has determined.[56]

That is why, he goes on to say, Aristotle supposed we ought to assign *electio* either to the "appetitive intellect" or to the "intellective appetite," phrases meant to indicate the intertwining of intellect and will in *liberum arbitrium*. (Of this pair, Aquinas opts for "intellective appetite"—the will understood as preceded by certain acts of intellect—as the more appropriate candidate for the faculty to which *liberum arbitrium* is to be assigned.) Although he thinks that if we take *liberum arbitrium* to be a faculty rather than one of the powers of a faculty, then it is just the will itself, he emphasizes that *liberum arbitrium* is the will understood as interwoven with and dependent on intellect.[57]

Finally, that will has the ability to do otherwise even in acts of *electio* does not stem from the fact that the will may simply choose not to follow intellect,[58] or may act in some other way as a homunculus independent of intellect. It concerns instead the relations between intellect and will. Insofar as the will has control over itself, this is mediated by the intellect. It is also limited, since there are intellective apprehensions which are not preceded by or dependent upon acts of will. Will may not always succeed, for example, in getting intellect to stop thinking about something, because something in the environment causes the thought to recur repeatedly in the intellect, as in the case described above of the prisoner who wants not to think about what his hearing keeps calling to his mind, namely, the torture of his fellow prisoners. But, within a limited range, will can be effective at controlling intellect, for example, by being able in some circumstances to redirect the attention of the intellect, and in that way the will can also have indirect control over itself.

Of course, the will's directing intellect in any of these ways will depend on intellect's presenting will's doing so as good in these circumstances. That is why a human agent's control over her own actions is a function of intellect and will and is an emergent power or property, resulting from the dynamic interaction between intellect and will, rather than a static power localized in the structure of one particular faculty. Given the nature of Aquinas's account of freedom, it makes more sense to attribute freedom to a human being with regard to willing or acting than to take freedom as a property of one particular component, whether will or intellect.

4. Freedom and the Will's Ability to Do Otherwise

Aquinas supposes that human beings have control over their own actions and that this control is manifest, perhaps even specially evinced, in certain acts of *electio* involving the ability to do otherwise. It is also important to recognize that for Aquinas the powers that give a human being control over her actions aren't themselves grounded in an ability to do otherwise. What produces such control is the nature of human intellect and will and their interaction. As long as these are functioning normally (and that, as we have seen, precludes will's being causally determined by anything outside the willer), an agent has control over her actions and freedom with respect to her willing and acting, even if she cannot do otherwise.

Some sign of this attitude on Aquinas's part can be found in what he says about the limits of *liberum arbitrium*. Something can be outside the power of *liberum arbitrium* in two ways. First, it can exceed the efficacy of the motive powers. For example, flying by flapping one's arms is not within the power of human *liberum arbitrium*, because flying exceeds human powers of movement. Secondly, and this is the important point for our purposes, acts which we do under the sudden impetus of some passion, such as wrath or concupiscence, are outside the power of *liberum arbitrium* because they occur quickly, before reason can deliberate about them. An agent may be able to avoid letting passion have such effects by paying careful attention; but an agent cannot always be paying careful attention. In unguarded moments, such passions can arise without the process of reason, even tacit reason, necessary to choice; and the agent in acting on such a passion is consequently unable to do otherwise on that occasion. If Aquinas supposed that *liberum arbitrium* were identical to free will or if he thought that the ability to do otherwise were essential to free will, he should go on to say here that such acts aren't sinful or blame-worthy in any respect since they occur unfreely. What he in fact says is that they are sinful, but constitute only venial sins since their suddenness and their taking us by surprise provide us with some excuse.[59]

In *De malo* (QDM) Aquinas argues at length that it is heretical to suppose that the will is moved of necessity to will whatever it wills, because such a supposition undermines all attributions of praise and blame, removes the impetus to deliberation, exhortation and precept, and so on. But in that very question he also grants that the will sometimes wills what it wills of necessity. This happens when what is willed is so altogether good that intellect can't find any description under which to present it as not good—as in the case of happiness. But it also happens in other sorts of cases, as when intellect establishes very clearly that one course of action is in every respect superior to any other available.[60] So Aquinas ends his discussion of this point with the conclusion that although the will is sometimes moved of necessity, it isn't always so moved.

What Aquinas means us to understand here, we might suppose, is that what the will wills is free only when the will is not moved of necessity. But such an interpretation would be a mistake. In arguing that the will does will some things of necessity, Aquinas explains that there are two relevant sorts of necessity. One is the necessity of coercion, which would occur if some cause outside the agent causally produced in the will a volition for some particular thing.[61] This, Aquinas says, is incompatible with freedom. (In fact, as we saw earlier, there can be no such coercion of will for Aquinas, because he thinks that it is conceptually impossible for any necessity of this sort to operate on the will.) But there is also the necessity of natural inclination. This is the sort by which the will wills, for example, things whose goodness is overwhelmingly apparent to the agent. Necessity of this sort, according to Aquinas, is not repugnant to the will and doesn't take away its freedom.[62] Siding with Augustine, he says "Freedom . . . is opposed to the necessity of coercion, but not to the necessity of natural inclination."[63]

That is why Aquinas thinks that there can be freedom of will on the part of the redeemed in heaven, who no longer have the ability to will evil.[64] Their inability to will anything but the good stems not from any extrinsic coercion being exercised on their wills but rather from the clear view their intellects have of the nature of the good.

> Where there is no defect in apprehending and comparing, there can be
> no volition for evil with regard to those things which are ordered to the
> end, as is clear in the case of the blessed.[65]

Their intellects can no longer find descriptions under which to present as good things that are really evil. And so, although the blessed cannot will evil, they nonetheless will freely whatever they will.

Elsewhere Aquinas contrasts the necessity of coercion with the necessity of the end. When someone is compelled by an extrinsic cause in such a way that he cannot do otherwise than he does, this is necessity of coercion, and it is altogether repugnant to the will. But necessity of the end is different. It arises, for example, when the end desired can be attained in only one way, as when crossing the sea requires using a ship. This is in no way repugnant to the will, on Aquinas's view. But, Aquinas concludes, the necessity of natural inclination is similar in the relevant respects to necessity of the end, and so necessity of natural inclination is also not repugnant to the will. For this reason as well as others, he maintains that "natural necessity doesn't take away the freedom of the will."[66]

Clearly, then, Aquinas doesn't suppose that human freedom even as regards willing consists in or depends on the ability to do otherwise. Aquinas would consequently reject what is called the Principle of Alternative Possibilities (PAP). PAP has many different formulations, but they all share this claim:

> (PAP) A person has free will with regard to (or is morally responsible for)
> doing an action A only if he could have done otherwise than A.[67]

Aquinas would reject this principle not only for bodily actions but even for acts of will.

Many contemporary philosophers also suppose that PAP is false. A standard strategy for showing that PAP isn't necessary for free will is what has come to be known as a Frankfurt-style counterexample.[68] In such an example, a person P does an action A in circumstances that incline most people to conclude that P is doing A freely, but (in the example) there is some mechanism that would have operated to bring it about that P would have done A if P had not done A by himself. In the actual sequence of events presented in the counterexample, however, the mechanism does not operate, and P does do A by himself. So the counterexample is designed to make us think that P does A freely in the actual sequence of events although it is not the case that P could have done otherwise than A.[69] Frankfurt-style counterexamples can be constructed either for bodily actions such as leaving a room or for mental actions such as deciding to leave a room.

Some libertarians defend PAP by arguing strenuously against Frankfurt-style counterexamples.[70] But Aquinas would presumably find such counterexamples to PAP acceptable. In the actual sequence of events, P's doing A is *not* brought about by any cause extrinsic to P, and nothing in the counterexample keeps us from supposing that it is only P's own intellect and will which are responsible for P's doing A.

These reasons for the rejection of PAP don't have the implication that libertarian free will is never accompanied by alternative possibilities. On the contrary, as we have seen, Aquinas emphasizes human ability to do otherwise, for example in his account of *liberum arbitrium*. It may in fact be true on his view that in most cases in which an agent acts with free will, the agent can do otherwise. The ability to do otherwise would then be what medieval logic calls "an associated accident," a non-essential property that accompanies its subject much or even all of the time. Nonetheless, as I have argued, on Aquinas's account human freedom with regard to willing isn't to be identified with the ability to do otherwise; it is possible for an agent to act freely even when she can't act otherwise than she does.

Even where there are alternative possibilities available, on Aquinas's account of the will's relations to intellect they will be open to the agent only because she can be in a different intellective state from the one she is in fact in. For Aquinas, alternative possibilities for the will are dependent on alternative possibilities for the intellect; it is not possible for the determination of the intellect to be that doing A is what is good now and for the will (with that determination of the intellect still in place) to will not to do A. But it may nonetheless be possible for the will to will not to do A because it may be possible for the agent's intellect to recalculate and to rescind the determination that doing A is good now.

5. Aquinas among the Libertarians

Although standard Frankfurt-style counterexamples are commonly thought to show that alternative possibilities aren't necessary for freedom, there are also analogues to Frankfurt-style counterexamples which show that alternative possibilities aren't sufficient for freedom either.

Consider, for example, Robert Heinlein's *The Puppetmasters*. In that story, an alien race of intelligent creatures wants to conquer the earth. Part of the alien plan for invasion includes a covert operation in which individual aliens take over particular human beings without being detected. When an alien "master" takes over a human being, the human being (say, Sam) has within himself not only his own consciousness but the master's as well. Since it is crucial to the alien plan that their taking over human beings be undetected in the early stages of the invasion, they are careful to make the behavior of people like Sam correspond to the behavior Sam would normally have engaged in had he not been infected with the alien. So when, under the control of the alien, Sam does some action A, it is also true that if there had been some reason sufficient for Sam in his uninfected state to do not-A, the alien would have brought it about that Sam in his infected state did not-A. In that case, then, there is a possible world in which Sam does otherwise than A. Sam has the ability to do otherwise, then; nonetheless, Sam isn't free with respect to his doing A.

In the standard Frankfurt-style counterexamples, the absence of alternative possibilities doesn't preclude an agent's acting on his own unimpeded intellect and will in the actual sequence of events. In the analogue counterexamples, the presence of an alternative possibility doesn't stem from any ability that the agent's own intellect and will have in the actual sequence. What the standard and analogue counterexamples together show, I think, is the correctness of Aquinas's position. In order to determine whether or not an agent is free, it is important to determine whether the intellect and will on which he acts are his own, not whether alternative possibilities are present or absent for him. For Aquinas, human freedom depends on human cognitive capacities and on the connection of the will to those capacities. Consequently, as long as human acts of will originate in those faculties, those acts count as voluntary and free, even if the agent couldn't have done otherwise in the circumstances or the act of will is necessitated by natural inclinations of intellect and will.

So Aquinas holds a view which is libertarian in some sense. It maintains that human beings have free will and that free will is incompatible with causal determinism. Nonetheless, this is a position that will strike some libertarians as highly unsatisfactory. For some medieval libertarians (and for some contemporaries), an act of will is free only in case the agent could have performed a different act of will in exactly the same set of circumstances with exactly the same set of beliefs and desires.[71] For such libertarians, the alternative possibilities available to the will need to be available to the will simultaneously, with the agent in the same state of mind. On this way of thinking about free will, to be free, the will needs to be unconstrained not only by causal influences outside the agent; it needs to be unconstrained even by the agent's intellect. On Aquinas's view, however, it isn't possible for the will to be unconstrained by the intellect, and what is necessary for freedom is that an agent's will not be causally determined by anything outside the agent. For Aquinas, there is an alternative possibility open to the will only in virtue of the fact that it is possible for the intellect to be in a different state.

Such different intuitions about what is needed for free will are reminiscent of medieval debates about the nature of the autonomy of a free will. Some Franciscans tended to suppose that a *free* will had to be independent of the intellect as well as of all external causal influence.[72] Aquinas thought that the will is free just because of its connection with the intellect. For my purposes here, what is most important to see in this dispute is the nature of Aquinas's position within the genus of libertarian theories of free will. One can hold an incompatibilist theory of free will, as Aquinas does, without accepting the principle of alternative possibilities; one can maintain that the will is free in a way incompatible with casual determinism without espousing the Franciscan version of libertarianism. What exactly to call Aquinas's position is not clear. It seems to me that it is a species of libertarianism, but one which grounds libertarian freedom in an agent's acting on his own intellect and will, and not in the alternative possibilities open to the agent.[73]

Notes

1. See, for example, Klaus Riesenhuber, "The Bases and Meaning of Freedom in Thomas Aquinas," *Proceedings of the American Catholic Philosophical Association* 48 (1974), 99–111, esp. p. 101.

2. Cf. J. Korolec, "Free Will and Free Choice," in *The Cambridge History of Later Medieval Philosophy*, ed. Norman Kretzmann, Anthony Kenny, Jan Pinborg, associate editor Eleonore Stump (Cambridge: Cambridge University Press, 1982), p. 630; David Gallagher, "Thomas Aquinas on the Will as Rational Appetite," *Journal of the History of Philosophy* 29 (1991), 570, n.26; and Daniel Westberg, "Did Aquinas Change His Mind about the Will?" *The Thomist* 58 (1994), 41–60.

3. Cf. David Burrell, *Freedom and Creation in Three Traditions* (Notre Dame, Ind.: University of Notre Dame Press, 1993); and Brian Davies, *The Thought of Thomas Aquinas* (Oxford: Clarendon Press, 1992), pp. 174–78.

4. *ST* I–II q.10 a. 1 and I q.82 a. 1.

5. *ST* I q.82 a.4.

6. *ST* I q.59 a.1 obj.3.

7. For a discussion of sensory cognition, see my paper "Aquinas on the Mechanisms of Cognition: Sense and Phantasia," in *Medieval Analyses in Language and Cognition*, ed. Sten Ebbesen and Russell L. Friedman (Copenhagen: Royal Danish Academy of Sciences and Letters, 1999).

8. See, e.g., *ST* I q.59 a.1 corpus. See also *ST* I q.83 a.1, I–II q.6 a.1, and *De veritate (QDV)* q.xxiv a.1.

9. See, e.g., the reference to Aristotle in *ST* I q.59 a.1 obj. 1.

10. See, e.g., *ST* I q.19 a.1 corpus.

11. See *ST* I–II q.9 a.1, *ST* I q.82 a.4, and *ST* I–II q.17 a.1.

12. Although faith is divinely infused, according to Aquinas, he also seems to suppose that faith results from such an action of the will on the intellect. See, e.g., *QDV* q.14 a.3 reply, ad 2 and ad 10. I have defended Aquinas's view that will can act on intellect in this way in "Intellectual Virtues: Wisdom and the Will to Believe," in *Aquinas's Moral Theory: Essays in Honor of Norman Kretzmann*, ed. Scott MacDonald and Eleonore Stump (Ithaca: Cornell University Press, 1999).

13. See *ST* I–II q.17 a.1 and a.6.

14. *ST* I–II q.9 a.2.

15. *ST* I q.81 a.3 and I–II q.10 a.3.

16. *ST* I q.81 a.3.

17. Cf. *ST* I–II q.9 a.1.

18. Cf. *De malo (QDM)* q.6 a.1, where Aquinas says that even as regards happiness, the exercise of the will is not necessary since a person can always will on a particular occasion not to think about happiness.

19. For the way in which intellect makes use of sensory cognition to apprehend particulars, see my paper "Aquinas's Account of the Mechanisms of Intellective Cognition," *Revue internationale de philosophie* 52 (1998).

20. See *ST* I q.82 a.2.

21. The ultimate good *simpliciter* is God, on Aquinas's account. Hence the sight of God in the beatific vision also moves the will necessarily.

22. *ST* I q.82 a.1.

23. *ST* I q.82 a.2.

24. *QDV* q.22 a.12.

25. There is something misleading about talk of intellect's cognizing or will's willing. Aquinas says, "We *can* say that the soul understands, in the same way that we can say that the eye sees; but it would be more appropriate to say that a *human being* understands *by means* of the soul" (*ST* I q.75 a.2 ad 2).

26. For Aquinas's general view that all acts of will must be preceded by an act of intellect, see, e.g., *ST* I q.82 a.4 ad 3.

27. *ST* I–II q.1 a.4, esp. obj.3 and ad 3.

28. *ST* I q.82 a.4; *QDV* q.22 a.12. Cf. also *QDM* q.6 a.1.

29. *ST* I–II q.17 a.1.

30. *ST* I–II q.50 a.5, I–II q.52 a.1, and I–II q.66 a.1.

31. Cf., e.g., *ST* I–II q.17 a.2 and a.5 ad 1.

32. This distinction is related to the distinction between external and internal actions. For a helpful discussion of this distinction, see David Gallagher, "Aquinas

on Moral Action: Interior and Exterior Acts," *Proceedings of the American Catholic Philosophical Association* 64 (1990), 118–29.

33. See, e.g., *ST* I–II q.6 a.4, and *QDV* q.24 a.1 ad 1. Cf. also *QDM* q.6 a.1 ad 22, where Aquinas says, "he who does what he does not want [to do] does not have free action, but he can have free will."

34. *ST* I–II q.10 a.3.

35. *ST* I–II q.17 a.1 ad 2.

36. Aquinas's position here is like his position as regards perception and intellection. The proper sense organ for sight is the eye, and yet, Aquinas thinks, it is a human being who sees, not the eye, and a similar point could be made about intellective cognition. See, e.g., *ST* I q.75 a.2 ad 2.

37. *ST* I–II q.6 a.2 and q.17 a.5.

38. *ST* I–II q.6 a.3 ad 3.

39. *ST* I–II q.6 a.1 sc.

40. *ST* I–II q.6 prooemium.

41. *ST* I–II q.6 a.7 ad 3.

42. *ST* I–II q.6 a.1 corpus.

43. *ST* I–II q.6 a.2.

44. *ST* I–II q.9 a.6. The exception to this claim about extrinsic principles is God, who can be an extrinsic cause without removing voluntariness since he is the extrinsic cause creating the will with its inclinations and its connections to the intellect. (See, e.g., *ST* I q.105 a.4 ad 2.)

45. *ST* I–II q.6 a.4.

46. *ST* I–II q.80 a.3. See also, e.g., *QDV* q.24 a.2, where he says, "If the judgment of the cognitive [faculty] is not in a person's power but is determined extrinsically (*aliunde*), then the appetite will not be in his power either, and consequently neither will [his] motion or activity."

47. I discuss the relationship of libertarianism and the ability to do otherwise at some length in "Libertarianism and the Principle of Alternate Possibilities," in *Faith, Freedom, and Rationality: Philosophy of Religion Today*, ed. Jeff Jordan and Daniel Howard-Snyder (London: Rowman & Littlefield, 1996), pp. 73–88.

48. *ST* I q.83 a.1 obj.2. See also *ST* I q.83 a.3, where Aquinas says, "we are said to have *liberum arbitrium* when we can receive one and reject another."

49. *ST* I q.83 a.3 sc.

50. *ST* I q.83 a.4.

51. *QDV* q.24 a.6.

52. See, e.g., *ST* I–II q.13.

53. See, e.g., *ST* I–II q.15 a.3 ad 3.

54. See also *Commentary Aristotle's Nichomachaean Ethics* III.v [434], where Aquinas says that the genus of *electio* is the voluntary; on his view, although "every [act of] *electio* is something voluntary, *electio* and the voluntary are not altogether the same, but the voluntary is in more [acts than *electio* is]." One reason for insisting that *electio* is not identical to the voluntary is this: [436] "Those things which we do quickly we say are voluntary, because their source is in us, but they are not said [to be done] with *electio*, because they don't arise from deliberation."

55. *ST* I q.19 a.10 obj.2.

56. *ST* I q.83 a.3.

57. *ST* I q.83 a.4.

58. Cf. *QDM* q.16 a.2, where Aquinas says, "evil cannot arise in an appetite in virtue of appetite's being discordant with the apprehension it follows."

59. *QDV* q.24 a.12.

60. *QDM* q.6 a.1.

61. God's grace does operate on the will with causal efficacy, but Aquinas's account of grace is complicated and it isn't at all clear that the operations of grace constitute an exception to his claim here.

62. *QDV* q.22 a.5; see also *QDV* q.24 a.10 obj.5 and ad 5.

63. *QDV* q.22 a.5 ad 3 in contrarium.

64. See, e.g., *QDM* q.16 a.5, where Aquinas says that there is no state in which human beings lack *liberum arbitrium*.

65. *QDV* q.22 a.6.

66. *ST* I q.82 a.1 corpus and ad 1.

67. For different versions of PAP and an assessment of their strengths and weaknesses, see, e.g., Thomas Flint, "Compatibilism and the Argument from Unavoidability," *Journal of Philosophy* 84 (1987), 423–40.

68. See, e.g., Harry Frankfurt, "Alternate Possibilities and Moral Responsibility," *Journal of Philosophy* 66 (1969), 829–39.

69. See my discussion in "Intellect, Will, and Alternate Possibilities," reprinted in *Perspectives on Moral Responsibility*, ed. John Martin Fischer and Mark Ravizza (Ithaca: Cornell University Press, 1993), pp. 237–62.

70. See, e.g., David Widerker, "Libertarian Freedom and the Avoidability of Decisions," *Faith and Philosophy* 12 (1995), 113–18, and "Libertarianism and Frankfurt's Attack on the Principle of Alternative Possibilities," *The Philosophical Review* 104 (1995), 247–61.

71. For the medieval positions in question, see Bonnie Kent, *Virtues of the Will: The Transformation of Ethics in the Late Thirteenth Century* (Washington, D.C.: Catholic University of America Press, 1995), esp. chs. 3 and 4.

72. For an example of a Franciscan position of the sort opposed to Aquinas's, see, e.g., *John Duns Scotus: Contingency and Freedom, Lectura I 39*, tr. A. Vos Jaczn, H. Veldhuis, A. H. Looman-Graaskamp, E. Dekker, and N. W. den Bok, The New Synthese Historical Library, vol. 42 (Dordrecht: Kluwer Publishing Co., 1994), pp. 116–17.

73. I am grateful to the faculty and students at the Thomas Institute in Cologne and to William Alston, David Burrell, Brian Leftow, and Timothy O'Connor for helpful comments on earlier drafts of this paper. I am especially indebted to Norman Kretzmann for many very useful comments and suggestions.

12

Being and Goodness

Parts of Aquinas's moral philosophy, particularly his treatments of the virtues and of natural law, are sometimes taken into account in contemporary discussions, but the unusual ethical naturalism that underlies all of his moral philosophy has been neglected. Consequently, the unity of his ethical theory and its basis in his metaphysics are not so well known as they should be, and even the familiar parts of the theory are sometimes misunderstood.

We think Aquinas's naturalism is a kind of moral realism that deserves serious reconsideration. It supplies for his virtue-centered morality the sort of metaethical foundation that recent virtue-centered morality has been criticized for lacking.[1] Moreover, it complements Aquinas's Aristotelian emphasis on rationality as a moral standard by supplying a method of determining degrees of rationality. And when Aquinas's naturalism is combined with his account of God as absolutely simple, it effects a connection between morality and theology that offers an attractive alternative to divine-command morality, construing morality not merely as a dictate of God's will but as an expression of his nature.[2] Finally, Aquinas's brand of naturalism illuminates a side of the problem of evil that has been overlooked, raising the question whether recent defenses against the problem are compatible with the doctrine of God's goodness.

Aquinas's ethics is embedded in his metaphysics, only the absolutely indispensable features of which can be summarized here. Consequently, we can't undertake to argue fully for his ethical theory in this essay. For our purposes it will be enough to expound the theory, to consider some of the objections it gives rise to, and to point out some of the advantages it offers for dealing with recognized issues in ethics and philosophy of religion.

1. The Central Thesis of Aquinas's Metaethics

The central thesis of Aquinas's metaethics is that *the terms 'being' and goodness' are the same in reference, differing only in sense.*[3] What does Aquinas mean by this claim, and what are his grounds for it?

It will be helpful to begin with an observation about terminology. Contemporary metaphysics uses cognates of some Latin words crucial to Aquinas's presentation of his theory, but the terms 'essence', 'actual', and 'exists', for example, have acquired meanings different from the meanings Aquinas understood the corresponding Latin terms to have. For instance, he does not identify essential characteristics with necessary characteristics; as he uses those terms, all essential characteristics are necessary, but not all necessary characteristics are essential. Furthermore, in Aquinas's usage what is actual is opposed to what is potential rather than to what is merely possible, as in standard contemporary usage. As he understands it, what is actual is, fundamentally, what is in being; and what is in being is, ordinarily, what exists. But, as we'll see, his conception of being is broader than the ordinary conception of actual existence.

Goodness is what all desire, says Aquinas, quoting Aristotle,[4] and what is desired is (or is at least perceived as) desirable. Desirability is an essential aspect of goodness. Now if a thing is desirable as a thing of a certain kind (and anything at all *can* be desirable in that way, as a means, if not as an end), it is desirable to the extent to which it is perfect of that kind—i.e., a whole, complete specimen, free from relevant defect.[5] But, then, a thing is perfect of its kind to the extent to which it is fully realized or developed, to the extent to which the potentialities definitive of its kind—its specifying potentialities—have been actualized. And so, Aquinas says, a thing is perfect and hence desirable (good of its kind) to the extent to which it is in being.[6] That's one way of seeing how it is true to say that a thing's goodness is its being.

Offering the same line of explanation from the standpoint of the thing rather than a desirer of the thing, Aquinas says that everything resists its own corruption in accordance with its nature, a tendency he interprets as its aiming (naturally) at being fully actual, not merely partially or defectively in being. Thus, since goodness is what all things aim at or desire, each thing's goodness is its full actuality.[7]

In another gloss on Aristotle's dictum Aquinas takes the sense of 'goodness' to be brought out in the notion of that in which desire culminates.[8] Now what is desired is desired either for the sake of something else, for the sake of something else and for its own sake, or solely for its own sake. What is desired solely for its own sake is what the desirer perceives as the desirer's final good, that for the sake of which it desires all the other things it desires, that in which the hierarchy of its desires culminates. But what each desirer desires in that way is the fulfillment of its own nature, or at least that which the desirer perceives as the very best for the desirer to have or be.[9] Each thing aims above all at being as complete, whole, and free from defect as it can be.[10] But the state of its being complete and whole just is that thing's being fully actual, whether or not the desirer recognizes it as such. Therefore, full actualization is equivalent to final goodness, aimed at or desired by every thing.[11]

Finally, Aquinas argues that every action is ordered toward being, toward preserving or enhancing being in some respect either in the individual or in its species: in acting all things aim at being. Therefore, again, being is what all desire; and so being is goodness.[12]

On Aquinas's view, these various arguments show that when the terms 'being' and 'goodness' are associated with any particular sort of thing, both terms refer to the actualization of the potentialities that specify that thing's nature. Generally, then, 'being' and 'goodness' have the same referent: the actualization of specifying potentialities. The actualization of a thing's specifying potentialities to at least some extent is, on the one hand, its existence as such a thing; it is in this sense that the thing is said to have *being*. But, on the other hand, the actualization of a thing's specifying potentialities is, to the extent of the actualization, that thing's being whole, complete, free from defect—the state all things naturally aim at; it is in this sense that the thing is said to have *goodness*. Like the designations 'morning star' and 'evening star', then, 'being' and 'goodness' refer to the same thing under two descriptions and so have different senses but the same referent.

This claim of Aquinas about being and goodness, his central metaethical thesis, is bound to give rise to several objections. But since effective replies to such objections depend on certain elements of Aquinas's metaphysics, we'll postpone considering them until we've presented those elements.

2. Full Actuality and Substantial Form

On Aquinas's view, every thing has a substantial form.[13] The substantial form of any thing is the set of characteristics that place that thing in its species and that are thus essential to it in Aquinas's sense of 'essential'.[14] Some of these essential characteristics determine the genus within which the thing's species belongs; the others differentiate the thing's species from other species of that genus. The thing's genus-determining characteristics (or simply its genus) and differentiating characteristics (or simply its differentia) together comprise its substantial form or specific essence, what is essential to it as a member of its species. All the characteristics making up the thing's substantial form are essential to it as an individual, but if there are individual essences as well, they will include characteristics over and above those constituting the substantial form.[15]

The substantial form as a set of essential characteristics invariably includes at least one power, capacity, or potentiality, because every form (any set of real rather than merely conceptual characteristics) is a source of some activity or operation.[16] Among the essential characteristics, the thing's differentia is a characteristic peculiar to and constitutive of the thing's species, the characteristic that can be identified as the thing's specifying potentiality (or potentialities). The differentia is thus the source of an activity or operation (or set of them) peculiar to that species and essential to every member of the species. As Aquinas puts it, the thing's specific nature includes the power to engage in a specific operation determining of and essential to that thing as a member of that species.[17]

It follows that a thing's form is perfected when and to the extent to which the thing performs an instance of its specific operation, actualizing its specifying potentiality.[18] A thing's operation in accord with its specific power brings into actuality what was not actual but merely potential in that thing's form. So in Aquinas's basic, metaphysical sense of 'perfect', a thing is perfect of its kind to the extent to which it actualizes the specifying potentiality in its form.[19] The derivative, evaluative sense of 'perfect' is explained by the connection between actuality and goodness: for something to be actual is for it to be in being, and 'being' and 'goodness' are the same in reference. Therefore, a thing is good of its kind to the extent to which it is actual.[20] Or, putting it another way, a thing is good of its kind (or perfect) to the extent to which its specifying potentiality is actualized, and bad of its kind (or imperfect) to the extent to which its specifying potentiality remains unactualized.[21]

3. From Metaethics to Normative Ethics

The specifying potentialities of a human being are in the cognitive and appetitive rational powers, intellect and will, which comprise its differentia, reason.[22] Although endowed with freedom of choice, a human will in association with its intellect is inclined toward goodness not just naturally (like the appetitive aspect of every other being) but also "along with an awareness of the nature of the good—a condition that is a distinguishing characteristic of intellect."[23] Rational beings are "inclined toward goodness itself considered universally" rather than naturally directed toward one particular sort of good-ness.[24] The operation deriving directly from the human essence, then, is acting in accordance with rationality, and actions of that sort actualize the specifying potentiality of human beings. A human being acting in accordance with rationality makes actual what would otherwise have been merely po-tential in his or her substantial form. By converting humanly specific poten-tiality into actuality, an agent's actions in accordance with rationality increase the extent to which the agent has being as a human being; and so, given the connection between being and goodness, such actions increase the extent to which the agent has goodness as a human being. Human goodness, like any other goodness appropriate to one species, is acquired in performing instances of the operation specific to that species, which in the case of hu-manity is the rational employment of the rational powers. The actions that contribute to a human agent's moral goodness will be acts of will in accor-dance with rationality.[25]

A thing's substantial form, the set of essential characteristics determining the thing's species, constitutes the nature of the thing. And so whatever actualizes a thing's specifying potentiality thereby also perfects the nature of the thing. Given what else we have seen of Aquinas's theory, it follows that in his view what is good for a thing is what is natural to it, and what is unnatural to a thing is bad for it. So, he says, the good is what is according to nature, and evil is what is against nature;[26] in fact, what is evil cannot be natural to anything.[27] As for human nature, since it is characterized essentially by a capacity for rationality, what is irrational is contrary to nature where human beings are concerned.[28]

Habits that dispose a person to act in accordance with nature—i.e., ra-tionally—are good habits, or virtues.[29] Vices, on the other hand, are habits disposing a person to irrationality and are therefore discordant with human nature.[30] Aquinas quotes with approval Augustine's appraisal of a vice as bad or evil to the extent to which it diminishes the integrity or wholeness of the agent's nature.[31]

It is an important consequence of this account of goodness and badness that no thing that exists or can exist is completely without goodness. This consequence can be inferred directly from the central thesis about being and goodness,[32] but some of its moral and theological implications are worth pointing out. Evil is always and only a defect in some respect to some extent; evil can have no essence of its own. Nor can there be a highest evil, an ultimate source of all other evils, because a *summum malum*, an evil devoid of all good, would be nothing at all.[33] A human being is defective, bad, or evil not because of certain positive attributes but because of privations of various forms of being appropriate to his or her nature.[34] And, in general, the extent to which a thing is not good of its kind is the extent to which it has not actualized, or cultivated dispositions for actualizing, the potentialities associated with its nature.[35] Every form of privation is covered by that observation—from physical or mental subnormality, through ineptitude and inattention, to debauchery and depravity. In each case some form of being theoretically available to the thing because of its nature is lacking.

These considerations put us in a better position to assess Aquinas's understanding of the difference in sense between 'being' and 'goodness'. It should be clear by now that being is to be considered both absolutely and in a certain respect. Considered *absolutely*, being is the instantiation of a certain substantial form, the mere existence of a thing of some sort. But since each substantial form also includes a specifying potentiality, when that potentiality is actualized, the thing actualizing it is more fully a thing of that sort, a better specimen. When being is considered in this second way, it is correct to say that *in a certain respect* there is an increase of being for that thing. The ordinary sense of 'being' is being considered absolutely, that is, a thing's mere existence as the instantiation of some substantial form. But since to be is to be something or other, even being considered absolutely entails the actualization to *some* extent of *some* specifying potentiality, and in this way everything that is is good (in some respect and to some extent).

4. Supervenience

Aquinas, then, may be added to the lengthening list of those who think that goodness supervenes on some natural property.[36] As we've seen, Aquinas would say in general that an object *a* has goodness (to any extent) as an *A* if and only if *a* has the property of having actualized its specifying potentiality (to that extent). In particular, moral goodness supervenes on rationality in such a way that if any human being is morally good (to any extent), that person has the property of having actualized his or her capacity for rationality (to that extent); and if any human being has that property (to any extent), he or she is morally good (to that extent). Goodness supervenes on actualization of specifying potentialities; human moral goodness supervenes on actualization of rationality.

The relationship Aquinas sees between goodness and natural properties is complex and can be shown most easily by analogy. Fragility supervenes on certain natural properties without being reducible to any one of them, as Campbell and Pargetter have argued.[37] In line with their argument we might say that x is fragile in virtue of chemical bonding A, y in virtue of B, and z in virtue of C. Fragility cannot be reduced to or identified with bonding A, or B, or C, but it supervenes on each of them. It may be that what is common to x, y, and z is that each has weak chemical bonds in crucial spots, but those weak bonds are chemically quite distinct in connection with A, B, and C. In that case it can be said that the characteristic of being fragile and the characteristic of having weak chemical bonds in crucial spots are coextensive, and that fragility supervenes on natural characteristics, and yet it must also be denied that fragility can be identified with any one of those characteristics.

The relationship between fragility and other characteristics in that analysis is like the relationship between goodness and natural characteristics in Aquinas's ethical naturalism. A thing's goodness and the actualization of the thing's specifying potentiality are coextensive. Goodness in general is not to be identified with a particular natural characteristic, however, because the natural characteristic that is the actualization of a specifying potentiality will vary from one species of things to another. And the same observation holds regarding being: what is required to be a fully actualized member of species X is different from what is required to be a fully actualized member of species Y. The degree of actualization of the specifying potentialities for an X is the degree of being as an X, and this is also the degree of goodness as an X. But the specifying potentialities for an X differ from the specifying potentialities for a Y. So being and goodness are identical, but neither is to be identified with any one particular natural characteristic on which it supervenes.

But is moral goodness in particular identical with the natural characteristic of actualized rationality? Since human beings are essentially rational animals, human moral goodness is coextensive with actualized rationality. But moral goodness (or badness) is a characteristic of all beings whose nature involves freedom of choice, whether or not they are human. And so not even moral goodness is necessarily coextensive with the actualization of rationality, the specifying potentiality for human beings in the actual world. Goodness as an X will, for every X, be identical with the actualization of an X's specifying potentialities, but there is no natural characteristic such that goodness (or even moral goodness) is identical with it (where identity of properties is taken to require at least necessary coextension).

5. Objections to the Central Thesis

On the basis of this exposition of Aquinas's central thesis against its metaphysical background we can reply to objections the thesis is almost certain to generate. (The first two of those we consider are in fact considered and rebutted by Aquinas himself.)

Objection 1: A thing's being and its being good are clearly not the same—

many things that are, aren't good—and so being and goodness are clearly not coextensive. But if the terms are identical in reference, as Aquinas claims they are, being and goodness would have to be coextensive.[38]

This first objection trades on the counterintuitive character of a corollary of the central thesis—viz., everything is good insofar as it is in being. Aquinas accepts that corollary, associating it particularly with Augustine.[39] But the corollary cannot be reduced to an absurdity simply by observing that there are things that aren't good. In accordance with the central thesis, a thing has goodness in a certain respect and to a certain extent simply by virtue of possessing a substantial form and thus existing as a thing of a certain sort. As we've seen, however, the sense of 'goodness' is not simply the possession of some substantial form but, in particular, the actualization of the specifying potentiality inherent in that form. Only to the extent to which a thing has actualized that potentiality is it true to say unqualifiedly that the thing is good. For instance, to call Hitler good (without identifying some special respect, such as demagoguery) is to imply that he is good as a human being, or as a moral agent, which is false in ways that Aquinas's practical morality could detail by indicating how this or that action or decree of Hitler's fails to actualize rationality.

Objection 2: Goodness admits of degrees, but being is all or nothing. No rock, desk, or dog is in being just a little; no dog is in being more than another dog. On the other hand, things clearly can increase or decrease in goodness, and one thing can be better or worse than another thing of the same kind. Therefore, 'goodness' and 'being' can't have the same referent.[40]

It may be right to say of existence, at least abstractly, that it's all or nothing. But since every instance of existence is existence *as* something or other, and since existence as something or other typically admits of degrees—being a more or less fully developed actualized specimen—it is by no means clear that being is all or nothing. Making the same observation from Aquinas's point of view, we might say that there's more to being than just existence. Where contingent beings are concerned, potentiality for existing in a certain respect is a state of being that is intermediate between actually existing in that respect and not existing at all in that respect, as we've seen.[41] Furthermore, the actualization of potentialities is often gradual, so that the being of the thing whose specifying potentiality is being actualized admits of degrees. Stages in the actualization of a thing's specifying potentiality certainly can be and often are described in terms of goodness rather than being. All the same, the degrees of goodness picked out in such ordinary descriptions are supervenient on degrees of being.

Objection 3: According to Aquinas's central thesis, the more being, the more goodness. In that case unrestrained procreation, for example, would be a clear instance of promoting goodness, since the increase of the human population is an increase of being and consequently of goodness. But that consequence is absurd.

Human beings who bring another human being into existence have not in virtue of that fact alone produced any goodness in any ordinary sense. If with Aquinas we take the basic sense of 'goodness' to be the actualization of a thing's specifying potentiality, then a human being produces goodness to the extent to which it actualizes its own or something else's specifying potentiality. Considered in itself, bringing children into the world does nothing to actualize any human being's specifying potentiality.[42] On the contrary, a man who fathered very many children would probably contribute to a *decrease* of goodness. He would be unable to have much parenting influence on the lives of his children or to give them the care they needed just because there were so many of them, and so it is at least a probable consequence of his unrestrained procreation that there would be more people whose chances of actualizing their specifying potentialities were unnaturally low.

But objection 3 is more complicated than the preceding objections just because goodness does supervene on being (in the way described in section 5 above). Consequently, whenever a thing has being in any respect, it also has goodness in some respect to some extent. If Ahasuerus, with his many wives and concubines, fathered, say, 150 children, he was partially responsible for the existence of 150 human beings and, consequently, for the goodness supervening on the being that constituted their existence. But neither we nor Aquinas would count Ahasuerus as a moral hero or even morally praiseworthy just because he fathered all those children.

Our rejoinder to objection 1 will help here. The small amount of goodness that must supervene on even the mere existence of a thing is not enough to call that thing good. In fact, if the thing falls too far short of the full actualization of its specifying potentiality, it is bad (or evil) considered as an instance of its kind, even though there is goodness in it. So insofar as Ahasuerus couldn't do what he ought to have done to help his children develop into good human beings, his unrestrained procreation couldn't count as the production of goodness; and to the extent to which his fathering so many children would be a factor in diminishing or preventing his care of them, it could count as producing badness.

Objection 4: According to Aquinas, loss of being is loss of goodness: badness (or evil) is the privation of goodness, which is a privation of being. In that case taking penicillin to cure strep throat would be a bad thing to do, since it would result in the destruction of countless bacteria. But that consequence is absurd.

Objection 4 gains a special strength from the fact that it forces a defender of Aquinas's position to take on the task of ranking natural kinds. The task may seem not just uncongenial but impossible for anyone who understands goodness as supervenient on being itself. In Jack London's story "To Build a Fire" either a man will save his life by killing his dog or the dog will continue to live but the man will die. Since in either case one being is left, it may look as if Aquinas's theory must be neutral on the question of which of those beings should survive. But a moral intuition that is at least widely shared would consider the case in which the dog dies and the man survives to be preferable.

Far from offending that intuition, Aquinas's theory can explain and support it because his metaphysics provides a systematic basis on which to rank natural kinds: the Porphyrian Tree, a standard device of medieval metaphysics inherited from Hellenistic philosophy. A Porphyrian Tree begins with an Aristotelian category (*substance* is the standard medieval example) and moves via a series of dichotomies from that most general genus through at least some of its species. (In theory, all its possible species can be uncovered by this means.) The dichotomies produce progressively more specific species by the application of a pair of complementary properties (differentiae) to a less specific species (a genus) already in the tree. In this way, for example, *substance* yields *corporeal substance* and *incorporeal substance* to begin the tree. Corporeal substances can in turn be divided into those capable and those incapable of growth and reproduction and other life processes; and corporeal substances capable of life processes can be divided into those capable and those incapable of perception—animals and plants, roughly speaking. Finally, those capable of perception can be divided into those capable and those incapable of rationality—human beings and other animals. In this schema, then, human beings are corporeal substances capable of life processes, perception, and rationality.

Since each dichotomy in the tree is generated by the application of complementary characteristics, and since (setting aside the complicated case of the first dichotomy) all the characteristics applied involve capacities, one of the species (or genera) encountered in any pair after the first is characterized by a capacity its counterpart lacks. But, given Aquinas's views on being and actuality, an increment in capacity (or potentiality) constitutes an increment in being, and, because of the supervenience of goodness on being, a species (or genus) with more capacities of the sort that show up in the differentiae will have potentiality more goodness than one with fewer. So, other things being equal, the goodness of a human life is greater than that of a dog's just because of rationality, the incremental capacity.[43]

We don't have to accept the universal applicability of the Porphyrian Tree in order to see that in it Aquinas does have a method for ranking at least some natural kinds relative to one another, and that the method is entirely consistent with his central thesis. Moreover, the method yields results that elucidate and support the intuitive reaction to the Jack London story: other things being equal, we value a human being more than a dog (or a colony of bacteria) because there's more to a human being than there is to a dog (or a colony of bacteria). Finally, although Aquinas subordinates all other species of animal to the human species, this feature of his theory cannot be interpreted as sanctioning wanton cruelty toward nonhuman animals or their gratuitous destruction. It is another corollary of his central thesis that any destruction of being is always prima facie bad in some respect and to some extent. Because some destruction may often be less bad than the only available alternative, it may often be rationally chosen. But unless there is some greater good (some enhancement of being) that can be achieved only by means of destruction, an agent who chooses to destroy will choose irrationally.

In expounding and defending Aquinas's metaethics we have been moving toward a consideration of his normative ethics, to which we now turn.

6. The Evaluation of Actions

Aquinas's normative ethics is constructed around a theory of virtues and vices, which are conceived of as habitual inclinations, or dispositions, toward certain sorts of actions. It will be helpful, therefore, to begin this consideration by looking briefly at his analysis and evaluation of human actions.[44]

A human action, strictly speaking, is one in which a human agent exercises the specifically human rational faculties of intellect and will.[45] (Absentminded gestures, consequently, are not human actions even though they are "actions associated with a human being."[46]) Every human action has an object, an end, and certain circumstances in which it is done.

An action's object, as Aquinas conceives of it, is fundamentally the state of affairs the agent intends to bring about as a direct effect of the action.[47] We might characterize the object as the immediate aim or purpose of the action. When Esther goes uninvited into the court of King Ahasuerus's palace, for instance, the object of her action is an audience with the king.

But in Aquinas's analysis of action, an action's object is distinguished from the action's end.[48] We might provisionally think of an action's end as the agent's motive for performing the action. So the end of Esther's action of coming to the palace is to persuade Ahasuerus to rescind his decree mandating the death of all the Jews in his kingdom.

Seen in this way, the *object* of an action is *what* the agent intends to accomplish as a direct result of her action, while its *end* is *why* she intends to accomplish it. Both the object and the end of an action are taken into account in determining the action's species, in determining what the action essentially is.[49] Given Aquinas's central thesis regarding being and goodness, then, it is not surprising to find him maintaining that the goodness or badness of any action is to be decided on the basis of an assessment of the action's object and end. If the contemplated states of affairs that the action aims at and that motivate the agent are good, the action is good; if either the object or the end is not good, the action is not good.

So far, this account of the goodness of actions seems to ignore the fact that certain types of actions are morally neutral. The object of pitching horseshoes is to get them to fall around a stake, a state of affairs that certainly seems to be neither morally good nor morally bad. Suppose the end of such an action on a particular occasion is to entertain a sick child, which we may suppose is morally good. Then it might seem that the action itself, pitching horseshoes to entertain a sick child, would have to be evaluated by Aquinas as not good; for although its end is good, its object is not.

This counterintuitive evaluation can be dispelled by taking into account Aquinas's concept of the *circumstances* of an action: When was the action done? Where? By whom? How? etc.[50] An action's circumstances are obviously not essential features of a type of action, but they are what might be called *particularizing* accidents, because any broadly conceived type of action is particularized or recognized as the particular action it is by attending to its circumstances. So, for example, part of what makes Esther's action the particular action it is, is its circumstances. She comes uninvited to the court of the king's palace at a time when Ahasuerus has decreed death for anyone who comes into the court of the palace without having been called by the king, unless the intruder "finds favor with the king." Furthermore, because it has been a month since the king last sent for her, Esther has reason to believe she is out of favor with the king. Finally, she comes there at a time when Ahasuerus has decreed the death of all the Jews in his kingdom, and Esther's intention is to speak for her people. It is on the basis of a consideration of these circumstances that the action of coming uninvited to the king, which seems morally neutral, is particularized as Esther's act of courage and altruism.[51]

The importance of a consideration of circumstances in Aquinas's evaluation of actions can be seen in the fact that he takes any and every action particularized by its circumstances to be either good or bad, even though the type of the action broadly conceived of may be morally neutral (his paradigms are picking a straw off the ground or taking a walk).[52]

Not all of an action's accidents are included among its circumstances. So, for example, Esther's action has the accidents of contributing to the death of Haman and of being commemorated in a book of the Bible. But on Aquinas's theory neither of those accidents can or should make any difference to an evaluation of Esther's action. An action's circumstances, he says, are those accidents of it that are related *per se* to the action being evaluated; all its other accidents are related to it only *per accidens*.[53]

By this distinction he seems to mean that the circumstances of Esther's particular action, the action being evaluated in our example, are features accidental to the *type* of action she performs, but not accidental to her particular action on that particular occasion. On the contrary, even our understanding of the object and end of her particular action is heavily influenced by what we know of its circumstances. In light of that knowledge we might want to revise our original broad assessment and say, more precisely, that the object of her action is a *dangerous and difficult* audience with the king, and that its end is a *resolute and self-sacrificial* attempt to get the king to rescind his edict.

The action's circumstances may be called its *intrinsic* accidents, the others its *extrinsic* accidents. The intrinsic accidents of Esther's action clarify and redefine our understanding of *what she does*, what she is responsible for; its extrinsic accidents—such as its being commemorated in a book of the Bible—obviously contribute nothing to such an understanding. Even the extrinsically accidental fact that her action has some causal relationship with Haman's death is not in any way a feature of what *she* does, because the connection between her action and his death is an unforeseeable and partly fortuitous chain of events, something she could not be held responsible for.

So Aquinas's evaluation of actions is based entirely on a consideration of *what* those actions *are* and not at all on a consideration of their extrinsic accidents. In that way it is a natural outgrowth of his central metaethical thesis. The object and end of an action determine the action's type and so, broadly speaking, they determine the being of the action; the action's circumstances determine the being of the particular action that is actually performed, and in doing so they clarify and refine our understanding of the particular action's object and end. A particular (actually performed) action, then, is good only in case both its object and its end as informed by its circumstances are good; otherwise the particular action is bad. The goodness of the action's object or end depends, in turn, on whether the contemplated state of affairs motivating or aimed at by the agent is good, as judged by the central thesis.

The end of Esther's action, for example, is to persuade the king to rescind his decree of death for all the kingdom's Jews. But the king's decree was irrational, on Aquinas's view, since it would have resulted in a great loss of being and hence of goodness without any greater good to justify that loss. Helping to bring about the rescinding of an irrational decree, however, is rational, other things being equal, and therefore morally good.[54] (Analogous things can be said about the object of Esther's action.)

7. Problems for a Simpleminded Application of the Thesis

In the story of Esther, her attempt to save her people involves her knowingly risking her life: "and if I perish, I perish." How, if at all, is the evaluation of her action in terms of its object and end affected by that circumstance of the action? Aquinas would, not surprisingly, find that aspect of her action praiseworthy. In discussing courage, he praises risking one's life in the defense of the common good as a prime example of that virtue.[55] But suppose that Esther succeeds in saving her people and dies in the attempt. Would Aquinas's theory still evaluate her action as good in that case?

The simpleminded reply to that question is an emphatic affirmative: Of course Esther's action is good even if it costs her her life; it saves thousands of lives at the expense of one. On balance there is a great surplus of being and consequently of goodness.

Although the affirmative reply seems right, the reason given for it is repugnant. If this simpleminded bookkeeping approach were what Aquinas's thesis about being and goodness required, the thesis would lead to results that are egregiously inconsistent with the rest of Aquinas's moral theory as well as repugnant to moral intuitions shared by most people in his time and ours. We can show this by considering applications of the simpleminded approach to three cases more complicated than our revised version of Esther's story. The first of them is a version of one of Aquinas's own examples.

The heaven case: Johnson is a murderer, and Williams is his innocent victim. But when Johnson murders him, Williams (unbeknownst to Johnson) is in a state of grace, and so goes to heaven. The ultimate end of human existence is union with God in heaven, and so by bringing it about that Williams achieves the ultimate end, Johnson brings about an increase of being (and consequently of goodness). In reality, then, Johnson's murder of Williams is morally justified.

Aquinas considers his version of the heaven case as an objection to his own claim that the deliberate killing of an innocent person is never morally justified.[56] His rejoinder to this objection is that the fact that Williams goes to heaven, the good that is supposed to justify Johnson's murder of Williams, is an accident that is related to Johnson's action only *per accidens*; Williams's going to heaven is an extrinsic accident of Johnson's action. Aquinas is apparently thinking along this line: Williams's spiritual condition and not Johnson's action is what causes Williams to go to heaven, and it is an extrinsic accident of Johnson's action that Williams was in that condition at the time of the murder. Since it is a feature of Aquinas's theory that an action is to be evaluated solely on the basis of what it is and not on the basis of any of its extrinsic accidents, his evaluation of Johnson's action would not take any account of the fact that Williams goes to heaven. What Johnson's action is, as far as the story goes, is simply the murder of an innocent person, which is of course not morally justifiable in Aquinas's theory.

Aquinas's treatment of the heaven case strikes us as satisfactory, but his conclusion that sending Williams to heaven is only an extrinsic accident of Johnson's action seems to depend on the fact that Johnson does not (presumably cannot) know that Williams is in a state of grace. If Johnson knew that killing Williams would result in Williams's going to heaven, it would at least be harder to deny that achieving that result was part of the end of Johnson's action and thus part of what Johnson's action was. We want to consider some cases in which there is no relevant ignorance on the part of the agent.

The hostage case: A madman takes five people hostage and threatens to kill them all unless Brown kills Robinson, an innocent bystander. Brown decides that killing Robinson is morally justified by the surplus of being (and consequently of goodness) that will result from using Robinson's death to save the lives of the five hostages.

In the hostage case the object of Brown's action is Robinson's death, and its end appears to be the saving of five lives. Aquinas's way of dismissing the counterintuitive moral assessment in the heaven case is clearly unavailable as a way of dealing with the hostage case. The good that appears to justify Brown's action is the action's *end*, which *must* be taken into account in evaluating the action. In considering how Aquinas would deal with the hostage case, it will be helpful to look more closely at his conception of the end of an action.

Since it is Aquinas's view that actions should be evaluated only on the basis of what they are and not on the basis of their extrinsic accidents, and since it is also his view that actions are to be evaluated on the basis of their ends, the state of affairs sought after as the end of the action must be intrinsic to the action itself. For that reason it seems clear that the notion of motive, although it is in some respects close to Aquinas's notion of end, is not interchangeable with it. A state of affairs counts as the end of an action if and only if the agent performs the action for the sake of establishing that state of affairs, *and* the agent *can* in fact establish that state of affairs *solely by* performing that action.

In the hostage case the good that is supposed to justify Brown's killing the innocent Robinson is the saving of five lives. But that good cannot be the end of Brown's action because it is not a state of affairs he can establish by killing Robinson. The survival of the hostages depends not on Brown's action but on the action of the madman, who can of course kill them all even if Brown meets his demand. Therefore, the survival of the hostages is not a state of affairs Brown can be said to establish solely by killing Robinson. And once this more precise notion of the end of an action has been introduced, the hostage case can be assimilated to the heaven case after all. In both cases, the good that is supposed to justify the killing of an innocent person turns out not to be an intrinsic part of the action being evaluated but rather only an extrinsic accident of it that is for that reason to be left out of account in the evaluation of the action. When Brown's action in the hostage case is evaluated in that way, it is evaluated simply as the deliberate killing of an innocent person; and since that state of affairs is unquestionably bad, the action itself is not morally justified.

But even if this attempt to defend Aquinas's evaluation of actions succeeds in the hostage case, it will apparently fail if we alter the form of the counterexample in one crucial respect.

The hospital case: Five patients in a hospital are waiting for donors to be found so that they can undergo transplant operations. One of them needs a heart; the second, a liver; the third, lungs; and the fourth and fifth each need a kidney. Every one of the five patients will be able to lead a normal life if, but only if, an organ donor can be found. Each of them will die very soon without a transplant operation. Jones, the skilled transplant specialist in charge of these patients, decides that killing Smith, a healthy, innocent person, is morally justified by the surplus of being (and consequently of goodness) that will result from using Smith's organs to save the five critically ill patients.[57]

The end of Jones's action, even on the more precise interpretation of 'end', is the saving of five lives. In the hospital case, unlike the hostage case, no other agent's action is needed to establish the state of affairs Jones aims at establishing, because he is a relevantly skilled specialist in charge of the five patients. And if the saving of their lives can in this case count as the end of Jones's action, then it must be taken into account in evaluating the action. For that reason, the tactic that was effective in defending Aquinas's evaluation of actions against the hostage case won't work against the hospital case.

But Aquinas's evaluation of actions requires taking into account the action's object as well as its end. Since the object and the end together make the action what it *is*, and since the goodness of anything is a function of its being, both object and end must be good if the action is to be good. But the object of Jones's action in the hospital case is the death of the innocent Smith and the removal of his organs, which is unquestionably morally bad. Aquinas would, more specifically, condemn the object of Jones's action in the hospital case as *unjust* (as we will explain in the next section).

But the sacrifice of one to save many in the hospital case is formally like our revised version of Esther's story. In order to understand Aquinas's evaluation of the hospital case and to see whether it applies also to Esther's courageous act of altruism, we need to understand something of Aquinas's theory of the virtues in general and of justice in particular.

8. Justice and Its Place in the Scheme of the Virtues

Assuming for now the metaphysical underpinnings of Aquinas's theory of the virtues—his accounts of intellect and will, passion and operation, disposition and habit—we can begin this brief synopsis by saying that (human) moral goodness is a kind of goodness attainable only by rational beings and, as we've seen, a rational being is good to the extent to which it actualizes its capacity for rationality. Summarizing drastically, we can say that moral virtue is the will's habit of choosing rationally in controlling passions and directing actions.[58] Of the cardinal virtues, prudence is the habit of skilfully choosing means appropriate for the attaining of ends and so is concerned with directing actions; in this way prudence links intellectual and moral virtues.[59] As for the cardinal virtues concerned with controlling passions, if the passions are of a sort that need to be controlled in order to keep them from thwarting rationality, the relevant habit is temperance. And if the passions are the sort that need to be controlled in order to keep them from deterring the agent from an action to which reason prompts him, the relevant habit is courage.[60] Finally, if what is at stake is the exercise of rationality not in the agent's governance of himself but in his actions affecting other people, the relevant habit is justice.[61]

In Aquinas's view, a society has a being of its own. Some things contribute to the being of a society, and others to its dissolution. In accordance with Aquinas's metaethics, the things that contribute to a society's being are part of the society's good, and the virtue of justice generally in the members of the society is directed toward establishing and preserving that common good. Aquinas, who follows Aristotle closely here, distinguishes distributive from commutative justice in respect of the rational moral principles to which the virtue conforms. Distributive justice is the rational regulation of the distribution of the society's worldly goods, aiming at a rational relationship in that respect between the society as a whole and any individual member of it.[62] Commutative justice, on the other hand, is the rational regulation of relationships among individuals or subgroups within the society. The basis of commutative justice in Aquinas's treatment of it seems to be that human beings considered just as persons are equals, and that it is therefore rational for them, considered just as persons, to treat one another as equals, and irrational for them to treat one another unequally, considered just as persons.[63]

A used-car dealer and his customer, considered just as persons, are equals. If the dealer deceives the customer about the defects of a car and so cheats him out of much of the purchase price, then in that particular exchange of worldly goods the dealer gets a greater share than the customer gets—which is contrary to reason because the dealer and the customer are equals in all relevant respects. The inequality of the trade is part of what makes it an instance of cheating, and cheating is morally bad because it contravenes the principles of commutative justice.[64]

So, whenever one person takes another's worldly goods, the action will be just only if it is rational. A necessary (though not also sufficient) condition of its being rational is its involving an even trade. A slanderer, for instance, takes away the victim's reputation, one of the more important worldly goods, and gives nothing in return; slander is thus a gross injustice.[65] Murder is perhaps the grossest injustice of all, since in depriving the victim of life, the greatest of worldly goods, the murderer is not only providing no worldly compensation but also rendering the victim incapable of receiving any such compensation.[66]

In the hospital case the object of Dr. Jones's action is characterized by exactly that sort of injustice. His taking of Smith's life and vital organs involves considerable benefit for his five patients, but there can be no compensatory worldly good for Smith. The injustice in the object of Jones's action is a sufficient condition for evaluating the action as morally bad, regardless of the beneficial aspects of its end.

We began our investigation of the simpleminded application of Aquinas's central thesis by considering a revised version of the story of Esther, in which she loses her life in saving her people. It should now be clear that the intuitive positive evaluation of such an act of self-sacrifice is not affected by our negative evaluation of Jones's sacrifice of Smith in the hospital case. Esther would not be guilty of any injustice if she gave up her own life for her people, although of course Ahasuerus would be guilty of injustice if he took her life in those circumstances. In fact, according to Aquinas's account of commutative justice it is impossible for Esther to be unjust to herself, because a person cannot take *for* herself an unfair share of worldly goods *from* herself. The reasons for disapproving of Jones's action in the hospital case do not apply to Esther's hypothetical self-sacrifice, and approval of her self-sacrifice need not and should not be based on the simpleminded bookkeeping application of Aquinas's central thesis.

9. Agent-Centered Restrictions in Aquinas's Ethics

These considerations give us reason to think that Aquinas's ethics is a deontological theory of morality that can handle the problem of agent-centered restrictions. Samuel Scheffler has recently described these restrictions as rendering "typical deontological views . . . apparently paradoxical."

> An agent-centred restriction is, roughly, a restriction which it is at least sometimes impermissible to violate in circumstances where a violation would serve to minimize total overall violations of the very same restriction, and would have no other morally relevant consequences. Thus, for example, a prohibition against killing one innocent person even in order to minimize the total number of innocent people killed would ordinarily count as an agent-centred restriction. The inclusion of agent-centred restrictions gives traditional deontological views considerable anti-consequentialist force, and also considerable intuitive appeal. Despite their congeniality to moral common sense, however, agent-centred restrictions are puzzling. For how can it be rational to forbid the performance of a morally objectionable action that would have the effect of minimizing the total number of comparably objectionable actions that were performed and would have no other morally relevant consequences? How can the minimization of morally objectionable conduct be morally unacceptable?[67]

While Aquinas's theory certainly endorses the truism that the good is to be maximized, it also interprets the nature of goodness in general and of good actions in particular in such a way that no action whose object is characterized by injustice can be rationally performed no matter how great a good is incorporated in the action's end. On this basis, a generalization of agent-centered restrictions can be endorsed and accommodated in Aquinas's teleological deontology.

The generalized version of Scheffler's example is a prohibition against perpetrating or permitting one injustice of uncompensatable suffering even in order to minimize the total number of injustices, and at this level of generality "the very same restriction" is the restriction against perpetrating or permitting injustice. Agent-centered restrictions that prohibit agents from perpetrating or permitting actions that constitute an injustice are rational for that very reason, regardless of the good to be achieved by performing those actions.

10. The Theological Interpretation of Aquinas's Central Thesis

Aquinas's central metaethical thesis has a theological interpretation more fundamental than any of its applications to morality. For since Aquinas takes God to be essentially and uniquely "being itself" (*ipsum esse*), it is God alone who is essentially goodness itself.[68] This theological interpretation of Aquinas's thesis regarding being and goodness entails a relationship between God and morality that avoids the embarrassments of both "theological subjectivism" and "theological objectivism"[69] and provides a basis for an account of religious morality preferable to any other we know of.[70]

The question "What has God to do with morality?" has typically been given either of two answers by those who think the answer isn't "Nothing."[71] God's will is sometimes taken to create morality in the sense that whatever God wills is good just because he wills it: consequently, right actions are right just because God approves of them and wrong actions are wrong just because God disapproves of them. This divine-command morality may be thought of as theological subjectivism (TS).[72] The second of these two typical answers takes morality to be grounded on principles transmitted by God but independent of him, so that a perfectly good God frames his will in accordance with those independent standards of goodness: consequently, God approves of right actions just because they are right and disapproves of wrong actions just because they are wrong (theological objectivism [TO]).

The trouble with TS is that by its lights apparently anything at all could be established as morally right or good by divine fiat. So, although TS makes a consideration of God's will essential to an evaluation of actions, it does so at the cost of depriving the evaluation of its moral character. Because it cannot rule out anything as absolutely immoral, TS seems to be a theory of religious morality that has dropped *morality* as commonly understood out of the theory. TO, on the other hand, obviously provides the basis for an objective morality, but it seems equally clearly not to be a theory of *religious* morality since it suggests no essential connection between God and the standards for evaluating actions. Furthermore, the status of the standards to which God looks for morality according to TO seems to impugn God's sovereignty.

So the familiar candidates for theories of religious morality seem either, like TS, to be repugnant to moral intuitions or, like TO, to presuppose moral standards apart from God, which God may promulgate but does not produce. For different reasons, then, both TS and TO seem inadequate as theories of religious morality; neither one provides both an objective moral standard and an essential connection between religion and morality.

On the conception of God as essentially goodness itself, however, there is an essential relationship between God and the standard by which he prescribes or judges. The goodness for the sake of which and in accordance with which he wills whatever he wills regarding human morality is identical with his nature. On the other hand, because it is God's very nature and not any arbitrary decision of his that thereby constitutes the standard for morality, only things consonant with God's nature could be morally good. The theological interpretation of the central thesis of Aquinas's ethical theory thus provides the basis for an objective religious morality.

11. Justice, Uncompensated Suffering, and the Problem of Evil

But a more pointed theological application of Aquinas's central thesis can be developed by combining the conception of God as perfect goodness itself with the impermissibility of certain actions as brought out in our generalized account of agent-centered restrictions. The rationality of agent-centered restrictions is a consequence of the irrationality of treating the victim of the initial action unjustly in such a way that even achieving that action's laudable end leaves the victim uncompensated, and it is the injustice of the uncompensated suffering that makes the action impermissible.[73] It follows that it is impossible that a perfectly good God would permit, much less perform, any action whose object involves a victim who is treated unjustly and left uncompensated, no matter how much other evil might be prevented thereby.

Nevertheless, many, perhaps most, attempts to solve the problem of evil portray God as permitting or even performing actions that appear to be impermissible in just that way. For instance, Richard Swinburne's "argument from the need for knowledge," which is certainly not idiosyncratic in its attempt to provide a morally sufficient reason for God's permitting natural evil, takes the initially attractive line that many natural evils "are necessary if agents are to have the *knowledge* of how to bring about evil or prevent its occurrence, knowledge which they must have if they are to have a genuine choice between bringing about evil and bringing about good."[74] But as this line is developed it turns out, not surprisingly, that in very many cases God must be portrayed as allowing some innocent person or persons to suffer without compensation so that others may learn to avoid or to prevent or mitigate such suffering on other occasions; "If God normally helps those who cannot help themselves when others do not help, others will not take the trouble to help the helpless next time."[75] Even if we suppose, as Swinburne does, that the knowledge gained in such a way cannot be gained otherwise, at least not efficaciously, God's role in this arrangement seems morally on a par with that of Dr. Jones in the hospital case—or worse, since the end of Jones's action is the prevention of death while the end of God's nonintervention is the alleviation of ignorance.

Swinburne deals with difficulties of this sort by stressing God's right to treat us as we have no right to treat one another.[76] But to say in this context that God has such a right is to imply that there would be no injustice on God's part if he exercised the right. Swinburne's claim, then, comes to this: if God were to do something that would be unjust by human standards, it would not count as unjust simply because God was its perpetrator. If this claim is not to convey the morally repulsive suggestion that anything whatever that God might do would count as good solely because God did it (including, e.g., breaking his promise to save those who put their trust in him), then there must be morally relevant features of God's nature and action for which there are no counterparts in human nature and action.

Swinburne sometimes suggests that God's being the creator of the world is just such a feature. This seems to be the most promising line to take in support of Swinburne's claim about God's rights, but we do not think it succeeds. A mother is also in a sense the creator of her child. While that relationship gives her rights over the child that others do not have, it is not nearly enough to justify her if she inflicts uncompensated suffering on her unwilling child. If she were to deny her daughter any college education in order to have money enough to send her son to Harvard, when her daughter also wants an education and receives no compensating benefits for failing to get one, the mother would be outrageously unfair. That she was in some sense the creator of the children would in no way lessen the unfairness. Of course, God is the creator of human beings in a much more radical sense than a mother is the creator of her children. But would the assessment of the mother's unfairness be at all softened if it turned out that she had built these children from scratch in a laboratory? We see no respect in which the degree of radicalness in the claim that one person created another could be a morally relevant consideration in evaluating the justice of the creator's treatment of his creatures.

Similarly, Plantinga has suggested that natural evils might be perpetrated by fallen angels, and that the good there is in the exercise of free will on their part might provide a morally sufficient reason for God to allow instances of natural evil, if, and only if, the world characterized by such an arrangement is one in which there is more good than evil.[77] On this view, an omniscient, omnipotent, perfectly good God might permit the inhabitants of Mexico City to suffer in an earthquake so that the good of freedom might thereby be achieved in the earthquake-causing activity of fallen angels, as long as the general preponderance of good over evil was not thereby destroyed.[78] Plantinga's Free Will Defense (FWD) has sometimes been challenged because it has been thought to impugn God's omnipotence, but as far as we know, the literature on FWD has not so far addressed the challenge that arises from Aquinas's sort of ethical theory, which provides grounds for doubting whether FWD preserves God's perfect goodness. As our earthquake example suggests, FWD does not explicitly rule out attributing to God an action Aquinas would consider unjust and hence immoral. If it does not, then, on Aquinas's view, the reason FWD assigns to God for permitting some instances of evil (especially natural, but also some kinds of moral evil) is not a *morally* sufficient reason.

But the issue should not be construed as tied particularly to Aquinas's ethics. If moral goodness includes agent-centered restrictions, both general and particular, then God's justice and individual human rights must be taken into account in any attempt to explain God's permitting moral or natural evil. And it may be more effective to raise the issue in terms of agent-centered restrictions, which have a "considerable intuitive appeal" and "congeniality to moral common sense" quite independently of their involvement in Aquinas's or any other ethical theory. Putting the matter in those terms, if a proposed solution to the problem of evil depends on implicitly rejecting generalized agent-centered restrictions as having no application to God, it will be important to ask what sort of ethical theory is presupposed by the proposal and to consider whether such a theory is consistent with whatever else is held to be true about God by the defender of theism against the argument from evil.

In correspondence with us Plantinga has said of FWD that agent-centered restrictions and the requirements of justice

> clearly are not excluded; they just aren't explicitly mentioned. If you are right (and I'm not convinced you aren't) in thinking that God couldn't permit an innocent to suffer without some compensating good (accruing to that very person), then a world in which innocents suffer without such compensation won't be a very good world. In fact, if such a state of affairs is so evil that no amount of good can outweigh it, then *no* good possible world would be one in which there is such uncompensated suffering of innocents. . . . But can't we mend matters simply enough, just by adding . . . that *a* [the possible world God actualizes in FWD] meets the agent-centered restrictions: that *a* contains no instances of uncompensated suffering of innocents . . . [?]

Plantinga is plainly right to insist that FWD doesn't explicitly rule out agent-centered restrictions, but adding them successfully requires saying more about the nature of the world in which innocents suffer but are compensated.

Worries raised by consideration of agent-centered restrictions are not allayed simply by stipulating compensation for the suffering of innocent victims, as can be seen by considering an adaptation of an episode from Dickens's *Tale of Two Cities*. An enormously rich French aristocrat habitually has his carriage driven at high speeds through the streets of Paris and is contemptuously indifferent to the suffering thereby inflicted on the lower classes. One day his carriage cripples a child. Seeing that the child has been seriously hurt, the aristocrat flings several gold coins to the grieving family. The family, to whom the coins represent a fortune, are entirely satisfied; but no one would suppose that the aristocrat has thereby exonerated himself. It's easy to find circumstances of this sort, in which victims may consider themselves compensated even though the perpetrator (or permitter) remains unjustified.

Insisting on an essential rather than a merely accidental connection between the suffering and the compensation will not guarantee justification. If a mother forces her son into months of semistarvation and sensory deprivation in order to impress on him the blessings of ordinary life, he will no doubt find intense pleasure in ordinary experiences thereafter. Here the compensation is essentially connected with the suffering. But even if the pleasure is so intense as to outweigh all the pains of the deprivation, the mother is not thereby justified.

What else is required can be seen in a slight variation on our hostage case. Even if a madman were threatening to cut off five other children's fingers unless you cut off your child's fingers, you would not have a morally sufficient reason to do so. Our claim is based, as before, on considerations of the injustice in the object of the action demanded of you. Rational agent-centered restrictions make that action impermissible. And yet it's not difficult to describe circumstances in which you would have a morally sufficient reason for acting in that way, in which you would be not only not blamed but even praised for it. If your daughter's fingers were caught in machinery in such a way that she would die horribly unless they were amputated at once, and no one but you could perform the action, goodness would require it of you. It seems clear that all that accounts for the difference in the moral status of the act of amputation in these latter circumstances is that it is now the indispensable (or best possible) means to *preventing a greater evil* for the child herself.

Given the constraints raised by considerations of agent-centered restrictions, then, if an agent is to be justified in allowing the suffering of an innocent victim, he must (among other conditions) believe (reasonably) that without such suffering greater harm would come to the victim. Analogously, the strictures we have derived from the central thesis of Aquinas's metaethics preclude only such solutions to the problem of evil as fail to show how

God's permitting innocent suffering can be the indispensable (or best possible) means of (at least) preventing greater harm to the victim.[79]

Notes

1. See, e.g., Robert B. Louden, "On Some Vices of Virtue Ethics," *American Philosophical Quarterly* 21 (1984), 227–236; Gregory E. Pence, "Recent Work on Virtues," *American Philosophical Quarterly* 21 (1984), 281–297.

2. See our article "Absolute Simplicity," *Faith and Philosophy* 2 (1985), 353–382; esp. 375–376.

3. Thomas Aquinas, *Summa theologiae* (ST) Ia q. 5, esp. a. 1. We are interpreting Aquinas's "*sunt idem secundum rem*" as "are the same in reference" and "*differunt secundum rationem*" as "differ in sense." Aquinas's treatment of this thesis about being and goodness is a particularly important development in a long and complicated tradition, on which see Scott MacDonald, "The Metaphysics of Goodness in Medieval Philosophy before Aquinas" (Ph.D. diss., Cornell University, 1986). See also Michael Hönes, "Ens et Bonum Convertuntur: Eine Deutung des scholastischen Axioms unter besonderer Berücksichtigung der Metaphysik und Ethik des hl. Thomas von Aquin" (inaugural diss., Albert-Ludwigs-Universität, Freiburg i. Br., 1968).

4. See, e.g., Thomas Aquinas, *Summa contra Gentiles* (SCG), I 37.4 (n. 306); III 3.3 (n. 1880); Aristotle, *Nicomachean Ethics* I 1, 1094a1–3.

5. Kinds must be broadly conceived of in this connection. For an exhibit at a plant pathology conference a stunted, diseased specimen of wheat may be perfect of its kind, just what's wanted. But the kind at issue in that case is not wheat but wheat-afflicted-by-wheat-mildew. Alternatively, it might be said that the goodness of an exhibit, like that of other artifacts, is related to the rational purposes of its users, in which case the kind at issue is not wheat but exhibit-specimen-of-mildewed-wheat.

6. *ST* Ia q. 5, a. 1

7. See, e.g., SCG I 37.4 (n. 306); *ST* IaIIae q. 94, a. 2. Rational agents have goals over and above their natural aims, and so the objects of their conscious desires are sometimes only perceived by them as good and not also actually good for them.

8. SCG III 3, passim.

9. See, e.g., *ST* IaIIae q. 1, a. 5.

10. When the thing described is a rational being, the object of its aim will include its *conception* of the fulfillment of its nature, which can be more or less mistaken. Objectively evil objects of desire are desired because they are perceived as good for the desirer to have.

11. What is meant by 'equivalent' here is spelled out in our discussion of supervenience in sec. 5.

12. *SCG III* 3.4 (n. 1881).

13. T. H. Irwin's "The Metaphysical and Psychological Basis of Aristotle's Ethics," in *Essays on Aristotle's Ethics*, ed. A. Rorty (Berkeley: University of California Press, 1980), pp. 35–53, is particularly useful for our purposes here because

of Aquinas's dependence on Aristotle. On the relevant role of substantial form in particular, see esp. pp. 37–39 of Irwin's article.

14. See above.

15. See, e.g., *ST* Ia q. 5, a. 5; IaIIae q. 85, a. 4; *Quaestiones disputatae de veritate* (*DV*), q. 21, a. 6.

16. See, e.g., SCG III 7.7 (n. 1916); *ST* IaIIae q. 55, a. 2. A contemporary counterpart of this view of forms might be seen in Sydney Shoemaker's "Causality and Properties," in *Time and Cause*, ed. Peter van Inwagen (Dordrecht: Reidel, 1980), pp. 109–135; reprinted in Shoemaker, *Identify, Cause, and Mind* (Cambridge: Cambridge University Press, 1984), pp. 206–233.

17. See, e.g., SCG I 42.10 (n. 343): "The differentia that specifies a genus does not complete the nature (*rationem*) of the genus; instead, it is through the differentia that the genus acquires its being in actuality."

18. See, e.g., *ST* IaIIae q. 49, a. 4, esp. ad 1.

19. *ST* IaIIae q. 3, a. 2: "Anything whatever is perfect to the extent to which it is in actuality, since potentiality without actuality is imperfect."

20. See, e.g., SCG III 16.3, 4 (nn. 1987 & 1988).

21. See, e.g., *ST* IaIIae q. 18, a. 1.

22. See, e.g., ibid., q. 55, aa. 1, 2; q. 63, a. 1.

23. *ST* Ia q. 59, a. 1. The awareness concomitant with a rational appetite can be distorted.

24. Ibid.; cf. SCG II 47 and DV q. 23, a. 1. See also our discussion in "Absolute Simplicity" sec. 5, 359–362.

25. See, e.g., SCG III 9.1 (n. 1928); *ST* IaIIae q. 18, a. 5.

26. *ST* IaIIae q. 18, a. 5, ad 1.

27. SCG III 7.6 (n. 1915): "Therefore, since badness or evil is a privation of that which is natural, it cannot be natural to anything."

28. See, e.g., *ST* IaIIae q. 71, a. 1.

29. See, e.g., *ST* IaIIae q. 55, aa. 1–4. For human beings, acting in accordance with rationality is their second actuality (as Aquinas says, following Aristotle). A newborn human being is only potentially a reasoning being. A mature human being acting in accordance with rationality, such as Aquinas when he is writing on ethics, is rationally exercising his rational powers; and that actual exercise of the specifying potentiality for human beings is their second, or more fully complete, actuality. But there is a state intermediate between the newborn's and that of the fully active mature human being—e.g., the state of Aquinas when he is asleep or in some other way not then actualizing his specifying potentiality. The sleeping Aquinas, unlike the philosophizing Aquinas, lacks the second actuality appropriate to human nature; but even the sleeping Aquinas has something the newborn infant lacks—an acquired disposition or habit to exercise his rational powers in certain ways. That is, the sleeping Aquinas has the being appropriate to human beings, but incompletely, in the condition picked out as first actuality (see, e.g., *ST* IaIIae q. 49, aa. 3, 4). Virtues are instances of first actuality relative to certain actions in accordance with rationality. Perfection as a human being (in this life) must include first actualities in part because the freedom associated with rational powers ranges over more alternatives than can be sorted out rationally and expeditiously on an occasion of action unless some disposition to

respond in one way rather than another is part of the agent's character. That's one reason virtues are essential ingredients in human goodness. (See, e.g., *ST* IaIIae q. 49, a. 4; q. 55, a. 1.)

30. *ST* IaIIae q. 54, a. 3: "And in this way good and bad habits are specifically distinct. For a habit that disposes [the agent] toward an action that is suited to the agent's nature is called good, while a habit that disposes [him] toward an action that is not suited to his nature is called bad."

31. *ST* IaIIae q. 73, a. 8, s.c.

32. See, e.g., SCG III 7, passim.

33. SCG III 15, passim.

34. See, e.g., *ST* Ia q. 5, a. 3, ad 2: "No being can be called bad or evil insofar as it is a being, but insofar as it lacks some sort of being—as a human being is called evil insofar as it lacks the being of virtue and an eye is called bad insofar as it lacks clarity of sight."

35. See, e.g., SCG III 20, 22.

36. For a helpful survey, examples, and much else of relevance, see Jaegwon Kim, "Concepts of Supervenience," *Philosophy and Phenomenological Research* 45 (1984), 153–177.

37. John Campbell and Robert Pargetter, "Goodness and Fragility," *American Philosophical Quarterly* 23 (1986), 155–165. "The relationship between fragility, fragility phenomena and the basis of the fragility is given by two identities. (1) being fragile = having some property which is responsible for being such that ⟨X is dropped, X breaks⟩, etc. and (2) the property which is responsible for object O's being such that ⟨O is dropped, O breaks⟩, etc. = having chemical bonding B. This explicates the 'because' relation for fragility, i.e., it tells us what is meant when we say that O is fragile because it has bonding B. And when we say that object N is fragile because it has bonding A, clause (1) remains unchanged and clause (2) is changed in the obvious way" (p. 161).

38. *ST* Ia q. 5, a. 1, obj. 1.

39. *ST* Ia q. 5, a. 1, s.c. (Augustine, *De doctrina christiana* I 32).

40. *ST* Ia q. 5, a. 1, obj. 3.

41. See n. 29 above.

42. The capacity for reproduction is a potentiality human beings share with all living things.

43. The *ceteris paribus* clause in this claim is important. Even though species *A* outranks species *B* in the way described, it is theoretically possible that a particular individual of species *B* might outrank an individual of species *A*. Suppose that there are angels, that angels constitute a species as human beings do, that the species *angel* outranks the species *human being*, and that Satan is a fallen angel. It is theoretically possible that Mother Theresa outranks Satan in the relevant sense even though the amount of being available to an angel is greater than that available to any human being. For if Mother Theresa has actualized virtually all of her specifying potentialities and Satan very few of his, it will be possible to ascribe more being and hence more goodness to Mother Theresa than to Satan.

44. For a clear, succinct presentation of some of this material in more detail, see Alan Donagan, "Aquinas on Human Action," in *The Cambridge History of*

Later Medieval Philosophy, ed. N. Kretzmann, A. Kenny, and J. Pinborg (Cambridge: Cambridge University Press, 1982), pp. 642–654.

45. Aquinas's "Treatise on Action" is contained in *ST* IaIIae qq. 6–17; qq. 18–21 are concerned with the evaluation of actions.

46. For this distinction, see *ST* IaIIae q. 1, a. 1.

47. On the object of an action, see, e.g., *ST* IaIIae q. 10, a. 2; q. 18, a. 2.

48. On the end of an action, see, e.g., *ST* IaIIae q. 1, aa. 1–3; q. 18, aa. 4–6. For our purposes here we are omitting some of the details of Aquinas's complex distinction between the object and the end of an action; for some of the complications see, e.g., *ST* IaIIae q. 18, a. 7.

49. On specifying an action, see, e.g., *ST* IaIIae q. 1, a. 3; q. 18, aa. 2, 5, 7.

50. On the circumstances of an action, see esp. *ST* IaIIae q. 7, passim.

51. On the role of circumstances in the evaluation of actions, see, e.g., *ST* IaIIae q. 18, aa, 3, 10, 11.

52. *ST* IaIIae q. 18, a. 8.

53. See, e.g., *ST* IaIIae q. 7, a. 2, ad 2.

54. On Aquinas's treatment of issues of this sort regarding decrees or laws see Norman Kretzmann, "*Lex iniusta non est lex*: Laws on Trial in Aquinas's Court of Conscience," *American Journal of Jurisprudence* 33 (1988).

55. See, e.g., *ST* IIaIIae q. 123, passim.

56. *ST* IIaIIae q. 64, a. 6, obj. 2 and ad 2.

57. For a well-known form of the problem in the hospital case, see Philippa Foot, "The Problem of Abortion and the Doctrine of Double Effect," in her *Virtues and Vices* (Berkeley: University of California Press, 1978), pp. 19–32.

58. See, e.g., *ST* IaIIae q. 60, passim. For a good discussion of the Aristotelian background, see L. A. Kosman, "Being Properly Affected: Virtues and Feelings in Aristotle's Ethics," in *Essays on Aristotle's Ethics*, ed. Rorty, pp. 103–116.

59. See, e.g., *ST* IaIIae q. 57, a. 5; q. 58, a. 4; IIaIIae qq. 47–56.

60. See, e.g., *ST* IaIIae q. 60, a. 4.

61. See, e.g., *ST* IaIIae q. 61, a. 2; IIaIIae qq. 57–71.

62. *ST* IIaIIae q. 61, a. 1.

63. *ST* IIaIIae q. 61, a. 2.

64. See, e.g., *ST* IIaIIae q. 77, passim.

65. See *ST* IIaIIae q. 73, passim; for comparisons of slander (or "backbiting") with theft or murder, see esp. a. 3.

66. On murder as a vice in opposition to commutative justice and the vice "by which a man does the greatest harm to his neighbor," see *ST* IIaIIae q. 64, passim.

67. Samuel Scheffler, "Agent-Centred Restrictions, Rationality, and the Virtues," *Mind* 94 (1985), 409–419; 409. In this article Scheffler is commenting on Philippa Foot's "Utilitarianism and the Virtues," *Proceedings and Addresses of the American Philosophical Association* 57 (1983), 273–283; also (a revised version) Mind 94 (1985), 196–209. For Scheffler's own resolution of the puzzle of agent-centered restrictions, see his book *The Rejection of Consequentialism* (Oxford: Clarendon Press, 1982).

68. See, e.g., *ST* Ia q. 2, a. 3 ("*Quarta via*"); q. 3, aa. 4, 7; q. 6, a. 3. Bonaventure, Aquinas's contemporary and colleague at the University of Paris, forthrightly

identifies God as the single referent of 'being' and 'goodness' in his own version of the central thesis, interpreting the Old Testament as emphasizing being, the New Testament as emphasizing goodness (see, e.g., *Itinerarium mentis in deun*, V 2).

69. See Norman Kretzmann, "Abraham, Isaac, and Euthyphro: God and the Basis of Morality," in *Hamartia: The Concept of Error in the Western Tradition*, ed. D. V. Stump et al. (New York: Edwin Mellen Press, 1983), pp. 27–50.

70. See our "Absolute Simplicity," 375–376.

71. This brief discussion of religious morality is adapted from "Absolute Simplicity."

72. For an interesting, sophisticated treatment of divine-command theories of morality, see, e.g., Philip Quinn, *Divine Commands and Moral Requirements* (Oxford: Clarendon Press, 1978).

73. Dostoevsky presents the classic case of this sort of acknowledgment near the conclusion of Ivan's harangue of Alyosha over the problem of evil: " 'Imagine that you are creating a fabric of human destiny with the object of making men happy in the end, giving them peace and rest at last, but that it was essential and inevitable to torture to death only one tiny creature—that baby beating its breast with its fist, for instance—and to found that edifice on its unavenged tears, would you consent to be the architect on those conditions? Tell me, and tell the truth.' 'No, I wouldn't consent,' said Alyosha softly" (*The Brothers Karamazov*, Bk. V, chap. 4).

74. Richard Swinburne, *The Existence of God* (Oxford: Clarendon Press, 1979), pp. 202–203.

75. Ibid., p. 210.

76. Ibid., pp. 216–218.

77. See, e.g., Alvin Plantinga, *The Nature of Necessity* (Oxford: Oxford University Press, 1974), pp. 192–193.

78. Something similar can be said about cases in which the justification for God's allowing one human being to treat another in a flagrantly unjust way (as occurs in murder or rape, for instance) is basically the freedom of the perpetrator.

79. For an attempt at a solution that sets out to avoid that sort of failure, see Eleonore Stump, "The Problem of Evil," *Faith and Philosophy* 2 (1985), 392–423. Ralph McInerny's "Naturalism and Thomistic Ethics" (*The Thomist* 40 [1976], 222–242) provides corrections of some misinterpretations of Aquinas's ethical naturalism. We are grateful for comments on earlier drafts of this paper by Richard Creel, James Keller, James Klagge, Scott MacDonald, Alvin Plantinga, Bruce Russell, Nicholas Sturgeon, Richard Swinburne, and Edward Wierenga.

13

♨

Law and Politics

Aquinas's political and legal theory is important for three reasons. First, it reasserts the value of politics by drawing on Aristotle to argue that politics and political life are morally positive activities that are in accordance with the intention of God for man. Second, it combines traditional hierarchical and feudal views of the structure of society and politics with emerging community-oriented and incipiently egalitarian views of the proper ordering of society. Third, it develops an integrated and logically coherent theory of natural law that continues to be an important source of legal, political, and moral norms. These accomplishments have become part of the intellectual patrimony of the West, and have inspired political and legal philosophers and religious and social movements down to the present day.

I. The Legitimacy of the Political Order

The challenge to which Aquinas responded was posed to medieval Christianity by the rediscovery of the full corpus of Aristotle's works, which except for some logical treatises had been unavailable to the West before the thirteenth century. Aristotle's *Politics* included descriptions and evaluations of a wide range of political experiences in fourth-century Greece that were different from the experience of the medieval feudal order. His *Metaphysics*, *Physics*, and *Nicomachean Ethics* contained analyses of human conduct and of the external world that contrasted with the approach to legal and scriptural texts that had predominated in the medieval "schools" (which were in the process of becoming the forebears of modern universities). Operating on the basic assumption that reason and revelation are not contradictory, that "grace does not contradict nature, but perfects it," Aquinas combined tradition,

Scripture, contemporary practice, and Aristotelian philosophical methods to produce a lasting and influential "Thomistic synthesis" in politics and legal theory. Central to that effort was his reliance on Aristotle's conception of teleology or final causes, which in Aquinas's thought became the working out of God's purposes in the nature of the universe and mankind that he had created.

Aquinas, however, is first a Christian, and his Aristotelianism is a Christian Aristotelianism. In contrast to Christianity, Aristotle had no conception of original sin, and, although he was not optimistic about the possibility of creating the ideal state, he was open to the possibilities of "constitutional engineering" and conscious of the wide variations in the political structures of the 158 Greek constitutions he had studied. For early Christianity and the Fathers of the Church, however, typified in the writings of St. Augustine (381–430), political life was corrupted by man's hereditary inclination to evil, and the state was a coercive institution designed to maintain a minimum of order in a sinful world. The ruler, even if he was a Christian, could only strive to moderate human power drives and impose a minimal justice on the earthly city that would make it possible for the members of the heavenly city to reach their eternal reward.[1] For the Aristotle of Book I of the *Politics*, on the other hand, man is *zoon politikon*—literally, a *polis*-oriented animal— and political life is a necessary part of his full development. "He who is unable to live in society, or has no need because he is sufficient to himself, is either a beast or a god."[2]

In his major political work *The Governance of Rulers* (*De regimine principum*, 1265–67), Aquinas correctly broadens the translation of *zoon politikon* to argue that "man is by nature a political and social animal" (Chapter 1) who uses his reason and faculty of speech to cooperate in building political communities that respond to the needs of the group and of the individuals who compose it. The political community will be a union of free men under the direction of a ruler who aims at the promotion of the common good. Government then has a positive role and moral justification. Infidel (e.g., Moslem) rulers can rule justly "since dominion and government are based on human law, while the distinction between believers and unbelievers is a matter of divine law, [and] the divine law which is based on grace does not abolish human law which is based on reason."[3]

Having said this, Aquinas then argues that the Church may for religious reasons take away the infidel's power to rule, so that the autonomy of the temporal rule is not absolute. On the question of church-state relations Aquinas is contradictory, since in some passages—notably in *The Governance of Rulers*, Chapter 15—he appears to argue for papal supremacy over all earthly rulers because "those who are responsible for intermediate ends [that is, the common good of the temporal community] should be subject to the one who is responsible for the ultimate end and be directed by his command," while in other places—ST IIaIIae.60.6 and In Sent II.44.2—he states that the civil ruler is subject to the spiritual only in religious matters (although in In Sent II.44.2 he makes an exception for the pope as possessing both spiritual and secular power). In theory, it would appear that Aquinas should be a dualist or advocate of the "indirect power" of the Church, defending a moral rather than a legal or political supremacy for the Church, but, as far as the texts go, he "waffles."

M. J. Wilks has argued that by admitting the legitimacy of temporal rule in a sacral age, Aquinas was initiating the process of secularization that would ultimately destroy the intellectual and ideological power of the Catholic church.[4] It is certainly true that Aristotle provided a rational justification for government different from that of revelation; but once the claims of reason, as exemplified by Aristotle, were admitted, there was always a possibility of conflict. For Aquinas, however, a belief that faith and reason were both valid and divinely legitimated sources of human knowledge meant that neither should be considered as dominating the other. (In fact, of course, as Aquinas implies in his discussion of divine law,[5] revelation acts as a kind of negative check on reason although, unless the pope is the sole interpreter of the divine law, this does not in itself argue for papal supremacy over the temporal ruler.)

II. Aquinas and Constitutionalism

In addition to re-legitimizing political life, Aquinas shifted the emphasis in thinking about the best form of government. Until the thirteenth century, it was assumed that monarchy was not only the best form of government but also the only one that was in accordance with divine intention. The Neoplatonic world view of "the great chain of being" coincided with the realities of the feudal structure to support a hierarchical structure in the universe and in society that was profoundly anti-egalitarian in its implications. The hierarchy of the angels under one God was reproduced on earth with various ranks in church, state, and society, each assigned to its position under a single monarch. As Aquinas says in *The Governance of Rulers*, Chapter I, "In everything that is ordered to a single end, one thing is found that rules the rest," and in Chapter 2, "In nature, government is always by one." Among the bees there is a "king bee," and one God has created and rules the universe. Thus monarchy is the best form of government.

Yet from Aristotle Aquinas had also derived a view of government as rule over free men who are able to direct themselves. Moreover, he admits that a monarch can be easily corrupted and there seems to be no remedy against the tyrant but prayer.[6] The solution, Aquinas suggests, is for the community to take action to get rid of the bad ruler if this is legally possible. (In his *Commentary on the Sentences*, written when he was a young man, Aquinas went further and argued for individual action against tyrants even to the extent of tyrannicide against usurpers, although not against legitimate rulers who abuse their power.) In two other places, Aquinas advocates a mixed constitution that combines monarchy with aristocracy (in its etymological sense of the rule of the virtuous) and democracy, involving an element of popular participation—a system that he describes as both modeled on the government established by Moses and recommended by Aristotle in the *Politics*.[7]

If these passages are combined with Aquinas's belief in the supremacy of law and his recognition of the special claims of the Church as concerned with man's ultimate end, it is easy to understand why Lord Acton described Aquinas as "the First Whig" or believer in the limitation of governmental power. We should add, however, that he was also one of the first to endorse popular participation in government, despite the fact that he was writing before the emergence of national representative institutions.[8] Aquinas may also have been familiar with republican institutions in the Italian city-states, and he cites in his writings the example of the Roman republic. In addition, his *Commentary on the Politics* familiarized students and intellectuals both with Aristotle's discussions of the commonwealth (*res publica*) "in which the multitude rules for the common benefit," and with Aristotle's definition of a citizen as one who rules and is ruled in turn,[9] this tending to undermine the dominant hierarchical and monarchical model.

The admixture of constitutional and republican elements in Aquinas's monarchism meant that centuries later, when neo-Thomists like Jacques Maritain and Yves Simon argued for a Thomistic basis for modern Christian Democratic theory, they did not have to look far to find texts to cite. This is not to say that Aquinas himself was a democrat. There is no mention of the need for explicit consent to law and government, and where he discusses participation, it is participation by corporate groups, not individuals, or by "the people" as a whole rather than through the individual voting and the majority rule of modern democracy.[10] Above all, the modern idea of religious freedom was completely alien to his thought. Heretics "have committed a sin that deserves not only excommunication by the church but their removal from the world by death [since] it is a much more serious matter to corrupt the faith that sustains the life of the soul than to counterfeit money, which sustains temporal life."[11] It is true that Aquinas admits that if there is "an error of reason or conscience arising out of ignorance and without any negligence, that error of reason or conscience excuses the will that abides by that erring reason from being evil";[12] but for him it was unthinkable that a heretic who had known the truth (as distinct from a Jew or "infidel") could be other than culpable for rejecting it.

Aquinas's view of women was also very different from that taken in modern liberal democratic theory. Contemporary feminist critics have focused on a single article in the *Summa theologiae* in which Aquinas argues that God created woman, not as a helpmate to man "since he can get more effective help from another man, but to assist in procreation."[13] Even more shocking to modern sensibilities, in the same article Aquinas rejects Aristotle's description of woman as "a misbegotten man," arguing that although, as Aristotle states, women are weaker and passive "because of some material cause or some external change such as a moist south wind, . . . woman is not something misbegotten but is intended by nature to be directed to the work of procreation."[14] He adds that woman is naturally subject to man in a mutually beneficial relationship "because man possesses more discernment of reason."

The most striking difference from modern liberalism is Aquinas's treatment of slavery. Here he is attempting to reconcile two conflicting traditions. On the one hand, Aristotle (in Book I, Chapter 5, of the *Politics*) argued that the enslavement of those who are incapable of living a moral life is justified by nature. On the other hand, the Fathers of the Church wrote that all men are equal by nature and viewed slavery as a consequence of sin. Aquinas's answer is to refer to Aristotle's argument, to describe slavery as an "addition" to the natural law "that has been found to be convenient both for the master and the slave," and to limit the master's rights over his slave in the areas of private and family life as well as the right to subsistence.[15] Yet it is not clear that he rejects Aristotle's view of natural slavery, and as late as the sixteenth century theologians at the court of Spain debated whether or not American Indians were natural slaves.[16]

In modern terms Aquinas's political thought in its original formulation (that is, before the neo-Thomist revisions) is closer to European or Latin American corporatist and integralist conservatism than to modern liberalism. In one area, however, there is less need for a drastic reformulation in order to come up with a theory that is still applicable today—and that is the Thomistic theory of natural law.

III. Natural Law

Next to the Five Ways of proving the existence of God (ST Ia.2), the Treatise on Law (ST IaIIae.90–97) is probably the best-known part of the *Summa theologiae*. Aquinas begins with a definition of law as "an ordination of reason for the common good promulgated by the one who is in charge of the community."[17] Two comments should be made about this definition. First, by defining law as an ordination of *reason* Aquinas is saying more than simply that it is rational in character. As is clear from his explanation, he has in mind a particular type of reason—reasoning that is teleological or goal-oriented: "whenever someone desires an end, reason commands what is to be done to reach it."[18] This rational command is not a mere act of the will. When the Roman law says "the will of the prince has the force of law," it is understood that that will "must be guided by reason. . . . Otherwise the will of the prince would be iniquity rather than law."

The second point is that for Aquinas, law is based on the community, since it is ordered to the common good and "making law belongs either to the whole people or to the public personage who has the responsibility for the whole people."[19] Thus even without organized representative institutions, the ruler is obliged to keep the common good in mind when he legislates, and corrupt governments are those that are directed at the private good of the ruler rather than the common good.

Aquinas then outlines his typology of laws. At the top of the hierarchy of laws is *the eternal law*, which he defines as "the rational governance of everything on the part of God as ruler of the universe,"[20] and identifies as divine providence.

Natural law, ranked below the eternal law, is defined by Aquinas as "the participation in the eternal law by rational creatures." That participation is through "a natural inclination to their proper action and ends."[21] What this means, as he explains in Question 94, is that reason has the capacity to perceive what is good for human beings by following the "order of our national inclinations."[22] These Aquinas lists as self-preservation, an end that human beings share with all substances, family life and bringing up offspring, which are shared with all animals, and the goals of knowing God and living in society, which are shared with all rational creatures. These goals in turn are seen as obligatory because practical reason perceives as a basic principle that "good is to be done and evil is to be avoided," which is a self-evident principle like the principle of non-contradiction.

The brief discussion of natural law in Question 94 has been the subject of considerable critical comment and debate. Jacques Maritain used it to argue that Aquinas believed that human beings come to know the natural law intuitively through natural inclination, and that when that knowledge is articulated in rational and universal terms, it becomes something else—*the law of nations (ius gentium)*.[23] It is clear from the text, however, that Aquinas means that knowledge of the natural law is rational knowledge that is based on our perception of natural goals or inclinations "that are naturally apprehended by reason as good." It is true that in an earlier discussion Aquinas describes *synderesis*, the capacity to understand the basic principles of morality, as beginning with "the understanding of certain things that are naturally known as immutable principles without investigation," but he then goes on to describe the way human beings make judgments on the basis of those principles "concerning what has been discovered by reasoning."[24] Applying this account to the discussion of natural law, it seems that human beings know quasi-intuitively that good is to be done and evil to be avoided, but that they use their reason to make judgments that identify the basic human goods that are the object of our natural inclinations.

Others besides Maritain have attempted to de-emphasize the rational and propositional character of Aquinas's theory. Michael Novak, for example, describes Aquinas's natural law theory as "the traditional pragmatism. . . . not a set of generalizations but a set of individual intelligent actions,"[25] and E. A. Goerner argues that natural law is only an imperfect, second-best standard of morality, while "natural right" (*ius naturale*) is the "equitable but unformulatable virtue of the prudent and the just."[26] Morton White also misrepresents Aquinas's theory of natural law when he describes it as deductive in character, on the model of a system of logic.[27]

Aquinas states explicitly that adultery, homosexuality, usury, drunkenness, gluttony, suicide, murder, lying, and the breaking of promises are opposed to nature and therefore forbidden by natural law.[28] His argument is not intuitive, pragmatic, or deductive, but teleological in terms of the nature and purposes of human beings in relation to a given type of action. Those purposes can come into conflict, as Aquinas recognizes, but he believes that such conflicts are not irreconcilable, and that apparent contradictions can be resolved by the use of reason, since the world has been created and continues to be guided by a rational and purposive God.

Aquinas built his theory of natural law by taking a number of Aristotelian concepts and combining them in a way that is different from the way they were used by Aristotle. Whether or not he was faithful to the spirit of Aristotle can be argued,[29] but a comparison of Aquinas's discussion of natural law with the relevant passages in Aristotle's writings reveals that Aquinas has combined quite disparate elements in Aristotle—the *phronesis* of the *Nicomachean Ethics*, the description of final causality in the *Physics*, the discussion of the natural basis of government, slavery, property, etc., in Book I of the *Politics*, the ambiguous treatment of natural justice (not natural law) in Book V of the *Ethics*, and the description of law as reason in Book III of the *Politics*—into a new synthesis that makes the determination of natural ends (based on natural inclinations) a central consideration in the development of a workable theory of natural law.

The originality of Aquinas's theory is evident when it is compared, for example, with discussions of natural law in Gratian's *Decretum, or Concordance of Discordant Canons*, the major source book for canon law in the thirteenth century. Gratian describes natural law as "what is contained in the Old and

New Testaments," following this with quotations from Isidore of Seville's *Etymologies* stating that "Divine laws come from nature" and, in a formulation borrowed from the introductory passages of the *Digest* of Roman law, "Natural law is the law that is common to all nations."[30]

For Aquinas *the law of nations* is related to natural law as "conclusions from principles," conclusions that enable people to relate to one another in all societies.[31] Aquinas therefore classifies the law of nations as a type of *human law,* that is, the particular applications of natural law derived by reason, while he calls the more specific and variable applications of human law "civil law" (from *civitas* = 'city'). Both varieties of human law are derived from natural law, and if human law disagrees with natural law, "it is no longer a law, but a corruption of law."[32]

When Aquinas discusses the application of natural law through human law, he allows for a good deal more flexibility than one might expect, given the absolute character of the prohibitions of natural law. Thus evils like prostitution, usury, and the widespread exercise of the religious rites of heretics or infidels may be tolerated "so as not to prevent other goods from occurring, or to avoid some worse evil."[33] The "secondary" precepts of natural law, which "follow as immediate conclusions from first principles," can be changed "in a few cases because some special reasons make its precepts impossible to observe,"[34] although, except for the mention of polygamy in the Old Testament, there is no further discussion of the difference between the two types of principles.

It is also possible for there to be additions to the natural law of "provisions that are useful to human life." In addition to slavery, already mentioned, property is cited as an addition to resolve the contradiction between the statement of Isidore of Seville, reflecting a common view of the Fathers of the Church, that "possession of all things and universal freedom are part of the natural law" and Aristotle's arguments in favor of the natural character of private property and slavery. For Aquinas, "neither separate possessions nor slavery resulted from nature, but they were produced by human reason for the benefit of human life."[35] Despite what appears to be a parallel treatment of the two cases of property and slavery, however, it is clear from other passages, cited earlier, that Aquinas is much more favorable to Aristotle's view of the natural law basis of private property (within limits such as a starving man's need for the means of subsistence)[36] than he is to his argument for natural slavery.

Two other concepts derived from Aristotle serve to provide flexibility in Aquinas's application of the natural law. The first is prudence, which he describes as a virtue by which human beings choose the right means for the attainment of ends that are identified by practical reason.[37] Some modern interpreters of Aquinas's political thought put great emphasis on prudence, particularly in the area of the conduct of international relations, where, it is claimed, the norms of natural law can be applied only in a modified way. Others are more insistent that even in the case of modern war, natural law prohibitions, against the killing of the innocent, for example, even indirectly, are still binding.[38]

Equity is a second source of flexibility that Aquinas derived from Aristotle's *Nicomachean Ethics* (V 10). Aquinas's word for equity is not its Latin cognate, *aequitas*, but Aristotle's original Greek term, *epieikeia*. This is the power of the ruler to depart from the letter of the law when its literal application would violate its spirit.[39] An example that Aquinas gives is the opening of the gates of a besieged city after the legal hours of closure in order to admit defenders of the city being pursued by the enemy. The exceptions, however, may not violate the divine law or the "general precepts" of natural law.[40]

In the area of sexual morality, which is part of the divine law, there is no departure from the Christian doctrine that sexual expression is permitted only within the bonds of monogamous marriage, although Aquinas admits that polygamy was tolerated in the Old Testament. Fornication and adultery are seriously wrong because they operate against the natural goals of family life, especially the upbringing of children. Because this is "the natural ordering of the sex act that is appropriate to mankind," masturbation, sodomy, and bestiality are also unnatural vices, in increasing order of seriousness.[41]

Did Aquinas believe that these sins should be made the subject of legislation? On the one hand, like Aristotle he believed that the object of government was to promote virtue. On the other hand, as noted above, he was also willing to allow for considerable legislative flexibility "to avoid greater evils," and human law can prohibit only "the more serious vices, especially those that harm others and which must be prohibited for human society to survive."[42]

On the other hand, Aquinas's discussion of sexual pleasure as divinely intended (and as more intense before the Fall) implies a more positive view of sexuality than earlier Christian writers had held.

The teleological approach to natural law also affected Aquinas's discussion of usury, which in the Middle Ages was defined broadly as the charging of interest for lending money. Citing Aristotle's discussion in Book I of the *Politics*, Aquinas asserts that because money is not in itself productive, but only a means of exchange, it is wrong to receive payment for a loan of money. But he admits that "human law allows usury, not because it considers it just, but to avoid interference with the useful activities of many people."[43]

There are two other issues where Aquinas's natural law theory has been relevant for public policy down to the present day, abortion and the just war. Deliberate abortion of the fetus is for Aquinas equivalent to murder, but only after "quickening" or "ensoulment," which Aquinas, following Aristotle, believed occurred forty days after conception in the case of males, and eighty days thereafter for females.[44] However, contrary to what some contemporary polemicists have argued, Aquinas believed that abortion even before ensoulment was a sin, although not the sin of murder. He did not discuss the case where the mother's life is directly threatened, but given his biblically based opposition to doing evil so that good may come of it (Romans 3:8), it is unlikely that he would have approved.

Aquinas was not the originator of the just war theory. Cicero had defended the wars of Rome as just, and Augustine had discussed the problem of the legitimate use of defensive violence by Christian rulers. What Aquinas did was to systematize its conditions, setting out three: declaration by the ruler whose duty it is to defend the commonwealth, a just cause (in particular, self-defense), and a right intention.[45] Possibly equally important was his description of what came to be known in ethics as the principle of "double effect."[46] In discussing whether killing an unjust aggressor in order to defend one's life would be using evil means to achieve a good end, Aquinas argues that one intends only the defense of one's own life but not the killing that may inevitably result, and that only the minimally necessary force may be used. This passage has been cited in connection with the debate on the morality of nuclear warfare, with the defenders of nuclear deterrence arguing that it is not immoral to target military objectives that may incidentally have the unintended (but inevitable) effect of killing innocent people.[47]

IV. Aquinas's Legacy

As we have seen, Aquinas's thought on the topics of this chapter continues to be influential to the present day. Initially, he was only one of many writers of *Summae*, and he was even regarded with some suspicion because of the Church's condemnation of the doctrines of the Latin Averroists.[48] Despite the fact that Aquinas expressly opposed the Averroists in detail, some propositions drawn from his works were condemned by the bishop of Paris in 1277 in a general condemnation of Averroism. In 1323, however, Aquinas was declared a saint; his writings were widely taught, especially by the Dominican order, to which he belonged; and when the Council of Trent assembled in the middle of the sixteenth century, his *Summa theologiae* was placed on the altar along with the Bible as a source from which to draw answers to the arguments of the Protestant reformers. In 1879, his teachings were declared to be the official philosophy of the Roman Catholic church by Pope Leo XIII, and, at least until the Second Vatican Council (1962–1965), they were the principal basis of theological and philosophical instruction at Catholic seminaries and in most Catholic universities.

His political ideas were developed by sixteenth-century Jesuit theorists such as Suarez and Bellarmine and through them influenced Grotius and other early writers on international law. His theory of natural law was adapted late in sixteenth-century England by Richard Hooker in his *Laws of Ecclesiastical Polity*, and through Hooker influenced John Locke. Aquinas's views on property, the family, and sexual morality have been widely cited in papal encyclicals; and a modernized version of his politics, which endorses democracy, religious pluralism, and human rights, has become the ideological basis of significant Christian Democratic parties in Germany, the Low Countries, Italy, Chile, Venezuela, and Central America. His statement on the invalidity of unjust laws was cited by Martin Luther King in his *Letter from Birmingham Jail*, and he has inspired many contemporary Catholic social theorists to argue for the establishment of a "communitarian" society that avoids the excessive individualism of capitalism and the collectivism of socialism.

Protestant Christians are critical of the excessive rationalism and optimism of Thomistic ethics, and of Aquinas's refusal to recognize that there are contradictions between a rationalistic teleological natural law theory and certain aspects of the message of Christ, such as sacrificial love, martyrdom, rejection of wealth and worldly possessions, and "turning the other check." Radicals are suspicious of Aquinas's emphasis on the "natural" character of social systems that, they insist, are subject to human control and conditioned by economic structures. At least until the twentieth-century Neo-Thomist changes in favor of democracy, freedom, human rights, and religious pluralism, liberals were suspicious of Thomism's clericalism, implicit authoritarianism, sexism, and hierarchical outlook that seemed to prefer order to freedom.

Recognizing that many of Aquinas's views on society and politics that are unacceptable today (such as his monarchism, his qualified acceptance of slavery, his attitudes toward Jews, his defense of the burning of heretics, his belief in the natural inferiority of women) were historically conditioned or the result of an uncritical acceptance of Aristotle, the modern reader, like a number of contemporary moral and social philosophers (such as John Finnis, Alasdair MacIntyre, and Alan Donagan),[49] can still find relevant Aquinas's belief in the human capacity to identify goals, values, and purposes in the structure and functioning of the human person that can be used to evaluate and reform social, political, and legal structures, and to make a sustained argument based on evidence and clear statements of one's assumptions and the conclusions derived from them. This belief, which is really a faith that the meaning of human life is, at least in part, accessible to human reason, is an important element in the continuing attraction of what some of his followers like to call the perennial philosophy (*philosophia perennis*).

Notes

1. Augustine, *The City of God*, Bk. XIV, ch. 28; Bk. XIX, chs. 6, 13.
2. Aristotle, *Politics*, I.2.
3. Aquinas, ST IIaIIa.10.10.
4. M. J. Wilks, *The Problem of Sovereignty in the Later Middle Ages* (Cambridge, 1963).
5. ST IaIIa 91.4.
6. Aquinas, *De regimine principum* 6.
7. In Sent II.44.2.exp.; ST IaIIae.95.4, 105.1.
8. The English Parliament dates its foundation in its present form to 1265, the year Aquinas began to write *De regimine principum.*
9. Aquinas, "Commentary on the Politics," in R. Lerner and Huhsin Mahdi (eds.), *Medieval Political Philosophy* (Ithaca, 1963).
10. ST IaIIae.105.1.
11. ST IIaIIae.11.3.
12. ST IaIIae.19.6.
13. ST IaIIae.92.1.
14. Aristotle, *On the Generation of Animals*, IV. 2.
15. ST IIaIIae.57.3, 94.5, ad 3, 104.5.
16. L. Hanke, *Aristotle and the American Indians* (Chicago, 1959).
17. ST IaIIae.90.4.
18. ST IaIIae.90.1.
19. ST IaIIae.90.2.
20. ST IaIIae.91.1.
21. ST IaIIae.91.2.
22. ST IaIIae.94.2.
23. J. Maritain, *Man and the State* (Chicago, 1951), ch. 4.
24. ST Ia.79.12.
25. M. Novak, *A Time to Build* (New York, 1967), p. 342
26. E. A. Goerner, "Thomistic Natural Right," *Political Theory* 2.
27. M. White, *Religion, Politics, and the Higher Learning* (Cambridge, Mass., 1959), pp. 124 ff.
28. ST IaIIae.94.3; IIaIIae.47.2, 64.5, 78, 88.3, 110.3, 154.2.
29. See, for example, H. V. Jaffa, *Thomism and Aristotelianism* (Chicago, 1952).
30. D.1.c.1 and 7, translated in P. E. Sigmund, *Natural Law in Political Thought* (Washington, D.C., 1981).
31. ST IaIIae.95.4.
32. ST IaIIae.94.1. Cf. Norman Kretzmann, "Lex Iniusta Non Est Lex," *The American Journal of Jurisprudence* 33 (1988).
33. ST IIaIIae.10.11, 78.1.
34. ST IaIIae.95.5.
35. ST IaIIae.95.5 obj. 3.
36. ST IIaIIae.66.7.
37. ST IaIIae.57.5. See also *Quaestiones disputatae de virtutibus in communi* 13.
38. For the two views see Novak, *A Time to Build.*
39. ST IIaIIae.120.

40. ST IaIIae.96.6, 97.4.

41. ST IaIIae.154.11.

42. ST IaIIae.96.1.

43. ST IIaIIae.78.1.

44. In Sent IV.31.2.

45. ST IIaIIae.40.1.

46. ST IIaIIae.40.7.

47. See P. Ramsey, *War and the Christian Conscience* (Durham, N.C., 1961), pp. 39 ff.

48. See Jan A. Aertsen, "Aquinas's Philosophy in Its Historical Setting," in Norman Kretzmann and Eleonore Stump (eds.), *The Cambridge Companion to Aquinas* (Cambridge, 1993).

49. J. Finnis, *Natural Law and Natural Rights* (Oxford, 1980); A. MacIntyre, *Whose Justice? Which Rationality?* (Notre Dame, 1988); A. Donagan, *The Theory of Morality* (Chicago, 1977).

14

ᴓᴡᴏ

Aquinas on Good Sense

Elizabeth, Anne, and Emma

I am concerned here with the virtue which Aquinas calls *prudentia*. But, as is almost always the case with Aquinas's technical vocabulary, the nearest English word to the Latin one would be a mistranslation: *prudentia* does not mean what we call prudence. Prudence suggests to us a certain caution and canniness, whereas *prudentia* is much nearer to wisdom, practical wisdom.

Fortunately, however, we have a nearly perfect English equivalent in Jane Austen's phrase 'good sense'. I take Jane Austen to be centrally concerned not with presenting the ethos of the new respectable middle class but rather with the failure of the new bourgeoisie to live satisfactory lives because of the inability of the older 'aristocratic' tradition to transmit to them a certain outlook and way of behaving and education that came down to the author via the remains of a Christian morality. The eighteenth-century ideal of civilized living collapsed because it involved the loss of this tradition, a tradition which (as Gilbert Ryle and others have pointed out) is, broadly speaking, Aristotelean.

Of course, no novel is a philosophical treatise, but much of Jane Austen's writing can usefully be seen as an exploration of this tradition and in particular of the notion of *prudentia*. Elizabeth Bennett (in *Pride and Prejudice*) is shown as having and growing in good sense, in contrast both to the silliness of her younger sisters, who think of nothing beyond present pleasure, and, on the other hand, to the pedantry of her elder sister, Mary, who thinks that book-learning is enough. She also stands in contrast to her witty and perceptive but almost purely voyeuristic father, who uses his intelligence to survey a life in which he refuses to become involved. Finally, there is a contrast with her friend Charlotte, who succumbs to worldly wisdom and marries the dreadful Mr Collins for 'prudential' reasons. All these people are presented as *morally* inferior (and thus ultimately unhappy) because they lack good sense. Anne Elliot (in *Persuasion*) is, of course, centrally concerned with what Aquinas regards as a major constituent of *prudentia*: making proper use of the counsel of others. And one aspect of the education of Emma (in *Emma*) is even more interesting, because this is not completed until at the end of the book Mr Knightley, who in part represents an alien imposed morality, is integrated into her life—he marries her and goes to live in *her* house together with the totally undisciplined father. The scuffles between the super-ego and the libido are being resolved in what begins to look more like virtue.

Conscience

Anyway, it is with good sense that we are concerned. A prominent part has been played in post-Renaissance moral thinking by the notion of conscience, and people are often shocked to discover that this plays so small a part in Aquinas's moral teaching. Like the notion of the sheer individual in abstraction from social roles and community, and like the idea of 'human rights' attaching to such an abstract individual, it was a notion for which nobody had a word in either classical or post-classical antiquity or in the Middle Ages. Aquinas does use the word *conscientia*, but for him it is not a faculty or power which we exercise, nor a disposition of any power, nor an innate moral code, but simply the judgement we may come to on a piece of our behaviour in the light of various rational considerations. Usually it is a judgement we make on our past behaviour, but it can be extended to judgement on behaviour about which we are deliberating. Plainly such judgements happen and they are important when they do; but what is meant in modern talk by conscience is normally something quite different. Nowadays we speak of someone 'consulting her conscience', rather as one might consult a cookery-book or a railway timetable. Conscience is here seen as a private repository of answers to questions, or perhaps a set of rules of behaviour. Someone who 'has a conscience' about, say, abortion or betting is someone who detects in herself the belief that this activity is wrong or forbidden and who would therefore feel guilty were she to engage in it.

To have a conscience, then, in this way of thinking is to be equipped with a personal set of guide-lines to good behaviour, and to stifle your conscience is not to pay attention to these guide-lines. Since following the guide-lines is often inconvenient or difficult, it is necessary to exert our will-power to do so. So the moral life, for this way of thinking, is an awareness of your rules of behaviour coupled with a strong will which enables you to follow these rules.

For most of those who think in this way, the verdict of conscience is ultimately unarguable. If someone says honestly: 'My conscience tells me this is wrong' she is thought to be giving an infallible report on the delivery of her inner source of principles which must call a halt to argument. It is believed that the reason why violating the consciences of others—i.e. coercing them to do what is contrary to their conscience—is a very grave evil is that there can be no rational appeal beyond conscience. For this reason there are 'conscience clauses', and for this reason a tribunal for conscientious objectors to war-service is essentially concerned to determine whether a person who claims to have a conscientious objection is telling the truth about the delivery of his conscience. Such a tribunal is not expected directly to consider the validity or otherwise of the objector's position: what matters is simply that it *is* the decision of his conscience. This concern for conscience *as such* is admirably expressed in Robert Bolt's play about Thomas More, *A Man for All Seasons*, though it is not an attitude that would have been shared by an old-fashioned thinker like St Thomas More himself. For this modern way of thinking there exists a *prima facie* right for individuals to follow their consciences, and hence societies in which, for example, there is no such provision for conscientious objection are seen as necessarily unjust and tyrannous.

In the tradition with which I am concerned, there exists no such right; for rights have a quite different foundation. On the other hand there is a principle of good sense in legal matters that even activities thought to be antisocial are not to be prohibited by the apparatus of the law if this will cause more social harm than tolerating them. A society that legally tolerates any number of devious and peculiar sexual or financial practices is not proclaiming its belief that these are harmless (still less that they are possible options for the good life); it is proclaiming its belief that, whatever harm they may do, sending in the police or opening the way for blackmail would be immensely more disruptive and dangerous to the general good. Similarly, much more harm would be done by imprisoning or forcibly conscripting people who genuinely believe that war (or *this* war) is unjust than by tolerating them. It is for this reason, and not because of the alleged absolute rights of conscience, that it is a bad thing not to respect conscientious objectors. It is not the strength and sincerity of my conviction that the use of nuclear weapons must always be evil, but rather the grounds for this conviction that make it morally right for me to refuse any co-operation with such use. Obviously, no members of a tribunal could accept these grounds without becoming conscientious objectors themselves; short of this they can only make a sensible, and therefore just, decision to tolerate me.

The truth of this can be seen, I think, if we ask ourselves whether there should be tribunals to judge whether a man really holds as a matter of conscience that he should strangle all Jewish babies at birth or that his children's moral education is best served by starving them or burning them with cigarette ends. It is, I think, a mark of the confusion that has prevailed in moral thinking that intelligent people can find it quite hard to give a reasoned answer to such questions. So let us turn from this to the Aristotelean tradition as developed by Aquinas.

Prudentia

In this view we come to decisions, the 'deliveries of conscience', by practical thinking, and such thinking, like so many human activities, can be done well or badly, 'conscientiously' or sloppily, honestly or with self-deception. The virtue which disposes us to think well about what to do is *prudentia*, good sense.

We should notice that, like most thinking, this would normally be a communal activity; we would ordinarily try to get the thing right by discussing the matter with others, by asking advice or arguing a case; we would have a background of reading books or watching Channel Four, of listening to preachers or parents or children, of criticizing the views and behaviour of others; and all these are things that can be done well or badly. One may foolishly accept advice from strong-minded friends, credulously follow the preacher or stubbornly resist a good argument—these are all things for which we could appropriately be blamed, and this shows that to be disposed *not* to behave like that is to have a virtue. We may on particular occasions pity the credulous, foolish or stubbornly unreasonable person, just as we might pity the coward or drug-addict, but ordinarily we would think it also proper to blame such people (and therefore, of course, proper to forgive them).

Unreasonableness, pig-headedness, bigotry, and self-deception are all in themselves blameworthy, and they are constitutive of the kind of stupidity that is a vice. That is why no stupid person can be good. In case anyone should think that this gives academics and intellectuals a moral advantage over ignorant peasants, let us remember that what is in question is not theoretical thinking and the handling of concepts and words, but practical shrewdness and common sense in matters of human behaviour. In this matter I think the 'ignorant' peasant may often have the edge over the professor. One of the hindrances to acquiring the virtue of good sense is living too sheltered a life. There is, of course, a sense of 'education' (rather different from the one in common use) in which the educated person does indeed have a moral advantage over the uneducated; if this were not so, education would not be a serious human activity.

It will be clear that in this Aristotelean view, conscience, the moral judgement I have come to, is in no sense infallible. For what I have called the modern position, the delivery of conscience is a base-line: moral questions concern simply whether and to what extent you follow your conscience. For the older point of view you can be praised or blamed for the moral principles you hold. People who have come to the conclusion (who have convinced themselves) that torture can be a good and necessary thing and who thus carry it out cheerfully without a qualm of conscience would, in accordance with the older view, be not less but more to blame than those who recognize that torture is evil, who do not want to do it, but nevertheless do it out of fear of reprisals should they fail in their 'duty'.

Concerning judgements of conscience, Aquinas asks two interesting questions in succession. Is it always wrong, he asks, not to do what you mistakenly think is right? (Is it always wrong to go against your conscience?) He says that it *is* always wrong to flout your judgement of conscience in this way—he holds, for example, that someone who had come to the conclusion that Christianity was erroneous would be wrong not to leave the Church. But then he asks the following question: Is it always right to do what you mistakenly think is right? (Is it always good to follow your conscience?) This is where he departs from the modern view: he says it is not necessarily right for you to do what you think is right, for you may have come to your decision of conscience carelessly, dishonestly or by self-deception. He holds, in fact, the disturbing view that you can be in the position of being wrong if you do *not* follow your conscience and also being wrong if you *do*. But, he argues, you can only have got yourself into this position through your own fault. It is only by continual failure in virtue, by the cultivation of excuses and rationalisations, that you have blinded yourself to reality. It is not at all uncommon for individuals through their own fault to have put themselves in positions in which the only courses left open to them are all bad. Then they simply have to choose the lesser evil, which does not on that account become good. Suppose, for example, that a government has established in a remote and desolate area a large set of factories for the wicked purpose of manufacturing nuclear weapons. Unemployed people from distant parts of the country get on their bikes and flock to this place to get jobs. Once this has happened the government may continue its genocidal activity or else it may throw these thousands of people out of work with no hope of work. It has put itself in the position where all its options, for which it would rightly be held responsible, are bad.

Thus, for Aquinas, a clear conscience is no guarantee of virtue. We should always, he says, fear that we may be wrong. We should have what he calls *sollicitudo* about this. As Oliver Cromwell (not always an assiduous disciple of St Thomas) said to the General Assembly of the Church of Scotland: 'I beseech you, gentlemen, in the bowels of Christ, to bethink you that you may be mistaken.'

Good sense is the virtue that disposes us to deliberate well, to exercise our practical reasoning well, and it presupposes that we have some good intention, that we intend an end that is in itself reasonable. The *intentio finis*, intending the end, is an *actus voluntatis*, a realisation or actualisation of the power we call the will, the power to be attracted by what we intellectually apprehend as good. (We should be on our guard against translating '*actus voluntatis*' as an 'action' or performance of the will: that primrose path leads to the dualistic notion of an interior performance of the will, an intention, accompanying the exterior action. The *actus voluntatis* here is the condition or state of being attracted to some good, which is *actus* in that it fulfills the potentiality of the will as the oak fulfills the potentiality of an acorn, not as the kick fulfills the potentiality of the leg. It must be said that Aquinas's own language is not always as guarded as it might be on this important point.)

It is in and by the will that we are in a state of intending an end; it is by the will, that is, that we find this end attractive *as an end*. The will is being actualised or exercised because we present the end to ourselves rationally (in language or other symbols). This is to be distinguished from being attracted to some good that presents itself to us simply as sensually apprehended. The latter attractions and appetites we share, more or less, with other, non-linguistic animals. Such animals can, of course, in Aquinas's view be moved by an end or purpose in what they do, they can act willingly (*voluntarie*); they cannot be said in his technical language (which I believe he invented) to *intend* that end. In modern English I think we would say that the dog intended to chase the rabbit, but all that we would mean is that the dog's seeing of the rabbit, its sensual apprehension of it as desirable, is the reason why it is chasing. We do not mean that the dog *has* this reason, for this would only be possible if the dog were able to *analyse* its situation in language, to see, as Aquinas puts it, 'the *end as end* to be pursued by these or those means'. So while we may certainly say the dog is willingly (*voluntarie*) chasing (as opposed to unwillingly, *involuntarie*, or without willing, *non-voluntarie*) we cannot say that the dog has the intention, *intentio*, of chasing it. Although it is acting willingly, *voluntarie*, it is not acting in terms of a state or condition of willing. Because it has no language it can have no will.

Synderesis

So, for Aquinas, good sense, good deliberation, does not concern itself with the *intentio finis*, the wanting of the end, but with the adjustment of the means to the end. The intellectual presentation of the end that we find attractive (which we want or intend) is not in the field of practical reasoning but of an intellectual disposition that Aquinas calls *synderesis*. This is a very peculiar word for a very peculiar and interesting concept. It is, for one thing, a piece of fake Greek that seems to have been invented by Latin-speaking medieval philosophers and does not occur in any classical Greek text. The clue to understanding it, I believe, is to see that, for Aquinas, in the sphere of practical action *synderesis* is related to deliberation in the way that, in the theoretical sphere, *intellectus* is related to reasoning.

Aquinas thought that in any kind of true knowledge, any *scientia*, there must be certain first principles that are simply taken for granted; they are not part of the subject of the *scientia* itself. Keynesians do not argue with Milton Friedmanites about whether $1 + 1 = 2$; economists take for granted truths that are argued to by philosophers of mathematics. The statistical study of economics is permeated by the truths of arithmetic but it is not about them. Economics is done in terms of arithmetic, it does not seek to establish these truths. The economist needs the arithmetical *habitus* or skill, but what he is engaged in is something different. Now, as I understand him, Aquinas would think of the economist as having *intellectus* with regard to the arithmetical principles he takes for granted but exercising his *ratio*, reasoning, about his own particular topic. We should notice that the arithmetical truths are not *premisses* from which truths of economics are deduced; they are terms within which, in the light of which (to use Aquinas's own metaphor), the argument is conducted. Aquinas frequently says that *intellectus* is the *habitus* of first principles, while reason, *ratio*, is concerned with how to draw conclusions in the light of these principles in some particular field.

'First principles' must be a relative term, for what are the first principles of one science (economics or chemistry) will be the conclusions of another (mathematics). Aquinas did not think there could be an infinite regress of sciences, each treating as arguable what the one below it took for granted. We must, he thought, eventually arrive at some first principles that nobody could think of as arguable, as the conclusion of a reasoned argument. He instances the principle of non-contradiction: that the same proposition cannot simultaneously be *both* true and false. And indeed this cannot be argued since any argument, to be an argument at all, must take this for granted; it must be conducted in terms of, in the light of, this. (This principle must not be confused with the principle called the 'excluded middle', which says that a proposition must be *either* true or false: this can be rationally denied and all multi-valued logics start from rejecting it.) So the absolutely ultimate first principle in theoretical reasoning, the principle in terms of which any reasoning whatever must take place, is something like the principle of non-contradiction, and *intellectus* in its ultimate sense is the *habitus* or settled disposition to conduct argument in terms of this principle: that is, the disposition simply to conduct argument, to use definite meaningful symbols, at all.

Now Aquinas sees *synderesis* as parallel in practical reasoning to *intellectus* in theoretical reasoning. Practical reasoning begins with something you want;

it takes for granted that this is wanted and deliberates about the means of achieving it. The intellectual grasp of the aim as aim (not the attraction to it and intention of it, which is the actualisation of will, but the understanding of it) is *synderesis*. The deliberation takes place in terms of this end presented to us as understood by *synderesis* and found attractive as an end, intended by us in virtue of our being able to want rationally (because we have a reason), and it concludes to an action or decision to act.

But, of course, what might be the starting point of one deliberation may be a conclusion come to in a previous one. We do not, says Aristotle, deliberate about aims; but what we aim at, what we have *synderesis* of intellectually and intend as a matter of will, may be the result of a previous deliberation. In each bit of practical reasoning, if we take them separately, it is by *synderesis* that we intellectually grasp what by the will we intend, find attractive (i.e. good), and it is by practical reasoning (preferably disposed by good sense) that we decide what we will do about it.

Now, just as with an hierarchy of sciences in theoretical reasoning we get back to some ultimate first principles that we simply grasp by *intellectus* (principles which cannot be the conclusion of any previous reasoning) like the principle of non-contradiction, so in practical reasoning there is *synderesis* not only of relative first principles but also of some ultimate first principle such as that the good is what is to be wanted (which could not itself be the conclusion of some previous practical reasoning). Just as all theoretical reasoning is conducted in terms of, in the light of, the principle of non-contradiction (which lies at the root of all symbolism, or language) so all practical reasoning is conducted in terms of, in the light of, the practical principle of seeking what is in some respect good (which lies at the root of all meaningful human action—what Aquinas calls an *actus humanus* as distinct from a mere *actus hominis*). Practical reasoning is practical reasoning because it is conducted in this light, just as theoretical reasoning is theoretical reasoning because it is conducted in the light of non-contradiction.

Synderesis, then, in its ultimate sense is the natural dispositional grasp of this ultimate practical principle; and we should remember that in neither the theoretical nor the practical case is the principle a premiss of some syllogism, although it can be stated as a proposition. It is rather the principle in virtue of which there is any syllogism at all.

Practical Reasoning

Another way of putting this is to say that just as the *intellectus* of the ultimate first theoretical principle is the natural (and unacquired) disposition to be 'truth-preserving' in reasoning, so the *synderesis* of the ultimate first practical principle is the natural (and unacquired) disposition to be 'satisfactoriness-preserving' in deliberation. I owe these terms to Dr Anthony Kenny and what follows draws heavily on his *Will, Freedom and Power* (Oxford, 1975), especially chapter 5. Kenny notes that theoretical argument has a truth-preserving logic: its concern is that we should not move from true premisses to a false conclusion. Now he suggests that practical thinking is to be governed by a satisfactoriness-preserving logic which will ensure that we do not move from a satisfactory premiss to an unsatisfactory conclusion. Take the thinking: 'I want to get this carpet clean; the Hoover will do it; so, to the Hoover!' We should notice that the first clause expresses an intention (the *intentio finis*) and the last, in the optative mood, may be replaced simply by the action of using the Hoover. This action taken as the conclusion of a piece of practical reasoning (i.e., done for a reason) is itself meaningful. It has become an act of cleaning the carpet because of the intention with which it is being done. What, to a less informed observer, might seem to be the same act might have had other meanings and been a different human action: if, for instance, I used the Hoover because I wanted its noise to irritate my hated neighbour. In that case there would be a different piece of practical reasoning exhibiting the meaning of my action, exhibiting, that is, the intention with which it is being done.

The intention with which it is done centrally defines a human act as the sort of human act it is. Thus, if you accidentally drop a five pound note and I pick it up, I may do so with the intention of keeping it for myself or with the intention of giving it back to you. The first intention specifies my action as one of stealing, and the second as one of restitution. My intention or motive in picking up the note is not an occurrence inside my head which causes me to pick up the money in the way that an agent brings about an event (as 'efficient cause'); it is what Aquinas calls a 'final cause' in virtue of which I, the agent, do the action and in virtue of which the action has its 'form', its specification. It is the practical reasoning, exhibiting the intention with which the action is done, that shows what, in human terms, the action *counts* as or is. Nobody, of course, suggests that whenever you act meaningfully you go through some particular chain of reasoning in your mind. That would be no more true of practical thinking than it is of theoretical thinking. We can act or think quite reasonably without going through syllogisms or other arguments. But in both cases it is possible to spell out the thought in some such way in order to show whether it is really a valid piece of reasoning or a muddle. A muddle in theoretical thinking can lead to your being mistaken; a muddle in practical thinking can lead to your not doing or getting what you want, what you intended.

Some philosophers, Alasdair MacIntyre, for example (*After Virtue* [London, 1981], chapter 12), hold that the conclusion of a practical syllogism is *always* a meaningful action (or meaningful inaction) rather than a proposition, but this seems unnecessarily restrictive. It is clear that the conclusion is not a theoretical proposition (in the indicative mood) but it may well be not simply an action but (in the optative mood) a plan of action or, as Aquinas prefers to see it, a command addressed (in the imperative mood) either to others or to oneself.

The logic of practical reasoning differs from that of theoretical reasoning most evidently in being based not on necessity but on sufficiency. Its conclusion is an action or proposal of action which will be sufficient to attain the aim expressed in the major premiss; one that will sufficiently preserve the satisfactoriness of the original aim; what will be excluded are practical conclusions which do not thus preserve satisfactoriness. In theoretical reasoning, on the other hand, the conclusion will be what is necessarily entailed by the premisses; what will be excluded will be conclusions which are not thus necessarily entailed, which may be false when the premisses are true.

Thus one common form of theoretical reasoning goes like this: 'If p then q; but p; therefore q'. 'If he's from Blackburn then he's from the north; but he is from Blackburn; so he's from the north'. One form which would be excluded would be: 'if p then q; but q; therefore p'. 'If he's from Blackburn, he's from the north; but he's from the north; so he's from Blackburn'. Plainly this is not necessary, for he may be from Stockton or Carlisle.

Now contrast this with a piece of practical reasoning: 'If I use the Hoover the carpet will be cleaned; but I want the carpet clean; so I'll use the Hoover'. This provides a practical conclusion sufficient for my purposes. It is not however necessitated. There may be many other practical conclusions which would attain my aim, which would preserve the satisfactoriness of getting the carpet clean. The shape of this valid practical reasoning resembles, however, the shape of invalid theoretical reasoning. We seem to be arguing: 'if p then q; but q; therefore p'. But such a form of reasoning is only invalid if we are seeking a necessitated conclusion; in practical reasoning we are never doing this; we look simply for an action which will be sufficient for our purposes.

One very important contrast between theoretical and practical reasoning is that if we have a valid piece of theoretical reasoning no number of extra premisses will render it invalid. Thus I may argue as follows: 'All clergymen are wrong about the meaning of life; but all bishops are clergymen; therefore all bishops are wrong about the meaning of life'. This conclusion remains valid however many other things I may find to say about clergymen or bishops: it makes no difference whether or not they play the piano nicely or have long furry ears and prehensile tails or are (some of them) my best friends or whatever. In this argument, so long as the original premisses are true the conclusion is necessarily true. This does not go for practical reasoning. Take the argument: 'If I take this train it will get me to London; but I want to get to London; so I'll take the train'. This conclusion is practically valid so far as it goes but it ceases to be so if we add: 'I am always sick in trains' or 'This train is about to be blown up by crazed fascists'. In such a case the meaning of the action of boarding the train is no longer to be seen simply as going to London but also as becoming sick or being killed, which I may not want at all.

Thus the logic of theoretical reasoning can provide us with formulae which tell us what it is reasonable and what it is unreasonable to *think*, given certain premises. Practical reasoning, concerned with what it is reasonable to do, is not closed off by any such formulae. If we are to think well practically we must have an eye to all the relevant additional premises which may serve to invalidate a conclusion. Actions done for reasons can be done for an indefinite number of reasons. And no single reason necessarily compels you to the action; there could be others dissuading you. It is just this multi-facetedness of actions done for reasons that, in St Thomas's view, lies at the root of our freedom. No particular reason, no particular good that is sought, can necessitate our action; only the vision of the ultimate infinite good, God, can thus necessitate us.

Good sense, then, for St Thomas the disposition to do our practical reasoning well, involves a sensitive awareness of a multitude of factors which may be relevant to our decision. It involves, he says, bringing into play not merely our purely intellectual (symbol-using) powers but our sensuous apprehension of the concrete individual circumstances of our action. In his view, since our rather limited form of intelligence can only deal in the meanings of words and other symbols (for him our thinking is conceived on the model of our talking), and since no concrete individual can be the meaning of a symbol, we grasp the particular individual not by our intelligence but only by our sense powers. Thus, for him, you cannot identify a particular individual simply by describing it in words (any such words could be referring to another individual); in the end you have to point at it or single it out by some such bodily act. He concludes from this that if we are to be good at practical decision-making, if we are to have good sense, we need to exercise well our sensual, bodily apprehension of the world; so we need to be in good bodily health as well as clear in our ideas. The depression (*tristitia*) which for him comes principally from not getting enough fun out of life is likely to impede the virtue of good sense just as it impedes the sensual virtues of courage or chastity.

Aquinas's treatment of the ancillary dispositions that attend on the virtue of *prudentia* is one of the most interesting and, I think, original parts of his treatment, but I cannot discuss it here. I will conclude with a glance at one important topic: what is the difference between good sense and cunning?

Cunning and Good Sense

The *logic* of practical reasoning is neutral as between good and bad ends; the same canons of argument apply to thinking about how to get your uncle his Christmas present and thinking about how to murder him. But, in Aquinas's view, practical reasoning itself is not thus neutral. Good sense, which perfects our practical reasoning, directs it towards good ends. The cunning practised by the one seeking apparently good but actually evil ends is not misdirected prudence but a degenerate form of practical reasoning, a false prudence. There are more ways of being unreasonable than being illogical.

Aquinas gives us a clue to the difference between cunning and good sense in one of his many comparisons between practical and theoretical reasoning. It is like the difference between dialectical argumentation and *scientia*. By true *scientia* we know that something is true and really why it is true. The characteristic cry of the one with *scientia* is: 'Yes, I see, of course, that has to be so'. *Scientia* traces facts back to their first principles by argumentation. Now consider this argument: 'All slow-witted people are subjects of the Queen of England; all the British are slow-witted; so all the British are subjects of the Queen of England'. This is a perfectly valid argument and it comes to a true conclusion although both its premisses are manifestly false. It is not true that all slow-witted people are subjects of the Queen; nor is it true that all the British are slow-witted. There is nothing logically odd about deriving a true conclusion from false premisses; as we have seen, it is deriving false conclusions from true premisses that has to be excluded by a 'truth-preserving' logic. But although the falsity of the premisses does not make the argument illogical it does make the argument unscientific. We would be misled to say: 'Yes, I see, the British must necessarily be subjects of the Queen because they are slow-witted'. We would be using the wrong middle term to connect being British and being subject to the Queen. What the correct middle term would be it is a little hard to say—one would need to know something about how the House of Hanover established its legitimacy in Britain.

It is not merely false premisses but also 'improper' or irrelevant premisses that render an argument unscientific. Thus if we were to substitute going out in the midday sun for slow-wittedness you might, for all I know, have true premisses but nonetheless you will not have truly explained the matter since it is not because of this propensity that the British (or at least Englishmen) are subject to the Queen. If your premisses are either untrue or irrelevant or both but your argument is logically valid and your conclusion true, you have what Aquinas would call a piece of merely dialectical reasoning. *Scientia* is distinguished from dialectical argument by its aim, which is a *true* comprehension of the order of the world, one the premisses of which are both true and 'proper'. Now, in a similar way, good sense is distinguished from cunning by its aim, which is acting well, pursuing ends which constitute or contribute to what is *in fact* the good life for a human being.

Thus good sense, for Aquinas, is not mere cleverness but presupposes the moral virtues, the dispositions that govern our appetites and intentions, for it is concerned not merely with what seems good to me but with what is in fact good for me; and it is the lynch-pin of humane and reasonable living because without it none of these goods will be attained.

15

Aquinas on the Passions

Following Aristotle's lead, medieval philosophers generally accepted, first, a distinction between the cluster of principles and capacities that account for movement and sensation, known as the *sensitive* part of the soul, and the cluster of principles and capacities that account for thought and volition, known as the *intellective* part of the soul;[1] and second, a distinction between the apparatus of powers whereby information about the world is acquired and assimilated, known as the *cognitive* or *apprehensive potencies*, and the apparatus of powers whereby one engages the world, known as the *appetitive potencies*.

These distinctions cut across each other. The intellective and sensitive parts of the soul each have cognitive and appetitive faculties; cognition and appetition take place in both the intellective and sensitive parts. There are thus four fundamental departments into which psychological experience may be divided. The principle of cognition in the intellective part of the soul is the intellect itself, where thinking and reasoning take place. The principle of appetition in the intellective part of the soul is the will, responsible for volition and choice; the will is literally 'intellective appetite.' The principle of cognition in the sensitive part of the soul is called 'sensing,' where sensation and perception occur.

My focus is on Aquinas's treatment of the fourth department of psychological experience: the principles of appetition in the sensitive part of the soul, namely the eleven kinds of *passions of the soul*: the six concupiscible passions of love and hate, desire and aversion, and joy and sorrow; the five irascible passions of hope and despair, confidence and fear, and anger.[2] Aquinas's account of the nature and structure of the passions as psychological phenomena, developed in his *Summa theologiae* (especially in IaIIae.22–48), is a model of the virtues of medieval scholasticism. This essay concentrates on making sense of Aquinas's theory. The first section explores his analysis of the nature of the passions, and the second takes up the structure of the passions by considering the complex ways in which they are related to one another. At this point we turn to exploring the ways in which passions can be controlled by us (if at all). The third section deals with the extent to which Aquinas's theory renders us passive with regard to our passions, and the fourth examines his account of how reason controls the passions. I hope to show that Aquinas deserves a distinguished place in debates over the passions or emotions.

1. The Nature of the Passions

Aquinas gives the theoretical background to his analysis of the passions in *Summa theologiae* Ia.77.3. Passions are *potencies*; a passion is something the soul is *able* to experience, where the modality is interpreted as roughly akin to the modern notions of an 'ability' or 'capacity.' Now these modern notions correspond to a fundamental distinction among kinds of potencies: abilities correspond to *active* potencies, capacities to *passive* potencies. I have the ability, or the active potency, to climb trees. Water has the capacity, or passive potency, to be heated—say, to make tea. Active potencies enable their possessor to 'do' something, whereas passive potencies enable their possessor to 'suffer' or 'undergo' something. This intuitive sense is captured in the idea that the reduction of a potency to act[3] requires a cause or explanation: those potencies whose actualization is due to an internal principle are active potencies; those potencies whose actualization is due to an external principle are passive potencies. The grammatical voice of the verb used to express the act in question is often a linguistic test of the kind of potency involved. Thus we can offer as paradigms:

The act of an active potency is φ-ing.

The act of a passive potency is being X-ed.

Acts have *objects*, and therefore so do the potencies that are individuated by the acts.[4] An acorn has an active potency for growth, for absorbing nutrients from the surrounding soil and converting them to upward growth (stem, seedling, sapling . . .). Yet the acorn's potency is not for unlimited growth. Oak trees stop growing when they reach their adult form, which limits their potency. To reach the full adult height is the 'goal' of the acorn, the culmination and terminus of its growth. Biochemical processes are the efficient cause of the acorn's growth, whereas its formal and final cause are its end. This end is the object of the act, and hence the object of the acorn's potency for growth. The point may be summarized as follows:

[OAP] The object of an active potency is the act's end.

Now consider the case of vision, which is a passive potency. (Here the linguistic test offered above is misleading: 'seeing' is in the active voice but is a passive potency.) The act of seeing, which is the exercise of the passive potency of vision, comes about from an external principle or cause and exists so long as the external principle is reducing the potency to act, just as water's capacity to be heated is actualized by a fire so long as it actively heats up the water. The external principle acts as the formal and final cause of the actualization of the passive potency—its end.[5] As above, the end is the object of the act. Hence the object of seeing is the thing seen; the object of being heated is heat (more exactly being hot), which is imparted by the fire. The point may be summarized as follows:

[OPP] The object of a passive potency is the act's external principle.

Acts are themselves distinguished by their objects, which determine the kind of act in question.

Since the actuality (or realization) of an active potency is an act that is defined by reference to its end, there are as many kinds of potencies as there are distinct ends. These are roughly of two kinds: *activities*, where the goal of the act is the act itself, such as dancing or walking; *performances* or *achievements*, where the end or completion of the act is the state that obtains at or after the temporal limit of the act, such as winning the race or being married.[6] Both activities and achievements are kinds of actions.

Since the actuality (or realization) of a passive potency is an act that is defined by reference to an external principle, according to [OPP], such acts must therefore be occurrent *states* of the subject: the external principle exercises its influence on the subject, causing a change within it in some way, one that persists so long as the external principle continues to exercise its influence. The subject of a passive potency may be put into a state by the exercise of a passive potency that persists after the potency is no longer being exercised, but the state is not properly the exercise of the passive potency; it is instead the result of its exercise. Jones has a passive potency to be beaten with a stick; his passive potency is actualized just as long as Smith is beating him with a stick. Once Smith is done, Jones has been beaten with a stick and is no longer actualizing his potency to be (actively) beaten; his bruised condition is the actualization not of his potency to be beaten but rather of his potency to have been beaten, a different matter altogether. Since the passive potency is actualized only by an external principle, the acts of passive potencies are examples of what the subject *suffers* or *undergoes*; they are not actions, but passions.

So it is with the passions of the soul. They are passive potencies, the actualization of which is a matter of the soul's being put into a certain state: being angered by a remark about one's ancestry, for example. Anger, joy, sorrow, fear, desire—these are all states of the sensitive appetite, conceptually on a par with the pangs of hunger originating in the vegetative part of the soul.[7] (This fits well with the common view that the sensitive part of the soul is essentially passive, whereas the intellective part is essentially active.) Three consequences follow from this point. First, for Aquinas, the surface grammar of passion-statements is misleading, just as it is for perception-statements: hating, like seeing, is grammatically active but describes a state of the subject induced by some external agency. Second, the grammatical formulation of a passion-statement may conceal an ambiguity. A remark such as

I want a sloop

may be interpreted either as a *description* of a state experienced by the subject (referring to the presence of the passion of desire in the sensitive appetite) or as a *report* of a choice or decision (referring to an act elicited by the intellective appetite, that is, the will). Aquinas regiments the distinction between these two interpretations, introducing specialized terminology (in ST IaIIae qq. 8–17) for reporting acts of the will so as to avoid such ambiguities (the vocabulary of 'intention,' 'choice' or 'election,' 'consent,' and the like). Third, passions are individuated by their objects in line with [OPP] above, as any passive potency is, so that the formal difference between, say, fear and love is a matter of the distinct objects each has.[8]

In general, then, we can say that the passions of the soul are *objectual intentional states* of the sensitive appetite. The sense of this claim can be unpacked by considering a structural parallel between the cognitive and appetitive potencies of the sensitive part of the soul, at the core of which is an analogy between *experiencing a passion* and *having a perception*: the passions are a kind of 'appetitive perception.'[9]

What happens when Jones sees a sheep? The act of seeing the sheep is the actualization of Jones's passive potency of vision. Technically, the sense organ (Jones's eye) receives the form of the sheep without the sheep's matter, and the inherence of the form of the sheep in Jones's sense organ simply is the actualization of Jones's faculty of vision. That is what it is to see a sheep. The inherence of the dematerialized form of the sheep in Jones's sense organ actualizes his faculty of vision in a particular way, distinct from the way in which a dematerialized form of an elephant would actualize it. The different ways in which the faculty of vision may be actualized are classified and understood by reference to the external principles that produce them, whereas the form of the sheep, when it inheres in ordinary matter (flesh and bone and wool) and makes it a sheep rather than an elephant, is classified and understood directly through itself. Jones's act of seeing is therefore *intentional*: it is directed 'toward' something, which, as defined above, is the object of the passive potency—in this case, the sheep. It always makes sense to ask *what* someone is seeing, hearing, touching, and so on.[10] Furthermore, given the underlying Aristotelian mechanism, the act of seeing is *objectual*: Jones receives, and can only receive, forms from particular things.[11] What kinds of things can be seen? What is the most general characterization of the object of vision as such, that is, *qua* object of vision? The answer to this question specifies the *formal object* of vision.[12] The answer can appear trivial— as in the reply "the formal object of vision is the visible"—but often a nontrivial specification of the formal object is available: the formal object of vision, for example, is *color* (more precisely it is *the colored*).

Now consider the parallel for sensitive appetite. What happens when Jones loathes a sheep? There are two questions at stake: about the intentionality of the passion (what it is that is loathed) and about the character of the passion (what makes the passion loathing rather than loving). I start with the first. The act of loathing the sheep is the actualization of Jones's passive potency of loathing (*odium*). Technically, the actualization of Jones's potency for loathing requires some form's inhering in the sensitive appetite once it has been apprehended and assimilated: the preceding cognition 'supplies' the sensitive appetite with the form toward which the passion is directed.[13] A physiological account of passion is available, just as it is for perception. The inherence of the form of the sheep in Jones's sensitive appetite has as its material element some somatic condition (ST IaIIae.22.2 ad3).[14] Jones loathes sheep, and seeing one chills the blood around his heart. Thus passions, like perceptions, are intentional in character: they are directed toward something, which, as defined above, is the object of the passive potency, in this case the sheep. It always makes sense to ask *what* someone loathes, loves, or hopes for, and so on. Furthermore, since the sensitive appetite depends upon sensitive cognition, the act of loathing is thereby *objectual*: Jones receives, and can only receive, forms from particular things. He can, in a derivative way, loath all of sheepdom, but this is a matter of loathing any particular sheep that comes along, not a matter of loathing sheephood or sheepness.[15]

The formal object of a potency is the most general characterization which anything that counts as the object of the potency can fall under; it is the condition any object must satisfy in order to be intelligible as an object of the potency, whether the potency be active or passive.[16] Something must be colored in order to be visible at all; the response to the question "What do you see?" cannot be "A colorless object." The formal object of the appetitive faculties is the *good*, as the formal object of the cognitive faculties is *the true*; the formal object of the sensitive appetite is *the sensible good*, and that of the intellective appetite, the will, is *the immaterial good* (ST Ia.80.2).[17] In keeping with [OPP], the nature of any passion is given as a formal object falling under *the sensible good*. The differentiae of formal objects define distinct kinds of potencies defined through those formal objects. Thus the concupiscible passions (love and hate, desire and aversion, joy and sorrow) have the common formal object *sensible good or evil taken absolutely*, and the irascible passions (hope and despair, confidence and fear, anger) have the common formal object *sensible good or evil taken as difficult or arduous* (ST Ia.81.2).

The analogy with perception breaks down at this point. Aquinas argues in several cases that the formal object of a given passion, such as loathing, must also be the cause of loathing (ST IaIIae.26.1). The parallel claim in the case of perception is plausible: the formal object of vision, namely, the visible, is also what causes the act of vision to take place. Likewise it may be the case that Jones loathes the very sheep in front of him as a palpable evil. But, strictly speaking, Aquinas admits that the efficient cause of Jones's loathing is his perception or cognition of the sheep as an evil.[18] This marks a sharp difference between the objects of perception and passion: perception is always of what is present, whereas passions need not be. Smith's insulting letter to Jones causes Jones's anger at Smith, though Smith may be nowhere in the vicinity when his letter is read by Jones. Perception, on the other hand, requires the presence of its object for its actualization. The passions have *targets* at which they are aimed, and these *targets* may not be present (or indeed exist at all).[19]

To summarize the results of Aquinas's analogy between perception and passion: the passions are physiologically based potencies of the sensitive appetite, the proximate efficient cause of which is a perception, whose actualities are objectual intentional states; they are targeted at some individual that must fall under a given formal object, which defines their nature.

Aquinas therefore explains the passions of the soul as complex psychophysiological states that, like beliefs, are intentional and objectual.[20] The passions involve feelings, which are mental states known primarily through their phenomenological and qualitative properties, but they are not explicable solely in terms of feelings. (If they were, the passions would be analogous to sensations rather than perceptions.) Furthermore, Aquinas's account of the nature of the passions rules out classifying 'objectless' psychological experiences as passions: nonspecific emotions such as angst or dread on the one hand, and moods on the other hand.[21] By the same token, each of the eleven kinds of passions of the soul Aquinas identifies must have a target. For example, joy (*gaudium*) is a matter of rejoicing *over* something; sorrow (*tristitia*) is also directed at something and in this regard is more similar to grief than to sadness; and so on for the rest of the passions.[22] Yet so far all we have is a disorderly heap of passions. What kind of logical structure do the various passions of the soul exemplify?

2. The Structure of the Passions

Aquinas offers a taxonomic account of the passions. That is to say, he separates the passions into kinds that are distinguished by various forms of contrariety. But the taxonomy of the passions is not the strict taxonomic division ideally given in biology; the passions are not divided into pairs of coordinate species that are exclusive and exhaustive, defined by opposite differentiae. Instead, the different passions are specified by a multiplicity of criteria that allow several coordinate kinds at the same level and different modes of opposition between different pairs of passions, which are traditionally arranged in pairs (each of which is called a 'conjugation') at the same level—except for anger, which has no contrary. All in all, things are fairly messy, and a good deal the more interesting for it.[23]

From section 1 above we know that the differentiae of formal objects define the distinct kinds of potencies that are defined through those formal objects. The formal object of the appetitive faculties is *the good* and the formal object of the sensitive appetite, as a subordinate appetitive faculty, is *the sensible good* (ST Ia.80.2). Not too much emphasis should be put on 'sensible' here, I think. Aquinas only means that, as the sensitive appetite depends on sensitive apprehension (perception), its object must be capable of being perceived. He certainly does not mean to exclude nonpresent targets of the passions, and he carefully allows some passions to be directed at things in virtue of the kind of thing they are.[24]

In *Summa theologiae* Ia.81.2 and again in IaIIae.23.1, Aquinas begins his discussion of the passions by dividing them into two broad kinds. The concupiscible passions have the formal object *sensible good or evil taken absolutely*, whereas the irascible passions have the formal object *sensible good or evil taken as difficult or arduous*. In explaining the distinction in his earlier discussion, Aquinas appeals to the claim that natural substances on the one hand pursue what appears good and avoid what appears evil, and on the other hand resist and overcome contrary forces and obstacles that prevent the attainment of good or the avoidance of evil. Aquinas offers two arguments in support of his distinction (ST Ia.81.2):

These two impulses are not reduced to one principle [for the following reasons]:

[First], because sometimes the soul occupies itself with unpleasant things, against concupiscible impulse, so that it may fight against contrary [forces] in line with the irascible impulse. Accordingly, the irascible passions even seem to be incompatible with the concupiscible passions—the arousal of concupiscence diminishes anger, and the arousal of anger diminishes concupiscence, as in many instances.

[Second], this point is also clear in virtue of the fact that the irascible is the champion and defender of the concupiscible, so to speak, when it rises up against whatever gets in the way of suitable things that the concupiscible desires, or it attacks harmful things from which the concupiscible flies. (And for this reason all the irascible passions arise from concupiscible passions and terminate in them: e.g., anger is born from sorrow and, taking revenge, terminates in joy.)

I shall return to the details of these two arguments shortly. But perhaps the most remarkable thing about these arguments is that Aquinas gives them at all. Imagine the analogous case for metaphysics: after dividing the genus *animal* by the differentia *rational*, further arguments are given to establish that rational animals really are not the same as irrational ones! The explanation, presumably, is that the distinction between the formal objects of the concupiscible and irascible appetites is not a strict differentia, as would be, say, *sensible good or evil taken absolutely* and sensible good or evil taken relatively *(non-absolutely)*. But then why didn't Aquinas distinguish them in this manner?[25] (The problem is not isolated to this case; it holds for the definitions of all the passions by their formal objects, which are opposed only within a conjugation.) Aquinas does not say, but I think the only plausible answer is that this is how he found the passions—not organized into mutually exclusive and exhaustive classes of phenomena, but clustering around types of formal objects that are not strictly contradictory. The ideal of a strict taxonomy is a Procrustean bed for a scientist who is sensitive to the nuances of the phenomena. For example, the irascible passions have an internal complexity absent from concupiscible passions. Jones's anger at Smith is more than his aversion to Smith (he doesn't simply avoid him); it involves a shift of focus to seeing Smith as an obstacle that none of the concupiscible passions can account for. Likewise, hope is more than future-oriented desire, since it includes the consciousness of its (possible) realization. In addition to such complexity, the passions will also have richly nuanced interrelations—sorrow giving rise to anger, as Aquinas notes.

This reconstruction has the consequence that Aquinas's account of the passions and their structure is not, appearances to the contrary, a matter of definition. Instead, he is engaged in a scientific (or proto-scientific) enterprise: that of arranging his data in the most general classes possible consistent with illuminating analysis. The justification for the definitions Aquinas does offer is not his arbitrary fiat but the fruitfulness with which they help us understand the passions as psychological phenomena. In other words, the taxonomic structure he articulates has no independent explanatory value; its worth is cashed out in its fidelity to the phenomena it seeks to explain and in the utility of its classification scheme. Aquinas is thus proposing a 'scientific taxonomy' to account for the structure of the passions.

We can appreciate the distinctive character of Aquinas's explanation by contrasting it with two other accounts, one modern and one contemporary, which take fundamentally different approaches. Consider first the compositional theory of the passions proposed by Descartes, who identifies six 'primitive' passions—wonder, love, hate, desire, joy, and sadness—the combination of which generates all the passions we experience.[26] These primitive passions are like chemical elements; they are mixed and blended in different proportions and modes to produce the rich variety of emotional textures we encounter in psychological experience. Aquinas's model is biological rather than chemical. He takes the passions to be essentially different from one another, so that they are related causally rather than by mixture.

Yet Aquinas does not define the passions solely in terms of their causal role in psychological experience, as a functionalist theory does. Instead, he allows for a sharp distinction between the passions and their effects, so that causal connections among the passions are a matter for investigation rather than analytic truth. In his parenthetical remark at the end of the second argument in the passage given above, for example, he says that "anger is born from sorrow and, taking revenge, terminates in joy." One of the merits of Aquinas's account is that such claims can be made and perhaps falsified. Functionalist theories can also allow for contingent connections between causally defined items, but were two passions to have the same causal inputs and outputs, a functionalist account could not distinguish them, whereas Aquinas's scientific taxonomy could. He examines the causes and effects of each of the passions carefully, showing how each is embedded in a causal nexus, but he does not reduce them to mere roles in this nexus. Rather, each passion has a definition in terms of its intrinsic features, which partially explains the causal relations in which it can stand.[27]

How satisfactory is Aquinas's taxonomy? There is, I think, no obvious way to answer this question, other than to consider whether it can in fact account for all our psychological experiences in an illuminating way. Rage, wrath, annoyance, and irritation all seem to be classified under the heading of 'anger' (ira); they are presumably distinguished, though not essentially distinguished, by their degree of intensity. Likewise, fright, fear, timidity, and reticence are all forms of 'fear' (*timor*). The adequacy of Aquinas's taxonomic classification depends on how useful such classifications are. They are at least plausible.[28] For our purposes here it is enough to have shown that despite the disrepute into which taxonomic theories have fallen outside of biology, there is no prima facie reason to rule them completely out of court. Further evaluation will depend on a closer look at the details of his theory. With this in mind, consider Aquinas's arguments for distinguishing the concupiscible passions from the irascible passions.

Aquinas's distinction between the concupiscible and the irascible passions runs contrary to the trend of affective psychology, stemming from Locke, which holds that only concupiscible passions, and indeed perhaps only desires, are needed for adequate psychological explanations.[29] These 'push-pull' theories, typically based on the claim that pleasure and pain alone are the sole motivating psychological factors, are incompatible with Aquinas's analysis. But his two arguments for the distinctness of the irascible passions from the concupiscible passions are based on the claims that (a) the two kinds of passion act independently[30] and can interfere with each other, and (b) they are both required to explain psychological experience, since they are directed at different objects. These claims can be made plausible by an example. Suppose that Jones shows Rover a bone and then teases him by almost, but not quite, letting him have it. After a while Rover will no longer pursue the bone, even when it is available, but direct his energies to attacking Jones and chewing his ear off. According to Aquinas, Rover becomes gripped by the passion of anger *as well as* by the desire for the bone, and after sufficient provocation Jones becomes the sole and unfortunate focus of Rover's attention. According to Lockean psychology, either Rover should immediately pursue the bone as soon as it becomes available—which, after teasing, does not happen—or the original desire to pursue the bone is *replaced* by the desire to chew Jones's ear off, and then replaced again by the desire for the bone. Slightly more sophisticated versions of Lockean psychology allow for a new desire to arise in Rover—the desire to chew off Jones's ear—*concurrent* with and outweighing Rover's (standing) desire for the bone. But no matter which explanation the Lockean theory adopts, a basic question is unanswered and indeed unaddressed. What prompts Rover to adopt the desire to attack Jones *at all*? Jones is not edible, as the bone is. Jones is not a natural target of canine aggression. Why does Rover attack Jones rather than merely circumventing him as quickly as possible? The answer is familiar from experience. Rover attacks Jones because Jones is a present evil, a threat to Rover's pursuit of pleasure, an obstacle to be overcome. But that is precisely to allow Aquinas's point that obstacles or difficulties themselves can be objects of passions. Furthermore, they are certainly not desires on a par with the simple push-pull model. The burden, therefore, is on the Lockean to explain how desires alone can account for (a) and (b) in ordinary cases.

The rest of Aquinas's discussion (ST IaIIae.23.2–4) is concerned with differentiating the six kinds of concupiscible passions and the five kinds of irascible passions: that is, with describing the kinds of opposition relating the formal objects that define each of these eleven passions. Aquinas lays out the two kinds of opposition (ST IaIIae.23.2):

> Passion is a kind of motion, as stated in Physics 3.3 [202a25]. Therefore, one must take the contrariety of passions according to the contrariety of motions or changes. Now there are two kinds of contrariety in motions or changes, as stated in Physics 5.5 [229a20]:
>
> (a) according to the [subject's] approach to or withdrawal from the same terminus
>   This contrariety belongs properly to changes—that is, generation (which is a change to being) and corruption (which is a change from being). The other kind is
>
> (b) according to the contrariety of the termini
>   This contrariety belongs properly to motions. For example, whitening (which is the motion from black to white) is opposed to blackening (which is the motion from white to black).

A subject can be changed by its relation to a single terminus, as in (a); in such cases the subject acquires or loses something, where such acquisition and loss are opposed processes. If we have not a single terminus but two 'poles' of the change, as in (b), we can describe the subject as moving from one terminus to the other, or the other way around; the direction of movement yields different motions.[31] Aquinas immediately applies these cases to the passions:

> Therefore, two kinds of contrariety are found in the passions of the soul:[32]
>
> (a*) according to the [subject's] approach to or withdrawal from the same terminus
>
> (b*) according to the contrariety of objects, i.e. of good and evil
>   Only (b*) is found in the concupiscible passions, namely [contrariety] according to the objects, whereas (a*) and (b*) are both found in the irascible passions.

Why shouldn't there be the motion of 'worsening' (from good to evil) and the contrary motion of 'bettering' (from evil to good)—parallel to whitening and blackening—for both kinds of passions? Aquinas offers the following explanation:

> The reason for [the claim that only (b*) is found in the concupiscible passions] is that the object of the concupiscible, as stated above [in ST Ia-IIae.23.1], is sensible good or evil taken absolutely. Yet good *qua* good cannot be a terminus that change is directed away from but only one that it is directed towards, since nothing evades good *qua* good; rather, all things strive for it. Likewise, nothing strives for evil as such; rather, all things evade it, and for this reason evil does not have the nature of a terminus that change is directed towards but only [the nature] of a terminus that change is directed away from. Therefore, every concupiscible passion in respect of good is [directed] towards it (as in love, desire, and joy); every [concupiscible] passion in respect of evil is [directed] away from it (as in hate, aversion or abhorrence, and sorrow). Therefore, contrariety according to the approach to or withdrawal from the same terminus, [namely (a*)], cannot exist in the concupiscible passions.

It is one of Aquinas's fundamental principles that all of creation tends toward the good. In the case of creatures that have at least sensitive abilities, he takes this principle to have the consequence that all action is directed to the (apparent) good. Since the passions are part of the affective structure of living creatures, they tend toward something only to the extent that it is seen as a good. Hence there cannot be any passion that tends toward (apparent) evil. In terms of motion, no creature can, in any of its passions, withdraw from the good. Pursuit of the (apparent) good is automatic and innate. Hence (a*) is impossible.[33] The concupiscible passions are grouped into conjugations as pairs of contrary opposites with regard to good and evil (as Aquinas lists them above), that is, with respect to (b*): love/hate, desire/aversion, joy/ sorrow.

The argument given in the preceding paragraph does not turn on any special feature of the concupiscible passions. Thus it seems as though (a*) cannot hold for any of the passions, including the irascible passions. Yet Aquinas says that it does hold for the irascible passions. How is this possible? He continues his explanation (ST IaIIae.23.2):

> The object of the irascible is sensible good or evil—not taken absolutely but under the aspect of difficulty or arduousness, as stated above [in ST IaIIae.23.1]. Now the arduous or difficult good has a nature such that (i)

something tends to it insofar as it is good (which pertains to the passion *hope*), and (ii) something recedes from it insofar as it is arduous or difficult (which pertains to the passion *despair*). Likewise, the arduous evil has a nature such that (i) it is shunned insofar as it is evil (and this pertains to the passion *fear*); and (ii) it has a nature such that something tends to it as something arduous through which it avoids being subjected to something evil (and *confidence* tends to it in this fashion). Therefore, in the irascible passions we find both (a*) [contrariety] according to the approach to or withdrawal from the same terminus, as between confidence and fear, and again (b*) contrariety according to the contrariety of good and evil, as between hope and fear.[34]

These four irascible passions are grouped into the conjugations hope/despair and confidence/fear according to (a*) rather than (b*) like the concupiscible passions; Aquinas describes (a*) for each irascible conjugation of (i)–(ii). The answer to the question raised above, then, is that irascible passions characterize approach and withdrawal not in terms of good or evil but in terms of the surmountability or insurmountability of the difficulties associated with the (good or evil) object. Hope is the passion that sees its object as a surmountable (attainable) difficult good, so that the difficult good 'approaches' the agent's possession; despair is the passion that sees its object as an insurmountable (unattainable) difficult good, so that the difficult good 'withdraws' from the agent's possession. Likewise, confidence is the passion that sees its object as a surmountable (avoidable) difficult evil, and fear the passion that sees its object as an insurmountable (unavoidable) difficult evil.

Irascible passions also include contrariety of type (b*). Aquinas only mentions and does not explain one of the two pairs, hope/fear, but his reasoning is not hard to uncover. Hope and fear regard their (difficult) objects as likely to be possessed by the agent—hope directed at the good and fear at the evil. We can invert the reasoning for the other pair, confidence/despair: each regards its (difficult) object as likely not to be possessed, confidence doing without the evil and despair doing without the good.

There is an exceptional irascible passion: anger. Aquinas argues (ST Ia-IIae.23.3) that it has no contrary of any sort. Anger has for its object a difficult evil already present which it strives to attack and overcome (revenge). Since the evil is present, there is no movement of withdrawal, so (a*) is impossible. Likewise, the opposite of present evil is an obtained good—but, as Aquinas remarks, "this can no longer have the aspect of arduousness or difficulty"; nor does any motion remain after the acquisition of a good (except for the repose of the appetite in the acquired good, which pertains to joy, a concupiscible passion). The other four irascible passions are defined by the variety of contrary oppositions they bear to one another, but anger is defined solely in terms of its formal object, without any other kind of passion opposed to it.

The various kinds of contrariety among the irascible passions (including the lack of contrariety for anger) defines each formal object and specifies the essence of each kind of irascible passion. The situation is not so clear-cut in the case of the concupiscible passions, each conjugation of which is characterized by contrariety of the sort described in (b*). Why are there three *distinct* conjugations of concupiscible passions rather than just one? In taking up this question (ST IaIIae.23.4) Aquinas exploits the technical resources available in the theory of motion:

> Every mover in some fashion either draws the patient[35] to itself or repels it from itself. In drawing [the patient] to itself [the mover] does three things in it. First, [the mover] imparts to it an inclination or aptitude to tend to [the mover]. For example, an airborne light body imparts lightness to a body generated [by it], through which [the generated body] has an inclination or aptitude to be airborne also. Second, if the generated body is outside its proper place, [the mover] imparts *movement towards its place*. Third, [the mover] imparts repose in its place to it once it arrives there, since something reposes in its [proper] place by the same cause whereby it is moved to that place. A similar account holds for repulsion.
>
> Now in the motions of the appetitive part, the good has a 'power of attraction' (so to speak) and evil a 'power of repulsion.' Therefore, first of all the good causes in the appetitive potency a certain inclination or aptitude or affinity towards the good. This pertains to the passion *love*. The corresponding contrary is *hatred* in the case of evil. Second, if the good is not yet possessed, it imparts [to the patient] a motion towards attaining this beloved good. This pertains to the passion of *desire or cupidity*. The opposite in the case of evil is *aversion* or *abhorrence*. Third, once the good has been acquired, it imparts to the appetite a certain repose in the acquired good. This pertains to *pleasure* or *joy*; the opposite in the case of evil is *pain* or *sorrow*.

Each thing has its proper place, to which it moves when possible; even when not moving toward its proper place (for example, when prevented from doing so), it has a natural aptitude toward its proper place. The proper place for a stone is the center of the earth. When a stone is released in the air, unless a contrary (violent) motion is imparted to it, the stone will tend downward toward the center of the earth. Nor does it lose this tendency when not exercising it. The theory of motion he relies on may be quaint, but the point of Aquinas's comparison should be evident: the three conjugations of concupiscible passions differ in representing the simple tendency to move toward the good (love) or away from evil (hate); actual motion toward the good (desire) or away from evil (aversion); and the 'repose' found in the possession of the good (joy) or evil (sorrow). The first conjugation represents the purely evaluative aspect of the passions; the second, their motivating features; the last, the enjoyment taken in attaining the desired and loved object or the sorrow in not avoiding the hated object. Aquinas concludes, on the basis of his analogy with movement, that love/hate is the start of all passions and joy/sorrow the end of all, with desire/aversion and all the irascible passions denoting kinds of affective movement (ST Ia-IIae.25.1–2).

Aquinas's overall taxonomic structure of the sensitive appetite may therefore be represented, in first approximation, in tabular form.

Passions

Concupiscible Passions		*Irascible Passions*
Love—Hate	[simple tendency]	Hope—Despair
Desire—Aversion	[movement]	Confidence—Fear
Joy—Sorrow	[repose]	Anger

These are the most general classifications Aquinas identifies within the sensitive appetite, where each class is singled out by the kinds of contrariety it bears to the other passions and its role in the stages of motion. These, of course, are consequences of the formal object of each passion.

Much more could be said about the elements of this structure; the account given here is not simplified, but certain complexities have been put to one side, and it is certainly incomplete.[36] But rather than pursue these issues, I want to focus the discussion by considering the sense in which the passions are *controllable* by us. (This will mean a focus on humans to the exclusion of other animals.) There are two sides to this question. First, since the passions are by definition passive potencies, their passivity might be thought to prevent our exercise of control over them. We are no more than the passive subjects of our passions; their actualization is involuntary—a spasm of desire is on all fours with a sneeze, and loathing is like digestion. Second, modern discussions of the emotions recognize that they are, to at least some extent, 'cognitively penetrable': they are affected by shifts in belief and related desires[37] But how can the passions be affected by anything taking place in the higher faculties, posterior to the act of the sensitive appetite? I take up each question in the next two sections.

3. Passions and Passivity

The passions are passive potencies: objectual intentional states of the sensitive appetite elicited by an external principle, defined by their formal objects and structured as described in the preceding section. Nonhuman animals, having no higher faculties, are clearly at the mercy of their passions, which determine their actions completely. But since the analysis of the sensitive part of the human soul is continuous with that of the sensitive soul belonging to nonhuman animals, why should the case be any different for us? The passivity of the passions seems to militate against the possibility of human control.

Aquinas holds that the passivity of the passions goes only so far. He is careful to avoid what Robert Gordon has termed "the two fallacies" that attend discussions of "the passivity of the emotions."[38] These fallacies are, first, passivity of this sort entails that we are ultimately at the mercy of our passions; second, passivity entails that the passions are not voluntary.[39] These seem to be the core intuitions underlying the worry that passivity prevents control. We'll look at each in detail in this section.

First, given that fear, for instance, is a way (or the product of a way) of being acted upon, it does not follow that we are completely passive with regard to fear—that fear overwhelms us or that we are subject to the vagaries of our affective experience. Now distinguish two questions: (i) whether we are entirely passive with respect to experiencing fear; (ii) whether we are entirely passive in the face of the fear we happen to be experiencing. Even if we were to grant (i) to be the case (discussed more fully below), there are serious complications for (ii). It is true that the sensitive appetite is passive with respect to the external principle that puts it into the state it is in—namely, fear. Because the sensitive appetite is a part or faculty of the soul as a whole, we can even say that the entire soul is *per accidens* passive with regard to fear. But the qualification *per accidens* is important. From the fact that the sensitive appetite is passive with regard to its external principle it does not follow that the soul as a whole is passive with regard to the state of its sensitive appetite—that fear, the state of the sensitive appetite, is an active cause putting the entire soul into some given state. If a soldier is wounded in his hand, the damage inflicted to his hand licenses our asserting that he (as a whole) has been wounded; we pass from a strict assertion about a part to a general claim about the whole, which is very different from saying that the wound in his hand causes damage to the rest of his body. His wounded hand is not a cause of the wound with regard to the rest of the soldier's body, or to his whole body, which is the fallacy in question. In like manner, the passivity of the passions does not make us passive with respect to our passions.

This argument depends on two assumptions. First, it supposes that the sensitive part of the soul is a proper part of the whole soul, an assumption that holds for humans but fails for animals. (Animals are therefore passive with respect to their passions: they cannot but act on them.)[40] Second, it supposes that the intellective part of the soul contributes to the condition of the soul as a whole—that is, that motivation is not exhausted by the sensitive appetite; since the will is intellective appetite and operates in close conjunction with the intellect, this assumption is well founded.[41] For Aquinas, the will can be and typically is at least a partial co-cause of the state of the soul as a whole. We have to *choose* something as well as *want* it to be motivated by it in the relevant way.

Yet even if it is in general fallacious to move from the passivity of the passions to our passivity vis-à-vis the passions, Aquinas recognizes that we often explain actions by referring to the motives of the agent, where a passion is cited as the sole motive for action. For example, when we say that Jones struck Smith out of anger, we explain Jones's action (striking Smith) by referring to the passion he is experiencing (anger). It seems as though passions do completely explain actions, Aquinas's insistence notwithstanding.

Aquinas takes such 'explanations' of action to conflate two very different cases: the rare circumstances in which people are literally overcome by their passions, and the ordinary case in which some degree of cognitive and volitional control is retained. He describes the difference between these cases as follows (ST IaIIae.10.3):

The influence of a passion on a man occurs in two ways. First, such that a man does not have the use of his reason, as happens in the case of those who become crazed or maddened through vehement anger or desire—as with any other bodily disorder, for passions of this sort don't happen without a bodily change. And the explanation of such cases is the same as for brute animals, which follow the impulse of their passions of necessity: there is no movement of reason within them and consequently none of will. [Second], at times reason is not totally devoured by passion but preserves the free judgment of reason with regard to something, and in line with this preserves some movement of the will.[42] Therefore, to the extent that reason remains free and not subject to passion, so too the movement of the will that remains does not of necessity tend towards that to which the passion inclines it.

Thus either (i) there is no movement of the will in the man, but rather he is dominated by the passion alone; or (ii) if the movement of the will is [in the man], then he doesn't follow the passion of necessity.

Passions that literally overwhelm reason and will can reduce humans to the level of brute animals, so that they are not 'acting' at all, strictly speaking, but merely reacting blindly to circumstances.[43] This is one interpretation of what is going on when Jones strikes Smith. Jones is so overcome with rage that he lashes out blindly and only later, when he 'returns to his senses,' learns what he has done.

More common, however, are cases in which the agent is not overwhelmed by a passion but rather 'goes along' with it. Aquinas says that the will gives its *consent* to a passion (ad1). In this instance, "reason is not totally devoured by passion," and at least in principle the faculties of the intellective part of the soul could dictate action contrary to the passion. If not blinded by an overwhelming rage, Jones could refrain from striking Smith. When we explain his striking Smith by citing his (nonoverwhelming) anger, we simultaneously describe the state of Jones's soul and report on a choice Jones has made. The description may pick out something passive, but the report does not. The sense in which Jones's anger is a passion doesn't make him passive with respect to it. The explanation of a human action by passion, then, does not run contrary to Aquinas's analysis—not, at least, once it is understood in this way.

The second fallacy identified by Gordon is to conclude that passions, in virtue of their passivity, are not voluntary.[44] There is a clear sense in which the passions are subject to our control. The will's consent to a passion is required, in normal circumstances, for the passion to serve as a basis for action. But a related issue here is less clear. Aquinas recognizes that we seem to *excuse* actions by referring to the motives of the agent, where a passion is cited as the motive for action. Jones struck Smith, his lawyer might protest, only because Smith made him angry with his insults. Even if a choice is somehow involved, his anger (deliberately incited by Smith) makes his action less culpable. Jones did not simply walk up to Smith and strike him, after all; he was provoked. Thus Jones's anger is at least one of the background circumstances in which Jones made his choice to strike Smith. Jones's action is therefore not as purely voluntary as his deciding in cold blood to strike Smith would be. Aquinas seems to endorse this line of thought (ST Ia-IIae.9.2): "Accordingly, something seems fitting to a man when he is in a passion that doesn't seem so apart from the passion—for instance, something seems good to an angry man that doesn't seem so when he is calm."[45] The passions influence our behavior (even if they do not determine it), and so our actions under the influence of the passions are not entirely voluntary. Or so it might be argued.

Aquinas attacks this question with his analysis of the *voluntary*, the *nonvoluntary*, and the *involuntary*. He sets forth two requirements for voluntary action (ST IaIIae 6.1 and 2):

(1) The principle of action is *within* the agent.
(2) The end of the action is known *as* the end

Aquinas points out (6.1 ad1) that the internal principle of an action need not be the first principle of the action; there may be an external principle that occasions the action of the internal principle (as passions are prompted by circumstances), or the operation of the internal principle in itself requires the prior action of other principles (as the passions ordinarily need the will to operate). Now the action generated by the internal principle must have an end, as noted in section 1 above, which must be known as the end for the action to be voluntary; it must be seen as some kind of good, be it in fact real or merely apparent.[46] Failure to meet either (1) or (2) prevents an action from being voluntary; it renders it *nonvoluntary*. Yet these two requirements are ordinarily satisfied when someone acts on the basis of a passion. The influence of the passion does not prevent an action from being voluntary.

Aquinas recognizes that an action considered in itself, apart from the circumstances in which it is performed, might be opposed to the will; he calls such an action *involuntary* (see ST IaIIae.6.6). He discusses Aristotle's case of an action done out of fear, when the ship's captain jettisons the cargo during a storm (*Nicomachean Ethics* 3.1 [1110a9–11]). Technically, such an action is voluntary, for it satisfies (1) and (2). Throwing the cargo overboard, an action performed to avoid the greater evil of the ship's foundering (that is, done out of fear), is voluntary. Whether the cargo is thrown overboard depends solely on the captain; it is his command that determines the fate of the cargo. Yet the captain's action is involuntary. In other circumstances, or independent of these particular circumstances, the captain would not throw the cargo overboard—far from it; he is entrusted with its protection. Therefore, although his action is voluntary, it is involuntary in a respect (*secundum quid*). In such cases, the agent wills what he does not want to will. The correct moral, it seems, is that we are responsible for what is done out of fear, since the actions are voluntary, but the circumstances may be extenuating. So too with Jones's anger. Striking Smith does not seem like a good idea in other circumstances; were it not for Smith's provocation, Jones would not strike Smith at all. Jones is responsible for striking Smith but, perhaps, should be excused for doing so.[47]

The cases of anger and fear contrast sharply with concupiscence (ST IaIIae.6.7). Aquinas argues that concupiscence (*concupiscentia*) is simply voluntary. There is nothing of the involuntary in it, for the agent wills to have what he would will to have in other circumstances. The desired object would be chosen in other circumstances as well; hence there cannot be any extenuating circumstances for concupiscence.[48] Therefore, action on the basis of a passion is voluntary but may include an involuntary component. But even if it does, whether the involuntary component should free the agent from blame is a separate issue.

4. Reason and the Passions

Aquinas holds, *contra* Hume, that reason is and ought to be the ruler of the passions: since the passions *can* be controlled by reason they *should* be controlled by reason (ST IaIIae.24.3). But this bit of moralizing depends on reason's being able to control the passions in a more robust way than that described in section 3, where the cases under discussion do no more than somehow affect what seems good to the agent. Aquinas recognizes several external factors that can affect the content of the apparent good: bodily dispositions (ST IaIIae.17.7 ad2); the physiological states of the organs involved in the somatic reaction associated with the passion (ST IaIIae.10.3); the condition of the recipient in the attendant circumstances as well as the condition of the object itself (ST IaIIae.9.2), and so on. Yet none of these ways in which the content of the apparent good can be affected is under the control of reason, except indirectly. Digestion is just as 'controllable' by reason, since it too is a process that proceeds largely autonomously but can be influenced by bodily disposition, the state of the stomach, what is eaten and the circumstances in which it is eaten, and so on. Aquinas needs to explain the way in which passions can be controlled in a robust sense: how beliefs and reasons can influence the passions themselves (if they can), as opposed to merely influencing action based on the passions. In short, Aquinas needs to explain how the passions are cognitively penetrable.

The mere presence of the higher faculties in humans is not enough to explain the cognitive penetrability of the passions. For the passions might be caused by their external principles regardless of our beliefs, as the sense of taste responds to hot peppers no matter what our cognitive state may be. Instead, there must be some means by which the cognitive and the appetitive faculties can interact.[49] The intellect must be connected to the sensitive appetite, in some fashion yet to be determined, so that belief can directly affect desire.

Aquinas describes the connection between perception and passion in the case of nonhuman animals (ST Ia.78.4):

If an animal were moved only according to what is pleasant and unpleasant to sense, it would only be necessary to postulate in the animal the apprehension of forms that sensing perceives, in which [the animal] takes pleasure or shudders at. But an animal must search out or avoid some things not only because they are suitable or unsuitable to the senses, but also according to some other uses and advantages or disadvantages. For example, a sheep seeing an approaching wolf runs away—not because of its unsightly color or shape, but as if it were a natural enemy. Likewise, a bird collects straw not because it pleases sense but because it is useful for building a nest. Thus it is necessary for an animal to perceive intentions [*intentiones*] of this sort, which the exterior senses do not perceive. There must be some distinct principle for the perception of this, since the perception of sensible forms takes place in virtue of a sensible transmutation, but not the perception of the aforementioned intentions. Therefore, the *proper sense* and the *common sense* are appointed for the reception of sensible forms . . . but the *estimative power* is appointed for apprehending intentions, which are not received through sensing.

Animals do not respond solely to the perceptible properties of the objects they encounter. They also respond to such objects as useful or useless, as harmful or harmless, which are not perceptible properties of these objects. Sheep run when they see wolves; birds gather straw for nests. The nonperceptible properties of an object are the *intentiones* associated with it.[50] The behavior of sheep and birds, Aquinas maintains, cannot be explained solely in terms of the perceptible properties of wolves or straw. The intentions associated with wolves and straw, however, provide the beginnings of an explanation. We need to postulate a faculty for the reception of these nonperceptible properties—the estimative power.[51] While Aquinas does not here spell out the connection to the passions, the link should be obvious: when a sheep receives the intention of enmity from the wolf in the estimative power, it has the passion *avoidance* (or perhaps *fear*), which is the proximate cause of and explanation for the sheep's flight. Animals subsume perceived objects under the formal objects of the passions by the estimative power.

Aquinas does not explain the mechanics of the connection between the estimative power and the sensitive appetite, but the details are of no interest for our purposes; sheep necessarily respond to certain intentions with certain passions, whether this is in the end due to their physiology, conditioning, or a mixture. Matters are more complicated in the case of humans (who are themselves more complicated), as Aquinas immediately points out (ST Ia.78.4):

It should be noted that there is no difference as regards sensible forms between man and the other animals, for they are similarly transmuted by the exterior senses. But there is a difference as regards the aforementioned intentions, for other animals perceive intentions of this sort only by a kind of natural instinct, whereas man does so through a kind of combination. And so [the power] that is called the natural *estimative* in other animals is called the *cognitive* in man, which discloses intentions of this sort through a kind of combination. Accordingly, it is also called *particular reason*. Physicians assign a determinate organ for this [faculty], namely the middle part of the head, for it combines individual intentions just as intellective reason [combines] universal intentions.

The natural estimative power, common to all animals, is replaced in humans by the cogitative power: particular reason. Aquinas is unhelpful as to its nature. Localized in the middle part of the head, particular reason is said to 'combine' intentions: more exactly, it combines individual intentions, as reason (in the intellective faculty) combines universal intentions. This faculty is the mediating link between cognition and the passions. We can make some headway on understanding particular reason by looking at what Aquinas says later (ST Ia.81.3):

[The irascible and the concupiscible appetite] obey reason with respect to their own acts. For in other animals the sensitive appetite is apt to be moved by the estimative power; for example, a sheep that esteems a wolf as inimical is afraid. But the cogitative power takes the place of the estimative power in man, as stated above [in ST Ia.78.4]. Some call it 'particular reason' because it combines individual intentions. Accordingly, the sensitive appetite in man is apt to be moved by it. Yet particular reason itself is apt to be moved and guided in accordance with universal reason. Singular conclusions are thus drawn from universal propositions in logic. And so it is clear that universal reason commands the sensitive appetite (which is divided into the concupiscible and the irascible) and that the [sensitive] appetite obeys [reason]. Now because deducing singular conclusions from universal principles is not the work of the simple intellect but of reason, the irascible and the concupiscible are said to obey reason rather than to obey the intellect. Also, anyone can experience this in himself: by applying some universal considerations, anger or fear or the like can be mitigated—or even stirred up.

Particular reason is a faculty that stands apart from all the other cognitive faculties and receives their input. It deals with singular propositions. Now it is a fundamental thesis of Aquinas's philosophy of mind that sense deals with particulars and intellect with universals; reason joins universal concepts together in propositional judgment.[52] But singular propositions can follow from universal ones, and particular reason is the faculty that draws such inferences.

Furthermore, particular reason may supply singular propositions that are combined with other propositions, singular or universal, to draw conclusions. As he says, "particular reason is moved and guided by universal reason."[53]

Aquinas's remark at the end of the passage confirms this interpretation. From the singular proposition "This is a lion" (provided by sensible apprehension) and the universal proposition "All lions eat human beings" (known to the intellect), the particular reason draws the conclusion "This lion eats human beings"—a singular proposition that should trigger a response of fear. Other universal considerations, such as "All lions prefer eating humans to anything else," should in the appropriate way increase my fear. Alternatively, the intellect can be left out of account, and I can lessen my fear by combining "This is a lion" with the singular proposition "This is Chicago, the well-known vegetarian lion."[54] In either case, particular reason is the place where the logical 'combinations' take place.

In replying to an objection, Aquinas lists the psychological faculties that are directly linked to the sensitive appetite the way particular reason is (ad2):

> Now intellect or reason is said to rule the concupiscible and irascible "with a politic rule" [Politics 1.2 (1254b2)], because the sensitive appetite has something belonging to it that can resist reason's command. For the sensitive appetite is apt to be moved not only by the estimative power in other animals and by the cogitative power in man, but also by the imaginative power and by sensing.[55] Accordingly, we experience that the irascible and the concupiscible struggle against reason, in that we sense or imagine something pleasurable that reason forbids, or [something] unpleasant that reason enjoins. Yet the fact that the irascible and the concupiscible struggle against reason in some instance does not stop them from obeying it.

Reasons and beliefs, then, can directly affect the sensitive appetite through imagination and particular reason. These cognitive faculties are naturally linked to sensitive appetite, and, just as sensitive apprehension does, they provide content for the passions. The cognitive penetrability of the passions depends on the mediating activity of the imagination and of particular reason.

The truth of this general claim is compatible with the passions being more or less open to reasoning and persuasion on any given occasion. People may persist in the fear of flying even while mumbling the air-safety statistics to themselves; weakness of the will is possible; other factors (such as organic dysfunction) may intervene. The passions are recalcitrant; they are not slaves to reason's commands but free citizens (mostly) following the ruler's advice. Yet the difficulties that stand in the way of making the passions completely rational are minor compared to the importance of Aquinas's basic claim that reasons and beliefs *can* affect the passions. The passions are not, after all, similar to our reaction to hot peppers. They can be affected by reasons and beliefs. Their cognitive penetrability will turn out to be fundamental to Aquinas's moral and theological psychology, since this allows people to perfect themselves through the virtues.

How sensitive apprehension, imagination, and particular reason actually interact with sensitive appetite, though, is left obscure. All Aquinas says is that "the sensitive appetite in man is apt to be moved by [particular reason]," and "the sensitive appetite is apt to be moved not only by . . . the cognitive power in man, but also by the imaginative power and by sensing." All well and good, but how do they do it?

Aquinas has no real answer to this question, and that, I think, is one of the virtues of his account. He describes psychological activity at a high level of abstraction, where the relation among psychological faculties is characterized functionally: sensitive apprehension, imagination, and particular reason are treated as so many *inputs* to sensitive appetite. This is the level of abstraction common in contemporary cognitive science. Aquinas does suggest where the answer may be found: in the realization of the functional system he mentions the physiological basis, the middle part of the head, where, he vaguely suggests, the interface among the faculties might be. But he does not pursue the matter, leaving it to future neurophysiologists if any should be interested, preferring to concentrate instead on the substantive claims made in his functional psychology. In this regard, Aquinas (and scholastic philosophy of mind generally) is far superior to its successors. Descartes's account of the passions and their somatic bases, for instance, is shot through with his attempts to identify the underlying neurophysiological mechanism in terms of brain-pores and animal spirits. Neurophysiology is not psychology, though, and all the latter demands are functional mechanisms, which may be physiologically instantiated in one way or another. Aquinas should not be blamed for not giving an account of how the interaction among the various psychological departments takes place; he was, rightly, more concerned with the logic of such interaction than with the nuts and bolts of how it worked.

Conclusion

Aquinas's account of the nature and structure of the passions as psychological phenomena is as fine a piece of philosophical analysis as the Middle Ages had to offer. And, apart from its historical merits, I have tried to argue that his theory is attractive in its own right. His emphasis on a faculty psychology and scientific taxonomy is a more sophisticated philosophical approach to psychological inquiry than that found in the early modern period, bearing remarkable similarities to contemporary questions and accounts being developed in cognitive science. The subtlety and penetration of Aquinas's analysis of the passions is unparalleled, and the questions he addresses are still philosophically pressing and acute. His discussion deserves to be taken seriously by anyone concerned with the issues he examines, not just by those with primarily historical or systematic interests. That is his genuine philosophical legacy to us, and it is a rich legacy indeed.

Notes

1. The sensitive and intellective parts of the soul sit astride another fundamental cluster of principles accounting for nourishment, growth, and reproduction, known as the vegetative part of the soul. There are psychological experiences founded solely on the vegetative part: for instance, hunger, thirst, and sexuality (as mere physical reactivity). But medieval philosophers, along with modern psychologists, do not classify these together with the passions of the soul or emotions; they are more primitive motivational forces, now called 'drives' or 'urges,' which I discuss only incidentally in what follows.

2. All translations are my own; I use the Marietti edition of ST. The term 'passion' is cognate to the Latin *passio*, and as such is a term of art with no relation to the ordinary English word: there need be nothing vehement, forceful, or heartfelt about Aquinas's passions. For a critique of the traditional terminology, see Eric D'Arcy's introduction in ST (Black-friars, 19:xxiii).

3. *Acts* are not to be confused with *actions*. The latter are a special case of the former, namely, realizations of potencies where the principle is within the agent.

4. Potencies are individuated by their corresponding acts because potencies and acts are not capable of definition: the division potency/act is a transcendental division of being, on a par with the division of being into the ten categories and hence unable to be captured in a genus-species hierarchy (which is what makes Aristotelian definition possible). Yet because act is *prior* to potency, potencies can be distinguished by their corresponding acts. This doctrine is at the root of the pair of distinctions mentioned at the beginning of this essay: cognitive and appetitive potencies are distinguished by their objects, and the object of appetite is the good, whereas the object of cognition is the real (or the true), as Aquinas argues in ST Ia.80.1 ad1; the sensitive and intellective parts of the soul are themselves distinguished by their objects, which, for Aquinas, differ as particular and universal, respectively.

5. In the case of vision, the external principle is also the *efficient* cause of the passive potency's reduction from potency to act. The efficient cause actualizing a passive potency may differ from its formal and final cause, however; see the discussion at the end of section 1.

6. This distinction, taken from Aristotle's *Nicomachean Ethics* 2.5 and 10.4, is reflected in the different kinds of tensed statements that can be made about the acts in question. For a discussion and application of the point to the case of the

passions, see Anthony Kenny, *Action, Emotion, and Will* (London: Routledge & Kegan Paul, 1963), chap. 7; Ronald de Sousa, *The Rationality of Emotion* (Cambridge: MIT Press, 1987), chap. 8.

7. Aquinas holds that there are analogues to the passions pertaining to the purely intellective part of the soul—call them pseudopassions. These pseudopassions, unlike the passions, do not involve any somatic reactions or indeed any material basis at all. They are located in the intellective appetite as rational acts of will. Angels and disembodied human souls experience only these pseudopassions; animals experience only passions; living human beings alone are capable of both. The *amor intellectualis Dei* is a pseudopassion, one that may be deeply held. Likewise, the dispassionate drive to destroy something evil, the reflective judgment that something—for example, smallpox—should be eradicated, is a pseudopassion. On a more prosaic level, the desire to stop smoking is typically a pale pseudopassion, quite unlike the passion (the craving) for nicotine. The account given here applies strictly to the passions, not the pseudopassions, which play a major role in Aquinas's theology and merit investigation in their own right.

8. I explore this point in detail in the next section.

9. The parallel between emotions and perceptions has been exploited, with some degree of success, by several contemporary philosophers; see, e.g., de Sousa, *The Rationality of Emotion*, chap. 5.

10. There is a sense in which someone can 'see' without seeing anything, namely, while looking for something. (This is perhaps more plausible for hearing than for seeing, as in the case of a person listening for something: "Quiet—I thought I heard a burglar upstairs! Listen!") In such cases one is still looking or listening *for* something, and so the directedness of the act is preserved. Furthermore, they are cases in which a person sees or hears many things and rejects each in turn as not the object in question: "This noise is just the furnace (not the burglar), that one is the cat meowing (not the burglar)," and so on. The sensing is clearly intentional, with an intellectual 'filter' on the input.

11. This is not to be confused with the claim that the received form is itself particular or individual. The point here is that there are no 'forms' of states of affairs, propositional objects, abstract entities, and the like. Forms are received from individuals rather than complexes—independent of whether the content of the perception is singular or universal, and also of whether the received form by means of which perception takes place is singular or universal.

12. The terminology was not fixed. Aquinas usually says 'object' rather than 'formal object.' The formal object of a cognitive potency is usually called its 'per se object' or 'primary object.'

13. See ST Ia.81.2: "The sensitive appetite is an inclination that follows upon the sensitive apprehension (just as natural appetite is an inclination that follows upon the natural form)." See also ST Ia.80.2 and elsewhere for this claim. The sensitive appetite receives not only the form from perception but also the associated *intentiones* (ST IaIIae.22.2), as discussed in section 4.

14. In ST IaIIae.44.1 Aquinas begins his reply by remarking: "In the case of the passions, the formal element is the motion of the appetitive potency and the material element is a bodily change, where one is proportionate to the other;

accordingly, the bodily change appropriates the nature of and a resemblance to the appetitive motion." Aquinas examines the somatic reactions associated with each of the passions in considerable detail: e.g., the several articles of ST IaIIae.44 are devoted to the effects of fear. Vital spirits are concentrated in the higher region, deflected from the heart, which is contracted; this chills the rest of the body and may produce trembling, the chattering of teeth, and fluttering in the stomach. Depending on the kind of fear, blood may rush into the head to produce blushing (if the object is shameful) or away from the head to produce paleness (if the object is terrifying). If the onset of fear is sudden and sharp, control over bodily limbs and functions will be lost. Knocking knees, shuddering, heaving chest, difficult breathing, voiding of the bowels or bladder—all these accompany a general paralysis.

15. ST IaIIae.29.6 clarifies this point: "Hatred in the sensitive part [of the soul] can therefore be directed at something universally, namely, because something is hostile to an animal because of its common nature and not only in virtue of the fact that it is a particular thing—for instance, the wolf [is hostile] to the sheep. Accordingly, sheep hate the wolf generally." Sheep do not hate wolfhood but all wolves *qua* having a wolf-nature inimical to sheep, which is to say that the sheep's hatred is directed at any given wolf. This is akin to hatred *de dicto* rather than *de re*, in contemporary terminology, although sheep do not hate (or do anything else) under descriptions. Only particular things are the objects of passions; see QDV 25.1 resp. This much said, Aquinas is liberal about what may count as a 'particular thing': in ST IaIIae.42.4 he describes the ways in which someone might, e.g., fear fear itself.

16. The medieval notion of 'formal object' has passed directly into the contemporary debates over the emotions, apparently by way of Kenny, *Action, Emotion, and Will*, p. 189: see, e.g., de Sousa, *The Rationality of Emotion*, pp. 121–23.

17. When Aquinas says that the formal object of the appetite is *the good*, for example, he means that any item that counts as an object of appetite must be characterized as good, not that goodness itself (whatever that may be) is the object of appetite. See note 15 above.

18. It is not clear whether Aquinas holds that (a) Jones perceives the sheep as an evil, or (b) Jones perceives the sheep and thereafter judges or esteems it as an evil; the neutral word 'cognition' covers both alternatives. See the discussion of *intentiones* in section 4. Furthermore, according to Aquinas, Jones's loathing of the sheep is ultimately due to some form of love; the efficient cause of *love* is the cognition of something as good (ST IaIIae.27.2), and love, surprisingly, is the ultimate cause of hatred (ST IaIIae.29.2), on the grounds that you can only hate what in some fashion you care about.

19. The terminology is derived from Wittgenstein, *Philosophical Investigations* I §476; see de Sousa, *The Rationality of Emotion*, pp. 115–16. The targets of passions need not exist: e.g., I can fear the (nonexistent) burglar or love the dear departed.

20. Aquinas's theory of the passions is therefore *cognitivist* in much the sense described in Robert Kraut, "Feelings in Context," *Journal of Philosophy* 83 (1986): 642–52: "Cognitive processes are somehow essential to emotion," where such processes include "complexity, intentional focus, susceptibility to appraisal" and issue in theories that explain emotions in terms of belief and desire (p. 643).

Kraut, among others, defends a 'feeling theory' of the emotions, which is strictly incompatible with the account Aquinas provides. The debate is well known in the modern literature (see de Sousa, *The Rationality of Emotion*, chaps. 3–5).

21. This means not that Aquinas denies the existence of such psychological phenomena but that his account of them does not depend on treating them as passions. Anxiety, e.g., is a matter of the proper physiological conditions for fear being present (or at least some of them) without the corresponding form in the sensitive appetite. He also uses the theory of the four humors to provide a purely physiological account of moods.

22. This is not to deny that there may be corresponding 'objectless' forms of these passions, as some have argued that anxiety is nonspecific fear, but—as suggested in the preceding note—whatever these phenomena may be, they are not passions.

23. Most of the following discussion is drawn from ST IaIIae.23.1–4.

24. See note 15 above on this last point. Aquinas's restriction of the passions to the sensible good, understood as the demand that the target of the passion be perceptible even if not perceived, is connected with his distinction between sensory and intellective goods (and perhaps the distinction between passions and pseudopassions as well: see note 7).

25. For the matter, why didn't Aquinas distinguish them as *sensible good taken absolutely* and *sensible evil taken absolutely*? He uses the opposition between good and evil as one of the contrarieties that give structure to the interrelations among the passions; why not use it from the beginning?

26. René Descartes, *Les passions de l'âme* §69. In §68 he rejects Aquinas's taxonomy of the passions on the grounds that (1) the soul has no parts; (2) he does not see why concupiscence and anger should have any explanatory primacy; (3) Aquinas's account does not give equal recognition to all six primitive passions.

27. Aquinas's discussion of the causes, the effects, and often the remedies for each passion are wide-ranging, penetrating, and occasionally humorous, as when he considers in ST IaIIae.40.6 whether youth and inebriation are causes of hope (they are), or in ST IaIIae.48.3 whether anger notably interferes with the ability to reason (it can). Aquinas investigates serious questions of all sorts, such as whether transport and jealousy (*extasis* and *zelus*) are effects of love (ST Ia-IIae.28.3–4), whether someone can hate himself (ST IaIIae.29.4), whether sympathy from friends can help alleviate sorrow (ST IaIIae.38.3), whether love is the cause of fear (ST IaIIae.43.1).

28. I don't know how to prove that they are any more than plausible, however. Consider the following remark in John Haugeland, *Artificial Intelligence: The Very Idea* (Cambridge: MIT Press, 1985), p. 234, about fear and anger: "What I call EMOTIONS, on the other hand, are more measured, more discriminating. The point is not that they are less powerful—*fear and anger are not fright and rage watered down*—but rather they are more intelligent, more responsive to argument and evidence" (my emphasis). Haugeland rejects Aquinas's classification of rage and anger, or fright and fear, under the same heading. Which theory is right? How do we tell?

29. See John Locke, *Essay concerning Human Understanding* 2.20, for his claim

that the passions are simply ideas of pleasure and pain. Jones's hope, e.g., is simply mental pleasure generated by the occurrent idea of "a probable future enjoyment of a thing, which is apt to delight him" (2.20.9).

30. This claim is too strong: irascible passions depend on concupiscible passions, since they presuppose some kind of conative attitude toward whatever is regarded as difficult or arduous. That is why Aquinas holds that the irascible passions arise from and terminate in the concupiscible passions. He treats these relations among kinds of passions at length in ST IaIIae.25.

31. Aquinas's distinction between (a) and (b) reflects a real difference in physics. In the case of substantial change, generation and corruption do not involve, in addition to being, a 'real' terminus of nonbeing. That is to say, there is no readily identifiable substrate persisting through the entire change. In accidental change, however, there are two opposed forms that successively inhere in the persisting substrate. Aquinas argues, as we shall see, that concupiscible passions can only involve something like substantial change, whereas irascible passions have features similar to both substantial and accidental change.

32. Aquinas inverts the order of presentation here, giving (b*) before (a*).

33. This argument also rules out the motion of 'worsening' (contrary to the motion of 'bettering'). Aquinas is playing fast and loose with (b*) when it comes to the concupiscible passions: he characterizes them in terms of their motions with regard to each member of a single pair of contradictorily opposed termini— namely, good (motion toward) and evil (motion away from)—not in terms of motions *between* contradictorily opposed termini. Love, for example, is not a motion *from evil* to good but only a motion to good.

34. Aquinas again inverts the order of presentation here, giving (b*) and then (a*).

35. The 'patient' is the item that suffers or undergoes the action of the mover (formed on analogy with 'agent').

36. This account does no more than scratch the surface of Aquinas's account of the passions. Among the complexities it ignores are these. (1) There are kinds of passion subordinate to those listed here. For instance, *amor* (love) is divided into *amor amicitiae* and *amor concupiscentiae*; anger comprises wrath, ill-will, and rancor. (2) Joy is a kind of pleasure and sorrow a kind of pain; more exactly, pleasure and pain are generic terms applying equally to body and soul, whereas joy and sorrow apply strictly to the soul. These passions are nevertheless named after joy and sorrow as the most 'exalted' form of the passion. Similar remarks apply to love and 'dilection,' desire and cupidity, and others. (3) The formal object of each passion needs to be spelled out in precise detail.

37. The notion of 'cognitive penetrability' used here is taken from Zenon Pylyshyn, *Computation and Cognition* (Cambridge: MIT Press, 1984).

38. Robert M. Gordon, *The Structure of Emotions* (Cambridge: Cambridge University Press, 1987), chap. 6, esp. pp. 117–21.

39. See ibid., chap. 6, on the extent of these fallacies in contemporary philosophical work on the emotions.

40. Aquinas's story here is more complex than I have made it out to be, for reasons he expounds in ST Ia.80.1. As a part of his metaphysics he holds

(F) Form is the principle of action

But for animals and humans (F) does *not* automatically reduce to.

(F*) The determinate form of a thing is the principle of its action

Now (F) is not equivalent to (F*) because, in the case of creatures that have sensitive or intellective abilities, in addition to the determinate form that, say, an elephant has (the form that makes it to be the kind of thing it is, namely, an elephant), additional forms are acquired through the cognitive or apprehensive powers. When the elephant sees a mouse, its sense organs transmit the mouse-phantasm to its sensitive soul; the behavior of the elephant is fixed by its determinate form and how the acquired form interacts with the determinate form: mouse-phantasm combined with elephant-form produces trumpeting and rearing, a response that likely involves a mixture of physiological structure and conditioned responses ('habits').

41. To say this does not explain *how* the higher powers (intellect and will) interact with the passions. The case of intellect is discussed in section 4 below.

42. See also ST IaIIae.17.7 ad2 for this point.

43. In terms of the famous distinction Aquinas draws in ST IaIIae.1.1, such blind reactions are not *actiones hunianae* but merely *actiones hominis*.

44. Gordon's explanation of the fallacious character of this inference turns on the sense in which we may have control over purely passive responses, so that experiencing the passive response can reasonably be described as voluntary (*The Structure of Emotions*, pp. 119–20). He is certainly correct that passivity does not rule out control. My eyes must see whatever is in front of them, but I can open or close them at will, change the direction of my gaze, and so on. I can likewise put myself in frightening situations so as to feel fear—freely walking into a haunted house, say. For that matter, we can exercise similar control over the functions of the vegetative part of the soul: my stomach digests whatever is in it, but I control whether something is in it, as well as what and when. Yet the mere possibility of exercising control over passive responses does not mean that we can always exercise such control, and hence that such actions are always voluntary. Whether we can dominate our passions so completely depends on the extent to which they are subject to the higher faculties of the intellective part of the soul (see section 4). Yet this is a less interesting way of taking the question. Surely what matters is not whether we have voluntary control over experiencing the passions but whether the action that is (at least partially) caused by the passions is voluntary—and that is the question under discussion here.

45. See also ST IaIIae.17.7 ad2.

46. To be known as the end of an action—to fall under the *ratio finis*—is to be seen as some sort of good. Animals may know their ends, but humans know their ends as ends. It's one matter to be hungry and so tear apart the wrapping and eat the food within, and quite another to recognize one's tearing apart the wrapping as an action that has the food within as an end, as Aquinas notes in ST IaIIae.6.2 (he adopts Aristotle's practice of referring to the thing that is the end as itself 'the end'). The ability to recognize an end as an end is in turn dependent on something more fundamental, namely, the capacity for self-reflection: one has to conceptualize oneself as an agent engaged in an action to

recognize an end as an end, and that, in its turn, depends on having a conception of oneself.

47. Whether Jones should in fact be excused for striking Smith is another question, one that pertains to moral theory rather than an account of the passions. (Aquinas will say that there is no general principle that defines exculpating circumstances.) For our purposes it is enough to note that Aquinas preserves the force of both intuitions: that Jones was in control of his actions when he struck Smith (he acted voluntarily) and that Jones was provoked (his action was involuntary in a respect). Gordon's second fallacy is thereby avoided, and the reason why people are tempted by the fallacious inference is explained.

48. Why the asymmetry? Aquinas thinks there is a moral distinction to be drawn between Jones's being provoked by Smith and Brown's being enticed by Green. I suspect he has not distinguished three cases: (i) Brown would choose Green apart from the enticing circumstances; (ii) Brown would desire Green but not choose Green apart from the enticing circumstances; (iii) Brown would neither choose nor desire Green apart from the enticing circumstances. Aquinas's argument depends on understanding the baseline as in (i), but the parallel to the case of Jones and Smith is (ii) or (iii). Surely circumstances can make something seem desirable just as much as they can make something seem provocative.

49. The particular case of the interaction between cognition and appetite in the intellective part of the soul—that is, between intellect and will—has been exhaustively studied in Aquinas. The connection between perception (sensitive cognition) and passion (sensitive appetite) has been granted to be largely one way, the latter depending on the former. It is the link between intellective cognition and sensitive appetite that remains obscure.

50. These *intentiones* are problematic. Does a wolf 'give off' an intention of harmfulness? Does an elephant therefore find the wolf dangerous? Are such intentions located in the object, the subject, or relationally between the two? See Katherine Tachau, *Vision and Certitude in the Age of Ockham* (Leiden: E. J. Brill, 1988), for an account of medieval philosophical attempts to grapple with *intentiones*.

51. The name for this faculty, the *vis aestimativa*, is linked to 'evaluating' (*aestimatio*) and to 'esteem' (*aestimare*). This nicely captures the nonjudgmental assessment of objects as useful or useless, harmful or harmless, and so on.

52. See Peter King, "Scholasticism and the Philosophy of Mind: The Failure of Aristotelian Psychology," in *Scientific Failure*, ed. Tamara Horowitz and Allen I. Janis (London: Rowman & Littlefield, 1994), pp. 109–38, for a discussion of Aquinas's philosophy of mind. My identification of 'particular reason' in this passage with the faculty of drawing singular conclusions is based on Aquinas's connection between particular and universal reason in the latter part of the passage; his initial description of particular reason as the faculty that "combines individual intentions" certainly seems unlike any inferential ability. Scott MacDonald has proposed that universal reason may draw singular conclusions which then affect the intention-combining faculty, in part on the grounds that the combination of intentions is a much lower-level function than syllogistic inference.

53. Nothing in the passage cited above forces us to identify the particular

reason Aquinas is discussing here with the faculty of drawing singular conclusions.

54. More exactly, the individual intention "This lion is dangerous" is combined with "This lion, namely Chicago, is not dangerous." Here 'combination' seems to mean 'is replaced by.' Aquinas owes us an account of the forms of combination.

55. A parallel listing is given in ST IaIIae.17.7: "Whatever is due to the power of the soul follows upon an apprehension. Now the apprehension of the imagination, although it is particular, is governed by the apprehension of reason, which is universal, just as a particular active power [is governed] by a universal active power. On this score the act of the sensitive appetite is subject to the command of reason. . . . Sometimes it also happens that a movement of the sensitive appetite is suddenly aroused upon the apprehension of the imagination or of sensing. In this case, the movement is outside the command of reason, although it could have been prevented if reason had foreseen it. Accordingly, the Philosopher says that reason controls the irascible and the concupiscible not 'with a tyrannical rule,' which is that of a master over his slave, but 'with a politic or regal rule' [Politics 1.2 (1254b2–5)], which is over free men who are not completely subject to command." Sensitive apprehension, imagination, and particular reason directly affect the sensitive appetite; presumably the first two also provide input to the particular reason.

A Chronological List of Aquinas's Writings

Works sometimes ascribed to Aquinas may well be texts of which he was not the author in any sense. What follows is a list of Aquinas's writings with respect to which there is not too much scholarly controversy concerning authenticity. They are cited by Latin titles commonly used for them, together with English translations of these. But note that we cannot always be sure of the titles which Aquinas gave to his writings (notably, in the case of the *Summa theologiae* and the *Summa contra Gentiles*). Within each category below, works are cited in roughly chronological order of composition, though in some cases this order is uncertain. For detailed discussions concerning the dating of Aquinas's writings, see Jean-Pierre Torrell, *Saint Thomas Aquinas: The Person and His Work* (Washington, D.C.: Catholic University of America Press, 1996).

General Theological Treatises

Scriptum super libros "Sententiarum" (*Commentary on the "Sentences" of Peter Lombard*: c. 1252–57).
Summa contra Gentiles, sometimes referred to as *Summa contra Gentes* (*Summary against the Pagans* [sc., people neither Jewish nor Christian]: c. 1259–65).
Summa theologiae, sometimes referred to as *Summa theologica* (*Summary of Theology*: c. 1265–73).
Compendium theologiae (*Compendium of Theology*: c. 1265–73).

Disputed Questions

Questiones disputatae De veritate (*Disputed Questions on Truth*: c. 1256–59).
Questiones disputatae De potentia (*Disputed Questions on the Power [of God]*: c. 1265–66).
Questio disputata De anima (*Disputed Question on the Soul*: c. 1265–66).

Quaestio disputata De spiritualibus creaturis (*Disputed Question on Spiritual Creatures:* c. 1267–68).

Questiones disputatae De malo (*Disputed Questions on Evil:* c. 1266–70).

Questiones disputatae De virtutibus (*Disputed Questions on the Virtues:* c. 1271–72).

Questio disputata De unione verbi incarnati (*Disputed Question on the Union of the Incarnate Word:* c. 1271–72).

Quaestiones de quodlibet I–XII (*Quodlibetal Questions I–XII* [concerning a very large range of topics]: c. 1252–56 and c. 1268–72).

Biblical Commentaries

Super Ieremiam et Threnos (*Commentaries on Jeremiah and Lamentations:* c. 1248–52).

Expositio super Isaiam ad litteram (*Commentary on Isaiah:* c. 1248–54).

Expositio super Job ad litteram (*Commentary on Job/Literal Exposition on Job:* c. 1261–65).

Catena aurea (*The Golden Chain* [commentary on the Gospels drawing on quotations from the church fathers]: c. 1262–64).

Lectura super Matthaeum (*Commentary on Matthew:* c. 1269–70).

Lectura super Ioannem (*Commentary on John:* c. 1270–72).

Expositio et lectura super Epistolas Pauli Apostoli (*Commentaries on the Letters of St. Paul:* dating very difficult to establish, possibly 1265–73).

Postilla super Psalmos (*Commentary on the Psalms:* c. 1273).

Commentaries on Aristotle

Sententia libri De anima (*Commentary on Aristotle's "On the Soul":* 1267–68).

Sententia libri De sensu et sensato (*Commentary on Aristotle's "On Sense"* [and "On Memory"]: c. 1268–69).

Sententia super Physicam (*Commentary on Aristotle's "Physics":* c. 1268–69).

Sententia super Meteora (*Commentary on Aristotle's "Meteorology":* c. 1268–70).

Sententia libri Politicorum (*Commentary on Aristotle's "Politics":* c. 1269–72).

Expositio libri Peri hermeneias (*Commentary on Aristotle's "On Interpretation"* ["De Interpretatione"]: c. 1270–71).

Expositio libri Posteriorum (*Commentary on Aristotle's "Posterior Analytics":* c. 1270–72).

Sententia super Metaphysicam (*Commentary on Aristotle's "Metaphysics":* c. 1270–72).

Sententia libri Ethicorum (*Commentary on Aristotle's "Nichomachean Ethics":* 1271–72).

Sententia super librum De caelo et mundo (*Commentary on Aristotle's "On the Heavens":* c. 1272–73).

Sententia super libros De generatione et corruptione (*Commentary on Aristotle's "On Generation and Corruption":* c. 1272–73).

Other Commentaries

Expositio super librum Boethii De trinitate (*Commentary on Boethius's "De Trinitate":* c. 1257–59).

Expositio in librum Boethii De hebdomadibus (*Commentary on Boethius's "Hebdomads"* [actually, Boethius's third theological tractate]: c. 1257–59).
Expositio super Dionysium De divinis nominibus (*Commentary on [Pseudo-]Dionysius's "The Divine Names"*: c. 1261–68).
Expositio super librum De causis (*Commentary on the "Book of Causes"*: c. 1272).

Polemical Writings

Contra impugnantes Dei cultum et religionem (*Against Those who Impugn the Cult of God and Religion*: 1256).
De perfectione spiritualis vitae (*On the Perfection of the Spiritual Life*: 1269–70).
De unitate intellectus contra Averroistas (*On the Unicity of the Intellect against the Averroists*: 1270).
Contra doctrinam retrahentium a religione homines a religionis ingressu [commonly referred to as *Contra retrahentes*] (*Against the Teachings of Those Who Prevent Men from Entering the Religious Life*: 1271).
De aeterntate mundi (*On the Eternity of the World*: c. 1271).

Treatises and Other Works on Assorted Topics

De ente et essentia (*On Being and Essence*: c. 1252–56).
De principiis naturae (*On the Principles of Nature*: c. 1252–56, possibly earlier).
Contra errores Graecorum (*Against the Errors of the Greeks*: c. 1263–64).
De regno ad regem Cypri (*On Kingship, to the King of Cyprus*: c. 1267).
De substantiis separatis (*On Separate Substances*: c. 1271).
De mixtione elementorum (*On the Mixture of Elements*: c. 1270).

Liturgical and Related Works

Collationes in decem praecepta (*Homilies on the Ten Commandments*: c. 1261–73).
Officium de festo Corporis Christi (*Office for the Feast of Corpus Christi*: c. 1264).
Collationes in orationem dominicam, in Symbolorum Apostolorum, in salutatem angelicam (*Homilies on the Lord's Prayer, the Apostles's Creed, and the Angelic Greeting*: c. 1268–73).
Hymn *Adoro Te* (commonly referred to by its Latin title: date unknown).

Bibliography

1. Primary Sources

The most authoritative listing of Aquinas's works in English is I. T. Eschmann, "A Catalogue of St. Thomas's Works: Bibliographical Notes," in *The Christian Philosophy of St. Thomas Aquinas*, by Étienne Gilson (New York: Random House, 1956). It is supplemented by "A Brief Catalogue of Authentic Works," in *Friar Thomas D'Aquino*, by James A. Weisheipl (Oxford: Basil Blackwell, 1974; republished with Corrigenda and Addenda, Washington, D.C.: Catholic University of America Press, 1983).

The definitive edition of Aquinas's writings is currently being published by the Leonine Commission, established by Pope Leo XIII in 1880, which has now produced volumes containing Aquinas's most important works: *Sancti Thomae Aquinatis Doctoris Angelici, Opera Omnia, Iussu Leonis XIII* (Rome: Vatican Polyglot Press, 1882–). Publications of Aquinas's writings prior to the Leonine edition include the Parma edition (*Opera Omnia* [Parma: Fiaccadori, 1852–73]) and the Vivès edition (*Opera Omnia* [Paris: Vivès, 1871–82]). Most of Aquinas's writings have also been published in manual size by the Casa Marietti (Turin and Rome). Students of Aquinas should also consult R. Busa, *Index Thomisticus* (Stuttgart and Bad Cannstatt: Frommann-Holzboog, 1974–80), which provides a text of Aquinas's writings and a useful, if somewhat unwieldy, way to search for terms used by him.

A substantial amount of Aquinas's writing still remains untranslated into English. There are, however, some currently available English editions of a number of his more important works. To date, the best English edition of the *Summa theologiae* (with notes and commentaries) is the Blackfriars edition, 61 vols., Latin and English with notes and introductions (London: Eyre and Spottiswoode; New York: McGraw-Hill Book Co., 1964–80). Unfortunately, however, this translation is sometimes unreliable. For a more literal rendering of the text, see *St. Thomas Aquinas, "Summa theologica,"* translated by the Fathers of the English Dominican Province (originally published by Burns, Oates, and Washbourne in London in 1911 and now available from Christian Classics, Westminster, Md., 1981). This edition may be found on the Internet at http://www.newadvent.org/summa. A searchable concordance to it can be found on the Internet at http://www.gocart.org/summa.html. Also worth consulting is Timothy McDermott, ed., *St. Thomas Aquinas, "Summa theologiae.": A Concise Translation* (London: Eyre and Spottiswoode, 1989).

For a reliable translation of the *Summa contra Gentiles*, see *On the Truth of the Catholic Faith,* trans. by Anton Pegis, James F. Anderson, Vernon J. Bourke, and Charles J. O'Neil (New York: Doubleday, 1955–57, reprinted as *Summa contra Gentiles* (Notre Dame, Ind.: University of Notre Dame Press, 1975). An annotated translation of the *Summa contra Gentiles* by Joseph Rickaby (with some abridgments) is available on the Internet at http://www.nd/departments/maritain/etext/gc.html.

Other English translations of Aquinas's writings include:

(a) Disputed Questions

Disputed Questions on Virtue (Quaestio disputata De virtutibus in communi and Quaestio disputata De virtutibus cardinalibus). Trans. Ralph McInerny. South Bend, Ind.: St. Augustine's Press, 1999.

On Charity (Quaestio disputata De caritate). Trans. Lottie H. Kendzierski. Milwaukee: Marquette University Press, 1984.

On Evil (Questiones disputatae De malo). Trans. Richard Regan. New York and Oxford: Oxford University Press, 2001.

On Spiritual Creatures (Quaestio disputata De spiritualibus creaturis). Trans. M. C. Fitzpatrick and J. J. Wellmuth. Milwaukee: Marquette University Press, 1949.

On the Power of God (Quaestiones disputatae De potentia). Trans. English Dominican Fathers. 3 vols. London: Burns, Oates, and Washbourne, 1932–34.

Quodlibetal Questions 1 and 2. Trans. Sandra Edwards. Toronto: Pontifical Institute of Medieval Studies, 1983.

The Soul (Quaestio disputata De anima). Trans. J. H. Robb. Milwaukee: Marquette University Press, 1984.

Truth (Quaestiones disputatae De veritate). Trans. Robert W. Mulligan, J. V. McGlynn, and R. W. Schmidt. 3 vols. Chicago: Henry Regnery Co., 1952–54.

(b) Commentaries on Scripture

Commentary on Saint Paul's Epistle to the Ephesians. Trans. Matthew L. Lamb. Albany, N.Y.: Magi Books, 1966.

Commentary on Saint Paul's Epistle to the Galatians. Trans. F. R. Larcher. Albany, N.Y.: Magi Books, 1966.

Commentary on Saint Paul's First Letter to the Thessalonians and the Letter to the

Philippians. Trans. F. R. Larcher and Michael Duffy. Albany, N.Y.: Magi Books, 1969.

Commentary on the Gospel of John (Lectura super Ioannem). Trans. James A Weisheipl and F. R. Larcher. 2 vols. Albany, N.Y.: Magi Books, 1980; Petersham, Mass.: St. Bede's Publications, 1998.

The Literal Exposition on Job (Expositio super Job as litteram). Trans. Anthony Damico. Atlanta: Scholars Press, 1989.

(c) Commentaries on Aristotle

A Commentary on Aristotle's "De anima" (Sententia libri De anima). Trans. Robert Pasnau. New Haven: Yale University Press, 1999.

Commentary on Aristotle's "Metaphysics" (Sententia super Metaphysicam). Trans. John P. Rowan. Notre Dame, Ind.: University of Notre Dame Press, 1995.

Commentary on Aristotle's "Nicomachean Ethics" (Sententia libri Ethicorum). Trans. C. I. Litzinger. 2 vols. Notre Dame, Ind.: University of Notre Dame Press, 1964.

Commentary on Aristotle's "Physics" (Sententia super Physicam). Trans. R. Blackwell. New Haven: Yale University Press, 1963.

Commentary on the "Posterior Analytics" of Aristotle (Expositio libri Posteriorum). Trans. F. R. Larcher. Albany N.Y.: Magi Books, 1970.

On Interpretation (Expositio libri Peri hermeneias). Trans. Jean T. Oesterle. Milwaukee: Marquette University Press, 1962.

(d) Other Commentaries

Commentary on the "Book of Causes" (Expositio super librum De causis). Trans. Vincent A. Guagliardo, Charles R. Hess, and Richard C. Taylor. Washington, D.C.: Catholic University of America Press, 1996.

Saint Thomas Aquinas, The Divisions and Methods of the Sciences. Questions V and VI of His Commentary on the "De Trinitate" of Boethius (Expositio super librum Boethii De trinitate). Trans. A. Maurer. Toronto: Pontifical Institute of Medieval Studies, 1986.

Saint Thomas Aquinas, Faith, Reason, and Theology. Questions I–IV of His Commentary on the "De Trinitate" of Boethius (Expositio super librum Boethii De trinitate). Trans. A. Maurer. Toronto: Pontifical Institute of Medieval Studies, 1987.

(e) Other Writings

On Being and Essence (De ente et essentia). Trans. Joseph Bobik. Notre Dame, Ind.: University of Notre Dame Press, 1965.

Aquinas on Matter and Form and the Elements (Translations of "De principiis naturae" and "De mixtione elementorum"). Trans. Joseph Bobik. Notre Dame, Ind.: University of Notre Dame Press, 1998.

On There Being Only One Intellect (De unitate intellectus contra Averroistas). Trans.

Ralph McInerny. In *Aquinas against the Averroists* by Ralph McInerny. West Lafayette, Ind.: Purdue University Press, 1993.

Compendium of Theology (Compendium theologiae). Trans. Cyril Vollert. St Louis, Mo., and London: B. Herder Book Co., 1949.

The Sermon Conferences of St. Thomas Aquinas on the Apostle's Creed (Collationes in Symbolorum Apostolorum). Trans. Nicholas Ayo. Notre Dame, Ind.: University of Notre Dame Press, 1988.

Readers might like to note that Thérèse Bonin maintains an updated Web site listing currently available English translations of Aquinas at: http://www.home.duq.edu/~bonin/thomasbibliography.html. The Thomas Institute in Utrecht also lists translations into English of Aquinas and provides one of the most helpful Internet research sites for students of Aquinas. It can be found at http://www.ktu.nl/thomas/.

2. Useful Selections from Aquinas in English

Baldner, Steven E, and William E. Carroll. *Aquinas on Creation*. Toronto: Pontifical Institute of Medieval Studies, 1997.

Clark, Mary T. *An Aquinas Reader*. Rev. ed. New York: Fordham University Press, 2000.

Martin, Christopher, ed. *The Philosophy of Thomas Aquinas*. London: Routledge, 1988.

McDermott, Timothy, ed. *Aquinas: Selected Philosophical Writings*. Oxford and New York: Oxford University Press, 1993.

McInerny, Ralph. *Thomas Aquinas: Selected Writings*. Harmondsworth: Penguin Books, 1998.

Pegis, Anton C., ed. *Introduction to St. Thomas Aquinas*. New York: Modern Library, 1945.

3. Bibliographical Works

Bourke, Vernon J. *Thomistic Bibliography: 1920–1940. The Modern Schoolman* 21 (suppl.) (1945).

Ingardia, Richard. *Thomas Aquinas: International Bibliography, 1977–1990*. Bowling Green, Ohio: Philosophy Documentation Center, 1993.

Mandonnet, P., and J. Destrez. *Bibliographie Thomiste*. 2d ed., revised by M.-D. Chenu. Paris: Vrin, 1960.

Miethe, Terry L., and Vernon J. Bourke. *Thomistic Bibliography, 1940–1978*. Westport, Conn.: Greenwood Press, 1980.

The *Bulletin Thomiste* (1940–65), continued in *Rassegna di Letteratura Tomistica* (1966–   ), receives all Thomistic publications and is a useful research tool with respect to Thomistic bibliography.

4. General Studies and Introductions to Aquinas

Aertsen, Jan. *Nature and Creature: Thomas Aquinas's Way of Thought*. Leiden: E. J. Brill, 1988.

Anscombe, G.E.M., and P. T. Geach. *Three Philosophers*. Oxford: Basil Blackwell, 1961.

Barron, Robert. *Thomas Aquinas: Spiritual Master*. New York: Crossroad Publishing Co., 1996.

Chenu, M. D. *St. Thomas d'Aquin et la théologie*. (Paris: Éditions du Seuil, 1959.

——. *Towards Understanding Saint Thomas*. Trans. A. M. Landry and D. Hughes. Chicago: Henry Regnery Co. 1964.

Chesterton, G. K. *St. Thomas Aquinas*. London: Hodder and Stoughton, 1943.

Copleston, F. C. *Aquinas*. Harmondsworth: Penguin Books, 1955.

Davies, Brian. *The Thought of Thomas Aquinas*. Oxford: Clarendon Press, 1992.

——. *Aquinas*. London and New York: Continum, 2002.

Elders, Leo J. *The Philosophical Theology of St. Thomas Aquinas*. Leiden: E. J. Brill, 1990.

Gilson, Étienne. *The Christian Philosophy of St. Thomas Aquinas*. New York: Random House, 1956.

Inglis, John. *On Aquinas*. Belmont, Calif.: Wadsworth, 2002.

Kenny, Anthony. *Aquinas*. Oxford: Oxford University Press, 1980.

Kretzmann, Norman, and Eleonore Stump. *The Cambridge Companion to Aquinas*. Cambridge: Cambridge University Press, 1993.

Ralph. McInerny, *St. Thomas Aquinas*. Notre Dame, Ind.: University of Notre Dame Press, 1982.

——. *A First Glance at St. Thomas Aquinas: A Handbook for Peeping Thomists*. Notre Dame, Ind.: University of Notre Dame Press, 1990.

O'Meara, Thomas F. *Thomas Aquinas Theologian*. Notre Dame, Ind.: University of Notre Dame Press, 1997.

Pieper, Josef. *Guide to Thomas Aquinas*. Trans. R. Winston and C. Winston. Notre Dame, Ind.: University of Notre Dame Press, 1987.

Redpath, Peter A. *A Simplified Introduction to the Wisdom of St. Thomas*. Washington, D.C.: University Press of America, 1980.

Selman, Francis. *St. Thomas Aquinas: Teacher of Truth*. Edinburgh: T. and T. Clark, 1994.

Wippel, John F. *The Metaphysical Thought of Thomas Aquinas*. Washington, D.C.: Catholic University of America Press, 2000.

5. Material for Studying the Life of Aquinas

Ferrua, A., ed. *Thomae Aquinatis vitae fontes praecipuae*. Alba: Ed. Dominicane, 1968.

Foster, Kenelm, ed. *The Life of Thomas Aquinas*. London: Longmans, Green and Co.; Baltimore: Helicon Press, 1959.

Torrell, Jean-Pierre. *Saint Thomas Aquinas: The Person and His Work*. Washington, D.C.: Catholic University of America Press, 1996.

Tugwell, Simon, ed. *Albert and Thomas: Selected Writings*. New York, and London: Paulist Press, 1988.

Weisheipl, James A. *Friar Thomas D'Aquino*. Oxford: Basil Blackwell, 1974; republished with Corrigenda and Addenda, Washington, D.C.: Catholic University of America Press, 1983.

6. Other Relevant Reading on Aspects of Aquinas's Writings

Aertsen, Jan A. "The Convertibility of Being and Good in St. Thomas Aquinas." *New Scholasticism* 59 (1985).

―――. "The Philosophical Importance of the Doctrine of the Transcendentals in Thomas Aquinas." *Revue Internationale de Philosophie* 52 (1998).

Aillet, Marc. *Lire la Bible avec S. Thomas: Le passage de la "littera" à la "res" dans la "Somme théologique."* Fribourg: Éditions Universitaires Fribourg Suisse, 1993.

Ashworth, E. J. "Signification and Modes of Signifying in Thirteenth Century Logic: A Preface to Aquinas on Analogy." *Medieval Philosophy and Theology* 1 (1991).

―――. "Analogy and Equivocation in Thirteenth-Century Logic: Aquinas in Context." *Medieval Studies* 54 (1992).

Barbellion, Stéphane-Marie. *Les "preuves" de l'existence de Dieu: Pour une relecture des cinq voies de saint Thomas d'Aquin.* Paris: Les Éditions du Cerf, 1999.

Bird, Otto. "How to Read an Article in the *Summa*." *New Scholasticism* 27 (1953).

Blanchette, Oliva. *The Perfection of the Universe according to Aquinas: A Theological Cosmology.* University Park, Pa.: Pennsylvania State University Press, 1992.

Boland, Vivian. *Ideas in God according to Saint Thomas Aquinas: Sources and Synthesis.* Leiden: E. J. Brill, 1996.

Bowlin, John. *Contingency and Fortune in Aquinas's Ethics.* Cambridge: Cambridge University Press, 1999.

Boyle, Leonard E. *The Setting of the "Summa Theologiae" of Saint Thomas.* Étienne Gilson Series 5. Toronto: Pontifical Institute of Medieval Studies, 1982.

Brown, Patterson. "St. Thomas; Doctrine of Necessary Being." *Philosophical Review* 73 (1964).

Burrell, David. *Aquinas, God, and Action.* London and Henley, 1979.

―――. *Knowing the Unknowable God.* Notre Dame, Ind.: University of Notre Dame Press, 1986.

―――. *Freedom and Creation in Three Traditions.* Notre Dame Ind.: University of Notre Dame Press, 1993.

Cajetan, Thomas de Vio. *Commentary on Being and Essence,* tr. L. H. Kendzierski and F. C. Wade, SJ. Milwaukee, Wis.: Marquette University Press, 1964.

Callus, Daniel A. *The Condemnation of St. Thomas at Oxford.* Aquinas Society of London Aquinas Paper No. 5. London, 1955.

Cessario, Romanus. *The Godly Image: Christ and Salvation in Catholic Thought from Anselm to Aquinas.* Petersham Mass.: St. Bede's Publications, 1990.

Clarke, W. N. "St. Thomas' Essence-Existence Doctrine." *New Scholasticism* 48 (1974).

―――. "What Is Most and Least Relevant in the Metaphysics of St. Thomas Today?" *International Philosophical Quarterly* 14 (1974).

Congar, Yves. *Thomas d'Aquin: Sa vision de théologie et de l'Église.* London: Variorum Reprints, 1984.

Corbin, Michel. *Le chemin de la théologie chez Thomas d'Aquin.* Paris: Beauchesne, 1974.

Craig, William Lane. "Aquinas on God's Knowledge of Future Contingents." *Thomist* 54 (1990).

Crowe, Michael Bertram. "Peter of Ireland: Aquinas's Teacher of the Artes Liberales." in *Arts liberaux et philosophie au Moyen Age*. Montreal: Institu d'Études Médiévale; Paris: Librairie Philosophique J. Vrin, 1969.

Davies, Brian. "Classical Theism and the Doctrine of Divine Simplicity." In *Language, Meaning, and God*, ed. Brian Davies. London: Geoffrey Chapman, 1987.

———. "The Mystery of God: Aquinas and McCabe." *New Blackfriars* 77 (1996).

———. "Aquinas, God, and Being." *Monist* 80 (1997).

Dodds, Michael J. *The Unchanging God of Love: A Study of the Teaching of St. Thomas Aquinas on Divine Immutability in View of Certain Contemporary Criticism of This Doctrine*. Fribourg: Éditions Universitaires Fribourg Suisse, 1986.

Doig, James C. *Aquinas on Metaphysics*. The Hague: Martinus Nijhoff, 1972.

Donagan, Alan. "Thomas Aquinas on Human Action." In *The Cambridge History of Later Medieval Philosophy*, N. Kretzmann, A. Kenny, and J. Pinborg. Cambridge: Cambridge University Press, 1982.

Dubarle, Dominique. *L'ontologie de Thomas d'Aquin*. Paris: Les Éditions du Cerf, 1996.

Eco, Umberto. *The Aesthetics of Thomas Aquinas*. London: Radius, 1988.

Elders, Leo J. *The Metaphysics of Being of St. Thomas Aquinas in a Historical Perspective*. Leiden: E. J. Brill, 1993.

Elders, Léon *Autour de Saint Thomas d'Aquin: Receuil d'études sur sa pensée philosophique et théologique*. 2 vols., Paris: FAC-Éditions, Brugge: Uitgeverji Tabor, 1987.

Fabro, C. *Participation et causalité selon Saint Thomas d'Aquin*. Louvain: Publications Universitaires de Louvain, 1961.

Finnis, John. *Aquinas*. Oxford: Oxford University Press, 1998.

Fogelin, Robert J. "A Reading of Aquinas's Five Ways." *American Philosophical Quarterly* 27 (1990).

Gallagher, David. "Free Choice and Free Judgment in Thomas Aquinas." *Archiv für Geschichte der Philosophie* 76 (1994).

———. ed., *Thomas Aquinas and His Legacy*. Washington, D.C.: Catholic University of America Press, 1994.

Gauthier, René-Antoine. "*Somme contre Les Gentils*": *Introduction*. Paris: Éditions Universitaires, 1993.

Geach, Peter. *God and the Soul*. London: Routledge and Kegan Paul, 1969.

Geiger, Louis-Bertrand. *Penser avec Thomas d'Aquin*. Fribourg: Éditions Universitaires Fribourg Suisse; Paris: Les Éditions du Cerf, 2000.

Gilby, Thomas. *The Political Thought of Thomas Aquinas* Chicago: University of Chicago Press, 1958.

Gilson, Etienne. *Being and Some Philosophers*. 2d ed. Toronto: Pontifical Institute of Medieval Studies, 1952.

Goris, Harm J. M. *Free Creatures of an Eternal God: Thomas Aquinas on God's Infallible Foreknowledge and Irresistible Will*. Leuven: Peeters, 1996.

Haldane, John J. "Aquinas on Sense-Perception." *Philosophical Review* 92 (1983).

Hall, Douglas C. *The Trinity: An Analysis of St. Thomas Aquinas's "Expositio" of the "De Trinitate" of Boethius*. Leiden: E. J. Brill, 1992.

Hankey, W. J. *God in Himself: Aquinas's Doctrine of God as expounded in the "Summa Theologiae."* Oxford: Oxford University Press, 1987.

Henle, R. J. *Saint Thomas and Platonism*. The Hague: Martinus Nijhoff, 1956.

Hibbs, Thomas S. *Dialectic and Narrative in Aquinas.* Notre Dame, Ind.: University of Notre Dame Press, 1995.

Hillgarth, J. N. *Who Read Aquinas?.* Étienne Gilson Series 13. Toronto: Pontifical Institute of Medieval Studies, 1992.

Hughes, Christopher. *On a Complex Theory of a Simple God.* Ithaca: Cornell University Press, 1980.

Jenkins, John. "Expositions of the Text: Aquinas's Aristotelian Commentaries." *Medieval Philosophy and Theology* 5 (1996).

———. *Knowledge and Faith in Thomas Aquinas.* Cambridge: Cambridge University Press, 1997.

Jordan, Mark. "The Intelligibility of the World and the Divine Ideas in Aquinas." *Review of Metaphysics* 38 (1984).

———. *Ordering Wisdom: The Hierarchy of Philosophical Discourses in Aquinas.* Notre Dame Ind.: University of Notre Dame Press, 1986.

———. *The Alleged Aristotelianism of Thomas Aquinas.* Étienne Gilson Series 15. Toronto: Pontifical Institute of Medieval Studies, 1992.

Keenan, James F. *Goodness and Rightness in Thomas Aquinas's "Summa Theologiae."* Washington, D.C.: Georgetown University Press, 1992.

Kenny, Anthony. *The Five Ways.* London: Routledge and Kegan Paul, 1969.

———. *Aquinas on Mind.* London and New York: Routledge, 1993.

——— ed. *Aquinas: A Collection of Critical Essays.* London and Melbourne: Macmillan, 1969.

Kent, Bonnie. "Transitory Vice: Thomas Aquinas on Incontinence." *Journal of the History of Philosophy* 27 (1989).

Kerr, Fergus. "Aquinas after Marion." *New Blackfriars* 76 (1995).

Klima, Gyula. "The Semantic Principles Underlying Saint Thomas Aquinas's Metaphysics of Being." *Medieval Philosophy and Theology* 5 (1996).

Knasas, John F. X. "Aquinas: Prayer to An Immutable God." *New Scholasticism* 57 (1983).

Konyndyk, Kenneth J. "Aquinas on Faith and Science." *Faith and Philosophy* 12 (1995).

Kretzmann, Norman. "Goodness, Knowledge, and Indeterminancy in the Philosophy of St. Thomas Aquinas." *Journal of Philosophy* 80 (1983).

———. *The Metaphysics of Theism.* Oxford: Clarendon Press, 1997.

———. *The Metaphysics of Creation.* Oxford: Clarendon Press, 1999.

Leftow, Brian. "Aquinas on Time and Eternity." *American Catholic Philosophical Quarterly* 64 (1990).

———. "Souls Dipped in Dust." In *Soul, Body, and Survival*, ed. Kevin Corcoran Ithaca: Cornell University Press, 2001.

Lisska, Anthony J. *Aquinas's Theory of Natural Law: An Analytic Reconstruction.* Oxford: Clarendon Press, 1996.

Lockey, Paul, ed. *Studies in Thomistic Theology.* Houston: Center for Thomistic Studies, 1995.

Lonergan, Bernard. *Verbum: Word and Idea in Aquinas.* Ed. D. B. Burrell. Notre Dame, Ind.: University of Notre Dame Press, 1967.

MacDonald, Scott. "Aquinas's Parasitic Cosmological Argument." *Medieval Philosophy and Theology* 1 (1991).

———. "Ultimate Ends in Practical Reasoning: Aquinas's Aristotelian Moral Psychology and Anscombe's Fallacy." *Philosophical Review* 100 (1991).

———. "Aquinas's Libertarian Account of Free Choice." *Revue Internationale de Philosophie* 52 (1998).

———. "Practical Reasoning and Reasons-Explanations: Aquinas's Account of Reason's Role in Action." In *Aquinas's Moral Theory: Essays in Honor of Norman Kretzmann*, ed. Scott MacDonald and Eleonore Stump. Ithaca: Cornell University Press, 1999.

MacDonald, Scott, and Eleonore Stump, eds. *Aquinas's Moral Theory: Essays in Honor of Norman Kretzmann*. Ithaca: Cornell University Press, 1999.

Makin, Stephen. "Aquinas, Natural Tendencies, and Natural Kinds." *New Scholasticism* 63 (1989).

Martin, C.F.J. *Thomas Aquinas: God and Explanations*. Edinburgh: Edinburgh University Press, 1997.

Masterson, Patrick. "Aquinas' Notion of God Today." *Irish Theological Quarterly* 44 (1977).

Maurer, Armand. *Being and Knowing: Studies in Thomas Aquinas and Later Medieval Philosophers*. Toronto: Pontifical Institute of Medieval Studies, 1990.

McCabe, Herbert. *God Matters*. London: Geoffrey Chapman, 1987.

———. "The Logic of Mysticism—I." In *Religion and Philosophy*, ed. Martin Warner. Royal Institute of Philosophy Supplement 31. Cambridge: Cambridge University Press, 1992.

———. "Aquinas on the Trinity." *New Blackfriars* 80 (1999).

McInerny, Ralph *Ethica Thomistica: The Moral Philosophy of Thomas Aquinas*. Washington, D.C.: Catholic University of America Press, 1982.

———. *Being and Predication*. Washington, D.C.: Catholic University of America Press, 1986.

———. *Boethius and Aquinas*. Washington, D.C.: Catholic University of America Press, 1990.

———. *Aquinas on Human Action: A Theory of Practice*. Washington, D.C.: Catholic University of America Press, 1992.

———. *Aquinas and Analogy*. Washington, D.C.: Catholic University of America Press, 1996.

Merriell, D. Juvenal. *To the Image of the Trinity: A Study in the Development of Aquinas' Teaching*. Toronto: Pontifical Institute of Medieval Studies, 1990.

Mondin, B. *St. Thomas Aquinas's Philosophy in the Commentary on the Sentences*. The Hague: Martinus Nijhoff, 1975.

O'Rourke, Fran. *Pseudo-Dionysius and the Metaphysics of Aquinas*. Leiden: E. J. Brill, 1992.

Owens, Joseph. *St. Thomas Aquinas on the Existence of God, Collected Papers of Joseph Owens*. Edited by John R. Catan. Albany: State University of New York Press, 1980.

Pasnau, Robert. "Aquinas on Thought's Linguistic Nature." *Monist* 80 (1997).

———. *Theories of Cognition in the Later Middle Ages*. Cambridge: Cambridge University Press, 1997.

———. *Thomas Aquinas on Human Nature*. Cambridge: Cambridge University Press, 2002.

Patfoort, Albert. *Thomas d'Aquin: Les clés d'une théologie*. Paris: FAC-Éditions, 1983.

Pegis, Anton Charles. *St. Thomas and the Problem of the Soul in the Thirteenth Century*. Toronto: Pontifical Institute of Medieval Studies, 1934.

Penelhum, Terence. "The Analysis of Faith in St. Thomas Aquinas." *Religious Studies* 13 (1977).

Persson, Per Erik. *Sacra Doctrina: Reason and Revelation in Aquinas*. Oxford: Basil Blackwell, 1970.

Pesch, Otto Hermann. *Thomas von Aquin: Grenze und Grosse mittelalterlicher Theologie*. Mainz-Weisenau: Matthias-Grünewald-Verlag, 1988. Translated into French under the title *Thomas d'Aquin: Limites et grandeur de la théologie médiévale* (Paris: Les Éditions du Cerf, 1994).

Pieper, Josef. *The Silence of Saint Thomas*. Trans. John Murray and Daniel O'Connor. Chicago: Henry Regnery Co., 1965.

Pinto de Oliveira, Carlos-Josaphat, ed., *"Ordo sapientie et amoris": Image et message de Saint Thomas d'Aquin à travers les récentes études historiques, herméneutiques, et doctrinales*. Fribourg: Éditions Universitaires Fribourg Suisse, 1993.

Principe, Walter H. *Thomas Aquinas' Spirituality*. Étienne Gilson Series 7. Toronto: Pontifical Institute of Medieval Studies, 1984.

Putnam, Hilary. "Thoughts Addressed to an Analytical Thomist." *Monist* 80 (1997).

Radcliffe, E. S. "Kenny's Aquinas on Dispositions for Human Acts." *New Scholasticism*, 58 (autumn 1984).

Redpath, Peter A. *The Moral Wisdom of St. Thomas: An Introduction*. Lanham, N.Y.: University Press of America, 1983.

Reilly, James P., Jr. *Saint Thomas on Law*. Étienne Gilson Series 12. Toronto: Pontifical Institute of Medieval Studies, 1990.

Ryan, Thomas F. *Thomas Aquinas as Reader of the Psalms*. Notre Dame, Ind.: University of Notre Dame Press, 2000.

Schmidt, R. W. *The Domain of Logic according to Saint Thomas Aquinas*. The Hague: Martinus Nijhoff, 1966.

Schoot, Henk J. M. *Christ, the "Name" of God: Thomas Aquinas on Naming Christ*. Leuven: Peeters, 1993.

———, ed. *Tibi Soli Peccavi: Thomas Aquinas on Guilt and Forgiveness*. Leuven: Peeters, 1996.

Sentis, Laurent. *Saint Thomas d'Aquin et le mal: Foi chrétienne et théodicée*. Paris: Beauchesne, 1992.

Sigmund, Paul E. *St. Thomas Aquinas on Politics and Ethics*. New York: W. W. Norton, 1988.

Sillem, Edward. *Ways of Thinking about God: Thomas Aquinas and Some Recent Problems*. London: Darton, Longman, and Todd, 1961.

Somme, Luc-Thomas. *Fils adoptifs de Dieu par Jésus Christ*. Paris: Vrin, 1997.

Stubbens, Neil. "Naming God: Maimonides and Aquinas." *Thomist* 54 (1990).

Stump, Eleonore. "Atonement according to Aquinas." In *Philosophy and the Christian Faith*, ed. Thomas V. Morris. Notre Dame, Ind.: University of Notre Dame Press, 1988.

———. "Atonement and Justification." In *Trinity, Incarnation, and Atonement*, ed.

Ronald J. Feenstra and Cornelius Plantinga, Jr. Notre Dame, Ind.: University of Notre Dame Press, 1989.

———. "Faith and Goodness." In *The Philosophy in Christianity*, ed. Godfrey Vesey. Cambridge: Cambridge University Press, 1989.

———. "Intellect, Will, and the Principle of Alternate Possibilities." In *Christian Theism and the Problems of Philosophy*, ed. M. Beaty. (Notre Dame, Ind.: University of Notre Dame Press, 1990.

———. "Aquinas on the Foundations of Knowledge." *Canadian Journal of Philosophy*, supplementary volume 7 (1992).

———. "Aquinas's Account of the Mechanisms of Intellective Cognition." *Revue Internationale de Philosophie* 52 (1998).

———. "Aquinas on the Mechanisms of Cognition: Sense and Phantasia." In *Medieval Analyses in Language and Cognition*, ed. Sten Ebbesen and Russell L. Friedman. Copenhagen: Royal Danish Academy of Sciences and Letters, 1999.

Theron, Stephen. "*Esse.*" *New Scholasticism* 53 (1979).

Thomas, J. L. H. "The Identity of Being and Essence in God." *Heythrop Journal* 27 (1986).

Torrell, Jean-Pierre. *Saint Thomas d'Aquin, maître spirituel.* Fribourg: Éditions Universitaires Fribourg Suisse; Paris: Les Éditions du Cerf, 1996.

———. La "*Somme de théologie*" *de saint Thomas d'Aquin.* Paris: Les Éditions du Cerf, 1998.

———. *Récherches thomasiennes.* Paris: Vrin, 2000.

Tugwell, Simon. "Prayer, Humpty Dumpty and Thomas Aquinas." In *Language, Meaning, and God*, ed. Brian Davies. London: Geoffrey Chapman, 1987.

Valkenberg, Wilhelmus G.B.M. *Words of the Living God: Place and Function of Holy Scripture in the Theology of St. Thomas Aquinas.* Leuven: Peeters, 2000.

van der Ploeg, J. "The Place of Holy Scripture in the Theology of St. Thomas." *Thomist* 10 (1947).

Van Steenberghen, Fernand. *Le problème de l'existence de Dieu dans les écrits de S. Thomas D'Aquino.* Louvain-La-Neuve: Éditions de l'Institut Supérieur de Philosophie, 1980.

———. *Thomas Aquinas and Radical Aristotelianism.* Washington, D.C.: Catholic University of America Press, 1980.

Velde, Rudi A. te. *Participation and Substantiality in Thomas Aquinas.* Leiden: E. J. Brill, 1995.

Velecky, Lubor. *Aquinas' Five Arguments in the "Summa Theologiae" Ia 2,3.* Kampen: Kok Pharos Publishing House, 1994.

Vos, Arvin. *Aquinas, Calvin, and Contemporary Protestant Thought.* Washington, D.C.: Christian University Press, 1985.

Wawrykow, Joseph P. *God's Grace and Human Action: "Merit" in the Theology of Thomas Aquinas.* Notre Dame, Ind.: University of Notre Dame Press, 1995.

Wéber, Édouard-Henri. *Le Christ selon Saint Thomas d'Aquin.* Paris: Desclée, 1988.

Weisheipl, James A. *Thomas D'Aquino and Albert His Teacher.* Toronto: Pontifical Institute of Medieval Studies, 1980.

Westberg, Daniel. *Right Practical Reason: Aristotle, Action, and Prudence in Aquinas.* Oxford: Clarendon Press, 1994.

White, Victor. *God the Unknown.* London: Harvill Press, 1956.

----. *Holy Teaching: The Idea of Theology according to St. Thomas Aquinas.* Aquinas Society of London Aquinas Paper No. 33. London, 1958.

Williams, A. N. *The Ground of Union: Deification in Aquinas and Palamas.* New York and Oxford: Oxford University Press, 1999.

Williams, C. J. F. *What Is Existence?* Oxford: Clarendon Press, 1981.

----. *Being, Identity, and Truth.* Oxford: Clarendon Press, 1992.

----. "Being." In *A Companion to the Philosophy of Religion*, ed. Philip L. Quinn and Charles Taliaferro. Oxford: Basil Blackwell, 1997.

Wippel, John F. *Metaphysical Themes in Thomas Aquinas.* Washington, D.C.: Catholic University of America Press, 1984.

----. "Substance in Aquinas's Metaphysics." *Proceedings of the American Catholic Philosophical Association* 61 (1987).

----. "Thomas Aquinas and Participation." In *Studies in Medieval Philosophy*, ed. J. F. Wippel. Washington, D.C.: Catholic University of America Press, 1987.

----. "Truth in Thomas Aquinas (Part I and Part II)." *Review of Metaphysics* 43 (1989).

----. *Thomas Aquinas on the Divine Ideas.* Étienne Gilson Series 16. Toronto: Pontifical Institute of Medieval Studies, 1993.

----. "Thomas Aquinas on Demonstrating God's Omnipotence." *Revue Internationale de Philosophie* 52 (1998).

----. *The Metaphysical Thought of Thomas Aquinas.* Washington, D.C.: Catholic University of America Press, 2000.

Wissink, J.B.M., ed. *The Eternity of the World in the Thought of Thomas Aquinas and His Contemporaries.* Leiden: E. J. Brill, 1990.